The Wider Island of Pelops

Professor Christopher Mee

The Wider Island of Pelops

Studies on Prehistoric Aegean Pottery
in Honour of Professor Christopher Mee

Edited by

David Michael Smith, William G. Cavanagh
and Angelos Papadopoulos

ARCHAEOPRESS ARCHAEOLOGY

ARCHAEOPRESS PUBLISHING LTD
Summertown Pavilion
18-24 Middle Way
Summertown
Oxford OX2 7LG

www.archaeopress.com

ISBN 978-1-80327-328-0
ISBN 978-1-80327-329-7 (e-Pdf)

Cover: View of Mt. Taygetos from the Neolithic - Bronze Age settlement at Kouphovouno.
In foreground, pithos fragment, Phylakopi, Melos (NAM acc. no. 26505).

This book is available direct from Archaeopress or from our website www.archaeopress.com

Contents

Preface

The Wider Island of Pelops offers readers a snapshot of current research in the field of ceramic studies across the prehistoric Aegean. It captures a wide gamut of theoretical, contextual, and scientific approaches and, in so doing, serves as a fitting tribute to Professor Christopher Mee, who through his own research contributed so much to our understanding of prehistoric Aegean pottery, its myriad functions, and its utility in conveying social and cultural meaning.

The volume is, in part, formed of contributions offered to a two-day conference held in honour of Chris at the Upper House of The British School at Athens (BSA) across September 18th and 19th, 2017. This meeting was organised by two of Chris' former students at the University of Liverpool, David Smith and Angelos Papadopoulos, with generous support from the director and administrative staff of the BSA, to whom the editors of this volume are indebted, and with the help of funding from the Institute for the Study of Aegean Prehistory (INSTAP).

The remainder of the papers included here were offered to the volume subsequently, by friends and colleagues who had worked with Chris, and others who have followed his research. These include contributions by Robin Barber, Julien Beck and colleagues, Lisa French†, Walter Gauss, Mercouris Georgiadis, Chrysanthi Gallou and colleagues, Margarita Nazou and Aris Papayiannis. The seventeen papers which make up this volume are united by their common ceramic focus and, collectively, cover the broad histories of the Neolithic and Bronze Age, and the myriad and shifting relationships that linked the settlements of the Peloponnese to so many others beyond its limits.

Across almost a decade of fieldwork at the Laconian site of Kouphovouno, Chris Mee proved himself to be an inspiring colleague and leader. His co-directors in that project, Bill Cavanagh and Josette Renard (**Chapter Four**), here utilise the architecture and objects uncovered during the recent excavations (1999-2007) to explore the theme of 'territoriality' in the Peloponnese during the Neolithic period. The analysis of identity expression at Middle Neolithic Kouphovouno at the level of structure, village, *terroir*, and territory, provides the foundation for discussion of a Late Neolithic site characterised by very different forms of material culture, patterns of settlement, and horizons of cultural influence and exchange. Framed by the ebb and flow of multiple small-scale population movements which served to foment social and technological innovation, ceramics adopted a new significance in the negotiation of tensions and the furtherance of opportunities arising from the contextual dynamics of tradition and transformation within, and beyond, the Neolithic community.

The Neolithic cave site of Alepotrypa at Diros has long served as a keystone for our interpretation of the rich and complex later Neolithic Laconian landscape. New excavations and survey in the area of Ksagounaki have furthered our understanding of the period in the immediate hinterland of Alepotrypa, and now important work by Stella Katsarou and Andreas Darlas (**Chapter Eleven**) has begun to populate the, previously obscure, Final Neolithic coast of the western Mani peninsula. The caves and rock shelters of this region evidence a deep history of human activity reaching back into the Palaeolithic period, although two caves in particular, Skoini 3 and Skoini 4, are highlighted for the extraordinary contribution that they make to our understanding of death, meaning-making and social reproduction during the final phase of the Neolithic. Based on the evidence of a highly unusual male-female double burial in Skoini 3 and a second, likely also male-female, at Skoini 4, Katsarou and Darlas recognise a communal concept of the afterlife expressed through the mortuary reproduction of household metaphors, the observation of which served to regulate power dynamics amongst the living, and monumentalise the 'wild' Maniote landscape through the dead.

The prehistoric landscape of the southern Peloponnese is addressed in rather different fashion by Lisa French † (**Chapter Six**), whose own contribution considers the place of Mycenae in the Argive Plain during the Neolithic and Early Helladic period, with reference to a modest assemblage of EN-EH pottery recovered from historic excavations and survey across the acropolis of Mycenae itself, and at several sites in its hinterland.

A short distance to the southeast of Mycenae, the comprehensive study by Eva Alram-Stern and colleagues of LN to EH I pottery from a series of well-defined contexts revealed by Katie Demakopoulou's recent excavations at Midea offers important insight into the economy of the site, and its place in the socio-technological landscape of the wider Argive Plain (**Chapter One**). The examination of ceramic shape and decorative categories is complimented by the results of a programme of thin section petrography and Scanning Electron Microscope (SEM) analyses which provide important material and technological detail to our understanding of ceramic production and consumption at the site. Networks of knowledge and practice emerge from the analysis of diachronic patterns in fabric and firing choices, as does the existence of circulatory networks which afforded the people of Early Helladic Midea access to products from at least as far afield as Aegina, on the Saronic island of Kolonna, *c.* 75km to the west.

As the final results of the Dutch excavations at Geraki (1995-2009), in Laconia, progress toward publication, Joost Crouwel provides a conspectus of the FN and EH pottery assemblage (**Chapter Five**). The FN settlement is remarkable in Laconia, and indeed, the wider Peloponnese, for the monumental fortification wall by which it was enclosed; the associated ceramic assemblage is relatively modest, but demonstrates affinities in shape and surface treatment with other important Final Neolithic sites both within, and beyond, Laconia. Very low quantities of probable EH I material (including fruitstands, bowls and mat-impressed bases) evidence a phase of occupation absent from the built record as currently known, and offer something to the discussion of the elusive Laconian EH I period. A far larger volume of pottery, and a wider repertoire of shapes, belong to EH II; most of those vessels which make up the assemblage seem entirely at home in the Laconian-northeastern Peloponnesian tradition — and none more so than those in the eponymous, elaborate and, seemingly, defiantly Laconian, Geraki Ware — raising intriguing questions around the modes by which the community at Geraki engaged with sites further afield.

The third, and final, contribution to focus on the FN and Early Bronze Age (EBA) moves beyond the Peloponnese, to Attica, where recent excavations have made it one of the most closely explored regions of Greece, and offer an unprecedented opportunity to analyse social and cultural identity within a 'small-world' or 'micro-regional' framework. Here, incorporating data from Kontra Gliate and Thorikos, Margarita Nazou (**Chapter Twelve**) addresses the definition of a ceramically, and socio-culturally, discrete, Attica. The modern region, and its borderlands and coastscapes, emerge from her analysis as ceramically heterogenous; better understood to consist of multiple stylistic (or socio-cultural) zones which emerge as the result of a complex interaction of shared knowledge and practice, and idiosyncratic responses to multiple and various pressures, imperatives and opportunities over time. For now, much about the region remains obscured by difficulties of chronology, and by inequivalence in the archaeological record across the Attic interior, although as Nazou makes clear, these are surely only temporary barriers to understanding, which are already well on their way to being broken down.

The Argolic Gulf would seem to offer similar potential for the application of a small-world framework, although the extraordinary results of recent work by Julien Beck and colleagues undertaken at Lambayanna in the Argolic bay of Kiladha, make clear the folly of restricting analysis to dry land (**Chapter Three**). Located close to the famous 'Fournoi Cluster' of the Stanford University Argolid Exploration Project, underwater survey has revealed a substantial, and hitherto unknown, EH I-II settlement, fortified at least at its western (seaward) limit by a monumental wall. Terracotta rooftiles hint at the existence of monumental architecture elsewhere in the settlement, while a substantial assemblage of ceramics, and ground and chipped stone, as with other elements of the site, invites comparison with the EH II type site of Lerna on the western coast of the Gulf. Lambayanna is one of a number of Bronze Age sites to be discovered submerged off the Peloponnesian coast (with the EH settlement at Salandi, a short distance to the north, and the remarkable LN-PG site of Pavlopetri off the Laconian Malea peninsula, **Chapter Seven**). These discoveries promise much, although there is, as yet, no evidence at Lambayanna of the elusive ceramic EH III.

The EH III 'gap' in the Peloponnese has long presented a challenge to archaeologists; Chris Mee among them. In Laconia, at least, the visibility of the period has been improved somewhat by the work of Emilia Banou and Ioanna Efstathiou-Manolakou, by the recent underwater survey at Pavlopetri, and by the work of the Ephorate of Antiquities of Laconia. To be included among this latter, are recent excavations at the EH-LH site of Karavas Soustianon, the results of which are presented here by Aris Papayiannis (**Chapter Fourteen**). EH architecture is largely absent from the site, probably as the result of extensive levelling activity during the later Bronze Age, but stratified fills, and several pits, have, collectively, yielded a substantial, and important, volume of EH III pottery. Much of this material can be paralleled at Lerna IV, although the absence at Karavas of wheelmade classes (including Fine Gray-Burnished) is a notable point of distinction. The rarity of pattern-painted decoration within the Karavas assemblage is particularly significant, given its identification as a key marker for EH III, and may go some way toward explaining why the phase has, historically, proved so difficult to recognise from surface collection.

The EH III period also features large in Walter Gauss' analysis of the parallel Early and Middle Helladic histories of the key sites of Korakou in the Corinthia and Kolonna on Aegina (**Chapter Eight**). Kolonna, of course, stands apart from the vast majority of mainland sites as a monumental survivor of the major socio-structural and economic changes which characterised the later EH and the transition to the Middle Bronze Age. Notwithstanding hints of monumental architecture at EH Korakou, Gauss' reassessment of the stratigraphy and ceramic material from Carl

Blegen's early excavations makes clear differences between the two, as currently understood, and draws on the EH-MH transition, at which both sites may have suffered destruction, as a crucial point of divergence in their respective trajectories. This might reasonably be considered to represent the organic rhythms of settlement in two distinct, if connected, parts of southern Greece, but Gauss highlights too the distorting effects of methodology in the history of excavation, and proposes that, with the future excavation of EH and MH Korakou, the two sites might prove to have been not so different after all.

The transition to the Middle Bronze Age is also addressed by Robin Barber (**Chapter Two**), this time in the first of two contributions to present material from the Cycladic site of Phylakopi on Melos. Here, Barber considers the chronological relationship between the beginning of the Middle Bronze Age in the Cyclades and on the mainland and, more specifically, on the relationship between pottery of the Cycladic 'Geometric' and Aeginetan-mainland Matt-painted styles, following a proposal first put forward by Robert Buck that the former predated the latter and, likely, served as its inspiration. Supported by new data from recent excavations at Akrotiri, Barber makes a renewed case for the identification at Phylakopi of Duncan Mackenzie's proposed Phase II-i, a 'transitional' phase between EC III and the MC period.

A rather different set of questions is asked of Phylakopi by David Smith (**Chapter Sixteen**), who presents a diachronic analysis of cooking vessels and culinary practice at the site, based on the restudy of material recovered during the 1896-1899 excavations of the British School at Athens; an important lens through which to view the networks within which Phylakopi operated, and the manner in which those connections were integrated into the socio-cultural identities of its inhabitants. Early Cycladic practices emerge from analysis as fairly typical of the wider archipelago, with important ceramic parallels from Dhaskalio and Akrotiri; subsequent contact with Middle Minoan Crete prompts the reproduction of Minoan cooking shapes by Melian potters, and, more rarely, the arrival to Phylakopi of genuine Cretan imports, suggesting the adoption of Cretan cooking styles, if not, necessarily, the introduction of Cretan cuisine, and not, it seems, to the detriment of Melian practices. During the Late Cycladic, and particularly during LH III, the presence of rare shapes, such as the 'Mycenaean' griddle pan, align at least some components of dining at Phylakopi with those of 'palatial' centres on the mainland and Crete, suggesting the sometime reproduction of perceived 'elite' dining behaviour and, together with the earlier Minoanising component, offering an important perspective on the complex and cross-scale choices which underpinned the emergent phenomena of 'Minoanisation' and 'Mycenaeanisation' in the later Bronze Age settlement.

The contributions of Gauss, Barber and Smith illustrate the rich rewards to be won through the mining of unpublished ceramic material from historic excavations. Angelos Papadopoulos' discussion of Mycenaean ceramics and other material recovered during the late 19th century AD British Museum excavations at Episkopi-Bamboula (Kourion Site D) on Cyprus, represents something of a cautionary tale, illustrating the difficulties that might accompany any attempt to do so (**Chapter Thirteen**). Navigating an incomplete and, sometimes, contradictory paper record, and the uncertainty arising from problematic storage in the years immediately following excavation, Papadopoulos is, nevertheless, able to tease out important detail from the Cyprus Museum 'share' of this otherwise little-known assemblage, and further illuminate the economic and social networks which connected mainland Greece and Cyprus during the Late Bronze Age.

Mercouris Georgiadis (**Chapter Nine**) and Iphiyenia Tournavitou (**Chapter Seventeen**) transport us to the island of Kythera, and to the remarkable peak sanctuaries at Leska and Ayios Georgios sto Vouno, respectively. The two sites each present a very different perspective on the peak sanctuary phenomenon as it was adopted, or adapted, outside of Crete. The site at Leska, in the west of the island, has yielded no trace of architecture, nor any metal objects. It has, however, yielded a MM-LM I ceramic assemblage in Kytheran fabrics which included Minoanising drinking, serving and cooking vessels, and rare examples of more specialised shapes (ring-handled basins, rhyta and braziers), attesting to the importance of consumption — although not, it appears, the act of cooking itself — in ritual practice at the site, and the role played by the communities of Kythera in articulating the connection between Crete and the Peloponnese.

A similar articulatory role can be recognised at Ayios Georgios sto Vouno, which dominates views from the site of Kastri, and across the southeastern part of the island, and which yielded a far larger, and much more varied, material assemblage than its western Kytheran counterpart. The evidence from this site, and from others on Crete, are used by Tournavitou to re-examine the use of fire in peak sanctuary ritual. The distinction of ritual from more pragmatic concerns (heat, light) is, now, a difficult undertaking, although historical and ethnographic examples of fire ritual provide potential parallels for their use in the Bronze Age Aegean, and, fires emerge from Tournavitou's analysis as a relatively common feature of the peak sanctuary record. From site to site, however, the evidence for prehistoric fire or pyre use is highly variable, and oftentimes uncertain, and the manner in which they may have been deployed as ritual apparatus, including for the destruction of ceramics and other votive objects, is far from clear. The latter practice may have been observed only relatively sporadically, perhaps dictated by atypical circumstance rather than by religious orthodoxy, although we are reminded, too, of the variety of ways in which fire has been incorporated into historic and modern ritual, which may leave no material trace.

The excavation of the Mycenaean palace at Ayios Vasileios by Adamantia Vasilogamvrou and colleagues represents one of the most important excavations of recent times, and offers a compelling response to long-standing uncertainty over the location of a 'palatial' centre in Laconia. With work ongoing, the site has already yielded a wealth of material — including a large number of Linear B tablets — which promises to reframe the political geography of the region, and illuminate the relationships that the Eurotas Valley enjoyed with the wider Aegean during the Middle and Late Helladic periods. In **Chapter Ten**, Eleftheria Kardamaki and colleagues examine the middle and later palatial ceramic assemblage of LH IIIA2 to LH IIIB2 (-IIIC Early) from the area of the North Cemetery and the court, addressing the chronological relationship between the Argive and Laconian ceramic sequences, and clarifying key differences in the representation of particular shapes and decorative schema at Ayios Vasileios compared to other sites in Laconia, and to contemporary Argive centres. The causal factors which underpin these differences — economic, political or social, or some combination thereof — for now, remain obscure; their resolution contingent on further excavation and ever more refined analyses.

The final Mycenaean period, LH IIIC, is considered from opposite ends of the Peloponnese by Jeremy Rutter (**Chapter Fifteen**) and Chrysanthi Gallou (**Chapter Seven**). At Aigeira, on the southern shore of the Corinthian Gulf, analysis of material from a number of substantial, and well stratified, LH IIIC deposits has resulted in the identification of five distinct LH IIIC ceramic phases. Rutter's detailed analysis of this assemblage offers a complex picture of the settlement's shifting priorities, practices, and, perhaps ideologies, through its final settlement phase. Hand manufactured (including coil-built) vessels in several imported and local fabric classes are shown to appear during the earlier part of the sequence (APP 1-3) alongside more typical wheel-thrown Mycenaean shapes, in an assemblage characterised by conservatism of shape and an unexpected heterogeneity of ceramic technologies. Low numbers of sherds belonging to the later sequence, APP 4 and APP 5, hint at change, but are, currently, too few to make clear their significance. Distinctions in the form and decoration of vessels intended for private and public use make clear the retained value of ceramics for framing social interaction.

Gallou and colleagues offer a contemporary view from southern Laconia, exploring themes of connectivity and communication at the transition from the Late Bronze Age to the Iron Age. During the post-palatial flux of the late 12th and early 11th centuries BC, several Laconian coastal sites, including Epidauros Limera, enjoyed a period of relative prosperity; the latter buoyed by integration within both Peloponnesian and wider Aegean, Attic, Cycladic and Cretan networks and, perhaps, by the arrival of migrants displaced from former palatial centres, whose influence is manifest in ceramic innovation. The authors also present important new ceramic evidence for post-palatial occupation at the now-submerged settlement of Pavlopetri, a site which, along with Epidauros Limera, provides a rare example of survival on the Laconian coast after LH IIIC Middle. The LH IIIC Late to Protogeometric material from Epidauros Limera makes clear the survival of Cretan, Cycladic, Dodecanesian and mainland relationships, and characterises the site as something of a Postpalatial cultural melange. It was, the authors propose, a combination of strategic advantage, deeply-rooted and far-reaching socio-economic networks, socio-cultural commonality and an emergent resilience to the most disruptive effects of the dissolution of palatial power structures, which allowed the harbour settlements of southern Laconia to adapt and thrive, at the threshold of the first millennium BC.

D.M.S and W.G.C.

List of Contributors

Eva Alram-Stern

Institute for Oriental and European Archaeology Austrian Academy of Sciences, 11-13 Hollandstrasse, 1020, Vienna, Austria.

Robin Barber

The British School at Athens, 52 Souedias, GR 10676, Athens, Greece.

Julien Beck

Département des sciences de l'Antiquité, Université de Genève, Faculté des Lettres, 5, rue de Candolle, CH – 1211 Genève 4.

Clare Burke

Institute for Oriental and European Archaeology Austrian Academy of Sciences, 11-13 Hollandstrasse, 1020, Vienna, Austria.
Department of Archaeology, University of Sheffield, Minalloy House, 10-16 Regent Street, Sheffield, S1 3NJ, United Kingdom.

William Cavanagh

Department of Archaeology, University of Nottingham, Nottingham, NG7 2RD, United Kingdom.

Joost Crouwel

University of Amsterdam, Amsterdam Archaeological Centre, PO box 94203, 1090 GE Amsterdam.

Andreas Darlas

Ephorate of Palaeoanthropology-Speleology, 34B Ardittou, GR 11636, Athens, Greece.

Peter M. Day

Department of Archaeology, University of Sheffield, Minalloy House, 10-16 Regent Street, Sheffield, S1 3NJ, United Kingdom.
Institute of Nanoscience and Nanotechnology, N.C.S.R. 'Demokritos', Patriarchou Grigoriou E & 27 Neapoleos, GR 15341, Athens, Greece.

Katie Demakopoulou

Director Emerita, National Archaeological Museum Athens, 28 Oktovriou 44, GR 10682, Athens, Greece.

Patrizia Birchler Emery

Département des sciences de l'Antiquité, Université de Genève, Faculté des Lettres, 5, rue de Candolle, CH – 1211 Genève 4.

Elizabeth French†

The British School at Athens, 52 Souedias, GR 10676, Athens, Greece.

Chrysanthi Gallou

Department of Archaeology, University of Nottingham, Nottingham, NG7 2RD, United Kingdom.

Walter Gauss

Austrian Archaeological Institute of the Austrian Academy of Sciences, Athens Branch, 26 Leoforos Alexandras, GR 10683, Athens, Greece.

Mercouris Georgiadis

Department of History and Archaeology, National and Kapodistrian University of Athens.

Vasco Hachtmann

Institute for Prehistory, Early History and Near Eastern Archaeology, University of Heidelberg.

Jon Henderson

Department of Archaeology, School of History, Classics and Archaeology, University of Edinburgh.

Nektarios Karadimas

Aegeus, Society for Aegean Prehistory, 6 Litous, GR 15124, Athens, Greece.

Eleftheria Kardamaki

Institute for Oriental and European Archaeology Austrian Academy of Sciences, 11-13 Hollandstrasse, 1020, Vienna, Austria.

Stella Katsarou

Ephorate of Palaeoanthropology-Speleology, 34B Ardittou, GR 11636, Athens, Greece.

Despina Koutsoumba

Ephorate of underwater antiquities, 30 Kallisperi, GR 11742, Athens, Greece.

Margarita Nazou

National Hellenic Research Foundation, 48 Vasileos Konstantinou, GR 11635, Athens, Greece.

Angelos Papadopoulos

College Year in Athens, Greece, 5 Plateia Stadiou, GR 11635, Athens, Greece.

Aris Papayiannis

Institute of Transbalkan Cultural Cooperation (ITCC-ΙΔΙΠΟΣ)

Ephorate of Antiquities of Thesprotia, 68 Kyprou, GR 46100, Igoumenitsa, Thesprotia, Greece.

Josette Renard

Université Paul Valéry - Montpellier, ArScAn — Protohistoire égéenne, UMR 7041 Maison de l'Archéologie et de l'Ethnologie, Boîte 16, 21 allée de l'université, F-92023 Nanterre Cedex, France.

Jeremy Rutter

Department of Classics, Dartford College, Hanover, New Hampshire 03755-3562, USA.

David Michael Smith

Department of Archaeology, Classics and Egyptology, University of Liverpool, 12-14 Abercromby Square, Liverpool, L69 7WZ, United Kingdom.

Elias Spondylis

Ephorate of Underwater Antiquities, 59 Dionysiou Areopagitou and Erechthiou, GR 11742, Athens, Greece.

Iphiyenia Tournavitou

Department of History, Archaeology, and Social Anthropology, University of Thessaly, GR 38221 Volos, Greece.

Adamantia Vasilogamvrou

Director Emerita of Antiquities, Ministry of Culture.

Sofia Voutsaki

Groningen Institute of Archaeology (GIA), Groningen University, Poststraat 6, 9712 ER Groningen, The Netherlands.

List of Abbreviations

14C   Carbon-14
16C   Carbon-16
18C   Carbon-18
acc. no.   accession number
AD   *Anno Domini*
APP   Aigeira Pottery Phase
ARF   Argillaceous Rock Fragment
ASCSA   American School of Classical Studies at Athens
BC   Before Christ
BIAA   British Institute of Archaeology at Ankara
BM   British Museum
BP   Before Present
BSA   British School at Athens
c.   *circa*
cal.   calibrated
cat. no.   catalogue number
CD   Compact Disc
cf.   *conferatur* (compare)
cm   centimetres
CM   Cyprus Museum
e.g.   *exempli gratia*
EB   Early Bronze
EBA   Early Bronze Age
EC   Early Cycladic
EDS   Energy Dispersive Spectroscopy
EH   Early Helladic
EIA   Early Iron Age
EM   Early Minoan
EMP   Early Matt-Painted
EN   Early Neolithic
EPCA   Ephorate of Prehistoric and Classical Antiquities
EPG   Early Protogeometric
ESAG   Swiss School of Archaeology in Greece
et al.   *et alii*
FCP   Franchthi Ceramic Phase
fig.   figure
FM   Furumark Motif
FN   Final Neolithic
FS   Furumark Shape

FSA   Fellow of the Society of Antiquaries
g   grams
GPS   Geographical Positioning System
ha   hectares
i.e.   *id est*
INSTAP   Institute for the Study of Aegean Prehistory
kg   kilograms
km   kilometres
LB   Late Bronze
LBA   Late Bronze Age
LC   Late Cycladic
LH   Late Helladic
LM   Late Minoan
LN   Late Neolithic
m   metres
m2   square metres
MBA   Middle Bronze Age
MC   Middle Cycladic
MH   Middle Helladic
MM   Middle Minoan
MN   Middle Neolithic
MNI   Minimum Number of Individuals
NSCR   National Centre for Scientific Research ('Demokritos')
MYBE   Mycenae-Berbati NAA fabric group
n.   note
NAA   Neutron Activation Analysis
no.   number
OES   Optical Emission Spectroscopy
PG   Protogeometric
pl.   plate
PPNA   Pre-Pottery Neolithic A
s.v.   *sub voce* (under the heading)
SCE   Swedish Cyprus Expedition
SEM   Scanning Electron Microscopy
SEM-EDS   Scanning Electron Microscopy with Energy Dispersive Spectroscopy
SM   Submycenaean
SMP   Soft Matt-Painted
TIR   Tiryns NAA fabric group
σ   sigma error

Professor Christopher Mee (1950-2013)

To strive, to seek, to find, and not to yield.

Spanning a total of four decades, Chris' contribution to Greek archaeology was broad in scope and ambition, and significant both for the understanding that it delivered and the friendships which formed in its wake.

Chris was born in Hereford in August 1950, and demonstrated an early aptitude for academia, earning a top-ten county ranking for his eleven-plus exam and, by virtue of it, a free place at the Hereford Cathedral School (where he would come to serve as House Monitor).

His first experience of archaeology came whilst a pupil at Hereford, with enrolment on an extramural course on the topic of prehistoric, Roman and early Medieval archaeology at Hereford Teacher Training College, taught by city archaeologist, Ron Shoesmith, and Stan Stanford, who was then extramural-supervisor at Birmingham University. Chris' enthusiasm for the subject drove him very quickly toward the field; a move which saw a part of every Saturday given over to the processing of midden material recovered during excavations beneath the Medieval city walls. Before long, he was given the chance to excavate a sondage of his own, although his efforts therein would prove entirely fruitless. Afternoons were spent at the county library thumbing the *Transactions of the Woolhope Naturalists' Field Club*, among other local journals, as well as the first issues of *Current Archaeology* and, during his final year of sixth form, he undertook an archaeological survey of the Roman villa at Spoonley Wood in Sudeley, organised with the help of his Classics teacher, Harry Rhodes, which provided opportunity to hone drafting skills on state plans of mosaic floors and standing architecture.

Oxbridge entrance exams resulted in a call to interview at Cambridge, although Chris chose instead to take up a place reading Classics at the University of Bristol. Fate, perhaps, had intervened, since it was during his first year of studies here that he was introduced to Christa, who was reading French and shared a room with one of Chris' departmental colleagues. At Bristol, his passion for the Greek past was fostered by the likes of Nicholas Hammond, Wills Professor of Greek and President of the Hellenic Society (1965-1968) and John Cook, Chair of Ancient History and Archaeology and former Director of the British School at Athens (1946-1954), whose experience of the eastern Aegean seems certain to have informed Chris' own academic proclivities.

Supported by a postgraduate scholarship from Bristol (1971-1973), Chris undertook his first visit to Greece in 1972, as the country creaked and groaned beneath the weight of military dictatorship. He was, by that time, enrolled at Bedford College, University of London, under the supervision of Nicolas Coldstream, and was admitted as a student at the British School at Athens, where he remained, engaged in doctoral research, until late November. His studies through the following year were supported by a scholarship from the Greek Ministry of Education (1973-1974), and throughout by monies from the Central London Research Fund. Chris spent July 1973 at Nauplion, working alongside Elizabeth French on the study of the Late Helladic pottery recovered from the Citadel House at Mycenae during William Taylour's 1968 campaign (Taylour 1969). Late in the season, he made the short journey to Mycenae itself to assist in the excavation of a group of intact LH IIIB-C vessels exposed in a remnant baulk of the earlier British works during the course of service excavations led by Spyridon Iakovides and George Mylonas (see Catling 1974). In September 1973, he and Christa were married.

Chris' first foray into Laconian archaeology came in May 1974, as the newlyweds joined Hector Catling for the second season of excavation at the Late Helladic mansion on the Menelaion Ridge above Sparta. In October, he travelled with Christa to assume the position of Institute Scholar at the British Institute of Archaeology at Ankara (BIAA). Outside respective institutional responsibilities, their time was spent travelling throughout eastern and southern Anatolia, and Chris was able to develop his understanding of the Mycenaean presence on the eastern Aegean littoral, working alongside Elizabeth French on the study of the Late Helladic pottery from the sites of Tarsus, Kazanli and Mersin, then stored in the Adana Museum, and on other groups from Miletos (at Akköy) and Aphrodisias (see Hall *et al.* 1976: 15; Mee 1978: 121).

Much of his doctoral study was finalised in the BIAA library during the earlier part of 1975, and so Chris and Christa returned to Greece during the summer; travelling together to Nauplion with Elizabeth French and William Taylour for a further three-week study of material from Mycenae, before Chris ventured northward to the Langadas Basin and Ken Wardle's excavation in the Late Bronze Age-Early Iron Age settlement at Assiros Toumba (see Wardle, Halstead and Jones 1980: 234, n.28).

Following submission of his thesis, *The Dodecanese in the Bronze Age* (two volumes; later adapted for publication as *Rhodes in the Bronze Age*), in October, Chris returned with Christa to Athens, spending the session as David Student at the British School (1975-1976) before his appointment as Robin Barber's successor to the Assistant Directorship, under Hector Catling. May 1976 saw a month-long stay at Aphyssou for the Menelaion excavation study season, working in the shadow of the Taygetos alongside Paul Halstead, then a doctoral student at Cambridge, and Bedford College alumnus, Bill Cavanagh. In November, as Assistant Director-elect, he was briefly required to assume the responsibilities of the Knossos Fellow, as incumbent Fellow, Roger Howell, returned to the Greek mainland to study material recovered during the University of Minnesota excavations at Nichoria. His short residency on Crete resulted in yet more fieldwork, this time in the excavation of a probable Late Minoan chamber tomb at Lower Gypsadhes, Knossos, which yielded a small quantity of LM IB-IIIA1 pottery though had seemingly been abandoned during construction following the collapse of its roof (see Catling 1977: 11).

On his succession to the Assistant Directorship on December 1st 1976, Chris was immediately confronted with a heavy administrative workload, as well as responsibility over the then recently established Summer Course in the Archaeology and Topography of Ancient Greece; a legacy of Robin's tenure, in the successful execution of which he was ably assisted by Christa (as Byzantine expert), Bill, who was resident at the School throughout the summer of 1977 finalising his doctoral study of prehistoric and Early Iron Age Attic burial practices, and Bill's wife, Lena, then Director's Secretary. Autumn brought travel to northern Greece and, in November, through a combination of chance, good fortune, and an aptitude for appearing to all others as if they were supposed to be there, Chris and Christa found themselves packed into a crowded lecture theatre at the University of Thessaloniki, as Manolis Andronikos formally announced to an astonished press his identification of the Tomb of Phillip at Vergina.

The role also presented Chris new research opportunities, including collaborations with Richard Jones, then Research Officer (and later, Director) of the new Fitch Laboratory, on the analysis by optical emission spectroscopy (OES) of LH IIIA2-C pottery from the chamber tomb cemeteries of Moschou and Macra Vunara at Ialysos (Jones and Mee 1978; Jones, Mee and Catling 1978; Mee 1978), and with Bill on an analysis of the phenomenon of tomb reuse on the Greek mainland, Crete and the Dodecanese during LH IIIC (Cavanagh and Mee 1978). This latter would mark the beginning of what would become an extraordinary academic partnership.

Chris and Christa travelled again to the eastern Aegean in February 1978 to undertake research for a co-authored guidebook to the history and archaeology of the island of Kos; an easy-going work struck through with subtle good humour, which included a warning to prospective travellers that the orchestra of the Roman theatre at Kardamena 'is now patrolled by a large pig'. May through June placed both, along with Bill (then Macmillan Student) and numerous other members of the British School (many redirected from the Menelaion excavation), at the rescue excavation of the Knossos North Cemetery, a large swathe of which had been placed under immediate threat by the granting of approval to the University of Crete for the construction of a new Medical Faculty on the site. Duties on the summer school, and a short period of study at Rhodes Museum followed, before Chris ceded the post of Assistant Director to Tony Spawforth and returned with Christa to the UK in December as a new father to daughter Catherine, and Lecturer in Classical Archaeology at the University of Liverpool, following the departure of Christiane Sourvinou-Inwood.

It was in post at Liverpool that Chris embarked upon the research which today occasions such high regard.

Chris' first major fieldwork project was, by his own account, motivated by the desire to escape a particularly bitter Liverpool winter. In reality, his arrival at Liverpool had coincided with a shift which saw students based in the Department of Ancient History and Classical Archaeology for the first time, and with the commencement of a new BPhil in Classical Archaeology (beginning October 1980) and Chris was concerned both to establish a suitable research project and to provide for his new students an in-house venue in which they might gain first-hand experience of Greek archaeology. The endeavour was a collaborative one, undertaken with two other recent arrivals at the university, Hamish Forbes and Lin Foxhall, and was located on Methana; a discrete, semi-arid peninsula of approximately 50km2 projecting into the Saronic Gulf from the eastern Argive coastline. Hamish had, from 1972 to 1974, carried out ethnographic research into Methanite agricultural practices (see Forbes 1976; 1982; 2007) and so had become familiar with the peninsula, and its archaeological remains, such as he had encountered them in the field. The terrain was unforgiving; the Methanite landscape characterised by a challenging volcanic relief dominated by andesitic and dacitic domes and lava flows, and by the extensive use of terracing to maximise the agricultural availability of soils across the poorly watered, and largely unmechanised, interior. It was these difficulties, however, which invited questions about the ancient occupation of the peninsula and the character of its socio-cultural and economic relationships with the Peloponnesian interior at its east and the islands of the Saronic Gulf to the west. Following a successful permit application to the Attic Ephorate, the Methana Survey Project was born.

Chris undertook a brief trip to the peninsula during the summer of 1981 to conduct a preliminary reconnaissance, identifying suitable facilities in the main town - called Methana officially, though Loutra by the locals on account of its hot springs - and confirming the presence of several obvious and interesting sites. He returned the following year, accompanied by Lin and Hamish, to carry out a programme of selective sampling which yielded a still larger number of findspots, with a greater topographical and chronological range than anticipated, and confirmed Methana's archaeological potential. Chris' appointment at Liverpool had been made permanent in October 1981 and the Methana Project developed even as major UGC cutbacks in university financing forced John V.H. Eames' early retirement and presented Chris with the need to cover additional teaching on the Roman world. Intensive survey proper was begun in 1984, taking place over three seasons between 1984 and 1986, with a fourth (study) season in 1987, during which time Chris was appointed to the Charles W. Jones Lectureship in Classical Archaeology at Liverpool (October 1985). The project was headquartered in an old-fashioned hotel, with kitchen facilities in which guests could prepare their meals and a large garden — complete with roaming chickens — where the survey team could eat a mid-day meal in the shade of mature trees on their return from an arduous day's survey on steep slopes typically clothed in aggressive vegetation. It followed in the wake of Stanford's pioneering Argolid Exploration Project (1972; 1979-1983) and the Melos Survey Project (1974-1976), and positioned Chris and colleagues at the forefront of a wave of methodological and theoretical development in landscape archaeology and archaeological survey which swept across the field of Mediterranean archaeology over the decade and saw contemporary Peloponnesian projects in the Eurotas (1983-1989), Nemea (1984-1986) and Berbati (1988-1990) Valleys.

Skills and protocols honed on Methana in response to the difficult landscape and its (pre-)historic modification (devised — according to Chris — to protect the field team from 'sudden death, or at least serious loss of blood', see Forbes and Mee 1997: 4) would be called

upon again, and soon. Less than five years later, and with the final report of the Methana Survey still some way off, Chris, then Head of Department at Liverpool, turned his attention to central Laconia, and to the problem of those so-called 'small rural sites' identified in large numbers by the British-Dutch Laconia Survey (1983-1989) on which Bill, by then at the University of Nottingham, had shared directorial duties with Joost Crouwel of the University of Amsterdam; another long-time friend of Chris' encountered first during his stint as site supervisor for the 1973 and 1974 seasons of the Menelaion campaign. The resultant Laconia Rural Sites Project (1992-1995) saw Bill and Chris, together with Liverpool geographer and Methana veteran, Peter James, deploy a battery of complementary non-intrusive techniques — geophysical prospection, soil and environmental analyses, and ultra-intensive systematic surface sampling — to a select number of these sites in an attempt to better resolve their structural character and the wider socio-economic landscapes within, and upon, which they operated. The innovative interdisciplinary research undertaken here, and on Methana, ultimately yielded a body of work still hugely important for the insight it delivers into the natural and anthropogenic modification of the Greek landscape and the diachronic networks and occupational strategies of two very different regions of the Peloponnese.

Closer to home, 1993 saw the publication, with Jenny Doole, of a comprehensive illustrated catalogue of the extensive collections of Aegean material culture (EN to LH IIIC) held in the (now) World Museum Liverpool and the University's own Garstang Museum of Archaeology, while 1994 brought with it recognition of excellence in both teaching and research in the form of election as a Fellow of the Society of Antiquaries (FSA) in March. Chris succeeded Graham Shipley as editor of the *Annual of the British School at Athens* in January 1997 (volume 92). This responsibility he would keep to 2002 (volume 97), alongside his work on a succession of co-authored publications which emerged during the later decade, among which are to be found the final volume of the Methana survey (Mee and Forbes 1997), a contribution to the Corpus of Cypriote Antiquities detailing the collections of the Garstang Museum of Archaeology and Liverpool's Williamson Art Gallery (Mee and Steel 1998) and, in the same year, *A Private Place: Death in Prehistoric Greece* (Cavanagh and Mee 1998): the first and definitive study of the Palaeolithic to Late Bronze Age Aegean mortuary record, named for a line in Marvell's *To His Coy Mistress*.

Throughout, Chris had sought to develop a long-term programme of systematic excavation in Laconia, although the Laconia Rural Sites Project had failed to bear fruit as far as the identification of potential targets, as had been the hope. The 1989 publication by Josette Renard (then affiliated to the University of Clermont-Ferrand and the Centre national de la recherche scientifique) of Neolithic and Early Helladic remains recovered by Otto von Vacano's wartime trial soundings on the east of the tell at Kouphovouno (*Le site Néolithique et Helladique Ancien de Kouphovouno, Laconie. Fouilles de O.-W von Vacano, 1941*), however, presented an alternative prospect within the Sparta basin. The site, although obscure, was not entirely unknown, having been included among those sites extensively surveyed first by Helen Waterhouse and later by Richard Hope-Simpson (1960) and, more recently, by Emilia Banou (1996; 2000). Such was the quantity, and quality, of material visible at the surface mid-century that the site was singled out as perhaps the 'most important Neolithic settlement in Laconia' (Hope-Simpson and Waterhouse 1960: 74). No other contemporary Laconian open site had then been subject to systematic excavation and the very great potential of Kouphovouno to illuminate the Neolithic and Bronze Age occupation of the region was clear.

The Kouphovouno Project, a *synergasia* between the British School at Athens and the 5th Ephorate of Prehistoric and Classical Antiquities (EPCA) (now the Ephorate of Antiquities of Laconia) under the directorship of Chris, Bill and Josette, had its inaugural field season in mid-June 1999 in the form of an intensive surface survey which continued until mid-August. This afforded Chris the opportunity to apply the multidisciplinary methodological techniques pioneered by the Laconia Rural Sites Project to a large, multi-period site, supported, again, by Peter James who, with Alison Jones, oversaw the analysis of cores and soil samples, and by Chris' former doctoral student, Neil Brodie, who directed the geophysical survey. The inception of the project was a boon to Liverpool, Nottingham, and Clermont-Ferrand, and to the student bodies of all three institutions wherefrom large numbers of the field team were drawn. The project was based at a campsite on the national Sparta-Mystras road, which boasted both a swimming pool (supplied from the mountains and always ice-cold as a result) and an on-site taverna(!), as well as an extremely affable proprietor, Mr Panagiotis Kapetaneas, who would each summer turn over his storage space for conversion to the project's incident room, his fields to a swamp of tents, and his trees to a network of hammocks which provided for the team shady respite from the, often extreme, heat of the Laconian summer. Similar relief was sought in weekend excursions to Gytheio on the southern coast, or treks (often led by Chris at pace) through the Langadhiotissa Pass from Parori and up into the cooler elevations of the Taygetos massif, occasionally overnighting in the bunkhouse at Varvara. Five seasons of excavation and two study seasons (2004 and 2007) followed, during

which time Chris was awarded the title of Charles W. Jones Professor of Classical Archaeology (July 2000), made Sub-Dean of the Faculty of Arts (August 2000), and subsequently assumed the duties of Head of the School of Archaeology, Classics and Egyptology at Liverpool (from January 2003).

The excavations at Kouphovouno delivered an extraordinary quantity of pottery, not least that recovered from an impressive 4.5m deep sondage cut through the entire stratigraphic sequence on the west side of the tell. It was Chris' diligent reading of this material, a ceramic yield weighing in the hundreds of kilograms, in the two *apothiki* of the 5th EPCA at Sparta that prompted him to turn his academic attention toward the production and consumption of pottery in Laconia and the wider Peloponnese during the Neolithic and Early Helladic periods, and to the social and economic networks within which it circulated; an avenue of research which promised at once new perspective on the surface record and the illumination of some of the darkest corners of Laconian prehistory. These themes quickly found expression in Oliver Dickinson's festschrift, *Autochthon* (2005), wherein was posed the damning question: 'why were most Final Neolithic potters so incompetent?' (Cavanagh and Mee 2005: 31) and gained a louder voice in Chris' own contribution to his 2007 volume, co-edited with Josette Renard, *Cooking up the Past: Food and Culinary Practices in the Neolithic and Bronze Age Aegean*.

In 2008, Chris and Bill were honoured with a festschrift of their own; a volume in recognition of their contribution to date, edited by former doctoral students Chrysanthi Gallou, Mercouris Georgiadis and Gina Muskett, and filled with contributions from a cast of long-time friends and colleagues in whose own works Bill and Chris are often cited in gratitude. The same year saw Chris offer a chapter on the Mycenaean Aegean to Cynthia Shelmerdine's *Cambridge Companion to the Aegean Bronze Age*. In January 2010, Chris returned to the British School at Athens in an official capacity as Visiting Fellow; a four-month post which provided time and chance to work at Athens and Sparta on the publication of the Middle and Late Neolithic pottery assemblages from Kouphovouno. Accompanied by Christa, who undertook her own work on the School's early archive, it also permitted Chris to finalise his textbook, *Greek Archaeology: A Thematic approach* (2011); a work which, unsurprisingly, champions an interdisciplinary narrative and a joined-up perspective on the Greek past: a call for 'ever-closer union' by a man who had, throughout his academic career, bridged the divide between Classical and prehistoric Aegean archaeology.

A contribution on death and burial to Eric Cline's *Oxford Handbook of the Bronze Age Aegean* (2010) appeared in the same year, although Kouphovouno and Laconia continued to form the focus of Chris' later works. Included among these are contributions to Jerry Rutter's (2011) festschrift, *Our Cups are Full*, and an editorial turn, in partnership with Geraki Project field-director Mieke Prent, for the proceedings of a 2010 conference on Early Helladic Laconia within a special issue of the journal of the Netherlands Institute at Athens, *Pharos* (2012). Several studies have also appeared posthumously which have delivered truly important insight into Early Bronze Age mainland chronology (Cavanagh, Mee and Renard 2016) and the agricultural strategies of Greece's Neolithic farmers (Vaiglova *et al.* 2014); indeed, recent work has positioned Kouphovouno as one of the earliest sites in Europe to utilise selective manuring as a means to increase crop yields, transforming the landscape of the Sparta basin from terra incognita to a hub of agricultural innovation.

What has become clear in the course of writing this account is how thoroughly inadequate it has proved in conveying the warmth and wit of the man himself. Those who have offered their own memories of Chris invariably recollect his relaxed affability, kindness, and good humour, and an enviable capacity for keeping his head when all about were losing theirs, despite whatever doubt or turmoil may have run beneath the surface. To his students, he was a man of calm authority, whose lectures presented a model for clarity of structure and presentation and were rightly favoured as a result. He played the saxophone. He was immensely proud of his family.

Chris ended his career as Emeritus Professor, a title conferred in August 2012 following his retirement from the Charles W. Jones Chair of Classical Archaeology, and the forthcoming publication of the excavations at Kouphovouno will represents Chris' final academic contribution to the study of Greek prehistory. His legacy at Liverpool and beyond is, however, assured, thanks to the foundation of an eponymous annual lecture series and the creation of a travel award intended to allow current students to begin to forge their own path through the Mediterranean, as Chris himself had done more than 40 years previously.

D.M.S.

Acknowledgements.

Thanks are due to all of those who, collectively, have offered their own, invariably affectionate, recollections of Chris or have aided in clarifying his various appointments, and particularly to Prof. Bill Cavanagh, Prof. John Davies, Prof. Hamish Forbes, Dr John Gait, Mrs Christa Mee, Ms. Clare Morgan-Jones at Hereford Cathedral School, Prof. Christopher Tuplin, and Mr David Walters.

Christopher Mee: A Bibliography

Barker, G., C. Mee, W. Cavanagh, R. Schon and S.M. Thompson
2000. Responses to 'The hidden landscape of Prehistoric Greece'. *Journal of Mediterranean Archaeology* 13: 100-123.
Bienkowski, P., C.B. Mee and E. Slater
2005. *Writing and Ancient Near Eastern Society: Papers in Honour of Alan R. Millard* (Library of Hebrew Bible/Old Testament Studies 426). New York and London: T & T Clark.
Cavanagh, W.G. and C.B. Mee
1978. The reuse of earlier tombs in the LH IIIC period. *The Annual of the British School at Athens* 73: 31-44.
1990. The location of Mycenaean chamber tombs in the Argolid, in R. Hägg and G.C. Nordquist (eds) *Celebrations of Death and Divinity in the Bronze Age Argolid. Proceedings of the Sixth International Symposium at the Swedish Institute at Athens, 11-13 June, 1988* (Skrifter utgivna av Svenska institutet i Athen., 4o, 40): 55-63. Stockholm: the Swedish Institute at Athens.
1994. The Laconia Rural Sites Project. *Archaeological Reports* 40: 19.
1995a. Mourning before and after the Dark Age, in C. Morris (ed.) *Klados: Essays in Honour of J.N. Coldstream* (Bulletin of the Institute of Classical Studies Supplement 63): 45-61. London: University of London Institute of Classical Studies.
1995b. The Laconia Rural Sites Project. *Archaeological Reports* 41: 14-15.
1998. *A Private Place: Death in Prehistoric Greece* (Studies in Mediterranean Archaeology 125). Jonsered: Paul Åström.
1999. Building the Treasury of Atreus, in P. Betancourt, V. Karageorghis, R. Laffineur, and W.-D. Niemeier (eds) *Meletemata: Studies in Aegean Archaeology Presented to Malcolm H. Wiener as he Enters his 65th Year* (Aegaeum 20): 93-102. Liège: the University of Liège.
2005. Reflections on Neolithic Laconia, in A. Dakouri-Hild and S. Sherratt (eds) *Autochthon: Papers Presented to O.T.P.K. Dickinson on the Occasion of his Retirement* (British Archaeological Reports International Series 1432): 24-37. Oxford: Archaeopress.
2007. Functional analysis of survey sites, in R. Westgate, N. Fisher and J. Whitley (eds) *Building Communities. House, Settlement and Society in the Aegean and Beyond. Proceedings of a Conference Held at Cardiff University, 17-21 April 2001* (The British School at Athens Studies 15): 11-17. London: the British School at Athens.
2009. Perati kai Para Pera, in D. Daniilidou (ed.) Δώρον. Τιμητικός τόμος για τον Σπύρο Ιακωβίδη (Ακαδημία Αθηνών, Κέντρον Ερεύνης της Αρχαιότητος Σειρά Μονογραφίων 6): 169-189. Athens: the Academy of Athens.
2011. Minding the gaps in Early Helladic Laconia, in W. Gauss, M. Lindblom, R.A.K. Smith and J.C. Wright (eds) *Our Cups are Full. Pottery and Society in the Aegean*

Bronze Age. Papers presented to Jeremy B. Rutter on the Occasion of his 65th Birthday (British Archaeological Reports International Series 2227): 40-50. Oxford: Archaeopress.

2015. 'In vino veritas': raising a toast at Mycenaean funerals, in Y. Galanakis, T. Wilkinson and J. Bennett (eds) *ΑΘΥΡΜΑΤΑ: Critical Essays on the Archaeology of the Eastern Mediterranean in Honour of E. Susan Sherratt*: 51-56. Oxford: Archaeopress.

2016. The MH cemetery at Kouphovouno, Sparta, Lakonia, in E. Papadopoulou-Chrysikopoulou, V. Chrysikopoulos and G. Christakopoulou (eds) *Achaios. Studies Presented to Professor Thanasis I. Papadopoulos*: 45-52. Oxford: Archaeopress.

Cavanagh, W.G., C.B. Mee and P. James

2005. *The Laconia Rural Sites Project* (The British School at Athens Supplementary Volume 35). London: the British School at Athens.

Cavanagh, W.G., C.B. Mee and J. Renard

2000. Kouphovouno. *Archaeological Reports* 46: 40.

2001. Kouphovouno (Messénie). *Bulletin de Correspondance Hellénique* 125(2): 645-648.

2002a. Kouphovouno. *Archaeological Reports* 48: 31-32.

2002b. Kouphovouno (Laconie). *Bulletin de Correspondance Hellénique* 126(2): 583-589.

2003a. Kouphovouno. *Archaeological Reports* 49: 31-32.

2003b. Kouphovouno (Laconie). *Bulletin de Correspondance Hellénique* 127(2): 554-563.

2004a. Kouphovouno. *Archaeological Reports* 50: 27-28.

2004b. Kouphovouno (Laconie). *Bulletin de Correspondance Hellénique* 128-129(2.1), 854-865.

2005. Kouphovouno. *Archaeological Reports* 51: 29-30.

2006a. Kouphovouno (Laconie). *Bulletin de Correspondance Hellénique* 130(2) : 722-727.

2006b. Kouphovouno. *Archaeological Reports* 52: 39.

2007a. Kouphovouno (Laconie). *Bulletin de Correspondance Hellénique* 131(2) : 972-980.

2007b. Kouphovouno. *Archaeological Reports* 53: 24-27.

2008a. Kouphovouno. *Archaeological Reports* 54: 34-36.

2008b. Excavations at Kouphovouno, Laconia: results from the 2001 and 2002 seasons. *The Annual of the British School at Athens* 102: 11-101.

2016. Early Bronze Age chronology of Mainland Greece: a review with new dates from the excavations at Kouphovouno. *The Annual of the British School at Athens* 111: 35-49.

Cavanagh, W.G., C.B. Mee, J. Renard, N. Brodie, F. Froelich, P.A James, M. Kousoulakou and A. Karabatsoli

2004. 'Sparta before Sparta': report on the intensive survey at Kouphovouno, 1999-2000. *The Annual of the British School at Athens* 99: 49-128.

Cavanagh, W.G., A. Lagia and C.B. Mee

2016. Mortuary practices in the Middle Bronze Age at Kouphovouno: vernacular dimensions of the mortuary ritual, in A. Dakouri-Hild and M.J. Boyd (eds) *Staging Death. Funerary Performance, Architecture and Landscape in the Aegean*: 207-225. Berlin: de Gruyter.

Evely, D., T. Killen, C.B. Mee, A. Peatfield and M. Popham

1994. New fragments of Linear B tablets from Knossos. *Kadmos: Zeitschrift für vor- und frühgriechische Epigraphik* 33(1): 10-21.

Forbes, H. and C.B. Mee

1997. Introduction, in C.B. Mee and H. Forbes (eds) *A Rough and Rocky Place: the Landscape and Settlement History of the Methana Peninsula, Greece. Results of the Methana Survey Project sponsored by the British School at Athens and the University of Liverpool* (Liverpool Monographs in Archaeology and Oriental Studies): 1-4. Liverpool: Liverpool University Press.

Forbes, H., C.B. Mee and L. Foxhall

1996. Six hundred years of settlement history of the Methana peninsula: an interdisciplinary approach. *Dialogos: Hellenic Studies Review* 3: 72-94.

Foxhall, L., C.B. Mee, H. Forbes and D. Gill

1987. The Ptolemaic base of Methana. *American Journal of Archaeology* 93(2): 247-248.

Gill, D., C.B. Mee and G. Taylor

1997. Appendix 4. Artefact catalogue, in C.B. Mee and H. Forbes (eds). *A Rough and Rocky Place: the Landscape and Settlement History of the Methana Peninsula, Greece. Results of the Methana Survey Project sponsored by the British School at Athens and the University of Liverpool* (Liverpool Monographs in Archaeology and Oriental Studies): 282-343. Liverpool: Liverpool University Press.

Hall, S.A., D. French, S. Mitchell, B. Aksoy, S. Diamant, M. Balance, G.E. Bean, G. Carlson, M.F. Charlesworth, D.F. Easton, E. French, P. Gerstenblith, Ü. Göker, G. Hillman, C. Mee, S. Payne, A. Sheppard, H.M. Thomas, J.M. Wagstaff, J.M. Reynolds and M.H. Crawford

1976. Report of the Council of Management and the Director for 1975. *Anatolian Studies: Journal of the British Institute at Ankara* 26: 3-19.

James, P.A., C.B. Mee and G. Taylor

1994. Soil erosion and the archaeological landscape of Methana, Greece. *Journal of Field Archaeology* 21(4): 395-416.

Jones, R. and C.B. Mee

1978. Spectrographic analysis of Mycenaean pottery from Ialysos on Rhodes: results and implications. *Journal of Field Archaeology* 5(4): 461-470.

1986a. Provenance studies of Aegean Middle Bronze Age pottery, in R.E. Jones (ed.) *Greek and Cypriot Pottery: A Review of Scientific Studies* (Fitch Laboratory Occasional Paper 1): 411-437. Athens: the British School at Athens.

1986b. Provenance studies of Aegean Late Bronze Age pottery, in R.E. Jones (ed.) *Greek and Cypriot Pottery: A Review of Scientific Studies* (Fitch Laboratory Occasional Paper 1): 439-521. Athens: the British School at Athens.

Jones, R., C.B. Mee and H.W. Catling

1978. Analyses of Late Mycenaean pottery from Rhodes and Cyprus. *Archaeophysika* 10: 156.

Mee, C.B.

1975. The Dodecanese in the Bronze Age. Unpublished PhD dissertation, Bedford College, University of London.

1978. Aegean trade and settlement in Anatolia in the second millennium BC. *Anatolian Studies: Journal of the British Institute at Ankara* 28: 121-156.

1980. The first Mycenaeans in the eastern Aegean. *Bulletin of the Institute of Classical Studies* 27: 135-136.

1982. *Rhodes in the Bronze Age: An Archaeological Survey.* Warminster: Aris and Phillips.

1984. Mycenaeans and Troy, in L. Foxhall and J.K. Davies (eds) *The Trojan War. Its Historicity and Context* (Papers of the First Greenbank Colloquium, Liverpool, 1981): 45-56. Bristol: Bristol Classical Press.

1985. Indelicato, S.D., Piazza pubblica e palazzo nella Creta Minoica. *The Town Planning Review* 56(1): 118.

1987a. Dietz, S., Excavations and surveys in southern Rhodes. The Mycenaean period. Results of the Carlsberg Foundation excavations in Rhodes, 1902-1914. *The Classical Review* 37(1): 109-110.

1987b. Mountjoy, P.A., Mycenaean decorated pottery: a guide to identification. *Antiquity* 61(223): 501-502.

1987c. Mountjoy, P.A., Orchomenos V. Mycenaean pottery from Orchomenos, Eutresis and other Boeotian sites. *The Journal of Hellenic Studies* 107: 255.

1987d. Melas, E.M., The islands of Karpathos, Saros and Kasos in the Neolithic and Bronze Age. *The Antiquaries Journal* 67(1): 141-142.

1988a. The LH IIIB period in the Dodecanese, in S. Dietz and I. Papachristodoulou (eds) *Archaeology in the Dodecanese*: 56-58. Copenhagen: the National Museum of Denmark.

1988b. A Mycenaean thalassocracy in the eastern Aegean?, in E.B. French and K.A. Wardle (eds) *Problems in Greek Prehistory*: 301-306. Bristol: Bristol Classical Press.

1988c. Coleman, J.E., Excavations at Pylos in Elis. *The Classical Review* 38(1): 174-175.

1993. Soles, J.S., Minoan funerary practices: the Prepalatial cemeteries at Mochlos and Gournia and the house tombs of Bronze Age Crete. *The Classical Review* 43(2): 365-366.

1994a. Maran, J., Bronze Age Thessaly: Die deutschen Ausgrabungen auf der Pevkakia-Magula in Thessalien, III: Die Mittlere Bronzezeit. *The Classical Review* 44(2): 374-375.

1994b. Benzi, M., Rodi e la civiltà micenea. *The Journal of Hellenic Studies* 114: 220-221.

1994c. Walberg, G., Middle Minoan III - a time of transition. *The Classical Review* 44(2): 417-418.

1996a. Shaw, J.W. and M.C. Shaw, Kommos. An excavation on the south coast of Crete. Volume 1: the Kommos region and houses of the Minoan town. Part 1: the Kommos region, ecology and Minoan industries. *The Classical Review* 46(2): 335-336.

1996b. Rehak, P., The role of the ruler in the prehistory of the Aegean. Proceedings of a panel discussion at the annual meeting of the Archaeological Institute of America, New Orleans, Louisiana, 28 December 1992. *The Classical Review* 46(2): 380-381.

1997a. Davies, W.V. and L. Schofield, Egypt, the Aegean and the Levant: interconnections in the second millennium B.C. *The Classical Review* 47(1): 218.

1997b. Antonova, I., V. Tostikov and M. Treister, The gold of Troy: searching for Homer's fabled city. *The Classical Review* 47(2): 437.

1997c. Shipley, G. and J. Salmon, Human landscapes in Classical antiquity. *Landscape History* 19(1): 96-97.

1998a. Anatolia and the Aegean in the Late Bronze Age, in E. Cline and D. Harris-Cline (eds) *The Aegean and the Orient in the Second Millennium: Proceedings of the 50th Anniversary Symposium, Cincinnati, 18-20 April 1997* (Aegaeum 18): 137-148. Liège: the University of Liège.

1998b. Gender bias in Mycenaean mortuary practices, in K. Branigan (ed.) *Cemetery and Society in the Aegean Bronze Age* (Sheffield Studies in Aegean Archaeology 1): 165-170. Sheffield: Sheffield Academic Press.

1998c. Özgünel, C., Mykenische Keramik in Anatolien. *American Journal of Archaeology* 102(1): 216-217.

1998d. Nixon, L. and S. Price, The Sphakia Survey (Crete). *Antiquity* 72(277): 725.

1998e. Ruud, I.M., Minoan religion: a bibliography. *The Classical Review* 48(1): 214-215.

1998f. Shaw, J.W and M.C. Shaw, Kommos an excavation on the south coast of Crete. Volume 1: the Kommos region and houses of the Minoan town. Part 2: the Minoan hilltop and hillside houses. *The Classical Review* 48(1): 134-135.

1999. Regional survey projects and the prehistory of the Peloponnese, in J. Renard (ed.) *Le Péloponnèse. Archéologie et Histoire: Actes de la rencontre internationale de Lorient (12-15 mai 1998)*: 67-79. Rennes: Rennes University Press.

2000a. Cook, J.M. and R.V. Nicholls, Old Smyrna excavations: the temples of Athena. *The Classical Review* 50(2): 663-664.

2000b. Whittaker, H., Mycenaean cult buildings: a study of their architecture and function in the context of the Aegean and Eastern Mediterranean. *The Journal of Hellenic Studies* 120: 190-191.

2001. Nucleation and dispersal in Neolithic and Early Helladic Laconia, in K. Branigan (ed.) *Urbanism in the Aegean Bronze Age* (Sheffield Studies in Aegean Archaeology 4): 1-14. Sheffield: Sheffield Academic Press.

2002. Buoyant at the crossroads of Aegean and Greek archaeology. *Antiquity* 76(291): 261-264.

2005. Methana, in S. Hornblower and A. Spawforth (eds) *The Oxford Classical Dictionary, Third Edition*: 969. Oxford: Oxford University Press.

2007a. The production and consumption of pottery in the Neolithic Peloponnese, in C.B. Mee and J. Renard (eds) *Cooking up the Past: Food and Culinary Practices in the Neolithic and Bronze Age Aegean*: 200-224. Oxford: Oxbow Books.

2007b. Hope-Simpson, R. and D.K. Hagel, Mycenaean fortifications, highways, dams and canals. *American Journal of Archaeology* 111(2): 374-375.

2008a. Mycenaean Greece, the Aegean and beyond, in C.W. Shelmerdine (ed.) *The Cambridge Companion to the Aegean Bronze Age*: 363-386. Cambridge: Cambridge University Press.

2008b. Marangou, L., C. Renfrew, C. Doumas and G. Gavalas, Markiani, Amorgos. An Early Bronze Age fortified settlement. *The Journal of Hellenic Studies* 128: 243-244.

2008c. Mycenaeans on the Bronze Age world stage. *Omnibus* 55: 31-33.

2009. Interconnectivity in Early Helladic Laconia, in W.G. Cavanagh, C. Gallou and M. Georgiadis (eds) *Sparta and Laconia: from Prehistory to Pre-Modern. Proceedings of the conference held in Sparta, organised by the British School at Athens, the University of Nottingham, the 5th Ephoreia of Prehistoric and Classical Antiquities and the 5th Ephoreia of Byzantine Antiquities 17–20 March 2005* (The British School at Athens Studies 16): 43-53. London: the British School at Athens.

2010a. Cohesion and diversity in the Neolithic Peloponnese: what the pottery tells us, in W. Cavanagh and S. Hodkinson (eds) *Being Peloponnesian. Proceedings from the Conference Held at the University of Nottingham 31st March–1st April 2007* (Centre for Spartan and Peloponnesian Studies Online Publication 1): 1-11. Nottingham: Centre for Spartan and Peloponnesian Studies, University of Nottingham.

2010b. Death and burial, in E. Cline (ed.) *The Oxford Handbook to the Aegean Bronze Age*: 277-290. Oxford: Oxford University Press.

2011. *Greek Archaeology: A Thematic Approach*. Malden: Wiley-Blackwell.

2012a. Early Bronze Age Laconia: an overview, in C. Mee and M. Prent (eds) Early Helladic Laconia. Proceedings of the Round Table Conference held 16 January 2010 at the Netherlands Institute at Athens. Pharos. *Journal of the Netherlands Institute at Athens* 18(1):: 141-145.

2012b. Methana, in S. Hornblower, A. Spawforth and E. Eidinow (eds) *The Oxford Classical Dictionary, Fourth Edition*: 942. Oxford: Oxford University Press.

2014a. The Late Neolithic rhyta from Kouphovouno in the Peloponnese, Greece. *Journal of Prehistoric Religion* 24: 7-18.

2014b. Broodbank, C., The making of the middle sea. A history of the Mediterranean from the beginning to the emergence of the Classical world. *The Classical Review* 64(2): 569-570.

Mee, C. B., H. Bowden, L. Foxhall, D.W.J. Gill, T. Koukoulis and G. Taylor

1997. Catalogue of sites, in C.B. Mee. and H. Forbes (eds) *A Rough and Rocky Place: the Landscape and Settlement History of the Methana Peninsula, Greece. Results of the Methana Survey Project sponsored by the British School at Athens and the University of Liverpool* (Liverpool Monographs in Archaeology and Oriental Studies): 118-120. Liverpool: Liverpool University Press.

Mee, C.B. and W.G. Cavanagh

1984. Mycenaean tombs as evidence for social and political organization. *Oxford Journal of Archaeology* 3: 43-64.

1990. The spatial distribution of Mycenaean tombs. *The Annual of the British School at Athens* 85: 225-243.

1998. Diversity in a Greek landscape: the Laconia Survey and Rural Sites Project, in W.G. Cavanagh and S.E.C. Walker (eds) *Sparta in Laconia: the archaeology of a city and its countryside. Proceedings of the 19th British Museum Classical Colloquium held with the British School at Athens and King's and University Colleges, London 6-8 December 1995* (The British School at Athens Studies 4): 141-148. London: the British School at Athens.

2000. The hidden landscape of Prehistoric Greece: a view from Laconia and Methana. *Journal of Mediterranean Archaeology* 13(1): 102-107.

Mee, C.B., W.G. Cavanagh and J. Renard

2014. The Middle-Late Neolithic transition at Kouphovouno. *The Annual of the British School at Athens* 109: 65-95.

Mee, C.B., and J. Doole

1993. *Aegean Antiquities on Merseyside. The Collections of Liverpool Museum and Liverpool University* (National Museums and Galleries on Merseyside Occasional Papers, Liverpool Museum No. 7). Liverpool: National Museums and Galleries on Merseyside.

Mee, C.B. and H. Forbes

1997a. *A Rough and Rocky Place: the Landscape and Settlement History of the Methana Peninsula, Greece. Results of the Methana Survey Project sponsored by the British School at Athens and the University of Liverpool* (Liverpool Monographs in Archaeology and Oriental Studies). Liverpool: Liverpool University Press.

1997b. Survey methodology, in C.B. Mee and H. Forbes (eds) *A Rough and Rocky Place: the Landscape and Settlement History of the Methana Peninsula, Greece. Results of the Methana Survey Project sponsored by the British School at Athens and the University of Liverpool* (Liverpool Monographs in Archaeology and Oriental Studies): 33-41. Liverpool: Liverpool University Press.

Mee, C.B., D. Gill, H. Forbes and L. Foxhall

1991. Rural settlement changes in the Methana peninsula, Greece, in G. Barker and J. Lloyd (eds) *Roman Landscapes: Archaeological Survey in the Mediterranean Region* (Archaeological Monographs of the British School at Rome 2): 223-232. London: the British School at Rome.

Mee, C.B. and P. James

2000. Soils and site function: the Laconia Rural Sites Project, in P. Halstead and C. Frederick (eds) *Landscape and Land Use in Postglacial Greece* (Sheffield Studies in Aegean Archaeology 3): 162-175. Sheffield: Sheffield University Press.

Mee, C.B., G. Konstantinopoulos and E. Kollias

1996. Rhodes, in G. Campbell (ed.) *The Grove Encyclopaedia of Classical Art and Architecture, Volume 2*: 439-442. Oxford: Oxford University Press.

Mee, C.B. and C. Mee

1979. *Kos*. Athens: Lycabettus.

Mee, C.B. and W.E. Mierse

1996. Kos, in G. Campbell (ed.) *The Grove Encyclopaedia of Classical Art and Architecture, Volume 1*: 623-624. Oxford: Oxford University Press.

Mee, C.B. and J. Renard

2007. *Cooking up the Past: Food and Culinary Practices in the Neolithic and Bronze Age Aegean*. Oxford: Oxbow Books.

Mee, C.B. and E. Rice

1998. Rhodes, in S. Hornblower and A. Spawforth (eds) *The Oxford Companion to Classical Civilization*: 598-599. Oxford: Oxford University Press.

2005. Rhodes, in S. Hornblower and A. Spawforth (eds) *The Oxford Classical Dictionary, Third Edition*: 1315-1316. Oxford: Oxford University Press.

2012. Rhodes, in S. Hornblower, A. Spawforth and E. Eidinow (eds) *The Oxford Classical Dictionary, Fourth Edition*: 1278-1279. Oxford: Oxford University Press.

2014. Rhodes, in S. Hornblower and A. Spawforth (eds) *The Oxford Companion to Classical Civilization, Second Edition*: 662-663. Oxford: Oxford University Press.

Mee, C.B. and A. Spawforth

2001a. *Greece: An Oxford Archaeological Guide*. Oxford: Oxford University Press.

2001b. *Αρχαιολογικός οδηγός της ηπειρωτικής Ελλάδας*. Athens: Leadercom.

Mee, C.B. and L. Steele

1998. *Corpus of Cypriote Antiquities 17: the Cypriote Collections in the University of Liverpool and the Williamson Art Gallery and Museum* (Studies in Mediterranean Archaeology 20.17). Jonsered: Paul Åström.

Mee, C.B. and G. Taylor

1997. Prehistoric Methana, in C.B. Mee and H. Forbes (eds) *A Rough and Rocky Place: the Landscape and Settlement History of the Methana Peninsula, Greece. Results of the Methana Survey Project sponsored by the British School at Athens and the University of Liverpool* (Liverpool Monographs in Archaeology and Oriental Studies): 42-56. Liverpool: Liverpool University Press.

Vaiglova, P., A. Bogaard, M. Collins, W.G. Cavanagh, C.B. Mee, J. Renard, A. Lamb, A. Gardeisen and R. Fraser

2014. An integrated stable isotope study of plants and animals from Kouphovouno, southern Greece: a new look at Neolithic farming. *Journal of Archaeological Science* 42: 201-215.

Vaiglova, P., F. Rivals, A. Bogaard, R. Fraser, A. Gardeisen, W. Cavanagh, C.B. Mee, J. Renard and A. Lamb

2014. Interpreting ancient crop and animal management strategies at Neolithic Kouphovouno, southern Greece: results of integrating crop and animal stable isotopes and dental micro- and mesowear, in G. Touchais, R. Laffineur and F. Rougemont (eds) *PHYSIS: L'environnement naturel et la relation homme-milieu dans le monde Égéen Protohistorique. Actes de la 14e Rencontre égéenne internationale, Paris, Institut National d'Histoire de l'Art (INHA), 11-14 décembre 2012* (Aegaeum 37): 287-296. Liège: the University of Liège.

Further bibliography

Banou, E. 1996. *Beitrag zum Studium Lakoniens in der mykenischen Zeit* (Quellen und Forschungen zur antiken Welt 20). Munich: Tuduv-Verlagsgesellschaft mbH.

Banou, E. 2000. Middle Helladic Laconia: new evidence. *Studi Micenei ed Egeo-Anatolici* 42(2): 175-199.

Catling, H. 1974. Archaeology in Greece, 1973-1974. *Archaeological Reports* 20: 3-41.

Catling, H. 1977. The Knossos area, 1974-1976. *Archaeological Reports* 23: 3-23.

Hall, S.A., D. French, S. Mitchell, B. Aksoy, S. Diamant, M. Balance, G.E. Bean, G. Carlson, M.F. Charlesworth, D.F. Easton, E. French, P. Gerstenblith, Ü. Göker, G. Hillman, C. Mee, S. Payne, A. Sheppard, H.M. Thomas, J.M. Wagstaff, J.M. Reynolds and M.H. Crawford 1976. Report of the Council of Management and the Director for 1975. *Anatolian Studies: Journal of the British Institute at Ankara* 26: 3-19.

Forbes, H.A. 1976. We have a little of everything. The ecological basis of some agricultural practices in Methana, Trizinia. *Annals of the New York Academy of Sciences* 268: 109-126.

Forbes, H.A. 1982. Strategies and Soils. Technology, Production and Environment in the Peninsula of Methana, Greece. Unpublished PhD dissertation, University of Pennsylvania.

Forbes, H. 2007. *Meaning and Identity in a Greek Landscape: an Archaeological Ethnography*. Cambridge: Cambridge University Press.

Taylour, W.D. 1969. Mycenae, 1968. *Antiquity* 43(170): 91-97.

Wardle, K., P. Halstead and G. Jones 1980. Excavations at Assiros, 1975-9: a settlement site in central Macedonia and its significance for the prehistory of south-east Europe. *The Annual of the British School at Athens* 75: 229-267.

Waterhouse, H.E. and Hope Simpson, R. 1960. Prehistoric Laconia, part 1. *The Annual of the British School at Athens* 55: 67-107.

The Late-Final Neolithic and Early Helladic I Pottery from Midea in the Argolid: Continuity and Change

Eva Alram-Stern, Clare Burke, Katie Demakopoulou and Peter M. Day[1]

Introduction

Midea, a well-known Mycenaean citadel, situated at the eastern border of the Argive Plain (Figure 1.1), was excavated from 1983 to 2009 through a joint Greek-Swedish excavation programme, under the direction of Dr Katie Demakopoulou (Demakopoulou 2012). The material on which this article concentrates comes from two adjacent trenches, A and Aa, located on the Northwest Terrace of the Upper Acropolis (Demakopoulou *et al.* 2005; 2006/2007; 2008; Demakopoulou and Alram-Stern, in preparation).

Although the site is perhaps better known for its later remains, excavation recovered Late and Final Neolithic (LN and FN) pottery, as well as Early Helladic I and II (EH I and EH II) types, from a variety of stratified, undisturbed deposits, and as residual material in later contexts. This rich assemblage provides a valuable opportunity to examine both the first phases of occupation at the settlement, and its wider relationships and connections.

This paper summarises the Neolithic-EH I pottery from Midea, and offers comment on aspects of its morphology, surface modification, fabric, and production technology. These data are used to examine the potential use and the distribution of pottery during the Neolithic and EH I periods. Although only a small proportion of the material comes from closed contexts,

all diagnostic sherds have been recorded to show the range of shapes and macroscopic fabrics present at the site. This has been complemented by further analysis of selected sherds using thin section petrography and scanning electron microscopy (SEM).

Archaeological features and chronology

An important discovery for our understanding of Neolithic and Early Helladic activity at the site was a space defined by two walls, probably a room, located in Trench A, with one portion of wall being attached to a massive double-faced megalithic wall that may have formed part of a fortification system. Within this possible room an assemblage of large pottery fragments and intact vessels was recovered, primarily consisting of EH II types (Alram-Stern 2018; Burke *et al.* 2018; Demakopoulou *et al.* 2006/2007: 23-24). Next to this wall there was a rock-cut tomb (Grave 1) and a FN pit grave (Grave 2, Figure 1.2), accompanied by a sealed deposit in the area of Grave 2 containing abundant LN pottery. This positioning, and the find types recovered, suggest that the FN Grave 2 cut through an earlier LN layer ('LN Deposit') (Demakopoulou *et al.* 2006/2007: 21-23). To the east of these features, in Trench Aa, excavation revealed a layer in which EH I pottery was abundant (Demakopoulou *et al.* 2008: 7-13) (Figure 1.2).

Grave 2 represents the only closed FN context identified at the site and contained the skeleton of a woman, aged 40-50 years old, buried in a contracted position (M. Schultz, personal communication). 14C analysis indicates a date for this burial during the earliest FN (MAMS 27718: 4357–4274 cal. BC (1σ), 4442–4261 cal. BC (2σ)), synchronous with the start of the FN period at Franchthi Cave, which is dated to *c.* 4310 cal. BC (Vitelli 1999: 138, table 9). It predates significantly the Attica-Kephala culture, which current data places in the early 4th millennium BC (Tsirtsoni 2016: 454, table 1; 459-460). Of particular note were two red burnished sherds recovered from the floor of the grave, one belonging to the body of a pithoid jar with plastic decoration, the other the base of a jar; both are dated to the FN and were sampled for petrographic analysis (Figure 1.4d; Figure 1.5b: sample MID 13/12).

In terms of pottery proportions, from a total of *c.* 3100 diagnostic LN-EH II sherds, around 2000 belong to EH II type vessels, whilst the remaining 1100 can be divided as nearly two thirds corresponding to LN and FN pottery and one third belonging to EH I (Table1).

[1] Acknowledgements: This project was generously funded by the Austrian Science Fund, Stand-Alone Project no. P24798-G18. We are grateful to the Ephorate of Antiquities of Argolida for giving permission for the research and providing facilities for the macroscopic study of the pottery. Permission for sampling and analysis was kindly provided by the Directorate of Conservation of Ancient and Modern Monuments of the Hellenic Ministry of Culture and Sports. Furthermore, we would like to thank the Austrian Academy of Sciences Institute for Oriental and European Archaeology including our collaborators María Antonia Negrete Martínez and Constanze Moser as well as Anno Hein and Vassilis Kilikoglou Institute of Nanoscience and Nanotechnology, N.C.S.R. 'Demokritos', Thanassis Karabotsos of The University of West Attica and all those who kindly offered comparative analytical material and data. We are grateful to everyone who granted access to ceramic material and facilitated the work as part of our broader study: Joseph Maran (Tiryns), Daniel Pullen, James Wright, Jack Davis and John Cherry (Tsoungiza and Nemea Valley Archaeological Project 204), John Lavezzi, James Wiseman and John Cherry (Ancient Corinth), Ioulia Tzonou-Herbst (Korakou) and Anthi Theodorou-Mavrommatidi (Epidauros). CB and PD are especially indebted to the 4th Ephorate of Prehistoric and Classical Antiquities, Nafplion, specifically Alcestis Papadimitriou and Angeliki Kossyva for generously offering material from Ephorate excavations at sites in the Argolid and their continued patience and support with publication.

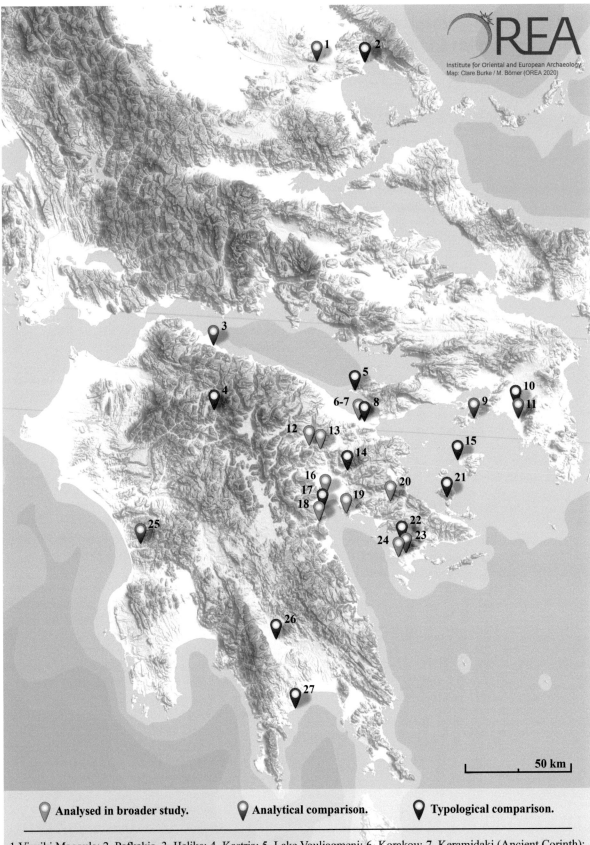

Figure 1.1. Map of the northeastern Peloponnese, with comparative sites and sites mentioned in the text (© Clare Burke).

Analysed in broader study.   Analytical comparison.   Typological comparison.

1. Visviki Magoula; 2. Pefkakia, 3. Helike; 4. Kastria; 5. Lake Vouliagmeni; 6. Korakou; 7. Keramidaki (Ancient Corinth); 8. Gonia; 9. Salamis; 10. Athens; 11. Kontopigado; 12. NVAP 204; 13. Tsoungiza; 14. Prosymna; 15. Aegina-Kolonna; 16. Lempetzi (Argos); 17. Lerna; 18. Spiliotakis (Monopori); 19. Talioti; 20. Epidavros Apollon Maleatas; 21. Methana; 22. Franchthi; 23. Delpriza; 24. Agios Pantelimonas; 25. Ayios Dhimitrios; 26. Kouphovouno; 27. Makrovouni

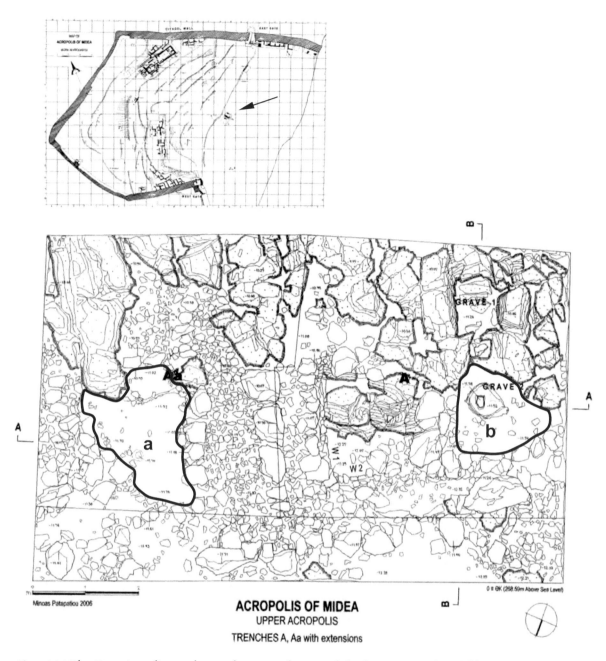

Figure 1.2. Midea, Upper Acropolis, Trenches A and AA, areas of graves and closed contexts are indicated: (a) area with Early Helladic I destruction layer; (b) Late Neolithic fill (after Demakopoulou 2006. Drawing: M. Patapatiou).

The Late and Final Neolithic period pottery wares and forms

The Late Neolithic period

The LN pottery from Midea is best represented in the 'LN Deposit'. With the exception of a single FN sherd, the deposit contained exclusively LN type pottery and, like the LN material at Midea generally, contained a good proportion of fine wares (34%), a trend comparable to other sites including Kouphovouno (Mee 2007: 210-215). These fine wares are dominated by deep bowls, a common LN vessel shape. In terms of surface finish, a total of 70 fragments from the 'LN

Deposit' belong to Pattern Painted pottery, of which 14 fragments are Polychrome Ware, and seven fragments are Bichrome Ware.

Comparable Polychrome and Bichrome Pattern Painted wares are most common in the later phase of the LN period (Dousougli 1998: 110-124; Katsipanou-Margeli 2018: 62-64; Phelps 2004: 96-102; Vitelli 1999: 40-42, 51-52). The class is characterized by the presence of red painted surface decoration typically surrounded by a dark brown on a buff or orange surface (Figure 1.3). At Midea, characteristic motifs comprise vertical and diagonal lines, often bordered by wavy lines, as well as triangles and maeandroid designs. These patterns

Table 1.1. Chronological chart of the periods mentioned in the text.

Absolute Chronology BC (Manning 1995, Pullen 2011, Tsirtsoni 2016)	Periodization Greek mainland Peloponnese	Argolid	Korinthia	Attica Boiotia Euboia
2200 2450/2350	EH IIB	Lerna IIIC–D		Lefkandi I
2750/2650	EH IIA	Lerna IIIA–C early	Tsoungiza EH II Developed Tsoungiza EH II Initial	
3100	EH I	Talioti	Tsoungiza EH I Perachora X-Z	Eutresis III–IV Tsepi
4000	Younger Final Neolithic = Chalcolithic	Halieis Franchthi 5b FN Lerna II	Tsoungiza FN	Athens N. Slope Tharrounia IIb
4500	Final Neolithic = Chalcolithic	Franchthi 5a Prosymna		Attica-Kephala Tharrounia II
4900	Late Neolithic II („late")	LN Lerna II Franchthi 4	Gonia	Tharrounia Ib
5500	Late Neolithic I („early")	Franchthi 3		Tharrounia Ia

are well known in the northeastern Peloponnese and suggest that Midea was part of a network of interaction, which include Gonia and Lerna, within which similarly decorated pottery was produced in different locations, some of which may have circulated (for Gonia, see Figure 1.3b: cf. Phelps 2004: fig. 44:21; for Lerna, Figure 1.3c: cf. Vitelli 2007: 334 fig. 75d).

At Midea, the Polychrome and Bichrome wares are dominated by hemispherical bowls most likely associated with the consumption of food. The similar style and size of these bowls may reflect a desire for standardisation considered meaningful when used in commensal acts (Figure 1.3a) (Halstead 2012: 40-42). In addition, the LN deposit around Grave 2 also produced

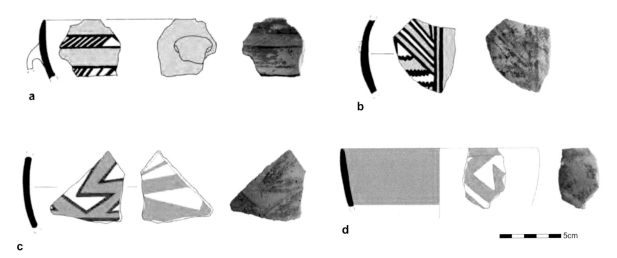

Figure 1.3. Late Neolithic pottery from Midea: (a-c) Polychrome, (d) Bichrome (photos: Kostas Xenikakis; drawings: Constanze Moser, © ORFA).

88 fragments of burnished pottery and five of Pattern Burnished pottery, one Grey Ware fragment and one sherd with fine incised decoration, most again deriving from bowls. There are good parallels for this assemblage within the material from Franchthi Ceramic Phase (FCP) 4 (Vitelli 1999: 38-63), whilst the general dominance of bowls clearly indicates the importance of dining at Midea during the LN period.

The macroscopic fabric of the fine ware vessels is mostly red (2.5YR 4/6), sometimes pink (7.5YR 8/4), with many moderately sorted, small to fine white inclusions, small grey, and small red rounded to angular inclusions and pores (Macroscopic Group 2). However, the Polychrome and Bichrome wares are characterized by two more distinct macroscopic fabrics. The first is very fine grey (7.5YR 5/0 – 10YR 4/1) or pink (7.5YR 6/4 – 10YR 6/3) with only rare inclusions visible to the naked eye; the second is also grey or pink, but with small red inclusions (Macroscopic Group 1. Figure 1.5A: MID 13/10; for

petrography, see Figure 1.9A). There are very strong similarities between the macroscopic fabrics of the Polychrome ceramics and the probably synchronous, Burnished and Pattern Burnished wares. In contrast, there is a clear difference between the macroscopic fabrics of the LN fine wares and those of coarser vessels. It is particularly notable that the coarse, most often pithoid, vessels from the LN deposit around Grave 2 were macroscopically comparable to the typical FN fabrics from Midea, implying a degree of technological continuity in the manufacture of coarse pottery between the LN and FN periods. This will be discussed in more detail in the technology section below.

The Final Neolithic period

FN pottery is frequent in nearly all contexts and has been identified with the help of comparable material from other sites. The presence of earlier FN activity, synchronous with the construction of the grave, is

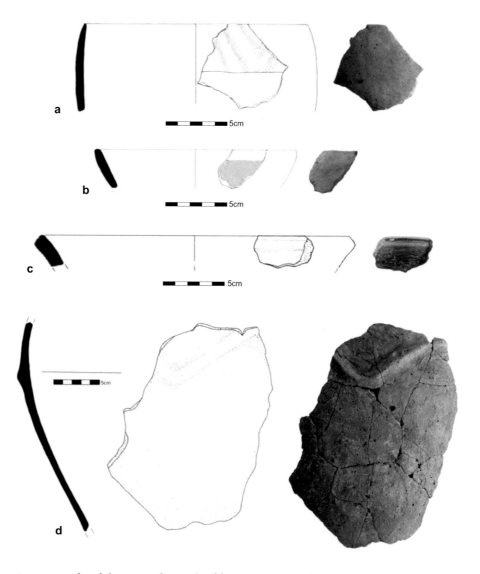

Figure 1.4. Final Neolithic pottery from Midea: (a) Fine Incised Ware; (b) Crusted Ware; (c) rolled rim bowl (d) jar with plastic decoration (photos: Kostas Xenikakis, Clare Burke; drawings: Constanze Moser, © OREA).

suggested by the recovery of Fine Incised Ware (Figure 1.4a) (Vitelli 1999: 70, 252, fig. 53h) and Crusted Ware (Vitelli 1999: 68-70, 248 fig. 51) (Figure 1.4b) paralleled in the earlier FN of Franchthi Cave.

A small number of Fine Incised Ware sherds were recorded at Midea, belonging to deep bowls, displaying fine linear zigzag or triangular incisions under the rim or on the upper part of the body, on a smoothed or burnished surface. Incised wares are characterised by local variation (e.g., at Kastria: Katsarou and Sampson 1997: 232-256), with the shape and decoration of those from Midea being comparable to 'Prosymna Incised Ware' well-known from the nearby site (Phelps 2004: 105-106) (Figure 1.4a). The similarity in form and decoration evident in examples from Midea and from nearby sites in the Argolid suggests that these bowls conformed to a regional style, circulating among groups of people who shared similar consumption practices.

Crusted Ware represents another distinctive component of the FN ceramic record at Midea, fragments of which are characterised by the addition of broad bands of white crusted paint below the rim on an otherwise wiped or slightly burnished surface. Crusted wares have a wide distribution over the Peloponnese and the Greek mainland generally, making the identification of close parallels more difficult (Phelps 2004: 108-111; Franchthi: Vitelli 1999: 68-70, 73-74; Lerna: Vitelli 2007: 354–355, fig. 85; Pefkakia: Weisshaar 1989: 21-22; Ayios Dimitrios: Zachos 2008: 17). All examples from Midea belong to hemispherical or deep bowls (Figure 1.4b), and three are again, macroscopically comparable to the LN macroscopic fine fabrics (Macroscopic Groups 1 and 2) described above.

Although a variety of FN fine wares are attested at Midea, the assemblage is dominated by burnished and unburnished coarse wares, sometimes bearing plastic decoration in the form of single and multiple bands (Figure 1.4d, sample 12) with a similar dominance of coarse wares having been recognised in the FN ceramic profiles of other Peloponnesian sites (Mee 2007: 215-216). The most common forms at Midea are bowls and jars, although low numbers of pithoid vessels, pans and scoops are also present. The characteristic macroscopic fabric for this pottery is low fired with red or black fracture with many (7.5-15%) small to fine white inclusions, small grey inclusions and red inclusions, pores that are not readily visible in dark fabrics (Macroscopic Group 3. Figure 1.5B-C: MID 13/12, MID 13/22). However, five sherds are of the fine grey and pink macroscopic fabric with red inclusions characterised as LN Macroscopic Group 1, suggesting some continuity in fabric technology between the LN and FN.

The presence at Midea of so-called Heavy Burnished Ware including some belonging to rolled rim bowls, may indicate settlement also during the later phases of the Final Neolithic period (Alram-Stern 2014: 312-313, 314 fig. 6; Katsipanou-Margeli 2018: 81-82). One example of a Heavy Burnished Ware rolled rim bowl was particularly striking within the assemblage due to its unusual red macroscopic fabric and brownish red, highly burnished surface, and may well represent an import to the site (Figure 1.4c, sample MID 13/3: for petrography, see Figure 1.10).

A characteristic form related to Macroscopic Group 3 is the so-called 'cheese-pot', of which 39 fragments have been identified (Figure 1.6). These bowls are characterised by a row of perforations under the rim. They appear around the start of the 5th millennium BC and are most frequent throughout the Aegean during the 4th millennium BC (Alram-Stern 2014: 313-315 fig. 7; Katsipanou-Margeli 2018: 78-81), surviving in EH I as pans with perforated rims of the type reported at Kontopigado (K. Kaza-Papageorgiou and V. Hachtmann, personal communication).

These 'cheese-pots' appear in a variety of forms at Midea, as is common at other FN sites. They include deep, hemispherical bowls (Figure 1.6b-d) (Vitelli 1999: 242 fig. 48b), large coarse bowls (Vitelli 2007: 362 fig. 89a-b, 368 fig. 92a), deep bucket-like vessels (Alram-Stern 2006: 56 no. 74), storage jars (Papathanassopoulos 2011: 159, no. 106), pans (Figure 1.6a) (Alram-Stern 2006: 56 nos. 82-83; Pantelidou Gofa 2013; 2016: 227-232, pl. 106-109) and large, asymmetrical vessels (Vitelli 1999: 292 fig. 73b; 2007: 370 fig. 93, 372 fig. 94). Some are decorated with incision (Figure 1.6c) and have a lug handle (Figure 1.6b) or a rolled rim. The pans are commonly produced in a coarse macroscopic fabric with frequent white inclusions (Figure 1.6a; see also samples MID 13/20 (Figure 1.5c) and MID 13/11 (Figure 1.9D)) with an unfinished exterior and a smoothed interior. In contrast, bowls with perforations are often of a medium fine to medium coarse fabric and may be burnished on both interior and exterior.

The characteristic feature of these pots, a row of holes below the rim, appears on a variety of vessel forms, from shallow coarse ware pans to semi-fine bowls. If these holes are to be interpreted as a functional feature common to a variety of vessel types, they may have been used for fixing a cover of cloth or animal hide which was tightened over the mouth of the vessel. Such an interpretation has been already suggested by Elizabeth Banks (Vitelli 2007: 123), who interpreted these vessels either as drums (Vitelli 2007: 123) or as containers of warm coals and ashes (Banks 2015: 84). However, such covers may have a less specialised function, serving simply to protect the vessel contents during storage or transportation. This interpretation has ethnographic analogies from modern Greece and Lena Cavanagh (personal communication) recalls seeing cloth covers

Figure 1.5. Images of macroscopic fabrics. A: Sample MID 13/10 Late Neolithic polychrome bowl. B: Sample MID 13/12 Final Neolithic jar with plastic decoration. C: Sample MID 13/22 Final Neolithic burnished jar with plastic decoration. D: Sample MID 13/20 Final Neolithic cheese-pot (© C. Burke).

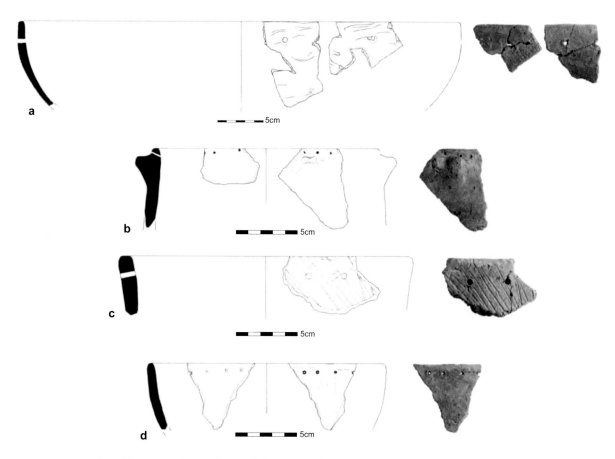

Figure 1.6. Final Neolithic pottery from Midea: (a-d) cheese-pots (photos: Kostas Xenikakis; drawings: Constanze Moser, © OREA).

being tied to baskets in order to protect food during transport as a child in mid-20th century Central and Southern Greece.

The Early Helladic I wares and forms

A second closed context, a level excavated in 2006, besides much LN and FN material, contained a considerable number of pottery fragments dated to EH I. The stratigraphy, as well as the lesser degree of fragmentation of the EH I material, indicates that this pottery forms part of a destruction horizon.

In total, 186 diagnostic EH I sherds have been recorded at Midea. No complete EH I vessels were recovered and so vessel profiles have been reconstructed with reference to parallels from other sites. The most common forms are bowls (Figure 1.7), including examples of types known from Tsoungiza such as deep to medium bowls (Figure 1.7a), hemispherical bowls (Figure 1.7b), flaring rim bowls with flattened lip (Figure 1.7c), and bowls with inturned rims (Pullen 2011: 72-74, form 5-8). Their surface is usually red slipped and burnished, however, rare unburnished and, very rarely, unslipped, examples are also present. Other characteristic shapes are fruitstands, large shallow bowls/fruitstands, askoi and jars. A single example of a frying pan is also noted. Parallels for these shapes come from Tsoungiza (Pullen 2011: 56-87), Talioti (Weisshaar 1990) and Lake Vouliagmeni in Corinthia (Fossey 1969).

In contrast to the previous period, with very few exceptions, the EH I macroscopic fabrics were fired from pink to red (2.5YR 5/8 – 5YR 7/6 – 7.5YR 6/4) with a grey core, and contained visible white and sparkling white inclusions, and less commonly, red clasts (Figure 1.7a; MID 13/35; for micrograph, see Figure 1.13B). They were grouped according to their texture, being fine (Macroscopic Group 4), medium fine (Macroscopic Group 5) and medium coarse (Macroscopic Group 6). Equal numbers of bowls, askoi and jars were produced in Macroscopic Group 4, Macroscopic Group 5, and Macroscopic Group 6. However, it was particularly notable that the fruitstand assemblage was dominated by the fine Macroscopic Group 4 (Figure 1.12), providing an early indication of a possible shared origin (discussed in more detail in the technology section, below). The fabric of the frying pan was characterised by a higher proportion of red inclusions, and was assigned to Macroscopic Group 7. In addition to these macroscopic fabrics, it was possible to identify a distinctive fragment of a large bowl with out-turned rim, characterised by gold mica inclusions (Figure 1.7d; MID 13/29: for micrograph see Figure 1.14A), otherwise unknown in the local material, which petrography confirmed as an import from Aegina.

The most characteristic EH I shapes at Midea are the fruitstand and the large shallow bowl (many of which may be the bowls of fruitstands which have become detached). These vessels display a limited repertoire of types, but differ quite considerably in their diameter (0.22-0.64m) (Figure 1.8). They are characterised by either a downward or an outward turned rim, with incised decoration on the interior (for parallels from Talioti, see Weisshaar 1990: pls. 2-6; also at Tsoungiza, Pullen 2011: 65-72, Form 1) (Figure 1.8a-b). In addition to these two rim types, there are also shallow bowls

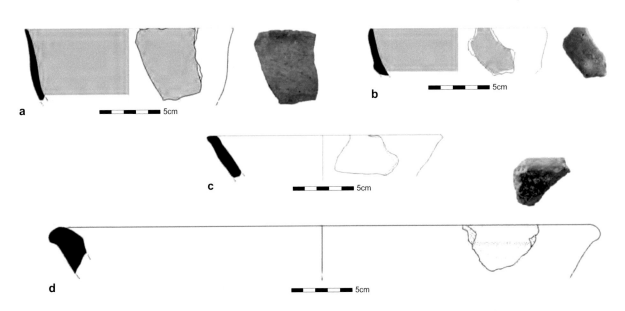

Figure 1.7. Early Helladic I pottery from Midea: (a-c) bowls; (d) bowl with everted rim
(photos: Kostas Xenikakis; drawings: Constanze Moser, © OREA).

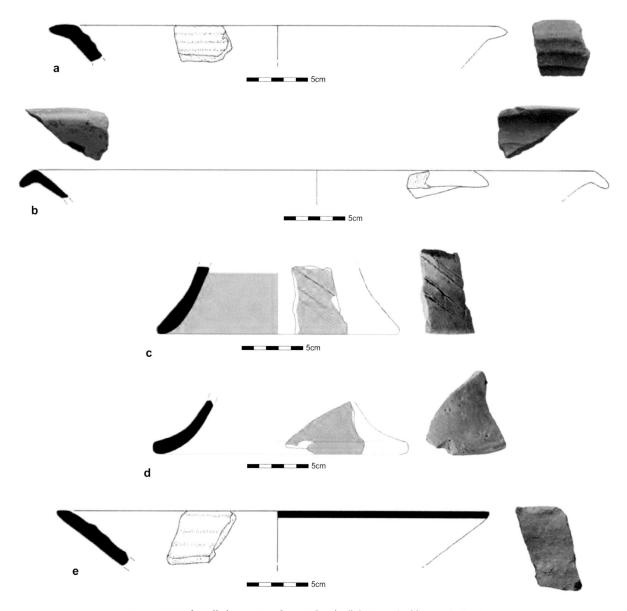

Figure 1.8. Early Helladic I pottery from Midea: (a-d) fruitstands; (e) large shallow bowl
(photos: Kostas Xenikakis, Clare Burke; drawings: Constanze Moser, © OREA).

with flattened or simple spreading rims known from Talioti (Weisshaar 1990: 28 pl. 4:9,11) and Makrovouni Magoula in the Argolid (Dousougli 1987: 183, 184 fig. 12:46-47) (Figure 1.8e). Most have a red painted, usually unburnished, interior and often an untreated exterior.

As noted above, the shallow bowls and fruitstands belonged predominantly to the fine-grained Macroscopic Group 4 (MID 13/35: for petrography, see Figure 1.13A) and only rarely appear in the medium fine Macroscopic Group 5 and coarse Macroscopic Fabric 6. Furthermore, the presence of fruitstands and shallow bowls, and in a comparatively high number (45 examples) at Midea suggests the participation of the community in particular dining practices requiring these vessels (discussed by Burke *et al.* 2020), which has analogies in Attica, the Cyclades and Crete during Early Bronze I (Burke *et al.* 2020; Day and Wilson 2004;

Pantelidou Gofa 2016: 110-119, pl. 44-51; Rambach 2000: 193-196; Wilson and Day 2000).

Potting technology of the Midea assemblage

Methodology

To complement the typological and macroscopic study, petrographic analysis was undertaken at the University of Sheffield, Department of Archaeology on a total of 126 samples, of which 29 belonged to the Neolithic period (including two samples which could only be assigned as FN-EH I), and 19 samples belonging to EH I type pottery. The aim of this analysis was to provide insights into the diachronic trends of pottery production and consumption represented within the ceramic assemblage at Midea, and to position these results in relation to wider patterns of behaviour indicated by a recent larger study of EH pottery in the northeastern Peloponnese (Burke 2017; Burke *et al.* 2016; Burke *et al.* 2018; Burke *et al.* 2020. For a map of comparative sites within the larger analytical study, see Figure 1.1). Petrographic fabrics were defined based on four primary criteria: the identification of aplastic inclusion types, the frequency, size and shape of aplastic inclusions, the appearance of the micromass (including optical activity and colour), and the character of any visible voids.

Firing conditions were estimated based on macroscopic observations of vessel colour, the presence or absence of visible firing cores, the presence of primary calcite, the degree of optical activity of the micromass under the polarising light microscope, and through microstructural analysis using Scanning Electron Microscopy (SEM). SEM was undertaken at the Technological Educational Institute, University of Western Attica and the National Centre for Scientific Research (NCSR) 'Demokritos' Athens, to examine the vitrification of the ceramic microstructure and to estimate relative equivalent firing temperature ranges. These were estimated based upon standards established by Maniatis and Tite (1981) and Kilikoglou (Day and Kilikoglou 2001). These results were compared to similar material previously analysed from other sites in the northeastern Peloponnese (Burke 2017).

Representative samples were selected from across the visible range of technological, chronological and typological variability present in the assemblage, relating to macroscopic fabrics, surface modification types, and vessels forms, to allow investigation of diachronic change in technological choice. Although not all periods were represented evenly (especially in relation to LN type pottery), it was possible to sample a range of vessel types and wares (including FN cheese-pots, globular and deep bowls and jars and EH I fruitstands, bowls and jars), with a range of surface modifications (primarily burnishing, but also incision, slipping and appliqué).

Geological Overview

The geology of the Argolid region is characterised by the interaction of the Tripolis and Pindos geological zones. The area around Midea is dominated by the sedimentary geology of Lower and Middle Cretaceous argillaceous shales, cherts, sandstones and coarser clastic sediments. These are accompanied by Upper Cretaceous limestones which form the mountains around the Argive Plain, occasionally interspersed with red clays and chert. The hill of Midea itself consists of Lower Cretaceous to Paleocene limestones, hornstones, and marls, bordered to the south by Upper Pliocene to Pleistocene undivided flysch containing shales, calcite,

marls, sandstones and ophiolitic bodies. To the east lies Upper Triassic to Middle Jurassic carbonate rocks of chert, limestone and dolomites (Papastamatiou *et al.* 1970; Papavassiliou *et al.* 1984; Zangger 1993: 8; Zaronikos *et al.* 1970).

Neolithic fabrics

The Neolithic fabrics are dominantly characterised by the practice of tempering clay pastes with mudstones, siltstones and grog (crushed pottery added to the clay paste, see Figure 1.9).

Grog was identified in both LN and FN type pottery and although, as expected, there is not a 1:1 macro-micro correlation, the grog inclusions broadly corresponded to the red inclusions noted in Macroscopic Groups 1, 2 and 3. Variation in the type and abundance of different rock inclusions across the samples, suggests the use of different raw material sources in their manufacture. Some of these inclusion types appear to be naturally present in the base clay, whilst others appear to have been added as temper, alongside the grog. In addition to grog and argillaceous rock fragments (ARFs), the most common inclusion types are calcite, sandstone, siltstone and/or chert. All are compatible with the sedimentary geology within a 4km radius of Midea, and suggest local production of these vessels. Importantly, these fabrics also display a degree of variability in their coarseness, degree of optical activity, and the nature of the grog within the paste which indicates a lack of standardisation and likely reflects the contribution of multiple potters who shared the grog tempering tradition.

The most characteristic difference between the grog-based petrographic fabrics is in relation to their coarseness, with several LN and FN vessels manufactured in a particularly fine fabric with well sorted grog, mudstone and siltstone. These finer fabrics occur alongside more common coarse grog fabrics, which although sharing grog temper have less well sorted inclusions, and a broader range of inclusion types that include sandstone and quartzite compatible with the local geology. Although present in small numbers, the strong similarity between grog tempered LN and FN samples is striking (see Figure 1.9), and lends support to those macroscopic fabric observations outlined above suggesting a degree of continuity between LN and FN ceramic production practices.

It is particularly interesting to note that different samples sometimes contain grog fragments that look the same, suggesting either that the grog temper originated from a single vessel and was added to the paste of a variety of new pots, or that the grog temper came from different vessels that were made with the same paste recipe. Additionally, some fragments of grog

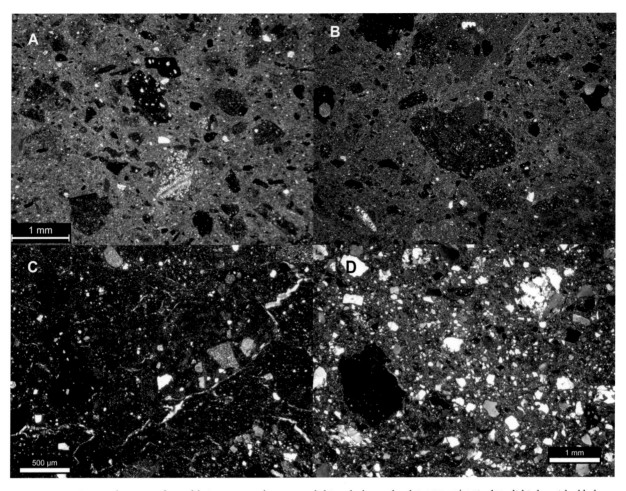

Figure 1.9. Micrograph images of grog fabric. A: MID 13/10 Late Neolithic polychrome bowl, B: MID 13/21 Final Neolithic burnished hole mouthed jar, C: MID 13/23 burnished globular bowl, D: MID 13/11 Final Neolithic cheese-pot (© C. Burke).

have a similar appearance to the surrounding matrix of the sample in which they sit, suggesting the recycling of pottery produced by the same potter or more likely the recycling of pottery made in the same pottery paste recipe tradition. The variability noted in these fabrics supports the idea that there was no standardised or consistent approach to the choice of raw materials in terms of geological resources for pottery production around Midea, and that instead it was the use of grog that formed a fundamental aspect of potting practice. Indeed, there are also examples of secondary grog (grog within grog), testifying to the continuous recycling of vessels used by the community during the Neolithic at Midea.

A non-standardised approach is also indicated by the absence of evidence for particular fabrics being chosen for the manufacture of particular wares or vessel types, confirming the macroscopic and typological observations outlined above. This suggests that the choice of raw materials was unrelated to the intended function of the vessel and that particular paste recipes were not used for particular wares. Although the addition of temper may reflect a rather more practical desire to control the plasticity and workability of the clay, and to prevent significant cracking during

drying and firing that might lead to vessel failure, this is not an entirely satisfactory explanation for its use. There is considerable ethnographic evidence to show that the choice of raw materials in pottery making is rarely related to functional considerations, but instead embedded within the learnt practice and broader traditions of the potters themselves (Day 2004; Gosselain 1998). The use of grog, in particular, may have also had social or symbolic motivations. This is especially evident when we see that it was often added with other materials, such as mudstone, which would have performed in a similar way and were theoretically as readily available to Neolithic potters considering their abundance in the landscape and the pottery fabrics. Alongside its more functional properties, the use of grog may reflect an attempt to link the past to the present, and there is, for example, ethnographic evidence for the recycling of pottery sherds by potters attempting to link the successful production of older vessels with the production of new ones, imbuing the new vessels with the success of the old (Gosselain and Livingstone Smith 2005: 41).

These results from Midea are consistent with trends across the wider Aegean, with the use of grog being primarily considered as a FN technology with limited evidence for continuation into the Early Bronze Age, attested at sites across the Greek mainland and Crete, including Salamis (Whitbread and Mari 2014), Visviki Magoula (Pentedeka 2015), Alepotrypa (Pentedeka 2018), Youra (Quinn *et al.* 2010), Tsoungiza (Burke 2017), Helike (Iliopoulos *et al.* 2011); Kavousi (Day *et al.* 2005), Phaistos (Mentesana 2016) and Knossos (Tomkins 2002). The wide distribution of this practice clearly testifies not only to a shared potting tradition across different production locations, but also to the transfer of knowledge between different communities during the Neolithic and into the Early Bronze Age periods. Certainly, there is extensive ethnographic research into crafting (e.g., Gosselain and Livingstone Smith 2005; Lemonnier 2002; 2012; Stark *et al.* 2008) that has demonstrated the socially embedded nature of crafting activity, and the way in which 'technological' knowledge is related to wider worldviews and specific cultural understandings about the 'correct' or 'best' way to undertake a craft. Certainly, psychological and anthropological studies repeatedly demonstrate that human cognition and behaviour is derived from a combination of subconsciously and consciously learnt behaviour which form shared ways of doing and thinking, or what Mauss termed *habitus* (2009 [1934]), later developed into practice theory by Bourdieu (1972) and considered further through Wenger's communities of practice (Lave and Wenger 1991; Wenger 1998). As such, technological practice is based on repeated, embodied actions on the material world and cannot be isolated from its social context (Lemonnier 2002; 2012). The motivations and ideas behind the crafting and use of pottery are culturally contingent (Burke and Spencer-Wood 2018: Lemonnier 2002; 2012; van der Leeuw 2002) and the fundamental role of social norms and values in framing crafting behaviour help to explain why there is such wide variation in how

pottery is made and its nature across time and space as it reflects and, indeed, contributes to the wide variety of cultural contexts in which learning and craft take place. As such, the wide acceptance of grog tempering in the Neolithic Aegean suggests that it was embedded within concepts that were recognised and shared by large numbers of potters, irrespective of their location or of the other raw materials with which they made their vessels.

In addition to grog-based pastes, it has been possible to identify two other distinct fabrics within the Neolithic material sampled from Midea. The first is a Sandstone to Low Grade Metamorphic fabric which we will address more fully in the discussion of the EH I type pottery, but which appears to have a long history and relates to an important community of practice in the Argolid region. The second is a Serpentinite fabric represented by the high quality burnished rolled rim bowl discussed above (Sample MID 13/3; see Figure 1.4c and Figure 1.10).

This bowl is macroscopically distinctive, possessing an even red burnished surface and an unusual red fabric which lacks the firing core so often present in other Neolithic vessels from Midea. Petrographic analysis has revealed this bowl belongs to a serpentinite fabric and, unlike the other fabrics containing serpentinite at Midea such as the Sandstone to Low Grade Metamorphic fabric discussed below, and a mudstone breccia fabric associated with EH II type pottery (Burke *et al.* 2018), this sample contains no other rock fragments that could aid in identifying its provenance. Serpentinite fabrics have been identified at a number of comparative sites in the northeastern Peloponnese (Burke 2017), however, none of these appear to be a match for the sample from Midea. The provenance of this sample is currently unknown, but it does appear inconsistent with the geology immediately in the area of Midea suggesting it is likely imported.

Figure 1.10. Sample MID 13/3 A: image of macroscopic fabric; B: micrograph of serpentinite inclusions (© C. Burke).

Figure 1.11. Sample MID 13/2 A: SEM image showing an unvitrified microstructure (x4000 magnification); B: image of the dark grey-black fracture of the ceramic (© C. Burke).

Final Neolithic firing

All of the FN grog-tempered samples examined using SEM belong to burnished vessels with mottled light to dark surfaces, indicative of exposure to mixed firing atmospheres. The samples also have a dark core or are black across the whole break (Figure 1.11), suggesting incomplete oxidation and/or incomplete combustion of any organic material within the ceramic, consistent with a short firing duration. These features were observed more generally within the FN material.

SEM-EDS analysis revealed low calcareous microstructures consistent with initial to extensive vitrification, suggestive of equivalent firing temperature ranges up to 900°C, and microstructures with no vitrification consistent with equivalent firing temperatures below 750-800°C (Figure 1.11). Low firing temperature ranges at around or below 800°C were also indicated within samples by the high degree of optical activity within the micromass and the presence of primary calcite which begins to degrade at around and above this temperature threshold.

Whilst it is difficult to establish with certainty whether low firing temperature ranges reflect purposeful practice or poorly controlled firing, the mottled colours and incomplete oxidation of the ceramics would seem to suggest the latter. It is worth noting that low firing temperature ranges would have been needed to ensure preservation of the burnished surfaces of these vessels, as vitrification resulting from high firing temperatures would destroy the burnished sheen.

Early Bronze Age fabrics

The EH I pottery sampled from Midea is characterised by a narrow range of fabrics. However, the fragmentary nature of the assemblage and some mixed contexts made recognition of definitively EH I material difficult at times. The sampled material is dominated by fruitstands, as an accepted characteristic shape of this date, but other bowl types and jars are included, benefiting from comparison with contemporary material published in the region.

As already noted, the EH I type material is dominated by the presence of a distinctive macroscopic fabric (Macroscopic Group 4; see Figure 1.12). This correlates to a distinct petrographic fabric, first recognised in the Neolithic samples, containing sandstone grading into low-grade metamorphic rock fragments, accompanied by rare serpentinite and degraded basic igneous inclusions (Figure 1.12). These inclusions can be sourced to those Upper Pliocene-Pleistocene flysch outcrops which contain sandstones and ophiolitic bodies located in the area south of Midea and in the Talioti Valley.

As discussed in detail elsewhere (Burke *et al.* 2018; Burke *et al.* 2020), this fabric has a number of key features relating to the types of raw materials, firing practices, typology and its distribution patterns (also discussed by Weisshaar 1990; Dousougli 1987) that link it to an important centre of production in the Argolid. It appears in a category of red firing and/or red slipped pottery, and was commonly used for the production of fruitstands in particular. Importantly, it becomes the most abundant fabric group for a wide

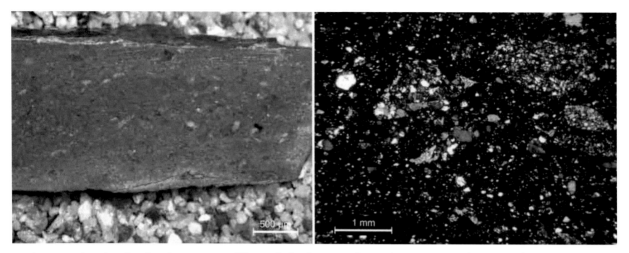

Figure 1.12. Sample MID 13/35. The macroscopic fabric and related petrographic Sandstone to Low Grade Metamorphic fabric at Midea (© C. Burke).

range of EH II pottery types at many of the Argive sites we have examined, including Midea, suggesting that its associated potting centre became the dominant supplier in the area.

The second significant fabric associated with EH I type pottery is characterised by the presence of intermediate volcanic rock fragments (predominantly andesite) and matches Gauss and Kiriatzi's FG1 (2011) from the island of Aegina, *c.* 75km east of Midea. As noted above, these imports are clearly identified in the hand specimen by the presence of gold mica (Figure 1.13).

Andesite fabrics have also been identified in comparable EH I and EH II material at Tsoungiza (Burke *et al.* 2016) and Delpriza (Burke 2017), and EH II material at Korakou (Burke 2017), as well as in Attica associated with EH I-II and II pottery from Kontopigado-Alimos (Tsai and Day work in progress) and EH II Koropi (Douni and Day work in progress), highlighting the wide distribution of vessels from the island during this time. At Midea, and comparative sites, andesite fabrics are commonly found in bowl shapes which are characterised both by

the presence of gold mica and their thick red-brown slipped and highly burnished surface treatment. It is interesting to note that analysis at Midea and elsewhere shows that similar bowl forms were made locally at all of the sites studied (Burke 2017), which serves to highlight the effort of importation from Aegina, and it may have been that the quality of the finish of the Aeginetan examples was a contributing factor in their clear desirability for consumers. As andesite grinding stones were also circulated during this time it is likely that the two products may have travelled together from the island to the mainland.

Early Bronze Age firing

The Sandstone to Low Grade Metamorphic MG4 fabric displays a range of characteristics related to firing. The vessels commonly have a red surface which is sometimes slipped also in a red colour, suggesting firing in a predominantly oxidising atmosphere. However, there are examples with mottled surface colours suggestive of exposure to mixed atmospheric conditions during firing, and others exhibiting a thick

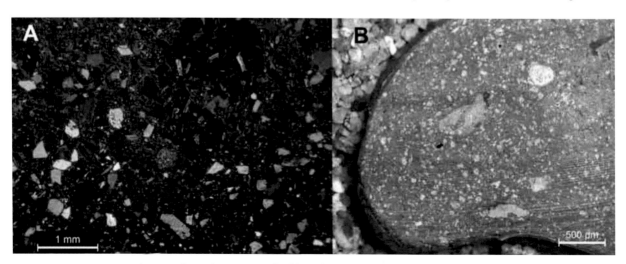

Figure 1.13. Sample MID 13/29 A: photomicrograph of the andesite fabric; B: image of macroscopic fabric (© C. Burke).

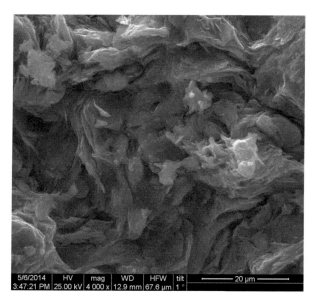

Figure 1.14. SEM image of MID 13/31 (x4000 magnification) displaying an unvitrified microstructure suggestive of firing below 750°C (© C. Burke).

Figure 1.15. SEM image of MID 13/29 (x4000 magnification) displaying an unvitrified microstructure (© C. Burke).

grey core with sharp borders indicative of incomplete oxidation of the vessel due to fast firing (Figure 1.12).

SEM analysis has revealed samples with predominantly non-vitrified microstructures (Figure 1.14). However, comparative samples of the same fabric from other sites testify to equivalent firing temperature ranges up to 950°C (Burke 2017; Burke *et al.* 2018).

The presence of uneven surface colours, thick firing cores, and evidence for a range of firing temperatures may indicate the use of poorly controlled and/or fast firing techniques (Burke 2017; Burke *et al.* 2018). The analysis of the same fabrics from a number of sites and phases demonstrates the existence of a long-practiced firing tradition that continued into EB II, contrasting with the centres of production and technological practices responsible for the characteristic high quality dark slipped pottery of EH II (Burke *et al.* 2016; Burke *et al.* 2018; Burke *et al.* 2020).

Finally, turning to the Aeginetan import, the optical activity of the micromass and the presence of a burnished surface provided an early indication that this vessel was fired at low firing temperature ranges. This was confirmed by SEM analysis which identified the presence of non-vitrified microstructures consistent with equivalent temperature ranges below 750°C (see Figure 1.15).

This result corroborates SEM analysis of the same fabric at Kolonna on Aegina (Gauss and Kiriatzi 2011: 271) and other sites in the northeastern Peloponnese (Burke 2017). As already discussed in relation to the Neolithic, low firing temperatures allow the preservation of the burnished finishes of these vessels.

Conclusion

This new ceramic evidence suggests that the Upper Acropolis of Midea saw activity from at least the later part of the LN period, i.e. early 5th millennium BC. According to both 14C dating and pottery typology, the FN use of the site begins in the earliest part of the FN period (4300 BC) and continues later into the 4th millennium BC.

The LN pottery is characterised by a high proportion of fine ware, while that of the FN period is dominated by coarse ware. The style of decoration visible in the LN and FN Pattern Painted and Fine Incised wares indicates the involvement of Midea in local northeastern Peloponnesian networks of interaction, which perhaps found expression in dining activity at the site. A comparatively common special form in the material of Midea is the cheese-pot with a row of perforations under the rim. It has been suggested that these perforations had a functional purpose for fixing a cover over the vessel which was most probably used during food production. In early EH I, we see the appearance of the fruitstand and the large shallow bowl at Midea and at other sites in the Argolid, such as Makrovouni and Talioti, these widespread changes most likely reflect a shared change in consumption and potentially dining practices across the northeastern Peloponnese and further afield.

Macroscopic fabric analysis has identified similarities within the coarse and fine ware assemblages at Midea indicative of continuity between LN and FN production traditions. It has also indicated a major shift in practice between the FN and the start of the EBA, represented by the introduction of new shapes and new macroscopic fabrics.

The petrographic results support these macroscopic observations, adding detail about raw materials and technological practices used in the production of pottery consumed by the community at Midea. The analyses have demonstrated that potters local to Midea took part in the pan-Aegean wide technological practice of grog tempering during the Neolithic and confirmed a change between the FN and EBA, represented by the decline of the grog tempering tradition alongside the rise of an important community of practice in the Argolid region, most likely in the area of the Talioti Valley. Although as a characteristic shape, fruitstands are potentially over-represented in the sampled material from Midea, it is worth noting that the Talioti potting community appears to have been particularly focused on the production of fruitstands, with over 90% of the fruitstands sampled within the broader EBA study belonging to this fabric group, their broad consumption possibly related to specific dining practices (Burke *et al.* 2020). The Argive centre of production rose to prominence over the course of the EBA to become the predominant source of pottery for surrounding settlements (Burke *et al.* 2020; also discussed from a macroscopic perspective by Weisshaar 1990). Importantly, the identification of a potential FN import (albeit from an as yet unknown location) and the presence of EH I type pottery from Aegina demonstrates the early access that Midea had to wide reaching networks of contact and exchange.

Analysis has also shown that much of the Neolithic pottery from Midea was fired in variable conditions at low temperature ranges, a choice possibly related to the preferential use of burnishing as a method of surface modification. A similar choice may account for the likely low firing temperature of the Aeginetan sample, given that on Aegina, too, burnishing constituted a common finishing method for early exports (Burke 2017; Burke *et al.* 2018). In contrast, the Sandstone to Low Grade Metamorphic fabric exhibits variable firing temperature ranges and features consistent with the technological tradition of fast firing, prevalent at this Argive centre of production irrespective of surface finish (Burke 2017; Burke *et al.* 2018). These results make clear that firing practices were a product of specific understandings and practices tied into the wider *chaîne opératoire* and traditions of pottery production.

Bibliography

Alram-Stern, E. 2006. Die prähistorische Keramik, in E. Alram-Stern and S. Deger-Jalkotzy (eds) *Die österreichischen Ausgrabungen von Aigeira in Achaia, Aigeira I. Die Mykenische Akropolis. Faszikel 3. Vormykenische Keramik, Kleinfunde, Archäozoologische und Archäobotanische Hinterlassenschaften, Naturwissenschaftliche Datierung* (Veröffentlichungen der Mykenischen Kommission 24. Sonderschriften des Österreichischen Archäologischen Institutes 43): 15-88. Vienna: the Austrian Academy of Sciences.

Alram-Stern, E. 2014. Times of change: Greece and the Aegean during the 4th millennium BC, in B. Horejs and M. Mehofer (eds) *Western Anatolia before Troy. Proto-Urbanisation in the 4th Millennium BC? Proceedings of the International Symposium Held at the Kunsthistorisches Museum Wien, Vienna, Austria, 21-24 November 2012* (Oriental and European Archaeology 1): 305-327. Vienna: the Austrian Academy of Sciences.

Alram-Stern, E. 2018. Early Helladic II pottery from Midea in the Argolid: forms and fabrics pointing to special use and import, in B. Horejs and E. Alram-Stern (eds) *Pottery Technologies and Sociocultural Connections between the Aegean and Anatolia during the 3rd Millennium BC* (Oriental and European Archaeology 10): 161-181. Vienna: the Austrian Academy of Sciences.

Banks, E.C. 2015. *Lerna VII. The Neolithic Settlement.* Princeton: the American School of Classical Studies at Athens.

Bourdieu, P. 2009 [1977]. *Outline of a Theory of Practice.* Cambridge: Cambridge University Press.

Broodbank, C. 1993. Ulysses without sails: trade, distance, knowledge and power in the early Cyclades. *World Archaeology* 24(3): 315-331.

Burke, C. 2017. Crafting Continuity and Change: Ceramic Technology of the Early Helladic Peloponnese, Greece. Unpublished PhD dissertation, University of Sheffield.

Burke, C. and S. Spencer-Wood (eds) 2018. *Crafting in the World: Materiality in the Making.* New York: Springer.

Burke, C., P. Day, E. Alram-Stern, K. Demakopoulou and A. Hein 2018. Crafting and consumption choices: Neolithic-Early Helladic II ceramic production and distribution, Midea and Tiryns, Mainland Greece, in B. Horejs and E. Alram-Stern (eds) *Pottery Technologies and Sociocultural Connections between the Aegean and Anatolia during the 3rd Millennium BC* (OREA 10): 145-159. Vienna: the Austrian Academy of Sciences.

Burke, C., P.M. Day and A. Kossyva 2020. Early Helladic I and Talioti pottery: is it just a phase we're going through? *Oxford Journal of Archaeology* 39(1): 19-40.

Burke, C., P.M. Day and D. Pullen 2016. The contribution of petrography to understanding the production and consumption of Early Helladic ceramics from Nemea, Mainland Greece, in M.F. Ownby, I.C. Druc and M.A. Masucci (eds) *Integrative Approaches in Ceramic Petrography:* 104-115. Salt Lake City: University of Utah Press.

Day, P.M. 2004. Marriage and mobility: traditions and the dynamics of the pottery system in twentieth century East Crete, in P.P. Betancourt,

C. Davaras and R. Hope Simpson (eds) *Pseira VIII. The Archaeological Survey of Pseira Island, Part 1* (Prehistory Monographs 11): 105-139. Philadelphia, Pennsylvania: INSTAP Academic Press.

Day P.M. and V. Kilikoglou 2001. Analysis of ceramics from the kiln, in J.W. Shaw, A. Van de Moortel, P.M. Day and V. Kilikoglou (eds) *A LM IA Ceramic Kiln in South-Central Crete: Function and Pottery Production* (Hesperia Supplement 30): 111-133. Princeton: the American School of Classical Studies at Athens.

Day, P.M., L. Joyner, E. Kiriatzi and M. Relaki 2005. Appendix 3: Petrographic analysis of some Final Neolithic-Early Minoan II pottery from the Kavousi area, in D.C. Haggis. *Kavousi I. The Archaeological Survey of the Kavousi Region* (Prehistory Monographs 16): 177-195. Philadelphia, Pennsylvania: INSTAP Academic Press.

Day, P.M. and D.E. Wilson 2004. Ceramic change and the practice of eating and drinking in Early Bronze Age Crete, in P. Halstead and J.C. Barrett (eds) *Food, Cuisine and Society in Prehistoric Greece* (Sheffield Studies in Aegean Archaeology 5): 45-62. Oxford: Oxbow Books.

Demakopoulou, K. 2012. *The Mycenaean Acropolis of Midea.* Athens: Ministry of Culture and Tourism, Archaeological Receipts and Expropriations Fund.

Demakopoulou, K. and E. Alram-Stern, in preparation. *Pre-Mycenaean Midea. The Late Neolithic to Middle Bronze Age Settlement. Excavations on the Acropolis of Midea. Results of the Greek-Swedish Excavation of Midea.*

Demakopoulou, K., N. Divari-Valakou, M. Nilsson and A.L. Schallin, 2006-2007. Excavations in Midea 2005. *Opuscula Atheniensia: Annual of the Swedish Institute at Athens* 31-32: 7-29.

Demakopoulou, K., N. Divari-Valakou, M. Nilsson, A.L. Schallin and K. Nikita 2008. Excavations in Midea 2006. *Opuscula: Annual of the Swedish Institutes at Athens and Rome* 1: 7-30.

Demakopoulou, K., N. Divari-Valakou, A. L. Schallin, L. Sjögren and M. Nilsson 2005. Excavations in Midea 2004. *Opuscula Atheniensia: Annual of the Swedish Institute at Athens* 30: 7-34.

Dousougli, A. 1987. Makrovouni-Kefalari Magoula-Talioti. Bemerkungen zu den Stufen FHI und II in der Argolis. *Prähistorische Zeitschrift* 62(2): 164-220.

Dousougli, A. 1998. Άρια Αργολίδος. Χειροποίητη κεραμική της νεότερης νεολιθικής και της χαλκολιθικής περιόδου (Υπουργείο Πολιτισμού Δημοσιεύματα του Αρχαιολογικού Δελτίου 66). Athens: Ministry of Culture, Archaeological Receipts and Expropriations Fund.

Fossey, J.M. 1969. The prehistoric settlement by Lake Vouliagmeni, Perachora. *The Annual of the British School at Athens* 64: 53-69.

Gauss, W. and E. Kiriatzi 2011. *Pottery production and Supply at Bronze Age Kolonna, Aegina: An Integrated Archaeological and Scientific Study of a Ceramic Landscape.* Vienna: the Austrian Academy of Sciences.

Gosselain, O. 1998. Social and technical identity in a clay crystal ball, in M. Stark (ed.) *The Archaeology of Social Boundaries*: 79-106. London and Washington: Smithsonian Institution Press.

Gosselain, O. and A. Livingstone Smith 2005. The source. Clay selection and processing practices in Sub Saharan Africa, in A. Livingstone Smith, D. Bosquet and R. Martineau (eds) *Pottery Manufacturing Processes: Reconstruction and Interpretation* (British Archaeological Reports International Series 1349): 33-48. Oxford: Archaeopress.

Halstead, P. 2012. Feast, food and fodder in Neolithic-Bronze Age Greece. Commensality and the construction of value, in S. Pollock (ed.) *Between Feasts and Daily Meals: Toward an Archaeology of Commensal Spaces* (eTopoi: Journal for Ancient Studies Special Volume, 2): 21-51. Berlin: Edition Topoi.

Iliopoulos, I., V. Xanthopoulou and P. Tsolis-Katagas 2011. A petrographic assessment of houseware and storage pithoi in the Early Helladic settlement of Helike, Achaea, Greece, in D. Katsonopoulou (ed.) *Helike IV: Ancient Helike and Aigialeia. Protohelladika: the Southern and Central Greek Mainland*: 127-142. Athens: the Helike Society.

Katsarou, S. and A. Sampson 1997. Φάσεις I-III. Η νεολιθική κεραμική, in A. Sampson (ed.) *Το Σπήλαιο των Λιμνών στα Καστριά Καλαβρύτων: Μία προϊστορική θέση στην ορεινή Πελοπόννησο* (Εταιρεία Πελοποννησιακών Σπουδών 7): 77-273: Athens: the Society of Peloponnesian Studies.

Katsipanou-Margeli, B. 2018. The stratigraphic and pottery sequence of Trench B1 at Alepotrypa Cave: a first approach to the investigation of ceramic and chronological associations, in A. Papathanasiou, W.A. Parkinson, D.J. Pullen, M.L. Galaty and P. Karkanas (eds) *Neolithic Alepotrypa Cave in the Mani, Greece. In Honor of George Papathanassopoulos*: 33-90: Oxford: Oxbow Books.

Lave, J. and E. Wenger 1991. Learning in doing: social, cognitive, and computational perspectives, in J. Lave and E. Wenger. *Situated Learning: Legitimate peripheral participation.* Cambridge: Cambridge University Press

Lemonnier, P. (ed.) 2002. *Technological Choices: Transformation in Material Cultures since the Neolithic.* London: Routledge.

Lemonnier, P. 2012. *Mundane Objects: Materiality and Non-Verbal Communication* (UCL Institute of Archaeological Critical Cultural Heritage Series 10). California: Left Coast Press.

Maniatis, Y. and M.S. Tite 1981. Technological examination of Neolithic-Bronze Age pottery from Central and Southeast Europe and from the Near-East. *Journal of Archaeological Science* 8: 59-76.

Mauss, M. 2009[1934]. *Techniques, Technology and Civilization* (edited and with an introduction by N.

Schlanger). New York and Oxford: Durkheim Press and Berghahn Books.

Mee, C. 2007. The production and consumption of pottery in the Neolithic Peloponnese, in C. Mee and J. Renard (eds) *Cooking up the Past. Food and Culinary Practices in the Neolithic and Bronze Age Aegean*: 200-224. Oxford: Oxbow Books.

Mentesana, R. 2016. The Final Neolithic-Early Bronze Age Transition in Phaistos, Crete: an Investigation of Continuity and Change in Ceramic Manufacture. Unpublished PhD dissertation, University of Sheffield.

Pantelidou Gofa, M. 2013. Ανασκαφή Τσέπι Μαραθώνος. *Πρακτικά της εν Αθήναις Αρχαιολογικής Εταιρείας* 165(2010): 171-175.

Pantelidou Gofa, M. 2016. *Τσέπι Μαραθώνος. Ο αποθέτης 39 του προϊστορικού νεκροταφείου* (Βιβλιοθήκη της εν Αθήναις Αρχαιολογικής Εταιρείας 310). Athens: the Archaeological Society of Athens.

Papastamatiou, J., D. Vetoulis, A.A. Tataris, G. Christodolou, J. Bornova, N. Lalechos and G.D. Kounis 1970. *Geological Map of Greece. 1:50,000. Argos*. Athens: Institute for Geology and Subsurface Research.

Papathanassopoulos, G.A. 2011. *Το νεολιθικό Διρό. Σπήλαιο Αλεπότρυπα, Τόμος I*. Athens: Melissa Publishing House.

Papavassiliou, C., D. Bannert, H. Risch, U. Pflaumann and G. Katsikatsos 1984. *Geological Map of Greece. 1:50,000. Lygourion*. Athens: Institute of Geology and Mineral Exploration.

Pentedeka, A. 2015. Technological and provenance study of the Visviki Magoula ceramic assemblage, in E. Alram-Stern and A. Dousougli-Zachos (eds) *Visviki Magoula/Velestino. Die deutschen Grabungen des Jahres 1941* (Beiträge zur ur- und frühgeschichtlichen Archäologie des Mittelmeer-Kulturraumes 36): 222-297. Bonn: Rudolf Habelt.

Phelps, W.W. 2004. *The Neolithic Pottery Sequence in Southern Greece* (British Archaeological Reports International Series 1259). Oxford: Archaeopress.

Pullen, D.J. 2011. *Nemea Valley Archaeological Project I. The Early Bronze Age Village on Tsoungiza Hill*. Princeton: the American School of Classical Studies at Athens.

Quinn, P., P.M. Day, V. Kilikoglou, E. Faber, S. Katsarou-Tzeveleki and A. Sampson 2010. Keeping an eye on your pots: the provenance of Neolithic ceramics from the Cave of the Cyclops, Youra, Greece. *Journal of Archaeological Science* 37(5): 1042-1052.

Rambach, J. 2000. *Kykladen I. Die frühe Bronzezeit. Grab- und Siedlungsbefunde* (Beiträge zur ur- und frühgeschichtlichen Archäologie des Mittelmeer-Kulturraumes 33). Bonn: Rudolf Habelt.

Sampson, A. (ed.) 1997. *Το Σπήλαιο των Λιμνών στα Καστριά Καλαβρύτων: Μία προϊστορική θέση στην ορεινή Πελοπόννησο*. Athens: the Society of Peloponnesian Studies.

Stark, M., B. Bowser and L. Horne (eds) 2008. *Cultural Transmission and Material Culture. Breaking Down Boundaries*. Tucson: Arizona University Press.

Tomkins, P. 2002. The Production, Circulation and Consumption of Ceramic Vessels at Early Neolithic Knossos, Crete. Unpublished PhD dissertation, University of Sheffield.

Tsirtsoni, Z. (ed.) 2016. *The Human Face of Radiocarbon. Reassessing Chronology in Prehistoric Greece and Bulgaria, 5000-3000 cal BC* (Maison de l'Orient et de la Méditerranée 69). Lyon: House of the Orient and the Mediterranean-Jean Pouilloux.

Van der Leeuw, S.E. 2002. Giving the potter a choice, in P. Lemonnier (ed.) *Technological Choices: Transformation in Material Cultures since the Neolithic*: 238-288. London: Routledge.

Vitelli, K.D. 1999. *Franchthi Neolithic Pottery, Volume 2, The Later Neolithic Ceramic Phases 3 to 5* (Excavations at Franchthi Cave, Greece, Fascicle 10). Bloomington and Indianapolis: Indiana University Press.

Vitelli, K. D. 2007. *Lerna. A Preclassical Site in the Argolid: Results of Excavations conducted by the American School of Classical Studies at Athens, Volume V. The Neolithic Pottery from Lerna*. Princeton: the American School of Classical Studies at Athens.

Weisshaar, H.-J., 1989. *Die deutschen Ausgrabungen auf der Pevkakia-Magula in Thessalien I. Das späte Neolithikum und das Chalkolithikum*, (Beiträge zur ur- und frühgeschichtlichen Archäologie des Mittelmeer-Kulturraumes 28). Bonn: Rudolf Habelt.

Weisshaar, H.-J. 1990. Die Keramik von Talioti, in U. Jantzen (ed.) *Tiryns, Forschungen und Berichte XI*: 1–34. Mainz: Philipp von Zabern.

Wenger, E. 1998. *Communities of practice: Learning, meaning, and identity*. Cambridge: Cambridge University Press.

Whitbread, I.K. and A. Mari 2014. Provenance and proximity: a technological analysis of Late and Final Neolithic ceramics from Euripides Cave, Salamis. *Journal of Archaeological Science* 41: 79-88.

Wilson, D.E. and P.M. Day 2000. EM I chronology and social practice: pottery from the early palace tests at Knossos. *The Annual of the British School at Athens* 95: 21 63.

Zachos, K. 2008. *Ayios Dhimitrios. A Prehistoric Settlement in the Southwestern Peloponnese: the Neolithic and Early Helladic Periods* (British Archaeological Reports, International Series 1770). Oxford: Archaeopress.

Zangger, E. 1993. *The Geoarchaeology of the Argolid* (Argolis II). Berlin: Gebr. Mann.

Zaronikos, J.N., A.A. Tataris, G.A. Kallergis and G.D. Kounis 1970. *Geological Map of Greece. 1:50,000. Nafplion*. Athens: Institute of Geology and Mineral Exploration.

Kouphovouno and the Cyclades: A Note

R. L. N. Barber

A recent survey of the radiocarbon chronology of mainland Greece, based on analyses of samples from excavations at Kouphovouno conducted by Bill Cavanagh, Chris Mee and Josette Renard (Cavanagh *et al.* 2016), has implications for the Cyclades. These lie in the suggested priority of the beginning of the Middle Cycladic (MC) period over the Middle Helladic (MH) and are particularly relevant to a proposal by Robert Buck (1964: 290), in the only full study of MH Matt-painted pottery so far published, that Cycladic 'Geometric' pottery (as defined by Edgar 1904: 93-102) was of earlier origin and its likely source of inspiration.

The close similarity of the early 'Geometric' pottery of Phylakopi, and other Cycladic islands, to the Matt-painted pottery of the Saronic island of Aegina and many Middle Helladic sites on mainland Greece is undeniable — the distribution of the barrel jar shape[1] (Buck 1964: 247-248, shape C1), with characteristic Geometric decoration, provides a striking example — but it is noteworthy that obvious differences in styles of painting and, in some instances, the results of clay analysis, suggest multiple production centres, even though many of the mainland pieces are thought to come from Aegina (Philippa-Touchais 2002: 37).

The Cyclades enter the Kouphovouno-based framework via three samples from Phase A of recent excavations at Akrotiri, dated to *c.* 2280-2130 BC (2σ) (*c.* 2205-2140 BC (1σ)).[2] Although the integrity of Akrotiri Phase A is questionable (Sotirakopoulou 2016: 355-356), and its wholesale assignation to a Middle Cycladic phase highly improbable given the apparently secondary nature of the deposits, and the fact that it contains elements which must be EC III in date (Knappett and Nikolakopoulou 2008: 3, table I; Nikolakopoulou *et al.* 2008: 313; Nikolakopoulou 2019b: 149-150, for reference to finds of DFI (Dark-faced Incised), which are diagnostic of early EC IIIB; for EC III, cf. also Renfrew

and Evans 2007: 176). It also appears to lack some classic MC features.

Nevertheless, even if Akrotiri Phase A were an integrated group, with the samples from the early end of the spectrum represented by the pottery, the dates could be applied to contexts no later (and quite possibly earlier) than early EC IIIB (= Phylakopi I-ii), the first point at which 'Geometric' pottery is found at Phylakopi. If they were associated with the later end, they would probably relate to the early phase of the Second City there (Phylakopi II-i), with the suggested absolute dates (Cavanagh *et al.* 2016: 46, table 5) pointing to an origin of the Geometric style some 200 years earlier (presumably, still in early EC IIIB).

As regards the later pottery spectrum in Akrotiri Phase A, again as viewed from Melos, it is coming to seem increasingly likely that we have been wrong to dismiss Mackenzie's phase II-i of the Second City at Phylakopi (Barber 1983: 77-78) and that a number of elements can be identified as probably belonging to it (Barber 2017: 75).[3] The most probable explanation[4] of this is that there was a long phase, best termed for the moment 'transitional' (end of City I / early City II at Phylakopi), between classic EC III and classic MC. Phase A at Akrotiri certainly includes, as well as the earlier material, a considerable number of elements which, at Phylakopi, would be assigned to such a transitional stage.

A, perhaps somewhat risky, historical speculation is prompted by the presence, for instance, of Combination Ware (one of the main features of the transition) in I-iii levels at Phylakopi. This indicates that the transition had begun before the end of the First City there and that, at Akrotiri, the clearance represented by backfilling of the rock-cut chambers might have been the result of an episode contemporary with the destruction of Phylakopi I.

Returning to the relationship between Cycladic 'Geometric' and mainland Matt-painted pottery, which was the primary stimulus for this note, we should not forget the indications (MacGillivray 1984), independent of the radiocarbon chronology, which point to

---

[1] Illustrations of Cycladic 'Geometric', Aeginetan and mainland Matt-painted barrel jars: Phylakopi: Atkinson *et al.* (1904: pl. viii, no. 4); Paros: Rubensohn (1917: 58, fig. 62; 61, fig. 67, etc.); Thera: Nikolakopoulou (2019a: 215, table 3.1 (3/4), shape G1; 2019b: 64, no. 339, pl. 24); Orchomenos: Sarri (2010: pl. 77, nos. 1, 2 (= col.pl. 5, nos. 5, 6)); Eutresis: Goldman (1931: 147 fig. 201; 149, fig. 205); Aegina, Kolonna: Siedentopf (1991: pl. 16f); Argos: Philippa-Touchais (2002: 27, fig. 23, no. 71); Lerna: Caskey (1955: pl. 12b).
[2] The samples in question, derived from a compressed seed block from Pillar Pit 67N, are discussed in Nikolakopoulou (2019a: 37-38), and appear in Cavanagh *et al.* (2016: 46, table 5). I am most grateful to Professor Christos Doumas who invited me to Akrotiri several years ago to look at the material, and to Dr Irene Nikolakopoulou who showed me some of the pottery from these excavations.

[3] To the Combination Ware and Thick Linear style pottery mentioned there should be added the 'Geometric pottery with designs in matt black' discussed by Edgar (1904: 102-106), now known as Soft Matt-Painted (SMP).
[4] I hope shortly to address this matter further.

associations of Cycladic 'Geometric' pottery with mainland contexts earlier than MH. This position has received some further tentative support in discussion of recent finds from Kolonna on Aegina (Gauss and Smetana 2008: 338). Thus, even without the Akrotiri dates, there is a good case for continuing to uphold Buck's view.

Finally, one may enquire the reasons for the mainlanders' enthusiasm for contact with the Cyclades (perhaps particularly Melos) as demonstrated by the pottery. It may have lain partly in the trading activities of the islanders, bringing to the mainland products whose nature and sources we cannot identify. But the most obvious tangible commodity of value which the Cyclades possessed was Melian obsidian, of great importance to mainland communities where the use of metals was not yet highly developed.[5]

Bibliography

Atkinson, T.D., R.C. Bosanquet, C.C. Edgar, A.J. Evans, D.G. Hogarth, D. Mackenzie, C. Smith and F.B. Welch 1904. *Excavations at Phylakopi in Melos* (Society for the Promotion of Hellenic Studies Supplementary Paper no. 4). London: Macmillan.

Barber, R.L.N. 1983. The definition of the Middle Cycladic period. *American Journal of Archaeology* 87(1): 76-81.

Barber, R. 2017. Phylakopi on Melos and the National Archaeological Museum, in M. Lagogianni-Georgakarakos (ed.) *Odysseys*: 71-78. Athens: Ministry of Culture, Archaeological Receipts and Expropriations Fund.

Buck, R.J. 1964. Middle Helladic mattpainted pottery. *Hesperia: the Journal of the American School of Classical Studies at Athens* 33(3): 231-313.

Caskey, J.L. 1955. Excavations at Lerna, 1954. *Hesperia: the Journal of the American School of Classical Studies at Athens* 24(1): 25-49.

Cavanagh, W., C. Mee and J. Renard 2016. Early Bronze Age chronology of mainland Greece: a review with new dates from the excavations at Kouphovouno. *The Annual of the British School at Athens* 111: 35-49.

Edgar, C.C. 1904. IV. The pottery, in Atkinson, T.D., R.C. Bosanquet, C.C. Edgar, A.J. Evans, D.G. Mackenzie, C. Smith and F.B. Welch 1904. *Excavations at Phylakopi in Melos* (Society for the Promotion of Hellenic Studies Supplementary Paper no. 4): 80-176. London: Macmillan.

Gauss, W. and R. Smetana 2008. Aegina Kolonna and the Cyclades, in N. Brodie, J. Doole, G. Gavalas and C. Renfrew (eds) *Horizon. A Colloquium on the Prehistory of the Cyclades*: 325-338. Cambridge: McDonald Institute for Archaeological Research.

Goldman, H. 1931. *Excavations at Eutresis in Boeotia.* Cambridge, Mass: Harvard University Press.

Knappett, C.J. and I. Nikolakopoulou 2008. Colonialism without colonies? A Bronze Age case study from Akrotiri, Thera. *Hesperia: the Journal of the American School of Classical Studies at Athens* 77(1): 1-42.

MacGillivray, J. A., 1984. The relative chronology of Early Cycladic III, in J. MacGillivray and R.L.N. Barber (eds) *The Prehistoric Cyclades. Contributions to a Workshop on Cycladic Chronology*: 70-77. Edinburgh: Department of Classical Archaeology, The University of Edinburgh.

Nikolakopoulou, I. 2019a. *Akrotiri, Thera. Middle Bronze Age Pottery and Stratigraphy, Volume I. Stratigraphy, Ceramic Typology and Technology, Weaving Equipment* (Βιβλιοθήκη της εν Αθήναις Αρχαιολογικής Εταιρείας 318). Athens: the Archaeological Society at Athens.

Nikolakopoulou, I. 2019b. *Akrotiri, Thera. Middle Bronze Age Pottery and Stratigraphy, Volume II. The Pottery Catalogue. Plates and Drawings* (Βιβλιοθήκη της εν Αθήναις Αρχαιολογικής Εταιρείας 319). Athens: the Archaeological Society at Athens.

Nikolakopoulou, I., F. Georma, A. Moschou and P. Sofianou 2008. Trapped in the middle: new stratigraphic and ceramic evidence from Middle Cycladic Akrotiri, Thera, in N. Brodie, J. Doole, G. Gavalas and C. Renfrew (eds) *Horizon. A Colloquium on the Prehistory of the Cyclades*: 311-324. Cambridge: McDonald Institute for Archaeological Research.

Philippa-Touchais, A. 2002. Aperçu des céramiques mésohelladiques à décor peint de l'Aspis d'Argos. I. La céramique à peinture mate. *Bulletin de Correspondance Hellénique* 126(1): 1-40.

Photos-Jones, E. and A. J. Hall 2014. *Eros, Mercator and the Cultural Landscape of Melos in Antiquity: the Archaeology of the Minerals Industries of Melos.* Glasgow: Potingair Press.

Renfrew, C. and R.K. Evans 2007. The Early Bronze Age pottery, in C. Renfrew, N. Brodie, C. Morris and C. Scarre (eds) *Excavations at Phylakopi in Melos 1974-77* (The British School at Athens Supplementary Volume 42): 129-180. London: the British School at Athens.

Rubensohn, O. 1917. Die prähistorischen und frühgeschichtlichen Funde auf dem Burghügel von

---

[5] The extensive mineral wealth of Melos (comprising aluminium silicates (clays), sulphur and sulphates (alum)), have a variety of possible applications, including as pigments (white Melian Earth), mordants (substances that fix dyes) for the textile industry (alum), fumigants (sulphur), or medicines/therapeutic products (alum/sulphur) (Photos-Jones and Hall 2014). These may also have contributed to the island's importance in prehistoric times. Dr Photos-Jones (personal communication) has pointed out that the intensive working of Melian obsidian (a glass of volcanic origin) by the island's inhabitants, in the Neolithic and Early Bronze Age, would have inevitably resulted in minor cuts and bleeding. Alum is a group of minerals (not a single mineral) of which Melos has a substantial number. These were extracted extensively in the Roman period, in the southeast of the island. Alum group minerals are astringent and, as such, can act as haemostatics (substances capable of stopping haemorrhage). It seems not unlikely that the obsidian workers of Melos may have discovered this and made commercial, as well as personal, use of their discovery. Although not yet demonstrated archaeologically, this suggestion gains credence from references to alum in the Linear B tablets (Photos-Jones and Hall 2014: 54-55).

Paros. *Mitteilungen des Deutschen Archäologischen Instituts, Athenische Abteilung* 42: 1–98.

Sarri, K. 2010. *Orchomenos IV. Orchomenos in der mittleren Bronzezeit* (Bayerische Akademie der Wissenschaften, Philosophisch-Historische Klasse Abhandlungen, Neue Folge, Heft 135). Munich: the Bavarian Academy of Sciences and Humanities.

Siedentopf, H.B. 1991. *Alt-Ägina IV,2: Mattbemalte Keramik der Mittleren Bronzezeit, unter Mitarbeit von Wolfgang Wohlmayr.* Mainz: von Zabern.

Sotirakopoulou, P. 2016. *The Pottery from Dhaskalio. The Sanctuary on Keros and the Origins of Aegean Ritual: the Excavations of 2006-2008, Volume IV.* Cambridge: McDonald Institute for Archaeological Research.

A Submerged EH II Settlement at Lambayanna in the Argolid: the Preliminary Results of the 2015 Survey[1]

Julien Beck, Patrizia Birchler Emery and Despina Koutsoumba

Introduction

The Bay of Kiladha Project represents a joint research collaboration between the University of Geneva, under the aegis of the Swiss School of Archaeology in Greece (ESAG), and the Ephorate of Underwater Antiquities, and has, since 2012, carried out a programme of study focused on the prehistoric landscape today submerged below the small bay of Kiladha in the Southern Argolid, close to the well-known site of Franchthi Cave. In the summer of 2013, an experimental underwater coring system was deployed at Lambayanna beach, a few hundred metres to the north of Franchthi Cave (Figure 3.1) (Beck and Koutsoumba 2014). Lambayanna had been chosen as a test site because it was understood to be devoid of archaeological remains by the local port authorities and by the Ephorate of Underwater Antiquities. Yet, upon snorkelling a few tens of metres from the shore, it became clear that there were built stone features on the sea floor, including, at some considerable distance from the coastline, a number of apparently massive constructions. A preliminary plan of the site was created with the help of a standard GPS.

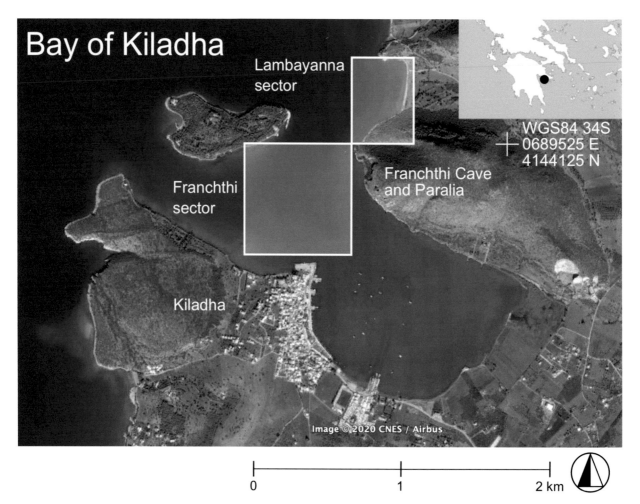

Figure 3.1. Map of the Bay of Kiladha showing the areas of the underwater survey.

[1] The authors wish to thank the former directors of the Ephorate of Underwater Antiquities, A. Simosi and P. Kalamara, as well as the former director of the Swiss School of Archaeology in Greece, K. Reber, for their support.

In 2014, the Bay of Kiladha formed an integral part of the University of Geneva's *Terra Submersa* Expedition; a project designed to map the submerged prehistoric landscapes of the Eastern Argolic Gulf. Data was collected with the help of the world's largest solar-powered boat, *PlanetSolar*, and the Hellenic Centre for Marine Research oceanographic research vessel, *Alkyon* (Beck and Koutsoumba 2015; Beck *et al.* 2017; Sakellariou *et al.* 2015). Over the course of the season, a dive team was also deployed to explore the seabed along the modern coastline, with special attention given to Lambayanna beach. This work revealed that the features first observed in 2013 formed part of a submerged settlement represented by walls of different sizes and orientations, and a large quantity of EH II potsherds which provided the architectural remains with a preliminary date.

An intensive survey was undertaken in 2015 (Beck and Koutsoumba 2016). On this occasion, numerous walls and buildings were discovered, and more than 5800 potsherds and other objects were recovered. As a result of the identification of an unexpectedly large number of built structures, and because submerged pottery is required to undergo desalination as part of an extended conservation process, the study of the 2015 finds is still in progress, and so only a preliminary report can be presented here.

The site

The pebble beach of Lambayanna stretches for a distance of *c.* 350m on a roughly north-south orientation. It is flanked at its northern end by a small rocky cliff surmounted by the church of Ayios Yannis Lambayannas, which gives the beach its name, and at its southern end by rocks which mark the beginning of the path to Franchthi Cave. The visible remains, formed mostly of collapsed stones from the foundations of walls and buildings, are almost entirely located in the centre of the beach, extending to the north up to *c.* 100m from the cliff, and to the south up to *c.* 100m from the rocks. They are limited to the east by a 30m wide sandbar along the beach and, to the west, continue to a distance of up to *c.* 100m from the shore (Figure 3.2b), covering a total area of approximately 1.2ha, at depths below sea level of between 1m and 3m.

The 2015 survey

Due to the limited time available, it was decided that the survey should adopt a simple 20m by 20m square grid to allow coverage of most of the area between the cliff to the north and rocks to the south. The survey area was not extended to the south of the visible remains due to the presence of a large number of beachrock formations which were thought to have acted as a natural barrier

to any expansion of the settlement southward. This theory was subsequently proved wrong by the discovery of EH II pottery within the beachrock. In total, the grid extended across an area of 100m by 280m (2.8ha), which was divided into 70 squares designated K10 to O23 (see Figure 3.2a). The grid itself was marked at the surface by buoys which were set at the corners of each square, and snorkelers (at depths of less than 2.5m, mainly in rows M-O) or divers (at depths of more than 2.5m, mainly in rows K-L) were instructed to undertake total collection of all relevant objects within each square. Finds were thus recorded collectively, square by square, with no attempt to locate their individual findspots more precisely within a given square. To attempt to do so would have taken a great deal of additional time, and would have provided very little additional meaningful data, as the finds were not in situ, but rather had been transported by post-depositional processes such as the collapse of built structures and, later, wave action. Each square was surveyed by a team of two to seven snorkelers or divers for between 30 and 90 minutes (the exact duration being dependant on the number of finds, and the time required to collect them).

In parallel, each square was explored for built structures, but it soon became apparent that there were too many to allow for the creation of a proper record in the time available. Therefore, only general observations were recorded, and a rough sketch of each square was made to identify those areas with concentrations of stones indicative of the presence of collapsed structures (Figure 3.2b).

The architectural remains

To judge from the high concentration of stones in squares K-O/10-18, the settlement covered a surface area of at least 1.2ha (Figure 3.2b). These stones represent collapse from the foundations of walls and buildings, many of which are still partly intact. The walls differ in length, width, orientation and building technique; although similar orientations, mainly to the north and north-west, are common, as well as the use of herringbone masonry so typical of EH architecture. Building plans were rectilinear or apsidal, as is usually the case for the EH mainland, and some of the longest walls were preserved for more than 10m. Paved surfaces made of carefully joined flat stones probably belonged to open areas or streets.

The settlement appears to have been fortified, based on the identification of a number of large wall foundations and three massive circular and horseshoe-shaped structures at the western, seaward, edge of the site (Figure 3.2b). The existence of a large wall made of flat stones had already been noted during the 2014 season (locus 100, see Beck and Koutsoumba 2015). Oriented

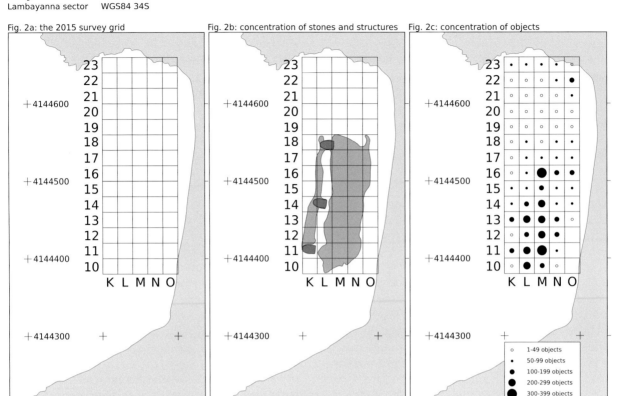

Bay of Kiladha 2015
Lambayanna sector   WGS84 34S

Fig. 2a: the 2015 survey grid

Fig. 2b: concentration of stones and structures

Fig. 2c: concentration of objects

○ 1-49 objects
• 50-99 objects
● 100-199 objects
⬤ 200-299 objects
⬤ 300-399 objects

Figure 3.2. Plans of the survey grids of the Lambayanna sector: (a) 2015 grid (b) concentration of stones and structures (c) concentration of objects.

north-south, it measured a maximum of *c.* 2.3m wide and was traced for a length of approximately 7m, joining at its southern end the northernmost horseshoe-shaped structure. During the 2015 season, another large wall with the same orientation and width, but made of rounded stones, was found to join the southernmost horseshoe-shaped structure.

The largest of the monumental horseshoe-shaped structures measures *c.* 18m by 10m. The outer limit, where preserved, is formed of carefully aligned boulders and the interior space appears to be subdivided by one or more rectilinear and/or circular walls. The structures are set at a distance of *c.* 55-60m apart, forming a line *c.* 150m in length. Their function remains a mystery.

The objects (Figure 3.3)

A total of 5851 objects were catalogued, almost all of which could be dated to EH II. Very few objects are more recent, and those that are consist overwhelmingly of potsherds: some are modern, probably thrown from fishing boats moored off the beach, though others can be dated to the Archaic, Classical, or Byzantine periods, and could also come from a small site to the south and south-east of Ayios Yannis Lambayannas church, as they were mostly found at the northern end of the bay,

close to the small rocky cliff. Of the remainder, the most productive survey squares were located further south (K-O/10-16, see Figure 3.2c).

Most of the finds consist of potsherds and terracotta fragments (5591), but other classes of object are also present, including stone implements (173), among which are a large number of ground stone tools (pounders, saddle querns, a fragment of an Ayios Kosmas-type andesite mortar and a single celt), a few obsidian blades and two nuclei, and animal bones and antlers. Potsherds form the greatest part of the material assemblage (5116). The terracotta assemblage, though far smaller (475), provides a representative range of standard EH II artefacts — including ladles, stands, spindle whorls, so-called 'anchors' (see Forsén 2008), hearths and roof tiles.[2] The surfaces of all potsherds are worn to different degrees: some are covered by

---

[2] Due to the special treatment required by those objects recovered from the seabed (i.e., their storage in water and prompt transfer to the Ephorate of underwater antiquities in Athens, for the purpose of desalination and conservation), it has not proved possible to carry out anything other than preliminary analysis of the assemblage. It has not been possible, for example, to weigh any of the artefacts, as they were always wet, nor has there been any attempt to join those fragments that seem to belong to the same object, or to undertake analyses of the fabrics represented. The final study of the finds in Athens will yield more complete results.

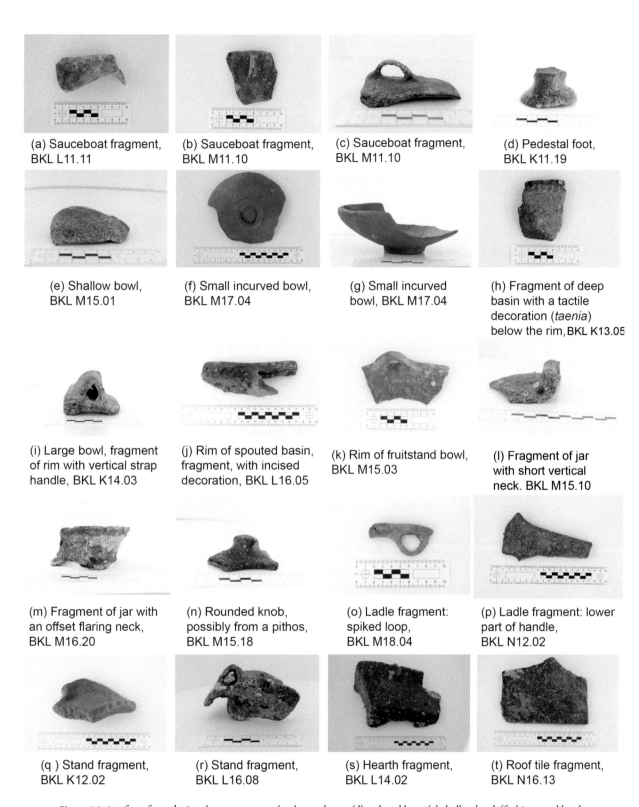

(a) Sauceboat fragment, BKL L11.11

(b) Sauceboat fragment, BKL M11.10

(c) Sauceboat fragment, BKL M11.10

(d) Pedestal foot, BKL K11.19

(e) Shallow bowl, BKL M15.01

(f) Small incurved bowl, BKL M17.04

(g) Small incurved bowl, BKL M17.04

(h) Fragment of deep basin with a tactile decoration (*taenia*) below the rim, BKL K13.05

(i) Large bowl, fragment of rim with vertical strap handle, BKL K14.03

(j) Rim of spouted basin, fragment, with incised decoration, BKL L16.05

(k) Rim of fruitstand bowl, BKL M15.03

(l) Fragment of jar with short vertical neck. BKL M15.10

(m) Fragment of jar with an offset flaring neck, BKL M16.20

(n) Rounded knob, possibly from a pithos, BKL M15.18

(o) Ladle fragment: spiked loop, BKL M18.04

(p) Ladle fragment: lower part of handle, BKL N12.02

(q) Stand fragment, BKL K12.02

(r) Stand fragment, BKL L16.08

(s) Hearth fragment, BKL L14.02

(t) Roof tile fragment, BKL N16.13

Figure 3.3. Artefacts from the Lambayanna sector: (a-c) sauceboats, (d) pedestal base, (e) shallow bowl, (f-g) incurved bowl, (h) basin, (i) strap handle, (j) spouted basin, (k) fruitstand, (l-m) jars, (n) knob, (o-p) ladles, (q) hearth, (r) roof tile.

marine organisms and seriously damaged; others still have almost smooth surfaces. None preserve any trace of paint or slip; relief decoration (in the form of different kinds of tænia band with impressed decoration) are better attested, albeit very unevenly.

The potsherds presented in this chapter represent only a very small part of the total collection. They consist almost exclusively of diagnostic bases and rims, with a smaller number of handles. Numerous body fragments, some of them rather large (commonly 20cm by 20cm, or even 20cm by 30cm), have also been recovered, but not yet thoroughly examined. Unfortunately, no vase was found intact, and very few are preserved sufficiently to provide a whole profile; those that are belong, invariably, to small bowls. The following provides a general overview of the main ceramic shapes and object types recovered from the EH settlement.

The pottery

Sauceboats

The sauceboats from Lambayanna are very badly preserved. Of the 20 fragments that could be confidently assigned to this category during preliminary observation, all are either highly diagnostic fragments of spouts, or body sherds preserving part of the characteristic horizontal or vertical handle. Most of the fragments belong to sauceboats of Lerna Type 2, although one could be an early Type 3 and two could be Type 3 (see Wiencke 2000: 585-587). All three types are characteristic of the EH II developed phase (Tsoungiza, see Pullen 2011: 348-352), or Lerna IIIA late to IIIC early. As the Lerna Type 2 sauceboat is the most common type in the Southern Argolid (see Pullen 1995: 21-22; Wiencke 2000: 588-589, with references), it is not surprising that it should also be the most common at Lambayanna.

The poor state of preservation makes it impossible to determine the shapes of the bases for these sauceboats, although both ring feet and pedestal bases have been found during the survey. Among the best preserved fragments, 18 pedestal bases and 45 ring bases have a maximum diameter of *c.* 6.5cm, with a standard height of 3.5-4cm for the pedestal bases. Three of the pedestal bases are clearly smaller, with a diameter of *c.* 4cm at the base and a height of *c.* 2.5-2.8cm. Similar bases appear on bowls or saucers during EH II (see Pullen 2011: 352; Wiencke 2000: 604-605), making it impossible now to recognise the typical type of base for the sauceboats at Lambayanna.

Small bowls

Small bowls, or saucers, are another very typical EH II shape at Lambayanna. As noted, those numerous fragments of small ring or pedestal bases recovered during the survey could belong either to small bowls/saucers or sauceboats. Examples of slightly hollow bases are more likely to belong to small bowls (for EH II bowl types, see Pullen 2011: 72-76, 177-180, 353-356; Wiencke 2000: 595-604). Rim fragments are more diagnostic and come variously from shallow, incurved, inturned and flaring types. Very small examples could, conceivably, belong to ladles. Very few complete profiles have been preserved, although included among the small number that have survived are a miniature shallow bowl with a slightly hollow base, an incurving bowl with a ring foot,

and a shallow bowl with slightly incurving rim and ring foot.[3]

Large bowls or basins

Bowls with a rim diameter larger than 20cm have been found on several EH II sites (Wiencke 2000: 538). These bowls can be shallow or deep, and possess a broad variety of rim types: inturned, flattened and thickened, including the so-called T-rims. They may be undecorated or, very commonly, feature a taenia band or impressed decoration just below the exterior rim. Vertical strap handles and ledge lugs attached at the rim, or just below it, are also common. Some feature a spout. Many of these types are attested at Lambayanna, but the majority of fragments belong to large inturned bowls with tænia decoration. A number preserve diagonal impressed decoration and there is one example of a spouted basin. Of note among this otherwise rather homogenous group of EH II bowls, is a fragment from the horizontal, offset rim of a fruitstand bowl, on top of which a vertical strap handle is attached. The type dates from EH I, forming a characteristic shape of the so-called Talioti group, and has a close parallel at Makrovouni (Dousougli 1987: 182, no. 42; 184, fig. 42; Weisshaar 1990: 5-7, pl. 2.10).

Jars

With many of the large body fragments not yet thoroughly studied, and no complete profiles recovered, the jar assemblage at Lambayanna is, for the moment, represented only by a few rather well-preserved necks. Jars with offset flaring necks are predominant, although short necked, vertical or slightly splayed types have also been recognised. Several examples of flat or recessed bases, measuring *c.* 15cm in diameter, have been recovered which could also belong to these types. Examples of ledge lugs and vertical strap handles may also be associated, although both types could also belong to large bowls, and the latter also to the saddle-type stand.

Pithoi and other shapes

A number of rim fragments of very large vessels (with reconstructed rim diameters of 50cm-60cm), several rounded knobs and a body fragment with an impressed plastic band attest to the presence of pithoi within the Lambayanna settlement. Other shapes, such as jugs, askoi, pans and plates, are more difficult to identify with certainty, but probable examples are represented variously by handles, flat bases, and fragments of large spouts.

---

[3] The terminology used here follows that of Pullen (2011: 352-356).

Other objects

Ladles

Ten ladle fragments have been identified within the survey assemblage. Several additional fragments of small open shapes could derive from the bowls of ladles, however, given their poor state of preservation it is not possible to categorise them certainly as such, rather than as miniature bowls.

Ladles are a common shape at all sites during EH I and EH II. The EH II examples are both more elaborate and longer (up to 23cm) than their predecessors and are thus fragile and seldom found in one piece (see Pullen 2011: 85-86, 370). Of the ten fragments identified, seven belong to the lower, heavier part of the handle (with a broad quadrangular section evolving into a thinner circular section), whereas the other three belong to the top of the handle, which forms a loop. The loop can be rounded, or oval and topped by a knob. Both types are attested at Lambayanna, although the latter by only one example. This type is also attested at Tiryns (Müller 1938: 36, pl. XXII,7), and recalls the 'wishbone' handles of the Final Neolithic scoops of Tsoungiza. Closer EH I parallels are found among the Talioti group (Pullen 2011: 26; 32 fig. 2.12 nos. 13, 15-16; Weisshaar 1990: 9, pl. 10, nos. 15 and 21).[4]

Stands

Large numbers of saddle type stands (Pullen 2011: 195-196) are attested at Lambayanna, of which one example is decorated with an impressed taenia band at the rim of the arch, and another preserves its handle. Several cylindrical legs attest to the presence of the intermediate type (Wiencke 2000: 607), although there are no certain examples of the knobbed square (Dokos) type (Wiencke's Type 1, see 2000: 607; also Pullen 2011: 194-195). A single knob with a rather flat head, could plausibly belong to the latter type, although similar knobs are attested on stands of the intermediate type.

Spindle whorls and anchor

The terracotta assemblage includes a total of five objects related to textile production: four conical spindle whorls and a fragment of a so-called anchor (Carington Smith 2000: 248-263; Forsén 2008). The conical spindle whorls include the common EH convex-sided short and standard, and conical-sided standard types, as defined at Lerna and Tsoungiza (Pullen 2011: 591-603; 618-627). The anchor, an object associated by many scholars with spinning or weaving, is represented by the point of one of the two 'flukes' which rose vertically either side of, and parallel to, the central shank (see Pullen 2011: 628, no. 844).

Hearths

EH II hearths are, typically, circular in shape, although both the keyhole (or 'horseshoe') and, more rarely, the figure-of-eight type, are also known in the Argolid (see Pullen 1995: 38-39; 2011: 371-372).[5] The three fragments found at Lambayanna can be confidently assigned to the keyhole type, although their surface is so worn that it is no longer possible to determine if any possessed relief or impressed decoration on the rim.

Roof tiles

A total of 12 fragments belong to terracotta roof tiles, all of the common flat EH type. The tiles vary in thickness, although no example exceeds 1.5cm. The largest tile fragment is preserved to a minimum length of 26cm; an additional fragment, surviving to a minimum length of 18cm, preserves two intact corners. These dimensions are consistent with those tiles identified on other EH II Argive sites.[6]

Chronologically, the pottery from squares K-O/10-18 is consistent with a date in EH II developed (Lerna IIIA late - IIIC early, or EH IIA).[7] The assemblage is typical of the material *koine* of the period, attested on many other sites in the Peloponnese, and elsewhere in mainland Greece. The Lambayanna assemblage shares most of its characteristics with other sites in the Argolid and the Corinthia, with the keyhole-shaped hearth and Ayios Kosmas type mortar suggesting that the site enjoyed access to one or more Cycladic-Saronic networks (Konsolaki-Giannopoulou 2011: 277-278; Runnels 1988: 14-15).

Discussion

It is clear from the preliminary study of the architecture and objects from Lambayanna that, for now, we are able only to discuss the settlement in terms of positive evidence — that is, based on the presence of specific categories of object — rather than addressing the implications of any apparent absence. As a result, our understanding of the site to date is, necessarily, limited. For example, it is not yet possible to present a distribution map of architecture and objects in each square of the grid, something that would potentially

---

[4] Note that Weisshaar assigns this particular shape to both the earlier and later phase of the Talioti group.

[5] The keyhole type is also attested at Ayia Irini on Kea (Wilson 1999) and, closer to the Argolid, at Kavo Vasili on Poros (see Konsolaki-Giannopoulou 2011: 277-278).

[6] At Lerna, tiles vary in length between 18cm and 35cm, and in width between 13cm and 27cm (Wiencke 2000: 253). Those fragments identified during the Stanford University Argolid Exploration Project are discussed by Pullen (1995: 39; cf. also Jazwa 2018: 169, table 2).

[7] As noted, the earliest material appears to belong to EH I (the loop of a ladle and the rim of a fruitstand bowl) and the latest is modern. There is, interestingly, no pottery (or other object) which can be dated to the Middle or Late Helladic period, although Mycenaean pottery has been found close to the church of Ayios Yannis Lambayannas (Runnels and Munn 1994: 508-509).

enable us to discern discrete zones of activities inside the settlement.[8]

That said, the presence of an EH II settlement at Lambayanna is totally consistent with the results of the Stanford University Argolid Exploration Project, as a high level of EH II activity was observed in and around the modern village of Fournoi (the so-called 'Fournoi cluster', see Jameson *et al.* 1994; Runnels *et al.* 1995), less than 4km to the east of the site. Such proximity makes it clear that these sites were linked, even if the nature of their relationship is less obvious. As a coastal site during the EH, did the Lambayanna settlement serve as a regional harbour through which local products were exported overseas? Was it an urban centre, surrounded by smaller, rural sites (the 'Fournoi cluster') engaged in specialised economic activity?

When considering such questions, one must remember that we have no idea how far the site extended to the north, south and east. It is likely that much more of the site remains hidden under marine sediment and, as yet, we have no way of knowing its total size, or its importance at the local and regional level. Its architecture, as far as one can tell from that currently visible, is entirely typical of EH II, with the exception of the three massive circular and horseshoe-shaped structures at the west of the site. These structures are exceptional in terms of both their size and building techniques; they are much bigger than those horseshoe-shaped towers identified at Lerna, of which the largest measured only 5m x 3m in size (Wiencke 2000: 120-121) and, with their careful construction and internal walls, they differ as well from the recently identified stone piles or cairns on other contemporary sites (see for example Smith 2017: 112-115; Tartaron *et al.* 2006; Tartaron *et al.* 2011: 626). There is, as yet, no trace of a 'corridor house' at Lambayanna.

Most of those objects recovered during the survey are also typical of EH II, and many can be dated relatively closely within the phase. The categories of objects attested are, similarly, entirely typical for the period in the Southern Argolid. More unexpected is the identification of material belonging to EH I, which, despite its relative rarity, suggests a pre-EH II foundation for the site.

Conclusion

Much more detailed quantitative and qualitative analyses of the architecture and objects from the 2015 survey are necessary if we are to fully understand the

character of the site at Lambayanna. In the meantime, it is already possible to assert that in the Bay of Kiladha, an area that was densely settled during EH II, there was a coastal settlement which, by EH II developed, covered an area of at least 1.2ha. The site was apparently fortified. The finds point to a typical range of food production and consumption activities; there is some evidence of textile production as well.

In addition to the ongoing study of the 2015 finds mentioned above, future work will focus on the resolution of the geographical and chronological extent of the settlement through geophysical survey and underwater excavation.

Bibliography

Beck, J. and D. Koutsoumba 2014. Baie de Kiladha 2013. *Antike Kunst* 57: 162-165.

Beck, J. and D. Koutsoumba 2015. Baie de Kiladha 2014: Expédition Terra Submersa. *Antike Kunst* 58: 187-190.

Beck, J. and D. Koutsoumba 2016. Baie de Kiladha 2015. *Antike Kunst* 59: 153-156.

Beck, J., D. Sakellariou and D. Koutsoumba 2017. Submerged Neolithic landscapes off Franchthi Cave: the measurements from the Terra Submersa Expedition and their implications, in A. Sarris, E. Kalogiropoulou, T. Kalayci and L. Karimali (eds) *Communities, Landscapes, and Interactions in Neolithic Greece, Proceedings of the International Conference, Rethymno 29-30 May, 2015* (International Monographs in Prehistory Archaeological Series 20): 261-268. Ann Arbor: International Monographs in Prehistory.

Carington Smith, J. 2000. The spinning and weaving implements, in C. Ridley, K.A. Wardle and C.A. Mould. *Servia I. Anglo-Hellenic Rescue Excavations 1971-73* (The British School at Athens Supplementary Volume 32): 207-263. London: the British School at Athens.

Dousougli, A. 1987. Makrovouni – Kefalari Magoula – Talioti. Bemerkungen zu den Stufen FH I und II in der Argolis. *Praehistorische Zeitschrift* 62: 164-220.

Forsén, J. 2008. The ever-intriguing "terracotta anchors" of the Early Bronze Age, in C. Gallou, M. Georgiadis and G.M. Muskett (eds) *Dioskouroi: Studies Presented to W.G. Cavanagh and C.B. Mee on the Anniversary of their 30-Year Joint Contribution to Aegean Archaeology* (British Archaeological Reports International Series 1889): 55-58. Oxford: Archaeopress.

Jameson, M.H., C.N. Runnels and T.H. van Andel 1994. *A Greek Countryside: the Southern Argolid from Prehistory to the Present Day*. Stanford: Stanford University Press.

Jazwa, K.A. 2018. The construction of Early Helladic II ceramic roofing tiles from Mitrou, Greece: influence and interaction. *Mediterranean Archaeology and Archaeometry* 18(2): 153-173.

Konsolaki-Giannopoulou, E. 2011. Η πρωτοελλαδική κατοίκηση στο νησί του Πόρου (Σαρωνικός κόλπος),

---

[8] Even if objects are not completely in situ (see above), the general correlation between surviving architecture and locations of high finds density (Figures 3.2b and 3.2c) suggests that movement from initial site of deposition may not have been very great and indicates that a general understanding of the settlement's organisation might therefore be possible.

in D. Katsonopoulou (ed.) *Helike IV. Ancient Helike and Aigialeia. Protohelladika: the Southern and Central Greek Mainland*: 273-292. Athens: the Helike Society.

Müller, K. 1938. *Tiryns IV. Die Urfirniskeramik*. Munich: Bruckmann.

Pullen, D.J. 1995. The pottery of the Neolithic, Early Helladic I and Early Helladic II periods, in C.N. Runnels, D.J. Pullen, and S. Langdon (eds) *Artifact and Assemblage. The Finds from a Regional Survey of the Southern Argolid, Greece. Volume I: the Prehistoric and Early Iron Age Pottery and the Lithic Artifacts*: 6-42. Stanford: Stanford University Press

Pullen, D.J. 2011. *Nemea Valley Archaeological Project, Volume 1. The Early Bronze Age Village on Tsoungiza Hill*. Princeton: the American School of Classical Studies at Athens.

Tartaron, T.F., D.J. Pullen and J.S. Noller 2006. Rillenkarren at Vayia: geomorphology and a new class of Early Bronze Age fortified settlement in Southern Greece. *Antiquity* 80(307): 145-160.

Tartaron, T.F., D.J. Pullen, R.K. Dunn, L. Tzortzopoulou-Gregory, A. Dill and J.L. Boyce 2011. The Saronic Harbors Archaeological Research Project (SHARP): investigations at Mycenaean Kalamianos, 2007-2009. *Hesperia: the Journal of the American School of Classical Studies at Athens* 80(4): 559-634.

Runnels, C.N. 1988. Early Bronze Age stone mortars from the Southern Argolid. *Hesperia: the Journal of the American School of Classical Studies at Athens* 57(3): 257-272.

Runnels, C.N. and M.H. Munn 1994. Appendix A. A register of sites, in M.H. Jameson, C.N. Runnels and T.H. van Andel. *A Greek Countryside: the Southern Argolid from Prehistory to the Present Day*: 415-538. Stanford: Stanford University Press

Runnels, C. N., D.J. Pullen and S. Langdon (eds) 1995. *Artifact and Assemblage. The Finds from a Regional Survey of the Southern Argolid, Greece. Volume I: the Prehistoric and Early Iron Age Pottery and the Lithic Artifacts*. Stanford: Stanford University Press.

Sakellariou, D., J. Beck, G. Rousakis, P. Georgiou, I. Panagiotopoulos, L. Morfis, K. Tsampouraki-Kraounaki and A. Zavitsanou 2015. Submerged prehistoric landscapes off Franchthi Cave, East Argolic Gulf: preliminary results, in *Proceedings of the 11th Panhellenic Symposium on Oceanography and Fisheries, "Aquatic Horizons: Challenges and Perspectives", Mytilene, Lesvos Island, Greece 13-17 May 2015*: 993-996. Athens: Hellenic Centre for Marine Research.

Smith, D.M. 2017. Recent research in Early Helladic southern Greece. *Archaeological Reports* 63: 107-129.

Weisshaar, H.-J. 1990. Die Keramik von Talioti, in *Tiryns XI*: 1-34. Mainz: Philipp von Zabern.

Wiencke, M.H. 2000. *Lerna IV. The Architecture, Stratification and Pottery of Lerna III*. Princeton: the American School of Classical Studies at Athens.

Wilson, D.E. 1999. *Keos IX. Ayia Irini: Periods I-III. The Neolithic and Early Bronze Age Settlements. Part I. The Pottery and Small Finds*. Mainz: Philipp von Zabern.

Tradition, Transition, and the Impact of the New in Neolithic Greece[1]

William Cavanagh and Josette Renard

Introduction

Certain specific themes from Chris Mee's work find echoes in the papers gathered here in his honour. Thus, his early work on Mycenaean finds in the Dodecanese and Anatolia are classic studies of the spread and adoption of cultural traits, such as architecture, burial forms or pottery, into an alien context. The survey on Methana, on the other hand, took a closely defined and culturally distinctive geographical territory, and reflected on its fluctuating history of identification and reaction to the larger powers that impinged on its history. Turning to his more recent articles, and to our excavations at Kouphovouno, we wish to draw attention to his argument on the transition from the Middle Neolithic (MN) to the Late Neolithic (LN) period at Kouphovouno (Mee *et al.* 2014), and his review of the so-called 'rhytons' (Mee 2014). These, too, touched on just those themes which run through much of his work: style and identity, and how these change through time.

It is our intention to explore these themes in the light of his work at Kouphovouno and under the broad head of territoriality. Territories are human and social constructs, if with an undertow of instinctive behaviour (Delaney 2005). In the context of the early Neolithic, it is natural to assume a fundamental transformation from the wide-ranging occupation of the landscape experienced by the Mesolithic forager to that of the farmer occupying a MN village such as Kouphovouno, a transformation which had developed over at least a millennium from the time of the earliest Neolithic settlements in the Peloponnese.

There is a complex relationship between territoriality and ethnicity (Hahn 2017). In both cases, there is a sense of the insider looking out, and of the outsider looking in. But, in contrast to ethnicity, territoriality can be expressed at a multiplicity of scales from the domestic space of a room or a building, to a neighbourhood, to cultivated land, a settlement and its domains, and even larger landscapes. It is governed by protocols of seeking and granting permission, symbolized by barriers such as doors, fences, ditches, and including sometimes natural features such as rivers and mountains. It sets the scene for acceptable behaviour in the home, in public, between guest and host, between friend and foe. We wish here to emphasise the layered nature of the occupation of space and how the people of the time may have seen themselves and each other. This perspective incorporates the insights provided by social psychology into processes such as the formation of group norms, stereotypes and schemas for action and the formation, sharing and transformation of attitudes and values (see, for example, Hogg and Vaughan 2018). A social psychology of the past is not open to the archaeologist as its methodologies cannot be applied, we do not have the wherewithal to conduct cognitive experiments. But the insights gained from that discipline can help place in context the varying settings (what we have termed territories) of group interaction which archaeologists do observe. What does archaeology of the MN and LN at Kouphovouno tell us about the expression and reach of relationships in Neolithic communities?

Middle Neolithic Kouphovouno: structures, village, *terroir* and territories

Let us start with the site itself. Our initial surface survey combined artefact collection with coring and geophysical survey. We concluded that the site covered at least 4ha, and reached its largest extent in the MN; a finding which received some further support from the excavations in Areas C and G. The estimation of population based on the areal extent of a site is fraught with difficulties, but a rough rule of thumb suggests a minimum of 250 people per hectare, which would imply the presence of at least 1000 souls when the village reached its maximum. This is a conservative estimate.[2]

[1] The loss of Chris Mee as a friend and a colleague afflicted us both deeply and it is a pleasure tinged with great sadness to offer this contribution in his honour. Our common project at Kouphovouno has been supported by many individuals, too many to name individually, and institutions. Particular thanks are owed to the members of the Archaeological Service of the Greek Ministry of Culture and to the staff of the British School at Athens and the many institutions who helped finance it: the British Academy, the British School at Athens, the Society of Antiquaries of London, the Institute for Aegean Prehistory, the Universities of Liverpool, Lorient, Clermont-Ferrand and Nottingham, the École française d'Athènes, the French Ministry of Foreign Affairs, and the Royal Geographical Society. We must extend our thanks to the anonymous referee, though their report urged that this chapter was so bad that it should not be published. So bracing a critique has, we hope, led us to clarify and, here and there, extend our argument and for this we are grateful. We have generally, if not always, followed their recommendations. All errors, of course, are our own.

[2] See Whitelaw (2001; 2017) for reviews based on very extensive, multi-period research; Cessford (2005) suggests an even denser concentration for the Neolithic settlement at Çatal Hüyük.

Our excavated areas covered approximately 6% of the whole site; just a small proportion, but sufficient to indicate a dense distribution of buildings consistent with a population that could be considered large by Middle Neolithic standards. The excavations revealed clusters of small structures, several of which may have formed a single habitation unit — we cannot be sure — typically with an interior footprint of 3.5-7m2, set around more open spaces and separated by narrow passages (Figure 4.1; Renard and Cavanagh 2017). This pattern of settlement raises a question mark over the nature of households in the community and the division between private and public space. We have presented elsewhere evidence to suggest that, as well as the cooking and serving of food, pot firing was carried out in the courtyards which served these 'households' (Ballut *et al.* 2017). There are hints (and no more than hints) in the pottery record that, against a picture of overwhelming homogeneity, slight differences of style can be recognised from one part of the site to another (cf. from Area C, Figure 4.2a-b, and from Area G, Figure 4.2c-d). Differences of style from household to household and restricted continuities of style have

been recognised in other Neolithic communities, such as the Linearbandkeramik of central Europe where 'certain stylistic characteristics are confined to single houses or small groups of buildings or can occur in successive houses on the same farmstead' (Pechtl 2015: 561). In other words, a certain territoriality was expressed in the village itself. As a parallel, argued on grounds of both architecture and pottery analysis, we would refer to Kotsakis's argument that Sesklo, in Thessaly, was divided in a way which resulted, effectively, in the creation of different communities, one living at the centre and another on the periphery of the site (Andreou *et al.* 2001: 263). These observations on the overall size of the settlement, on the disposition of structures within the village, and on activities conducted in them reflect a territoriality of kin-group or neighbourhood within the larger village.

Such a sense of unity and division may have expressed itself not only within the village but also in the fields that surrounded the settlement. Isotope analysis has confirmed that the agricultural regime required a very intensive investment of effort in weeding, watering and

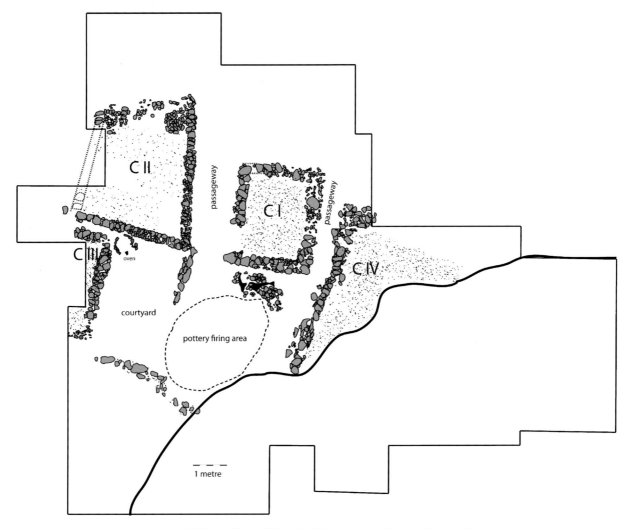

Figure 4.1. Middle Neolithic Buildings CI-CIV and courtyard in Area C at Kouphovouno.

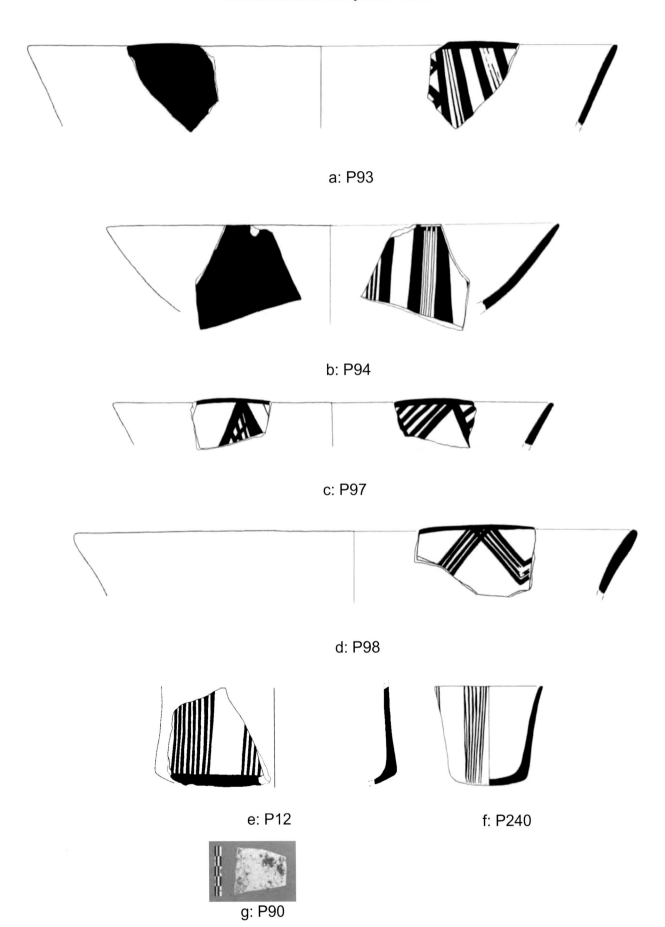

a: P93

b: P94

c: P97

d: P98

e: P12   f: P240

g: P90

Figure 4.2. *Pedestal bowls of phase MNγ from Areas C (a: Kouphovouno P93 b: P94) and G (c: Kouphovouno P97 d: P98). Carinated bowls from phase MNα (e: Kouphovouno P12) and MNζ (f: Kouphovouno P240). g: Kouphovouno P90 of MNβ, import from Central Greece? (Scale 1:3).*

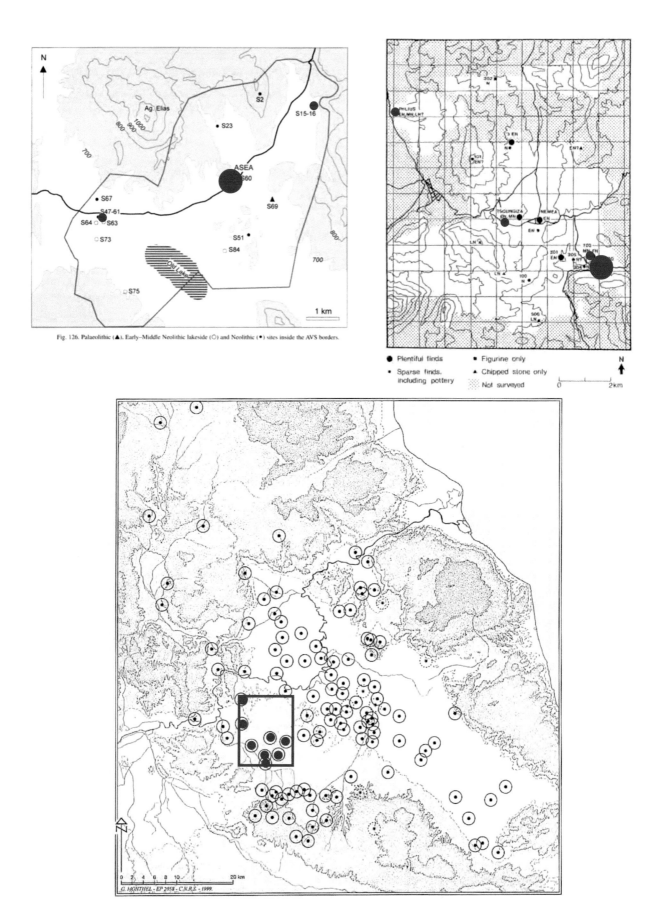

Figure 4.3. *Middle Neolithic sites located in the Asea Valley Survey (after Forsén and Forsén 2003: 186), the Nemea Valley Archaeological Project (after Wright et al. 1990: 586 fig. 2) and in Thessaly (after Perlès 2001: 138, fig. 7.8). The box drawn on the map of Thessaly indicates an area approximately the same as that on the Nemea Valley Archaeological Project map.*

manuring plots to yield a maximum return of wheat and legumes from smallholdings. At the same time, barley was cultivated in fields with less concentrated effort, perhaps in outfields further from the settlement (Vaiglova *et al.* 2014). We cannot, yet, reconstruct the details, but these different agricultural regimes raise questions about the organisation of production – intensive investment in the cultivation of wheat and pulses would surely reflect household production, but the extensive cultivation of barley need not have followed the same model.

Beyond the village and its fields, however, would have lain a wooded landscape, which would have served to isolate the village. Note the very different densities found in the occupation of territories in the Peloponnese on the one hand, and in Thessaly on the other. The results of intensive surveys have confirmed the relative sparsity of Middle Neolithic settlement in the peninsula – not a sherd of MN pottery was found on Chris Mee's Methana Survey, not a sherd on the Laconia Survey. Others, in the Asea and Nemea Valleys, recognised a number of a central sites each associated with one or two satellites. Contrast these with the very dense distribution of communities in Thessaly, where each village must have had a clearly demarcated boundary with its neighbours (Figure 4.3).

This observation raises larger questions of visibility and representativeness in archaeological survey, but their pursuit would lead us too far from the main theme of this chapter. Here we would simply make a small number of points. We believe that the total destruction of early ceramics on archaeological sites is not a given, but varies from region to region and culture to culture; the hard, well-fired and distinctive MN *Urfirnis* fabrics survive well in Greece and have turned up regularly on small, relatively short-lived, sites (Johnson 2004). There is no question that alluvial sediments can cover whole archaeological landscapes (e.g., Zangger 1993), but again the effects of this need to be assessed for each survey area — in much of inland Greece thick accumulations of Holocene alluvial sediment can be restricted to very specific landscapes. Thus, in the Laconia Survey and Methana Survey areas, the geomorphologists found only very limited areas of Holocene alluviation. Certainly, much of Greece is still not fully explored and, as such, current understanding is liable to change; note, for example, recent evidence for a previously unsuspected density of settlement in Western Thessaly (Orengo *et al.* 2015). Furthermore, the problem of visibility also affects multiperiod sites, even those which have been extensively explored over many years; thus, coring combined with 14C dating has revealed a millennium of Early and Middle Neolithic occupation at Dikili Tash, previously unrecognised (Lespez *et al.* 2017). The problems of visibility in survey

archaeology are not to be underestimated, but we would still contend that the marked difference between Thessaly and the Peloponnese in settlement density represents an archaeological reality. The more loosely knit and sparsely occupied pattern in the Peloponnese implies a different attitude to claims over, and partition of, the land.

But this territoriality of dispersion was not, at the same time, one of isolation; on the contrary, the pottery shows that these communities were in close contact with one another. The uniformity of pottery styles in the Peloponnese has long been recognised — Vitelli says of Lerna that the sherds are immediately recognizable as of 'the same kind' as those at contemporary sites around the Peloponnese (Vitelli 2007: 91; see also, Cullen 1985a; 1985b). Phelps saw the MN *Urfirnis* style as a creation of the northeastern Peloponnese, which later spread to the central, south and western Peloponnese (2004: 64); and it is very much a Peloponnesian style, its distribution outside the Peloponnese is sporadic and as a minor component alongside other styles (Phelps 2004: 61-64). Generally, pottery seems to be made locally, and imports are rare, though more scientific analyses are needed to confirm this impression. Cullen has explored differences in decorative syntax at Peloponnesian sites (Cullen 1985a: 326-331) and argued that the exchange of marriage partners or raiding between communities might offer a mechanism whereby designs and techniques were moved from one community to another. As at other sites, there are minor traits evident in the shapes and decoration of *Urfirnis* pottery which are specific to Kouphovouno; we might mention a preference for sets of vertical lines on carinated bowls (Figure 4.2e-f), a specific decorative schema on collar jars, the relative rarity of very tall pedestals for shallow bowls, or the absence of tall necks on the jars. These distinctions might seem subtle to us, but, given the sophistication of the *Urfirnis* style, we can be sure that consumers at the time would have been sensitive to every local variant. They were expressions of specific local identities, themselves framed by the territorial geography of the period. At Kouphovouno, it is noteworthy that these specific motifs continue throughout the site's MN occupation. We have distinguished seven MN phases covering perhaps some 300-400 years (Mee *et al.* 2014: 82, fig. 13) and, although there are changes in the typology of the pottery, the specific local characteristics listed above persist through all of them.

The minimalist view holds that a common pottery style, such as the *Urfirnis* style, need not imply racial, tribal, linguistic or cultural unity. All the same, the assemblages at each site are united not only by the similarity in decoration and employment of closely similar techniques in forming and firing the vessels, but also by the uniformity of the repertory of shapes, such as pedestalled bowls, carinated bowls, collar jars, piriform bowls, and others. These elaborately decorated vessels are plainly for the consumption of food in a context of social display (Mee 2007; Urem-Kotsou and Kotsakis 2007). It came as a surprise, therefore, to learn that there were differences in the subsistence remains from Kouphovouno and Franchthi: thus, free-threshing wheat (*Triticum aestivum/durum*) predominated at Kouphovouno, whilst glume wheats (*Triticum monococcum* and *Triticum dicoccum*) were dominant at Franchthi and, indeed, at most Neolithic sites on the Greek mainland. Halstead (2014) has highlighted the considerations which informed cereal crop choice among recent pre-mechanised farmers in the Mediterranean. In the faunal assemblage from Franchthi Cave, cattle are hardly present (Morgan 2014), whereas at Kouphovouno they contribute a significant proportion to food resources (Cantuel 2010; Cantuel *et al.* 2008). These data help illustrate the point that the picture of cultural unity suggested by the uniform pottery style in fact masks differences between one community and another as they adapted agriculture to local ecological conditions[3] or, indeed, in the cultural signals embedded in the consumption of food (Urem-Kotsou and Kotsakis 2007). What, then, the *Urfirnis* style seems to represent is not a uniformity in the subsistence economy and the way of life bound in with that economy, but rather shared conventions of social intercourse both within and between communities. Of course, as indicated above, scholars have already suggested that commensality and hospitality were important in Neolithic Greece; a community of custom governing the serving of food will have served to define the larger territory of the Peloponnese.

Certainly, a picture of peasants closed to the outside world and tied to their fields is increasingly undermined by new evidence. For much of Neolithic Europe, the evidence of aDNA (Brandt *et al.* 2015) and isotope analysis (Neil *et al.* 2017; Pellegrini *et al.* 2016) has weakened the notion of static, conservative villagers hardly moving beyond the boundaries of their immediate surroundings. These broader links of association are clearly signalled in the archaeology of our region. Initial analysis of the MN pottery at Kouphovouno suggests imported pottery is far from common — we can point to one MN sherd (Figure 4.2g) the fabric of which, Ian Whitbread confirms, is unlike anything else from Kouphovouno.[4] Elsewhere, however, thin-section

petrographic and chemical analyses have shown that pottery could travel considerable distances in the EN and MN periods (Tomkins and Day 2001; Quinn *et al.* 2010). Certainly, other materials confirm wide-ranging contacts, notably obsidian from Melos, and the honey flints, whose origins are not clear, but which certainly also travelled a long way to reach the Peloponnese. Catherine Perlès' model, supported by the Franchthi material, saw an indirect supply of obsidian and of honey flint via exchanges mediated through groups of specialists moving from village to village and organised on a regional basis (Perlès 2004: 137; developed further in Perlès 2005). This adds another level of territoriality, which we might call intercalation: groups of people, evidently different from those settled in the region, moving within and through the territories of the MN Peloponnese.

The territoriality signalled through long-ranging contacts is not confined to the procurement of chipped-stone artefacts. Another sign of a shared culture can be recognised in the split-leg figurines, which are found throughout the Peloponnese (Corinth, Franchthi, Lerna, Akratas, Nemea, Aria, Kouphovouno and Alepotrypa) and Central Greece (Thespiai and Otzaki), and which have more remote parallels in Bulgaria (Rakitovo, Oussoé and Geo Milev) and Albania (Podgorie and Vashtëmi) and perhaps even northern Serbia (Donja Branjevina) (Budja 2003; Cavanagh and Renard 2014; Dousougli 1998: 124). The geography of these 'tokens' opens up a landscape of very wide-ranging links, possibly tied to the spread of Neolithic settlers throughout Europe. Such material markers are not uniformly distributed. In Greece, for example, so-called 'stamp-seals' considered by Reingruber (2008: 600) to identify an 'international spirit' connecting Europe and Anatolia, predominate in the north (although not in eastern Thrace, see Özdoğan 2017), but are extremely rare in Central Greece and the Peloponnese (at Eutresis, Nemea, and Kouphovouno). So the split-leg figurines, on the one hand, and the stamp-seals on the other, evidently reflect different, and only marginally overlapping, territorial enclaves widely dispersed across the Balkans, which used varying symbolic vocabularies.

So far we have tried to present a reconstruction of territoriality in MN Greece which operated in a nested or segmentary fashion: both unity and division within the settlement at one level, across the village and its fields at another; division and unity between primary and satellite settlements in a wider terrain, to shared and contrasted identities across the whole province of the Peloponnese and, finally, relationships with the wider world embracing Central and Northern Greece and the Balkans. The construction developed above forms the background to the next part of this article and Chris Mee'sargument for a gradual transition from the MN to LN in Southern Greece.

---

[3] See Allen (2017) for similar differentiation in cultivation regimes within the EN cultures of northern Greece and the Balkans.

[4] The decorative pellets have possible parallels from sites in Central Greece such as Chaironeia, Elateia, Halai, Orchomenos and others (Reingruber 2008: 194-196, 331; Tzavella-Evjen 2012: 63-64, 68, 69-70; Weinberg 1962). For 'white ware' sherds at Franchthi, see Vitelli (1993: 132).

Late Neolithic Kouphovouno: innovation and influence

The earlier literature on the changes which marked Greece at the start of the LN period, in 14C terms the later part of the 6th millennium cal. BC, is very extensive and we can mention it, in this context, only very briefly. Most scholars are agreed that the establishment of the LN marks a major watershed in Greek prehistory. Phelps has referred to the break-up of the old (MN) settlement pattern and its cultural unity (2004: 64) and, in very broad terms, there seems to be a major reorientation of economy and settlement pattern over this period (Alram-Stern 1996: 93-95; Cavanagh 1999; Demoule and Perlès 1993; Dousougli 1998: 161-166; Johnson 2004). In Northern Greece, the very large extended sites such as Makriyalos and Stavroupolis date to the final MN and LN (Andreou *et al.* 2001: 303; Pappa and Besios 1999). Vitelli has emphasised the impermanence of settlement implied by the sporadic occupation of Franchthi cave (1999: 99-102). At the same time, the gradual expansion into previously sparsely populated environments has been underlined (for example, Broodbank 2000: 120-142). Here, however, we wish to look at a much more restricted question: namely, how are we to understand the change in pottery styles and their territorial extent?

In terms of the pottery styles, the smooth, highly accomplished but rather slow-moving technological progression in the Peloponnese, marked by the gradual development of the EN-MN, gives way to different and markedly new practices. Discussing the new styles in (LN) Franchthi Ceramic Phase (FCP) 3, Vitelli notes certain continuities, but many more differences in potting techniques, and concludes that 'the FCP 3 potters had few, if any direct ties to the *Urfirnis* tradition' (1999: 35). All the same, the stratigraphic sequence at Kouphovouno points to a period when the production of MN *Urfirnis* pottery continues alongside the new LN Black and Grey Burnished wares, Matt-painted and Polychrome pottery; thus, in our earliest LN Phase, MN styles still make up some 70% of the assemblage side-by-side with the new types (Table 4.1).[5]

Chris Mee selected the appearance of Black Burnished pottery as the defining point for the earliest LN at Kouphovouno. It formed 4.5% of the registered pottery from context G2009, which we took to be the earliest LN level. As one moves through LN 1α, the earliest LN Phase at Kouphovouno, the proportion of Black Ware rises to over 20%, then to over 30% and ultimately, in Phase LN 1γ, to a peak at 70%. Similarly, Grey Ware, Matt-painted and Polychrome slowly form an increasing proportion of the pottery assemblages. The Red-on-Black and Grey-on-Grey wares, which mark the LN assemblages in Central and Northern Greece, appear in small quantities at Kouphovouno.

So, the first important observation is the gradual transformation of the pottery assemblage: the new LN types first appear in a rather sporadic fashion at Kouphovouno and then slowly come to dominate the ceramic assemblage, as we have just illustrated. A second observation is the widespread nature of the innovations, the '*koine*' and links with the Balkans. A further consideration is what we shall term redundancy:

Table 4.1. Proportions of MN Patterned, MN Scribble Burnished, MN Monochrome, LN Black Ware, LN Grey Ware, LN Matt-painted, LN White Slipped and LN Polychrome in the main contexts of Phase LN 1α at Kouphovouno.

Context	% MN P	%MN SB	%MN M	Σ MN	% BW	%GW	%MP	%WS	%POL
G2009	3.58	6.85	84.55	95%	4.49	0.46	0.08	0.00	0.00
G1205	8.06	6.59	74.11	89%	6.23	4.64	0.37	0.00	0.00
G1203	6.51	5.13	72.98	85%	12.43	2.76	0.20	0.00	0.00
G2003	6.12	4.66	65.31	76%	21.57	1.46	0.87	0.00	0.00
G1208	4.79	5.39	58.92	69%	23.11	6.35	1.20	0.00	0.24
G2001	6.74	3.83	54.10	65%	29.69	2.00	3.64	0.00	0.00
G1139	5.43	4.94	48.15	58%	26.17	10.37	4.69	0.00	0.25
G1136	6.43	3.43	35.14	45%	33.00	11.43	9.71	0.86	0.00
G2000	4.07	2.85	30.89	38%	50.81	3.25	6.50	0.41	1.22
Overall	5.61	5.30	63.27	74%	18.63	4.50	2.47	0.12	0.1

[5] The order is fundamentally stratigraphic based on two sequences: G2000s + G1139 and G1136 and the G1200s. The links between the two sequences are based on seriation and typology. Note that if we separated out the two sequences the argument for a gradual introduction of LN wares would still stand. The Kouphovouno data do not support the suggestion that MN pottery in these contexts is residual.

the fact that, in contrast with the preceding MN period, there developed in the LN pottery of the Peloponnese and, more generally, throughout much of mainland Greece, a tendency for the coexistence of a variety of styles and fabrics all used to produce a very similar assemblage of pottery shapes. Let us examine these in turn.

Scholars have recognised a 'cultural uniformity' in the distribution of Black and Grey Wares, Matt-painted and Polychrome pottery (Alram-Stern 1996: 912; Demoule and Perlès 1993: 392; Dousougli 1998: 60-65; Phelps 2004: 96; Weinberg 1970: 601), and Theocharis referred to a ceramic 'koine' (1981: 128) uniting, at least for a time at the beginning of the Late Neolithic period, Macedonia, Thessaly, Central Greece and the Peloponnese. But it has long been asserted that the Black Wares reflect an even more sweeping change which affected the whole of the Balkan peninsula from the Peloponnese to northern Serbia.[6]

Absolute Dating of the earliest Late Neolithic in Greece and Vinča

The situation in the northern Balkans has been succinctly summarised by Nikolov, who notes that around 5500/5450 BC 'plain dark ware "flooded" the whole of Thrace, the central Balkans and the Lower Danube' (2017: 97). Before looking to the 'Dark Ware phenomenon', however, we must consider recent work on the absolute chronology of the period under consideration. At Kouphovouno, we define the transition to the earliest LN by the first appearance of Black Ware (initially a trickle), dated to 5578-5303 cal. BC (95% probability; Mee *et al.* 2014: 82, fig. 13). This is broadly consistent with dates from Franchthi (FCP 3: 5722-5486 cal. BC, 95% probability, Mee *et al.* 2014: 83, table 7); Halai, where the earlier LN I phase is placed by Facorellis and Coleman at 5600-5480 cal. BC (2012: 329); Thessaly, where Reingruber and colleagues (2017: 45) have placed the LN-MN transition at approximately 5500 cal. BC; and at Dikili Tash, where the earliest LN is placed around 5400 cal. BC (Lespez *et al.* 2017: 53 and fig. 4.8).[7] So we place the first appearance of LN type ceramics in the whole of the Greek mainland a little before or a little after 5500 cal. BC. More dates from clearly stratified contexts might clarify whether one part of Greece developed these types earlier than another, but on current evidence it would be unwise to assign priority to one particular area. For the central European end of the connection, we can turn to the recent definitive review of the dating of the Vinča

Culture by Whittle and colleagues where it is established that 'the start of phase A began in 5405-5310 cal. BC (95% probability) 5365-5320 cal. BC (68% probability) and the use of Vinča A ceramics ended in 5205-5070 cal. BC (95% probability), probably in 5200-5130 cal. BC (68% probability). Vinča A ceramics were thus in use for a period of 125–295 years (95% probability; duration A; Fig. 38), probably for 140–230 years (68% probability)' (Whittle *et al.* 2016: 28). In other words, these dates give priority for the development of Black Wares to the southern/eastern Balkans, though the implications of the Vinča dates for the sequences in Macedonia, Thrace and Bulgaria still need to be worked through; sites dated to Karanovo III/Veselinovo and contemporary phases in Bulgaria-Thrace are earlier (Nikolov 2017: 76-77; Thissen and Reingruber 2017: 154-160).

'Black Wares' from the Peloponnese to the Danube

The 'koine' in Greece refers to Dark Burnished, Matt-painted, Polychrome and allied types[8]; to pursue our current theme, we shall take as our focus Dark Burnished or Black Ware. The first point to be made is that 'Black Ware' is an imprecise term; dark burnished pottery is found in different cultures and at different periods and in almost all cases they are unrelated. In this case, however, archaeologists are agreed that the connection across the Balkans is real; consensus is not proof, but the case for a connection is strong. The pottery so classified can vary from extremely fine, thin-walled, carefully finished vases such as the carinated bowls, to thick heavy vessels such as some of the pedestalled bowls (Figure 4.4). Hauptmann's emphasis on the obsidian-like sheen of the surface treatment (1981: 77) echoes Tsountas' description of Thessalian Γ1α, but some examples can have a dull finish (an issue complicated by wear and post-depositional changes).

Many commentators do not insist on a black-dark grey colour for classification (Phelps 2004: 70, 77), Dousougli treats Black and Grey Wares as a single category (1998: 65-66; also Sampson 2008a: 89; discussion in Bonga 2013: 135) and we sympathise with this view; for Sitagroi, Keighley writes that 'the surface of Dark Burnished ware ranges between brown and black or is reddish' (1986: 349); of Vinča, Milojčić notes that the vases are mainly black to dark grey, but some are brick red (1949: 268). Generally, the variation in colour is ascribed to effects in firing, though clay composition may also have contributed to this. Technical studies have demonstrated various techniques in their production, including the use of different qualities of fabric and different techniques to achieve the black colour, notably reduction, smudging and sometimes both, or coating with manganese paint (see, for

---

[6] For an excellent review of this question, see Bonga (2013: 133-139).
[7] Note that here the terminology used is not the same as that applied further south in Greece, evidently the system applied is that used in the Balkans whereby 'MN' overlaps with the southern Greek LN (Commenge-Pellerin and Tsirtsoni 2004: 54-56) and 'LN I' is a slightly later phase than our LN 1α. More dates are needed.

[8] For a recent thorough, and very useful, review of Greek LN pottery publications, see Bonga (2013).

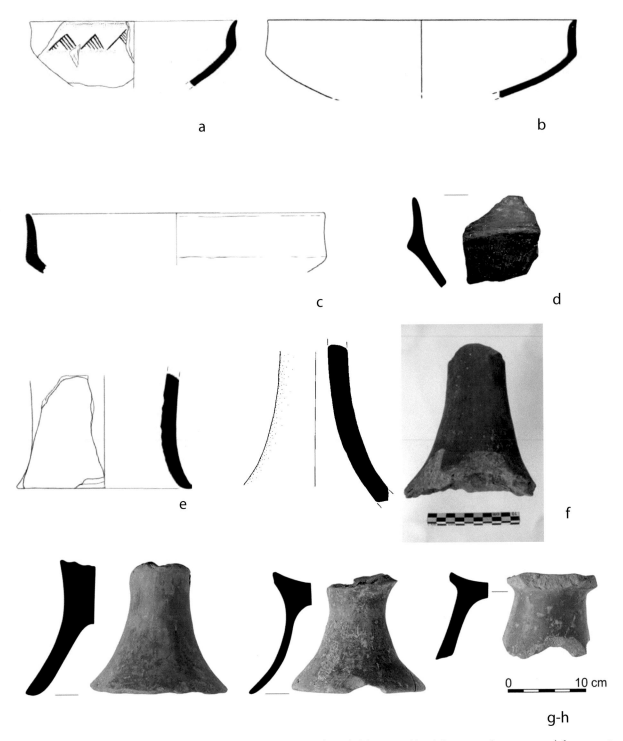

Figure 4.4. *LN Black Ware vases: (a) carinated bowl, Kouphovouno P342 (LN 1β); (b) carinated bowl, from Corinth Forum West (after Lavezzi 1978: 437 fig. 4:21); (c) carinated bowl, from Sitagroi (after Keighley 1986: 349, fig. 11.1:2-4) (d) carinated bowl, from Szederkény-Kukorica-dűlő (after Jakucs et al. 2016: fig. 8:6); (e) pedestal base, Kouphovouno P 343; (f) pedestal base, Kouphovouno P537 (g-h) three pedestal bases from Szederkény-Kukorica-dűlő (after Jakucs et al. 2016: fig. 10:7-9) (Scale a-c approx.1:3; e-h approx. 1:5).*

example, Hitsiou 2017; Papakosta 2011; Pentedeka 2015; Quinn *et al.* 2010; Schneider *et al.* 1991; Spataro 2017). At Kouphovouno, use of a variety of fabric types is indicated. Ian Whitbread's thin-section analysis is not finalised and the following observations must be considered provisional, but the Black Ware sample includes examples of a felsic group with pellets and a fine/very fine sandy matrix, a metamorphic group with

schist sand moderately sorted, and a calcareous group with limestone moderately sorted; these characteristics are also recognised on sherds dating to the MN period. At Franchthi, Vitelli noted of FCP 3 and 4 (broadly equivalent to Kouphovouno LN 1α-β) that most of the pots were likely made locally, but small numbers were probably brought to Franchthi (1999: 97-98). Elsewhere in LN Greece there are signs of increasingly specialised production and wide distribution. Pentedeka (2008; 2011; 2015) has identified fabrics of Black Burnished and Red-on-Black wares made in northeast Thessaly (perhaps, at least, at Magoula Tselma) and exported quite widely across Thessaly, for example to Visviki.[9] Increased numbers of imports from a wide range of sources are reported from Youra (Papakosta 2011; Quinn *et al.* 2010), and certainly by LN II, fine pottery from the area of Dimini was being exported over 200km into Macedonia (Hitsiou 2017).

There was also a transformation in the production of pottery in the northern and western Balkans. Spataro (2017) has documented the change in ceramic production in the Vinča Culture: innovations from the preceding Starčevo-Criş, particularly marked in the emergence of new Black Burnished pottery (the colour of which was achieved through reduction and sometimes by soot smudging), included the use of untempered fabrics employing fine loess or alluvial clays fired at high temperatures (≥ 850°C), and burnishing using a new *chaîne opératoire*. It is noteworthy that, despite similarities in appearance and some vase shapes indicative of links as far as the Peloponnese (Figure 4.4), the potters of northern Serbia/Romania followed different methods from their contemporaries further south. In contrast with Vinča, the neighbouring Danilo/Hvar culture sites adopted few of these innovations; they had Black Ware pottery decorated by burnishing to achieve a glossy surface, but did not copy the Vinča shapes and designs (Spataro 2017: 74-75).

Closer examination confirms the complex picture. To start from the southern periphery of this distribution, at Kouphovouno, at Franchthi and at other sites in the Peloponnese, there is a partial typological gap between *Urfirnis* and Black Ware, even though chronologically they overlapped. Classic MN shapes such as deep carinated bowls (as Phelps 2004: 190-191, figs. 16:10-15, 17:1-7), everted rim bowls (Phelps 2004: 192, fig. 18.1-14) and low collar-necked jars (Phelps 2004: 193-194 figs. 19.1-16 and 20.1-19)[10] are not made in LN Wares (with rare exceptions, such as the polychrome version of the MN deep carinated bowl shape noted by Vitelli 1999: 170, fig. 12g). Likewise, classic LN shapes such as the low rimmed, sharply carinated bowl thickened at the middle (as Phelps 2004: 200, fig. 26.1-12), shoulder bowl with a bead rim (as Phelps 2004: 201, fig. 27.8-

14) or the pedestalled vase with a bell-shaped bowl (as Phelps 2004: 204, fig. 30.13-19) are not made in *Urfirnis* (with rare exceptions, such as the LN-shaped carinated bowl in *Urfirnis* noted by Phelps 2004: 51, fig. 16.7; cf. Franchthi: Vitelli 1993: 177, fig. 85h; also at Theopetra, see Katsarou 2000: 244; and from Youra, Sampson 2008b: 19, fig. 2.7.18). The new LN shapes are found in the LN 1α phase at Kouphovouno side-by-side with *Urfirnis*, which dominated the assemblages. So, not only were there differences in technique but, to a degree, certain vase shapes were considered to belong to one tradition or another. The pedestalled bowls (or 'fruitstands') illustrate a more complex relationship. In the Peloponnese they develop out of a standard MN *Urfirnis* form (as Phelps 2004: 186, fig. 12.8-9 and 196, fig. 22.18-32). In the LN, the same type of cylindrical pedestal, though with a more flaring profile, is made in Black/Grey Ware (Figure 4.4e; cf., for example, Hauptmann 1981: 83, Beilage 7:48; Lavezzi 1978: 437, fig. 4.26; Sampson 2008a: 98 fig. 54.1102; Vitelli 1999: 28-29 fig. 7a-f); this seems to lead to the manufacture of a new, narrow necked form of pedestal with a flaring profile (Figure 4.4f), which may be linked with the development of a more bell-shaped bowl (as Phelps 2004: 204, fig. 30.14-19; cf. Vitelli 1999: 178, fig. 16n, 184, fig. 19h-j FCP 4.1 (= Kouphovouno LN 1β); Hauptmann 1981: 83, Beilage 7:47; Sampson 2008a: 93-94). This narrow-necked pedestal base comes closest to the Vinča culture types (Figure 4.4g-h; Milojčić 1949: 271, fig. 4.2) and it may be significant that it seems to develop later in the Greek LN sequence (end of LN 1α - LN1β at Kouphovouno; FCP 4.1 at Franchthi). Elateia produced fruitstands similar to those from Kouphovouno phase LN 1α (Weinberg 1962: 183, fig. 8.7-8, 10) with pedestal bases in the *Urfirnis* tradition (also found in Black on Red, Weinberg 1962: pl. 58f), as well as the bell-shaped bowls and narrow pedestals, but it is not clear if this second type occurred in Bothros 3 or only in later LN levels (see Weinberg 1962: 183 and 188-189, fig. 8.11-13, pl. 61b-d). Weinberg described Grey-Black Wares found in lower contexts as 'earlier and apparently unrelated' (1962: 186, n. 42 referring to 174-175), implying that Black Burnished is new to Elateia in what we would call early LN.[11]

At most sites in Greece there is agreement that Black Wares are a new introduction to a tradition otherwise characterised by broad continuity. Perlès has argued that, despite appearances, the occupants of LN Franchthi were descended from those of the MN (2004: 164-165) and the changes seen there in both pottery production and the working of obsidian were the result of social and economic factors. Lavezzi refers to a 'peaceful' transition from MN to LN at Corinth (2003: 68), but with marked changes in the ceramic

---

[9] FG 7 for Red-on-Black and LFG 6-9 Black Burnished, probably linked with eastern Thessaly (see Pentedeka 2015: 254-256, 270, 496).

[10] We would draw a distinction between the MN type of collar-necked jar with a low rim shaped like a dog-collar and the LN types varieties of which are discussed by Phelps (2004: 73, 80, 91-92); compare those at Franchthi (such as Vitelli 1999: figs. 1:a, 3:a, 4:a-c, 8:e-f, 10, 12a, 17:e-h, 20:a-b, 21:a-c, 21:e, 26:a-c, 37:d) which are frequently referred to by Vitelli as 'necked jars' (1999: 27-28, 32); the later types commonly had handles, which are not found on MN collar jars. The 'dog-collar' type is not completely unknown in LN (see, for example, Phelps 2004: figs. 33:21, 41:19).

[11] Although Weinberg preferred to place Bothros 3 in the latest MN (1962: 196).

repertoire. At Halai, O'Neill and colleagues report that 'In general, the finds suggest considerable continuity of material culture throughout the Neolithic occupation of Halai. There are no sharp breaks before the final abandonment that might indicate the arrival of new people or earlier episodes of abandonment' (O'Neill et al. 1999: 295). On the basis of the stratigraphy at Platia Magoula Zarkou and Makrychori, and their more general review of Thessalian pottery, Demoule et al. (1988) see the appearance of Black Burnished Ware as certainly new, but recognise a gradual evolution from the MN Sesklo to the Larisa-Tsangli periods in both the forms and decorative motifs of other pottery. At Servia too, Black Burnished pottery represents a new introduction alongside standard MN wares in Phase 6 at the site: 'the proportion of fine L.N. pottery steadily increases...By phase 7 it may be that M.N. pottery is no longer being manufactured...but although phase 6 is transitional, it does not seem that the new types developed at Servia' (Ridley and Wardle 1979: 213).

Researchers have also emphasised the differences between site assemblages at the time of the 'koine'. Thus, Vitelli has noted that not all features of the Larisa or Corinthian Black Burnished are present in FCP 3, and some first appear in FCP 4 in a different ware (1999: 35). Much the same is true of Kouphovouno, and other sites in the Peloponnese. In eastern Thessaly, Larisa Black Burnished Wares are the most common of the fine wares (for an overview of the Larisa types, see Hauptmann 1981: 75-96, Beilage 7), whereas in western Thessaly they are not frequent (Alram-Stern and Dousougli-Zachos 2015: 129); Black Burnished was well-represented at Varka (Sampson 1977), but it appears only in low numbers at Tharrounia and at other sites on Euboea (Cullen et al. 2013: 27; Phelps 2004: 76; Sampson 1993: 62). Slightly different assemblages have also been found in Boeotia (for example, Sampson 2008a: 89-111) and Thessaly. So, LN Black Burnished Ware means different things at different sites and at different times. The best illustration of this multiplicity of meanings comes from the innovative study of the LN assemblages of Makriyalos (Urem-Kotsou and Kotsakis 2007), which combines evidence from archaeological deposits, pottery, residue analysis, isotope analysis and bioarchaeology to distinguish different contexts of consumption, domestic and feasting. Larisa style pottery, and related classes, were prized and found in both household and feasting contexts. The carinated bowl is a common Black Ware shape, plainly related to those found from the Peloponnese to Serbia (Urem-Kotsou and Kotsakis 2007: 229 fig. 14.2), but Black Ware pedestalled bowls apparently did not feature. More generally in Macedonia whilst Dark Burnished carinated and bead-rimmed bowls are found as at Sitagroi (Figure 4.4c; Keighley 1986: 349, fig. 11.1.2-4), the pedestal bases, found in Dark and Pale Burnished fabrics, seem closer in form to those found at Selevac (Tringham and Krstić 1990: 298, fig. 9.1) than the types illustrated in Figure 4.4 (though wide open bowls with a thickened rim suggest a connection with the types found in southern Greece; see, for example, Keighley 1986: 349, fig. 11.4.7).

Before moving on to other considerations, we shall mention another distinct and widely distributed type of Black Ware pottery: the famous four-legged 'rhytons' which formed the subject of Chris Mee's article, mentioned above. They have earlier precedents outside Greece, where examples from Impressed Ware and contemporary contexts date to the first half of the 6th millennium BC (including at Smilčić, Crno vrilo, Vashtëmi, Barç, see Biagi and Spataro 2002; Mlekuž 2007; for the dating of Impressed Ware in the East Adriatic, see Forenbaher et al. 2013; and for Starčevo-Criş, see Thissen and Reingruber 2017: 163-165). The rhytons from Achilleion are very early in date — the earliest fragment in phase IIb would place the appearance of the shape before 6000 cal. BC (Gimbutas et al. 1989: 208-211) — but in appearance and decoration they are very different from the Black Ware LN series. The point we wish to stress here is that although earlier prototypes existed, the production of rhytons in Central Greece and the Peloponnese is a feature of the LN. This late adoption was not due to lack of contact in the earlier period; there are connections evident between the Peloponnese and the northwestern Balkan area in the MN. Rather, for whatever reason, there was felt a need for these curious vases in LN Greece which was not felt in the earlier period. Significantly, these rhytons are not reported from Danubian sites such as Vinča, but have a more pronounced eastern distribution (Mlekuž 2007: 268 fig. 1). The rhyton's adoption, therefore, also needs to be factored into an account of the innovations marking the LN period.

In summary, the case for ceramic innovation as a consequence of large-scale population movement faces several key challenges. First, it must address issues of chronology; second, at many sites pottery exhibits a gradual, rather than a sudden, transition; third, again from the ceramic perspective, it needs to explain the combination of wares whose origins and background seem to be different (notably Matt-painted, Polychrome and Black Ware); and fourth, that it should explain variation in pottery shapes and forms from region to region. The model does not rule out an effect from more sporadic movements of people. Common experience has now combined with the results of aDNA and isotope analysis to show that people in the Neolithic moved over long distances, and the abandonment of old settlements and the establishment of new in Late Neolithic Greece surely attests to some churning of the population. But these people did not bring with them a common cultural 'package'. Consequently, the adoption of a similar ceramic aesthetic (particularly that of the black, sometimes highly burnished, surface) and certain common shapes (notably carinated bowls and 'fruitstands') demands some other explanation. It is here that we return to the notion of territoriality to suggest that the transformation during the second half of the 6th millennium BC in LN Greece and the contemporary Balkans, saw a reworking of that sense of something held in common on which we have commented for the preceding period.

New networks and the reworking of territoriality

This transformation is also visible in those supply chains which linked groups across significant distances. The later 6th millennium BC saw the greatest diffusion of *Spondylus* shell ornaments through Europe. Chapman and Gaydarska suggest that the diffusion of such ornaments during this period (their Phase 2) was mediated through 'long-distance travellers' (2015: 645-646, 652, fig. 33.3). They have also argued that salt was traded widely in Neolithic Europe (Chapman and Gaydarska 2003). At the same time, we can recognise the circulation of the earliest copper trinkets in Europe (Heyd and Walker 2015: 674-675; for examples from Makriyalos Phase I, see Pappa and Besios 1999: 117); the sources of native copper exploited at the time have not been established, but the finds range across Moldavia, Hungary, Romania, Slovakia and Greece. The development of manganese-based paints, used on LN pottery all over Greece, indicate the exchange of special materials (or perhaps the knowledge of how to locate such materials); indeed, although there are variations of practice from Macedonia, to Thessaly, to Central Greece, and to the Peloponnese, a similar command of the firing of manganese and iron-based pigments allowing retention of a contrasting clay base suggests the existence of a technological community among potters throughout the '*koine*' (Bonga 2013: 129-132). As we have seen, scientific analysis has shown that prized pottery was moved considerable distances. Moreover, the working and the distribution of Melian obsidian changes in the Late Neolithic, but variously in the different regions of Greece (Perlès and Vitelli 1999: 97). These networks of exchange must have involved the movement of individuals on foot and by boat; their reception into villages and households would have required protocols of acceptance, and the exposure of individuals to the stimulus of new norms, stereotypes, and schemas of action would have marked the transformation of culture recognised in Greece.

The shapes of the new wares, including bowls with a sharply carinated profile and flaring rim, incurving bowls, often with bead rims, and pedestal bowls or 'fruitstands', are as important as the techniques used to make them. It is noteworthy that no shape is restricted to Black Ware; they appear in Grey Ware, Matt-painted and Polychrome and, during the earliest phase, were produced alongside *Urfirnis*. This brings us to our third observation, that which we have termed LN redundancy. Certainly in the MN Peloponnese it is possible to distinguish a variety of pottery wares, for example patterned and monochrome *Urfirnis* (presumably the difference in effort reflecting greater or lesser display), and functional varieties such as cooking pots, 'husking trays' and 'coarse *Urfirnis*'. But this differs from the variation we find in the LN, where the same shapes (including pedestal bowls, carinated bowls, incurved bowls, shoulder bowls, collar jars, piriform jars) are found in Black Ware, Grey Ware, Matt-painted and Polychrome. The new variation cannot be explained on functional grounds because the same shapes are found in all wares; nor is the difference simply between patterned and monochrome. As an alternative, we suggest that they conveyed different messages; Black Ware meant something different from Matt-painted, and that Polychrome projected yet another value.

How, then, would we account for the '*koine*', the sense that large areas of Greece came together in an exceptional manner at the beginning of the Late Neolithic? Let us first underline what was exceptional. For at least 1000 years prior, pottery production in the Peloponnese and, indeed, in various other regions of Greece, had followed a conservative tradition; each style evolving gradually from what went before. Here and there, specific types, such as the Impressed Wares of EN-MN northern Greece or the various EN-MN Black Wares (distinct in form and decoration from the LN Black Wares), went in or out of fashion. With the advent of the Late Neolithic, there was not only a radical change in the appearance of the pottery, but also in its wide distribution across much of the Balkans. A prominent, but not unique, expression of this is the adoption of Black Ware and a case can be made for the circulation of LN Black Burnished Wares within a territory stretching from Serbia in the north to the southern tip of the Peloponnese and across the Aegean islands. How are we to understand this expression of territoriality in the context of the Neolithic?

Contrast the more extensive links of the Peloponnesian Middle Neolithic: the split-leg figurines witness not so much direct imitation — for the Albanian and Bulgarian parallels look nothing like their Peloponnesian counterparts — as much as they evidence a common practice. Whatever beliefs lay behind the practice of splitting the figurines apart, and on this there are competing theories, it was the practice that was held in common, not the precise form and decoration of the physical object. In this case, territoriality was expressed as a shared perception of the act of breaking a clay figurine into pieces. Compare too, at a much later period, the broad spheres of interaction recognised by Maran in the later Early Bronze Age, which included an Aegean-West Anatolian zone, and an Adriatic-Ionian zone (not to mention the West Mediterranean Beaker zone) (Maran 1998: 432-450, pl. 71a) particularly associated with the metal trade. The earlier and later expressions of territoriality are not the same; each is a consequence of the particular conditions at the time of their emergence.

We would argue that different factors coincided to shape and frame these expressions in the LN. Firstly, some movement of population is clear. But, rather than a large, concerted mass movement, we would recognise very many small-scale displacements across the landscape resulting in a multi-cultural mix. There must have been a territorial context for such displacements and some 'political' accommodation through which such settlement and resettlement was able to take place within large regions. Crossing boundaries and moving into other people's territories is always a dangerous undertaking and the threat of violence must have been ever present. It is surely no coincidence that towards the end of the MN, and into the LN, arrowheads and projectile points become an ever more prominent element in the chipped stone assemblage; they are a sign of dangerous times. After all, signs of such violence are visible elsewhere in Neolithic Europe (Schulting and Wysocki 2005; Wahl and König 1987).

When faced with aggression and the need to negotiate a pact, symbolic and ceremonial objects would have been important. Bonga has underlined a number of observations about Black Ware vessels which point to their use in ceremonial activity, including evidence for fragmentation (also suggested for rhytons), frequent repairs (indicative of a particular value), and their use to hold cremation burials (2013: 153-154). The exchange of gifts and the sharing food are also important means for averting conflict, in addition to creating and maintaining social relations. The adoption of the rhyton could be placed in this context — the prominent ring handles mean that they could be passed from person to person and, indeed, Chapman (1988) has suggested that they contained salt, a substance which is, in many societies, a symbol of hospitality and, in others, a shield against malevolent forces. The rhytons, and Black Burnished pottery in general, presented a visual contrast with the Middle Neolithic painted styles such as *Urfirnis* or Red-on-White, (though, of course, black monochrome *Urfirnis* remains popular). For those communities sensitive to the appearance of their pottery, the difference must have been striking. Such pottery could, at first, have been used on ceremonial occasions. Its value lay in its use of a symbolic vocabulary that was recognised across different cultural groups stretching across the Balkans to the southern

Peloponnese. Black Ware rhytons, carinated bowls, pedestal bowls and other types could have been used at ceremonial meals as a token of shared values between groups engaged in various socio-political or economic relationships or rivalries, as has been suggested for Franchthi Cave or Makriyalos. The style's relative rarity at the earliest stage of its development, and the contrast it presented to conventional MN pottery, would have helped mark such ceremonial feasting as exceptional. If, initially, Black Ware enjoyed a special prestige, that may explain why it came to proliferate in LN assemblages in the Peloponnese. By the same token, with time, its symbolic power may have lost its cogency, and the ware may simply have come to signal a sense of common identity across the Peloponnese. Over time, the '*koine*' began to dissolve, and ceramic styles devolved into regional variants each with their own territorial distribution.

Conclusion

In conclusion, we have argued that a model of territorial partition across the Peloponnese and mainland Greece helps us to understand the material culture of those communities who occupied the land. Looking first at the MN, we highlighted different scales of territoriality from family divisions, to separate enclaves or neighbourhoods within the village, to divisions in the farmed fields, to major and subsidiary settlements, regional divisions, and vaguer but wider links across the whole of the Balkans. Such territories were not impermeable: individuals and small groups moved over considerable distances and served as agents of communication, facilitating the transfer of knowledge over the peninsula. This set the context for Chris Mee's analysis of the Kouphovouno finds and his observation of the gradual transition in pottery styles to the LN. We suggest that the realignment of population not only reworked the territorial fabric of Greece, but also presented communities of the time with challenges to their perception of access to land. Some settlements, such as Corinth, continued to flourish; we believe that Kouphovouno shrank in size, and other sites were abandoned, whilst new villages were established (Renard and Cavanagh 2017). People were on the move. This is the backdrop against which important innovations were made in the pottery of the time. The wide geographic reach, notably of Black Burnished Wares, no longer makes sense as a sign of a major ethnic movement: it varies too much (different forms, different assemblages) from site to site, it is frequently found as just one type of pottery among many and, where it appears, we see just the same sort of step-by-step transformation registered at Kouphovouno. We propose, therefore, that its initial wide distribution reflected, in part, a need for objects with widely recognised symbolic message across the whole of the Greek mainland, to help ease the tensions caused by disturbance in the territorial status quo. Furthermore, as borne out by the recent analytical work of researchers such as Areti Pentedeka, Elissavet Hitsiou, Patrick Quinn and Konstantina Papakosta, the value of at least the finest of the vases — the products of specialist craftsmen — made them suitable as gifts on ceremonial occasions.

Bibliography

Allen, S. 2017. Cultivating identities: landscape production by early farmers in the southern Balkans, in M. Gori and M. Ivanova (eds) *Balkan Dialogues: Negotiating Identity Between Prehistory and the Present*: 213-239. London: Routledge.

Alram-Stern, E. 1996. *Die Ägäische Frühzeit. 2. Serie, Forschungsbericht 1975-1993. 1. Band. Das Neolithikum in Griechenland mit Ausnahme von Kreta und Zypern* (Veroffentlichungen der Mykensichen Kommission 16). Vienna: the Austrian Academy of Sciences

Alram-Stern, E. and A. Dousougli-Zachos 2015. *Die deutschen Ausgrabungen 1941 auf der Visviki-Magula/ Velestino: die neolithischen Befunde und Funde.* Bonn: Rudolf Habelt.

Andreou, S., M. Fotiadis and K. Kotsakis 2001. The Neolithic and Bronze Age of northern Greece, in T. Cullen (ed.) *Aegean Prehistory: A Review* (American Journal of Archaeology Supplement 1): 259-319. Boston: Archaeological Institute of America.

Ballut, C., J. Renard, W. Cavanagh and R. Orgeolet 2017. Pottery firing structures in the early Mediterranean: micromorphological evidence and archaeological data from Middle Neolithic Kouphovouno (Southern Greece). *European Journal of Archaeology* 20(1): 98-119.

Biagi, P. and M. Spataro 2002. Il rhyton della caverna dell'edera di Aurisina (Trieste) e il problema della produzione e distribuzione dei rhyta neolitici nella regione adriatica. *Rivista di Archeologia* 25(2001): 5-11.

Bonga, L. 2013. Late Neolithic Pottery from Mainland Greece, ca. 5,300–4,300 B.C. Unpublished PhD dissertation, Temple University.

Brandt, G., A. Szécsényi-Nagy, C. Rotha, K. Werner and W. Haak 2015. Human paleogenetics of Europe – the known knowns and the known unknowns. *Journal of Human Evolution* 79: 73-92.

Broodbank, C. 2000. *An Island Archaeology of the Early Cyclades.* Cambridge: Cambridge University Press.

Budja, M. 2003. Seals, contracts and tokens in the Balkans Early Neolithic: where in the puzzle. *Documenta Praehistorica* 30: 115-130.

Cavanagh, W. 1999. Revenons à nos moutons. Surface survey and the Peloponnese in the Late and Final Neolithic, in J. Renard (ed.) *Le Péloponnèse. Archéologie et Histoire: Actes de la rencontre internationale de Lorient (12-15 mai 1998)*: 31-65. Rennes: Rennes University Press.

Cantuel, J. 2010. L'Exploitation de la Faune Durant le Néolithique en Grèce Continentale. Unpublished PhD dissertation, University of Clermont-Ferrand II.

Cantuel, J., A. Gardeisen and J. Renard 2008. L'exploitation de la faune durant le Néolithique dans le Bassin Égéen, in E. Vila, L. Gourichon, A.M Choyke and H. Buitenhuis (eds) *Archaeozoology of the Near East VIII: Proceedings of the Eighth International Symposium on the Archaeozoology of Southwestern Asia and Adjacent Areas*: 279–298. Lyon: House of the Orient and the Mediterranean-Jean Pouilloux.

Cavanagh, B. and J. Renard 2014. Neolithic figurines from Kouphovouno. *Journal of Prehistoric Religion* 24: 19-35.

Cessford, C. 2005. Estimating the Neolithic population of Çatalhöyük, in I. Hodder (ed.) *Inhabiting Çatalhöyük: Reports from the 1995-1999 Seasons* (British Institute of Archaeology at Ankara Monograph 38): 323-330. Cambridge: McDonald Institute for Archaeological Research.

Chapman, J. 1988. Ceramic production and social differentiation: the Dalmatian Neolithic and the Western Mediterranean. *Journal of Mediterranean Archaeology* 1(2): 3-25.

Chapman, J. and B. Gaydarska, 2003. The provision of salt to Tripolye mega-sites, in A. Korvin-Piotrovsky and V. Kruts (eds) *Tripolian Settlement-Giants: the International Symposium Materials*: 203-211. Kiev: Institute of Archaeology.

Chapman, J. and B. Gaydarska. 2015. *Spondylus gaederopus/ glycymeris* exchange networks in the European Neolithic and Chalcolithic, in C. Fowler, J. Harding and D. Hofmann (eds) *The Oxford Handbook of Neolithic Europe*: 639-656. Oxford: Oxford University Press.

Commenge-Pellerin. C and Z. Tsirtsoni (2004). Les récipients en céramique: formes et décors du Néolithique Moyen, in R. Treuil (ed.) *Dikili Tash, village préhistorique de Macédoine orientale I. Fouilles de Jean Deshayes (1961-1975), Volume 2* (Bulletin de Correspondance Hellénique Supplément 37): 27-61. Paris: the French School at Athens.

Cullen, T. 1985a. A Measure of Interaction Among Neolithic Societies: Design Elements of Greek Urfirnis Pottery. Unpublished PhD dissertation, Indiana University.

Cullen, T. 1985b. Social implications of ceramic style in the Neolithic Peloponnese, in W.D. Kingery (ed.) *Ancient Technology to Modern Science* (Ceramics and Civilization, Volume I): 77-100. Columbus: the American Ceramic Society.

Cullen, T., L.E. Talalay, D.R. Keller, L. Karimali and W.R. Farrand 2013. *The Prehistory of the Paximadi Peninsula, Euboea* (Prehistory Monographs 40). Philadelphia: INSTAP Academic Press.

Delaney, D. 2005. *Territory: A Short Introduction.* Malden: Blackwell.

Demoule, J-P., K. Gallis and L. Manolakakis 1988. Transition entre les cultures néolithiques de Sesklo et de Dimini: les catégories céramiques. *Bulletin de Correspondance Hellénique* 112(1): 1-58.

Demoule, J-P. and C. Perlès 1993. The Greek Neolithic: a new review. *Journal of World Prehistory* 7(4): 355-416.

Dousougli, A. 1998. Άρια Αργολίδος. Χειροποίητη κεραμική της νεότερης νεολιθικής και της χαλκολιθικής περιόδου (Υπουργείο Πολιτισμού Δημοσιεύματα του Αρχαιολογικού Δελτίου 66). Athens: Ministry of Culture, Archaeological Receipts and Expropriations Fund.

Facorellis Y. and J. Coleman 2012. Interpreting radiocarbon dates from Neolithic Halai, Greece. *Radiocarbon* 54(3-4): 319-330.

Forenbaher, S., T. Kaiser and P.T. Miracle 2013. Dating the East Adriatic Neolithic. *European Journal of Archaeology* 16(4): 589-609.

Forsén, J. and B. Forsén 2003. *The Asea Valley Survey. An Arcadian Mountain Valley from the Palaeolithic period until Modern Times* (Skrifter utgivna av Svenska institutet i Athen, 4o, 51). Stockholm: the Swedish Institute at Athens.

Gimbutas, M., S. Winn and D. Shimabuku 1989. *Achilleion. A Neolithic Settlement in Central Greece, 6400-5600 BC* (Monumenta Archaeologica 14). Los Angeles: Institute of Archaeology, University of California.

Hahn, H.P. 2017. Ethnicity as a form of social organisation: notes on the multiplicity of understandings of a contested concept, in M. Gori and M. Ivanova (eds) *Balkan Dialogues: Negotiating Identity Between Prehistory and the Present*: 38-51. London: Routledge.

Halstead, P. 2014. *Two Oxen Ahead: Pre-Mechanized Farming in the Mediterranean*. Hoboken: Wiley-Blackwell.

Hauptmann, H. 1981. *Die Deutschen Ausgrabungen auf der Otzaki-Magula in Thessalien III. Das späte Neolithikum und das Chalkolithikum* (Beiträge zur ur- und frühgeschichtlichen Archäologie des Mittelmeer-Kulturraumes 21). Bonn: Rudolf Habelt.

Heyd, V. and K. Walker 2015. The first metalwork and expressions of social power, in C. Fowler, J. Harding and D. Hofmann (eds) *The Oxford Handbook of Neolithic Europe*: 673-691. Oxford: Oxford University Press.

Hitsiou, E.S. 2017. *Pottery Production Technology and Long-Distance Exchange in Late Neolithic Makrygialos, Northern Greece* (British Archaeological Report International Series 2843). Oxford: British Archaeological Reports.

Hogg, M.A. and G.M. Vaughan 2018. *Social Psychology* (Eighth Edition). Harlow: Pearson Education.

Jakucs, J., E. Bánffy, K. Oross, V. Voicsek, C. Bronk Ramsey, E. Dunbar, B. Kromer, A. Bayliss, D. Hofmann, P. Marshall and A. Whittle 2016. Between the Vinča and Linearbandkeramik worlds: the diversity of practices and identities in the 54th-53rd centuries cal BC in Southwest Hungary and beyond. *Journal of World Prehistory* 29: 267-336.

Johnson, M. 2004. Early Farming in the Land of Springs: Settlement Patterns and Agriculture in Neolithic Greece. Unpublished PhD dissertation, Gothenburg University.

Keighley, J.M. 1986. The pottery of Phases I and II, in C. Renfrew, M. Gimbutas and E.S. Elster (eds) *Excavations at Sitagroi: a Prehistoric Village in Northeast Greece 1* (Monumenta Archaeologica 13): 345-390. Los Angeles: Institute of Archaeology, University of California.

Katsarou, S. 2000. Η μονόχρωμη κεραμική της Νεολιθικής ως προϊόν μίας διαδικασίας επιλογής, in N. Kyparissi (ed.) *Theopetra Cave: Twelve Years of Excavation and Research 1987-1998. Proceedings of the International Conference, Trikala, 6-7 November 1998*: 235-261. Athens: Ministry of Culture, Ephorate of Paleoanthropology-Speleology.

Lavezzi, J.C. 1978. Prehistoric investigations at Corinth. *Hesperia: the Journal of the American School of Classical Studies at Athens* 47(4): 402-451.

Lavezzi, J.C. 2003. Corinth before the Mycenaeans, in C.K. Williams and N. Bookidis (eds) *Corinth, The Centenary: 1896-1996* (Corinth: Results of Excavations Conducted by the American School of Classical Studies at Athens 20): 63-74. Princeton: the American School of Classical Studies at Athens.

Lespez, L., Z. Tsirtsoni, P. Darcque, D. Malamidou, H. Koukouli-Chryssanthaki and A. Glais 2017. Identifying the earliest Neolithic settlements in the southeastern Balkans: methodological considerations based on the recent geoarchaeological investigations at Dikili Tash (Greek Eastern Macedonia), in A. Reingruber, Z. Tsirtsoni and P. Nedelcheva (eds) *Going West? The Dissemination of Neolithic Innovations between the Bosporus and the Carpathians. Proceedings of the EAA Conference, Istanbul, 11 September 2014* (Themes in Contemporary Archaeology 3): 43-55. London: Routledge.

Maran, J. 1998. *Kulturwandel auf dem griechischen Festland und den Kykladen im späten 3. Jahrtausend v. Chr.: Studien zu den kulturellen Verhältnissen in Südosteuropa und dem zentralen sowie östlichen Mittelmeerraum in der späten Kupfer- und frühen Bronzezeit* (Universitätsforschungen zur prähistorischen Archäologie 53). Bonn: Rudolf Habelt.

Mee, C. 2007. The production and consumption of pottery in the Neolithic Peloponnese, in C. Mee and J. Renard (eds) *Cooking up the Past: Food and Culinary Practices in the Neolithic and Bronze Age Aegean*: 200-224. Oxford: Oxbow Books.

Mee, C. 2014. The Late Neolithic rhyta from Kouphovouno in the Peloponnese, Greece. *Journal of Prehistoric Religion* 24: 7-18.

Mee, C., B. Cavanagh and J. Renard 2014. The Middle–Late Neolithic transition at Kouphovouno. *The Annual of the British School at Athens* 109: 65-95.

Milojčić, V. 1949. South-eastern elements in the prehistoric civilization of Serbia. *The Annual of the British School at Athens* 44: 258-306.

Mlekuž, D. 2007. 'Sheep are your mother': rhyta and the interspecies politics in the Neolithic of the eastern Adriatic. *Documenta Praehistorica* 34: 267-280.

Morgan, C. 2014. Franchthi Cave, Archaeology in Greece Online. Record ID 4448, viewed 08 January 2018, <http://www.chronique.efa.gr/index.php/fiches/voir/4448/>.

Neil, S., J. Montgomery, J. Evans, G.T. Cook and C. Scarre 2017. Land use and mobility during the Neolithic in Wales explored using isotope analysis of tooth enamel. *American Journal of Physical Anthropology* 164(2): 371-393.

Nikolov, V. 2017. Thrace, post 6000 BC, in A. Reingruber, Z. Tsirtsoni and P. Nedelcheva (eds) *Going West? The Dissemination of Neolithic Innovations between the Bosporus and the Carpathians. Proceedings of the EAA Conference, Istanbul, 11 September 2014* (Themes in Contemporary Archaeology 3): 73-78. London: Routledge.

O'Neill, K., W. Yielding, J. Near, J.E. Coleman, P.S. Wren and K.M. Quinn 1999. Halai: the 1992-1994 field seasons. *Hesperia: the Journal of the American School of Classical Studies at Athens* 68(3): 285-341.

Orengo, H.A., A. Krahtopoulou, A. Garcia-Molsosa, K. Palaiochoritis and A. Stamati 2015. Photogrammetric re-discovery of the hidden long-term landscapes of western Thessaly, central Greece. *Journal of Archaeological Science* 64: 100-109.

Özdoğan, M. 2017. Neolithic assemblages and spatial boundaries as exemplified through the Neolithic of Northwestern Turkey, in M. Gori and M. Ivanova (eds) *Balkan Dialogues: Negotiating Identity Between Prehistory and the Present*: 197-212. London: Routledge.

Papakosta, K. 2011. Neolithic pottery: a characterisation study, in A. Sampson (ed.) *The Cave of Cyclops: Mesolithic and Neolithic Networks in the Northern Aegean, Greece, Volume II: Bone Tool Industries, Dietary Resources and the Paleoenvironment, and Archeometrical Studies* (Prehistory Monographs 31): 327-360. Philadelphia: INSTAP Academic Press.

Pappa, M. and M. Besios 1999. The Makriyalos Project: rescue excavations at the Neolithic site of Makriyalos, Pieria, Northern Greece, in P. Halstead (ed.) *Neolithic Society in Greece* (Sheffield Studies in Aegean Archaeology 2): 108-120. Sheffield: Sheffield Academic Press.

Pechtl, J. 2015. Linearbandkeramik pottery and society, in C. Fowler, J. Harding and D. Hofmann (eds) *The Oxford Handbook of Neolithic Europe*: 555-572. Oxford: Oxford University Press.

Pellegrini, M., J. Pouncett, M. Jay, M. Parker Pearson and M. Richards 2016. Tooth enamel oxygen "isoscapes" show a high degree of human mobility in prehistoric Britain. *Scientific Reports* 6: 34986 <https://doi.org/10.1038/srep34986>.

Pentedeka, A. 2008. Pottery Exchange Networks during Middle and Late Neolithic in Thessaly. Unpublished PhD dissertation, Aristotle University of Thessaloniki.

Pentedeka, A. 2011. Links of clay in Neolithic Greece: the case of Platia Magoula Zarkou, in A. Brysbaert

(ed.) *Tracing Prehistoric Social Networks through Technology: a Diachronic Perspective on the Aegean*: 106-125. London and New York: Routledge.

Pentedeka, A. 2015. Technological and provenance study of the Visviki Magoula ceramic assemblage, in E. Alram-Stern and A. Dousougli-Zachos. *Die deutschen Ausgrabungen 1941 auf der Visviki-Magula/Velestino: Die neolithischen Befunde und Funde* (Beiträge zur Ur- und Frühgeschichtlichen Archäologie des Mittelmeer-Kulturraumes 36): 222-297. Bonn: Rudolf Habelt.

Perlès, C. 2004. *Les Industries lithiques taillées de Franchthi (Argolide, Grèce), III: Du néolithique ancien au néolithique final* (Excavations at Franchthi Cave, Greece 13). Bloomington and Indianapolis: Indiana University Press.

Perlès, C. 2005. Réflexions sur les échanges dans le néolithique de Grèce, in P. Clancier, F. Joannès, P. Rouillard and A. Tenu (eds) *Autour de Polanyi. Vocabulaires, théories et modalités des échanges. Nanterre, 12-14 juin 2004, Colloques de la Maison René-Ginouvès*: 201-215. Paris: de Boccard.

Perlès, C. and K. Vitelli 1999. Craft specialization in the Neolithic of Greece, in P. Halstead (ed.) *Neolithic Society in Greece* (Sheffield Studies in Aegean Archaeology 2): 96-107. Sheffield: Sheffield Academic Press.

Phelps, W.W. 2004. *The Neolithic Pottery Sequence in Southern Greece* (British Archaeological Reports International Series 1259). Oxford: Archaeopress.

Quinn, P., P. Day, V. Kilikoglou, E. Faber, S. Katsarou-Tzeveleki and A. Sampson 2010. Keeping an eye on your pots: the provenance of Neolithic ceramics from the Cave of the Cyclops, Youra, Greece. *Journal of Archaeological Science* 37(5): 1042-1052.

Reingruber, A. 2008. *Die Deutschen Ausgrabungen auf der Argissa-Magula in Thessalien 2. Das frühe und das beginnende mittlere Neolithikum im Lichte transägäischer Beziehungen* (Beiträge zur Ur- und Frühgeschichtlichen Archäologie des Mittelmeer-Kulturraumes 35). Bonn: Rudolf Habelt.

Reingruber, A., G. Toufexis, N. Kyparissi-Apostolika, M. Anetakis, Y. Maniatis and Y. Facorellis 2017. Neolithic Thessaly: radiocarbon dated periods and phases. *Documenta Praehistorica* 44: 34-53.

Renard, J. and B. Cavanagh 2017. Kouphovouno (Laconia): some thoughts about the settlement pattern at the end of the Middle Neolithic, in A. Sarris, E. Kalogiropoulou, T. Kalayci and L. Karimali (eds) *Communities, Landscapes, and Interaction in Neolithic Greece. Proceedings of the International Conference, Rethymno, 29-30 May 2015* (International Monographs in Prehistory 20): 149-166. Ann Arbor: Berghahn Books.

Ridley, C. and K. Wardle 1979. Rescue excavations at Servia 1971-1973: a preliminary report. *The Annual of the British School at Athens* 74: 185-230.

Sampson, A. 1977. Ανασκαφές στο προϊστορικό οικισμό Βάρκας. *Αρχείο Ευβοϊκών Μελετών* 21: 5-60.

Sampson, A. 1993. *Σκοτεινή Θαρρουνίων: το σπήλαιο, ο οικισμός και το νεκροταφείο*. Athens: Ministry of Culture, Ephorate of Paleoanthropology-Speleology.

Sampson, A. 2008a. *The Sarakenos Cave at Akraephnion, Boeotia, Greece, Volume I: the Neolithic and the Bronze Age*. Athens: University of the Aegean and the Polish Academy of Arts and Sciences.

Sampson, A. 2008b. *The Cave of the Cyclops: Mesolithic and Neolithic Networks in the Northern Aegean, Greece, Volume I: Intra-Site Analysis, Local Industries, and Regional Site Distribution* (Prehistory Monographs 21). Philadelphia: INSTAP Academic Press.

Schneider, G., H. Knoll, C. Gallis and J-P. Demoule 1991. Transition entre les cultures néolithiques de Sesklo et de Dimini: recherché minéralogiques, chimiques et technologiques sur les céramiques et les argiles. *Bulletin de Correspondance Hellénique* 115(1): 1-64.

Schulting, R.J. and M. Wysocki 2005. "In this chambered tumulus were found cleft skulls ...": an assessment of the evidence for cranial trauma in the British Neolithic. *Proceedings of the Prehistoric Society* 71: 107-138.

Spataro, M. 2017. Innovation and regionalism in the Middle/Late Neolithic of south and south-eastern Europe (ca. 5,500-4,500 cal. BC): a ceramic perspective, in L. Burnez-Lanotte (ed.) *Matières à Penser: Raw Materials Acquisition and Processing in Early Neolithic Pottery Productions: Proceedings of the workshop of Namur (Belgium), 29-30 May 2015*: 61-80. Paris: the French Prehistoric Society.

Theocharis, D. 1981. *Νεολιθικός Πολιτισμός: σύντομη επισκόπηση της Νεολιθικής στον Ελλαδικό χώρο*. Athens: the National Bank of Greece Cultural Foundation.

Thissen L. and A. Reingruber 2017. Appendix: 14C database for Southeast Europe and adjacent areas (6600-5000 cal BC), in A. Reingruber, Z. Tsirtsoni and P. Nedelcheva (eds) *Going West? The Dissemination of Neolithic Innovations between the Bosporus and the Carpathians. Proceedings of the EAA Conference, Istanbul, 11 September 2014* (Themes in Contemporary Archaeology 3): 122-177. London: Routledge.

Tomkins, P. and P. Day 2001. Production and exchange of the earliest ceramic vessels in the Aegean: view from Early Neolithic Knossos, Crete. *Antiquity* 75(288): 259-260.

Tringham, R. and D. Krstić 1990. *Selevac: A Neolithic Village in Yugoslavia* (Monumenta Archaeologia 15). Los Angeles: University of California, Institute of Archaeology.

Tzavella-Evjen, H. 2012. *Χαιρώνεια* (Βιβλιοθήκη της εν Αθήναις Αρχαιολογικής Εταιρείας 275). Athens: the Archaeological Society at Athens.

Urem-Kotsou, D. and K. Kotsakis 2007. Pottery, cuisine and community in the Neolithic of north Greece, in C. Mee and J. Renard (eds) *Cooking up the Past: Food and Culinary Practices in the Neolithic and Bronze Age Aegean*: 225-246. Oxford: Oxbow Books.

Vaiglova, P., A. Bogaard, M. Collins, W. Cavanagh, C. Mee, J. Renard, A. Lamb, A. Gardeisen and R. Fraser 2014. An integrated stable isotope study of plants and animals from Kouphovouno, southern Greece: a new look at Neolithic farming. *Journal of Archaeological Science* 42: 201-215.

Vitelli, K. D. 1993. *Franchthi Neolithic Pottery. Volume 1: Classification and Ceramic Phases 1 and 2* (Excavations at Franchthi Cave, Greece 8). Bloomington and Indianapolis: Indiana University Press.

Vitelli, K.D. 1999. *Franchthi Neolithic Pottery. Volume 2: the Later Neolithic Ceramic Phases 3 to 5* (Excavations at Franchthi Cave, Greece 10). Bloomington and Indianapolis: Indiana University Press.

Vitelli, K.D. 2007. *Lerna V. The Neolithic Pottery from Lerna*. Princeton: the American School of Classical Studies at Athens.

Wahl, J. and H.G. König 1987. Anthropologisch-traumatologische Untersuchung der menschlichen Skelettreste aus dem bandkeramischen Massengrab bei Talheim, Kreis Heilbronn. *Fundberichte aus Baden-Württemberg* 12: 65-193.

Weinberg, S.S. 1962. Excavations at Prehistoric Elateia, 1959. *Hesperia: the Journal of the American School of Classical Studies at Athens* 31(2): 158-209.

Weinberg, S. S. 1970. The Stone Age in the Aegean, in I.E.S. Edwards, C.J. Gadd and N.G.L. Hammond (eds) *Cambridge Ancient History I, Part 1. Prolegomena and Prehistory* (Second Edition): 557-618. Cambridge: Cambridge University Press.

Whitelaw, T. 2001. From sites to communities: defining the human dimensions of Minoan urbanism, in K. Branigan (ed.) *Urbanism in the Aegean Bronze Age* (Sheffield Studies in Aegean Archaeology 4): 15-37. Sheffield: Sheffield Academic Press.

Whitelaw, T. 2017. The development and character of urban communities in prehistoric Crete in their regional context: a preliminary study, in Q. Letesson and C. Knappett (eds) *Minoan Architecture and Urbanism: New Perspectives on an Ancient Built Environment*: 114-180. Oxford: Oxford University Press.

Whittle, A., A. Bayliss, A. Barclay, B. Gaydarska, E. Bánffy, D. Borić, F. Draşovean, J. Jakucs, M. Marić, D. Orton, I. Pantović, W. Schier, N. Tasić and M. Vander Linden 2016. A Vinča potscape: formal chronological models for the use and development of Vinča ceramics in south-east Europe. *Documenta Praehistorica* 43: 1-60.

Wright, J.C., J.F. Cherry, J.L. Davis, E. Mantzourani, S.B. Sutton and R.F. Sutton Jr. 1990. The Nemea Valley Archaeological Project: a preliminary report. *Hesperia: the Journal of the American School of Classical Studies at Athens* 59(4): 579-659.

Zangger, E. 1993. *The Geoarchaeology of the Argolid* (Argolis 2). Berlin: Mann.

Final Neolithic and Early Helladic Pottery from Geraki[1]

Joost Crouwel

Introduction[2]

The acropolis hill of Geraki in east-central Laconia rises above the eponymous modern village to a maximum elevation of 309m above sea level (Figures 5.1-2). It offers a commanding view across a hinterland of fertile soils and pasture, and those major overland transport routes which thread through it to the southern Laconian coastline. Freshwater is provided by a series of springs dotted around its base and its summit preserves an ancient fortification wall, enclosing an area of approximately 240m by 160m (3.84ha). The site has long been identified with the ancient polis of Geronthrai and earlier scholars had noted evidence of both historic and prehistoric occupation (for the history of research, see Crouwel *et al.* 1995: 43-46; Gritsopoulou 1982: 47-130).

The Dutch Geraki Archaeological Project was designed to document in detail the history of occupation at Geraki. Initiated in 1995, it combined intensive surface survey, geomorphological analysis, and the study of standing architecture with a programme of site-wide test trenching and extended excavations at the northwest of the summit (up until 2009) (Figures 5.3-4). This work revealed evidence of prehistoric human activity beginning first in the Final Neolithic (FN) and continuing through the earlier Early Helladic (EH I-II), the Middle Helladic (MH) and the transition to the Late Helladic (MH III-LH IIA, often called the Shaft Grave period), as well as historic occupation from the Protogeometric to Hellenistic period. Remains of EH III date and those belonging to (most of) the Late Helladic or Mycenaean periods are notably absent, while typical Roman and Byzantine pottery is extremely scarce on the acropolis. During the Late Roman to Early Medieval period, and again during

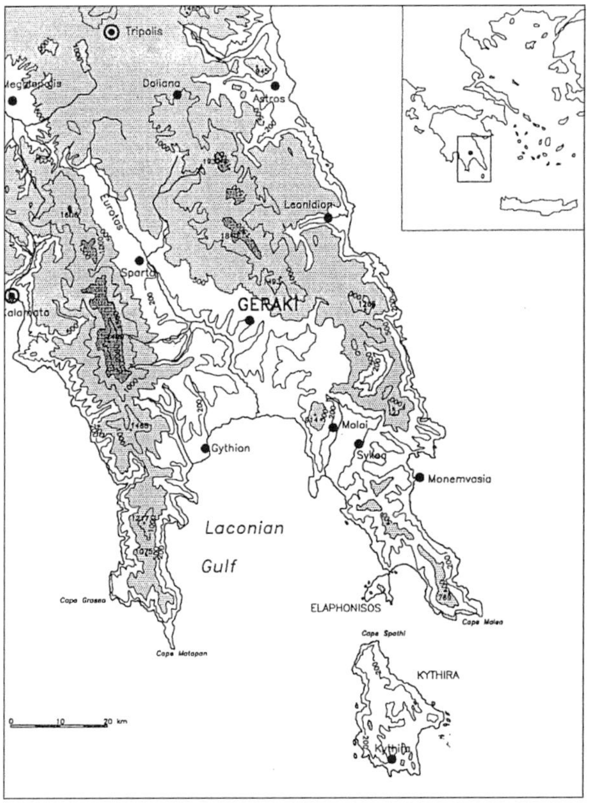

Figure 5.1. Map showing the location of Geraki in Laconia.

the second phase of the Greek Civil War (1946-1949), the circuit wall around the summit was repaired and re-used for defence. In other periods, activity on the site appears to have been largely agricultural, as is the case today. This paper concentrates on the FN and EH occupation of Geraki, and particularly on the pottery of these periods. It is very much an interim report, provided en route to the final publication of our work at Geraki.[3]

The absolute chronology of the periods in question is in a state of flux, with several recently published calibrated radiocarbon dates pushing back the date for the end of the FN and the beginning of the EH in south-central mainland Greece and adjacent islands from *c.* 3100 BC to sometime earlier in the fourth millennium BC, and refining somewhat the internal chronology of the EH period (see Cavanagh *et al.* 2016, with tables 3-5; Smith 2017: 107; for the traditional 'lower' chronology, see, among others, Pullen 2011: 14-16, table 1.2).

[1] Chris Mee and I first met and became friends in 1974, at Hector Catling's excavation of the Menelaion complex in Laconia. I miss him greatly as a friend and colleague.

[2] Acknowledgements: the Dutch work at Geraki was carried out with permission of the Greek Ministry of Culture and under the aegis of the Netherlands Institute at Athens. I am most grateful to my colleagues on the Geraki Project, and in particular to Mieke Prent (field director from 1995 and, since 2017, leader of the project), Stuart MacVeagh Thorne (stratigraphy) and Ayla Krijnen (ceramic analysis; who critically read a draft text of this paper). Many thanks are due also to Daniel Pullen and Vasif Şahoğlu for their observations on our FN and EH pottery during their brief stay in Geraki in 2005; to Aris Papayiannis and Eleni Stravopodi and her colleagues for showing me some of their finds from Karavas Soustianon and Kouveleïki Caves A and B respectively; and to Bill Cavanagh and Chris Mee for many discussions on the pottery from Kouphovouno and Geraki. I am also grateful to Eva van der Laan and Alma Reijling for help with the illustrations which are from the Geraki Archive.

[3] Preliminary reports are published in *Pharos: Journal of the Netherlands Institute at Athens*, volumes III-XVI and XVIII.2 (see Crouwel *et al.* 1995-1997; 1999; 2001; 2002; 2004a; 2004b; 2005-2007; 2009a; 2009b; 2012).

Figure 5.2. Geraki: seen from west.

The Final Neolithic period[4]

The first signs of human activity on the acropolis of Geraki date to the FN period (later 4th millennium BC).[5] This initial occupation is characterised, primarily, by the remains of a fortification wall (Wall 31) and by six discrete deposits of pottery, chipped and ground stone tools, and faunal and botanical remains, in the northwestern part of the summit (Field 17; see Figure 5.4). The double-faced and rubble-filled Wall 31 represents the first building phase at the site, Geraki I. It is also the first of a long sequence of defensive walls constructed at the site through its history. To date, the acropolis of Geraki is the earliest fortified settlement in the Peloponnese. A small number of hilltop sites with defensive walls of FN date are also known from Attica and the Cycladic islands (MacVeagh Thorne 2012: 117-122; Smith 2017: 120).

In addition to those six deposits noted, low numbers of FN potsherds have been identified, with varying degrees of certainty, across the acropolis, albeit mostly in contexts of later date. Of note is the identification of a further small deposit of FN pottery (Deposit 7), with a single intrusive EH II sherd, in a bedrock fissure, some metres to the west, in Field 17.

The pottery from these FN deposits is handmade and highly fragmentary, consisting of some 1000 small to large sherds of medium-coarse and, more often, coarse vessels that were used for food preparation, storage, and consumption (Figures 5.5-8).[6] A shallow, scoop-like, vessel is unique within the assemblage in preserving a complete profile (Figure 5.5, lower). Given the fragmentary nature of most of the FN sherds, it has often proved difficult to establish the shape of the vessels to which they originally belonged, although open shapes outnumber closed ones.

Most of the FN pottery is friable and easily broken, no doubt because of the relatively low temperatures at which it had been fired. This parallels very closely the characteristics of FN pottery from other open-air and cave sites, including Kouphovouno, just south of Sparta in the Eurotas Valley (Cavanagh *et al.* 2004: 91; Mee 2007: 215-216), Franchthi Cave in the Argolid (Vitelli 1999: 64-65, 70-98) and Ayios Dhimitrios in Elis (Zachos 2008: 16). Much of it has also fired very unevenly, with

---

[4] The term Final Neolithic is commonly, but not universally, used in the literature (among others, Phelps 2004: 7, n.2, where the FN equals his period IV in the Peloponnese; Cullen *et al.* 2013: 12-14; Papathanasiou *et al.* 2018; Pullen 2011: 19, n.1). Other scholars prefer the term 'Chalcolithic', which is widely used for northern Greece, in line with Balkan terminology (among others, Alram-Stern 2006, 2007 and 2014; Coleman 2011; Coleman and Facorellis 2018; Maran 1998: 7-8, 25, 74-75, 152-153), while 'Late Neolithic II' is also used, particularly by Greek archaeologists (Kaznesi and Katsarou 2003; Sampson 1997; Sotirakopoulou 2008).

[5] The absolute chronology of the end of the FN period and the beginning of the EH is still obscured by the so-called 'fourth millennium gap' (see especially Cavanagh *et al.* 2016: 47; Coleman 2011; Coleman and Facorellis 2018; Cullen *et al.* 2013: 13-14; Smith 2017: 107). Recent work by Cavanagh *et al.* (2016) has offered a mean date for the end of the period of 3257 BC (3,579–2,935 BC at 95% probability).

[6] The FN to EH II fabrics are being studied by Ayla Krijnen for her doctoral dissertation as well the final publication of our work at Geraki.

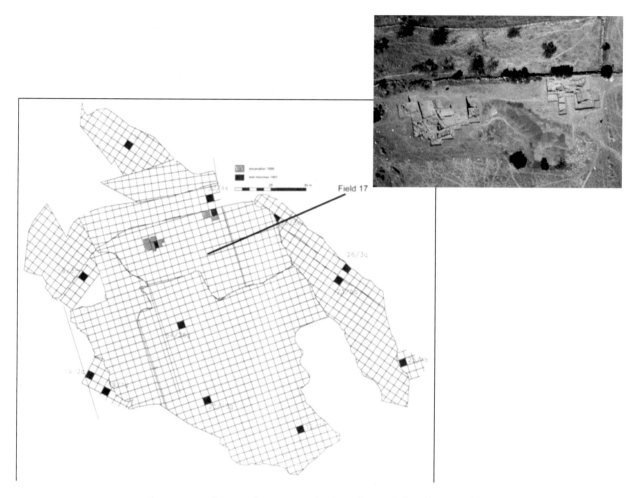

Figure 5.3. *Geraki, acropolis: position of trial trenches, including those in Field 17.*

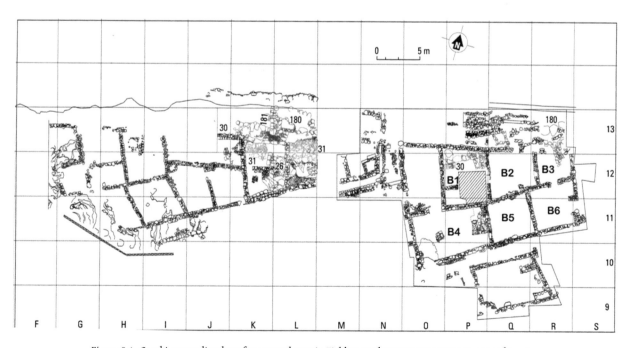

Figure 5.4. *Geraki, acropolis: plan of excavated area in Field 17. Each square represents an area of 5mx5m.*

dark colours (reds, browns, and blacks) predominating. The surfaces of vessels in the medium coarse category — comprised largely of bowls of varying size — are often slipped and burnished; a process which compacts the clay and produces a lustrous effect (Figure 5.6, upper and lower) (Pullen 2011: 25; Vitelli 2007: 7). The surface treatment of the coarse pottery — comprised largely of large bowls but also including some jars and pithoi — varies from minimally smoothed to slipped and burnished.

The assemblage offers many similarities to FN pottery from Alepotrypa Cave at Diros Bay on the northwest coast of the Mani peninsula in Laconia (see Papathanasiou *et al.* 2018). There are parallels too in material from Kouveleïki Caves A and B near Alepochori, a few kilometres south of Geraki (Kaznesi and Katsarou 2003; Koumouzelis 1995: 155-160), the open-air settlement at Kouphovouno (Cavanagh and Mee 2005: 31-32; Cavanagh *et al.* 2007: 27; Mee 2007: 215-220) and from Plakia (Laconia Survey site E48(80); Cavanagh 1996: 1-3; Shipley 1996: 339-340). These similarities also extend to sites in other parts of the Peloponnese and the Aegean islands, particularly in the identification at Geraki of *c.* 40 sherds from coarse bowls with a row of holes below the rim, of a type known as 'cheese-pots' (Figure 5.7), the function of which is still disputed (among others, Alram-Stern 2014: 313-314, fig. 7; Cullen *et al.* 2013: 30-31, 70; Katsarou 2018: 103-105; Katsipanou-Margeli 2018: 78-81; Mee 2007: 219; Phelps 2004: 115; Vitelli 1999: 104; Zachos 2008: 71-72), and in those coarse vessels, mainly bowls, with elaborate plastic decoration in the form of bands, with and without finger impressions or incisions, which are arranged in rectilinear patterns (Figure 5.8; also sherds from zembil 4141, Figure 5.9).

Other finds from Geraki have no clear published parallels. This includes the coarse asymmetrical scoop-like vessel[7] and a fragment, presumably from a coarse hole-mouthed jar, with elaborate plastic decoration (inv. nos. 7303/SF3 and 7303/SF8; Figure 5.5), as well as a circular incised lid[8] and a body sherd of coarse fabric, probably from a large bowl, combining a knob

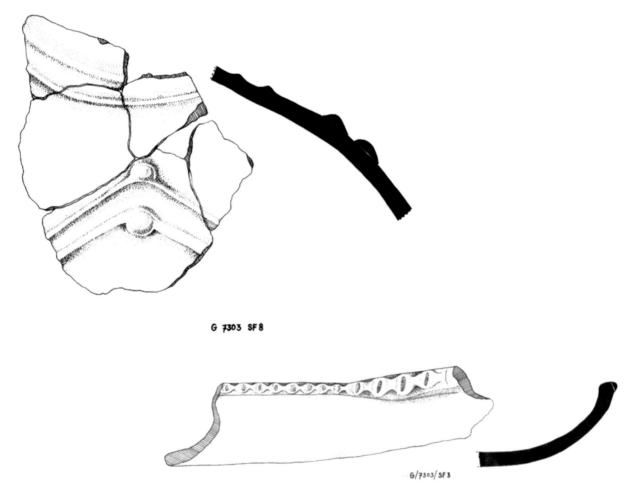

G 7303 SF 8

G/7303/SF 3

Figure 5.5. Geraki: fragment from Final Neolithic jar (inv. no. 7303/SF8) and scoop-like vessel (inv. no. 7303/SF3).

[7] But compare Katsarou (2018: 103, 105, no. 283), fragment of a 'scoop hybrid' from Alepotrypa Cave.
[8] But compare Immewahr (1971: 73, pl. 16, no. 255), thought to be the lid of an EC II pyxis.

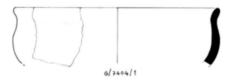

Figure 5.6. Geraki: fragments of Final Neolithic bowls (inv. nos. 7303/SF5 and 7404/1).

with elaborate incised and impressed decoration, both belonging to Deposit 7 (4141/3 and 4141/6; Figure 5.9, lowest row, extreme left and second from left).

Establishing a precise chronology of occupation at our site within the FN, a period of over a thousand years, is problematic. This is true for Laconia as a whole, from where no stratified sequence has been published to date. However, important chronological information is provided by a number of body sherds from small or medium-sized vessels found in contexts of later date in Field 17. These sherds are exceptional at Geraki in their fabric and surface treatment. Three are of medium-coarse fabric, their exterior slipped and burnished so as to produce a deliberate pattern of reddish brown colour (Figure 5.10). These sherds can be assigned to the so-called Pattern Burnished Ware known from elsewhere in southern mainland Greece and the adjacent islands. The standard decorative design consists of groups of parallel stripes, but more complex patterns also occur

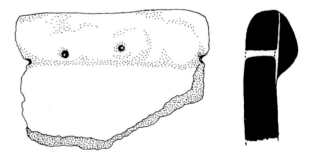

Figure 5.7. Geraki: sherd from Final Neolithic 'cheese-pot' (inv. no. 7312/3).

(among others, Alram-Stern 2007: 3-4; 2014: 311-312 with fig. 5, distribution map; Cullen *et al.* 2013: 29-31, 68-69; Phelps 2004: 106-108; Zachos 2008: 17, distribution map 3).[9]

---

[9] The sherds were identified by Eva Alram-Stern and Jeanette Forsén during a visit to Geraki in 1998.

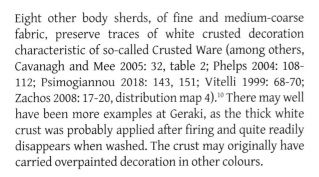

Figure 5.8. Geraki: sherds from Final Neolithic bowls (inv. nos. 7319/SF2, 7303/1, and 4786/SF2).

Eight other body sherds, of fine and medium-coarse fabric, preserve traces of white crusted decoration characteristic of so-called Crusted Ware (among others, Cavanagh and Mee 2005: 32, table 2; Phelps 2004: 108-112; Psimogiannou 2018: 143, 151; Vitelli 1999: 68-70; Zachos 2008: 17-20, distribution map 4).[10] There may well have been more examples at Geraki, as the thick white crust was probably applied after firing and quite readily disappears when washed. The crust may originally have carried overpainted decoration in other colours.

Pattern Burnished and Crusted Wares are considered to be characteristic of pottery belonging to an early phase of FN, often called the Attica-Kephala culture (among others, Cullen *et al.* 2013: 68, 93; Maran 1998: 135-139; Phelps 2004: 103-104). In Laconia, these categories are also represented at Alepotrypa Cave (Phelps 2004: 66, 104, 107, 109; Psimogiannou 2018: 143, 151) and Kouveleïki Cave A (Koumouzelis 1995: 157-158, figs. 16-18), but not at Kouphovouno (Cavanagh *et al.* 2004: 91; 2007: 63). The examples from the acropolis of Geraki appear to indicate occupation in the early FN. Pattern Burnished and Crusted Wares are, however, absent from those sizeable pottery deposits associated with the fortification wall at our site. These assemblages, and Wall 31, may therefore be tentatively assigned to a later phase of the FN. There is evidence to show that the FN settlement at Geraki, or at least that part of it represented by the fortification wall and its associated deposits, suffered a destruction by fire and was subsequently abandoned (MacVeagh Thorne 2012: 115, 121-122).

---

[10] The first such sherds from Geraki were recognized by Stuart MacVeagh Thorne.

Early Helladic I

No architectural remains or discrete deposits datable to EH I were found at Geraki. Only low numbers of potsherds from across the acropolis may be assigned — with varying degrees of certainty — to this period (traditionally *c.* 3100/3000-2650 BC, recently *c.* 3257(3579-2935) - 2951(3126-2778) BC, see Cavanagh *et al.* 2016; also Arvaniti and Maniatis 2018). All are isolated finds within (mostly) EH II (Early and Late) contexts. Despite this, the evidence seems sufficient to show that the acropolis of Geraki was reoccupied at some point in EH I.

At present, the EH I period is best documented in the northeast Peloponnese, Attica, and Central Greece (especially, Alram-Stern 2006: 34-39; Cullen *et al.* 2013: 71-74; Phelps 2004: 126-127; Pullen 2011: 41-139; Wiencke 2000: 631-632). Even here, sites with well stratified EH I material are rare, and it is often difficult to distinguish pottery of this period from that of the FN on the one hand, or EH II on the other. It is for this reason that the full publication of stratified EH I, as well as FN and EH II Early, material from Tsoungiza in the Corinthia is of particular importance (Pullen 2011: 41-139). The definition of EH I pottery at Tsoungiza relies heavily on the presence of a red slipped and (highly) burnished surface treatment, particularly on medium-

Figure 5.9. Geraki: Final Neolithic potsherds from trench 17/12h, zembil 4141.

Figure 5.10. Geraki: sherds of Final Neolithic Pattern Burnished Ware (inv. nos. 75/22. 69/23, 72/7, and 56/10).

coarse examples of the so-called fruitstand, flat-based bowls, and coarse bowls with mat-impressed bases (Pullen 2011: 65-72, 87-88).[11] It should be noted that the use of a burnished red, or red-brown, slip is already documented in the FN and continues into EH II Early (for discussion, see especially Cavanagh and Mee 2011: 41-48; Cullen *et al.* 2013: 28, 31, 42, 71-74; Tsoungiza pottery classes 2, 4 and 5, Pullen 2011: 62-62).

EH I pottery, as defined in the Argolid and Corinthia, has also been reported from various sites in Laconia (Banou 2012; Cavanagh 2012: 58; Cavanagh and Crouwel 2002: 128-130; Cavanagh and Mee 2011; Janko 2008a: 557-558; Maltezou 2016; Smith 2017: 107; Souchleris and Maltezou 2012; Zavvou 2012: 9, 21-22). It should be noted that no deposit of this period, or any other spanning the FN-EH I or EH I-II transitions, has been published to date. Altogether, the EH I period in Laconia remains elusive and the characteristics of its pottery insufficiently defined.

As for Geraki, the possible EH I sherds belong, mainly, to handmade, small and medium-sized bowls (saucers),

---

[11] Among the medium coarse bowls are small examples with profiles resembling the ubiquitous handleless saucers of EH II.

presenting a variety of profiles. They are usually produced in medium-coarse fabric, although fine and coarse examples are also known. The surfaces, red to red-brown in colour, are often well finished; burnished or polished to a lustre, with or without a visible slip.[12] The few pieces with bright red-orange slipped surfaces (including handle fragment inv. no. 7189/5, and an uncatalogued body sherd from the same zembil) are most unusual at Geraki, though recall similar finds from the sites in the northeast Peloponnese (Tsoungiza pottery classes 5 and 6, Pullen 2011: 61-62; Wiencke 2000: 329, 331).

The fruitstand, a shallow spreading bowl with an everted, often incised, rim on a high pedestal base, is a shape with a long history in mainland Greece (MN-EH II Late; see Wiencke 2000: 555-556). It is represented at Geraki by one relatively well-preserved example and 10 fragments of pedestal bases, of which some derive from well-defined contexts of FN and EH II Late date (Crouwel in Crouwel *et al.* 2004a: 22; Crouwel 2012: 131-132). At least one example may well date to EH I, when the shape appears to have been popular at Tsoungiza (Form 1, see Pullen 2011: 65-72). This fragment possesses an incised oblique line at the junction of the pedestal and the bowl, recalling the late EH I incised 'fruitstands' of the so-called Talioti group in the northeast Peloponnese (Douzougli 1987: 181-183, 208, nos. 42-51; Weisshaar 1990: pl. 5).[13]

Like the 'fruitstands', mat-impressed bases are attested on the Greek mainland already during the earlier part of the Neolithic (from the EN: see Wiencke 2000: 318-319). Some 20 fragments of coarse flat bases from Geraki preserve mat impressions on their underside (Figure 5.11). Some can be securely dated to the FN (Crouwel 2012: 133, no. 11), while none have been found in the various deposits of EH II Late. In view of the frequency of mat-impressed bases among the EH I pottery from Tsoungiza and elsewhere in the northeast Peloponnese (Pullen 2011: 88-89, 605-609), it is likely that some of the examples from Geraki might be dated similarly, although a FN or EH II Early date remains possible.

Geraki has also yielded four sherds from so-called 'frying pans'. These vessels are circular, with a flat or somewhat convex surface, low sides, and a projecting handle of varying type. The outside surface may be burnished and often carries incised, impressed or stamped decoration, or a combination thereof. Frying pans, of which the real function is still unknown, have been found in contexts of both EH I and EH II date across mainland Greece and in Laconia at Ayios Stephanos on the south-central

coast (MacGillivray 2008: 172-173, nos. 219 and 223; Taylour 1972: 240-241, no. HS 40) and Anthochori near Xirokambi in the Eurotas Valley (Maltezou 2016; Zavvou 2009: 39, fig. 4.30-31). These vessels have counterparts from the Cycladic islands, dating to Early Cycladic II (Coleman 1985; Form 22, Pullen 2011: 82-85, 370; Type 2 lid, Wiencke 2000: 575-576). One frying pan fragment from Geraki is decorated with two rows of impressed triangles or notches (Figure 5.12). This type of *Kerbschnitt* decoration is well-known during EH I and EH II on the Greek mainland, in the Cyclades, and on Crete, where it is used to decorate a variety of object types (among others, Wiencke 2000: 621, 623-624). The motif is present on a number of probable EH I-II Early frying pan fragments at Anthochori (Zavvou 2009: 39, fig. 4.31) and is represented elsewhere at Geraki on a stone pendant of EH II date (inv. no. 1104/SF3; Crouwel 1989).

Early Helladic II Early

The excavations in the northwestern part of the acropolis (Field 17) have demonstrated that two phases of defensive walling dating to the EH II period overlie the FN Wall 31 (Figure 5.4). The earliest of these, designated Geraki II, is represented by Wall 30 and dated to EH II Early.

Figure 5.11. Geraki: mat-impressed base of (?)Early Helladic I (inv. no. 7146/SF7).

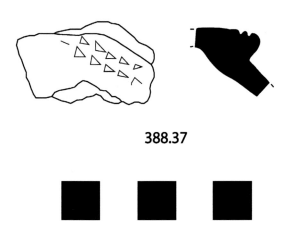

388.37

Figure 5.12. Geraki: sherd from 'frying pan' of Early Helladic I-II (inv. no. 388/37).

The pottery associated with the fortification Wall 30 comes largely from foundation fills and filling material that had fallen from its collapsed sections (trench 17/13k). The great majority of this, often very fragmentary, material may best be cautiously attributed to FN-EH I. It includes some sherds from cheese-pots, but none from the large bowls with elaborate plastic decoration well represented in those secure FN deposits noted above. There are also several sherds, mainly from saucers, and often with burnished red or red-brown surfaces, which may again only be cautiously dated to EH I-II Early. The remainder of this material is heterogenous in terms of its surface treatment, shape and decoration. It can be assigned to EH II and, more precisely, to EH II Early (see below). A similar mixture of much FN and EH I, and far less EH II Early, material was encountered in two other areas in Field 17 (trenches 17/12k and 17/13r), of which one preserved a neat stratigraphic sequence comprised of EH II Early below a floor of EH II Late and above deposits of the FN (deposits 1-3, see MacVeagh Thorne 2012: 111-113).

Like EH I, EH II Early (EH IIA, traditionally *c.* 2650-2450/2350 BC, recently *c.* 2951(3126-2778) - 2670(3126-2778) BC, see Cavanagh *et al.* 2016; also Arvaniti and Maniatis 2018) is best documented in the northeast Peloponnese. Well stratified deposits have been excavated at Lerna (phases IIIA and IIIB, both with sub-phases), the Unterburg at Tiryns (*Fundhorizonte* 1-4, representing EH II *Früh)* and Tsoungiza (EH II Initial and Developed, the latter with sub-phases), and (with the exception of Tiryns) fully published (Pullen 2011: 14-15, 37-39, 241, 900; Weisshaar 1983; Wiencke 2000: 641-653; also Wilson 2013: 412-413). There is also much stratified material of EH II Late (also called EH IIB) from Lerna (phases IIIC, with sub-phases, and IIID) and Tiryns (*Fundhorizonte* 5-8b, representing EH II *Entwickelt*), although the period is not represented at Tsoungiza. It should be noted that the subdivision of EH II into EH II Early and Late (EH IIA and IIB) is based largely on the

Lerna sequence and has been rejected by some scholars in favour of a tripartite chronological scheme for EH II in the southern and central Greek mainland. This does not affect the definition of EH II Early, which still corresponds with Lerna IIIA and IIIB, but divides EH II Late into two phases, Developed and Late, corresponding to Lerna IIIC and IIID respectively (Maran 1998: pl. 80; Wilson 2013: 412-431, tables 10 and 12).

The pottery of EH II Early at the key sites of Lerna, Tiryns, and Tsoungiza is characterised by the first appearance on vessels of fine fabric of light-firing and dark-firing slips commonly known as Light Painted and Dark Painted or *Urfirnis* (Classes 27 and 23-23, Pullen 2011: 162-167, 337-343; Wiencke 2000: 320-326), as well as ring bases and novel shapes such as the sauceboat. These innovations would become hallmarks of EH II as a whole.

While the surface finishes and pot shapes at Lerna and other sites in the northeast Peloponnese show continuity between EH II Early and Late, there is also evidence for typological and stylistic development between the two periods. Differences in the relative representation of particular shapes and treatments are clearly apparent too (see, especially, Wiencke 2000: 633-639).

In addition to Geraki, discrete deposits of EH II Early pottery (as defined at Lerna IIIA and IIIB) have only been firmly identified in Laconia at Kouphovouno (Cavanagh and Mee 2011: 44-46; Cavanagh *et al.* 2007: 27-40 with catalogue; Mee 2009: 45-52), although seriation analysis of pottery from Ayios Stephanos and from the area of the Laconia Survey has made it possible, in some cases, to distinguish between EH II Early and Late (Cavanagh and Mee 2011: 41-44; Janko 2008a: 560, 563-564; Janko 2008b). At Geraki, the identification of EH II Early pottery is based on stratigraphy, and on the identification of parallels among well dated material from Kouphovouno, Lerna, and other sites in the northeast Peloponnese. Some of the ceramic shapes attested at Geraki, such as the askos and saucer, have antecedents in EH I. Others, including the sauceboat, pyxis and spoon, first appear in EH II Early, as does the application of Light Painted and Dark Painted or *Urfirnis* surface treatments to shapes in fine fabrics, and the addition of a distinctive type of plastic decoration called Geraki Ware to shapes in coarse fabric.

Most of the pottery from Geraki assigned to EH II Early is indistinguishable in terms of surface treatment, shape and decoration from that found in the nine discrete destruction deposits of EH II Late at the site. A good example of this typological 'muddiness' is provided by three groups of joining sherds belonging to a so-called baking pan with a close parallel in a EH II Late deposit (inv. nos. 7214/SF2 and 2014/SF3; Figure 5.14, top row; see Crouwel in Crouwel *et al.* 2007: 6-10, 'baking dishes'). Baking pans were common in Central Greece throughout EH II (Form 27, see Pullen 2011: 372-373; Wiencke 2000: 535-536). The standard shape is large, low, and circular, and commonly manufactured in a friable coarse fabric characteristic of cooking pots (Figure 5.14, upper right). Examples often feature a dip in the rim, forming a wide opening, a horizontal interior ledge which is more carefully finished than the outside surface and, occasionally, one or two pre-firing holes through their wall.

Of note is a sizeable fragment belonging to a particular type of deep bowl which we have termed a 'krater' (Figure 5.14, lower left). This is the earliest example of a shape which is represented by some 60 rim sherds in the EH II Late deposits at Geraki (Crouwel in Crouwel *et al.* 2007: 10-12). Its characteristics include an everted rim (*c.* 35-40cm in diameter), flat-topped or downturned and with one or, less often, two sharp horizontal ridges below it. No bases or handles can be associated with this shape, which is usually made in medium-coarse and, less commonly, coarse fabric. At present, the 'krater' has no published close parallels from other sites in Laconia or elsewhere.

Some 20 coarse EH II Early body sherds bear the highly distinctive plastic decoration known as Geraki Ware. Well known from numerous pithoi, and a few fruitstands, belonging to the deposits of EH II Late, the decoration consists of low 'smear marks' or ridges, arranged in zigzag or other closely spaced patterns across much of the vessel's exterior surface. It was named Geraki Ware as it was unknown beyond our site when first identified in 1997. Since then, Geraki Ware has turned up during rescue excavations of the EH II settlement at the southwest edge of modern Sparta (Vasilogamvrou 2010) and that of Bozas on the northwest coast of the

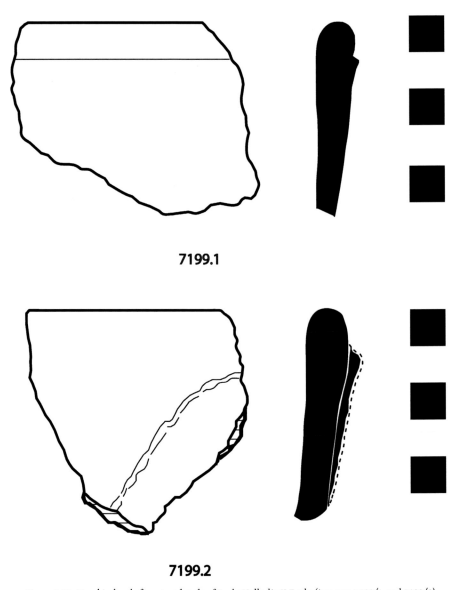

7199.1

7199.2

Figure 5.13. Geraki: sherds from two bowls of Early Helladic II Early (inv. nos. 7199/1 and 7199/2).

Malea peninsula (Zavvou 2012: 18-19). No examples of Geraki Ware have yet been identified outside Laconia. Excavation at Anthochori has yielded fragments of large, coarse, thick-walled bowls of probable EH II Early date decorated with low diagonal ridges reminiscent of Geraki Ware, but (in the words of the excavator) it is 'less careful, more simple and rough' (Zavvou 2009: 39, fig. 4.27) and applied to a different pot shape (also, Cavanagh and Mee 2011: 47; Zavvou 2012: 32).

There is little evidence at Geraki for ceramic features that occur in EH II Early but not in EH II Late. Two sherds belonging to vertical-walled bowls of coarse fabric (Figure 5.13), of which one has a ridge curving down from the rim, have well dated EH II Early counterparts at Kouphovouno (Cavanagh *et al.* 2007: 31, 37 fig. 17, 43, nos. A90-93) and among the surface material recovered by the Laconia Survey (Cavanagh and Crouwel 1996: 11, type 14, fig. 11.3.28).

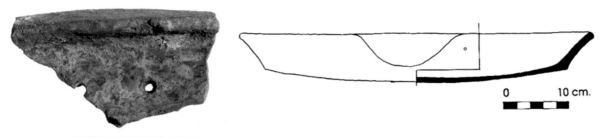

Figure 5.14. Geraki: fragments from 'baking pan' and 'krater' of Early Helladic II Early (inv. nos. 7214/SF2, 7108/4); reconstruction drawing of baking pan from Lerna (after Wiencke 2000: fig. II.74).

As observed above, the fine EH II Early pottery from Geraki includes surface treatments and shapes that are also represented at Kouphovouno and at other sites such as Lerna and Tsoungiza in the northeast Peloponnese. Indeed, this pottery already appears to display the ceramic uniformity and standardisation so characteristic of EH II Late in south central mainland Greece. On the other hand, the medium coarse and coarse assemblage of EH II Early (and EH II Late) at Geraki includes shapes and decorative treatments which appear distinctly local or regional, such as the 'krater' with horizontal ridge(s) below the rim, and the vessels in Geraki Ware (see also below).

Early Helladic II Late

The EH II Late occupation of Geraki is marked by a new building phase, termed Geraki III (EH IIB, traditionally c.2450/2350-2200/2150 BC, recently 2505(2586-2376)-2251(2399-2167) BC, see Cavanagh et al. 2016). This saw the EH II Early fortification, Wall 30, strengthened and widened by the addition of Walls 180/181 (Figure 5.4; MacVeagh Thorne 2012: 108; MacVeagh Thorne and Prent 2009: 235-236) and the construction between them of a small casemate room, as well as the addition of other rooms directly against the inner face of the enceinte.

The casemate room served largely as a storage space (Figures 5.4 and 5.15; trench 17/13q). It contained the remains of four pithoi with Geraki Ware decoration of which three were in situ and one contained charred grass peas. The fourth pithos possessed a spout just above its base, which suggests that it was used to hold liquids such as olive oil or wine. Other vessels recovered from the casemate include a so-called duck askos, a 'fruitstand' with Geraki Ware decoration (as well as a fragment of a second), and several saucers and bowls (Figure 5.16) (MacVeagh Thorne and Crouwel in Crouwel et al. 2004a: 5-24). The room also yielded an assemblage of tens of clay sealing fragments, several of them with stamped seal impressions, of which most had been used to seal the rim and cover of the storage vessels, thus safeguarding their contents (Weingarten et al. 2011).

A small part of a second storeroom was excavated some distance away, but still in Field 17. It yielded another Geraki Ware pithos in situ, a quantity of fava beans, two almost complete saucers and several clay sealing fragments with and without seal impressions (Figures 5.4 and 5.17, upper and lower left; trench 17/11i) (Weingarten et al. 1999).[14] Yet another probable storage area was excavated in a trial trench in the western part of the acropolis (Figure 5.4; trench 19/2a). It had been disturbed during the later occupation of the site and yielded large portions of two pithoi, one with Geraki Ware decoration (Figure 5.17, right), but no clay sealings.

These three storage areas are among nine contemporary deposits discovered during excavation across the acropolis (Prent in Weingarten et al. 2011; 158-162) which belong to a single destruction horizon. The destruction was the result of an extensive fire, which saw the accidental preservation of the site's clay sealing

---

[14] For the botanical remains from this context and from the casemate room, see Cappers in Crouwel et al. (1999a: 106-110), and Cappers and Mulder in Crouwel et al. (2004a: 25-33).

Figure 5.15. Geraki, acropolis: kite photograph of Field 17 (2001) and plan of Casemate Room.

assemblage, and which can be dated to EH II Late on the basis of ceramic parallels with the pottery of phase IIIC at Lerna (Wiencke 2000: especially 636-638; Wilson 2013: 412-414). Like Geraki, Lerna IIIC was a sizeable, fortified settlement, with a (larger) casemate room, rooms built against the inside of the enceinte, and evidence of seal use (Wiencke 2000). In addition, Lerna IIIC had a central building, Building BG, of the corridor house type, on higher ground somewhere away from the fortifications. Our fieldwork at Geraki, which included a geophysical survey (Brodie in Crouwel *et al.* 1996: 111-114), found no evidence for such an imposing building, but this may perhaps have to do with the eroded state of much of the summit of the acropolis (Weingarten in Weingarten *et al.* 2011: 156).[15]

The large amount of handmade pottery of EH II Late date from Geraki is made in a fairly limited range of

fine, medium and coarse fabrics and shapes and much appears to have been used for domestic purposes. The material is mostly fragmentary, although several pots are (almost) complete or could be entirely, or partially, restored.

The surface treatment, shapes, and decoration of the EH II Late ceramics appear to be much the same as those of EH II Early, but the assemblage is both larger and better preserved. There are also close affinities, particularly in the pottery of fine fabric, with finds from Ayios Stephanos and others in the area of the Laconia Survey (Cavanagh and Crouwel 1996; Janko 2008a: 558-565; MacGillivray 2008). There are indeed many EH II sites in Laconia (see especially, Banou 2012; Cavanagh and Crouwel 2002: 128-135; Janko 2008a: 558-565; Smith 2017: 113-114; Zavvou 2012), some of which also possess fortifications, though few on the scale of Geraki (MacVeagh Thorne *et al.* 2013; Smith 2017: 114).

Ceramic parallels between the fine Light Painted and, less commonly, Dark Painted or *Urfirnis* shapes at Geraki (including askoi, pyxides, saucers, and sauceboats) and those of sites beyond Laconia, such as Lerna, underline the remarkable degree of homogeneity and standardisation observed elsewhere in the EH II ceramic record (see especially, Maran 1998; Rutter 1993). On the other hand, some of the medium coarse and coarse pottery at Geraki, in both EH II Early and Late, exhibits

---

[15] Terracotta, mould-made roof tiles, characteristic of corridor houses and other important buildings, have not been identified at Geraki, but there are a number of schist fragments with holes like those used in roof construction at Lerna (for tiles, see Wiencke 2000: 197-203, 253-269, 630, n.8; for schist slabs, 2000: 198, 270-274, 630, n.8) and elsewhere in the Peloponnese.

Figure 5.16. Geraki: Early Helladic II Late pottery from the Casemate Room: 'duck askos' (inv. no. 1696/SF2), 'fruitstand' and fragment of another (inv. nos. 1723/SF1, 1724/SF2), two saucers (inv. nos. 1702/SF1, 1699/SF6) and bowl (inv. no. 1702/SF7).

Figure 5.17. Geraki, acropolis: EH II Late pithos in situ (inv. no. 156/SF2), saucer (inv. no 81/SF2), restored pithos (inv. no. 2110/SF1).

a distinctly local or regional character. In addition to the 'krater' with its horizontal ridge(s) below the rim, and to the Geraki Ware decoration, there is in EH II Late a preference for the addition of a band of light-coloured slip to the sharp ridge(s) of medium coarse 'kraters' and jars, and for the embellishment of medium coarse jug handles with an incised lozenge pattern, and for heavy ring bases of coarse bowls.

Post-destruction

After the devastating EH II Late fire destruction, the acropolis of Geraki appears to have been abandoned and, to judge from both the lack of immediate overbuilding and the severe erosion of the EH II remains (MacVeagh Thorne and Prent 2009: 238), remained so for quite some time before being reoccupied during the Middle Helladic period (MH). While ceramics of this period are abundant, pottery belonging exclusively to EH III (traditionally *c.* 2200/2150-2050/2000 BC, recently *c.* 2251(2399-2167) - 2157(2197-2016) BC, see Cavanagh *et al.* 2016) are absent.[16] This same absence is well-recognised in other parts of Laconia (Cavanagh 2012: 61-65, 71; Cavanagh and Mee 2011; 47-48; Mee 2012: 144). However, small numbers of unstratified, painted EH III potsherds have now been identified with varying degrees of certainty at a number of Laconian sites (see Banou 2012: 50-51; Crouwel 2014: 58-59; Smith 2017: 109, 114) and a quantity of unquestionable EH III pottery has very recently been discovered during rescue excavations at Karavas Soustianon, to the north of Sparta (see Aris Papayiannis, this volume; also, Rutter 2017: 22-23; Smith 2017: 114; Vasilogamvrou and Maltezou 2016). These new finds go a long way to filling the gap that had long intrigued Chris Mee, and continues to intrigue myself and others.

Bibliography

Alram-Stern, E. 2006. Die vormykenische keramik, in E. Alram-Stern and S. Deger-Jalkotzy (eds) 2006. *Aigeira I: Die Mykenische Akropolis. Faszikel 3: Vormykenische Keramik, Kleinfunde, Archäozoologische und Archäobotanische Hinterlassenschaften, Naturwissenschaftliche Datierung:* 19-88. Vienna: the Austrian Academy of Sciences.

Alram-Stern, E. 2007. Das Chalkolithikum in Südgriechenland. Versuch einer chronologischen und topographischen Gliederung, in F. Lang, C. Reinholdt and J. Weilhartzer (eds) *ΣΤΕΦΑΝΟΣ ΑΡΙΣΤΕΙΟΣ. Archäologische Forschungen zwischen Nil und Istros. Festschrift für Stefan Hiller zum 65. Geburtstag:* 1-10. Vienna: Phoibos.

Alram-Stern, E. 2014. Times of change: Greece and the Aegean during the 4th millennium BC, in B. Horejs and M. Mehofer (eds) *Western Anatolia before Troy. Proto-urbanisation in the 4th Millennium BC? Proceedings of the International Symposium held at the Kunsthistorisches Museum, Vienna, Austria 21-24 November 2012* (Oriental and European Archaeology 1): 305-327. Vienna: the Austrian Academy of Sciences.

Arvaniti, T. and Y. Maniatis 2018. Tracing the absolute time-frame of the Early Bronze Age in the Aegean. *Radiocarbon* 60(3): 751-773.

Banou, E. 2012. The Eurotas Valley and the Helos Plain in the Early Helladic period. Addressing some key issues on the basis of topography and pottery, in C. Mee and M. Prent (eds) *Early Helladic Laconia. Proceedings of the Round Table Conference held 16 January 2010 at the Netherlands Institute at Athens. Pharos. Journal of the Netherlands Institute at Athens* 18(1): 39-52.

Cavanagh, W.G. 1996. The Neolithic pottery, in W. Cavanagh, J. Crouwel, R.W.V. Catling and G. Shipley (eds) *Continuity and Change in a Greek Rural Landscape. The Laconia Survey Volume II. Archaeological Data* (The British School at Athens Supplementary Volume 27): 1-3. London: the British School at Athens.

Cavanagh, W.G. 2012. The Early Bronze Age in Laconia. A good story with a beginning, a middle and an end, in C. Mee and M. Prent (eds) *Early Helladic Laconia. Proceedings of the Round Table Conference held 16 January 2010 at the Netherlands Institute at Athens. Pharos. Journal of the Netherlands Institute at Athens* 18(1): 53-78.

Cavanagh, W.G. and J.H. Crouwel 1996. The Early Helladic period, in W. Cavanagh, J. Crouwel, R.W.V. Catling and G. Shipley (eds) *Continuity and Change in a Greek Rural Landscape. The Laconia Survey Volume II. Archaeological Data* (The British School at Athens Supplementary Volume 27): 5-16. London: the British School at Athens.

Cavanagh, W.G. and J.H. Crouwel 2002. The survey area in the prehistoric periods, in W. Cavanagh, J. Crouwel, R.W.V. Catling and G. Shipley (eds) *Continuity and Change in a Greek Rural Landscape. The Laconia Survey Volume I. Methodology and Interpretation* (The British School at Athens Supplementary Volume 26): 121-150. London: the British School at Athens.

Cavanagh, W.G. and C. Mee 2005. Reflections on Neolithic Laconia, in A. Dakouri-Hild and S. Sherratt (eds) *AUTOCHTHON. Papers presented to O.T.P.K. Dickinson on the Occasion of his Retirement* (British Archaeological Reports International Series 1432): 24-36. London: Institute of Classical Studies.

Cavanagh, W.G. and C. Mee 2011. Minding the gaps in Early Helladic Laconia, in W. Gauss, M. Lindblom, R.A.K. Smith and J.C. Wright (eds) *Our Cups are Full. Pottery and Society in the Aegean Bronze Age. Papers presented to Jeremy B. Rutter on the Occasion of his 65th Birthday* (British Archaeological Reports International Series 2227): 40-50. Oxford: Archaeopress.

---

[16] Very recently, a new chronological terminology has been proposed for what is traditionally called EH III, MH and LH I (see Rutter 2017).

Cavanagh, W.G., C. Mee and J. Renard 2004. 'Sparta before Sparta': report on the intensive survey at Kouphovouno 1999-2000. *The Annual of the British School at Athens* 99: 49-128.

Cavanagh, W.G., C. Mee and J. Renard 2007. Excavations at Kouphovouno, Laconia: results from the 2001 and 2002 seasons. *The Annual of the British School at Athens* 102: 11-101.

Cavanagh, W.G., C. Mee and J. Renard 2016. Early Bronze Age chronology of mainland Greece: a review with new dates from the excavations at Kouphovouno. *The Annual of the British School at Athens* 111: 35-49.

Coleman, J.E. 1985. 'Frying pans' of the Early Bronze Age Aegean. *American Journal of Archaeology* 89(2): 191-219.

Coleman, J.E. 2011. The Petromagoula-Doliana group and the beginning of the Aegean Early Bronze Age, in D. Katsonopoulou (ed.) *Helike IV: Ancient Helike and Aigialeia. Protohelladika: the Southern and Central Greek Mainland*: 13-44. Athens: the Helike Society.

Coleman, J.E. and Y. Facorellis 2018. The shadowy 'proto-Early Bronze Age' in the Aegean, in S. Dietz, F. Mavridis, Z. Tankosić and T. Takaoğlu (eds) *Communities in Transition. The Circum-Aegean Area during the 5th and 4th Millennia BC*: 33-66. Oxford: Oxbow Books.

Crouwel, J.H. 1989. A recently discovered Early Helladic pendant from Geraki, Lakonia, in P. Betancourt, V. Karageorghis, R. Laffineur and W.-D. Niemeier (eds) *Meletemata: Studies in Aegean Archaeology Presented to Malcolm H. Wiener as he Enters his 65th Year* (Aegaeum 20): 149-154. Liège: the University of Liège.

Crouwel, J.H. 2012. Early Helladic and Final Neolithic pottery in the area of the early fortification wall at Geraki, in C. Mee and M. Prent (eds) *Early Helladic Laconia. Proceedings of the Round Table Conference held 16 January 2010 at the Netherlands Institute at Athens. Pharos. Journal of the Netherlands Institute at Athens* 18(1): 125-140.

Crouwel, J.H. 2014. Geraki in Laconia in Late Helladic times, in Y. Galanakis, T. Wilkinson and J. Bennett (eds) *ΑΘΥΡΜΑΤΑ: Critical Essays on the Archaeology of the Eastern Mediterranean in Honour of E. Susan Sherratt*: 57-65. Oxford: Archaeopress.

Crouwel, J.H., M. Prent and H. Buitenhuis 2009b. Geraki. An acropolis site in Lakonia. Preliminary report on the fourteenth season (2008). *Pharos. Journal of the Netherlands Institute at Athens* 16: 1-30.

Crouwel, J.H., M. Prent, R. Cappers and T. Carter 1999a. Geraki. An acropolis site in Lakonia. Preliminary report on the fourth season (1998). *Pharos. Journal of the Netherlands Institute at Athens* 6: 93-118.

Crouwel, J.H., M. Prent, J. Fiselier and J.A.K.E de Waele 1997. Geraki. An acropolis site in Lakonia. Preliminary report on the third season (1997). *Pharos. Journal of the Netherlands Institute at Athens* 5: 49-83.

Crouwel, J.H., M. Prent, E. Langridge-Noti and J. van der Vin 2004b. Geraki. An acropolis site in Lakonia. Preliminary report on the ninth season (2003). *Pharos. Journal of the Netherlands Institute at Athens* 11: 1-34.

Crouwel, J.H., M. Prent, E. Langridge-Noti and J. van der Vin 2005. Geraki. An acropolis site in Lakonia. Preliminary report on the tenth season (2004). *Pharos. Journal of the Netherlands Institute at Athens* 12: 1-30.

Crouwel, J.H., M. Prent and S. MacVeagh Thorne 2007. Geraki. An acropolis site in Lakonia. Preliminary report on the twelfth campaign (2006). *Pharos. Journal of the Netherlands Institute at Athens* 14: 1-14.

Crouwel, J.H., M. Prent, S. MacVeagh Thorne, R.T.J. Cappers, S.A. Mulder, T. Carter, E. Langridge-Noti and L. van Dijk-Schram 2004a. Geraki. An acropolis site in Lakonia. Preliminary report on the eighth season (2002). *Pharos. Journal of the Netherlands Institute at Athens* 10: 1-81.

Crouwel, J.H., M. Prent, S. MacVeagh Thorne and J. van der Vin 2001. Geraki. An acropolis site in Lakonia. Preliminary report on the sixth season (2000). *Pharos. Journal of the Netherlands Institute at Athens* 8: 41-76.

Crouwel, J.H., M. Prent, S. MacVeagh Thorne and J. van der Vin 2002. Geraki. An acropolis site in Lakonia. Preliminary report on the seventh season (2001). *Pharos. Journal of the Netherlands Institute at Athens* 9: 1-32.

Crouwel, J.H., M. Prent, S. MacVeagh Thorne, G.-J. van Wijngaarden, N. Brodie and J.A.K.E. de Waele 1996. Geraki. An acropolis site in Laconia. Preliminary report on the second season (1996). *Pharos. Journal of the Netherlands Institute at Athens* 4: 89-120.

Crouwel, J.H., M. Prent, S. MacVeagh Thorne, G.-J. van Wijngaarden and C. Sueur 1995. Geraki. An acropolis site in Laconia. Preliminary report of the first season (1995). *Pharos. Journal of the Netherlands Institute at Athens* 3: 41-65.

Crouwel, J.H., M. Prent, S. MacVeagh Thorne, J. van der Vin and L. Smits 2006. Geraki. An acropolis site in Lakonia. Preliminary report on the eleventh season (2005). *Pharos. Journal of the Netherlands Institute at Athens* 13: 3-28.

Crouwel, J.H., M. Prent and D. G. Shipley 2009a. Geraki. An acropolis site in Lakonia. Preliminary report on the thirteenth season (2007). *Pharos. Journal of the Netherlands Institute at Athens* 15 (2007): 1-16.

Crouwel, J.H., M. Prent, J. van der Vin, P. Lulof and R. Dooijese 1999. Geraki. An acropolis site in Lakonia. Preliminary report on the fifth season (1999). *Pharos. Journal of the Netherlands Institute at Athens* 7: 21-49.

Cullen, T., L.E. Talalay, D.R. Keller, L. Karimali and W.R. Farrand 2013. *The Prehistory of the Paximadi Peninsula, Euboea* (Prehistory Monographs 40). Philadelphia: INSTAP Academic Press.

Douzougli, A. 1987. Makrovouni-Kefalari Magoula-Talioti: Bemerkungen zu den Stufen FH I und II in der Argolis. *Prähistorische Zeitschrift* 62: 164–220.

Gritsopoulou, T.A. 1982. *Ιστορία του Γερακίου*. Athens: Association of Gerakiotes in Attica.

Immerwahr, S. 1971. *The Athenian Agora, Volume XIII. The Neolithic and Bronze Ages*. Princeton: the American School of Classical Studies at Athens.

Janko, R. 2008a. Summary and historical conclusions, in W.D. Taylour and R. Janko (eds) *Ayios Stephanos. Excavations at a Bronze Age and Medieval Settlement in Southern Laconia* (The British School at Athens Supplementary Volume 44): 551-610. London: the British School at Athens.

Janko, R. 2008b. Appendix 1. Statistical ware-analysis of Early Helladic pottery deposits, in W.D. Taylour and R. Janko (eds) *Ayios Stephanos. Excavations at a Bronze Age and Medieval Settlement in Southern Laconia* (The British School at Athens Supplementary Volume 44): CD85-88. London: the British School at Athens.

Katsarou, S. 2018. When do the dead become dead? Mortuary projects from Ossuaries I and II, Alepotrypa Cave, in A. Papathanasiou, W.A. Parkinson, D.J. Pullen, M.L. Galaty and P. Karkanas (eds) *Neolithic Alepotrypa Cave in the Mani, Greece: in Honor of George Papathanassopoulos*: 91-126. Oxford: Oxbow Books.

Katsipanou-Margeli, B. 2018. The stratigraphic and pottery sequence of Trench B1 at Alepotrypa Cave: a first approach to the investigation of ceramic and chronological associations, in A. Papathanasiou, W.A. Parkinson, D.J. Pullen, M.L. Galaty and P. Karkanas (eds) *Neolithic Alepotrypa Cave in the Mani, Greece: in Honor of George Papathanassopoulos*: 33-90. Oxford: Oxbow Books.

Kaznesi, A. and S. Katsarou 2003. Η Νεολιθική κεραμική από τη Β Κουβελέικη σπηλιά Αλεποχοριού Λακωνίας. *Αρχαιολογικά Ανάλεκτα εξ Αθηνών* 32-34(1999-2001): 27-36.

Koumouzelis, M. 1995. Η Κεραμική από την Α' Κουβελεϊκή σπηλιά Αλεποχωρίου Λακωνίας. *Αρχαιολογικά Ανάλεκτα εξ Αθηνών* 22(1989): 143-159.

MacGillivray, J.A. 2008. The Early Helladic pottery, in W.D. Taylour and R. Janko (eds) *Ayios Stephanos. Excavations at a Bronze Age and Medieval Settlement in Southern Laconia* (The British School at Athens Supplementary Volume 44): 159-176. London: the British School at Athens.

MacVeagh Thorne, S. 2012. The early fortification walls of Geraki: Final Neolithic and Early Helladic, in C. Mee and M. Prent (eds) *Early Helladic Laconia. Proceedings of the Round Table Conference held 16 January 2010 at the Netherlands Institute at Athens. Pharos. Journal of the Netherlands Institute at Athens* 18(1): 105-124.

MacVeagh Thorne, S. and M. Prent. 2009. The walls of Geraki, in W.G. Cavanagh, C. Gallou and M. Georgiadis (eds) *Sparta and Laconia: from Prehistory to Pre-Modern. Proceedings of the Conference Held in Sparta, Organised by the British School at Athens, the University of Nottingham, the 5th Ephoreia of Prehistoric and Classical Antiquities and the 5th Ephoreia of Byzantine Antiquities 17-20 March 2005* (British School at Athens Studies 16): 235-242. London: the British School at Athens.

MacVeagh Thorne, S., M. Prent, A. Themos and E. Zavvou. 2013. Kastraki Keratitsas: preliminary results of the archaeological study of an Early Helladic fortification in Laconia. *Pharos. Journal of the Netherlands Institute at Athens* 19(2): 111-128.

Maltezou, A. 2016. Περιοχή Καραβά. *Αρχαιολογικόν Δελτίον* 66(2011)(Chr. Β΄1): 196-199.

Maran, J. 1998. *Kulturwandel auf dem griechischen Festland und den Kykladen im späten 3. Jahrtausend v. Chr.: Studien zu den kulturellen Verhältnissen in Südosteuropa und dem zentralen sowie östlichen Mittelmeerraum in der späten Kupfer- und frühen Bronzezeit* (Universitätsforschungen zur prähistorischen Archäologie 53). Bonn: Rudolf Habelt.

Mee, C. 2007. The production and consumption of pottery in the Neolithic Peloponnese, in C. Mee and J. Renard (eds) *Cooking up the Past: Food and Culinary Practices in the Neolithic and Bronze Age Aegean*: 200-224. Oxford: Oxbow Books.

Mee, C. 2009. Interconnectivity in Early Helladic Laconia, in W.G. Cavanagh, C. Gallou and M. Georgiadis (eds) *Sparta and Laconia: from Prehistory to Pre-Modern. Proceedings of the Conference Held in Sparta, Organised by the British School at Athens, the University of Nottingham, the 5th Ephoreia of Prehistoric and Classical Antiquities and the 5th Ephoreia of Byzantine Antiquities 17-20 March 2005* (British School at Athens Studies 16): 43-53. London: the British School at Athens.

Mee, C. 2012. Early Bronze Age Laconia: an overview, in C. Mee and M. Prent (eds) *Early Helladic Laconia. Proceedings of the Round Table Conference held 16 January 2010 at the Netherlands Institute at Athens. Pharos. Journal of the Netherlands Institute at Athens* 18(1): 141-145.

Papathanasiou, A., W.A. Parkinson, D.J. Pullen, M.L. Galaty and P. Karkanas (eds) 2018. *Neolithic Alepotrypa Cave in the Mani, Greece. In Honor of George Papathanassopoulos*. Oxford: Oxbow Books.

Phelps, B. 2004. *The Neolithic Pottery Sequence in Southern Greece* (British Archaeological Reports International Series 1259). Oxford: Archaeopress.

Psimogiannou, K. 2018. Patterns of pottery consumption, destruction and deposition at Alepotrypa Cave: the case of Chamber Z during the Neolithic period, in A. Papathanasiou, W.A. Parkinson, D.J. Pullen, M.L. Galaty and P. Karkanas (eds) *Neolithic Alepotrypa Cave in the Mani, Greece. In Honor of George Papathanassopoulos*: 127-157. Oxford: Oxbow Books.

Pullen, D.J. 2011. *Nemea Valley Archaeological Project I. The Early Bronze Age Village on Tsoungiza Hill*. Princeton: the American School of Classical Studies at Athens.

Rutter, J.B. 1993. Early Helladic pottery. Inferences about exchange and production from style and clay composition, in C. Zerner (ed.) *Wace and Blegen. Pottery as Evidence for Trade in the Aegean Bronze Age, 1939-1989. Proceedings of the International Conference held at the American School of Classical Studies at Athens, Athens, December 2-3, 1989*: 19-37. Amsterdam: J.C. Gieben.

Rutter, J.B. 2017. The temporal slicing and dicing of Minyan culture: a proposal for a tripartite division of a lengthier Greek Middle Bronze Age and the issue of nomadism at its beginning, in C.W. Wiersma and S. Voutsaki (eds) *Social Change in Aegean Prehistory*: 16-31. Oxford: Oxbow Books.

Sampson, A. 1997. *Το Σπήλαιο των Λιμνών στα Καστριά Καλαβρύτων: Μία προϊστορική θέση στην ορεινή Πελοπόννησο* (Society of Peloponnesian Studies Monograph Series 7). Athens: the Society of Peloponnesian Studies.

Shipley, G. 1996. Site catalogue of the survey, in W. Cavanagh, J. Crouwel, R.W.V. Catling and G. Shipley (eds) *Continuity and Change in a Greek Rural Landscape. The Laconia Survey Volume II. Archaeological Data* (The British School at Athens Supplementary Volume 27): 315-438. London: the British School at Athens.

Smith, D.M. 2017. Recent research in Early Helladic southern Greece. *Archaeological Reports* 63: 107-129.

Sotirakopoulou, P. 2008. The Cyclades, the east Aegean and western Asia Minor: their relations in the Aegean Late Neolithic and Early Bronze Age, in H. Erkanal, H. Hauptmann, V. Şahoğlu and R. Tuncel (eds) *The Aegean in the Neolithic, Chalcolithic and the Early Bronze Age. Proceedings of the International Symposium, Oct. 13-16, 1997, Urla - İzmir, Turkey* (Ankara University Research Centre for Maritime Archaeology 1): 533-557. Ankara: Ankara University Press.

Souchleris, L. and A. Maltezou. 2012. Κυπαρίσσι. Ανισόπεδος Κόμβος Λογκανίκου. *Αρχαιολογικόν Δελτίον* 67(Chr.): 99-111.

Taylour, W.D. 1972. Excavations at Ayios Stephanos. *The Annual of the British School at Athens* 67: 205-270.

Vasilogamvrou, A. 2010. *Νεώτερα στοιχεία για την Πρωτοελλαδική Λακωνία από τις πρόσφατες έρευνες της Ε΄ ΕΠΚΑ*. Paper delivered to the round table conference 'Early Helladic Laconia' held at the Netherlands Institute at Athens, January 16th, 2010.

Vasilogamvrou, A. and A. Maltezou 2016. Συκέα Μολάων. Θέση Μεγάλη Ρίζα-Βρανά, αγροτεμάχιο Π.

Ζουμπουλάκη. *Αρχαιολογικόν Δελτίον* 65(2010)(Chr. Β΄1α): 552.

Vitelli, K.D. 1999. *Franchthi Neolithic Pottery. Volume 2: the Later Neolithic Ceramic Phases 3 to 5* (Excavations at Franchthi Cave, Greece 10). Bloomington and Indianapolis: Indiana University Press.

Vitelli, K.D. 2007. *Lerna V. The Neolithic Pottery from Lerna*. Princeton: the American School of Classical Studies at Athens.

Weingarten, I., M. Prent, J.H. Crouwel and G. Vogelsang-Eastwood 1999. Early Helladic sealings from Geraki, Laconia. *Oxford Journal of Archaeology* 18(4): 357-376.

Weingarten, J., S. MacVeagh Thorne, M. Prent and J.H. Crouwel 2011. More Early Helladic sealings from Geraki in Laconia, Greece. *Oxford Journal of Archaeology* 30(2): 131-163.

Weisshaar, H.-J. 1983. Ausgrabungen in Tiryns 1981: Bericht zur frühhelladischen Keramik. *Archäeologicsher Anzeiger* 1983: 329-358.

Weisshaar, H.-J. 1990. Die Keramik von Talioti, in U. Jantzen (ed.) *Tiryns, Forschungen und Berichte XI*: 1–34. Mainz: Philipp von Zabern.

Wiencke, M.H. 2000. *Lerna IV. The Architecture, Stratification and Pottery of Lerna III*. Princeton: the American School of Classical Studies at Athens.

Wilson, D.E. 2013. Ayia Irini II-III, Kea. The phasing and relative chronology of the Early Bronze II settlement. *Hesperia: the Journal of the American School of Classical Studies at Athens* 82(3): 385-434.

Zachos, K. 2008. *Ayios Dhimitrios. A Prehistoric Settlement in the Southwestern Peloponnese: the Neolithic and Early Helladic Periods* (British Archaeological Reports International Series 1770). Oxford: Archaeopress.

Zavvou, E. 2009. Archaeological finds from the area of Anthochori, in W.G. Cavanagh, C. Gallou and M. Georgiadis (eds) *Sparta and Laconia: from Prehistory to Pre-Modern. Proceedings of the Conference Held in Sparta, Organised by the British School at Athens, the University of Nottingham, the 5th Ephoreia of Prehistoric and Classical Antiquities and the 5th Ephoreia of Byzantine Antiquities 17-20 March 2005* (British School at Athens Studies 16): 29-42. London: the British School at Athens.

Zavvou, E. 2012. Early Helladic Laconia after the time of H. Waterhouse and R. Hope Simpson, in C. Mee and M. Prent (eds) *Early Helladic Laconia. Proceedings of the Round Table Conference held 16 January 2010 at the Netherlands Institute at Athens. Pharos. Journal of the Netherlands Institute at Athens* 18(1): 1-37.

Understanding Mycenae

E.B. French †

Introduction

The outstanding problem remaining from the Mycenae Survey concerns the role and nature of the site in the Argive Plain, not only in the Middle and Late Bronze Age, which has already been much discussed, but also in the Neolithic and Early Bronze Age.[1] The text and drawings of David French's study of the Pre-Mycenaean pottery (forthcoming) are now awaiting final editing. From this work, by pinpointing the find spots within the site for diverse wares, and by comparing and contrasting these results with what we know of the occupation patterns in the region, some progress can be made and some ideas on how work might proceed suggested.

Mycenae in its setting

Even though I had known and worked on the site of Mycenae, and its environs, for over 50 years, it was not until I initiated the Mycenae Survey in 1991 that I had the opportunity to traverse the area in depth, to view the various pieces and types of evidence in combination, and to discuss and assess the resulting implications of that evidence with a team of specialist assistants.

The Knossos Survey had always impressed me, and I took a copy with me when I approached the Archaeological Society, in the redoubtable persons of Vasilis Petrakos and Spyros Iakovides, to seek permission to undertake the work at Mycenae. There, unlike Knossos, we had a unique starting point. Following the explosion of both public and academic interest in Mycenae occasioned by Schliemann's finds and their speedy publication, Ernst Curtius, of the German Institute, commissioned Bernhard Steffen to survey the site, including the acropolis in detail and the area around it. The published maps (Steffen 1884) are of unbelievable accuracy. During the Mycenae Survey, team members carried with them copies of the maps of the relevant sectors and checked carefully whether features first noted during the winter of 1881-1882 still existed. We soon became aware that a very high proportion of the features recorded by Steffen were still in existence and that new surface features were relatively rare.

There was, however, much evidence from the varied work of the previous century which, though perhaps recorded in a notebook or even published piecemeal, had not been added to area maps; most notably, those chamber tombs excavated by Tsountas, which numbered over 200. Databases of these known features were made over the winter before we began the field survey. At first, priority was given to those areas of study which assisted the doctoral work of two students of Professor Iakovides who were key members of the team — Anton Jansen, studying the road system, and Kim Shelton, studying the chamber tombs — though all features found in these areas were, of course, noted at the same time. The work was intended to be topographic and not a pottery collection survey, although any pottery encountered on the surface was noted; it was, however, remarkably rare.

Mycenae is a rocky outcrop lying immediately west of the lower hills of the Arachneion Range which edges the plain of Argos on the east. There are stream beds cutting deep ravines immediately to north and south. Routes in all directions, which often later became roads, have been traced radiating from the site, though they have almost disappeared where modern deep cultivation has taken place where the plain opens out to the southwest. From the site, the position would seem to dominate the plain, but it does not have full visual coverage of the plain and would have depended on Argos for full communication control. In the well-known opening passage in Aeschylus's *Agamemnon*, the night watchman lists the beacon stations which have brought the news of the fall of Troy. The positions of these beacons are either clear in the text or fairly easily identified; they are intercommunicating by plain sight and absolutely fully so by means of a fire beacon.

On the other hand, the site is not always easily identified from the plain to the west. It could hardly be seen from the main road below the site during the 1950s, until the creation of the vast modern carpark left a clear scar. The site was not identified by many early travellers and was not definitively rediscovered until Venetian times. The Argive Heraion, similarly, had only been rediscovered during a hunting expedition at the time of the War of Independence in the early 19th century AD.

In terms of resources, the site has an excellent water supply from the spring in the pass to the east, known as the Perseia Spring, and the water table was high

[1] It is my deep regret that I never had the chance to discuss the results of the Mycenae Survey with Chris. The only time he came through Mycenae during our work in the early 1990's was in order to discuss with me, as BSA Director, the permits he needed for his work in Laconia. I present here some of what we might have discussed.

in the plain until shortly after the middle of the 20th century AD, when an increase in the use of irrigation agriculture caused the present conditions. Good land lies close at hand, and the site also had good access to the higher upland grain bearing territory to the east. It enjoyed access also to grazing, and to a timber supply, though even in the Bronze Age, long timbers, together with the craftsmen who worked them, would doubtless have been sought from Arcadia, as they were until relatively recently, when such timber was still needed for local domestic building.

The central site is a rocky limestone hill, the citadel or acropolis. The slopes form terraces, and the underlying rock surface is very irregular, often offering startling surprises when reached at the bottom of a deep trench. On the east, the site stands at the outlet of a valley which runs between the mountains of Ayios Elias and Zara to the Berbati Plain and beyond towards the coast to the east. To the west, after a line of low hills, the plain slopes towards the railway and the modern road to Corinth, before rising again to the steeper slopes of the foothills of the Artemision range. The main route north runs through the Derveni pass to Nemea, but there are other, lesser, routes known to have been in use for many centuries. We are lucky to have good documentation of the pre-mechanised landscape for this part of the area, where the site itself lies in both written accounts and the visual record, in painting and, later, photographs. Fortuitously, two large windows in the site museum, looking to north and east, still frame a landscape which we can consider not greatly different from that of the later Bronze Age, but we cannot be certain that this applies also to the preceding millennia.

The landscape history of the southern part of the Argive Plain, now heavily cultivated, is less easy to reconstruct, though work has been done on this by Zangger (for example, 1993), and others. Recent papers, for example by Pullen (2018), have used the evidence of surface survey combined with that from excavations in an attempt to understand the habitation history of certain specific regions of the Peloponnese. I would like, ultimately, to see this done for the Argive Plain as a whole, and Mycenae in particular, using all possible sources of information.

While the work of the Survey was progressing, we tried to keep our close colleagues up to date with our ideas; in some cases, though, these fled like water from a duck's back in favour of entrenched opinions. For the Late Bronze Age, the evidence has been published in detail (French and Iakovides 2001) and I have also written a popular account (French 2002). Moreover, in a commissioned conference paper given here in Cambridge (French 2009), I considered the issue of town planning but, unfortunately, this publication seems not to have reached wide academic readership.

The sherd evidence from the Mycenae Survey is surprisingly slight and for the early periods that from excavation is largely without close contextual detail. Some points of significance can however be noted.

Neolithic and Early Bronze Age Mycenae

Neolithic material was avidly sought by Wace. He suggested (1957) that a vessel from unstratified material found near the Tomb of Aegisthus might be of this period, but this is not generally accepted. Two sherds datable to the period were positively identified by Caskey (1960: 159 n.8; Orlandos 1955: 74) in the Nauplion Museum, from among the material then recently found near Grave Circle A by the Archaeological Service, although they cannot now be traced from the numbering given. Mylonas (1957: 12 n.5) also mentions two possible Neolithic sherds recovered from near Grave Circle B that, again, have not been traced. Wace (1921-1923: pl. XIId), however, had previously published from the area at the foot of the Great Ramp a handle sherd that is now identified as Rainbow Ware (see Phelps 2004: 14, 31).

It was not until the very end of the 1966 season of excavation in the Citadel House Area that any concentration of material of this period was discovered (French and Taylour 2007: 2; French, forthcoming). At the end of the season, during cleaning in an area previously thought to consist of a soft bed rock ('stereo'), sherds, again of Rainbow Ware, began to appear. Luckily, they closely resembled examples of the type from Nemea exhibited in Corinth at that time, and even a dedicated Late Bronze Age specialist like myself could identify them. David French was enlisted to join the team for the museum work season of 1967 and, during the final two seasons of 1968 and 1969, great care was taken to preserve the many but various stray handmade wares from all levels, but particularly from the deepest ones immediately overlying the rock; keeping them separate with context notation, rather than assigning the unidentified to the 'sample basket'.

No other concentrations have been noted, but examples of five main wares of the period have been identified: Dark-faced Burnished, Rainbow, Patterned Red on Cream, *Urfirnis* (Monochrome, Patterned and Incised) and Black Burnished. All come from the rock terrace which lies at *c.* 242m above sea level on the west slope of the acropolis hill. It can most clearly be seen today as the eastern half within the circuit wall of Grave Circle A, before the deep drop of the rock to the west, and shows clearly both on Steffen's map of the acropolis and on de Jong's plan of the Grave Circle area (Wace 1921-1923: pl. 1). It extends a short way north to the base of the Great Ramp and further south under the Ramp House, the South House and Room 31 of the Cult Centre. All this is definite. At present, we have no idea of what may have been found in the lower levels of the extensive areas excavated by the Archaeological Society. But we do know that, so far, no Neolithic sherds have been identified (or even found and misidentified) amid the material from areas further up the slope excavated at any time by the British.

Our knowledge of sites of all phases of the Neolithic in the Argive Plain is still limited. There is a notable cave site at Kephalari, from where the Neolithic material is largely unpublished but called 'disturbed' when quoted (Felsch 1971: 2), as well as the excavated site at Lerna (Banks 2016; Vitelli 2007). In addition, I myself have visited one open site, close to Dalamanara near the road between Argos and Nauplion: a low mound in the plain, to me reminiscent of a number of magoula type sites in Thessaly, to which we went long ago with the Ephor Nikolas Verdelis and others. It has been suggested that the early levels at Lerna may belong to a site of this type. The relationship between caves and open 'farming' sites is intriguing and has begun to be discussed (Pullen 2018). A functional differentiation would make an easy solution, but at present there is no evidence even to suggest it. So how would Mycenae fit in?

The evidence from the Early Bronze Age is more complex. Sherds of the Early Helladic (EH), as they had already named it (in what their colleagues called 'The Immortal Bilge', Wace and Blegen 1918), were found by Wace and Blegen from the start of the British work at Mycenae in 1920, and are listed passim in Wace et al. (1921-1923). Among the find spots of EH material, the most striking one to us now is the area of the later palace, including in the debris deposit in the fill under the East Lobby of the Grand Staircase; itself a much later structure (as we now know), but where earlier material had been used in the terrace fill. This deposit is particularly interesting for the material it also yielded of the Early Palatial period, which included fresco fragments (French and Shelton 2005) and important dietary evidence in the form of bone and shell material; evidence which would seem to imply a building of some elite status. Could the evidence from the Early Bronze Age be similarly interpreted? Certainly, the choice of location at the top of the hill would seem to have some significance. What has not yet been checked in detail is to which of the phases now distinguished for the EH period the material from these deposits is to be assigned. This, of course, will form an important part in discussion of this type of site, which seems to make its first appearance during the period.

On the lower slopes, the area with stray finds is much increased to include most of that excavated under the designation of the Prehistoric Cemetery. No tombs definitely of EH date have been identified, but a single large dish found at the base of the Great Ramp by the Archaeological Society (Mylonas 1961: 155 fig. 9) might

be supposed to have come from one, based on its state of preservation. Similarly, some of the EH III pottery excavated by Stamatakis from the Grave Circle area and illustrated by Wace et al. (1921-1923) should be interpreted as having derived from tombs, indicating that the extensive, largely Middle Helladic (MH), cemetery over the west slope had been established before the end of the previous period. David French's study has identified all the usual categories of vessel among this scattered material. Wace (1932: 19) found traces of EH occupation on the summit of the Kalkani hill which was reconfirmed by the Survey. We also found another, similar, satellite site at Gourmades (Iakovides and French 2003: 60, Map 10, site H3:2b) located between Mycenae and Priphtiani (formerly Monasteraki).

Among the sites of many types which have been variously described in readily available literature (for example, Pullen 2008), we may note key examples. At Lerna, by later EH II, the site is well fortified and crowned with a major building from which the find of sealings would seem to indicate an administrative role. Unfortunately, the preceding phase, EH I, is missing in the stratigraphy (Wiencke 2000: 27), and we cannot therefore easily trace the ultimate origins of this notable advance. There are a variety of other sites situated on slight rises. One in particular, Makrovouni, impressed me when I visited it with members of the Stanford University Argolid Exploration Project for it lies not far upstream from Argos. However, what to me is of most interest is that at Tiryns too, the other so-called palace site of the Late Bronze Age Argive Plain, there is notable EH occupation on the top of the hill (for example, Weisshaar 1981; 1982; 1983). Also upstream, adjacent to Tiryns, is a river management facility, the so-called Kophini Dam. Dr Nikolas Verdelis, who excavated much of it, was certain that it had been constructed originally in the EH period, though undoubtedly enlarged and reinforced in Mycenaean times. If he was mistaken in this interpretation, then the very large quantity of EH pottery that he found must, at least, indicate the presence here of another large site which would have been somewhat similarly situated to Makrovouni.

The proliferation of sites across the Argive Plain is striking, and we may ask if they were independent, or if they reflect a feudal system of some kind. In relation to hierarchical position, it is interesting to note that the plain was divided in the Homeric texts into a North and a South Kingdom which suits the Late Bronze Age pattern well. But that, in Frankish and Ottoman times, the division was between East and West, which does not seem to reflect the pattern of any earlier period.

In a lecture given here in Cambridge in 2001, Professor Joseph Maran mentioned a plan to plot sherd find spots across the whole site at Tiryns, as we have been attempting to do at Mycenae. He now informs me that, unfortunately, this has not yet been carried out. At Mycenae there remains much work to do on the early pottery and other material from the Archaeological Society's excavations; not least, we should attempt to define more closely the exact period of expansion onto the crown of the citadel from a detailed restudy of the excavation and pottery notebooks. Then we could produce some more definitive suggestions to assist this preliminary assessment of the occupation history of the Argive Plain.

Bibliography

Banks, E. 2016. *Lerna VII. The Neolithic Settlement.* Princeton: the American School of Classical Studies at Athens.

Caskey, J.L. and E.G. Caskey 1960. The earliest settlement at Eutresis, supplementary excavations 1958. *Hesperia: the Journal of the American School of Classical Studies at Athens* 29(2): 126-167.

Felsch, R.C.S. 1971. Neolithische Keramik aus der Höhle von Kephalari. *Athenische Mitteilungen* 86: 1-12.

French, D.H. Forthcoming. *Well Built Mycenae. The Helleno-British excavations within the citadel at Mycenae 1959-1969, Fascicule 8: the Pre-Mycenaean Pottery.* Oxford: Oxbow Books.

French, E.B. 2002. *Mycenae: Agamemnon's Capital. The Site in its Setting.* Stroud: Tempus.

French, E.B. 2009. Town planning in palatial Mycenae, in S. Owen and L. Preston (eds) *Inside the City in the Greek World: Studies of Urbanism from the Bronze Age to the Hellenistic Period* (University of Cambridge Museum of Classical Archaeology Monographs 1): 55-61. Oxford: Oxbow Books.

French, E. and K. Shelton 2005. Early palatial Mycenae, in A. Dakouri-Hild and S. Sherratt (eds) *Autochthon: Papers presented to O.T.P.K. Dickinson on the occasion of his retirement, Institute of Classical Studies, University of London, 9 November 2005* (British Archaeological Reports International Series 1432): 175-184. Oxford: Archaeopress.

French, E.B. and W.D. Taylour 2007. *Well Built Mycenae. The Helleno-British excavations within the citadel at Mycanae 1959-1969, Fascicule 13. The Service Areas of the Cult Centre.* Oxford: Oxbow Books.

Iakovides, S. and E. French 2003. *Archaeological Atlas of Mycenae* (Βιβλιοθήκη της εν Αθήναις Αρχαιολογικής Εταιρείας 229). Athens: the Archaeological Society at Athens.

Mylonas, G.E. 1957. *Ancient Mycenae: the Capital City of Agamemnon.* Princeton: Princeton University Press.

Mylonas, G.E. 1961. Ἡ Ἀκρόπολις τῶν Μυκηνῶν. Ἀρχαιολογική Ἐφημερίς 1958: 153-207.

Orlandos, A. 1955. Mycenae. Το Ἔργον της εν Αθήναις Ἀρχαιολογικής Εταιρείας 1955: 69-74.

Phelps, W.W. 2004. *The Neolithic Pottery Sequence in Southern Greece* (British Archaeological Reports International Series 1259). Oxford: Archaeopress.

Pullen, D. 2008. The Early Bronze Age in Greece, in C.W. Shelmerdine (ed.) *The Cambridge Companion to the Aegean Bronze Age*: 19-46. Cambridge: Cambridge University Press.

Pullen, D. 2018. Caves and the landscape of Late Neolithic to Early Helladic I Greece: Comparing excavation and survey data from the Peloponnese, in S. Dietz, F. Mavridis, Ž. Tankosić and T. Takaoğlu (eds) *Communities in Transition. The Circum-Aegean Area during the 5th and 4th Millennia BC* (Monographs of the Danish Institute at Athens 20): 314-322 Oxford: Oxbow Books.

Steffen, B. 1884. *Karten von Mykenai.* Berlin: Dietrich Reimer.

Vitelli, K. D. 2007. *Lerna V. The Neolithic Pottery from Lerna.* Princeton: the American School of Classical Studies at Athens.

Wace, A.J.B. 1932. *Chamber Tombs at Mycenae* (Archaeologia 77). Oxford: the Society of Antiquities.

Wace, A.J.B. 1957. Mycenae 1939-1956, 1957: part I. Neolithic Mycenae. *The Annual of the British School at Athens* 52: 195-196.

Wace A.J.B., W.A. Heurtley, W. Lamb, L.B. Holland and C.A. Boethius 1921-1923. The report of the school excavations at Mycenae, 1921-1923 [corrected title: the report of the school excavations at Mycenae, 1920-1923]. *The Annual of the British School at Athens* 25: 1-434.

Wace, A.J.B. and C.W. Blegen 1918. The pre-Mycenaean pottery of the mainland. *The Annual of the British School at Athens* 22: 175-189.

Weisshaar, H.-J. 1981. Ausgrabungen in Tiryns 1978–1979: Bericht zur frühhelladischen Keramik. *Archäeologicsher Anzeiger* 1981: 220-256.

Weisshaar, H.-J. 1982. Ausgrabungen in Tiryns 1980: Bericht zur frühhelladischen Keramik. *Archäeologicsher Anzeiger* 1982: 440-466.

Weisshaar, H.-J. 1983. Ausgrabungen in Tiryns 1981: Bericht zur frühhelladischen Keramik. *Archäeologicsher Anzeiger* 1983: 329-358.

Zangger, E. 1993. *The Geoarchaeology of the Argolid* (Argolis 2). Berlin: Mann.

Localism and Interconnectivity in a Post-Palatial Laconian Maritime Landscape (Late Helladic IIIC to Submycenaean/Early Protogeometric)[1]

Chrysanthi Gallou, Jon Henderson, Elias Spondylis and William Cavanagh

Πολλά τα καλοκαιρινά πρωιά να είναι
που με τι ευχαρίστησι, με τι χαρά
θα μπαίνεις σε λιμένας πρωτοειδωμένους·
να σταματήσεις σ' εμπορεία Φοινικικά,
και τες καλές πραγμάτειες ν' αποκτήσεις,
σεντέφια και κοράλλια, κεχριμπάρια κ' έβενους,
και ηδονικά μυρωδικά κάθε λογής,
όσο μπορείς πιο άφθονα ηδονικά μυρωδικά·
σε πόλεις Αιγυπτιακές πολλές να πας,
να μάθεις και να μάθεις απ' τους σπουδασμένους.
(Kavafis, *Ithaki*)

Introduction

By focusing on the Southern Peloponnese during the 11th century BC,[2] we wish to emphasise the role of coastal communities in the process of transformation that Greece underwent at the transition from the Late Bronze Age to the Iron Age. Chris Mee helped to illuminate this process in his publications on Rhodes in the Bronze Age (Jones and Mee 1978; Mee 1982) and the suggestion of a role for Methana in the Early Iron Age (Mee and Taylor 1997: 53, 57), both parts of the broader Aegean network. In 1964, Vincent Desborough presented a downbeat picture of Laconia at this time, seeing Monemvasia as 'remote' and Amyklai as problematic and difficult to date (Desborough 1964: 87-90). A major corrective came with Katie Demakopoulou's epic body of work on the LH IIIC period in Laconia (Demakopoulou 1968; 1982; 2007;

2009) which has chronicled the increasing number of LH IIIC finds from Laconia and refined our understanding of the pottery typology of the period. Other significant recent advances to our understanding of Laconian LH IIIC Late/Submycenaean include Penelope Mountjoy's work on the development of Mycenaean pottery in the region (Mountjoy 1999; 2008; 2009), Birgitta Eder's work on the western Peloponnese (Eder 1998; 2001; 2006; 2009), and the discovery of LH IIIC late-Submycenaean finds from a chamber tomb at Peristeri (Tsasi) excavated by Themos and Zavvou in 2004 (Demakopoulou 2009: 121-122; Themos 2007: 460-463). More generally, recent work has emphasised the connections between different areas of Greece during the 11th century BC. Contributions are too many to summarise here, although several new monographs and collections of papers are noteworthy (including Deger-Jalkotzy 2014; Deger-Jalkotzy and Bächle 2009; Eder and Jung 2005; Iacono 2013; Jung and Mehofer 2013; Ruppenstein 2007; Sherratt 2003; 2012; Papadopoulos 2014; Papadopoulos et al. 2011; Papadopoulos and Smithson 2017a).

Two cases of interconnectivity in the latest Mycenaean world

Rather than attempting to provide an overview of the current state of Late Mycenaean studies, we intend to introduce the theme in a more selective way, and draw attention to two instances of interconnectivity between different parts of the Aegean. The relatively well-appointed Subminoan Tomb 200 in the North Cemetery at Knossos held the cremation of what was probably, but not certainly, a woman, accompanied by a necklace of 81 solid-cast, barrel-shaped gold beads

[1] It is a great pleasure to dedicate this offering to Chris Mee, a close friend and an inspiring colleague. We are also most grateful to Dr Simosi and colleagues in the Ephorate of Underwater Archaeology for their assistance and collaboration in the survey at Pavlopetri and post-excavation study, the staff and successive directors of the 5th Ephoreia of Prehistoric and Classical Antiquities and of the Sparta Museum, the directors and staff of the British School at Athens. The pottery drawings are the work of Denitsa Denova. We are grateful to Gemma Watson for her assistance with the plans of Pavlopetri. We are very grateful to the anonymous referee who saved the text from errors and helped us clarify our argument. We have, probably ill-advisedly, not followed their advice and avoided the most speculative of our suggestions, but even if wrong-headed we trust our more controversial suggestions will stimulate debate.
[2] By '11th century BC' we refer to the periods identified as LH IIIC Late and Submycenaean, adopting roughly the conventional chronology. Both the relative and the absolute dates are controversial and still hotly debated (see, for example, Papadopoulos et al. 2011; Papadopoulos 2017a: 19-23; Ruppenstein 2007; Toffolo et al. 2013; Wardle et al. 2014).

(Coldstream 1996: 539; Coldstream and Catling 1996: 194). A necklace of 140, almost identical, gold beads was found in Kerameikos Submycenaean stone cist Grave 136 in Athens, there associated with exotic beads of rock-crystal, glass and amber (Ruppenstein 2007: 24); a pair of dress pins implies that this was a female burial, although we cannot be certain. A necklace of 68 similar gold beads was associated with the double cremation of a young male and possibly a girl of 12-14 years old in Agora Tomb 80 (T80-3, see Papadopoulos 2017b: 907; Papadopoulos and Smithson 2017b: 489, 490 fig. 2.376), and a further example comprised of 87 beads was found with a child's skeleton in Tomb 147 at Perati (Iakovidis 1969-1970: 122, pl. 36β M199). The same type was represented in the great Tiryns Treasure, which must have been deposited at approximately the same time (Maran 2006: 129-142), and additional gold beads, some shaped like pomegranates, were found in Kamini Tombs B and E (Vlachopoulos 2006: 386, 402, 435, pls. 41, 54, 83-84). The beads are unique to the LH IIIC late-Submycenaean period and, unlike beaten gold Bronze Age types, they convey the metal's mass, perhaps its value in exchange, as well as serving as a means to display status. Indeed, the largest of the 68 beads from Agora Tomb 80 weighed 2.68g. The Tiryns Treasure has been interpreted as a collection of *keimelia* ('heirlooms' or 'family treasure') belonging to a family with a dynastic claim to power (Maran 2006). Tomb 200 at Knossos was linked by shared access with a warrior burial in Tomb 201, whose offerings echoed those of the Tiryns Treasure in the inclusion of a Cypriot bronze stand and a bronze sword, but differed from it in the inclusion of a supreme example of heroic *keimelion*: the latest boar's tusk helmet yet known to archaeology. This triangulation of finds from Knossos, Naxos, Athens and Tiryns, points not only to exchange between regions of the Aegean linked by the sea, but also to a shared ideology reflected in commonly acknowledged symbols of status, the attribution of similar value to prized possessions from the past, and the provision of gifts, and perhaps dowry, as a means of mediating relationships between different communities.

A second example concerns the more recent discovery of two cremations at the site of Ancient Epidauros in the Argolid; the first held in a LH IIIC late amphora or hydria, and the second in an Early-Middle Protogeometric Attic cremation urn closed with a bronze bowl (Piteros 2009). Although there are some LH IIIC cremations recorded from the Argolid (Palaiologou 2013; Piteros 2001), the standard Argive rite from the Submycenaean period onward was inhumation.[3] The rite and the pottery indicate that those buried at Ancient Epidauros originated from Attica.[4] The

bronze bowl also has a story to tell. The hemispherical type, of which the earliest example in Greece comes from the Submycenaean cemetery on Salamis, does not develop out of the Mycenaean tradition, but rather comes from Cyprus; the custom of closing cremation urns with bronze bowls of this type is well known in Iron Age Athens, though the example from Epidauros predates its earliest appearance there (Ruppenstein 2007: 206).

Finds of the period, like the above, trace not only the movement of objects but also movements of people and the forging of alliances.

Southern Laconia in a regional and overseas context: transitional LH IIIB2/IIIC Early to LH IIIC Middle

The end of LH IIIB, conventionally around 1200 BC, saw the loss of Mycenaean power in Laconia, with extensive horizons of destruction witnessed in the great mansion at the Menelaion (Catling 2009), Pellana (Spyropoulos 2013: 262) and Palaiopyrgi (Spyropoulos 2013: 101, 115); the palace at Ayios Vasileios was probably destroyed a century earlier, with the latest Mycenaean pottery identified so far at the site dating to the earliest LH IIIC horizon, roughly equivalent to Mountjoy's transitional LH IIIB2/IIIC Early (Kardamaki 2017: 74; Kardamaki *et al.*, this volume; Vasilogamvrou 2013; 2014; 2015a; 2015b). In LH IIIC, Laconia sees a precipitous decline in site numbers and population density, even more marked in the Eurotas Valley (Cartledge 2002: 58-61, fig. 8; Cavanagh and Crouwel 2002: 148; Janko 2008: 600).[5] An influx of refugees from the formerly powerful administrative centres of inland Laconia and beyond fuelled a rise in economic prosperity and population growth at certain southern Laconian sites during this period of crisis. Those southern Laconian coastal sites that continued to be occupied, or were re-occupied, from the transitional LH IIIB2/C Early and/or LH IIIC Early period onwards are listed in Table 7.1. The most important coastal sites during this period seem to have been the harbour towns at Ayios Stephanos in the Helos Plain, and Epidauros Limera and Pavlopetri on the Malea peninsula. Asopos (Bozas) might also have enjoyed significant interregional maritime connections at various points during the Bronze Age, as suggested by the discovery of a sealing and storage vessels of EBA date and LH IIIC pottery sherds (Zavvou 2007: 419-421; 2012a: 18-19; 2012b: 558), but further systematic exploration is needed. The same applies to the coastal sites at Mavrovouni and Kranae near Gytheion (see Banou 1996: 58-60), and

---

[3] Traces of burning or 'pyres' were found in association with Submycenaean burials in Γ21 and Γ31 at Mycenae, although while some bones had been affected by fire, the descriptions make clear these are burials in single graves, not cremations (Desborough 1973; French 2009: 152-153).

[4] For a similar cremation urn, see Kerameikos PG Grave 13; for a

belly-handled amphora closed with a bronze bowl, see Kerameikos PG Grave 48 (Kraiker and Kübler 1939: 186-187, pls. 54 and 58; Kübler 1943).

[5] Though excavation continues to reveal new sites, such as the LH IIIB-C site at Mouchteika, Karavas (Maltezou, 2016: 198-199), not many sites have been excavated in Laconia and it is possible that the depopulation may be overstated. A clear understanding of population movement during the final phase of the Bronze age awaits the discovery and publication of new sites. We are grateful to the referee for drawing our attention to this site.

Table 7.1. *LH IIIC and Submycenaean coastal sites in southern Laconia. This table excludes data from the unpublished University of Athens Epidauros Limera Survey. Question marks identify sites for which data are unclear or debateable.*

Site	Transitional IIIB2/IIIC	IIICe	IIICm	IIICl	SubMyc	SubMyc/EPG
Asopos: Bozas		x				
Asteri: Karaousi		x	x			
Ayioi Apostoloi: Trypalia	x					
Ayios Stephanos	x	x		?		
Cranae		x				
Diamonia: Kastelli		x				
Epidauros Limera	x	x	x	x	x	x
Mavrovouni		x				
Krokees				x?		
Pavlopetri	x	?		x	x	x
Peristeri (Tsasi)	?	x	x	x	x	
Phoiniki			x			
Sykia	x	x				
Xeronisi		x				
Zarax: Armakas Cave		x				

Gerakas on the east coast of the Malea peninsula, where the Armakas Cave has yielded a fragmentary LH IIIC Early deep bowl (FS 284) with linear decoration and a thin band inside the rim, that has close parallels from Kanakia on Salamis (Efstathiou-Manolakou 2009: 11, fig. 2.9).

The harbour town at Ayios Stephanos suffered a serious decline from LH IIIA, especially in LH IIIA2 and LH IIIB (Janko 2008: 595-598). This decline at Ayios Stephanos coincides, at least partially, with a period of prosperity at the palace at Ayios Vasileios,[6] and the site was revived (possibly accompanied by an influx of population from central Laconia) at some point after that palace had been destroyed (Janko 2008: 598-600, figs. 14.10-11; Mountjoy 2008: 315; Taylour and Janko 2008: 13, 14, 43, 48, 67). However, this LH revival was short-lived and the settlement was abruptly abandoned, with parts of it destroyed by fire, before the start of LH IIIC Middle (Janko 2008: 598, 605).[7] The material culture from this brief LH IIIC Early recovery hints at the existence of some external links, most notably in the form of a violin-bow fibula with incised decoration (HS 277, see Taylour 1972: 246, pl. 51d) and in similarities with the pottery from the Menelaion, Pylos, Ayios Kosmas in Attica, and Tiryns and Iria in the Argolid (Janko 2008: 599-600; Mountjoy 1999: 153, 282, 285, fig. 96 no. 196; 2008: 379, deep bowls fig. 6.12, nos. 3153, 3159-61, 3164 and 3179; for the deep bowls from the Menelaion, see Catling 2009: 383-394). The violin-bow fibula, HS 277, is of Kilian's type IIIB with a four-sided rectangular cross section to the bow decorated with parallel incised lines; the same type is found in the Argolid at Mycenae and Tiryns, and has parallels in Italy

---

[6] Janko dates the period of recession at Ayios Stephanos from the pottery in Area Epsilon, which Mountjoy places in LH IIIA2 Early (Mountjoy 2008: 302-314). Some caution is needed here as the fill is mixed and includes some later pots. Vitale (2011) has suggested a slightly later date for this pottery in LH IIIA2 Middle. With caution, the putative 'destruction' deposit at Ayios Stephanos would fall close to the major construction phases of the Western Stoa at Ayios Vasileios and Menelaion Mansion 2 (Kardamaki 2017: 114). The palace at Ayios Vasileios was burnt down some time later, at the end of LH IIIA2 or in LH IIIB1 (Kardamaki et al., this volume). The length of the time interval between construction and destruction at Ayios Vasileios is difficult to estimate; perhaps as little as a generation, though potentially much longer, especially if the LH IIIA2 style in the southern persisted longer than it did in the northern Peloponnese.

[7] Note, though, the LH IIIC Late-looking FS 59 amphoriskos in Mountjoy (2008: 378 no. 3695, fig. 6.39). For the similarities shared between this amphoriskos and LH IIIC Middle examples from Achaia and Mycenae, see Deger-Jalkotzy (2003: 62 n. 21).

from Montata in Emilia and Peschiera, Boccatura del Mincio near Verona (Eles Masi 1986: 4-5, fig. 2.27; Jung 2006: 189; Kilian 1985: 149 fig. 2: IIIB1). The example from Peschiera is decorated with lozenges incised with dots. A further parallel may exist in a decorated fibula from Hrustovaca Pecina in Serbia noted by Eles Masi (1986: 5). Industrial activity is attested at Ayios Stephanos in LH IIIC Early in the form of metalworking over hearths, although no furnaces, or slags indicative of smelting, have been found (French 2008: 447, 450-451; Janko 2008: 586). Whether metal products were intended for local consumption is far from certain. After the abandonment of Ayios Stephanos only two of its neighbouring sites continued to be occupied: Asteri (Karaousi), until LH IIIC Middle, and Peristeri (Tsasi) until Submycenaean/Early Protogeometric (Demakopoulou 2007: 162; 2009: 121-122; Janko 2008: 600; Mountjoy 1999: 289-290, no. 223, fig. 99). Ceramic evidence from both sites suggests that they maintained internal connections with Epidauros Limera on the Malea peninsula.

Epidauros Limera, on the eastern Maleatic coast, was first occupied in the Final Neolithic, and from the Early Mycenaean period was established as one of the most important harbour towns in the southeastern Peloponnese, with strong regional and overseas links. Although no LH residential remains have yet been excavated (or reported), pottery from the Mycenaean chamber tombs that were excavated in the area during the first half of the 20th century AD clearly confirm the site's uninterrupted occupation from the transitional MH III/LH I to the Submycenaean/Early Protogeometric (EPG) period (Gallou 2009; 2020). Thanks to its geographical location, Epidauros Limera developed close connections with inland Laconia, the eastern Peloponnese, Attica, the Aegean islands, Kythera and Crete. After the collapse of the Mycenaean palatial administration it, like Ayios Stephanos, probably received an influx of refugees and settlers from former centres in central Laconia (Cartledge 2002: 59). The positive effect of the integration of displaced populations into the local community may be seen in developments in the port's ceramic production from the transitional LH IIIB2/IIIC Early period onwards. Alongside maintaining local traditions and introducing their own innovations, its potters were heavily influenced by Minoanisms, shared common ceramic traits with the Argolid and Messenia (Demakopoulou 1968: pl. 79δ no. 68; Mountjoy 1999: 251 and n.145, 279, 282, 345, 352), and mediated external influences on ceramic production both on the peninsula, as evidenced, for example, by the Minoan traits on vases from the nearby site of Sykea,[8] and beyond.[9]

In LH IIIC Early, the site's continuing overseas contacts are manifest in Minoan-inspired pots and actual Cretan imports, including a FS 251 spouted mug (SM 5418) and an imported FS 174 Octopus Style stirrup jar (SM 5421) with parallels from Mouliana and Isopata on Crete (Demakopoulou 1968: 166-167, pl. 74δ-ε no. 37; 179, pl. 78β right, no. 59; Hallager 2007: 192 fig. 3f; Mountjoy 1999: 283, 285 no. 195, fig. 96). Economic prosperity peaked in LH IIIC Middle, and a distinctive local ceramic workshop was established which specialised in the manufacture of dark-ground amphoriskoi with narrow reserved bands (e.g., SM 5444, Demakopoulou 1968: 181, pl. 79γ no. 66; 2007: 164; Mountjoy 1999: 251, 287 no. 215, fig. 97), and stirrup jars and ring-based kraters with a star flanking ray pattern (e.g., stirrup jars SM 5419 and 5425, Demakopoulou 2007: 162; Mountjoy 1999: 252, 290 nos. 220-221, fig. 98). Probable exports of the former type have been identified at Asine and Perati, both of which provide parallels for an FS 122 lekythos (SM 5460) from Epidauros Limera (for SM 5460, see Demakopoulou 2007: 164; Mountjoy 1999: 287 no. 217, fig. 97; for Asine, see Mountjoy 1999: 161 no. 328, fig. 42; for Perati, Mountjoy 1999: 287 no. 215, fig. 97, 587 no. 425, fig. 218). Exported stirrup jars and kraters with the star flanking ray pattern circulated locally (for example, at Asteri (Karaousi)), regionally (at Palaia Epidauros, Asine and Perati) and overseas (at Naxos, see Demakopoulou 1982: 118; 2007: 163-164; Mountjoy 1999: 165 no. 341, fig. 44, 252, 290; Vlachopoulos 2006: 346-347; 2012: 148). Another vase from Tiryns with a spout swollen at mid-length and decoration comprised of blobs and panels is similar to the locally-produced Octopus Style stirrup jar SM 5440 from Epidauros Limera which, itself, incorporates Naxian traits in the form of an 'eye' painted in the barred ovals or almonds on its back (Demakopoulou 1968: 168, pl. 74γ no. 38; Mountjoy 1999: 165, 290 no. 219). Cretan, Argive and Naxian imports reached the port too, including an Octopus Style stirrup jar SM 5426 from Crete, and Close Style stirrup jar SM 5441 from the Argolid (Demakopoulou 1968: 163; 1982: 118; 2007: 162; D'Agata 2007: 101; Gallou, 2020: 221, fig. 4.157; Hallager 2007, 192 n.4; Mountjoy 1999: 251, 290 no. 222, fig. 99).[10] A rare strainer jug with twisted handle, SM 3314, has Attic and Rhodian parallels (Mountjoy 1999: 287 no. 218, fig. 97, 290, 589, 1040-1043, 1068).[11]

On the western coast of the Malea peninsula, just off the Pounta shore near the modern village of Viglafia opposite Elaphonisos, is located the now-submerged harbour town at Pavlopetri (Henderson et al. 2011). The underwater architectural remains (Figure 7.1) were first reported by Phokion Negris (Negris 1904) and

---

[8] The large FS 170 collar-necked jar with an overhang on the false mouth opposite the spout and banding all over the body (Steinhauer 1979: pl. 189δ) and the slightly later FS 63 collar-necked jar with a horned motif, (Mountjoy 1999: 251, 283).
[9] For example, the Solid Painted three-handled alabastron from the cave on the Leodakianaki plot at Geraki which has parallels from

Skyros (see Efstathiou-Manolakou 2009: 15, fig. 2.19).
[10] For discussion of the LH IIIC Close Style, see Vlachopoulos (2012: 143-151).
[11] For the origin and development of the LH III strainer jug, see Vlachopoulos (2012: 107-110).

were, once more, brought to public attention in 1967 by Nicholas Flemming. In 1968, the site was surveyed by an archaeological team from the University of Cambridge and, since 2009, the site has been the subject of survey and study by the Pavlopetri Underwater Archaeology Project, a joint collaboration, directed by Elias Spondylis, between the Ephorate of Underwater Antiquities of the Hellenic Ministry of Culture and Sports and the University of Nottingham, under the auspices of the British School at Athens (Gallou and Henderson 2012; Harding 1970; Harding et al. 1969). Three chamber tombs and an extensive cemetery of cist graves have been recorded underwater, while a large necropolis of rock-cut tombs lies on the Pounta shore, of which one example, of EH date, was excavated by the local Ephorate in 2004 (Zavvou 2012a: 22-23). The site was first occupied in the Final Neolithic and it continued to be used, without interruption, until around 1000/900 BC. Survey has also brought to light evidence for activity in the Archaic, Classical, Hellenistic, Roman and Late Antique periods.

No sherds of post-palatial date were recognised by the 1968 survey, and it was suggested that the site was abandoned at the end of LH IIIB (Harding 1970: 249; Harding et al. 1969: 135). However, the raised concave base of a deep bowl illustrated in the 1969 report (Harding et al. 1969: 137, fig. 15.16) may belong to the LH IIIC Early type FS 284. The recent survey has produced ceramic evidence (as yet unpublished) that confirms post-palatial occupation at the site. Significantly, no unambiguously LH IIIC material has been reported yet from the nearby Mycenaean sites at Tsegianika: Kyla, Megali Spilia, Trypalia, or Elaphonisos (see Gallou 2008, with further bibliography; see Efstathiou-Manolakou 2009: 14-15, for the caves at Trypalia (with LH IIIB-IIIC early deep bowls) and Mavri Spilia), suggesting that the LH IIIA-B villages and farmsteads in the environs of Pavlopetri were abandoned by the transitional LH IIIB2/IIIC Early period. Further, no post-palatial material has been published from the wider region of Vatika.

The show must go on: coastal Laconia in the 11th century BC

By the end of LH IIIC Middle, all coastal sites in southern Laconia were abandoned, with the exception of Epidauros Limera and Pavlopetri. The situation (at least on current evidence) is similarly dramatic in inland Laconia, with the exception of continued activity at the Amyklaion in the Sparta Valley (LH IIIC to Late-Submycenaean), Sparta (Submycenaean; see Themos 2002: 169), Pellana in the north Eurotas Valley (LH IIIC Late to Submycenaean), Peristeri (Tsasi; LH IIIC Late to Submycenaean/EPG) in the Helos Plain, and Phoinikia near the west Maleatic coast (SM 6432; Demakopoulou 2007: 166; Mountjoy 1999: 293 no. 239, fig. 100). An LH IIIC Late triple askoid vessel decorated with semi-

circles, stripes and a triangle with fringe fill, allegedly from a looted chamber tomb on the hill of Karneas near Krokeai, is dated to LH IIIC Middle by Demakopoulou (Demakopoulou 1982: 108-109, pl. 55 no. 123; 2007: 166, fig. 19) and LH IIIC Late by Mountjoy (1999: 293), who cites unpublished parallels from Palaiokastro in Arcadia. Some uncertainty exists over the provenance of this composite vessel due to its registration in the inventory of the Archaeological Museum of Sparta as deriving 'from a looted Mycenaean chamber tomb from the area of Neapolis Voion (1956)' (Zavvou 2002: 214 n. 16).[12] If the multiple vessel was discovered at Krokeai, then it might be associated with a very brief re-occupation of this part of the Helos Plain and could perhaps be linked to the LH III Late-looking amphoriskos HS 3695 from nearby Ayios Stephanos (dated by Mountjoy to LH IIIC Early, see 2008: 378, fig. 6.39). If the vessel was found in the area of Neapolis Voion, which seems to be most plausible, it could have been removed from one of the graves at Pavlopetri, the only site with evidence for 11th century BC occupation in the Vatika region.

It needs to be emphasised that the Mycenaean and Iron Age pottery from Pavlopetri came from the sea floor and has been subject to abrasion and erosion over a very long time. On many of the sherds, the painted decoration has been worn away and, consequently, it can be difficult to date them securely. For this reason, most sherds cannot be assigned with certainty to LH IIIC. A number of examples can, however, be placed in LH IIIB-C, including basins (FS 294) (cf. Catling 2009: 376-377; Popham et al. 2006: 195); shallow bowls (a Laconian speciality: Catling 2009: 377, 408-409; Mountjoy 1999: 213; 2008: 384); deep bowls, including one painted monochrome in and out; jugs with pierced handles (which, at the Menelaion, are dated LH IIIB-C: Catling 2009: 239, 261 figs. 275, 310) and kylikes, of which most could only be dated to LH III, but one with a swollen stem seems to be LH IIIC.

A number of pieces can also be assigned to the latest period of interest to us here (for findspots, see Figure 7.1; for illustrations, see Figure 7.2).[13] A large fragment of a Submycenaean amphoriskos with horizontal handles (PAV09-178, Figure 7.2a) is decorated with a wavy line set in a reserved panel at handle level, thicker and thinner bands above and below the panel, and solid paint on the neck and lower body. The clay is fine brown with a few red inclusions (7.5YR7/6, inside and outside) and, importantly, the lustrous black paint has the metallic sheen characteristic of Spartan Protogeometric, offering clear evidence that the origins of the paint technique can be found in the Submycenaean period. The vessel is similar to

---

[12] Banou (1996: 47-48, n.79) reports that the excavator found this tomb empty.

[13] This information comes courtesy of the research team.

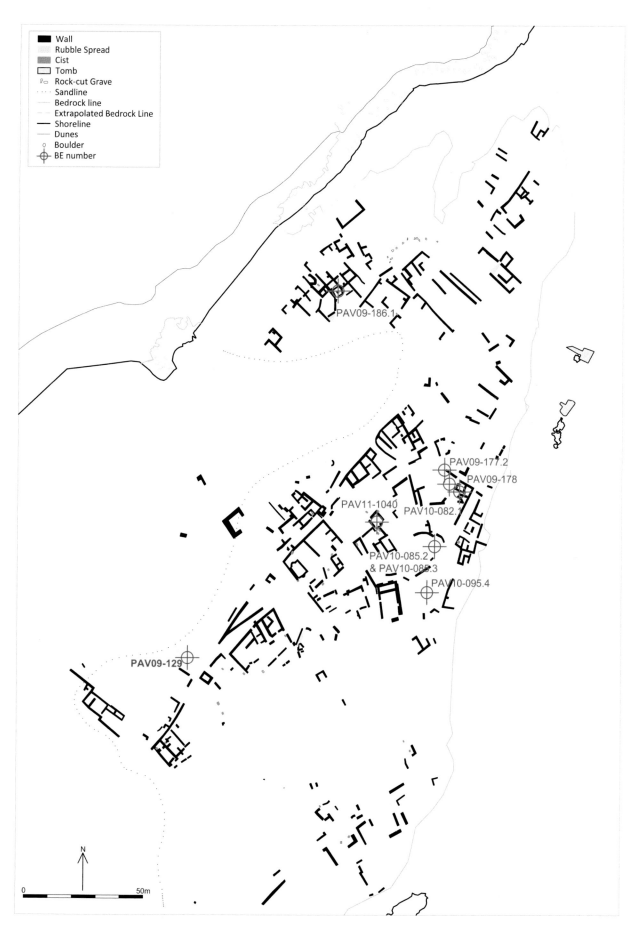

Figure 7.1. Plan of the underwater site of Pavlopetri, indicating the find spots of the vases illustrated in Figure 7.2.

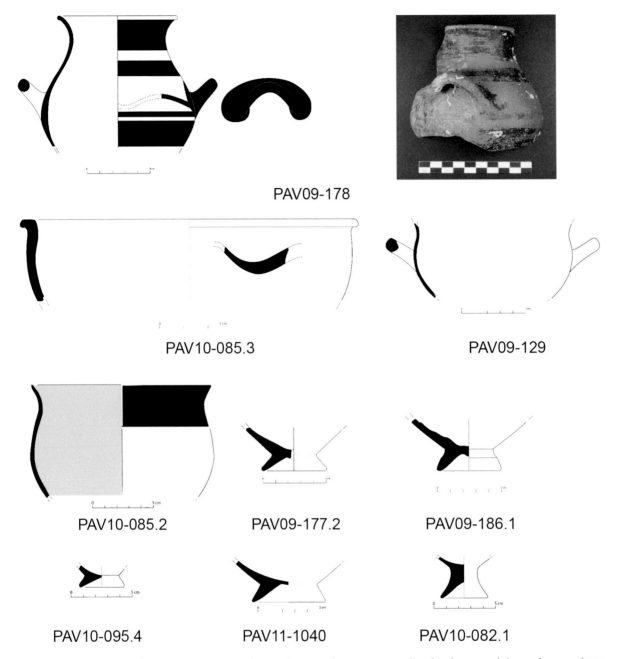

PAV09-178

PAV10-085.3

PAV09-129

PAV10-085.2

PAV09-177.2

PAV09-186.1

PAV10-095.4

PAV11-1040

PAV10-082.1

Figure 7.2. Submycenaean and Protogeometric pottery from Pavlopetri: Submycenaean amphoriskos (PAV09-178), krater fragment (PAV10-085.3) [LH IIIC/Submycenaean?], skyphos/deep bowl (PAV09-129) [LH IIIC/Submycenaean?], skyphos/deep bowl (PAV10-085.2) [LH IIIC/Submycenaean?], conical bases from open shapes (PAV09-177.2, PAV09-186.1, PAV10-095.4 and PAV11-1040) [Submycenaean/Protogeometric?], conical base of skyphos (PAV10-082.1) [Protogeometric?]. Scale approximately 1:3. Drawings by Denitsa Nenova.

amphoriskoi from Nichoria (see Mountjoy 1999: 363 no. 144, fig. 126) and the Kerameikos in Athens[14] — an example from Athens, Agora T64-1 (Papadopoulos and Smithson 2017b: 430; Papadopoulos and Strack 2017: 720), suggests that the Pavlopetri amphoriskos might belong to the very end of Submycenaean or the start of the PG.

Open shapes with a greater or lesser probability of a Submycenaean or Protogeometric date include a fragment of a krater (PAV10-085.3, Figure 7.2). It is poorly preserved and might be LH IIIC or Submycenaean, although the shape continues into PG as the krater Type M from Amyklai (Coulson 1985: 78, no. 286, fig. 9, pl. 13i). Deep bowl/skyphos fragments include PAV09-129 (FS 285/6, Figure 7.2) with only traces of black paint preserved on the exterior. It can be compared with the Submycenaean example from Pellana (Mountjoy 1999: 294 no. 249, fig. 101), although there is no evidence for the distinctive conical base and it could be earlier in date. PAV10-085.2 (Figure 7.2), with a deep band below

14 Parallels for the decorative schema include vessels from Kerameikos Grave 33 (Kraiker and Kübler 1939: 19, pl. 18) and for the shape, include others from Grave 108 (Kraiker and Kübler 1939: 7) and, especially, Grave 22 (Kübler 1943: pl. 4.925 [EPG]).

the rim, might be LH IIIC but could well be later; it is not clear if the handles were horizontal or vertical (cf. Eder 2006: 217-218, pl. 54.26; 227, pl. 62.151; Nichoria: P125, Coulson 1983: 126 fig. 3.10, 189, pl. 3.10; Naxos: Vlachopoulos 2006: 401 MN1776, drawing 30, pl. 53). Conical bases from open shapes (including PAV09-177.2, PAV09-186.1, PAV10-095.4 and PAV11-1040, Figure 7.2), range in diameter between 4cm and 6cm and probably come from skyphoi/kantharoi/cups. Parallels include examples from Olympia (Eder 2006: 228-236, pls. 63-65), Nichoria (Coulson 1983: 185, fig. 3.3, pl. 3.5; Mountjoy 1999: 363 no. 148, fig. 126) and Amyklai (Coulson 1985: 59, fig. 11) and the stem fragment of a PG open vase from Kastri on Kythera (Morgan 2011). The thick base of PAV10-082.1 is paralleled in PG skyphoi from, for example, Lefkandi (Lemos 2002: pl. 14.6), and in Cretan bell skyphoi (see Coldstream 1996: 378-384, fig. 60 no. G79; cf. also the PG krateriskos from Pellana, Spyropoulos 2013: 380-381, pls. 176, 177, 986, 987). The clay of PAV10-082.1 (Figure 7.2i) is quite coarse for a skyphos, but not impossibly so.

On the southeast Laconian coast, the chamber tombs at Epidauros Limera contained much of the known 11th century BC pottery from Laconia. LH IIIC Late is mainly represented by examples of FS 59, FS 106, FS 115, FS 137, FS 162, FS 175 and FS 285, and the Submycenaean by examples of FS 60 and FS 110 (Demakopoulou 2009: 118; Gallou 2020: 222-231; Mountjoy 1999: 293 nos. 245-246, fig. 101). External influence on local pottery production, imports, and exports, highlight the site's unbroken connections with its Peloponnesian and Aegean partners. A LH IIIC Late FS 175 stirrup jar (SM 5430) with dark-ground body decoration, elaborate triangles and a loop round the base of the false neck and the spout was imported from Asine (Figure 7.3a-b; Demakopoulou 2009: 118; Mountjoy 1999: 293 no. 240, fig. 100). Another example of the same shape (SM 5441) — of which only fragments from the shoulder survived, and which has not yet been identified in the storerooms of the Sparta Museum — has dot fringed apse motifs on the shoulder and arrived to the site either from Asine (Demakopoulou 1968: 170, pl. 74γ no. 40) or, more probably, from Attica, where a similar example comes from Chamber Tomb 10 at Athens 47 Syngrou Street (see Mountjoy 1999: 613 no. 566, fig. 234; also, Pantelidou 1975: 70, pl. 14, who stresses the preference of local potters to add dots around the motifs). A LM IIIC Late/Subminoan stirrup jar with cross-hatched triangles (SM 5432) reached the port from Crete (Figure 7.4a-b; Demakopoulou 1968: 172-173, pl. 75β right; Mountjoy 1999: 293 no. 241, fig. 100; cf. also Day 2011: 292-293, fig. 9.17, K116.4; Seiradaki 1960: 16-18, pl. 6a) at the same time as another Cretan stirrup jar (SM 3339) reached Pellana, probably via the southern Peloponnese (Demakopoulou 1982: 115-116, pl. 57; 2009: 119; Dickinson 1992: 114; Mountjoy 1999: 252, 293 no.

242, fig. 100; cf. Gypsades: Hood et al. 1959: 208, 241 fig. 27 nos. VII.6-7, 248).[15]

Further evidence of external contact is provided by a rare LH IIIC Late FS 97 alabastron (SM 5547) with dark-ground body, reserved base and outward pointing handles, decorated with a mixture of foliate band and necklace (Mountjoy 1999: 252, 291 no. 232, fig. 99; not currently located in the storerooms of the Sparta Museum). The type evolved in LH IIIC Early, perhaps under Cretan influence (Mountjoy 1999: 252), and is commonly found in the Dodecanese. Of those several examples that have been identified on the mainland, some can be dated to LH IIIC Middle/Late (see Mountjoy 1999: 161 no. 331, fig. 43 (Tiryns); 291; Papadopoulos and Papadopoulou-Chrysikopoulou 2017: 27-28, fig. 20b, pl. 15d; Petropoulos 2007: 255-256; Vlachopoulos 2012: 100-101). The LH IIIC Middle based alabastra from Tiryns and from Tomb Γ at Aplomata on Naxos, offer good parallels for the later Epidauros Limera vase (Mountjoy 1999: 161; Vlachopoulos 2006: 121). Mountjoy's proposed LM IIIC Early influence may be seen on the unusual Type 7 straight-sided pyxis from Karphi (see Day 2011:142, 144, 286, fig. 9.15, K80.8; Seiradaki 1960: 19, fig.). The detection of Cretan, Cycladic, Dodecanesian and mainland influences on the LH IIIC Late Epidauros Limeran pottery, imports, and local inventions, suggest that the harbour acted as a melting pot in which diverse ceramic traditions were integrated, adapted and redistributed.

Few funerary gifts are assigned a Submycenaean or transitional Submycenaean/EPG date. The FS 60 amphoriskos SM 3309, with biconical body and decoration of dot-fringed stacked triangles, is typical of this period (Figure 7.5; Demakopoulou 1982: 119, pl. 62.141; 2009: 118, fig. 8; Mountjoy 1999: 252, 293 no. 245). In shape, the FS 110 wide necked jug SM 5458, with two zones of zigzag, resembles examples from ancient Elis (Demakopoulou 1968: 185, pl. 82γ no. 79; Eder 2001: 18, pls. 2b no.1 and 11c no.3; Mountjoy 1999: 252, 293 no. 246, fig. 101; it has not been possible to identify SM 5458 in the storerooms of the Sparta Museum). The only known ring-vase (FS 196) from Laconia is SM 15652 (Figure 7.6a-b; Gallou, 2020: 230-231). It features a baseless hollow annular shape, a horizontally placed funnel-shaped spout (rim missing), a single vertical basket handle (missing) stretching from the base of spout to the opposite side of the ring, two tiny lugs on either side of the body (one preserved) and very scanty traces of black paint. LH III ring-vases usually feature a vertical or oblique spout with splaying or spreading lip (Furumark 1972: 617-618; Vlachopoulos 2012: 138); monochrome versions have been dated to LH IIIC

---

[15] For a cluster of links between Knossos in particular, and these vases from Epidauros Limera and Pellana, and Argos and Salamis, see D'Agata (2007: 101, table 3).

Figure 7.3a-b. Imported LH IIIC Late FS 175 stirrup jar (SM 5430) with dark ground body decoration and elaborate triangles, from Epidauros Limera.

Figure 7.4a-b. Imported LM IIIC Late/Subminoan stirrup jar (SM 5432) with cross-hatched triangles, from Epidauros Limera.

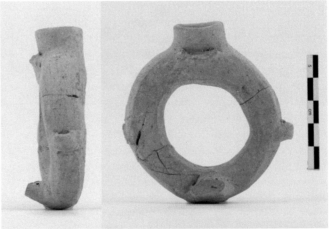

Figure 7.5. Submycenaean FS 60 amphoriskos (SM 3309) decorated with dot-fringed stacked triangles, from Epidauros Limera.

Figure 7.6a-b. Submycenaean or Submycenaean/ Early Protogeometric ring askos (SM 15652), from Epidauros Limera.

Late (Mountjoy 1999: 184-185, 439, 460, 792, 1147). The example from Epidauros Limera is distinguished by the position of its spout which is paralleled in the Submycenaean ring-vase from Kerameikos Grave 146 (see Kraiker and Kübler 1939: 112-113; Ruppenstein 2007: 156-157, fig. 16, pl. 38); we have not been able to identify any closer parallels. Ruppenstein classifies the Kerameikos ring-vase among novelties without a predecessor in the Submycenaean period or a successor in the Protogeometric period, and sees an evident Cypriot ancestry (Ruppenstein 2009: 331). A similar Cypriot ancestry could apply to the Epidauros Limera vase which, because of its cruder manufacture and peculiar features (horizontal spout, lugs), may be dated to the Submycenaean period or to the transition to the EPG.

Finally, 'a fragmentary pot with incised decoration' reported as coming from outside one of the Epidauros Limera chamber tombs explored in 1955 (Vanderpool 1955: 226) has been identified by Carla Antonaccio as a PG jug which 'bears witness to a visit made centuries after the construction and primary use of the tomb' (Antonaccio 1998: 57). Unfortunately, the recovery circumstances of the pot do not allow for clear inferences, but certainly this pot may bridge the all-important transition from the Mycenaean to the EIA period on the south-east Laconian coast.

Conclusions

The harbour towns of southern Laconia (Epidauros Limera, Kastri, Pavlopetri and Ayios Stephanos) have long histories going back to the FN period. They flourished under Minoan influence, but seem to have more mixed histories under the Mycenaean palaces. A classic case of gift exchange between Mycenaean kings in LH IIIA2-IIIB1 is evident in the quarrying and transport of massive blocks of *Rosso Antico* and grey-green stone from quarries in the Mani to Mycenae, where they graced the façade of the Treasury of Atreus. These cargoes would seem to be a diplomatic gift from a Laconian ruler to the *wanax* at Mycenae. A best-guess candidate for that ruler would be a king based at Ayios Vasileios. Although identification is dependent on the chronology of the palace's destruction (see n. 6) and the construction date of the Treasury (also uncertain), if not from Ayios Vasileios, then a ruler from where? Interestingly, at about this time or a little earlier (LH IIIA2 Early), one of the major Bronze Age southern Laconian harbour towns, Ayios Stephanos, was eclipsed, and its long history of maritime exchange interrupted. The decline of the port may be ascribed, in part, to geomorphological effects, since it is possible that the northern side of the promontory could have begun to silt up from the Eurotas by this time (Janko 2008: 554, 591), but the chronology is vague, and deltaic fill was evidently deposited after Classical times (Bintliff 2008;

Janko 2008: 554). Could this period of decline (LH IIIA2 Early) be explained as the result of interference by the palace at Ayios Vasileios in maritime affairs? Evidence for such a palatial interest may be provided by Epidauros Limera, whose port thrived at the very time that Ayios Stephanos was eclipsed, and which maintained connections both with the centres in the Sparta Valley and overseas (for LH IIIA2 Early pottery from the site, see Demakopoulou 1968; Gallou 2020: 178-198; Kountouri 1996-1997: 497-503; Mountjoy 1999: 250-251, 265-278). A Mycenaean ruler could well have exercised power over the ports of southern Laconian, and palatial interests may have favoured Epidauros Limera as one of the most important harbours. The site was ideally situated for maritime contacts with the northeast Peloponnese, Crete and the rest of the Aegean; let us not forget, that for any cargo sent via Ayios Stephanos towards these destinations, merchant sailors would have had to navigate the notoriously difficult passage around Cape Malea, with its unpredictable weather and powerful storms. Moreover, the harbour town at Epidauros Limera would likely have been easily accessible from central Laconia.[16] This model of palatial interference into the operations of the southern Laconian harbour towns fits with the picture of positive palatial investment in maritime infrastructure claimed at Pylos (Zangger 2008) and Korphos Kalamianos, a harbour installation newly founded in LH IIIB under palatial patronage (Pullen 2015). Perhaps palatial interest in maritime matters could have its downside too. Certainly, after the palace at Ayios Vasileios burnt down, the fortunes of Ayios Stephanos revived and the settlement flourished for another century (LH IIIB-IIIC Early). The mansion at the Menelaion was also in operation in LH IIIB2, with indications of administrative control, which seems to imply the existence of a rival centre in central Laconia (neither Ayios Vasileios nor the Menelaion, but somewhere else(?)), which could have made its presence felt in the south. More generally, the rise and fall of various palatial powers had consequences for the demographic structure of our region, as it did for the Aegean and most of the Mediterranean, in the later 13th-11th centuries BC; it is difficult to avoid the conclusion that mass migration was one of these consequences, and one in which the harbour towns played their part.

The survival of Epidauros Limera and Pavlopetri suggests that sites with good harbours maintained their maritime connections and, as a result, were more resilient, continuing as refuges, likely under the direction of strong, local sea-orientated groups. Both occupied strategic coastal positions on either side of the Malea peninsula and offered safe haven to passing ships

---

[16] If one accepts that the later road network was based on an earlier Bronze Age one. For a thorough investigation of the regional Classical road network, see Pikoulas (2012: 487-488).

at a time of increasing population movement and social dislocation. Between 3000 BC and 1000 BC, the town at Pavlopetri probably subsided relative to the sea level by 1.6m-2m (N. Flemming and D. Sakellariou, personal communication). If this was the case, the centre of Pavlopetri would have remained dry, but the sea would have invaded the bay behind Pavlopetri Island and the reef that links the island to the shore. This could have had the effect of creating a sheltered stretch of water that might have improved the effectiveness of the harbour as a haven for ships. Elias Spondylis reports that archaeological and geological indications from the submerged settlement at Pikri indicate that, when the average sea level reached 2.5m below the current one, the settlement in this area was destroyed. The date of this destruction is unclear and further archaeological evidence is needed to resolve the question (Spondylis *et al.* 2012).

Port sites, open to the sea and part of long-established networks, were better placed to weather the political and economic instability that accompanied the decline of the major Aegean palatial centres than those sites in the Laconian countryside, which were, apparently, more heavily invested in the centralised palace economies. Settlement and exchange was clearly more fragmented at this time, but good harbours, particularly in a time of increased mobility, would still be needed and seafaring, as a pragmatic skill, would still be practiced. Indeed, if anything, the end of the second millennium BC was a time of consolidation in ship design with established technological knowledge communicated through practice and action into EIA Greece (Wachsmann 1998: 251-254); significantly, there was no hiatus or re-introduction of technologies. The assemblage from the Point Iria wreck (Phelps *et al.* 1999), dating to *c.* 1200 BC and consisting of Cypriot pithoi, stirrup jars, jugs and LH/LM IIIB2 pithoid jars, alongside a few decorated Mycenaean fine ware vases (Lolos 1999), clearly demonstrates that maritime trade and contact continued during this period, albeit at a reduced level compared with that exemplified in the exotic, royally-appointed cargo of the Uluburun wreck a century earlier. Smaller communities involved in maritime trade continued, and perhaps even prospered to a degree, once they were free from palatial control (Broodbank 2013: 464-465).

The reworking of relationships in the LH IIIC-Submycenaean period across the Mediterranean world sets the scene for our review of the 11th century BC finds from coastal Laconia. The transformation of cross-cultural relations in the Mediterranean during this period has stimulated recent discussion using, inter alia, the vocabulary of material entanglement and postcolonial discourse (see papers in Maran and Stockhammer 2012). With a relatively small repertoire of finds, it is difficult to say how far harbour towns such

as Epidauros Limera, Ayios Stephanos and Pavlopetri engaged in exchanges beyond the Aegean. The fibula from Ayios Stephanos and pins from Peristeri (Demakopoulou 2009: 122, fig. 26) hint at links with Italy and the Balkans, although both types could also identify connections with Crete, the Peloponnese and Central Greece. The three pins from Peristeri lay at the shoulders and on the breast of the deceased. It has been suggested that they secured the shroud, but two might have served as dress pins and, to judge from the published photograph, they make a matching pair. Found in both male and female graves in Greece, such pins form part of a wider pattern of change in dress and personal ornamentation which, by the Protogeometric period at the latest,[17] becomes formalised in the wearing of the peplos (Catling 1996a; 530; Catling 1996b: 555; Desborough 1972: 295; Kilian-Dirlmeier 1984: 80-83; Lemos 2002: 108-109; Ruppenstein 2007: 221-228). Perhaps we can read this as an example of 'naturalisation', whereby a foreign type of artefact is adopted and adapted, over time, to create a new cultural icon.[18] It is not impossible that routes westward passed through our area on to Messenia, Elis, the Ionian Islands and the Adriatic, but stronger evidence is needed before we can assert this with confidence. At present, the indications of links between southern Laconia and the outside world seem to point southwards to Crete and northwards overland to central Laconia and northwards and eastwards by sea to the Argolid, Attica and the Aegean islands. As far as Crete is concerned, the story whereby mainland Greece and Crete came to be united by shared cultural norms (and shared genetic ancestry according to recent aDNA analysis, see Lazaridis *et al.* 2017) is an extremely long one, and one in which the harbours of Pavlopetri, Ayios Stephanos, Epidauros Limera and Kastri played an important part. The Cretan imports to Laconia of the 12th-11th centuries BC, that period which saw closer connection between the regions of the 'Greek' Aegean, prompt some thoughts on more specific exchanges. Imported LM IIIC stirrup jars, for example, follow on from the palatial trade in olive oil represented by Transport Stirrup Jars (as, for example, at the Menelaion, see Catling 2009: 369), and even these earlier exchanges included elements of both centralised control and private entrepreneurship (Haskell *et al.* 2011; Knapp and Demesticha 2017: 79-88). Plainly, perfumed oil was still prized in LH IIIC, but it was a commodity no longer manufactured in palatial workshops, and production and exchange were mediated through different networks. We indicated

---

[17] Kerameikos Submycenaean Grave 136, noted earlier, may be among the earliest examples.

[18] Claims of a foreign origin for Submycenaean dress pins are controversial: discussions reviewing earlier literature can be found in Ruppenstein, who argues against a Mycenaean ancestry to the dress pins of Iron Age Greece (2007: 224-225), and Papadopoulos who supports the theory of an internal development from the Bronze Age (Papadopoulos 2017b: 915-917).

through the examples in our introduction that shared attitudes to objects from the past (such as the Tiryns ring and the Knossos boar's tusk helmet) and similar tokens of wealth (such as gold beads) reflected the development of broadly shared cultural attitudes. The handful of finds from Pavlopetri and Epidauros Limera cannot support a superstructure of elaborate inference, but their evident links with Crete, the Argolid, Attica and the Aegean islands confirm that southern Laconia was integrated into the same cultural world. Shared beliefs, of course, do not rule out material interests and it seems likely that a prime motive in the movement of these goods was a commercial one. Greece of the 11th century BC is not only at the event horizon of the transformation 'from palace to polis', but also from Bronze Age to Iron Age — can it be a coincidence that Southern Laconia boasts some of the richest iron ore deposits in the Aegean?

Bibliography

Antonaccio, C. 1998. The Archaeology of Ancestors, in C. Dougherty and L. Kurke (eds) *Cultural Poetics in Archaic Greece: Cult, Performance, Politics*: 46-70. Cambridge: Cambridge University Press.

Banou, E. 1996. *Beitrag zum Studium Lakoniens in der mykenischen Zeit* (Quellen und Forschungen zur antiken Welt 20). Munich: Tuduv.

Bintliff, J.L. 2008. The regional geology and early settlement of the Helos Plain, in W.D. Taylour and R. Janko (eds) *Ayios Stephanos. Excavations at a Bronze Age and Medieval Settlement in Southern Laconia* (The British School at Athens Supplementary Volume 44): 527-550. London: the British School at Athens.

Broodbank C. 2013. *The Making of the Middle Sea. A History of the Mediterranean from the Beginning to the Emergence of the Classical World*. London: Thames and Hudson.

Cartledge, P. 2002. *Sparta and Lakonia: A Regional History, 1300-362 B.C.* (Second Edition). London: Routledge.

Catling, H.W. 1996a. The objects other than pottery in the Subminoan tombs, in J.N. Coldstream and H.W. Catling (eds) *Knossos North Cemetery: Early Greek Tombs* (The British School at Athens Supplementary Volume 28): 517-537. London: the British School at Athens.

Catling, H.W. 1996b. The Dark Age and later bronzes, in J.N. Coldstream and H.W. Catling (eds) *Knossos North Cemetery: Early Greek Tombs* (The British School at Athens Supplementary Volume 28): 543-574. London: the British School at Athens.

Catling, H.W. 2009. *Sparta: Menelaion I. The Bronze Age* (The British School at Athens Supplementary Volume 45). London: the British School at Athens.

Cavanagh, W.G. and J.H. Crouwel 2002. The survey area in the prehistoric periods, in W. Cavanagh, J. Crouwel, R.W.V. Catling and G. Shipley (eds) *Continuity and Change in a Greek Rural Landscape. The Laconia Survey Volume I. Methodology and Interpretation* (The British School at Athens Supplementary Volume 26): 121-150. London: the British School at Athens.

Coldstream, J.N. 1996. The Protogeometric and Geometric pottery, in J.N. Coldstream and H.W. Catling (eds) *Knossos North Cemetery Early Greek Tombs* (The British School at Athens Supplementary Volume 28): 311-420. London: the British School at Athens.

Coldstream, J.N. and H.W. Catling (eds) 1996. *Knossos North Cemetery Early Greek Tombs I-IV* (The British School at Athens Supplementary Volume 28). London: the British School at Athens.

Coulson, W.D.E. 1983. The pottery, in W.A. McDonald, W.D.E. Coulson and J. Rosser (eds) 1983. *Excavations at Nichoria in Southwest Greece, III. Dark Age and Byzantine Occupation*: 61-259. Minneapolis: University of Minnesota Press.

Coulson, W.D.E. 1985. The Dark Age pottery of Sparta. *The Annual of the British School at Athens* 80: 29-84.

D'Agata, A.L. 2007. Evolutionary paradigms and Late Minoan III. On a definition of LM III C Middle, in S. Deger-Jalkotzy and M. Zavadil (eds) *LH III C Chronology and Synchronisms II: LH III C Middle. Proceedings of the International Workshop Held at the Austrian Academy of Sciences at Vienna, October 29th and 30th, 2004* (Österreichische Akademie der Wissenschaften Philosophisch-Historische Klasse Denkschriften 362, Veröffentlichungen der Mykenischen Kommission 28): 89-118. Vienna: the Austrian Academy of Sciences.

Day, L.P. 2011. *The Pottery from Karphi: A Re-examination* (The British School at Athens Studies 19). London: the British School at Athens.

Deger-Jalkotzy S. 2003. Stratified pottery deposits from the LH IIIC settlement at Aigeira/Achaia, in S. Deger-Jalkotzy and M. Zavadil (eds) *LH IIIC Chronology and Synchronisms. Proceedings of the International Workshop Held at the Austrian Academy of Sciences at Vienna, May 7th and 8th, 2001* (Österreichische Akademie der Wissenschaften Philosophisch-Historische Klasse Denkschriften 310, Veröffentlichungen der Mykenischen Kommission 20): 53-75. Vienna: the Austrian Academy of Sciences.

Deger-Jalkotzy, S. 2014. A very underestimated period: the Submycenaean phase of early Greek culture, in D. Nakassis, J. Gulizio and S.A. James (eds) *KE-RA-ME-JA: Studies Presented to Cynthia W. Shelmerdine* (Prehistory Monographs 46): 41-52. Philadelphia: INSTAP Academic Press.

Deger-Jalkotzy, S. and A.E. Bächle (eds) 2009. *LH III C Chronology and Synchronisms III: LH III C Late and the Transition to the Early Iron Age. Proceedings of the International Workshop Held at the Austrian Academy of Sciences at Vienna, February 23rd and 24th, 2007* (Österreichische Akademie der Wissenschaften

Philosophisch-Historische Klasse Denkschriften 384, Veröffentlichungen der Mykenischen Kommission 30). Vienna: the Austrian Academy of Sciences.

Demakopoulou, K. 1968. Μυκηναϊκά αγγεία εκ θαλαμοειδών τάφων περιοχής Αγίου Ιωάννου Μονεμβασίας. Αρχαιολογικόν Δελτίον 23(1968)(Α΄): 145-194.

Demakopoulou, K. 1982. Το Μυκηναϊκό Ιερό στο Αμυκλαίο και η ΥΕ ΙΙΙ Γ Περίοδος στη Λακωνία. Unpublished PhD dissertation, National and Kapodistrian University of Athens.

Demakopoulou, K. 2007. Laconia and Arcadia in LH III C Middle: pottery and other finds, in S. Deger-Jalkotzy and M. Zavadil (eds) *LH III C Chronology and Synchronisms II: LH III C Middle. Proceedings of the International Workshop Held at the Austrian Academy of Sciences at Vienna, October 29th and 30th, 2004* (Österreichische Akademie der Wissenschaften Philosophisch-Historische Klasse Denkschriften 362, Veröffentlichungen der Mykenischen Kommission 28): 161-174. Vienna: the Austrian Academy of Sciences.

Demakopoulou, K. 2009. Laconia in LH III C Late and Submycenaean: evidence from Epidauros Limera, Pellana, the Amyklaion and other sites, in S. Deger-Jalkotzy and A.E. Bächle (eds) *LH III C Chronology and Synchronisms III: LH III C Late and the Transition to the Early Iron Age. Proceedings of the International Workshop Held at the Austrian Academy of Sciences at Vienna, February 23rd and 24th, 2007* (Österreichische Akademie der Wissenschaften Philosophisch-Historische Klasse Denkschriften 384, Veröffentlichungen der Mykenischen Kommission 30): 117-132. Vienna: the Austrian Academy of Sciences.

Desborough, V.R.d'A. 1964. *The Last Mycenaeans and their Successors. An Archaeological Survey c. 1200–c. 1000 B.C.* Oxford: Clarendon Press.

Desborough, V.R.d'A. 1972. *The Greek Dark Ages*. London: Benn.

Desborough, V.R.d'A. 1973. Late burials from Mycenae. *The Annual of the British School at Athens* 68: 87-101.

Dickinson, O.T.P.K. 1992. Reflections on Bronze Age Laconia, in J.M. Sanders (ed.) *ΦΙΛΟΛΑΚΩΝ. Lakonian Studies in Honour of Hector Catling*: 109-114. London: the British School at Athens.

Eder, B. 1998. *Argolis, Lakonien, Messenien: vom Ende der Mykenischen Palastzeit bis zur Einwanderung der Dorier* (Österreichische Akademie der Wissenschaften, Philosophisch-Historische Klasse, Veröffentlichungen der Mykenischen Kommission 17). Vienna: the Austrian Academy of Sciences.

Eder, B. 2001. *Die Submykenischen und Protogeometrischen Gräber von Elis* (Βιβλιοθήκη της εν Αθήναις Αρχαιολογικής Εταιρείας 209). Athens: the Archaeological Society at Athens.

Eder, B. 2006. Die spätbronze- und früheisenzeitliche Kermik, in H. Kyrieleis (ed.) *Olympische Forschungen XXXI. Anfänge und Frühzeit des Heiligtums von Olympia:*

Die Ausgrabungen am Pelopion 1987-1996: 141-246. Berlin: Walter de Gruyter.

Eder, B. 2009. The Late Bronze Age/Early Iron Age transition in western Greece: Submycenaean studies, in S. Deger-Jalkotzy and A.E. Bächle (eds) *LH III C Chronology and Synchronisms III: LH III C Late and the Transition to the Early Iron Age. Proceedings of the International Workshop Held at the Austrian Academy of Sciences at Vienna, February 23rd and 24th, 2007* (Österreichische Akademie der Wissenschaften Philosophisch-Historische Klasse Denkschriften 384, Veröffentlichungen der Mykenischen Kommission 30): 133-149. Vienna: the Austrian Academy of Sciences.

Eder, B. and R. Jung. 2005. On the character of social relations between Greece and Italy in the 12th/11th C. BC, in R. Laffineur and E. Greco (eds) *Emporia: Aegeans in the Central and Eastern Mediterranean. Proceedings of the 10th International Aegean Conference/10e Rencontre égéenne internationale, Athens, Italian School of Archaeology, 14-18 April 2004* (Aegaeum 25): 485-495. Liège and Austin: University of Liège.

Efstathiou-Manolakou, I. 2009. Archaeological investigations in the caves of Laconia, in W.G. Cavanagh, C. Gallou and M. Georgiadis (eds) *Sparta and Laconia: from Prehistory to Pre-Modern. Proceedings of the Conference Held in Sparta, Organised by the British School at Athens, the University of Nottingham, the 5th Ephoreia of Prehistoric and Classical Antiquities and the 5th Ephoreia of Byzantine Antiquities 17-20 March 2005* (The British School at Athens Studies 16): 5-20. London: the British School at Athens.

Eles Masi, P. von 1986. *Le fibule dell'Italia settentrionale* (Prähistorische Bronzefunde XIV,5). Munich: C.H. Beck.

French, E. 2008. The Late Helladic small finds, in W.D. Taylour and R. Janko (eds) *Ayios Stephanos. Excavations at a Bronze Age and Medieval Settlement in Southern Laconia* (The British School at Athens Supplementary Volume 44): 445-470. London: the British School at Athens.

French, E. 2009. Mycenae: LH III C Late: what little there is, in S. Deger-Jalkotzy and A.E. Bächle (eds) *LH III C Chronology and Synchronisms III: LH III C Late and the Transition to the Early Iron Age. Proceedings of the International Workshop Held at the Austrian Academy of Sciences at Vienna, February 23rd and 24th, 2007* (Österreichische Akademie der Wissenschaften Philosophisch-Historische Klasse Denkschriften 384, Veröffentlichungen der Mykenischen Kommission 30): 151-161. Vienna: the Austrian Academy of Sciences.

Furumark, A. 1972. *Mycenaean Pottery. Volume 1: Analysis and Classification. Volume 2: Chronology*. Stockholm: the Swedish Institute at Athens.

Gallou, C. 2008. 'Between Scylla and Charybdis': the archaeology of Mycenaean Vatika on the Malea peninsula, in C. Gallou, M. Georgiadis and G. Muskett (eds) *Dioskouroi: Studies presented to W.G. Cavanagh and C.B. Mee On The Anniversary of Their 30-Year Joint Contribution to Aegean Archaeology* (British Archaeological Reports International Series 1889): 292-321. Oxford: Archaeopress.

Gallou, C. 2009. Epidaurus Limera: the tale of a Laconian site in Mycenaean times, in W.G. Cavanagh, C. Gallou and M. Georgiadis (eds) *Sparta and Laconia: from Prehistory to Pre-Modern. Proceedings of the Conference Held in Sparta, Organised by the British School at Athens, the University of Nottingham, the 5th Ephoreia of Prehistoric and Classical Antiquities and the 5th Ephoreia of Byzantine Antiquities 17–20 March 2005* (The British School at Athens Studies 16): 85-93. London: the British School at Athens.

Gallou, C. 2020. *Death in Mycenaean Lakonia: A Silent Place*. Oxford: Oxbow Books

Gallou, C. and J. Henderson 2012. Pavlopetri, an Early Bronze Age harbour town in south-east Laconia, in C. Mee and M. Prent (eds) Early Helladic Laconia. Proceedings of the Round Table Conference held 16 January 2010 at the Netherlands Institute at Athens. Pharos. *Journal of the Netherlands Institute at Athens* 18(1): 79-104.

Hallager, B.P. 2007. Problems with LM/LH III B/C synchronisms, in S. Deger-Jalkotzy and M. Zavadil (eds) *LH III C Chronology and Synchronisms II: LH III C Middle. Proceedings of the International Workshop Held at the Austrian Academy of Sciences at Vienna, October 29th and 30th, 2004* (Österreichische Akademie der Wissenschaften Philosophisch-Historische Klasse Denkschriften 362, Veröffentlichungen der Mykenischen Kommission 28): 189-202. Vienna: the Austrian Academy of Sciences.

Harding, A. 1970. Pavlopetri: a Mycenaean town underwater. *Archaeology* 23: 242-250.

Harding, A., G. Cadogan and R. Howell 1969. Pavlopetri: an underwater Bronze Age town in Laconia. *The Annual of the British School at Athens* 64: 113-142.

Haskell, H.W., R.E. Jones, P.M. Day and J.T. Killen 2011. *Transport Stirrup Jars of the Bronze Age Aegean and East Mediterranean* (Prehistory Monographs 33). Philadelphia: INSTAP Academic Press.

Henderson, J., C. Gallou, N. Flemming and E. Spondylis 2011. The Pavlopetri Underwater Archaeology Project: investigating an ancient submerged town, in J. Benjamin, C. Bonsall, C. Pickard and A. Fischer (eds) *Submerged Prehistory*: 207-218. Oxford: Oxbow Books.

Hood, S., G. Huxley, N. Sandars and A.E. Werner 1959. A Minoan cemetery on upper Gypsades (Knossos Survey 156). *The Annual of the British School at Athens* 53-54: 194-262.

Iacono, F. 2013. Westernizing Aegean of LH IIIC, in M.E. Alberti and S. Sabatini (eds) *Exchange Networks and Local Transformations: Interaction and local change in*

Europe and the Mediterranean from the Bronze Age to the Iron Age: 60-79. Oxford: Oxbow Books.

Iakovidis, S. 1969-1970. Περατή, το νεκροταφείον. Τρεις τόμοι: Α΄ Οι τάφοι και τα ευρήματα — Β΄ Γενικαί παρατηρήσεις — Γ΄ κατάλογοι, πίνακες (Βιβλιοθήκη Αρχαιολογικής Εταιρείας 67). Athens: the Archaeological Society at Athens.

Jones, R.E. and C. Mee. 1978. Spectrographic analyses of Mycenaean pottery from Ialysos on Rhodes: results and implications. *Journal of Field Archaeology* 5(4): 461-470.

Janko, R. 2008. Summary and historical conclusions, in W.D. Taylour and R. Janko (eds) *Ayios Stephanos. Excavations at a Bronze Age and Medieval Settlement in Southern Laconia* (The British School at Athens Supplementary Volume 44): 551-610. London: the British School at Athens.

Jung, R. 2006. Χρονολογία Comparata. *Vergleichende Chronologie von Südgriechenland und Süditalien von ca. 1700/1600 bis 1000 v.u.Z* (Veröffentlichungen der Mykenischen Kommission 26). Vienna: the Austrian Academy of Sciences.

Jung, R. and M. Mehofer 2013. Mycenaean Greece and Bronze Age Italy: cooperation, trade or war? *Archäologisches Korrespondenzblatt* 43(2): 175-193.

Kardamaki, E. 2017. The Late Helladic IIB to IIIA2 pottery sequence from the Mycenaean palace at Ayios Vasileios, Laconia. *Archaeologia Austriaca* 101: 73-142.

Kilian, K. 1985. Violinbogenfibeln und Blattbügelfibeln des griechischen Festlandes aus mykenischer Zeit. *Prähistorische Zeitschrift* 60: 145-203.

Kilian-Dirlmeier, I. 1984. *Nadeln der frühhelladischen bis archaischen Zeit von der Peloponnes* (Prähistorische Bronzefunde XIII,8). Munich: C.H. Beck.

Kountouri, E. 1996-1997. Ένα σύνολο Μυκηναϊκών αγγείων από την Επίδαυρο Λιμηρά Λακωνίας, in T. Gritsopoulos and C. Kotsonis (eds) Πρακτικά Ε΄ Διεθνούς Συνεδρίου Πελοποννησιακών Σπουδών, Αργος - Ναύπλιον, 6-10 Σεπτεμβρίου 1995. Τόμος Α΄: Ολομέλεια (Πελοποννησιακά – Παράρτημα 22): 491-513. Athens: the Society of Peloponnesian Studies.

Kraiker, W. and K. Kübler 1939. *Kerameikos: Ergebnisse der Ausgrabungen I. Die Nekropolen des 12. bis 10. Jahrhunderts*. Berlin: Walter de Gruyter.

Kübler, K. 1943. *Kerameikos: Ergebnisse der Ausgrabungen IV. Neufunde aus der Nekropole des 11. und 10. Jahrhunderts*. Berlin: Walter de Gruyter.

Knapp, A.B. and S. Demesticha 2017. *Mediterranean Connections. Maritime Transport Containers and Seaborne Trade in the Bronze and Early Iron Ages*. New York: Routledge.

Lazaridis, I., A. Mittnik, N. Patterson, S. Mallick, N. Rohland, S. Pfrengle, A. Fürtwangler, A. Peltzer, C. Posth, A. Vasilakis, P.J.P McGeorge, E. Konsolaki-Yannopoulou, G. Korres, H. Martlew, M. Michalodimitrakis, M. Özsait, N. Özsait, A. Papathanasiou, M. Richards, S.A. Roodenberg,

Y. Tzedakis, R. Arnott, D.M. Fernandes, J.R. Hughey, D.M. Lotakis, P.A. Navas, Y. Maniatis, J.A. Stamatoyannopoulos, K. Stewardson, P. Stockhammer, R. Pinhasi, D. Reich, J. Krause and G. Stamatoyannopoulos 2017. Genetic origins of the Minoans and Mycenaeans. *Nature* 548: 214-218.

Lemos, I.S. 2002. *The Protogeometric Aegean: the Archaeology of the Late Eleventh and Tenth Centuries BC* (Oxford Monographs on Classical Archaeology). Oxford: Oxford University Press.

Lolos, Y.G. 1999. The cargo of pottery from the Point Iria Wreck: character and implications, in W. Phelps, Y. Lolos and Y. Vichos (eds) *The Point Iria Wreck: Interconnections in the Mediterranean, ca. 1200 BC: Proceedings of the International Conference, Island of Spetses, 19 September 1998*: 43-58. Athens: the Hellenic Institute of Marine Archaeology.

Maltezou, A. 2016. Περιοχή Καραβά. *Αρχαιολογικόν Δελτίον* 66(2011)(Chr. Β΄1): 196–199.

Maran, J. 2006. Coming to terms with the past: ideology and power in Late Helladic IIIC, in S. Deger-Jalkotzy and I.S. Lemos (eds) *Ancient Greece: From the Mycenaean Palaces to the Age of Homer* (Edinburgh Leventis Studies 3): 123-150. Edinburgh: Edinburgh University Press.

Maran, J. and P.W. Stockhammer (eds) 2012. *Materiality and Social Practice: Transformative Capacities of Intercultural Encounters*. Oxford: Oxbow Books.

Mee, C. 1982. *Rhodes in the Bronze Age: An Archaeological Survey*. Warminster: Aris and Phillips.

Mee, C. and G. Taylor 1997. Prehistoric Methana, in C. Mee and H. Forbes (eds) *A Rough and Rocky Place: the Landscape and Settlement History of the Methana Peninsula, Greece. Results of the Methana Survey Project sponsored by the British School at Athens and the University of Liverpool* (Liverpool Monographs in Archaeology and Oriental Studies): 42-56. Liverpool: Liverpool University Press.

Morgan, C. 2011. Kythera Island Project – 2010. *Archaeology In Greece Online*, Report 1946, viewed 11 May 2018, < https://chronique.efa.gr/?kroute=report&id=1946>.

Mountjoy, P.A. 1999. *Regional Mycenaean Decorated Pottery*. Rahden: Marie Leidorf.

Mountjoy, P.A. 2007. A definition of LH III C Middle, in S. Deger-Jalkotzy and M. Zavadil (eds) *LH III C Chronology and Synchronisms II: LH III C Middle. Proceedings of the International Workshop Held at the Austrian Academy of Sciences at Vienna, October 29th and 30th, 2004* (Österreichische Akademie der Wissenschaften Philosophisch-Historische Klasse Denkschriften 362, Veröffentlichungen der Mykenischen Kommission 28): 221-242. Vienna: the Austrian Academy of Sciences.

Mountjoy, P.A. 2008. The Late Helladic pottery, in W.D. Taylour and R. Janko (eds) *Ayios Stephanos. Excavations at a Bronze Age and Medieval Settlement in Southern Laconia* (The British School at Athens Supplementary Volume 44): 299-387. London: the British School at Athens.

Mountjoy, P.A. 2009. LH III C Late: an east Mainland - Aegean koine, in S. Deger-Jalkotzy and A.E. Bächle (eds) *LH III C Chronology and Synchronisms III: LH III C Late and the Transition to the Early Iron Age. Proceedings of the International Workshop Held at the Austrian Academy of Sciences at Vienna, February 23rd and 24th, 2007* (Österreichische Akademie der Wissenschaften Philosophisch-Historische Klasse Denkschriften 384, Veröffentlichungen der Mykenischen Kommission 30): 289-312. Vienna: the Austrian Academy of Sciences.

Negris, Ph. 1904. Vestiges antiques submergés. *Mitteilungen des Deutschen Archäologischen Instituts, Athenische Abteilung* 29: 340-363.

Palaiologou, H. 2013. Late Helladic IIIC cremation burials at Chania of Mycenae, in M. Lochner and F. Ruppenstein (eds) *Brandbestattungen von der mittleren Donau bis zur Ägäis zwischen 1300 und 750 v. Chr: Akten des internationalen Symposiums an der Österreichischen Akademie der Wissenschaften in Wien, 11-12 Februar 2010* (Österreichische Akademie der Wissenschaften Denkschriften der philosophisch-historischen Klasse 448; Mitteilungen der Prähistorischen Kommission 77; Veröffentlichungen der Mykenischen Kommission 32): 249-279. Vienna: the Austrian Academy of Sciences.

Pantelidou, M. 1975. Αι προϊστορικαί Αθήναι. Unpublished PhD dissertation, University of Athens.

Papadopoulos, J.K. 2014. Greece in the Early Iron Age: mobility, commodities, polities, and literacy, in B.A. Knapp and P. van Dommeln (eds) *The Cambridge Prehistory of the Bronze and Iron Age Mediterranean*: 178-195. Cambridge: Cambridge University Press.

Papadopoulos, J.K., B.N. Damiata and J.M. Marston 2011. Once more with feeling: Jeremy Rutter's plea for the abandonment of the term Submycenaean revisited, in W. Gauss, M. Lindblom, R.A.K. Smith and J. Wright (eds) *Our Cups are Full: Pottery and Society in the Aegean Bronze Age. Papers Presented to Jeremy B. Rutter on the Occasion of his 65th Birthday* (British Archaeological Reports International Series 2227): 187-202. Oxford: Archaeopress.

Papadopoulos, J.K. 2017a. Introduction, in J.K. Papadopoulos and E.L. Smithson 2017. *The Athenian Agora XXXVI. The Early Iron Age: the Cemeteries*: 1-34. Princeton: the American School of Classical Studies at Athens.

Papadopoulos, J.K. 2017b. Small finds other than pottery, in J.K. Papadopoulos. and E.L. Smithson 2017. *The Athenian Agora XXXVI. The Early Iron Age: the Cemeteries*: 899-971. Princeton: the American School of Classical Studies at Athens.

Papadopoulos, J.K. and S. Strack 2017. Pottery, in Papadopoulos, J.K. and E.L. Smithson 2017. *The*

Athenian Agora XXXVI. The Early Iron Age: the Cemeteries: 689-897. Princeton: the American School of Classical Studies at Athens.

Papadopoulos, J.K. and E.L. Smithson 2017a. *The Athenian Agora XXXVI. The Early Iron Age: the Cemeteries*. Princeton: the American School of Classical Studies at Athens.

Papadopoulos, J.K. and E.L. Smithson 2017b. Four cemeteries. A catalogue of tombs and their contents, in J.K. Papadopoulos and E.L. Smithson 2017. *The Athenian Agora XXXVI. The Early Iron Age: the Cemeteries*: 35-502. Princeton: the American School of Classical Studies at Athens.

Papadopoulos, T.I. and E. Papadopoulou-Chrysikopoulou 2017. *Excavations at the Mycenaean Cemetery at Aigion - 1967: Rescue Excavations by the Late Ephor of Antiquities, E. Mastrokostas*. Oxford: Archaeopress.

Petropoulos, M. 2007. A Mycenaean cemetery at Nikoleika near Aigon of Achaia, in S. Deger-Jalkotzy and M. Zavadil (eds) *LH III C Chronology and Synchronisms II: LH III C Middle. Proceedings of the International Workshop Held at the Austrian Academy of Sciences at Vienna, October 29th and 30th, 2004* (Österreichische Akademie der Wissenschaften Philosophisch-Historische Klasse Denkschriften 362, Veröffentlichungen der Mykenischen Kommission 28): 253-286. Vienna: the Austrian Academy of Sciences.

Phelps, W., Y. Lolos and Y. Vichos (eds) 1999. *The Point Iria Wreck: Interconnections in the Mediterranean, ca. 1200 BC: Proceedings of the International Conference, Island of Spetses, 19 September 1998*. Athens: the Hellenic Institute of Marine Archaeology.

Pikoulas, Y.A. 2012. *Το οδικό δίκτυο της Λακωνικής*. Athens: Horos.

Piteros, C. 2001. Ταφές και τεφροδόχα αγγεία τύμβου της ΥΕ ΙΙΙΓ στο Άργος, in N. Stampolidis (ed.) *Καύσεις στην Εποχή του Χαλκού και την Πρώιμη Εποχή Του Σιδήρου. Πρακτικά του συμποσίου, Ρόδος, 29 Απριλίου-2 Μαΐου 1999*: 99-120. Athens: the University of Crete.

Piteros, C. 2009. Αρχαία (παλαιό) επίδαυρος - Αγωγός Αποχέτευσης. *Αρχαιολογικόν Δελτίον* 55(2000)(Chr. Β΄1): 185-189.

Popham, M., E. Schofield and S. Sherratt 2006. 'Pots through the ages': vase shapes and their changes during the LH IIIC period, in D. Evely (ed.) *Lefkandi IV. The Bronze Age: the Late Helladic IIIC Settlement at Xeropolis* (The British School at Athens Supplementary Volume 39): 180-231. London: the British School at Athens.

Pullen, D.J. 2015. How to build a Mycenaean town: the architecture of Kalamianos, in A-L. Schallin and I. Tournavitou (eds) *Mycenaeans up to Date: the Archaeology of the Northeastern Peloponnese - Current Concepts and New Directions* (Skrifter utgivna av Svenska Intitutet i Athen, 4°, 56): 377-390. Stockholm: the Swedish Institute at Athens.

Ruppenstein, F. 2007. *Kerameikos: Ergebnisse der Ausgrabungen XVIII. Die Submykenische Nekropole: Neufunde und Neubewertung*. Munich: Hirmer.

Ruppenstein, F. 2009. The Transitional Phase from Submycenaean to Protogeometric: Definition and Comparative Chronology, in S. Deger-Jalkotzy and A.E. Bächle (eds) *LH III C Chronology and Synchronisms III: LH III C Late and the Transition to the Early Iron Age. Proceedings of the International Workshop Held at the Austrian Academy of Sciences at Vienna, February 23rd and 24th, 2007* (Österreichische Akademie der Wissenschaften Philosophisch-Historische Klasse Denkschriften 384, Veröffentlichungen der Mykenischen Kommission 30): 327-343. Vienna: the Austrian Academy of Sciences.

Seiradaki, M. 1960. Pottery from Karphi. *The Annual of the British School at Athens* 55: 1-37.

Sherratt, S. 2003. The Mediterranean economy: 'globalization' at the end of the second millennium B.C.E., in W.G. Dever and S. Gitin (eds) *Symbiosis, Symbolism and the Power of the Past: Canaan, Ancient Israel and Their Neighbors from the Late Bronze Age through Roman Palaestina. Proceedings of the Centennial Symposium, W.F. Albright Institute of Archaeological Research and American Schools of Oriental Research, Jerusalem, May 29-31, 2000*: 37-62. Winona Lake: Eisenbrauns.

Sherratt, S. 2012. The intercultural transformative capacities of irregularly appropriated goods, in J. Maran and P.W. Stockhammer (eds) *Materiality and Social Practice: Transformative Capacities of Intercultural Encounters*: 152-172. Oxford: Oxbow Books.

Steinhauer, G. 1979. Συκέα: ανασκαφή μυκηναϊκού τάφου. *Αρχαιολογικόν Δελτίον* 29(Chr. Β΄2): 294-295.

Spondylis, E., D. Koutsoumba and J. Henderson 2012. Παυλοπέτρι Λακωνίας. Ερευνητικό διάστημα 2009-2011. Lecture delivered to the international conference 'Το Αρχαιολογικό Έργο στην Πελοπόννησο', Tripoli 7-11 November 2012.

Spyropoulos, T. 2013. *Λακεδαίμων: '...ή τότε ποτέ ούσα ύφ'ήλίω νήσος ιερά...' (Πλάτωνος Κριτίας 115Β)*. Athens: Kardamitsas.

Taylour, W.D. 1972. Excavations at Ayios Stephanos. *The Annual of the British School at Athens* 67: 205-270.

Taylour, W.D. and R. Janko 2008a. The Bronze Age architecture and stratigraphy, in W.D. Taylour and R. Janko (eds) *Ayios Stephanos. Excavations at a Bronze Age and Medieval Settlement in Southern Laconia* (The British School at Athens Supplementary Volume 44): 13-119. London: the British School at Athens.

Themos, A. 2002. Οδός Γιτιάδα (Ο.Τ.97, οικόπεδο Π. Ντάρμου). *Αρχαιολογικόν Δελτίον* 52(1997) (Chr. Β΄1): 167-169.

Themos, A. 2007. Αναζητώντας το αρχαίο Έλος, in T. Gritsopoulos, K.L. Kotsonis and I.K. Giannaropoulou (eds) *Πρακτικά του Ζ΄ Διεθνούς Συνεδρίου Πελοποννησιακών Σπουδών, Πύργος, Γαστούνη, Αμαλιάδα, 11-17 Σεπτεμβρίου 2005. Τόμος Β΄: Αρχαιότης*

(Πελοποννησιακά Παράρτημα 27): 452-480. Athens: the Society of Peloponnesian Studies.

Toffolo, M.B., A. Fantalkin, I.S. Lemos, R.C.S. Felsch, W.-D. Niemeier, G.D.R. Sanders, I. Finkelstein and E. Boaretto 2013. Towards an absolute chronology for the Aegean Iron Age: new radiocarbon dates from Lefkandi, Kalapodi and Corinth. *PLoS ONE* 8(12): e83117.

Vanderpool, E. 1955. News letter from Greece. *American Journal of Archaeology* 59(3): 223-229.

Vasilogamvrou, A. 2013. Ανασκαφή στον Αγ. Βασίλειο Λακωνίας. *Πρακτικά της εν Αθήναις Αρχαιολογικής Εταιρείας* 165(2010): 65-80.

Vasilogamvrou, A. 2014. Ανασκαφή στον Αγ. Βασίλειο Λακωνίας. *Πρακτικά της εν Αθήναις Αρχαιολογικής Εταιρείας* 166(2011): 59-68.

Vasilogamvrou, A. 2015a. Ανασκαφή στον Αγ. Βασίλειο Λακωνίας. *Πρακτικά της εν Αθήναις Αρχαιολογικής Εταιρείας* 167(2012): 63-76.

Vasilogamvrou, A. 2015b. Ανασκαφή στον Αγ. Βασίλειο Λακωνίας. *Πρακτικά της εν Αθήναις Αρχαιολογικής Εταιρείας* 168(2013): 97-116.

Vitale, S. 2011. The Late Helladic IIIA2 pottery from Mitrou and its implications for the chronology of the Mycenaean mainland, in W. Gauss, M. Lindblom, R.A.K. Smith and J. Wright (eds) *Our Cups are Full: Pottery and Society in the Aegean Bronze Age. Papers Presented to Jeremy B. Rutter on the Occasion of his 65th Birthday* (British Archaeological Reports International Series 2227): 331-344. Oxford: Archaeopress.

Vlachopoulos, G. 2006. *Η Υστεροελλαδική Περίοδος στη Νάξο: τα ταφικά σύνολα και οι συσχετισμοί τους με το Αιγαίο Τόμος I. Τα Υστεροελλαδική IIIΓ ταφικά σύνολα της Νάξος* (Αρχαιογνωσία 4). Athens: the University of Athens.

Vlachopoulos, G. 2012. *Η Υστεροελλαδική IIIΓ Περίοδος στη Νάξο: τα ταφικά σύνολα και οι συσχετισμοί τους*

με το Αιγαίο Τόμος II. Νάξος και ο μυκηναϊκός κόσμος της μετανακτορικής περιόδου (Αρχαιογνωσία 10). Athens: the University of Athens.

Wachsmann, S. 1998. *Seagoing Ships and Seamanship in the Bronze Age Levant.* London: Chatham.

Wardle, K., T. Higham and B. Kromer 2014. Dating the end of the Greek Bronze Age: a robust radiocarbon-based chronology from Assiros Toumba. *PLoS ONE* 9(9): e106672.

Zangger, E. 2008. The port of Nestor, in J. Davis (ed.) *Sandy Pylos: An Archaeological History from Nestor to Navarino* (second, revised edition): 69-74. Princeton: the American School of Classical Studies at Athens.

Zavvou, E. 2002. Η περιοχή των αρχαιών Βοιών: τα πρώτα αποτελέσματα της έρευνας. *Λακωνικαί Σπουδαί* 16: 209–227.

Zavvou, E. 2007. Νέα στοιχεία για τις Λακωνικές πόλεις της δυτικής ακτής της χερσονήσου του Μαλέα, in T. Gritsopoulos, K.L. Kotsonis and I.K. Giannaropoulou (eds) *Πρακτικά του Ζ΄ Διεθνούς Συνεδρίου Πελοποννησιακών Σπουδών, Πύργος, Γαστούνη, Αμαλιάδα, 11-17 Σεπτεμβρίου 2005. Τόμος Β΄: Ἀρχαιότης* (Πελοποννησιακά Παράρτημα 27): 413-451. Athens: the Society of Peloponnesian Studies.

Zavvou, E. 2012a. Early Helladic Laconia after the time of H. Waterhouse and R. Hope Simpson, in C. Mee and M. Prent (eds) Early Helladic Laconia. Proceedings of the Round Table Conference held 16 January 2010 at the Netherlands Institute at Athens. Pharos. *Journal of the Netherlands Institute at Athens* 18(1):: 1-37.

Zavvou, E. 2012b. Η Χερσόνησος του Μαλέα, in A. Vlachopoulos (ed.) *Αρχαιολογία-Πελοπόννησος*: 556-563. Athens: Melissa Books.

Similarities and Differences between Korakou and Kolonna in the Early and Middle Bronze Ages[1]

Walter Gauss

The pioneering excavations of Carl Blegen at Korakou (1921) produced important evidence for the material culture of prehistoric Greece.[2] Likewise, the significance of Kolonna has been recognised since the late 19th century AD, even though only very little of the site had then been excavated.[3] Excavation and research since Blegen's time has demonstrated the importance of both sites to our understanding of the prehistory of the central Aegean.[4] As a first account of my own long-term interest and research, this paper offers a comparison of the two sites, and a discussion of their similarities and differences, particularly during the Early Helladic (EH) III period and the transition to the Middle Helladic (MH), when Kolonna developed into a principal hub for the central Aegean area (Gauss 2010; Klebinder-Gauss and Gauss 2015; Walter and Felten 1981). The first part of this contribution offers some general observations on both sites; the second, a comparative analysis of selected contexts at each; and the third part, a consideration of imports at Korakou from the perspective of Kolonna.

Both Korakou and Kolonna are coastal sites (Figure 8.1), situated in optimal, naturally protected, strategic locations. Positioned at the eastern end of the Corinthian Gulf, Korakou enjoys wide views over the gulf itself, as well as over large parts of the Corinthian hinterland. The island of Aegina is situated in a very happy geographic position at the centre of the Saronic Gulf, framed by the Peloponnesian and Attic coastlines and with the Cyclades to the south;[5] from its western coast, Kolonna looks towards the eastern Peloponnese and the Isthmus of Corinth. Korakou and Kolonna are, thus, harbour sites, although in neither case have their prehistoric ports been explored; from the late 19th century AD, it was assumed that Corinth (Korakou being then unknown) was the harbour site for Mycenae (Furtwängler and Loeschcke 1886: xiii). Notwithstanding Kolonna's importance as a maritime hub, research into the prehistoric harbour of the site has been largely neglected since Paul Knoblauch's studies of the 1960s and 1970s (Gerding 2013; Knoblauch 1969; 1973; Triantafillidis and Koutsoumba 2017; Triantafillidis and Tselentis 2015). Anchorages were probably available both north and south of the settlement at Kolonna;[6] mirroring the double configuration known from other sites of prehistoric and historic date, such as at Mikre Vigla on Naxos (Barber and Hadjianastasiou 1989: 139). To the south of Kolonna are located the Archaic seaward fortifications and ship-sheds (see, most recently, Gerding 2013). To the north, a mole or breakwater, now submerged, extends some 300m into the sea (Knoblauch 1969; 1973: 59-63). Its construction date is not clear and the assumption of a prehistoric, and specifically an MH, origin, though in my view both likely and very attractive, must be confirmed by future research.[7] If verified, this structure would have allowed safe anchorage immediately north of the Kolonna settlement, and would resolve the question of the prehistoric harbour's location. Its construction of large, undressed blocks does not exclude a prehistoric date, nor does the recognition that the sea level would need to have been at least 3.8m below its current depth for a prehistoric mole-breakwater to fulfil its function.[8]

---

[1] I am very grateful to the editors of this volume in honour of Chris Mee for their invitation to contribute a paper on Kolonna on Aegina, as well as for their patience and for their very thoughtful editing of the manuscript. First thoughts on the similarities and differences between Kolonna on Aegina and Korakou were presented at the conference 'Centennial Celebration of C.W. Blegen's 1915-1916 Excavations' at the American School of Classical Studies at Athens (ASCSA) on 3-5 September 2015. I would like to thank the antiquities service at Corinth and Corinth excavations, especially Ioulia Tzonou-Herbst and Guy Sanders, then director of the Corinth excavations, for making an inspection of the rich Early Helladic (EH) and Middle Helladic (MH) finds from Korakou possible, as well as for their hospitality and help. Photographs of the pottery from Korakou were taken by Petros Dellatolas and I owe many thanks again to the Corinth excavations for the possibility to publish the illustrations.
[2] Several additional publications by Carl Blegen and Alan Wace utilise evidence from Korakou. On the Late Helladic (LH) period at Korakou, see Davis (1979), Dickinson (1972) and Rutter (1974).
[3] For the history of excavation at Kolonna, see Gauss (2010). Excavation and study since the late 1960s has resulted in the publication of a number of monographs on various aspects of the prehistoric site (see, for example, Gauss and Kiriatzi 2011; Hiller 1975; Kilian-Dirlmeier 1997; Reinholdt 2008; Siedentopf 1991; Walter and Felten 1981).
[4] On Korakou, see particularly, Rutter (2003). Several studies, in addition to those listed in footnote 3, make clear the importance of Kolonna. These include Gauss (2010), Rutter (1993b: 776) and Maran (1992a: 324-328). On the identification of Aeginetan pottery at the site of Kiaphi Thiti in Attica, see Maran (1992b: 179-199) and for discussion of Aeginetan potting traditions, see Lindblom (2001: 22-44).

---

[5] On the geographical setting of Kolonna, see also Klebinder-Gauss and Gauss (2015).
[6] However, Knoblauch (1973: 81) rejects the possibility of a double harbour in the prehistoric period.
[7] See also, Knoblauch (1973: 85): 'Es bleibt die Frage noch zu beantworten, wann der große Wellenbrecher in der Nordbucht gebaut wurde. Es ist sicher, dass die Berechnungen mit Hilfe der linearen Strandverschiebung nicht realistisch ist (s. o. S. 83). Andererseits steht aber fest, dass der Wellenbrecher in der Nordbucht viel früher als die anderen Anlagen gebaut wurde.'
[8] 'Brauchbar wäre diese enorme Anlage also erst, wenn der

Figure 8.1. Aerial views of Korakou and Kolonna. Aerial views of Korakou and Kolonna.
Top: © American School of Classical Studies at Athens [hereafter ASCSA], Corinth Excavations, photo: J. Herbst;
bottom: © Salzburg University, Department Altertumswissenschaften/Klassische und Frühagaische Archäologie in
cooperation with IFFB Geoinformatik – Z_GIS der Universitat Salzburg

Both Korakou and Kolonna are medium sized sites. According to Blegen (1921: 1), the oval-shaped mound of Korakou measures c. 260m by 115m, covering an area of some 2.3ha. Kolonna occupies a roughly triangular-shaped peninsular of c. 3.5ha and is thus probably one-and-a-half times the size of Korakou. Both sites are characterised by a long history of superimposed occupation, with deposits ranging in depth between four and five metres. However, differences between Korakou and Kolonna in the extent and duration of their exploration, excavation methods, sampling strategies and classification systems, present problems when attempting to draw comparisons. Korakou was excavated by Carl Blegen and his team in only two seasons (1915 and 1916), with no further excavation carried out since then (Blegen 1921; Tzonou-Herbst 2010; 2013). Kolonna, alternatively, has a long history of excavation, beginning with the pioneering work of Valerios Stais and Adolf Furtwängler in the late 19th and early 20th centuries AD (Stais 1895a; 1895b),[9] and several excavation teams have since focused in part, or exclusively, on its prehistoric remains (see Gauss 2010; Gauss and Kiriatzi 2011: 20-21; Gauss and Klebinder-Gauss 2017). The size of the areas excavated at each site are also quite different. At Korakou, excavation extended across an area of c. 0.16ha (Blegen 1921: 1; Forsén 1992: 77) and yielded mostly LH remains; while excavation at Kolonna has subsumed an area almost seven times larger (c. 1.1ha), a large part of which consists of EH and MH architecture.

In terms of stratification, Blegen noted at Korakou, 11 successive levels of habitation in three main chronological groups: six levels attributed to the EH period, three to the MH period, and two to the LH period (Blegen 1921: 2-3; Forsén 1992: 77). To date, ten architectural phases have been distinguished at Kolonna

up to the beginning of the LH period, and several more LH (Mycenaean) phases of habitation must be assumed, but lack detailed recording and stratification. The earliest of these phases belongs to the Neolithic, four are EH and five are MH (Gauss 2010; Walter and Felten 1981). The MH phases, particularly, are characterised, principally, by successive building operations which modified the plan of the EH fortification walls. It is likely that Korakou also had one or more fortification walls, presumably of EH II (Tzonou-Herbst 2015; Tzonou-Herbst and Boyd 2015) and LH date (Rutter 1974: 414-420 and figs. 168-170.1; 2003: 80), but their existence and chronology must be verified by further research and, eventually, by excavation. Confirmation of the fortification wall and its date would certainly change the status of Korakou 'from an unprepossessing seaside town to a fortified port' (Rutter 2003: 80).

Regarding architectural remains, two successive EH II corridor houses and the remains of a further tiled building have been identified at Kolonna. No corridor house has yet been identified at Korakou. However, in trench P (level X), a fragment of an EH II roof tile was identified that can, perhaps, be taken as a further indication of the presence of an important EH II structure (see also, Blegen 1921: 175). The presence of a tiled EH II structure at Korakou would not be surprising should the site prove to have been fortified during the same period.[10]

The situation at Kolonna after the end of EH II is not clear, and the first EH III settlement phase, Kolonna IV, was evidently of limited extent.[11] According to the relatively few ceramic finds associated with this settlement, it should date to an early stage of EH III (Gauss and Smetana 2007b: 452; Walter and Felten 1981: 105-107). At a more advanced stage of EH III, a well-planned, fortified settlement was built above it. This settlement, Kolonna V, was destroyed in a massive fire. The floors of this destroyed settlement yielded some 120 complete, or almost complete, vessels (Gauss and Smetana 2003: 474-478; 2007b: 452; Walter and Felten 1981: 28-42, 108-117). The burnt remains of annual plants provide secure 14C evidence for a destruction date in the 22nd century BC (Wild et al. 2010: 1020, table 3).[12]

Wasserspiegel zwischen 3,55m und 4,05m - also mindestens 3,80m - tiefer läge als heute. Die Steinansammlungen westlich vor dem Kolonna-Hügel (Abb. 5) würden in diesem Fall ebenso aus dem Wasser ragen, wie alle von Ph. Négris angegebenen Felsriffe (Abb. 7)' (Knoblauch 1973: 60-61; also, Knoblauch 1969). On sea level change, see Knoblauch (1973: 54-55); Lambeck (1996); Poulos et al. (2009) and Triantafillidis and Koutsoumba (2017). For the Attico-Cycladic massif, Poulos and colleagues propose a steady-rate annual rise in central Aegean sea level of c. 0.9mm over the past 5000 years. This suggests an EH sea level some 4.5-5m lower than present (see Poulos et al. 2009: 13, table 1, 14). Based on this analysis, Triantafillidis and Koutsoumba (2017: 166) have also proposed a probable decennial rise of 1cm for the seas around Aegina since 3000 BC. It is worth noting that the submerged EH site of Lambayanna in the Bay of Kiladha (Beck and Koutsoumba 2017; Beck, Emery, and Koutsoumba, this volume) is today located at a depth of c. 1-3m, and the Bronze Age settlement of Pavlopetri in Laconia at a depth of c. 2-3m (Gallou and Henderson 2012; Harding et al. 1969; Henderson et al. 2011). Generalisation regarding sea level change, however, is difficult, if not impossible, given that the highly tectonic nature of the geology of Southern Greece means that any measurement of sea level change is strictly localised. Data drawn from the Attico-Cycladic massif may not, therefore, be readily transferrable to Laconia, or to the Corinthia (thanks to J.B. Rutter for his comments on this subject).

[9] For an overview and history of research, see also Gauss and Kiriatzi (2011).

---

[10] On the contrary, it would be surprising, if Korakou was fortified in EH II without a 'corridor house' or similar important structure. The close proximity of Korakou to other EH II sites, such as Corinth and Cheliotomylos, opens up further questions of their relationship with each other (for Corinth and Cheliotomylos, see Lavezzi 2003). A range of EH 'special finds' are known from Corinth and Korakou and have been discussed by Rahmstorf (for incised bone tubes, see 2006: 85, appendix 3, no. 4; for roller stamps, see 2006: 86, appendix 4, no. 1; for weights, see 2006: 87, appendix 5, nos. 15-16).

[11] The most important structure is the metallurgical installation built in the ruins of the former corridor house, for which, see Walter and Felten (1981: 23-28).

[12] The modelled calibrated date of the transition between ceramic Phase E (= Kolonna V destruction) and the succeeding ceramic Phase

At Korakou, the circumstances of the transition between EH II and EH III are unknown. Interestingly, Blegen notes traces of a site-wide destruction, presumably by fire, at the end of the EH period, but attributes no architectural remains or substantial floor deposits with certainty to it.[13] Given that no burnt botanical remains appear to have survived for 14C analysis, the absolute date of the destruction is similarly unclear. This absence of (published) information has led to discussion of whether the destruction should be ascribed to EH II or EH III (see Forsén 1992: 77-78, with further references; also, Weiberg and Lindblom 2014: 394 n.43). At Kolonna, the MH settlements basically follow the same layout as in EH III (Felten and Hiller 1996). The settlement is densely packed and houses share party walls. There is no evidence for apsidal structures with two exceptions, and these are not free-standing (Felten and Hiller 2004a: 1092). The site is characterised by the repeated strengthening of the fortification wall, the construction in the more advanced MH of a fortified extension to the settlement, and the construction of a monumental building at the centre of the settlement, the so-called Large Building Complex. At Korakou, relatively little is known about the layout of the settlement. Freestanding rectangular and apsidal buildings exhibit a different spatial organisation to that seen at Kolonna. The limited areas excavated reveal a densely packed settlement, although, to date, the site has yielded no signs of either monumental buildings or a fortification wall.

Local pottery production represents a major point of differentiation between the two sites. During the MH period, Aeginetan ceramics (including tableware, kitchenware and courseware) are likely distributed via Kolonna to sites throughout much of the central Greek mainland and the Peloponnese, and particularly to those around the Saronic Gulf (Gauss and Kiriatzi 2011: 242-243; Rutter 1993b: 777 fig. 12). To date, no pottery kilns or kiln wasters have been found that would indicate the existence of a prehistoric pottery workshop at Korakou. However, Instrumental Neutron Activation Analysis (INAA) and petrographic study has identified the Argolid and/or the northeastern Peloponnese as possible centres of Bronze Age pottery production (Attas 1982; Attas *et al.* 1987).

Blegen recovered some 100,000 sherds at Korakou (Blegen 1921: 4), of which the most numerous are Mycenaean (LH), with fewer EH and MH due to the limited extent of excavation. Indeed, the complete EH to LH stratigraphic sequence was identified only in a

single small pit, E.A, in the East Alley. The statistical tables compiled by Blegen offer a view of the quantities and proportions found therein (Blegen 1921: 127, table 1); for the sake of convenience, these have been recalculated as absolute numbers (Table 8.1): of a total yield of *c.* 7000 sherds, only *c.* 110 are of clear EH date and *c.* 1500 are clearly MH. Despite the limited extent of excavation, *c.* 50 complete, or almost complete, vessels of EH III and MH date were either published in the 1921 report or mentioned in later studies.[14]

At Kolonna, unfortunately, no comparable estimates of sherd numbers exist, but it is possible to extrapolate an approximate minimum total yield of several hundred thousand fragments based on sherd counts from recent excavation work, which was itself confined to a relatively small area of the site. So far, some 500 complete, or almost complete, vessels can be assigned to the EH III and MH periods.

The next part of this contribution will present discussion of selected deposits from Korakou side-by-side with the stratigraphic sequence at Kolonna. The best starting point for such a discussion at Korakou is the aforementioned Pit E.A. Here, Blegen uncovered an EH-LH sequence down to bedrock, although it remains to be established how continuous and complete this sequence was.[15] The pit was excavated in 19 arbitrary layers, designated levels I to XIX (Figure 8.2). The drawing of the pit's western section (Blegen 1921: 128, fig. 124) illustrates four distinct floor layers, of which two were attributed to House L and cleared as level II, and the remainder, lower down in the sequence, were cleared as levels IV and VIII. The fill underneath the lowest of these floors, which comprised levels IX and X, was used by Oliver Dickinson for his seminal definition of LH IIA and IIB (Dickinson 1972). The base of level X marks the beginning of a roughly horizontal layer of ash and debris of uneven thickness that was dug as levels XI and XII. Finally, another sloping layer of ash, again of varying thickness, was cleared as layers XIII to XVII. The finds from levels XII to XVI, basically sandwiched between the two ash layers, were characterised by Jack Davis as a homogenous deposit, and used in his important contribution defining LH I (Davis 1979: 236).[16] Levels XVII to XIX were not discussed in detail by Davis, who nevertheless noted EH and early MH material in levels XVII and XVIII (Davis 1979: 236). The deepest level, XIX, produced 80 sherds now known, mostly of

---

F (settlement phase Kolonna VI) is 2196 to 2111 BC (with 95.4% probability). Regarding the duration of the EH III period, see also Manning (1995: 151-153, 235 fig. 2).

[13] 'The last settlement of the first stratum (period) thus apparently came to an abrupt end in a general conflagration' (Blegen 1921: 2); '[...] the period ended at Korakou with the total destruction of the settlement' (Blegen 1921: 124).

[14] In total, more than 150 vessels of all prehistoric phases were mended (Blegen 1921: 4).

[15] The same question can be asked of Trench P. I am very thankful to J.B. Rutter, for his thoughts on the completeness of the stratigraphic sequence.

[16] Davis notes that level XII contained a few intrusive LH II sherds, and that level XVI was mixed with EH and early MH finds characteristic of the lower levels, XVII and XVIII. A mixing of strata/finds may also have occurred in levels XIV and XV, at least as far as it is possible to discern from the illustrated section of the stratigraphic sequence.

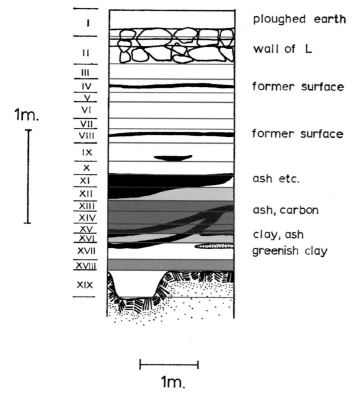

and cooking ware vessels (Figure 8.4.3-4),[24] and Pattern Painted sand-tempered fragments (Figure 8.4.5).[25] Wheelmade Grey Minyan pottery, including carinated fragments, were also represented, as were handmade imitations of true Grey Minyan. The Bichrome-painted krater rim should date to LH I, although other features are typical of an advanced MH date. The following level, XVII, contained some 560 fragments. Within this assemblage, a fragment belonging to the rim of a bridge-spouted jar is noteworthy (Figure 8.5.1)[26] as is as a Pattern Painted rim fragment of EH III date (Figure 8.5.2).[27] Regarding the chronology, most characteristic are a number of Aeginetan Bichrome-painted sherds (Figure 8.5.3-7)[28], several fragments of mainland Polychrome pottery (Figure 8.5.8-9)[29] and some red Solidly Painted open shapes (Figure 8.5.10-11).[30] Summarising the re-evaluated finds from levels XIX to XVII, one may conclude that there is clear evidence for EH II in level XIX, in addition to very few diagnostic EH III pieces. The presence in these levels of pottery of advanced MH and LH I date raises the possibility of contamination.

Figure 8.2. Stratigraphic section through the East Alley at Korakou (after Davis 1979, p. 237, fig. 2, based on C. Blegen, Corinth Notebook 85, p. 54; references according to information by S. Figueira and J. Sacher 13.7.2018).

EH II date. However, apart from three complete EH II profiles, of which two bore potmarks, there was at least one sand-tempered fragment (Figure 8.3.1),[17] a Matt-painted body sherd of possible of Aeginetan origin (Figure 8.3.3),[18] and two rim fragments of small open vessels in Grey Minyan and Yellow Minyan fabric, both with distinctive hollows on the interior of the rim (Figure 8.3.4-5).[19] Considered from the perspective of Kolonna, the range of finds from level XIX is quite surprising, as there sand-tempering is an MH feature,[20] and rims with a hollow on the interior are not found until the very end of the MH and the beginning of the LH. This latter view is supported by the ceramic analysis from Tsoungiza.[21] The next level up, XVIII, contained some 90 sherds. Characteristic of this group are a rim fragment from a Bichrome-painted Aeginetan krater (Figure 8.4.1),[22] Aeginetan Matt-painted (Figure 8.4.2)[23]

Early and Middle Bronze stratigraphy was also identified at Korakou in Trench P, in the western sector of the excavations, discussion of which is here limited to that material recovered from levels XI (bottom) to VIII (top).[31] Level XI contained some 50 sherds, many of EH II date, with a smaller number of EH III.[32] Noteworthy among this group are the rim of a highly burnished open vessel, presumably a bass bowl (Figure 8.6.1),[33] and a Solidly Painted body fragment in a mudstone-tempered fabric. This latter piece is from the belly or lower zone of a closed Pattern Painted vessel, identified by three parallel lines applied on top of the solid paint (Figure 8.6.2).[34] Level X, lying above XI, also yielded some 50 sherds; most can be dated to EH III, although a small number are later and suggestive of contamination. Noteworthy are several joining fragments of a bass bowl with pushed-up handles (Figure 8.7.1),[35] fragments of a closed mudstone-

---

[17] Lot 1916-19:04 (Figure 8.3.1) and Lot 1916-19:06 (Figure 8.3.2).

[18] Lot 1916-19:03.

[19] Lot 1916-19:01 (Figure 8.3.4) and Lot 1916-19:02 (Figure 8.3.5).

[20] Note that early sand tempering traditions have been recognised elsewhere, including in the EM IIB-MH I sand-tempered fabric on Kythera (Broodbank and Kiriatzi 2007), and in the EH IIB-EH III group FG5 at Eretria (Müller Celka *et al.* 2018: 206).

[21] For late MH kantharoi with hollowed rims and hollowed rims on narrow-necked jars, see Rutter (1990: 431, 445). Rutter also notes that 'the hollowed interior lip profiles of the goblets from Korakou, a feature characteristic of developed LH I goblets from Tsoungiza, [is] abandoned by the time the pottery from the LH IIA pit in EU 10 was being produced.' (1993a: 81, n.44).

[22] Lot 1916-18:014.

[23] Lot 1916-18:016.

[24] Lot 1916-18:01 (Figure 8.4.3) and Lot 1916-18:02 (Figure 8.4.4).

[25] Lot 1916-18:05.

[26] Lot 1916-17:030.

[27] Lot 1916-17:028.

[28] Fragments Lot 1916-17:01 to 014 are Aeginetan Matt-painted; illustrated are nos. 3 (Figure 8.5.3), 4 (Figure 8.5.4), 6 (Figure 8.5.5), 10 (Figure 8.5.6) and 11 (Figure 8.5.7).

[29] Lot 1916-17:016 (Figure 8.5.8) and Lot 1916-17: 017 (Figure 8.5.9).

[30] Lot 1916-17:019 (Figure 8.5.10) and Lot 1916-17: 20 (Figure 8.5.11).

[31] Regarding this excavation area, see also Maran (1998: 12 and n.75); Rutter (1982: 470-471); Weiberg and Lindblom (2014: 394 and n.43).

[32] Layer XI was not dealt with by Rutter (1982: 470-471) or Maran (1998: 12 and n.75).

[33] Lot 1915-11:01.

[34] Lot 1915-11:02.

[35] Lot 1915-10:01.

Figure 8.3. Pottery from Korakou East Alley level XIX (ASCSA, Corinth Excavations, photo: P. Dellatolas; The monument is under the jurisdiction of the Hellenic Ministry of Culture and Sports/Archaeological Resources Fund [hereafter YPPOA/TAPA]).

Figure 8.4. Pottery from Korakou East Alley level XVIII (ASCSA, Corinth Excavations, photo: P. Dellatolas. The monument is under the jurisdiction of the YPPOA/TAPA).

tempered vessel with incised plastic decoration (Figure 8.7.2),[36] and pithoi in the same fabric (Figure 8.7.3).[37] As noted above, level X yielded the only EH II roof-tile identified to date at Korakou.[38] The next level up, IX, included some 50 fragments, predominantly of EH III date, significant among which are a well-preserved bass bowl with pushed-up handles (Figure 8.8.1),[39] the rim of a pyxis in a mudstone-tempered fabric (Figure 8.8.2),[40] and the complete profile of a neck-handled tankard with incised decoration (Figure 8.8.3) originally published by Jeremy Rutter (CP132; Rutter 1982: 470, pl.

100.39). Initially, it was suggested that level IX should represent the equivalent of the earliest EH III subphase at Lerna, ceramic Phase IV.1 (Maran 1998: 12 and n.75; Rutter 1982: 470 n.10; 1995: 640–654; Weiberg and Lindblom 2014: 394 and n.43). However, the bass bowl with slightly pushed-up handles (Figure 8.8.1) from the same context indicates a more advanced date in EH III (see also, Forsén 1992: 77), equivalent to Lerna ceramic Phase IV.2 (Rutter 1995). If correct, then Trench P levels IX and X at Korakou can no longer be considered to represent stratified evidence of early EH III ceramic development. This view is, furthermore, underlined by the existence in the lower level XI of Pattern Painted pottery (Table 8.1) belonging to developed EH III.

The next level up, VIII, contained some 90 fragments of pottery, mostly of EH to advanced MH date, among which were also identified some clearly EH III fragments,

---

[36] Lot 1915-10:05.
[37] Lot 1915-10:03 (mended from five joining fragments, all from level X).
[38] On the distribution of corridor houses and EH II roof tiles, see Rutter (1993b: 762 fig. 3); for new EH finds, including evidence of monumental architecture, see Smith (2017).
[39] Lot 1915-09:01.
[40] Lot 1915-09:02.

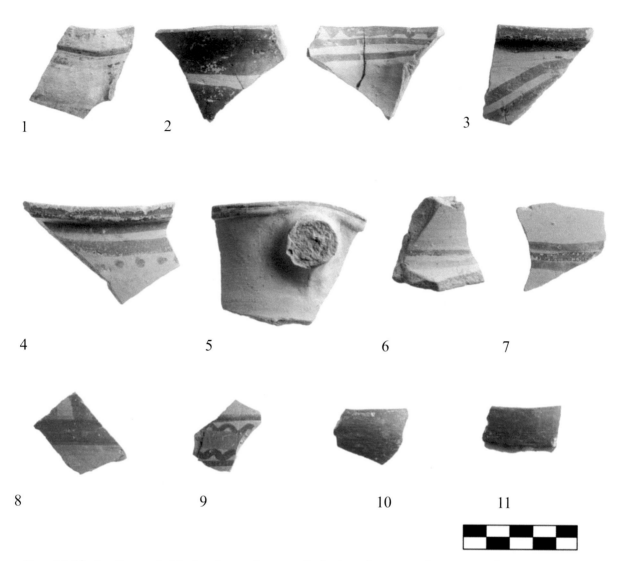

Figure 8.5. Selection of pottery froSelection of pottery from East Alley level XVII (ASCSA Corinth Excavations, photo: P. Dellatolas. The monument is under the jurisdiction of the YPPOA/TAPA).I.

Figure 8.6. Selection of pottery from Korakou Area P level XI.
(ASCSA, Corinth Excavations, photo: P. Dellatolas. The monument is under the jurisdiction of the YPPOA/TAPA).

1   2

3

Figure 8.7. Selection of pottery from Korakou Area P level X (ASCSA, Corinth Excavations, photo: P. Dellatolas. The monument is under the jurisdiction of the YPPOA/TAPA).

including the incised foot of a pedestal-footed cup (Figure 8.9.1).[41] Most interesting, are a number of Matt-painted fragments in a mudstone-tempered fabric (Figure 8.9.2),[42] some Aeginetan imports (Figure 8.9.3-4)[43] and Grey Minyan pottery with grooving on the exterior of the body (Figure 8.9.5).[44] Blegen notes the existence of a deep layer of ash and burnt debris at the base of level VIII.[45] It is possible that the completely preserved vessels from the preceding level IX form part of this destruction horizon, which might then be dated to an advanced stage of the EH III period, perhaps contemporary with the destruction of the Kolonna V settlement.[46]

The third part of this chapter will summarise initial observations on imports to Korakou, based on

---

[41] Lot 1915-08:09; see also, Rutter (1982: 471 no. 42, pl. 100.42).

[42] Lot 1915-08:08.

[43] Lot 1915-08:10 (Figure 8.9.3); Lot 1915-08:12 (Figure 8.9.4).

[44] Fragments Lot 1915-08:01-05 are Grey Minyan. Lot 1915-08:01 is illustrated (Figure 8.9.5).

[45] Forsén (1992: 77-78) suggests that this might be the site-wide destruction horizon noted by Blegen (1921: 2, 124).

[46] Forsén (1992: 77-78) has previously offered a similar interpretation. However, as Rutter (1982: 471 n.12) notes: 'In both his field notes and later pottery notes (Corinth Notebook 81 [1915] pp. 226-228, 361-363), Blegen records a deep layer of ash and burnt debris at the bottom of level P VIII. It is unfortunately unclear whether this burnt stratum is to be dated to the end of the early stage of EH III represented by the contents of P IX or to some later stage of EH III represented by the EH III material from P VIII. There is, of course, no way to tell whether the burnt destruction was restricted in scope or affected the site as a whole'.

Figure 8.8. Selection of pottery from Korakou Area P level IX (ASCSA, Corinth Excavations, photo: P. Dellatolas. The monument is under the jurisdiction of the YPPOA/TAPA).

Table 8.1. Sherd counts from the East Alley at Korakou.

Proportion of Different Wares found in Pit East Alley - Sherd Numbers																				Totals
Arbitrary Layers	I	II	III	IV	V	VI	VII	VIII	IX	X	XI	XII	XIII	XIV	XV	XVI	XVII	XVIII	XIX	
Painted LH III	89	150	177	145	7	0	0	0	0	0	0	0	0	0	0	0	0	0	0	568
Ephyrean Ware	1	0	1	12	7	50	12	7	1	0	0	0	0	0	0	0	0	0	0	91
Painted LH I-II	4	5	12	64	90	401	200	125	185	100	35	7	0	0	0	0	0	0	0	1228
Painted MH II	0	0	0	0	1	0	0	0	0	0	3	1	2	6	8	9	8	0	0	38
Black Monochrome	15	10	41	62	60	148	100	34	74	53	11	9	4	4	9	4	9	0	0	647
Red Monochrome	12	14	35	65	59	234	100	70	86	56	14	7	5	6	5	9	22	0	0	799
Buff Monochrome	9	95	90	100	114	375	300	96	182	174	65	101	87	108	128	110	148	12	0	2294
Gray Minyan	2	5	3	5	6	14	12	8	12	18	16	18	12	27	34	52	207	47	4	502
Mattpainted Ware	2	2	7	21	30	106	70	70	84	96	84	57	51	59	100	89	130	15	1	1074
Early Helladic Ware	0	0	0	0	0	0	0	0	0	0	0	0	0	1	0	10	12	21	69	113
Coarse Ware	3	11	9	6	5	55	20	8	33	30	8	23	10	12	20	33	39	13	13	351
Number of sherds	137	292	375	480	379	1383	814	418	657	527	236	223	171	223	304	316	575	108	87	7705

macroscopic inspection and from a Kolonna-centric point of view.[47] The number of Dark-on-Light Pattern Painted EH III sherds known from Kolonna is relatively small in comparison to those quantities known from sites like Lerna or Korakou.[48] Most examples appear to be of local Aeginetan manufacture and belong, almost exclusively, to closed shapes. Dark-on-Light Pattern Painted imports at Kolonna are even fewer in number; some, characterized by their lustrous appearance and fine fabric with almost no visible inclusions, are macroscopically indistinguishable from pattern-painted examples at Korakou, and may well derive from the same production centre. Scientific analyses of these examples at Kolonna have indicated an origin in the Argolid, or the northeastern Peloponnese or Corinthia (Gauss and Kiriatzi 2011: 158-163; Mommsen *et al.* 2001: 84-85).

Another distinctive fabric with mudstone inclusions is attested in Dark-on-Light Pattern Painted and Solidly Painted varieties at both sites during EH III. The production centre for this pottery may, again, have been located in the Argolid or the Corinthia. Interestingly, fragments of large, closed vessels with incised plastic decoration in this fabric are found at Korakou, and one complete vessel, and fragments of others, are known from Kolonna. At Lerna, one complete example of many similar vessels in this fabric has an elaborate decoration of incised plastic bands and has been interpreted by Rutter (1995: 289-290; 2008:

---

[47] For macroscopic analysis, see Gauss and Kiriatzi (2011: 42-67).
[48] Pattern Painted pottery at Kolonna seems limited mostly to small- and medium-sized closed vessels, whereas Pattern Painted open shapes are exceptionally rare.

1   2   3

4   5

Figure 8.9. Selection of pottery from Korakou Area P level VIII (ASCSA, Corinth Excavations, photo: P. Dellatolas. The monument is under the jurisdiction of the YPPOA/TAPA).

Figure 8.10. Aeginetan barrel jar and bowl from Korakou (inv. nos. CP303 and CP302) (ASCSA, Corinth Excavations, photo: P. Dellatolas. The monument is under the jurisdiction of the YPPOA/TAPA).

466) as a special vessel associated with ceremonial drinking events. At Korakou, mudstone temper seems to have been used in the manufacture of some MH Matt-painted pottery, whereas, at Kolonna, mudstone-tempered imports appear most commonly in EH levels.

The abundance of Middle Cycladic (MC) imports at Kolonna compared with their rarity at Korakou represents a very significant point of differentiation between the two sites. It would be very interesting to know if this is a site-specific phenomenon, or if the low visibility of MC pottery is also typical of neighbouring sites in the Corinthia.

No Aeginetan imports at Korakou can be identified, certainly, as being of EH III date, although this is rather unsurprising, given the more general rarity of Aeginetan EH III exports (Gauss and Kiriatzi 2011: 242, n.913–915).[49] The earliest clear Aeginetan imports identified to date at Korakou are a number of red

_____

[49] On a possible EH III import to Lerna, see also Rutter (1995: 149 no. P645, fig. 39). Rutter (1995: 420, 706, 749) identifies the piece as a possible Cycladic import, although the analysis of Dorais and Shriner (2002: 776) indicates an Aeginetan origin.

Figure 8.11. Aeginetan bowl from Korakou (inv. no. CP303) (ASCSA, Corinth Excavations, photo: P. Dellatolas.
The monument is under the jurisdiction of the YPPOA/TAPA).

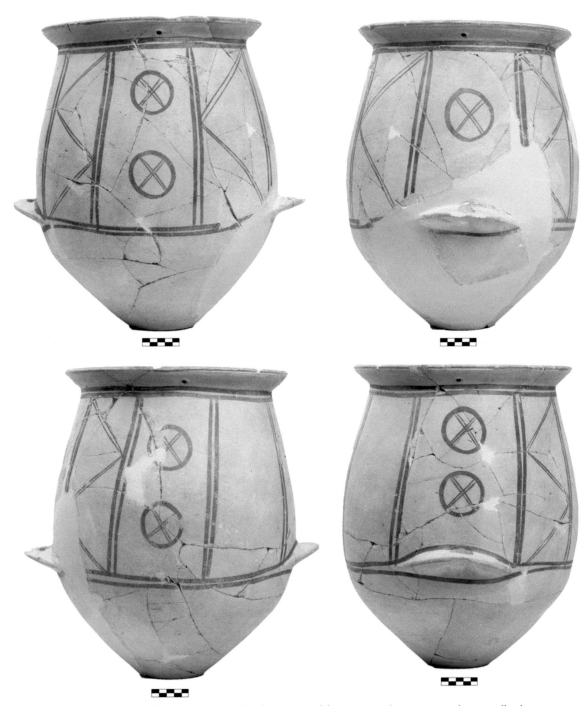

Figure 8.12. Aeginetan barrel Jar from Korakou (inv. no. CP302) (ASCSA, Corinth Excavations, photo: P. Dellatolas.
The monument is under the jurisdiction of the YPPOA/TAPA).

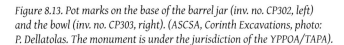

Figure 8.13. Pot marks on the base of the barrel jar (inv. no. CP302, left) and the bowl (inv. no. CP303, right). (ASCSA, Corinth Excavations, photo: P. Dellatolas. The monument is under the jurisdiction of the YPPOA/TAPA).

Solidly Painted bowls with straight or incurving rims from level XVII of the East Alley (Figure 8.5.10-11). Such vessels are attested in the stratigraphic sequence at Kolonna in the early MH period, from ceramic Phase H onwards.[50] They appear together with Aeginetan Matt-painted imports and, presumably, also with imported (so-called) kitchen wares. MH Aeginetan ceramic capabilities are, perhaps, best exemplified at Korakou by the Matt-painted barrel jar and Solidly Painted carinated bowl/cover of slightly more advanced MH date used to hold two infant burials in Trench R, level VI (Blegen 1921: 100-101) (Figures 8.10-13).[51] Both vessels have excellent parallels at Kolonna, and both bear a characteristic Aeginetan potter's mark (Figure 8.13).[52] Solidly-painted bowls with a carination at the shoulder make their first appearance in the Kolonna sequence in ceramic Phase H.[53] However, Matt-painted barrel jars are characteristic of the subsequent ceramic Phase I, which is associated with the middle phase of MH.[54] Aeginetan Matt-painted pottery is present in large quantities in all of those contexts at Korakou analysed to date, and would most certainly make up a large proportion of the imported pottery in any context preserved as excavated. In LH I, Aeginetan Bichrome Painted pottery is very common at Korakou and seems to far outnumber mainland Polychrome imports.

Finally, of the correlations evident between Korakou and Kolonna, this overview makes clear that there are similarities in the general development of both sites during the EH and MH periods. One obvious target for future research would be the clarification of when, how, and why, the developmental trajectories of the two sites diverged with time, and whether the development of Korakou mirrored that of other sites in the Corinthia. At Kolonna, the transition from the EH to the MH is crucial for the later development of the site, and the same can be argued for Korakou. In terms of the differences between the two sites, Kolonna would seem to be distinguished from Korakou by its ceramic economy, its fortifications and monumental architecture, as well as by the access it enjoyed to imports and valuable commodities in general. However, some of these apparent differences may be due to the very different histories of exploration undertaken at each site. If, in future, excavation were to be resumed at Korakou, an EH and MH sequence just as rich as that of Kolonna is certainly to be expected.

[50] Locally produced (Aeginetan) unpainted bowls with incurving rims make their first appearance in ceramic Phase G (Gauss and Smetana 2007a: 60; 2007b: 455). The analysis of the stratigraphic sequence thus far available indicates that locally produced (Aeginetan) red Solidly-Painted bowls with incurving rims make their first appearance slightly later, in ceramic Phase H (Gauss and Smetana 2007a: 62).

[51] For the location of Trench R, to the north of Trench P, see *Corinth Excavation Notebook* 81[1915]: 222. For the burial, see *Corinth Excavations Notebook* 84[1916]: 79 (dated 4.7.1916). For bowl CP302, see Blegen (1921: 18 fig. 25); for barrel jar CP303, see Blegen (1921: 19-20, 21 fig. 28).

[52] For CP302, see Wünsche (1977: 117 nos. 32-33, figs. 24-25); for CP303, see Siedentopf (1991: 55 no. 81, pl. 16). The barrel jar has a potter's mark of type F3 (Lindblom 2001: 49 fig. 14, 72-73), the bowl has a mark similar, but not identical, to type F26 (Lindblom 2001: 49 fig. 14, 74).

[53] Gauss and Smetana (2007a: 73 fig. 5, no. XXVII-38). On the deposition of vessels from this deposit, see Gauss and Smetana 2007a: 59 fig. C, 62-63).

[54] See, for example, the Matt-painted barrel jar pithos used for a child burial of settlement phase Kolonna IX (Gauss 2006: 441-442;

Siedentopf 1991: 56 no. 104, pl. 104). On the correlation of settlement phases and ceramic phases, see Gauss and Smetana (2007a; also, Wild *et al.* 2010). See also, the fragments of a large-sized Matt-painted barrel jar from the Large Building Complex at Kolonna (Felten *et al.* 2004b: 125 fig. 31 no. 12).

Bibliography

Attas, M. 1982. Regional Ceramic Trade in Early Bronze Age Greece: Evidence from Neutron Activation Analysis of Early Helladic Pottery from Argolis and Korinthia. Unpublished PhD dissertation, McGill University.

Attas, M., J.M. Fossey and L. Yaffe 1987. An archaeometric study of Early Bronze Age pottery production and exchange in Argolis and Korinthia (Corinthia), Greece. *Journal of Field Archaeology* 14(1): 77-90.

Barber, R.L.N. and O. Hadjianastasiou 1989. Mikre Vigla: a Bronze Age settlement on Naxos. *The Annual of the British School at Athens* 84: 63-162.

Beck, J. and D. Koutsoumba 2017. Bai de Kiladha 2016. *Antike Kunst* 60: 164-167.

Blegen, C.W. 1921. *Korakou. A Prehistoric Settlement near Corinth*. Boston and New York: the American School of Classical Studies at Athens.

Broodbank, C. and E. Kiriatzi. 2007. The first 'Minoans' of Kythera revisited: technology, demography, and landscape in the Prepalatial Aegean. *American Journal of Archaeology* 111(2): 241-274.

Davis, J.L. 1979. Late Helladic I pottery from Korakou. *Hesperia: the Journal of the American School of Classical Studies at Athens* 48(3): 234-263.

Dickinson, O.T.P.K. 1972. Late Helladic IIA and IIB: some evidence from Korakou. *The Annual of the British School at Athens* 67: 103-112.

Dorais, M.J. and C.M. Shriner 2002. An electron microprobe study of P645/T390: evidence for an Early Helladic III Lerna-Aegina connection. *Geoarchaeology* 17(8): 755-778.

Felten, F. and S. Hiller 1996. Ausgrabungen in der vorgeschichtlichen Innenstadt von Ägina-Kolonna (Alt-Ägina). Die Kampagnen 1993-1995. Ein Vorbericht. *Jahreshefte der Österreichischen Archäologischen Instituts in Wien* 65(B): 29-112.

Felten, F. and S. Hiller 2004a. Forschungen zur Frühbronzezeit auf Ägina-Kolonna 1993-2002, in E. Alram-Stern (ed.) *Die ägäische Frühzeit. 2. Serie. Forschungsbericht 1975 - 2002, 2. Band. Teil 2: Die Frühbronzezeit in Griechenland, mit Ausnahme von Kreta* (Veröffentlichungen der Mykenischen Kommission 21): 1089-1092. Vienna: the Austrian Academy of Sciences.

Felten, F., S. Hiller, C. Reinholdt, W. Gauss and R. Smetana 2004b. Ägina-Kolonna 2003. Vorbericht über die Grabungen des Instituts für Klassische Archäologie der Universität Salzburg. *Jahreshefte der Österreichischen Archäologischen Instituts in Wien* 73: 97-128.

Forsén, J. 1992. *The Twilight of the Early Helladics: A Study of the Disturbances in East-Central and Southern Greece towards the End of the Early Bronze Age* (Studies in Mediterranean Archaeology and Literature Pocketbook 116). Jonsered: Paul Åström.

Furtwängler, A. and G. Loeschcke 1886. *Mykenische Vasen. Vorhellenische Thongefässe aus dem Gebiete des Mittelmeeres*. Berlin: Asher.

Gallou, C. and J. Henderson 2012. Pavlopetri, an Early Bronze Age harbour town in south-east Laconia in C. Mee and M. Prent (eds) Early Helladic Laconia. Proceedings of the Round Table Conference held 16 January 2010 at the Netherlands Institute at Athens. Pharos. *Journal of the Netherlands Institute at Athens* 18(1): 79-104.

Gauss, W. 2006. Minos auf Ägina. Beobachtungen zu den Beziehungen Äginas zu Kreta, in E. Czerny, I. Hein, H. Hunger, D. Melman and A. Schwab (eds) *Timelines. Studies in Honour of Manfred Bietak, Volume II* (Orientalia Lovaniensia Analecta 149): 437-448. Leuven: Peeters.

Gauss, W. 2010. Aegina Kolonna, in E.H. Cline (ed.) *The Oxford Handbook of the Bronze Age Aegean (ca. 3000-1000 BC)*: 737-751. Oxford: Oxford University Press.

Gauss, W. and E. Kiriatzi 2011. *Ägina-Kolonna Forschungen und Ergebnisse V. Pottery Production and Supply at Bronze Age Kolonna, Aegina. An Integrated Archaeological and Scientific Study of a Ceramic Landscape* (Denkschriften der Gesamtakademie 65; Contributions to the Chronology of the Eastern Mediterranean 27). Vienna: the Austrian Academy of Sciences.

Gauss, G. and G. Klebinder-Gauss 2017. Äginetische Keramik: Produktion und Verbreitung in prähistorischer und historischer Zeit, in F. Lang, and W. Wohlmayr (eds) *50 Jahre Archäologie an der Paris Lodron-Universität Salzburg, Workshop Salzburg, 14 Dezember 2016* (ArchaeoPlus. Schriften zur Archäologie und Archäometrie an der Paris Lodron-Universität Salzburg 9): 23-34. Salzburg: University of Salzburg.

Gauss, W. and R. Smetana 2003. The Early Helladic III pottery from Aegina Kolonna, in M. Bietak (ed.) *The Synchronisation of Civilisations in the Eastern Mediterranean in the 2nd Millennium BC II. Proceedings of the SCIEM 2000 EuroConference. Haindorf, May 2-7, 2001* (Denkschriften der Gesamtakademie 29; Contributions to the Chronology of the Eastern Mediterranean 4): 471-486. Vienna: the Austrian Academy of Sciences.

Gauss, W. and R. Smetana 2007a. Aegina Kolonna. The stratigraphic sequence of the SCIEM 2000 Project, in F. Felten, W. Gauss and R. Smetana (eds) *Ägina-Kolonna Forschungen und Ergebnisse I. Middle Helladic Pottery and Synchronisms. Proceedings of the International Workshop held at Salzburg October 31st-November 2nd, 2004* (Ägina-Kolonna 1; Denkschriften der Gesamtakademie 42; Contributions to the Chronology of the Eastern Mediterranean 14): 57-80. Vienna: the Austrian Academy of Sciences.

Gauss, W. and R. Smetana 2007b. Early and Middle Bronze Age stratigraphy and pottery from Aegina Kolonna, in M. Bietak and E. Czerny (eds) *The Synchronisation* of Civilisations in the Eastern Mediterranean in the Second Millennium B.C. III. Proceedings of the SCIEM 2000 2nd EuroConference, Vienna, May 28 – June 1, 2003 (Denkschriften der Gesamtakademie 37; Contributions to the Chronology of the Eastern Mediterranean 9): 451-472. Vienna: the Austrian Academy of Sciences.

Gerding, H. 2013. Aigina, in D. Blackman, B. Rankov, K. Baika, H. Gerding and J. Pakkanen (eds) Shipsheds of the Ancient Mediterranean: 284-293. Cambridge: Cambridge University Press.

Harding, A., G. Cadogan and R. Howell 1969. Pavlopetri: an underwater Bronze Age town in Laconia. The Annual of the British School at Athens 64: 113-142.

Henderson, J., C. Gallou, N. Flemming and E. Spondylis 2011. The Pavlopetri Underwater Archaeology Project: investigating an ancient submerged town, in J. Benjamin, C. Bonsall, C. Pickard and A. Fischer (eds) Submerged Prehistory: 207-218. Oxford: Oxbow Books.

Hiller, S. 1975. Alt-Ägina IV, 1. Mykenische Keramik. Mainz: von Zabern.

Kilian-Dirlmeier, I. 1997. Alt-Ägina IV.3. Das mittelbronzezeitliche Schachtgrab von Ägina (Kataloge vor- und frühgeschichtlicher Altertümer 27). Mainz am Rhein: Von Zabern.

Klebinder-Gauss, G. and W. Gauss 2015. Opportunity in scarcity: environment and economy on Aegina, in A. Lichtenberger and C. von Rüden (eds) Multiple Mediterranean Realities. Current Approaches to Spaces, Resources, and Connectivities (Mittelmeerstudien 6): 67-91. Paderborn: Ferdinand Schöningh.

Knoblauch, P. 1969. Neuere Untersuchungen an den Häfen von Ägina. Bonner Jahrbücher 169: 104-116.

Knoblauch, P. 1973. Die Hafenanlagen der Stadt Ägina. Αρχαιολογικόν Δελτίον 27(1972)(Α΄): 50-85.

Lambeck, K. 1996. Sea-level change and shore-line evolution in Aegean Greece since Upper Palaeolithic time. Antiquity 70(269): 588–611.

Lavezzi, J.C. 2003. Corinth before the Mycenaeans, in C.K. Williams and N. Bookidis (eds) Corinth, The Centenary: 1896-1996 (Corinth: Results of Excavations Conducted by the American School of Classical Studies at Athens 20): 63-74. Princeton: the American School of Classical Studies at Athens.

Lindblom, M. 2001. Marks and Makers. Appearance, Distribution and Function of Middle and Late Helladic Manufacturers' Marks on Aeginetan Pottery (Studies in Mediterranean Archaeology 128). Jonsered: Paul Åström.

Manning, S.W. 1995. The Absolute Chronology of the Aegean Early Bronze Age. Archaeology, Radiocarbon and History (Monographs in Mediterranean Archaeology 1). Sheffield: Sheffield Academic Press.

Maran, J. 1992a. Die Deutschen Ausgrabungen auf der Pevkakia-Magula in Thessalien III. Die Mittlere Bronzezeit (Beiträge zur ur- und frühgeschichtlichen Archäologie des Mittelmeer-Kulturraumes 30-31). Bonn: Rudolf Habelt.

Maran, J. 1992b. Kiapha Thiti. Ergebnisse der Ausgrabungen II.2.. 2. Jt. v.Chr. Keramik und Kleinfunde (Marburger Winckelmann-Programm 1990). Marburg: Philipps University Marburg.

Maran, J. 1998. Kulturwandel auf dem griechischen Festland und den Kykladen im späten 3. Jahrtausend v. Chr.: Studien zu den kulturellen Verhältnissen in Südosteuropa und dem zentralen sowie östlichen Mittelmeerraum in der späten Kupfer- und frühen Bronzezeit (Universitätsforschungen zur prähistorischen Archäologie 53). Bonn: Rudolf Habelt.

Mommsen, H., W. Gauss, S. Hiller, D. Ittameier and J. Maran 2001. Charakterisierung bronzezeitlicher Keramik von Ägina durch Neutronaktivierungsanalyse, in E. Pohl, U. Recker and C. Theune (eds) Archäologisches Zellwerk. Beiträge zur Kulturgeschichte in Europa und Asien. Festschrift für Helmuth Roth zum 60. Geburtstag (Internationale Archäologie Studia honoraria 16): 79-96. Rahden: Leidorf.

Müller Celka, S., E. Kiriatzi, X. Charalambidou and N.S. Müller 2018. Early Helladic II-III pottery groups from Eretria (Euboea), in E. Alram-Stern and B. Horejs (eds) Pottery Technologies and Sociocultural Connections Between the Aegean and Anatolia During the 3rd Millennium BC (Oriental and European Archaeology 10): 197-213. Vienna: the Austrian Academy of Sciences.

Poulos, S.E., G. Ghionis and H. Maroukian 2009. Sea-level rise trends in the Attico-Cycladic region (Aegean Sea) during the last 5000 years. Geomorphology 107: 10-17.

Rahmstorf, L. 2006. Zur Ausbreitung vorderasiatischer Innovationen in die frühbronzezeitliche Ägäis. Prähistorische Zeitschrift 81(1): 49-96.

Reinholdt, C. 2008. Der frühbronzezeitliche Schmuckhortfund von Kap Kolonna. Ägina und die Ägäis im Goldzeitalter des 3. Jahrtausends v. Chr. (Ägina-Kolonna 2; Denkschriften der Gesamtakademie 46; Contributions to the Chronology of the Eastern Mediterranean 15). Vienna: the Austrian Academy of Sciences.

Rutter, J.B. 1974. The Late Helladic IIIB and IIIC periods at Korakou and Gonia in the Corinthia. Unpublished PhD dissertation, University of Pennsylvania.

Rutter, J.B. 1982. A group of distinctive pattern-decorated Early Helladic III pottery from Lerna and its implications. Hesperia: the Journal of the American School of Classical Studies at Athens 51(4): 459-488.

Rutter, J.B. 1990. Pottery groups from Tsoungiza of the end of the Middle Bronze Age. Hesperia: the Journal of the American School of Classical Studies at Athens 59(2): 375-458.

Rutter, J.B. 1993a. A group of Late Helladic IIA pottery from Tsoungiza. Hesperia: the Journal of the American School of Classical Studies at Athens 62(1): 53-93.

Rutter, J.B. 1993b. Review of Aegean Prehistory II: the Prepalatial Bronze Age of the southern and central Greek mainland. *American Journal of Archaeology* 97(4) 745-797.

Rutter, J.B. 1995. *Lerna III. The Pottery of Lerna IV.* Princeton: the American School of Classical Studies at Athens.

Rutter, J.B. 2003. Corinth and the Corinthia in the second millennium BC: old approaches, new problems, in C.K. Williams and N. Bookidis (eds) *Corinth, The Centenary: 1896-1996* (Corinth: Results of Excavations Conducted by the American School of Classical Studies at Athens 20): 75-83. Princeton: the American School of Classical Studies at Athens.

Rutter, J.B. 2008. The Anatolian roots of Early Helladic III drinking behavior, in H. Erkanal, H. Hauptmann, V. Şahoğlu and R. Tuncel (eds) *The Aegean in the Neolithic, Chalcolithic and the Early Bronze Age. Proceedings of the International Symposium, Oct. 13-16, 1997, Urla - İzmir, Turkey* (Ankara University Research Centre for Maritime Archaeology 1): 461-481. Ankara: Ankara University Press.

Siedentopf, H.B. 1991. *Alt-Ägina IV,2. Mattbemalte Keramik der mittleren Bronzezeit.* Mainz: von Zabern.

Smith, D.M. 2017. Recent research in Early Helladic southern Greece. *Archaeological Reports* 63: 107-129.

Stais, V. 1895a. Περί τῶν ἐν Αἰγίνη ἀνασκαφῶν. *Πρακτικά της εν Αθήναις Αρχαιολογικής Εταιρείας* 49(1894): 17–20.

Stais, V. 1895b. Προϊστορικοί συνοικισμοί ἐν Ἀττικῇ καὶ Αἰγίνῃ. *Αρχαιολογική Εφημερίς* 15(1895): 193-264.

Triantafillidis, I. and D. Koutsoumba 2017. The harbour landscape of Aegina (Greece), in J. Gawronski, A. van Holk and J. Schokkenbroek (eds) *Ships and Maritime Landscapes. Proceedings of the Thirteenth International Symposium on Boat and Ship Archaeology, Amsterdam 2012,* (International Symposium on Boat and Ship Archaeology 13): 165-170. Eelde: Barkhuis.

Triantafillidis, I. and V. Tselentis 2015. Management of underwater archaeological heritage: an environmental approach to the protection and preservation of the harbour complex of Aegina, in S. Fazlullin and M.M. Antika (eds) *SOMA 2013. Proceedings of the 17th Symposium on Mediterranean Archaeology, Moscow, 25-27 April 2013*: 202–212. Oxford: Archaeopress.

Tzonou-Herbst, I. 2010. Η πρώτη πόλη της Κορίνθου. Έρευνες στο Κοράκου 1915-2008, in T.A. Gritsopoulos, K.L. Kotsōnēs and I.K. Giannaropoulou (eds) *Πρακτικά του Η΄ Διεθνούς Συνεδρίου Πελοποννησιακών Σπουδών, Κόρινθος 26-28 Σεπτεμβρίου 2008* (Πελοποννησιακά – Παράρτημα 29): 47-56. Athens: the Society of Peloponnesian Studies.

Tzonou-Herbst, I. 2013. Η παράκτια Κορινθιακή πεδιάδα στη μυκηναϊκή περίοδο, in K. Kissas and W.-D. Niemeier (eds) *The Corinthia and the Northeast Peloponnese. Topography and History from Prehistoric Times until the End of Antiquity: Proceedings of the International Conference Organized by the Directorate of Prehistoric and Classical Antiquities, the LZ' Ephorate of Prehistoric and Classical Antiquities and the German Archaeological Institute, Athens, Held at Loutraki, March 26-29, 2009* (Athenaia 4): 35–44. Munich: Hirmer.

Tzonou-Herbst, I. 2015. From the mud of Peirene to mastering stratigraphy. Carl Blegen in the Corinthia and Argolid, in N. Vogeikoff-Brogan, J.L. Davis and V. Flourou (eds) *Carl W. Blegen: Personal and Archaeological Narratives*: 39-61. Atlanta: Lockwood Press.

Tzonou-Herbst, I. and M.J. Boyd 2015. Korakou's enclosure wall: geophysical survey and archival data. Paper delivered at the conference 'Οξυδερκεῖν at Korakou: a centennial celebration of C.W. Blegen's 1915-1916 excavations', The American School of Classical Studies at Athens, 4-6 September 2015.

Walter, H. and F. Felten 1981. *Alt-Ägina III,1. Die vorgeschichtliche Stadt. Befestigungen. Häuser. Funde.* Mainz: von Zabern.

Weiberg, E. and M. Lindblom 2014. The Early Helladic II-III transition at Lerna and Tiryns revisited: chronological difference or synchronous variability? *Hesperia: the Journal of the American School of Classical Studies at Athens* 83(3): 383-407.

Wild, E.M., W. Gauss and G. Forstenpointner, M. Lindblom, R. Smetana, P. Steier, U. Thanheiser and F. Weninger 2010. 14C dating of the Early to Late Bronze Age stratigraphic sequence of Aegina Kolonna, Greece. *Nuclear Instruments and Methods in Physics Research Section B: Beam Interactions with Materials and Atoms* 268(7-8) (Special issue: proceedings of the Eleventh International Conference on Accelerator Mass Spectrometry, Rome, Italy, September 14-19, 2008): 1013-1021.

Wünsche, R. 1977. *Studien zur äginetischen Keramik der frühen und mittleren Bronzezeit.* Munich: Deutscher Kunstverlag.

The Ceramic Assemblage of Leska on Kythera

Mercourios Georgiadis

Introduction

The late Middle to early Late Bronze Age is one of the best understood periods on Kythera, where it is represented by the settlement at Kastri (Coldstream and Huxley 1972) and the peak sanctuary of Ayios Georgios sto Vouno (Sakellarakis 1996; 2011; 2012; 2013a; 2013b; Tournavitou 2014), and by burials at Kastri and elsewhere (Bevan *et al.* 2002; Coldstream and Huxley 1972; Preston 2007). Archaeological surveys, both extensive and intensive, have provided data at a larger spatial scale in the northern (Paspalas and Gregory 2009) and central-eastern (Broodbank 1999; Broodbank and Kiriatzi 2007) parts of the island, while more or less specialised studies offer further perspective on the period (for example, Petrocheilos 1984; 1996).

The majority of archaeological material from this phase consists of ceramics, recovered from stratified, unstratified and closed contexts; a large volume of it from those sites noted above. Cretan cultural influence is apparent on Kythera already from late Early Bronze II (Broodbank and Kiriatzi 2007: 242-243, 253-254, 259, 261; Coldstream 1972c: 275-277; Coldstream and Huxley 1984: 107; Kiriatzi 2003: 129; 2010: 691) and continues at least until the end of the Cretan Neopalatial period, Late Minoan IB. Locally produced pottery displays many affinities with Crete in terms of the shapes, decoration and manufacturing techniques employed, and particularly in the treatment afforded to the clay and pottery production technology. Numerous pottery studies from Crete, and others from contemporary sites in Laconia, provide a template against which Kytheran material can be studied, while similarities between the Kytheran and Cretan ceramic tradition have allowed a better understanding of local practices and preferences. On Kythera itself, there are good stylistic analyses available from both Ayios

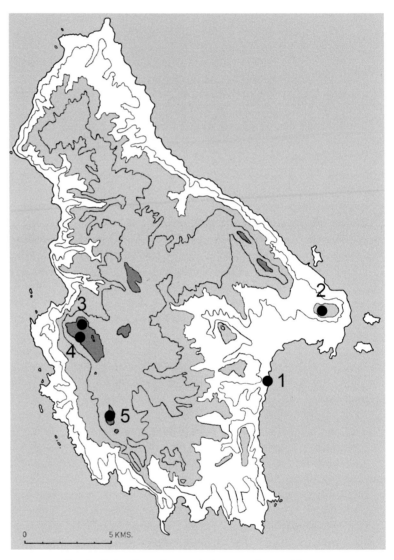

Figure 9.1. The island of Kythera, showing the key sites of Kastri (1); Agios Georgios sto Vouno (2); Leska (3); Katafygadi Cave (4); and Drymonas (5) (adapted from Coldstream and Huxley 1972: fig. 1).

Georgios sto Vouno and Kastri, while the latter site also offers stratified settlement data and closed burial contexts (Figure 9.1). The new ceramic data from Leska provides an opportunity to elucidate the character of the site and offer a new ceramic perspective on a lesser known part of the island. The site, moreover, has been identified as a peak sanctuary (Georgiadis 2012; 2014a; 2014b; 2016) and, for that reason, this paper will also address analogous assemblages from similar sites on Crete (Kyriakidis 2005; Tzachili 2016).

Kytheran ceramic production

Coldstream and Huxley (1972) provided a detailed analysis of the main clay fabrics employed on the island during the Middle Minoan (MM) and Late Minoan (LM) periods, and their use in the development of new vessel shapes and decorative styles, while surface survey undertaken by the Kythera Island Project (Broodbank 1999) recovered a large volume of sherds of low diagnostic value which required a more systematic study of island fabrics. Chemical analyses of defined fabric groups from Kastri (Kiriatzi 2003) has provided a clearer picture of clay sources. Those fine ceramics, without macroscopically-visible inclusions, were produced using clay from a source in the central-eastern part of the island, several kilometres to the west of Kastri. This same location provided the so-called Mudstone fabric, a fine clay with mudstone inclusions which increased durability and proved popular for the manufacture of medium and large coarse vessels. Red Micaceous, named for the colour of its clay and high silver mica content, is the most common coarse fabric employed during this period across Kythera and was derived from a source in the northern part of the island, between the modern villages of Potamos and Agia Pelagia. It is believed that the workshops which utilised these clays were situated a short distance from their sources. In the case of the Fine and Mudstone wares, it is possible that the workshop may have been located close to, or within, the settlement at Kastri. Chronologically, the Fine and Mudstone fabrics were already in use from the earlier Middle Bronze Age, while Red Micaceous is visible from MM III onwards. The latter largely replaced Mudstone as the main coarse ware at Kastri during the Neopalatial period (MM III-LM IB); Mudstone itself falling from use by the end of LM IA (Coldstream 1972c: 282, 289; Kiriatzi 2003: 125-126; 2010: 693-694). This chronology is based largely on the stratigraphic record of Kastri, despite the limited number of Protopalatial (MM I-II) contexts from the site, and has found support from Kiriatzi (2003). Finds from Ayios Georgios sto Vouno suggest that Red Micaceous fabric was already in use during MM I-II (Tournavitou 2014), although this observation was not based on stratigraphic data, but on stylistic analyses based on vessel shapes and decoration.

The pottery produced on Kythera shares a number of important characteristics with contemporary sites on Crete. These include similarities in the functional choice of clays, their preparation, levigation and mixture, and a shared technological preference for coarse clays where elasticity was required. The wheel can be identified on Kythera already from the early part of the 2nd millennium BC, and kilns (Coldstream 1972c: 277) were utilised to ensure greater control over firing conditions, greater uniformity, and a higher quality of finished product. As with these technical and technological decisions, so too vessel shape and decoration have close Cretan affinities, although specific regional associations are unclear, given parallels with sites in the west of the island and the area around Knossos. That said, Kytheran pottery production appears to be relatively eclectic, incorporating preferences for specific shapes and decorative motifs which owe little to influence from Cretan workshops.

Chemical analyses of pottery from Kythera have revealed that most of the Minoanising material recovered from contemporary sites on the southern and eastern Peloponnesian coast were imported not from Crete, but from Kythera; the island, it seems, serving as a node in those networks which linked Crete with the Greek mainland. Kytheran ceramics were desired for their quality — aesthetic or technical — and for the produce they contained, and were imported from the north of the island into Laconia and the Argolid (Bevan and Conolly 2013: 66; Catling 2009: 320-321; Cavanagh et al. 2022; Pentedeka et al. 2010: 34-35; Zerner 2008: 201-206).

The pottery assemblage from Leska

Leska is located in the western part of Kythera and represents the second highest peak of Mount Mermigkari, the tallest mountain on the island (Figure 9.2). An intensive survey carried out across the highest plateau of Leska produced an important concentration of MM-LM finds to the south-west of its summit (Georgiadis 2012). Bedrock in this area forms a relatively flat plateau and has retained much material in situ. Two trenches opened lower on the slope confirmed the discrete nature of the deposit, and the limited movement of material from the upper peak.

While the site itself extends over approximately 300m2 excavation was limited to an area of approximately 80m2. A total of six trenches were opened, the size and position of which were dictated by the presence of exposed bedrock outcroppings and the survival of soil to depth. Nevertheless, these trenches were sufficient to identify the boundaries of the site, roughly 20m by 15m, which included the summit and extended towards the south and southwest. Archaeological deposits, moreover, were relatively shallow, extending to a maximum depth of *c*. 0.5m below the present ground surface. Thus, Leska presents a very different character to the larger peak sanctuary at Ayios Georgios sto Vouno, where deposits extend across lower and steeper slopes and were located to a greater depth (Sakellarakis 1996; 2011). Ayios Georgios sto Vouno, moreover, produced a very rich ceramic assemblage (Tournavitou 2011; 2014) and traces of fire (Tournavitou, this volume). The absence of any architectural remains (walls or postholes) at Leska offers a broad parallel to Ayios Georgios sto Vouno, where a very small number of wall fragments may be contemporary.

Figure 9.2. Leska, view of the site from the east.

At Leska, more than 17,000 sherds were recovered during excavation, of which *c.* 13% were diagnostic in character. The vast majority were small and heavily abraded as a result of their exposure to the elements and, perhaps, anthropogenic activity. While breakage and weight also depend on the coarse or fine character of the sherds, an average sherd weight of 5.4g suggests a very long period of exposure. Until recently, there were no analogous data from sites sharing the same topographic characteristics and post-depositional conditions. However, publication of early excavations at the peak sanctuary of Vrysinas in central western Crete now provide a suitable parallel. Similarly located, on a plateau close to the summit of Agio Pneuma, sherds here are, on average, almost double the size of those from Leska, at *c.* 11.4g (Tzachili 2016: 31, fig. 7). This supports the identification of a far longer period of exposure at Leska. It may also explain the general lack of decoration on the Leska assemblage which, with traces on *c.* 0.76% of the total, is considerably lower than percentages from both Ayios Georgios sto Vouno (Tournavitou 2014) and Vrysinas (Tzachili 2016).

The local wares at Leska are the same as those noted for Kythera as a whole. Locally, fine wares have no visible inclusions and are attested in orange (7.5YR 6/6-7/8, reddish yellow) and buff (10YR 7/4, very pale brown) colours. Fine sherds constitute *c.* 66% of the diagnostic ceramic assemblage, with an average weight of *c.* 3.9g. Larger vessels, of course, are liable to produce a higher sherd count when exposed to the conditions noted above.

The coarse wares at Leska include both Mudstone and Red Micaceous varieties. Red Micaceous is the dominant coarse fabric at Leska, constituting *c.* 88.9% of the total coarse assemblage, with an average sherd

weight of 6.5g, and a colour range of red (2.5YR 5/6, red) to brown (7.5YR 5/4-5/6, brown - strong brown) (Coldstream 1972c: 279; Kiriatzi 2003: 125; Kiriatzi *et al.* 2012: 296). A number of misfired sherds are dark grey in colour (Gley 2 3/1- 4/1, very dark bluish grey- dark bluish grey). Mudstone constitutes *c.* 10.6% of the total coarse assemblage, with an average sherd weight of 8.5g, a buff colour (10YR 7/4, very pale brown) and, in some cases, an orange core (7.5YR 6/6, reddish yellow) (Coldstream 1972c: 279; Kiriatzi 2003: 124-125; 2010: 692). The angular mudstone/chert inclusions added in the fabric are red and reddish-brown in colour, and are found in different densities (semi-fine to semi-coarse).

Ceramic shapes

Open shapes

The ceramic assemblage from Leska is dominated by open vessels and, more specifically, by cups. Varying numbers of carinated, conical, bell, straight-sided, hemispherical and stemmed types, as well as tumblers, have been identified, all of which bear close affinities to examples from Ayios Georgios sto Vouno and Kastri.

The only shape from the contemporary Kytheran cup repertoire not represented at Leska is the Vapheio type. Vapheio cups were popular in both the settlement and cemetery at Kastri (Coldstream 1972c: 279, 280, 284-285), though they occur only rarely at Ayios Georgios sto Vouno (Tournavitou 2014: 33, 38-39). The shape is popular on contemporary sites in Laconia (William Cavanagh, personal communication; Rutter and Rutter 1976: 43, 53), though it is rare at Ayia Irini on Kea (Cummer and Schofield 1984: 142), where there is a strong influence of Minoan cultural elements on the local culture, and entirely absent from peak sanctuaries on Crete (Tournavitou 2014: 33).

Only two examples of carinated cups have been identified at Leska. The shape is attested at Kastri and Ayios Georgios sto Vouno (Coldstream 1972a: 94, fig. 38δ.1, 5-6; 180, fig. 54ω.23-24; Coldstream 1972c: 278-279; Tournavitou 2000: 298, fig. 1α) and is a common shape on the peak sanctuaries of Crete, and the island more generally, during the Protopalatial period (MM I-IIIA; see Betancourt 1985: 75, 77-78, 99, 105; Tzachili 2016: 72-74). Their presence at Leska suggests an early use date for this site, though, as at Ayios Georgios sto Vouno, a limited popularity for the shape.

The conical cup is the most popular vase type at this site, and perhaps the most common on contemporary sites on Kythera and Crete. The multifunctional and symbolic role of the shape has been discussed by Tournavitou (2009: 227) for both commensal and ritual activities on Kythera. It appears first during the Protopalatial period and becomes more popular during the Neopalatial. A large number are noted from the settlement and cemetery at Kastri, and the shape dominates at Ayios Georgios sto Vouno (Bevan et al. 2002; Coldstream 1972a; 1972b; 1972c; Tournavitou 2000; 2014). Deposits from Kastri have confirmed a chronological development of the rim and base over the course of the Neopalatial. Based largely on burial data, Bevan and colleagues (2002: 74-75) have suggested that cups with larger base diameters (3.5-4cm) belong to LM IA, and those with smaller diameters (3cm) can be placed in LM IB. All variants of the shape currently identified on Kythera are represented at Leska, with most examples dating to LM IA and LM IB. In addition, Leska has yielded a small assemblage of miniature variants (Georgiadis 2014a: 47) in the form of conical cups with a base diameter up to 2cm. Similar examples have been reported from Ayios Georgios sto Vouno (Tournavitou 2009: 215-219, figs. 18.1-18.4; 2014: 521, chart 6, 523-525, charts 8-10, 527-528, chart 12, 14, 530 chart 16, 533 chart 17).

With a curving body, bell cups could be considered as a further variant of the conical cup (Tournavitou 2014: 31-32, 303-305, fig. 9), although the prevalence of the shape at Kastri saw it treated as a distinct category by Coldstream (1972c: 285, 293). The type appears first in LM IA, when it has a straight rim, and continues in use into LM IB, with an upright rim. The shape appears relatively infrequently in the cemetery at Kastri and at Ayios Georgios sto Vouno (Bevan et al. 2002: 74 fig. 11; Tournavitou 2014: 31-32, 303-305, fig. 9) and only a small number have been recovered at Leska, of which the majority belong to LM IA, and fewer to LM IB.

The straight-sided cup is the second most popular cup type at Leska, as it is at Ayios Georgios sto Vouno

(Tournavitou 2014: 32), and is well represented at Kophinas (Spiliotopoulou 2015) and Vrysinas (Tzachili 2016: 105). This shape appeared first in MM IB and remained in use until the end of the MM III phase, with the exception of a small number of painted examples which appear later (Coldstream 1972c: 279-280; Tournavitou 2014: 33, 35-38). Several examples with surviving surfaces from Leska preserve traces of monochrome painted decoration. It is likely that the excavated examples from Leska belong to the Protopalatial and earliest Neopalatial periods.

The hemispherical cup is a similarly popular type at Leska, and is well represented at Kastri and Ayios Georgios sto Vouno (Bevan et al. 2002: 76-77, 88 fig. 20.245; Coldstream 1972a: 192, fig. 56ω.184; Tournavitou 2014: 40-41, 43). The hemispherical cup can possess a flaring rim (Type A) or an everted rim (Type B), corresponding to LM IA-B and LM IB, respectively. At Leska, c. 30% of cups can be attributed to Type A and c. 70% to Type B, suggesting an increase in the popularity of hemispherical cups at the end of the Neopalatial period.

Tumblers appear at Leska only in limited numbers, constituting less than 1% of the diagnostic ceramic assemblage. They are known within the settlement at Kastri, where they belong to LM IA, but are rare within the cemetery (Bevan et al. 2002: 77; Coldstream 1972c: 285, 294). They are rare within the local assemblage at Ayios Georgios sto Vouno, where they are presented as a straight-sided cup (Tournavitou 2014: 38-39, 318-319), and are attested at the Cretan peak sanctuaries of Juktas, Korakomouri and Traostalos (Kyriakidis 2005: 131-132 table 7; Tzedakis et al. 1999: 323).

A single example of a stemmed cup has been found at Leska. The shape, however, is extremely rare on Kythera, attested only from a handful of tombs in the Kastri area and in low numbers at Ayios Georgios sto Vouno, with all examples dated to LM IB (Bevan et al. 2002: 70, 73, 75, 85 fig. 17.144, 88 fig. 20.244; Coldstream 1972b: 243-244, fig. 87.3-4, pl. 75.3-4; Coldstream 1972c: 294; Tournavitou 2014: 47, 335-336, fig. 21.K353 and K354).

Bowls constitute c. 6% of the Leska ceramic assemblage, among which are included conical and pedestalled types, basins and ring-handled basins and kalathoi. These vessels likely served a variety of functions, including the transport, display, distribution and consumption of food stuffs. The conical bowl is the most frequent type, a shape well known from Kastri (Coldstream 1972c: 294). Representing c. 4% of the total ceramic assemblage, it is a larger version of the conical cup which appears most commonly in Red Micaceous fabric and, less commonly, in Mudstone. The shape is well represented within both the settlement and cemetery at Kastri (Bevan et al. 2002: 78; Coldstream 1972c: 281, 286, 294), but has not been identified at Ayios Georgios sto Vouno (Tournavitou 2014). Those examples from Leska can be dated to MM IIIB-LM IB.

Only two examples of pedestal bowls are noted. The type is present in earlier levels at MM IA Kastri (Coldstream 1972c: 277), and a small number of MM III-LM IA parallels are known from Ayios Georgios sto Vouno (Tournavitou 2014: 97, 448-449, fig. 81.K949 and K951, pl. 25.K949 and K951).

The basin enjoys only a limited presence at Leska (less than 1% of the assemblage), as it does at Kastri and Ayios Georgios sto Vouno (Coldstream 1972a: 104, 109, 114; Tournavitou 2014: 52, 342, 346). The Leska assemblage evidences a preference for the T-rim variant of MM IIIB-LM IB. Thus far, this vessel type has not been reported from any Cretan peak sanctuary (Tournavitou 2014: 53), suggesting that its use at Leska may represent a specific Kytheran idiosyncrasy.

The kalathos, while recognised at Leska, remains rare in the local assemblage (comprising less than 1%). The shape is present during LM IA and LM IB at Kastri, where examples are attested primarily, although not exclusively, as grave goods (Coldstream 1972a: 100; contra Bevan *et al.* 2002: 77-78, pl. 11), and are also noted, albeit infrequently, among the assemblage from Ayios Georgios sto Vouno (Sakellarakis 2013b: 67; Tournavitou 2011: 119, table 1).

The identification of the ring-handled basin at Leska was surprising, since the only other examples of this locally manufactured shape derive from burial contexts of LM IA and IB date at Kastri (Bevan *et al.* 2002: 65-66, 70, 78; Coldstream 1972b: 236, 247, 255; 1972c: 286). A very small number of sherds were noted from MM IIIB contexts within the settlement at Kastri and none at all were recovered from Ayios Georgios sto Vouno (Coldstream 1972a: 101; Preston 2007: 250). This shape is part of a skeuomorphic tradition in Kytheran ceramic manufacture, which has previously been identified (Bevan *et al.* 2002: 78, 93; Coldstream 1978: 392; Georgiadis 2014a: 46-47).

Two categories of specialised open shapes, rhyta and braziers, are also attested at Leska; both, ostensibly, are associated with ritual practice. Rhyta are identified by only three examples. Although associated with ritual activity, on both Crete and Kythera they appear in equal numbers in settlement, burial and sanctuary contexts (Betancourt 1985: 105; Coldstream 1972c: 282; Tournavitou 2006). On Crete, rhyta are attested at the peak sanctuaries at Atsipades, Prinias, Vrysinas, Xykefalo, Juktas, Zou Prinias, Traostalos and Kophinas, during the Protopalatial and Neopalatial periods (Jones 1999: 53-54 table 7; Kyriakidis 2005: 138, 139 fig. 32 and table 14; Morris and Peatfield 1995: 645-646; Peatfield 1992: 68).

The brazier, another rare shape at Leska attested by only a few examples, is often associated with fire-setting or the burning of incense (Muhly 1984). It is attested in both the settlement and cemetery at Kastri, and at Ayios Georgios sto Vouno, mainly during LM I (Coldstream 1972a: 123; Coldstream 1972c: 282, 288, 295; Tournavitou 2000, 2014: 97). It appears in low numbers in settlement contexts on Crete, although it is more common in peak sanctuary contexts (Tournavitou 2014: 99-100), with examples from Atsipades, Petsopha, Thylakas, Traostalos, Kophinas, Zou Prinias and Vrysinas (Chryssoulaki 1999: 316; 2001: 62-63; Jones 1999: 53-54 table 7, 59-74 table 10; Kyriakidis 2005: 137 fig. 30 and table 12, 139, 140 figs. 33 and 34 and table 15, 141 table 16; Papadopoulou and Tzachili 2010: 454, fig. 13 upper and middle row; Peatfield 1992: 70; 2007: 299).

Cooking vessels

This category is dominated at Leska by a single ceramic shape: the tripod cooking vase. Its identification as the second most popular shape in the local pottery assemblage (comprising *c.* 12% of total), after the conical cup, makes clear its central importance in those activities taking place at the site. The absence of evidence for fire at the site suggests however, that the act of cooking was undertaken elsewhere, as Peatfield (1992) has previously proposed for Atsipades, and that cooked food was carried to site within the tripod vase and subsequently transferred to other vessels for distribution and consumption.

The tripod vase also constitutes the second most popular shape at Ayios Georgios sto Vouno (Tournavitou 2014: 76), although the site offers fewer examples overall, and is represented in low numbers in the settlement at Kastri (Coldstream 1972c: 279, 282). This shape is found on Kythera in both of Betancourt's Neopalatial varieties, Type A and Type B (for the definition of these types, see Betancourt 1980). At Leska, both types appear predominantly in Red Micaceous fabric, and less often in Mudstone, with the Type A more popular (55% of the total tripod vessel count) than the Type B (45% of the total tripod vessel count). This ratio is in contrast to Ayios Georgios sto Vouno, where Type B vessels appear more popular (Tournavitou 2014: 77).

Tripod cooking vessels have also been identified at the Cretan peak sanctuary sites of Petsopha, Juktas, Kophinas, Korakomouri, Traostalos, Vrysinas and Atsipades (Jones 1999: 51-52 table 6; Kyriakidis 2005: 135-137, fig. 28, table 10; Morris and Peatfield 1995: 645; Peatfield 1992: 70; Spiliotopoulou 2015). For the most part, however, their frequencies remain unknown. Data are available only for Vrysinas, where, along with other cooking vessels, they account for 2-3% of the local assemblage (Tzachili 2003: 330; 2016: 48, 49-52, charts 3-4).

Closed Vessels

Closed shapes (jugs, jars and pithoi) account for some 15% of the total ceramic assemblage at Leska.

Low-necked jugs, ewers, low-spouted jugs and juglets are all attested, as is the bridge-spouted jar, which might be included in this category given its use for the serving of liquids and ritual activities (Tournavitou 2014: 14-15). On Crete, jugs are not attested in peak sanctuary contexts as frequently as one might think, although examples are known from Atsipades, Juktas, Petsopha, Spili Vorizi, Vrysinas, Korakomouri, Maza and Kophinas (Jones 1999: 51-52 table 6; Kyriakidis 2005: 133-134, table 9; Myres 1903: 378-380; Peatfield 2007: 299; Tzachili 2016: 46-47, 49-52, charts 3 and 4; Tzedakis *et al.* 1999: 323). All of those jug types attested at Leska find analogies in the assemblages of Kastri and Ayios Georgios sto Vouno (Coldstream 1972c: 281, 287, 295; Tournavitou 2014: 14-15). It is worth noting that, at both Leska and Ayios Georgios sto Vouno, juglets represent the most popular miniature shape, followed by the miniature conical cup mentioned earlier (Tournavitou 2009: 215-219, figs. 18.1 and 18.4; 2014: 549 chart 6, 550-551 charts 8-10, 552 chart 12, 553 chart 14, 554 chart 16, 555 chart 17, 558-559 charts 23-25; Georgiadis 2014a: 46-47). This jug size and shape is found only on a small scale and it does not imitate the larger variety. Similar examples are well known from a number of peak sanctuaries throughout Crete (Jones 1999: 51-52 table 6; Kyriakidis 2005: 160-161, table 25).

Jars are not common at Leska, although wide-mouthed, collar-necked, piriform and bridge-spouted variants are all attested, as are amphorae. To this group can also be added a small number of pithoi, which tend to be relatively small; no doubt as a result of the lower labour costs involved in carrying smaller examples to the summit of Leska. All of these shapes have parallels at Kastri and Ayios Georgios sto Vouno and, indeed, within the wider Kytheran repertoire (Coldstream 1972c: 281, 287, 295; Tournavitou 2014: 61-76), while jars and pithoi are also known from Atsipades, Karphi, Korakomouri, Philioremos, Traostalos, Vrysinas, Petsopha, Xykephalo, Juktas and Kophinas (Chryssoulaki 2001: 63; Jones 1999: 51-52 table 6; Kyriakidis 2005: 133-134, table 9; Peatfield 1992: 70; Tzachili 2003: 330-331; 2016: 32).

Decoration

The rarity of painted decoration at Leska is, as noted, a function of the very poor state of preservation exhibited by most of the assemblage. Nevertheless, where paint survives, the majority is black monochrome, with red-brown paint employed much less commonly. Painted decoration is attested principally on fine cups, i.e. conical, straight-sided and hemispherical types, and appears rarely on other open and closed shapes. Of the other forms of decoration visible at Leska, incision is mainly attested on rhyta, while finger impressions, relief bands and applied knobs are found on closed vases such as jugs, jars and pithoi, though overall they remain rare.

Discussion

Excavations undertaken on the arid, open summit of Mount Leska during 2011 produced an assemblage of local and Minoanising shapes manufactured in local fabrics. Closed shapes were rare, while open shapes, and particularly cups and tripod cooking pots, were prevalent. The character of this assemblage suggests the transport of pre-prepared foodstuffs to Leska and their consumption at the summit. The absence of animal bones at the site is surprising given the evidence for pastoral activity in the surrounding landscape, and the suitability of the wider region of Mount Mermigkari for use as upland pasture, and suggests that there may have existed social or religious proscriptions on the type of food which could be consumed there (Georgiadis 2012: 11). Given the relatively low numbers of closed vessels, jars and pithoi, it is likely that the serving and consumption of liquid played only a limited role in ritual activity. All vessels brought to the site seem to have been discarded on the surface once they had fulfilled their function, with no evidence for their curated burial or secondary treatment, a typical treatment attested in peak sanctuaries on Crete and Ayios Georgios sto Vouno (Kyriakidis 2005). This depositional process has almost certainly contributed to the poor condition of the assemblage.

There are clear parallels between the ceramics recovered at Leska, Ayios Georgios sto Vouno and Kastri. They all belong to the Kytheran ceramic tradition discussed by Coldstream and Huxley (1972) and Kiriatzi (2003; 2010) and all evidence the same ceramic fabrics, although their prevalence is dependent on the chronology and character of each site, and the circulation patterns of each fabric across the island. Similar preferences for particular shapes can be identified over time, although local idiosyncrasies are also visible, particularly in relation to the popularity of the bell cup and the addition of skeuomorphic features (Bevan *et al.* 2002; Georgiadis 2014a). The recovery of miniatures from a variety of sites (and contexts) also confirm a particular Kytheran preference for their use (Georgiadis 2014a).

The prevalence of drinking cups and cooking vessels supports the identification of feasting as a primary activity at both Leska and Ayios Georgios sto Vouno. The makeup of the ceramic assemblages from these two sites, alongside their topographic characteristics strongly suggest a cultic character. It seems that analogous activities were taking place at both Leska and Ayios Georgios sto Vouno, most likely sharing the same symbolic meaning. Thus, a degree of standardisation is apparent in the beliefs and practices observed on Kythera, as has been observed on Crete during the same period (Kyriakidis 2005).

Leska provides new ceramic data which enrich our understanding of the local potting traditions of Kythera during the MM and LM I periods. Furthermore, it provides a cultic assemblage important not only for what it can tell us of the ritual landscape and religious practices of Kythera, but of the island's position in the broader Aegean. The standardisation of pottery types consumed at the two Kytheran sanctuaries suggests the observation of similar ritual practices at both. It is possible that such practices may be specific to Kythera, although the analysis and publication of material from ritual sites on Crete, and elsewhere in the Aegean, should allow a clearer understanding of the degree to which Kythera exists in an extended network of belief.

Bibliography

Betancourt, P.P. 1980. *Cooking Vessels from Minoan Kommos. A Preliminary Report* (Occasional Paper 7). Los Angeles: Institute of Archaeology, University of California.

Betancourt, P.P. 1985. *The History of Minoan Pottery*. Princeton: Princeton University Press.

Bevan, A. and J. Conolly 2013. *Mediterranean Islands, Fragile Communities and Persistent Landscapes. Antikythera in Long-Term Perspective*. Cambridge: Cambridge University Press.

Bevan, A., E. Kiriatzi, C. Knappett, E. Kappa and S. Papachristou 2002. Excavation of Neopalatial deposits at Tholos (Kastri), Kythera. *The Annual of the British School at Athens* 97: 55-96.

Broodbank, C. 1999. Kythera Survey: preliminary report on the 1998 season. *The Annual of the British School at Athens* 94: 191-214.

Broodbank, C. and E. Kiriatzi 2007. The first 'Minoans' of Kythera revisited: technology, demography, and landscape in the Prepalatial Aegean. *American Journal of Archaeology* 111(2): 241-274.

Catling, H.W. 2009. *Sparta: Menelaion I. The Bronze Age* (The British School at Athens Supplementary Volume 45). London: the British School at Athens.

Cavanagh, W., C. Gallou, I. Spondylis and J. Henderson 2022. Southern Laconia in the Middle and earlier Late Bronze Age: pottery from Pavlopetri and other sites, in C. Wiersma and M.P. Tsouli (eds) *Middle and Late Helladic Laconia. Competing Principalities* (Publications of the Netherlands Institute at Athens 7): 33-46. Leiden: Sidestone.

Chryssoulaki, S. 1999. Ιερό κορυφής Τραόσταλου. *Κρητική Εστία* 7: 310-317.

Chryssoulaki, S. 2001. The Traostalos peak sanctuaries: aspects of spatial organisation, in R. Laffineur and R. Hägg (eds) *POTNIA. Deities and Religion in the Aegean Bronze Age. Proceedings of the 8th international Aegean Conference, Göteborg, Göteborg University, 12-15 April 2000* (Aegaeum 22): 57-66. Liège: the University of Liège.

Coldstream, J.N. 1972a. Deposits of pottery from the settlement, in J.N. Coldstream and G.L. Huxley (eds) *Kythera. Excavations and Studies Conducted by the University of Pennsylvania Museum and the British School at Athens*: 77-204. London: Faber and Faber

Coldstream, J.N. 1972b. Tombs: the finds, in J.N. Coldstream and G.L. Huxley (eds) *Kythera. Excavations and Studies Conducted by the University of Pennsylvania Museum and the British School at Athens*: 220-271. London: Faber and Faber.

Coldstream, J.N. 1972c. Kythera: the sequence of the pottery and its chronology, in J.N. Coldstream and G.L. Huxley (eds) *Kythera. Excavations and Studies Conducted by the University of Pennsylvania Museum and the British School at Athens*: 272-308. London: Faber and Faber.

Coldstream, J.N. 1978. Kythera and the southern Peloponnese in the LM I period, in C. Doumas (ed.) *Thera and the Aegean World I. Papers presented at the Second International Scientific Congress, Santorini, Greece, August 1978*: 389-401. London: Aris and Phillips.

Coldstream, J.N. and G.L. Huxley (eds) 1972. *Kythera. Excavations and Studies Conducted by the University of Pennsylvania Museum and the British School at Athens*. London: Faber and Faber.

Coldstream, J.N. and G.L. Huxley 1984. The Minoans of Kythera, in R. Hägg and N. Marinatos (eds) *The Minoan Thalassocracy: Myth and Reality. Proceedings of the Third International Symposium at the Swedish Institute in Athens, 31 May – 5 June 1982* (Skrifter Utgivna av Svenska Instituet I Athen 4°, 32): 107-112. Gothenburg: Paul Åström.

Cummer, W.W. and E. Schofield 1984. *Keos III. Ayia Irini: House A*. Mainz: von Zabern.

Georgiadis, M. 2012. Leska: a new peak sanctuary on the island of Kythera. *Journal of Prehistoric Religion* 33: 7-23.

Georgiadis, M. 2014a. The material culture of ritual sites from Minoan Kythera. *Journal of Prehistoric Religion* 34: 37-49.

Georgiadis, M. 2014b. The physical environment and the beliefs at Leska, a new peak sanctuary on Kythera, in G. Touchais, R. Laffineur and F. Rougemont (eds) *PHYSIS: L'environnement naturel et la relation homme-milieu dans le monde Égéen Protohistorique. Actes de la 14e Rencontre égéenne internationale, Paris, Institut National d'Histoire de l'Art (INHA), 11-14 décembre 2012* (Aegaeum 37): 481-484. Leuven: Peeters.

Georgiadis, M. 2016. Metaphysical beliefs and Leska, in E. Alram-Stern, F. Blakolmer, S. Deger-Jalkotzy,

R. Laffineur and J. Weilhartner (eds) *METAPHYSIS. Ritual, Myth and Symbolism in the Aegean Bronze Age. Proceedings of the 15th International Aegean Conference, Vienna, Institute for Oriental and European Archaeology, Aegean and Anatolia Department, Austrian Academy of Sciences and Institute of Classical Archaeology, University of Vienna, 22-25 April 2014* (Aegaeum 39): 295-302. Leuven: Peeters.

Jones, D.W. 1999. *Peak Sanctuaries and Sacred Caves in Minoan Crete: A Comparison of Artifacts* (Studies in Mediterranean Archaeology and Literature, Pocketbook 156). Jonsered: Paul Åström.

Kiriatzi, E. 2003. Sherds, fabrics and clay sources: reconstructing the ceramic landscapes of prehistoric Kythera, in K.P. Foster and R. Laffineur (eds) *METRON. Measuring the Aegean Bronze Age. Proceedings of the 9th International Aegean Conference/9e Rencontre égéenne internationale, New Haven, Yale University, 18-21 April 2002* (Aegaeum 24): 123-130. Liège: the University of Liège.

Kiriatzi, E. 2010. "Minoanising" pottery traditions in the southwest Aegean during the Middle Bronze Age: understanding the social context of technological and consumption practice, in A. Phillipa-Touchais, G. Touchais, S. Voutsaki and J. Wright (eds) *MESOHELLADIKA. The Greek Mainland in the Middle Bronze Age. Actes du colloque international organisé par l'Ecole française d'Athènes, en collaboration avec l'American School of Classical Studies at Athens et le Netherlands Institute in Athens, Athènes, 8-12 mars 2006* (Bulletin de Correspondance Hellénique Supplément 52): 683-699. Athens: the French School at Athens.

Kiriatzi, E., M. Georgakopoulou, C. Broodbank and S.W. Johnston 2012. Η ιστορία ενός τοπίου μέσα από τη μελέτη και ανάλυση κεραμικών και μεταλλουργικών ευρημάτων: το παράδειγμα της επιφανειακής έρευνας Κυθήρων, in N. Zacharias, M. Georgakopoulou, K. Polikreti, Y. Facorellis and T. Vakoulis (eds) *Πρακτικά 5ου Συμποσίου Ελληνικής Αρχαιομετρικής Εταιρείας, Αθήνα, 8-10 Οκτωβρίου 2008*: 289-304. Athens: Papazisis.

Kyriakidis, E. 2005. *Ritual in the Bronze Age Aegean. The Minoan Peak Sanctuaries*. London: Duckworth.

Morris, C.E. and A.A.D. Peatfield 1995. Pottery from the peak sanctuary of Atsipadhes Korakias, Ay. Vasiliou, Rethymnon, in N.E. Papadogiannakis (ed.) *Πεπραγμένα του Ζ Διεθνούς Κρητολογικού Συνεδρίου, Ρέθυμνον, 25-31 Αυγούστου 1991. Τόμος Α2: Τμήμα Αρχαιολογικό*: 643-647. Rethymno: the Historical and Folklore Society of Rethymno.

Muhly, P.M. 1984. Minoan hearths. *American Journal of Archaeology* 88(2): 107-122.

Myres, J.L. 1903. Excavation at Palaikastro II: § 13. The sanctuary-site of Petsofà. *The Annual of the British School at Athens* 9: 356-387.

Papadopoulou, E. and I. Tzachili 2010. Ανασκαφή στο ιερό κορυφής Βρύσινα νομού Ρεθύμνης, in M. Andrianakis and I. Tzachili (eds) *Αρχαιολογικό Έργο Κρήτης 1. Πρακτικά Της 1ης Συνάντησης Ρέθυμνο, 28-30 Νοεμβρίου 2008*: 452-463. Rethymno: School of Philosophy, University of Crete.

Paspalas, S.A. and T.E. Gregory 2009. Προκαταρκτικά συμπεράσματα της επιφανειακής έρευνας της Αυστραλιανής αποστολής στα Κύθηρα, 1999-2003, in V. Vasilopoulou and S. Katsarou-Tzeveleki (eds) *Από τα Μεσόγεια στον Αργοσαρωνικό. Β΄ Εφορεία Προϊστορικών και Κλασικών Αρχαιοτήτων. Το έργο μιας δεκαετίας, 1994-2003. Πρακτικά Συνεδρίου, Αθήνα, 18-20 Δεκεμβρίου 2003*: 549-560. Markopoulo: Municipality of Markopoulo, Mesogeia.

Peatfield, A.A.D. 1992. Rural ritual in Bronze Age Crete: the peak sanctuary at Atsipadhes. *Cambridge Archaeological Journal* 2(1): 59-87.

Peatfield, A. 2007. The dynamics of ritual on Minoan peak sanctuaries, in D.A. Barrowclough and C. Malone (eds) *Cult in Context: Reconsidering Ritual in Archaeology*: 297-300. Oxford: Oxbow Books.

Pentedeka, A., E. Kiriatzi, L. Spencer, A. Bevan. and J. Conolly 2010. From fabrics to island connections: macroscopic and microscopic approaches to the prehistoric pottery of Antikythera. *The Annual of the British School at Athens* 105: 1-81.

Petrocheilos, I.E. 1984. *Τα Κύθηρα. Από την Προϊστορική Εποχή ως τη Ρωμαιοκρατία* (Πανεπιστήμιο Ιωαννίνων Επιστημονική Επετηρίδα Φιλοσοφικής Σχολής. Δωδώνη: Παράρτημα 21). Ioannina: the University of Ioannina.

Petrocheilos, I.E. 1996. Επιφανειακή έρευνα στο Παλιόκαστρο Κυθήρων. *Πρακτικά της Αρχαιολογικής Εταιρείας* 148(1993): 154-161.

Preston, L. 2007. Bringing in the dead: burials and the local perspective on Kythera in the Second Palace Period. *Oxford Journal of Archaeology* 26(3): 239-260.

Rutter, J.B. and S.H. Rutter 1976. *The Transition to Mycenaean. A Stratified Middle Helladic II to Late Helladic IIA Pottery Sequence from Ayios Stephanos in Laconia* (Monumenta Archaeologica 4). Los Angeles: Institute of Archaeology, University of California.

Sakellarakis, Y. 1996. Minoan religious influence in the Aegean: the case of Kythera. *The Annual of the British School at Athens* 91: 81-99.

Sakellarakis, Y. 2003. Τα Κύθηρα στην τρίτη και δεύτερη χιλιετία π.Χ. *ΝΟΣΤΟΣ: περιοδική έκδοση του Ομίλου Κυθηρίων Πανεπιστημιακών* 2: 23-38.

Sakellarakis, Y. 2011. *ΚΥΘΗΡΑ. Το Μινωικό Ιερό Κορυφής στον Άγιο Γεώργιο στο Βουνό 1: τα Προανασκαφικά και η Ανασκαφή* (Βιβλιοθήκη της εν Αθήναις Αρχαιολογικής Εταιρείας 271). Athens: the Archaeological Society at Athens.

Sakellarakis, Y. 2012. Μινωικά χάλκινα μικροαντικείμενα, in Y. Sakellarakis (ed.) *ΚΥΘΗΡΑ. Το Μινωικό Ιερό Κορυφής στον Άγιο Γεώργιο στο*

Βουνό 2: Τα Ευρήματα (Βιβλιοθήκη της εν Αθήναις Αρχαιολογικής Εταιρείας 276): 213-238. Athens: the Archaeological Society at Athens.

Sakellarakis, Y. (ed.) 2013a. *ΚΥΘΗΡΑ. Το Μινωικό Ιερό Κορυφής στον ΄Αγιο Γεώργιο στο Βουνό 3: Τα Ευρήματα* (Βιβλιοθήκη της εν Αθήναις Αρχαιολογικής Εταιρείας 282). Athens: the Archaeological Society at Athens.

Sakellarakis, Y. 2013b. *ΚΥΘΗΡΑ. Ο ΄Αγιος Γεώργιος στο Βουνό: Μινωική Λατρεία. Νεότεροι Χρόνοι* (Βιβλιοθήκη της εν Αθήναις Αρχαιολογικής Εταιρείας 287). Athens: the Archaeological Society at Athens.

Spiliotopoulou, A. 2015. Νέα ματιά στο υλικό της κεραμικής και των ανθρωπόμορφων ειδωλίων από το ιερό κορυφής Κόφινα Αστερουσίων, in P. Karanastasi, A. Tzigounaki and C. Tsigonaki (eds) *Αρχαιολογικό ΄Εργο Κρήτης 3. Πρακτικά της 3ης Συνάντησης Ρέθυμνο, 5-8 Δεκεμβρίου 2013. Τομος Α΄: Εισηγήσεις φορέων - Ηράκλειο - Γενικά θέματα*: 281-292. Rethymno: the University of Crete and the Ephorate of Antiquities of Rethymno.

Tournavitou, I. 2000. Μινωικό ιερό κορυφής στα Κύθηρα: η κεραμεική, in T. Detorakis and A. Kalokairinos. *Πεπραγμένα του Η Διεθνούς Κρητολογικού Συνεδρίου, Ηράκλειο, 9-14 Σεπτεμβρίου 1996. Τόμος Α3: Προϊστορική και Αρχαία Ελληνική Περίοδος*: 297-316. Heraklion: the Society of Cretan Historical Studies.

Tournavitou, I. 2006. Ρυτά στα Μινωικά ιερά κορυφής: η περίπτωση των Κυθήρων, in E. Tabakaki and A. Kaloutsakis (eds) *Πεπραγμένα του Θ Διεθνούς Κρητολογικού Συνεδρίου, Ελούντα 1 - 6 Οκτωβρίου 2001. Τόμος Α1: Προϊστορική Περίοδος, Ανασκαφικα δεδομενα*: 391-408. Heraklion: the Society of Cretan Historical Studies.

Tournavitou, I. 2009. Does size matter? Miniature pottery vessel in Minoan Peak Sanctuaries, in A.L. D'Agata and A. van de Moortel (eds) *Archaeologies of Cult. Essays on Ritual and Cult in Crete in Honor of Geraldine C. Gesell* (Hesperia Supplement 42): 213-230. Princeton: the American School of Classical Studies at Athens.

Tournavitou, I. 2011. LM IB pottery from the colonies. Hagios Georgios sto Vouno, Kythera, in T.M. Brogan and E. Hallager (eds) *LM IB Pottery: Relative Chronology and Regional Differences. Acts of a Workshop held at the Danish Institute at Athens in Collaboration with the INSTAP Study Center for East Crete, 27-29 June 2007* (Monographs of the Danish Institute at Athens 11): 117-140. Athens: the Danish Institute at Athens.

Tournavitou, I. (Y. Sakellarakis, (ed.)) 2014. *ΚΥΘΗΡΑ. Ο ΄Αγιος Γεώργιος στο Βουνό 4: Κεραμεική της Εποχής του Χαλκού* (Βιβλιοθήκη της εν Αθήναις Αρχαιολογικής Εταιρείας 289). Athens: the Archaeological Society at Athens.

Trantalidou, K. 2013. Αρχαιοζωολογικά κατάλοιπα και ζητήματα της ορνιθοπανίδας, in Y. Sakellarakis (ed.) *ΚΥΘΗΡΑ. Το Μινωικό Ιερό Κορυφής στον ΄Αγιο Γεώργιο στο Βουνό 3: Τα Ευρήματα* (Βιβλιοθήκη της εν Αθήναις Αρχαιολογικής Εταιρείας 282): 463-563. Athens: the Archaeological Society at Athens.

Tzachili, I. 2003. Quantitative analysis of the pottery from the peak sanctuary at Vrysinas, Rethymnon, in K.P. Foster and R. Laffineur (eds) *METRON. Measuring the Aegean Bronze Age. Proceedings of the 9th International Aegean Conference/9e Rencontre égéenne internationale, New Haven, Yale University, 18-21 April 2002* (Aegaeum 24): 327-331. Liège: the University of Liège.

Tzachili, I. 2016. *Βρύσινας ΙΙ. Η Κεραμική της Ανασκαφής 1972-1973: Συμβολή στην Ιστορία του Ιερού Κορυφής*. Athens: Ta Pragmata.

Tzedakis, Y., S. Chryssoulaki, L. Vokotopoulos and A. Sfyroera 1999. Ερευνητικό πρόγραμμα 'Μινωικοί δρόμοι'. *Κρητική Εστία* 7: 317-326.

Zerner, C. 2008. The Middle Helladic pottery, with the Middle Helladic wares from Late Helladic deposits and the potters' marks, in W.D. Taylour and R. Janko (eds) *Ayios Stephanos. Excavations at a Bronze Age and Medieval Settlement in Southern Laconia* (The British School at Athens Supplementary Volume 44): 177-298. London: the British School at Athens.

Regional Diversities or Occupational Gap? Pottery Styles During the Late 14th and 13th Centuries BC at Ayios Vasileios[1]

Eleftheria Kardamaki, Vasco Hachtmann, Adamantia Vasilogamvrou, Nektarios Karadimas and Sofia Voutsaki

Introduction

The excavations at Ayios Vasileios have contributed immensely toward the infilling of a large gap in our knowledge of the Mycenaean Late Bronze Age through the addition of the palace of Laconia to the political map of southern Greece. Although the site had previously been considered significant (Cavanagh and Crouwel 2002: 149-150; Hope Simpson and Dickinson 1979: 110), and had even been identified as a likely candidate for a palace (Banou 1996: 37-39), we can now be certain that it will shed light on a number of longstanding research questions. The discovery of an archive containing Linear B tablets, and of structures with unique architectural features, for the first time in Laconia (Vasilogamvrou 2013; 2014; 2015a; 2015b), is of major importance for a fuller understanding of Mycenaean civilization as a whole.

However, excavation is a lengthy process and, so far, we have had only a glimpse of the extent of the palace and its surroundings. In fact, only one building complex has been excavated to any great extent; the so-called Building A, that, among many extraordinary items, contained a hoard of swords (see Vasilogamvrou 2013: pl. 50a). Further to the south, remains of a large court, oriented northwest-southeast, came to light. The court was surrounded to the south and, at least at the southern end of its west side, by deep stoas (Vasilogamvrou 2015b: 105) (Figure 10.1). In other excavated structures (Buildings Δ, B, see below), floors were poorly preserved or heavily damaged by Byzantine activity (Vasilogamvrou 2013: pl. 45; 2014: 62-64). Another significant find is the early Mycenaean cemetery with cist graves located to the north of Building A (North Cemetery). Based on the area excavated so far, it consists of 21 graves with some single, but mostly multiple, burials (Moutafi and Voutsaki 2016) (Figure 10.2). On the margins of the cemetery, ceramic deposits were excavated which yielded typical settlement material. Although these deposits were not found sealed by

any floors, some contain homogenous assemblages and, thus, offer valuable information regarding the chronology of the settlement. Notwithstanding the limitations mentioned above, the areas excavated so far provide some initial insights into the local typology.

In the present paper, we discuss pottery styles during the middle and late palatial periods (late 14th to the early 12th century BC)[2] in relation to chronological aspects, and demonstrate how the synchronization of styles from different regions can affect our reconstruction of the sequence of events during this crucial period in early European history. The first part of this period is considered to reflect the heyday, and greatest expansion, of the palaces, while the late 13th century BC is thought to evidence decline and instability, and is often viewed as the forerunner of the destructions at the end of LH IIIB (however, see Maran 2015: 280-283). Pottery from Ayios Vasileios dated to these phases will be considered against the background of a long-running discourse concerning the existence of a so-called *koine*, on the one hand, and of ceramic regionalism on the other (Sherratt 1980). Comparison with the Argolid has played a decisive role in this discussion. The principal reason for this is that the Argolid was a leading and innovative production centre which had a great impact on the distribution of Mycenaean styles in the Aegean; a fact also suggested by analytical studies (see Marketou *et al.* 2006: 48-49 for Argive/northeastern Peloponnesian imports to Rhodes). The second reason — closely related to the first — is that the LH IIIA–LH IIIB pottery styles from the Argolid have been the typo-chronological backbone for the dating of habitation and destruction events in many other regions of southern Greece, and beyond. Although, in many cases, direct comparison between settlement assemblages from the Argolid and elsewhere is not possible, the Argive ceramic sequence is often taken as indicative of the existence of an occupation hiatus, or a diverging local style, or both (Sherratt 1980). The situation is especially critical for the 13th century BC, and the problem of identifying the LH IIIB1 and LH IIIB2 horizons in settlements beyond the Argolid, and other sites in the northeastern Peloponnese, hampers a deeper understanding of what happened before, and around, the demise of Mycenaean palatial culture.

[1] We are grateful to Angelos Papadopoulos, David Smith and William Cavanagh, for their kind invitation to participate in a very stimulating pottery workshop dedicated to the memory of Christopher Mee. It is a great honour and a challenge for us to present a paper in memory of Christopher Mee, a pioneer archaeologist dedicated to exploring the human landscape. Aegean archaeology in general, and Laconian archaeology more specifically, have greatly benefited from his work. We hope that our contribution would have met his expectations.

[2] For LH IIIA2 Early and earlier deposits, see Kardamaki (2017).

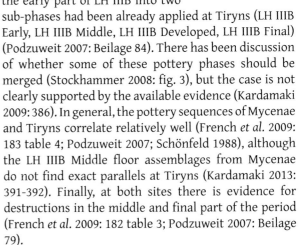

Figure 10.1. The area of the court of Ayios Vasileios including excavated parts of the South Stoa and West Stoa. Plan by Kostas Minakakis, Kostas Athanasiou and Eirini Koulogeorgiou.

The typology of LH IIIA2-LH IIIB2 in the Argolid

With the help of statistical analysis and typology, it has been possible to narrow down the relative dates of Argive floor deposits and fills (Kilian 1988: 120 fig. 2). While LH IIIA2 is divided into an early and late subphase (Furumark 1941: 101), the former is known only from funerary contexts in the Argolid (French 1965: 160; Vitale 2011: 342 table 5). The existence of an intermediate level between LH IIIA1 and LH IIIA2 cannot be excluded but has not been confirmed stratigraphically (French 1965: 160).[3] The semi-globular kylix, FS 257, with a decoration zone extending under the handles is considered to be indicative for a later subphase in LH IIIA2 (Mountjoy 1986: 88-90). The octopus, often with added white paint, represents one of the most popular motifs (French 1965: 165-166 figs. 2-3). In addition to the kylix, a wide range of other Pattern Painted, monochrome and plain open and closed vessels constitute typical LH IIIA2 table wares (French 1965).

For LH IIIB, there are two different chronological systems, at Mycenae and Tiryns respectively, built upon a rich stratigraphic sequence. At Mycenae, three pottery phases are distinguished (LH IIIB1, LH IIIB Mid, and LH IIIB2) with possible evidence for a further subdivision of LH IIIB1 (French 1966: 216-217; Mountjoy 1976: 82; Wardle 1969: 266). Initially understood aspart of LH IIIB1, LH IIIB Middle has been recently assigned to

the early part of LH IIIB2 (LH IIIB2 Early) (French and Taylour 2007; French et al. 2009;) following the new system of Vitale (2006) that distinguishes between LH IIIB2 Early and LH IIIB2 Late. The subdivision of the late as well as the early part of LH IIIB into two sub-phases had been already applied at Tiryns (LH IIIB Early, LH IIIB Middle, LH IIIB Developed, LH IIIB Final) (Podzuweit 2007: Beilage 84). There has been discussion of whether some of these pottery phases should be merged (Stockhammer 2008: fig. 3), but the case is not clearly supported by the available evidence (Kardamaki 2009: 386). In general, the pottery sequences of Mycenae and Tiryns correlate relatively well (French et al. 2009: 183 table 4; Podzuweit 2007; Schönfeld 1988), although the LH IIIB Middle floor assemblages from Mycenae do not find exact parallels at Tiryns (Kardamaki 2013: 391-392). Finally, at both sites there is evidence for destructions in the middle and final part of the period (French et al. 2009: 182 table 3; Podzuweit 2007: Beilage 79).

Throughout the 13th century BC, pottery development in the Argolid is characterized by constant innovation in shapes and motifs, the most conspicuous of which seem to coincide with destruction events. In LH IIIB1, the kylix with a shallow body and tall stem, decorated

---

[3] See Shelmerdine (1992: 495-497) and Vitale (2011) for a tripartite division of LH IIIA2 at Nichoria and Mitrou, respectively.

with whorl shells or hybrid as a single or running motif (Zygouries kylix) (FS 258A+B) appears. The same is true of the deep bowl with open style decoration (Group A) (French 1966). Its presence during LH IIIA2 has been postulated (French 1965: 178, 180 fig. 7.8; Mountjoy 1999: 129 fig. 29.213), but remains disputed (Schönfeld 1988: 173-174; see also, Thomas 2011). Both the Group A deep bowl and the kylix are quite common in the settlement assemblages (Wardle 1973: 305 fig. 4; Podzuweit 2007: Beilage 75). There is also some change in the plain table ware after LH IIIA2, with the introduction of the conical kylix, FS 274, that often has a polished surface treatment (Mountjoy 1976: 94). In LH IIIB2, there is a break in the pottery tradition of the pattern painted repertoire. The once popular kylix FS 258 vanishes rather suddenly (Podzuweit 2007: 211-212), following which the deep bowl, with its new and distinct variants (Close Style Group B deep bowl, rosette deep bowl; see Wardle 1973: 298) is the only common pattern-painted drinking/eating vessel. Towards the end of the phase, the Group B deep bowl becomes less frequent, and a variant with a thinner rim band is quite common (type C deep bowl: Kardamaki 2015: 84, 86 fig. 4.1).

The earliest Postpalatial phase at Tiryns and Mycenae is termed LH IIIC Early 1 (French 2011: 59-60, table 4; Kardamaki 2013; Podzuweit 2007), although at Mycenae an even earlier level is represented by terracing work in the Citadel House Area (Sherratt's 'Early': see French 2011). LH IIIC Early 1 is best equated with Rutter's Phase 1 (Rutter 1977; 2003a) and has many elements from Mountjoy's Transitional LH IIIB2-LH IIIC Early (Mountjoy 1999). Decisive in this respect is the absence of typical LH IIIC Early vessel types (carinated cup FS 240, painted angular bowl FS 295A), and the rarity of others (painted conical kylix FS 274; however, see Rutter 2003a: 197), and the presence of new deep bowl variants (Group A deep bowl with monochrome interior, medium band deep bowl) or cups (linear painted FS 215). Some of these vessel types may have appeared earlier but were still very rare (French et al. 2009: 195 fig. 8.5-6). The rosette deep bowl continues, but the type B deep bowl is now a rare exception. The definition of the Transitional phase by Mountjoy (actually very similar to Rutter's Phase 1), that shares features from both LH IIIB2 and LH IIIC Early, has reopened the discussion regarding the contemporaneity of the palace destructions (see below and Rutter 2003c: 255). The transitional phase postdates the destructions in the Argolid at Mycenae and Tiryns (cf. Iria, Mountjoy 1997: 117; 1999: 36), but should be contemporary with destructions elsewhere (Mountjoy 1999: 36). Major events assigned to the Transitional phase by Mountjoy include the destruction of the palace at Pylos and the destruction of the acropolis at Midea (although, see Demakopoulou 2003). The existence of a transitional phase between LH IIIB2 and LH IIIC Early has not found wide acceptance, and it has often been equated either with LH IIIB2 Late or LH IIIC Early 1 (French and Taylour 2007: v; Kardamaki 2013: 486-487, table 33; Vitale 2006: 200-201 tables 2 and 3). Most importantly, the use of LH IIIB2 should be avoided when discussing the wider geographical context, given that it is strongly bound in with the sequence in the Argolid (Rutter 2003a: 194; 2003b: 249-250).

Ayios Vasileios: the relevant contexts.

The following report is based on a comparison of the material excavated in two different sectors of the site, namely the North Cemetery and the area of the large court to the south. At the margins of the North Cemetery, traces of walls and built features were found, as well as pottery deposits from various Late Helladic phases (Figure 10.2). To the west (Figure 10.2A), a sequence of two thin layers contained homogenous pottery dating to LH IIIA. The material excavated is not plentiful and the formation process of these layers remains unknown. Nevertheless, because of their superimposition, they may provide valuable stratigraphic evidence. The pottery from these layers seems to coincide with a division of the two LH IIIA subphases in typological terms, indicated by the appearance of the stemmed bowl FS 304 and the monochrome kylix FS 264 in the upper layer (Figure 10.4.1-2. For the appearance of these shapes in LH IIIA2 early, see Vitale 2011: 332, 334). In any case, more stratified material is required to confirm this distinction. A second deposit found east of the cemetery (Figure 10.2B) contained mainly material of LH IIIA1 while fragments i.a. again of monochrome kylikes FS 264 (Figure 10.4.3-4) point at a formation of this deposit early in LH IIIA2. No layer dated exclusively to LH IIIB was excavated, and sherds of this phase are, in general, very rare in the area of the North Cemetery (Figure 10.5.1). After LH IIIA2, the next recognizable horizon is represented by find groups in which fragments of Mycenaean decorated pottery, almost exclusively, have monochrome painted interiors. One large concentration of this material, probably a homogenous deposit of LH IIIC Early date, was found northeast of the cemetery (Figure 10.2C).

Crucial information for the architectural history of the palace, its construction, destruction and post-destruction activities comes from the area of the court (Figure 10.1). The court and the stoas (parts of Buildings Δ and E) were built on top of an artificial platform, the latest pottery from which dates to LH IIIA2 Early (Kardamaki 2017; Vasilogamvrou et al. 2021). The floor of these structures was heavily burnt. In the West Stoa, the floor was sealed by a red layer — presumably part of the subfloor fill of the upper storey — that was superimposed by the collapsed debris from the upper floor that contained the Linear B archive (Petrakos 2016: 25; Vasilogamvrou 2015b: 107-109; Vasilogamvrou et al. 2021). The area has yielded only rarely primary

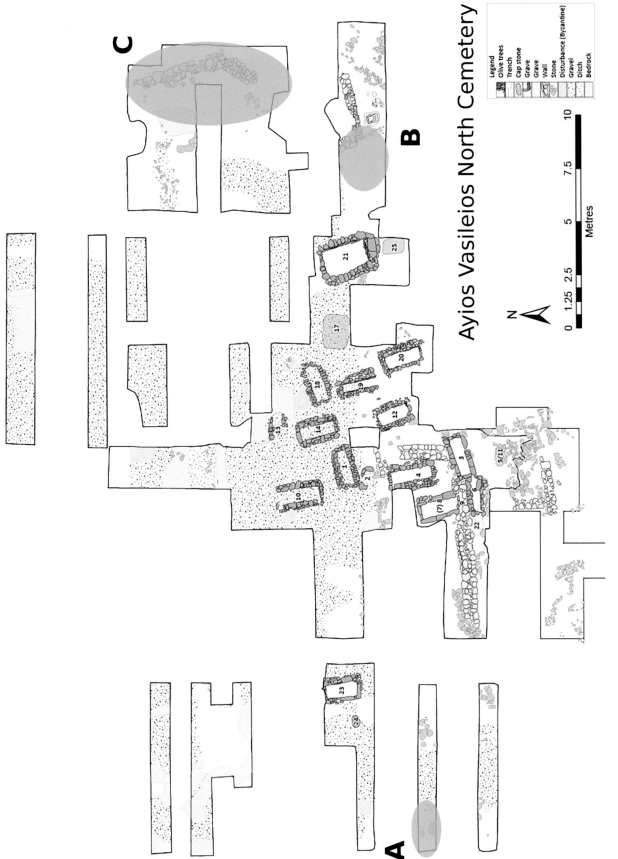

Figure 10.2. The North Cemetery. Ground plan by Eirene Koulogeorgiou, alterations by Vasco Hachtmann.

floor deposits. Part of the actual destruction deposit, comprising two groups of heavily burnt, fully or near fully preserved vessels, was found lying in situ on the floor of the South and West Stoas (Kardamaki 2017: 131 fig. 20.318–321) (Figure 10.6.1-3). A few well and fully preserved vessels (small dippers) were also discovered within the collapsed building debris from the first floor (Figure 10.6.4-5) or the red layer overlying the floor of the West Stoa, and may have been originally part of the upper floor assemblages. The rest of the material recovered in the red layer of the subfloor fill contained more or less abundant ceramic material of various phases, mainly LH IIIA and occasionally LH II; much of it in a fragmented state of preservation, although some well preserved. In the excavated part of the floor of the court and the South Stoa, a red layer overlying the floor was followed by another that was full of stone and mudbrick (Vasilogamvrou 2015a: 74, pl. 59a) (Figure 10.3). In some places, these layers were connected or interrupted by other layers of a different colour and consistency (grey layers or layers with stones, see Vasilogamvrou 2015b: 109). The complete stratigraphic sequence will, however, be presented elsewhere. The

interpretation of these layers in the court is still subject to study, but they may represent part of a levelling operation in the area after the destruction. One wall built directly on the floor of the court suggests an episode of rebuilding activity, during which levelling may have taken place (Vasilogamvrou 2015a: 74, pl. 58a). In several cases, Byzantine walls and structures (and especially the pits), representing the latest period of occupation, have disturbed the Mycenaean strata. The red layer identified on top of the floor of the court and South Stoa contained some typical LH IIIB1 sherds as the latest material. These sherds may derive from the time of use and destruction of the buildings and/or from post-destruction cleaning activities. The upper and highest Mycenaean layers in the area of the court and South Stoa above the red layer contained many fragments of deep bowls, best compared with Mountjoy's so-called LH IIIB2-LH IIIC Early transitional types.

The stylistically latest material in the group of the vessels found in situ on the floor (Figure 10.6.3), and in the building debris (Figure 10.6.4-5), of the West Stoa

Figure 10.3. The South Stoa and the court. Photo by Nektarios Karadimas.

seems to support a date in LH IIIB1, i.e. in the final part of this subphase (LH IIIB Middle).[4] While no painted LH IIIB1 pottery was found among these vessels (see below), the rim profile of some vessels (Figure 10.6.3)[5] and decoration (dotted rims) of some of those dippers (Figure 10.6.5) recovered from the destruction debris of the upper storey, could indicate a date in this phase. A date closer to the middle part of the 13th century BC (LH IIIB Middle) is provided by the presence of two sherds belonging to Group B deep bowls found within the building debris of the West Stoa.

The pottery typology at Ayios Vasileios during LH IIIA2 to LH IIIC Early in comparison to the Argolid

The following discussion will illustrate the general character of the LH IIIA2 and LH IIIC Early pottery assemblage from Ayios Vasileios, based on the evidence available so far. For each subphase (see above), the presence or absence of typical vessel types from the Argolid will also be discussed. Since most of the material from the area of the court comes from secondary deposits, part is comprised of early strays — especially in the post-destruction layers — that do not form an intelligible context, and contribute little to our understanding of the general character of these phases.

The LH IIIA2 table ware at Ayios Vasileios is dominated by plain and monochrome pottery, such as stemmed bowls (FS 304) (Figure 10.4.1 and 5), and semiglobular kylikes (FS 264) (Figure 10.4.2-3 and 6-7). Pattern painted pottery during LH IIIA2 Early is represented by goblets FS 255 with rock pendant, stemmed spirals, and other motifs that suggest they belong to the LH IIIA1 tradition (Kardamaki 2017). The kylix FS 256, a shape typical of LH IIIA2 Early (or LH IIIA2 Middle) (Mountjoy 1999: 129 fig. 29, 207), is not identified with certainty (see Kardamaki 2017: 127 fig. 16.267 for a possible early example). Similarly, kylix FS 257, the characteristic shape in the Argolid during LH IIIA2 Late, is very rare in the relevant deposits. It is possible that some disc bases and one or two rims without preserved decoration might come from this shape (Kardamaki 2017). The repertoire of plain vases is not very different here from that in the Argolid (French 1965: 182 fig. 8; see also, Thomas 2011). It includes carinated kylikes FS 267 (Figure 10.4.9), semiglobular kylikes (Figure 10.4.8) and goblets (in the early stage), angular bowls FS 295 and conical cups FS 204.

As noted above, fragments of characteristic LH IIIB1 shapes appear in the red layer overlying the floor of the court and the South Stoa. These consist, essentially, of rims of the pattern painted kylix FS 258B (Figure 10.5.2) and, possibly, of Zygouries kylix FS 258A, a very rare shape at Ayios Vasileios. It should be noted that further fragments of LH IIIB1 kylikes appear in the higher levels, mixed with material resembling that of the so-called Transitional LH IIIB2-LH IIIC Early phase. To the typical LH IIIB1 shapes, one may add dippers FS 236 with dotted rims (Figure 10.5.3) (Wardle 1969: 277 fig. 7.72),[6] and some rim fragments of the plain conical kylix FS 274 (Figure 10.5.5). There is no evidence for the use of Group A deep bowls. In the Argolid, the latter shape appears from the beginning of LH IIIB, and is probably in use already during LH IIIA2. It steadily increases in number towards the end of the subphase and, in LH IIIB2, it represents the most common variant of the shape (Podzuweit 2007: Beilage 23). Worth noting, in this respect, is the fact that examples of Group A deep bowls (Figure 10.5.1) are, in general, extremely rare in the material found in the North Cemetery and in the area of the court. Examples of Group B deep bowls, the typical LH IIIB2 shape in the Argolid, are very rare and appear twice in the destruction debris of the upper floor in the West Stoa, and once or twice in the upper layers above the floor of the court (French 1969: 82 fig. 7.6, 11-12). In the red layer above the floor of the court and the South Stoa, the majority of the painted sherds associated with LH IIIB1 kylikes belong to monochrome kylikes FS 264 (Figure 10.5.6-7).

Between the red layer and the post-destruction layer with the LH IIIB2-LH IIIC Early pottery, there were no cross joins. In both the North Cemetery and the area of the court, fragments of deep bowls are abundant. The shape is decorated with panel patterns, spirals, row motifs and wavy bands, and may have a medium or thin rim band on the exterior and a monochrome interior (Figure 10.5.8-14). Most of the deep bowl variants belong to Mountjoy's Transitional type 1 (Mountjoy 1999: 560-561, fig. 205.288) (Figure 10.5.9-10, 13-14) or the Group A deep bowl with monochrome interior (Figures 10.5.8 and 12) that was very common in the Argolid during LH IIIC Early (Kardamaki 2009). Mountjoy's Transitional type 1 appears to be common in the Argolid already in LH IIIB2 Late, but is assigned different names by different authorities ('deep bowl C', see Kardamaki 2009). The associated material from the post-destruction layers at Ayios Vasileios does not support a more precise dating in LH IIIB2 or LH IIIC Early 1. One rim could have belonged to a painted conical kylix FS 274, which is considered to be a typical LH IIIC Early feature in the Argolid (Podzuweit 2007: 76-77, pl. 42.1-7). Other typical LH IIIB2 or LH IIIC Early 1 types, well known from the Argolid (for example, the

---

[4] See Kardamaki (2017) for an original assumption of LH IIIA2 or LH IIIB Early for the date of destruction.

[5] For a similar vessel type and rim profile from the Temple Complex at Mycenae, LH IIIB Middle, cf. Moore and Taylour (1999: 39 fig. 13.68-1426 and 68-1427).

[6] For LH IIIA2 dippers with blobs, see Mountjoy (2008: 376 fig. 6.38.3680).

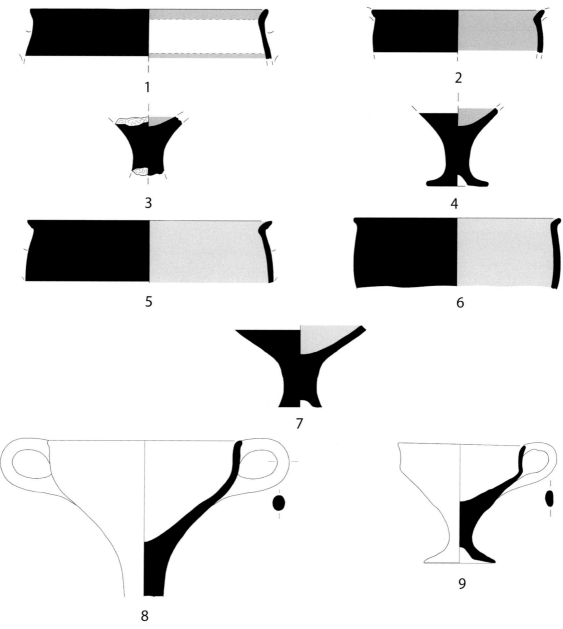

Figure 10.4. LH IIIA2 pottery from the North Cemetery (1-4), Building B (5, 7-9) and the fresco dump to the west of the court (6). Drawings: Vasco Hachtmann (nos. 1-4) and Anna Poelstra (nos. 5-9) (after Kardamaki 2017).

rosette deep bowl, deep bowl A, and linear painted cup FS 215) are absent or very rare.

Handmade and Burnished Ware in imitation of Italian shapes (see Kilian 2007), occurs for the first time in these layers, and in both sectors, the area of the court and the North Cemetery, albeit in negligible numbers. This ware is very well represented in the LH IIIC Early layers of Tiryns and Mycenae, and rare examples had already appeared in LH IIIB2 (Kilian 2007: 46). Hence, the latest material at Ayios Vasileios seems to combine features known in LH IIIB2 Late and LH IIIC Early 1 contexts in the Argolid.

Based on the stratigraphy and pottery typology presented above, the question arises whether the latest

post-destruction phase at Ayios Vasileios that shows features of the so-called Transitional phase of Mountjoy should, or could, be correlated in its greater part with LH IIIB2 Late in the Argolid sequence and, thus, dated to the later part of the 13th century BC.

Evidence from other Laconian sites

Additional evidence pertinent to the question discussed here comes from the other two major sites of the region: the Menelaion, located 12km to the north of Ayios Vasileios, and Ayios Stephanos, near the coast of the Laconian Gulf.

At the Menelaion, floor deposits dating to LH IIIA2 and LH IIIB1 have not been found. Fragments from

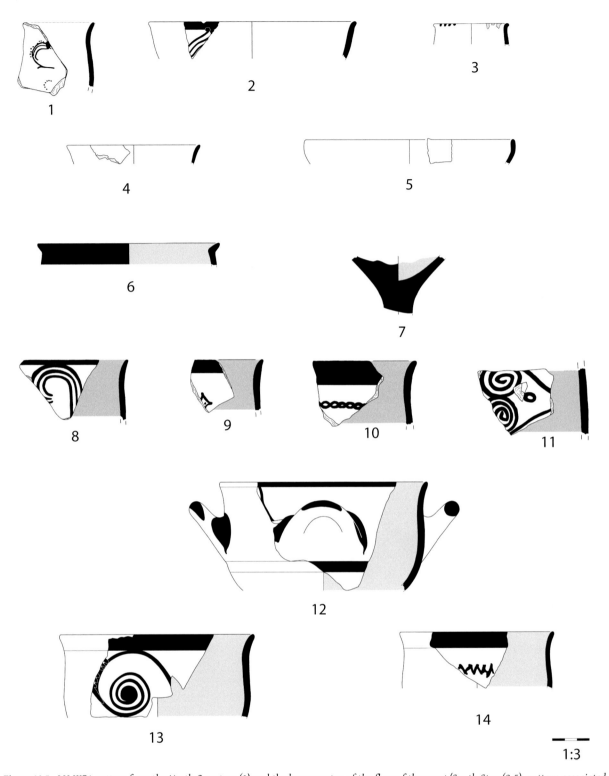

Figure 10.5. *LH IIIB1 pottery from the North Cemetery (1) and the layers on top of the floor of the court/South Stoa (2-5), pottery associated with LH IIIB1 fragments from the layers on top of the floor of the court/South Stoa (6-7), deep bowls from the so-called 'Postpalatial deposit' in the area of the North Cemetery (8-11), and the area of the court/South Stoa (12-14). Drawings: Vasco Hachtmann (nos. 1, 8-11) and Anna Poelstra (nos. 2-7, 12-14).*

vases typical for these subphases (kylikes 256/257, FS 258A+B) are very rare and appear only within secondary deposits that also contain later material (Catling 2009b: 169 fig. 173.WE28-30; 222 fig. 226.PE6-7). Catling has convincingly argued that the monochrome kylix FS 264, represented by several fragments in the wash levels of the hill, could reflect the local LH IIIA2 style (Catling 2009a: 359-360, 366, 452). The next phases recognised by Catling were dated to Transitional LH IIIB2-LH IIIC Early (often equated with LH IIIB2) and LH IIIC Early. Evidence for such a stratigraphic sequence was presented by Catling on the basis of Aetos South

Slope and the area of Building A, where the so-called Terrace Wall and the Bastion were built. Between the Terrace Wall and Building A, a roadway existed, the surface of which was sealed at some point by stones collapsed from the Terrace Wall. This collapse was attributed by Catling to an earthquake which claimed at least one victim (Catling 2009a: 212-218). On top of the debris of the collapsed wall, or in an area cleared of it, a number of structures and one floor were constructed. These represent the latest stage of occupation at the site during LH IIIC Early ('Squatter Occupation') (Catling 2009a: 236-238). The sherds found under the stones of the Terrace Wall, on the surface of the roadway, were dated by Catling to Transitional LH IIIB2-LH IIIC Early (Catling 2009a: 223). In both deposits, the roadway and the partial reoccupation, deep bowls of transitional types (types 1-3) are well attested (Catling 2009b: 257 fig. 261.AR45-47; 258 fig. 262.AR49-50 and 56; 272 fig. 276.AO23; 273 fig. 277.AO26-29). Based on the published material, however, Group A deep bowls with monochrome interior (and some other features more common during LH IIIC Early in the Argolid) appear only in the horizon of the reoccupation (Catling 2009b: 272 fig. 276.AO28). Noteworthy among these is a linear painted conical kylix FS 274 (Catling 2009b: 272 fig. 276. AO14). Handmade Burnished Ware is also reported only from these levels (Catling 2009b: 274 fig. 278). Typical LH IIIC Early shapes and Handmade Burnished Ware are also noted from a floor discovered close to the early Building B (LH IIB/LH IIIA1). The floor is built on top of earlier fills but yielded fragments from a monochrome carinated cup FS 240, a unique shape in Laconia (Catling 2009b: 271 fig. 275.AL12). This shape is supposed to emerge in imitation of Italian handmade cups, and appears in later stages of the early Postpalatial period (Stockhammer 2008: 57).

The evidence from the Menelaion is largely in accordance with that from Ayios Vasileios. At the latter site, too, the monochrome kylix FS 264 seems to be the most frequent LH IIIA2 shape, whereas pattern painted kylikes, as known from the Argolid, are rare. At the Menelaion, no layer was reported to include as the latest material exclusively LH IIIB1 kylikes. This absence may be accidental, since both LH IIIA2 and LH IIIB1 kylikes are represented by a few fragments scattered in later layers. As at Ayios Vasileios, the latest phases of occupation contain material that is best compared to Mountjoy's Transitional LH IIIB2-LH IIIC Early and there are rare examples of the Group B deep bowl (Catling 2009b: 211 fig. 215.NC54; 289 fig. 293.A115). However, Group A deep bowls seem to be more frequent at the Menelaion (Catling 2009b: 286 fig. 290.A65-69 and A75-78). In addition, some variants of rosette deep bowls without dotted rims have also been found (Catling 2009b: 290 fig. 294.A148-149). On the other hand, at Ayios Vasileios no sequence of Mountjoy's Transitional phase and LH IIIC Early has been identified. Moreover,

on present evidence, it seems that the Handmade Burnished Ware is far more frequent at the Menelaion than at Ayios Vasileios.

At Ayios Stephanos, the study of the stratigraphy and typology suggests the absence of LH IIIB1 or LH IIIB2 floors or layers (cf. Taylour and Janko 2008: 16, fig. 1.4). The LH IIIA2 pattern painted kylix FS 256/257 is much better represented at Ayios Stephanos than at Ayios Vasileios and there are also local variations that show affinities to Crete (Mountjoy 2008: 306-307, figs. 6.4-6.5; see also, Thomas 2011 for discussion). In all cases, the LH IIIA2 fills or floors are followed by Transitional or LH IIIC floors/layers, or the latter are found on top of even earlier levels (Mountjoy 2008: 362, fig. 6.33.3593-3597). The latest material is assigned to Transitional LH IIIB2-LH IIIC Early or LH IIIC Early on the basis of stylistic criteria, as the relevant material in most cases derives from the same layers (Mountjoy 2008: 315). LH IIIB1 sherds do occur but always within later layers (Mountjoy 2008: 376, fig. 6.38.3692). The most common variants of deep bowls are assigned either to the Transitional types or fit well within LH IIIC Early (Mountjoy 1999: 280 fig. 94.159, 163-165; 281 fig. 95.166–175; 286 fig. 97.200-212). Moreover, Group A deep bowls are absent or very rare as at Ayios Vasileios (Mountjoy 2008: 317-318, fig. 6.12.3162-3163; 321, fig. 6.14.3213 and 3218; 338, fig. 6.23.3353-3354). Noteworthy among the LH IIIC Early features is the painted conical kylix FS 274 (cf. Menelaion, above) and some closed shapes with distinct LH IIIC Early motifs (Mountjoy 2008: 340, fig. 6.24.3557; 362, fig. 6.33.3593 and 3595). No Handmade Burnished Ware has been reported from the site.

Analytical studies on the LH IIIA2-LH IIIB2 pottery from Laconia and the Argolid

Petrographic and chemical analysis has significantly broadened our view of the production, distribution and trade of pottery and goods across the Mycenaean world. Many of these analyses have focused, primarily, on determining the provenance of the material, but a more holistic approach based on the detailed description of fabric, typology and manufacture (chaînes opératoire) promises an even deeper understanding (see Alram-Stern et al., this volume). Neutron Activation Analysis (NAA) is the most reliable chemical method, as it enables the identification of more elements than other analytical procedures, and can measure with high precision (Perlman and Asaro 1969). In Laconia, significant analytical projects have focused on material from Ayios Stephanos and the Menelaion, although sherds from other sites, including Ayios Vasileios, have also been sampled for comparative purposes (with Optical Emission Spectroscopy (OES), see Jones and Tomlinson 2009). A total of 30 sherds from Ayios Stephanos were included in the Perlman and Asaro database and have since been statistically re-evaluated

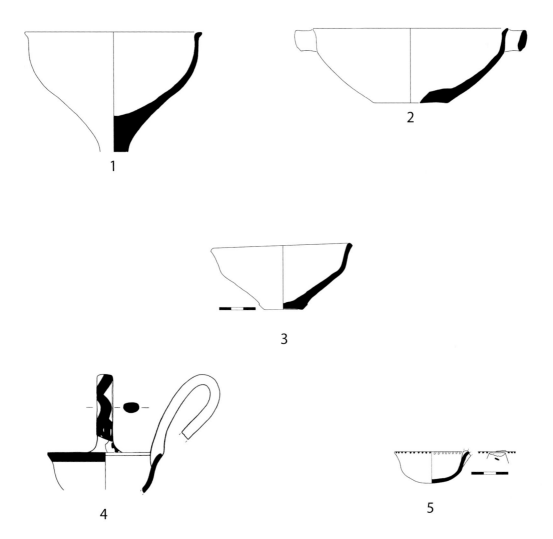

Figure 10.6. Pots found in situ on the floor of the South (1-2) and West Stoa (3); vessels from the building debris of the West Stoa (4-5). Drawings: Eleftheria Kardamaki (nos. 1-2; after Kardamaki 2017), Anna Poelstra (nos. 3, 5) and Reinhard Jung (no. 4).

(French *et al.* 2008; Mommsen *et al.* 2002). Focusing on provenance analyses of pottery of the LH IIIA2-LH IIIC Early phases, it was possible to establish various chemical groups in comparison with Mycenaean pottery from other regions, later pottery and, rarely, local clays. The results of these analyses help us to understand differences between the Argolid and Laconia beyond those of typology.

At Ayios Stephanos, this work revealed a coherent local group — identified through three independent analyses — that includes LH IIIC Early and, more rarely, LH IIIA/ LH IIIB Early sherds (mostly painted; French *et al.* 2008: CD-119). Among these, a fragment of a Zygouries kylix is noteworthy (Mountjoy 2008: 386-387). Such consistency, resulting in the clear distinction of two chronological groups (LH I/IIA on one hand, and LH III on the other), was not seen at the Menelaion. At the latter site, only a very few groups are restricted to specific wares. LH IIIC deep bowls, for instance, belong to two different chemical groups (Jones and Tomlinson 2009: CD-167). The first fits well with the LH III group

from Ayios Stephanos. The other is more diffuse and is represented by several wares from various phases (Jones and Tomlinson 2009: CD-167). This is difficult to explain, although the results of the ongoing analytical project at Ayios Vasileios will presumably provide important new insight. The variability of groups from the Menelaion may reflect the wider range of fabrics sampled there compared with Ayios Stephanos, or the existence of various workshops with long traditions, although it must be stressed that LH IIIA2 pottery from Ayios Stephanos is virtually absent from the sampled material.[7] Very little can be said about the location of production centres, but one important point is that the Laconian pottery was evidently not intended for export. The number of sherds found elsewhere and identified as Laconian by NAA — including from the Argolid, Troy (Mountjoy and Mommsen 2006), Qantir and, recently, Punta di Zambrone on the west coast of Calabria (Jung *et al.* 2015: 460) — is very small. For some

[7] For discussion of different pottery traditions identified at the Menelaion, see Lis (2017).

118

of these sherds, this may be an accidental similarity, but others may be real exports (Jones and Tomlinson 2009: CD-161). Conversely, imported LH IIIA2-LH IIIC Early pottery is very rare among the material from Laconia sampled so far. Samples which are clearly of Argive origin seem to be early, whereas the provenance of the early Mycenaean pottery, either from the Argolid (Mommsen *et al.* 2002) or the southern Peloponnese (French *et al.* 2008; Jones and Tomlinson 2009), is still uncertain.

The situation in the Argolid is very different, as has often been demonstrated on the basis of both analytical and archaeological arguments. Argive pottery is represented by two very well-known chemical profiles with various subgroups, identified with production centres in the southern Argolid (Tiryns/Asine, TIR) and the Argolid/northeastern Peloponnese (MYBE, the so-called Mycenae/Berbati clay paste represented across a wider region that included the northern Argolid and Corinth) (Demakopoulou *et al.* 2017). The Mycenae/Berbati group has been connected with one, or more, specialised workshops in the northern Argolid that produced decorated pottery for exchange, of which the pictorial kraters are the most conspicuous products (Mommsen and Maran 2001). Pottery from these workshops had a very wide distribution during LH IIIA2 and LH IIIB1, and was exported to the east and north Aegean, the Levant and Cyprus, Egypt, and Italy to the west (Bryan *et al.* 1997; Zuckerman *et al.* 2010). In some of these areas, MYBE pottery constitutes almost 90% of the imported pottery, whereas other mainland regions are represented only very rarely (Jung 2015).

The evidence presented above underlines the different ways in which production was organised in Laconia and in the Argolid. One important point of distinction is that in Laconia production was intended for local consumption, whereas the workshops of the were also aiming at export. Perhaps the production of innovative pattern painted pottery in the Argolid was stimulated by such processes, namely the desire to produce high quality decorated pottery that was appreciated as a valuable product in its own right. Finally, the fact that pottery of the two regions was very rarely exchanged is interesting. The rare Argive types were locally produced in Laconia (Ayios Stephanos, Zygouries kylix) and, to judge from macroscopic examination, the same is true of Ayios Vasileios. It seems that the results of the elemental analyses conducted so far reflect the conclusions of typological studies, according to which the Argive innovations, with a few exceptions, were rarely followed in Laconia during LH IIIA2 and LH IIIB Based on the limited distribution of characteristic LH IIIB2 Argive types, Sherratt argued for a 'decreased amount of contact between all areas of the Mycenaean world' (Sherratt 1980: 201). A lack of contact between

the Argolid and central Laconia, however, is only one possible explanation for a diverging regional pottery style during most of the Mycenaean palatial period. Even if we may assume that, from LH IIIA2 late onward, Argive ceramic innovations were largely rejected in household assemblages in central Laconia, considering other aspects of material culture (for example, wall paintings), one may draw a different conclusion. It should also be kept in mind that LH IIIA2 kylikes and closed shapes are very well represented in the Laconian cemeteries (Mountjoy 1999), but fewer LH IIIB1 kylikes are known (Demakopoulou 1971). Here we must consider the semiotic differences in pottery use between settlement and funerary contexts.

Discussion

The preceding discussion demonstrates that differences in pottery styles are not only relevant to comparison of the Argolid and Laconia, but that they also seem to exist between various sites within Laconia itself. For example, a more frequent use of the pattern painted kylix (FS 256/257) during LH IIIA2 is visible at Ayios Stephanos. At the beginning of LH IIIB1, pottery production and consumption at all three major Laconian sites seems to be more homogenous, even if the available evidence is very restricted in terms of the quality of deposits. The available material suggests that, contrary to the Argolid, relatively little use was made of the pattern painted kylix and, at the same time, there is no clear evidence that the Group A deep bowl was widely accepted in LH IIIB1. Due to the lack of relevant stratigraphic evidence, it remains unclear whether some of the Group A deep bowls from Ayios Stephanos and the Menelaion date to this subphase. Finally, at all three sites, the majority of the deep bowls exhibit advanced features described by Mountjoy as Transitional LH IIIB2-LH IIIC Early and not LH IIIB2. The LH IIIB2 variants of deep bowls common in the Argolid are either lacking, or very rare, in Laconia. The Group B deep bowl is virtually absent, and three out of four rosette deep bowls with rim preservation found at the Menelaion are not of the canonical LH IIIB2 type, since they lack the dotted rim (Catling 2009a: 391; 2009b: 194 fig. 198.SW15; 290 fig. 294.A148-149, A151). On the other hand, Group A deep bowls and the type C deep bowl with a medium band on the exterior rim (for which, see Kardamaki 2009) are attested at the Menelaion, however, stratified data are insufficient to permit a more accurate dating within LH IIIB and IIIC Early.

Taken together, the following scenarios may explain the variation of the pottery assemblages found at sites in Laconia compared to those of the Argolid: (a) a decline in occupation in Laconia is responsible for the limited evidence during LH IIIB1; a hiatus occurs in LH IIIB2, followed by reoccupation during LH IIIC Early 1 (or Transitional phase); (b) the changes reflect different pottery styles and there is no hiatus in LH IIIB2. In this case, the bulk of the pottery was the same in LH IIIB1 as in LH IIIA2 (Kardamaki 2017: 114) with the LH IIIB1 kylikes being rare exceptions; and the Transitional phase would be the Laconian equivalent of LH IIIB2 in the Argolid, with no recognisable distinction between LH IIIB2 Early and Late; (c) a combination of (a) and (b) is also possible. After a disastrous conflagration around the middle of LH IIIB, when the deep bowl was not yet fully adopted in ceramic assemblages in Laconia in favour of traditional types (e.g., the monochrome kylix), settlement activities at Ayios Vasileios may have declined. The same may be true for the Menelaion and Ayios Stephanos. The fact that the Group A deep bowl is missing at Ayios Vasileios but is attested at the Menelaion is still problematic. This may indicate regional differences within Laconia, or it may be resolved by further excavation at Ayios Vasileios. On the other hand, immediately after the destruction, around the middle of the LH IIIB phase, parts of the (former) palace may have been rebuilt, and new types of deep bowl that partly resemble Mountjoy's Transitional types may have become common. These new types would have largely continued into LH IIIC Early 1, making the distinction between later parts of LH IIIB (Argive LH IIIB2) and LH IIIC Early 1 very difficult.

While much more work is still required to be certain, it is the last two scenarios, (b) and (c), which reject the LH IIIB2 hiatus and favour a correlation of the Transitional period with LH IIIB2 and LH IIIC Early 1, which we currently consider to be most likely.

If correct, then the production and consumption of pattern painted pottery during the middle and late palatial period (LH IIIA2 Late-LH IIIB2) was quite different in Laconia compared with the Argolid, with the exception of Ayios Stephanos in LH IIIA2. The innovations of the Argive workshops were rarely adopted in Laconia. Instead, at Ayios Vasileios, and probably elsewhere, the bulk of the drinking and eating assemblages consisted of monochrome and plain wares. The differences went beyond the use of the pattern decoration. In LH IIIB1, the Pattern Painted kylix was used, however rarely, whereas the Group A deep bowl was not. Consistent with the absence of the Group A deep bowl from the LH IIIB1 layers at Ayios Vasileios is the absence of the krater FS 281 with horizontal handles. These two shapes are considered to be functionally complementary (Podzuweit 2007). This could suggest the existence of different drinking sets and consumption practices in the Argolid that were not yet shared in Laconia. On the other hand, it is perhaps no accident that at least a limited use of the LH IIIB1 kylix can be observed, since this shape — unlike the deep bowl — was not much different from the LH IIIA2 drinking vessels. The spread of the deep bowl occurred

later, perhaps, at some point during LH IIIB2, however, not all of the decorative systems used in the Argolid were accepted in Laconia.

At the moment, it is difficult to interpret the different use of the Pattern Painted pottery between regions, and what these differences could reflect. The leading role of the Argive workshops is beyond doubt. However, it should be remembered that this role is better understood when viewed from the perspective of inner-Argive communities, or of those east Aegean or Cypriote communities which received a large proportion of this pottery. In other regions of southern Greece, many of the innovative elements of the Argolid were rarely, if ever, imported or adopted. Perhaps the best-known example of such a differentiated use of drinking equipment comes from the destruction horizon of the palace at Pylos (Blegen and Rawson 1965) where deep bowls, and painted pottery in general, are extremely rare.

Bibliography

Banou, E. 1996. *Beitrag zum Studium Lakoniens in der mykenischen Zeit* (Quellen und Forschungen zur antiken Welt 20). Munich: Tuduv.

Bryan, N.D., E.B. French, S.M.A. Hoffman and V.J. Robinson 1997. Pottery sources in Bronze Age Cyprus: a provenance study by neutron activation. *Report of the Department of Antiquities, Cyprus* 1997: 31-64.

Catling, H. W. 2009a. *Sparta: Menelaion I. The Bronze Age. 1: Text* (The British School at Athens Supplementary Volume 45). London: the British School at Athens.

Catling, H. W. 2009b. *Sparta: Menelaion I. The Bronze Age. 2: Plates* (The British School at Athens Supplementary Volume 45). London: the British School at Athens.

Cavanagh, W.G. and J.H. Crouwel 2002. The survey area in the prehistoric periods, in W. Cavanagh, J. Crouwel, R.W.V. Catling and G. Shipley (eds) *Continuity and Change in a Greek Rural Landscape. The Laconia Survey Volume I. Methodology and Interpretation* (The British School at Athens Supplementary Volume 26): 121-150. London: the British School at Athens

Demakopoulou, K. 2003. The pottery from the destruction layers in Midea: Late Helladic III B2 Late or Transitional LH III B2/Late Helladic III C Early?, in S. Deger-Jalkotzy and M. Zavadil (eds) *LH IIIC Chronology and Synchronisms. Proceedings of the International Workshop Held at the Austrian Academy of Sciences at Vienna, May 7th and 8th, 2001* (Österreichische Akademie der Wissenschaften Philosophisch-Historische Klasse Denkschriften 310, Veröffentlichungen der Mykenischen Kommission 20): 77-92. Vienna: the Austrian Academy of Sciences.

Demakopoulou, K., N. Divari-Valakou, J. Maran, H. Mommsen, S. Prillwitz and G. Walberg 2017.

Clay paste characterization and provenance determination of Middle and Late Helladic vessels from Midea. *Opuscula. Annual of the Swedish Institutes at Athens and Rome* 10: 7-47.

French, E.B. 1965. Late Helladic III A2 pottery from Mycenae. *The Annual of the British School at Athens* 60: 159-202.

French, E.B. 1966. A group of Late Helladic III B1 pottery from Mycenae. *The Annual of the British School at Athens* 61: 216-238.

French, E.B. 1969. A group of Late Helladic III B2 pottery from Mycenae. *The Annual of the British School at Athens* 64: 71-93.

French, E.B. 2011. *Well Built Mycenae. The Helleno-British excavations within the citadel at Mycanae 1959-1969, Fascicule 16/17. The Post-Palatial Levels.* Oxford: Oxbow Books.

French, E.B. and W.D. Taylour 2007. *Well Built Mycenae. The Helleno-British excavations within the citadel at Mycanae 1959-1969, Fascicule 13. The Service Areas of the Cult Centre.* Oxford: Oxbow Books.

French, E.B., Ph. Stockhammer and U. Damm-Meinhardt 2009. Mycenae and Tiryns: the pottery of the second half of the thirteenth century BC – contexts and definitions. *The Annual of the British School at Athens* 104: 175-232.

French, E.B., S.M.A. Hoffmann, V.J. Robinson and J.E. Tomlinson 2008. Appendix 3. The Perlman and Asaro analyses of Late Helladic I-III sherds from the 1963 excavations: a statistical re-evaluation, in W.D. Taylour and R. Janko (eds) *Ayios Stephanos. Excavations at a Bronze Age and Medieval Settlement in Southern Laconia* (The British School at Athens Supplementary Volume 44): CD-118–123. London: the British School at Athens.

Furumark, A. 1941. *The Mycenaean Pottery: Analysis and Classification.* Stockholm: Victor Petterson.

Hope Simpson, R. and O.T.P.K. Dickinson 1979. *A Gazetteer of Aegean Civilisation in the Bronze Age, I. The Mainland and Islands* (Studies in Mediterranean Archaeology 52). Gothenburg: Paul Åström.

Jones, R.E. and J.E. Tomlinson 2009. Appendix G. Chemical analysis of Mycenaean pottery from Menelaion and its vicinity, in H.W. Catling. *Sparta: Menelaion I. The Bronze Age* (The British School at Athens Supplementary Volume 45): CD-147-169. London: the British School at Athens.

Jung, R. 2015. Imported Mycenaean pottery in the East: distribution, context and interpretation, in B. Eder and R. Pruzsinszky (eds) *Policies of Exchange. Political Systems and Modes of Interaction in the Aegean and the Near East in the 2nd millennium B.C.E. Proceedings of the International Symposium at the University of Freiburg, Institute for Archaeological Studies, 30th May-2nd June 2012* (Oriental and European Archaeology 2), 243–275. Vienna: the Austrian Academy of Sciences.

Jung, R., H. Mommsen and M. Pacciarelli 2015. From west to west: determining production regions of Mycenaean pottery of Punta di Zambrone (Calabria, Italy). *Journal of Archaeological Sciences: Reports* 3: 455-463.

Kardamaki, E. 2009. Ein neuer Keramikfund aus dem Bereich der Westtreppe von Tiryns. Bemalte mykenische Keramik aus dem auf der Westtreppenanlage deponierten Palastschutt. Unpublished PhD dissertation, University of Heidelberg.

Kardamaki, E. 2015. Conclusions from the new deposit at the Western Staircase terrace at Tiryns, in A-L. Schallin and I. Tournavitou (eds) *Mycenaeans up to Date: the Archaeology of the Northeastern Peloponnese – Current Concepts and New Directions* (Skrifter utgivna av Svenska Intitutet i Athen, 4°, 56): 79-97. Stockholm: the Swedish Institute at Athens.

Kardamaki, E. 2017. The Late Helladic IIB to IIIA2 pottery sequence from the Mycenaean palace at Ayios Vasileios, Laconia. *Archaeologia Austriaca* 101: 73-142.

Kilian, K. 1988. Mycenaeans up to date, trends and changes in recent research, in French, E.B. and K.A. Wardle (eds) *Problems in Greek Prehistory. Papers Presented at the Centenary Conference of the British School of Archaeology at Athens, Manchester, April 1986*: 115-152. Bristol: Bristol Classical Press.

Kilian, K. 2007. *Tiryns, Forschungen und Berichte XV. Die handgemachte geglättete Keramik mykenischer Zeitstellung.* Wiesbaden: Reichert.

Lis, B. 2017. Variability of ceramic production and consumption on the Greek mainland during the middle stages of the Late Bronze Age: the waterpots from the Menelaion, Sparta. *Oxford Journal of Archaeology* 36(3): 243-266.

Maran, J. 2015. Tiryns and the Argolid in Mycenaean times: new clues and interpretations, in A-L. Schallin and I. Tournavitou (eds) *Mycenaeans up to Date: the Archaeology of the Northeastern Peloponnese – Current Concepts and New Directions* (Skrifter utgivna av Svenska Intitutet i Athen, 4°, 56): 277-293. Stockholm: the Swedish Institute at Athens.

Marketou, T., E. Karantzali, H. Mommsen, N. Zacharias, V. Kilikoglou and A. Schwedt 2006. Pottery wares from the prehistoric settlement at Ialysos (Trianda) in Rhodes. *The Annual of the British School at Athens* 101: 1-55.

Mommsen, H. and J. Maran 2001. Production places of some Mycenaean pictorial vessels: the contribution of chemical pottery analysis. *Opuscula Atheniensia. Annual of the Swedish Institute at Athens* 25-26(2000-2001): 95-106.

Mommsen, H., Th. Beier and A. Hein 2002. A complete chemical grouping of the Berkeley Neutron Activation analysis data on Mycenaean Pottery. *Journal of Archaeological Science* 29(6): 613-637.

Moore, A.D and W.D. Taylour 1999. *Well Built Mycenae. The Helleno-British excavations within the citadel at Mycanae 1959-1969, Fascicule 10. The Temple Complex.* Oxford: Oxbow Books.

Mountjoy, P.A. 1976. Late Helladic III B1 pottery dating the construction of the South House at Mycenae. *The Annual of the British School at Athens* 71: 77-111.

Mountjoy, P.A. 1986. Mycenaean Decorated Pottery. A Guide to Identification (Studies in Mediterranean Archaeology 73). Gothenburg: Paul Åström.

Mountjoy, P.A. 1997. The destruction of the palace at Pylos reconsidered. *The Annual of the British School at Athens* 92: 109-137.

Mountjoy, P.A. 1999. *Regional Mycenaean Decorated Pottery*. Rahden: Marie Leidorf.

Mountjoy, P.A. 2008. The Late Helladic pottery, in W.D. Taylour and R. Janko (eds) *Ayios Stephanos. Excavations at a Bronze Age and Medieval Settlement in Southern Laconia* (The British School at Athens Supplementary Volume 44): 299-387. London: the British School at Athens.

Mountjoy, P. and H. Mommsen 2006. Neutron activation analysis of Mycenaean pottery from Troia (1988-2003 excavations). *Studia Troica* 16: 97-123.

Moutafi, I. and S. Voutsaki 2016. Commingled burials and shifting notions of the self at the onset of the Mycenaean Era (1700–1500 BCE): the case of the Ayios Vasilios North Cemetery, Laconia. *Journal of Archaeological Science: Reports* 10: 780-790.

Perlman, I. and F. Asaro 1969. Pottery analysis by neutron activation. *Archaeometry* 11(1): 21-52.

Petrakou, V. 2016. Άγιος Βασίλειος Λακωνίας. *Το Έργον της εν Αθήναις Αρχαιολογικής Εταιρείας* 62(2015): 24-26.

Podzuweit, C. 2007. *Tiryns, Forschungen und Berichte XIV. Studien zur spätmykenischen Keramik*. Wiesbaden: Reichert.

Rutter, J.B. 1977. Late Helladic III C pottery and some historical implications, in E.N. Davis (ed.) *Symposium on the Dark Ages in Greece, Sponsored by the Archaeological Institute of America, New York Society and Hunter College, City University of New York, April 30, 1977*: 1-20. New York: Hunter College.

Rutter, J.B. 2003a. The nature and potential significance of Minoan features in the earliest Late Helladic III C ceramic assemblages of the central and southern Greek mainland, in S. Deger-Jalkotzy and M. Zavadil (eds) *LH IIIC Chronology and Synchronisms. Proceedings of the International Workshop Held at the Austrian Academy of Sciences at Vienna, May 7th and 8th, 2001* (Österreichische Akademie der Wissenschaften Philosophisch-Historische Klasse Denkschriften 310, Veröffentlichungen der Mykenischen Kommission 20): 193-216. Vienna: the Austrian Academy of Sciences.

Rutter, J.B. 2003b. Report on the final discussion. III. Questions addressed by speakers at Vienna workshop on "Late Helladic III C chronology and synchronisms" (7-8 May, 2001), in S. Deger-Jalkotzy and M. Zavadil (eds) *LH IIIC Chronology and Synchronisms. Proceedings of the International Workshop*

Held at the Austrian Academy of Sciences at Vienna, May 7th and 8th, 2001 (Österreichische Akademie der Wissenschaften Philosophisch-Historische Klasse Denkschriften 310, Veröffentlichungen der Mykenischen Kommission 20): 249-251. Vienna: the Austrian Academy of Sciences.

Rutter, J.B. 2003c. Report on the final discussion. IV. Answers to these questions. Definitions, in S. Deger-Jalkotzy and M. Zavadil (eds) *LH IIIC Chronology and Synchronisms. Proceedings of the International Workshop Held at the Austrian Academy of Sciences at Vienna, May 7th and 8th, 2001* (Österreichische Akademie der Wissenschaften Philosophisch-Historische Klasse Denkschriften 310, Veröffentlichungen der Mykenischen Kommission 20): 255-256. Vienna: the Austrian Academy of Sciences.

Shelmerdine, C.W. 1992. The LH IIIA2–IIIB pottery, in W.A. McDonald and N.C. Wilkie (eds) *Excavations at Nichoria in Southwest Greece, II. The Bronze Age Occupation*: 495-521. Minneapolis: University of Minnesota Press.

Sherratt, E.S. 1980. Regional variation in the pottery of Late Helladic IIIB. *The Annual of the British School at Athens* 75: 175-202.

Schönfeld, G. 1988. Bericht zur bemalten mykenischen Keramik. Ausgrabungen in Tiryns 1982/83. *Archäologischer Anzeiger* 1988: 153-211.

Stockhammer, P. 2008. Kontinuität und Wandel. Die Keramik der Nachpalastzeit aus der Unterstadt von Tiryns. Unpublished PhD dissertation, University of Heidelberg.

Taylour, W.D. and R. Janko 2008. The Bronze Age architecture and stratigraphy, in W.D. Taylour and R. Janko (eds) *Ayios Stephanos. Excavations at a Bronze Age and Medieval Settlement in Southern Laconia* (The British School at Athens Supplementary Volume 44): 13-119. London: the British School at Athens.

Thomas, P.A. 2005. A deposit of LH IIIB1 pottery from Tsoungiza. *Hesperia: the Journal of the American School of Classical Studies at Athens* 74(4): 451-573.

Thomas, P.A. 2011. A deposit of LH IIIA2 pottery from Tsoungiza. *Hesperia: the Journal of the American School of Classical Studies at Athens* 80(2): 171-228.

Vasilogamvrou, A. 2013. Ανασκαφή στον Άγιο Βασίλειο Λακωνίας. *Πρακτικά της εν Αθήναις Αρχαιολογικής Εταιρείας* 165(2010): 65-80.

Vasilogamvrou, A. 2014. Ανασκαφή στον Άγιο Βασίλειο Λακωνίας. *Πρακτικά της εν Αθήναις Αρχαιολογικής Εταιρείας* 166(2011): 59-68.

Vasilogamvrou, A. 2015a. Ανασκαφή στον Άγιο Βασίλειο Λακωνίας. *Πρακτικά της εν Αθήναις Αρχαιολογικής Εταιρείας* 167(2012): 63-76.

Vasilogamvrou, A. 2015b. Ανασκαφή στον Άγιο Βασίλειο Λακωνίας. *Πρακτικά της εν Αθήναις Αρχαιολογικής Εταιρείας* 168(2013): 97-116.

Vasilogamvrou, A., E. Kardamaki and N. Karadimas 2021. The foundation system at the palace of Ayios Vasileios, Xirokambi, Laconia, in B. Eder and M. Zavadil (eds) *(Social) Place and Space in Early Mycenaean Greece. International Discussions in Mycenaean Archaeology October 5-8 2016, Athens* (Österreichische Akademie der Wissenschaften Philosophisch-Historische Klasse Denkschriften 528, Mykenische Studien 35): 341-364. Vienna: the Austrian Academy of Sciences Press.

Vitale, S. 2006. The LH IIIB-LH IIIC transition on the Mycenaean mainland: ceramic phases and terminology. *Hesperia: the Journal of the American School of Classical Studies at Athens* 75(2): 177-204.

Vitale, S. 2011. The Late Helladic IIIA2 pottery from Mitrou and its implications for the chronology of the Mycenaean mainland, in W. Gauss, M. Lindblom, R.A.K. Smith and J.C. Wright (eds) *Our Cups are Full.*

Pottery and Society in the Aegean Bronze Age. Papers presented to Jeremy B. Rutter on the Occasion of his 65th Birthday (British Archaeological Reports International Series 2227): 331-344. Oxford: Archaeopress.

Wardle, K.A. 1969. A group of Late Helladic III B1 pottery from within the Citadel at Mycenae. *The Annual of the British School at Athens* 64: 261–297.

Wardle, K.A. 1973. A group of Late Helladic III B2 pottery from within the Citadel at Mycenae: the Causeway Deposit. *The Annual of the British School at Athens* 68: 297-342.

Zuckerman, S, D. Ben-Shlomo, P.A. Mountjoy and H. Mommsen 2010. A provenance study of Mycenaean pottery from northern Israel. *Journal of Archaeological Science* 37(2): 409-416.

The Expansion of Mortuary Behaviour and Rites Across the Coastal Caves of the Mani Peninsula, Laconia, during the Final Neolithic: Evidence from the Burial Sites of Skoini 3 and Skoini 4[1]

Stella Katsarou and Andreas Darlas

Introduction

The aim of this paper is to discuss funerary behaviour in the caves along the western Mani littoral, southern Peloponnese, during the Final Neolithic (FN). The definition of this behaviour draws upon a pattern of funerary rites attested across the cluster of caves at Skoini, part of the west-facing coast at the northern exit of the Gulf of Oitylon. We argue for a strong link between the formation of cave contexts at FN Skoini and inhumation. We propose that the pattern of burial rites taking place here expressed the community's concept of the afterlife by translating household metaphors to this wild zone and monumentalizing the landscape through death, and also regulated power dynamics among the living.

Landscape profile and site range

Skoini is not an isolated case of cave use in the Gulf of Oitylon after the end of the Palaeolithic, the period when the human use of caves in this area is best attested (Darlas and Psathi 2016; Tourloukis *et al.* 2016). Neither does it represent an isolated new burial site on the peninsula, alongside the (so far single) mega-site at Alepotrypa Cave on Diros bay, further south (Papathanasiou *et al.* 2018). Rather, evidence from about twenty Holocene sites (Figure 11.1) along the coast shows that Skoini is part of a broader trend towards cave exploitation after the Palaeolithic, which extends throughout the densely populated western coast, and integrates Skoini with Diros. Spatially, the emerging data demonstrates that these communities were active across diverse cave types from the Middle Neolithic

(MN) to the Early Bronze Age (EBA). They aimed to acquire resources and exploit spaces suited to specific tasks which supported their household and settlement needs, and facilitated the expression of ceremonial and funerary behaviour in the lands beyond the confines of the villages.

This evidence for the widespread and multi-faceted human presence in the caves of the Mani through the Holocene, including the material from Skoini detailed below, is the added benefit from a large-scale reconnaissance programme ongoing since 1998 (Darlas and Psathi 2016). The programme has conducted surveys at more than 100 caves along the western coast of the Mani peninsula, and carried out test excavation at ten of them, with the objective of assessing the extent of the local Palaeolithic record, foragers' cave adaptations, and palaeoanthropological sequences. Observations have shown that landscape evolution and site-formation mechanisms that were in operation along the stepped profile of the coastline — which consists of an upper terrace, a vertical cliff, and a Tyrrhenian terrace just above current sea level (Dufaure 1975) — since the Pleistocene (Figure 11.2), facilitated a resumption in the exploitation of the caves used by Palaeolithic communities in the favourable conditions of the Neolithic.

The critical feature promoting human activities in the coastal caves of the western Mani was the scree accumulated since the last Glacial period on the Tyrrhenian terrace at the foot of the vertical cliff. At that time, the sea level was too far below the Tyrrhenian terrace to wash the scree away (Darlas 2007; 2012c; De Lumley and Darlas 1994). During the Neolithic, the scree remained unaffected by wave-washing and sea erosion, as the significant rise in sea level, to almost 5m below current level, was still below the height of the Tyrrhenian terrace. This scree enabled access to, and easier mobility between, adjacent higher caves and, together with the uninterrupted view across the sea, it was key to Holocene human activity in the precipitous caves of the western Mani. Sea level rise would have also enabled ready access from the coastline.

In this context, the evidence demonstrates that communities showed equal preference for both the

[1] Acknowledgements: the research was conducted by the Ephoreia of Palaeoanthropology-Speleology. Our warm thanks go to William Cavanagh for his invitation to join the colloquium in memory of Professor Chris Mee, and for providing insights during study. We are grateful to David Smith and the anonymous referee for their comments, and to the former whose detailed editing has greatly improved the paper. Conservator Panagiota Gioni has carried out the detailed recovery of the burial context. Anthropologist Eleni Stravopodi conducted preliminary identification of the human remains. Lithic specialist Ioanna Spiliotakopoulou reported on the chipped stone. Thanks are also due to Dimitris Chourdakis, who produced a detailed reconstruction of the double burial from Skoini 3, Eleni Stravopodi and Anastasia Papathanasiou for guidance through his project, and Dimitra Bakoyiannaki for producing the illustration of the pithos.

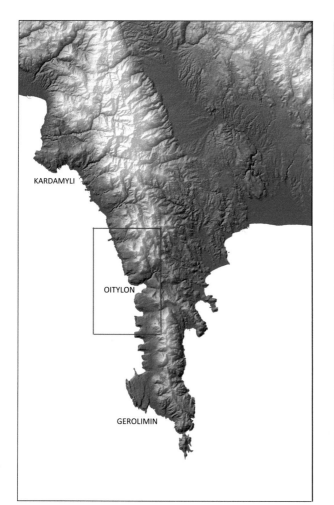 

Figure 11.1. Map of the area of research, illustrating the distribution of Neolithic and Early Bronze Age cave sites investigated by this project.

Figure 11.2. Typical Mani coastal step profile, north of the Gulf of Oitylon: upper terrace (1), vertical cliff (2), Tyrrhenian terrace (3), scree ('S')
(photo © Geotag Aeroview)

Figure 11.3. Kalamakia, Upper Cave: interior chamber, showing pottery and stone artifacts among stalagmite pillars and gours (photo: A. Darlas).

ubiquitous rockshelter, such as those at Skoini to be presented below, and for those rarer, but more intriguing, long and narrow underground caves which offered impressive subterranean chambers and winding passages (Figure 11.3).

Site preservation patterns, however, differ significantly between the enclosed subterranean cave and the exposed rockshelter. The latter was more likely to be affected by scree erosion after the Neolithic, which accelerated the loss of the original Holocene cultural landscape and resulted in low visibility in the number of identified sites. Geoarchaeological observations along the coast have revealed the partial or total loss of sediment in a significant number of rockshelters, wide-mouthed, and shallow caves, depending on scree preservation (Darlas 2007; 2012c). The phenomenon is best illustrated at Trimessi, 6.5km north of the Gulf of Oitylon, where the large surface scatter of Neolithic coarse pottery and poorly preserved ground stone observed below nine overhanging rockshelters, is indicative of marine erosional processes that totally undermined the protective scree and caused dispersal of the original cave fills. Whereas the caves at Trimessi lacked any intact Holocene sequence, the survival of

scree below the rock shelters at Skoini to the south, closer to the Gulf of Oitylon, protected the stratigraphy, and consequently permitted documentation of FN activities on that part of the coast.

Nevertheless, the narrow timeframe of the Holocene human presence in these rockshelter sites — which is limited to the FN — compared to the broader timespan of activities between the sixth (MN) and the third millennium BC (EBA) observed only in subterranean caves, raises further questions about bias in the archaeological visibility of Holocene sites along the Mani coast, and the impact of cultural preferences in the choice of cave spaces.

For the longest sequence of Holocene human activity within the Oitylon record, and its earliest activities, we point to surface evidence from Kalamakia on the southern coast of the Gulf of Oitylon and, more specifically, to that evidence from the long subterranean cave (Figure 11.3) located slightly higher than, and south of, the excavated Middle Palaeolithic site of Kalamakia (Darlas and De Lumley 2004). The earliest human practices known at this upper cave at Kalamakia date to the MN and bear witness to, most probably, ceremonial acts in the narrowest, and least accessible, chamber of the cave. Rituals here involved the use of decorated *Urfirnis* carinated bowls, found in large fragments on the floor of the chamber (Figure 11.4). Contemporary ritual use, involving the destruction of *Urfirnis* vessels, has so far been detected at Alepotrypa Cave, to the south (Psimogiannou 2018). The evidence for the diffusion of *Urfirnis*-related rites along the coast as far as Kalamakia may reflect the wider scale of ceremonial engagements in the MN between caves on the same coast. It may also imply the circulation of ritual equipment, either as small-scale transfer from a local workshop such as that attested at Alepotrypa (Pentedeka 2018), in line with suggested models of local *Urfirnis* distribution (Cullen 1985; Mee 2007), or as large-scale imports (Papathanasopoulos 2011: 57) from centres to the north, perhaps in Laconia or the Argolid (Koumouzelis 1995; Mee *et al.* 2014; Vitelli 1993; 2007).

There is a wider range of practices evident in the use of coastal caves by subsequent groups in the FN, which revolved around domestic, storage, and other functional purposes, as well as funerary use; all more easily identified than other ritual practices, which are also likely to have taken place. An explosion of activity took place during this period all along the coast, at new sites and at the old site of upper Kalamakia. The large, single-chambered Melitzia Cave (Darlas and Psathi 2016), which overlooked the Gulf of Oitylon from its eastern coast, the labyrinthine caves at Fournaki and Kolominitsa on the coast to the north of Skoini, as well as other rockshelters on either side of the gulf, provide surface evidence for expansion, and the intensive circulation of household and storage pottery on the coast. This evidence clearly illustrates a densely frequented landscape which hosted site-specific practices and facilitated social encounters outside settled villages as late as the mature EBA. Modes of use by FN and EBA groups also include rarely documented instances of technical works which aided the exploitation of natural water reservoirs inside several of the caves. The most indicative examples

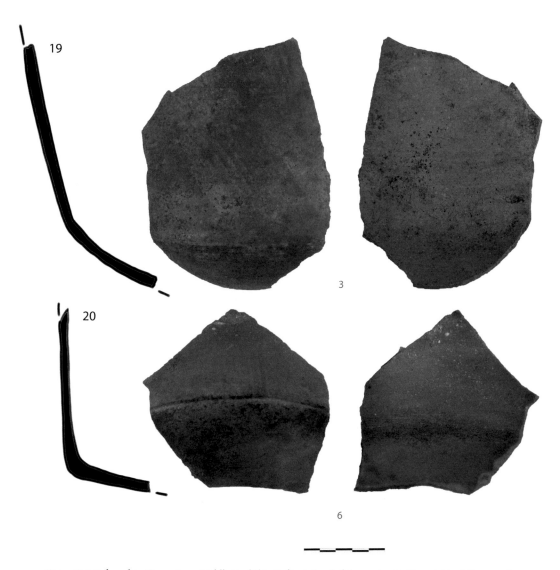

Figure 11.4. Kalamakia, Upper Cave: Middle Neolithic Urfirnis *bowls (illustration: D. Chourdakis, S. Katsarou).*

are the spring-fed lake that fills the rear chamber of Kolominitsa Cave (cf. Alepotrypa, Papathanasopoulos 2011) and the natural rimstones (gours) collecting drip water around the foot of stalagmite pillars at upper Kalamakia and Fournaki. Speleothem growth and formation inside the subterranean chambers of the coast (Boyd and Holmgren 2018) suggest that, for much of its history, and perhaps during the periods of human use discussed here, the dry and barren Laconian coastline preserved an extremely humid environment inside caves, which would have supplied prehistoric farming villages with prized water resources.

This picture of human expansion during the Neolithic and EBA into the caves north and south of the Gulf of Oitylon — discerned from the range of site variability and distribution, and of those human activities discovered through the cave research programme — requires us to reconsider the established picture of the wider area as one largely unexploited by farming communities, beyond those attested to the south by the important assemblage of Alepotrypa Cave (Papathanasiou *et al.* 2018) and the newly recorded open-air sites clustering outside it, and on the slope above Diros Bay (Papathanasopoulos 2011; Pullen *et al.* 2018). Mee (2010) had, indeed, made a point about the promising possibilities of a survey programme in the, then comparatively unexplored, Mani, for consideration alongside the prehistoric site densities and occupation patterns revealed by surveys conducted to the north, at the Laconian interior (Cavanagh 1996; Cavanagh and Crouwel 2002; Waterhouse and Hope Simpson 1960), and to the east, on the Maleas peninsula (Efstathiou-Manolakou 2009: 10-16). The data revealed during the survey discussed here confirms the crucial part caves play in making visible human activity, absent from open-air survey

material (cf. Pullen 2018; Pullen *et al.* 2018), during the Holocene in this area. It also provides the context for integrating the emblematic site at Alepotrypa, formerly regarded as an isolated case of cave use. Some less noted, sporadic, evidence of cave use in the Neolithic and Bronze Age at a few sites adjacent to, and south of, Diros (Efstathiou-Manolakou 2009: 7-8), now acquires significance through integration into this wider context of human exploitation revealed along the western coast.

Beyond chronological, cultural, and topographical information, the scale of the expansion of Neolithic and EBA activity over the Mani now provides the framework for exploring more comprehensive observations of the modes of social engagement with the landscape, communal taskscapes, and seasonal and symbolically-charged territories, which operated outside the context of the local sedentary centres.

Burials and rites at Skoini Cave 3 and Skoini Cave 4

Two events of funerary deposition revealed at caves Skoini 3 and Skoini 4 (Darlas 2012a, 2012b; Darlas and Psathi 2016) form the specific focus of the detailed description below. These two sites are the northernmost in a cluster of four, western-facing, rockshelters situated just north of the mouth of the Gulf of Oitylon (Figure 11.5). The southern two include Skoini 1, whose fill has been completely eroded, and the adjacent Skoini 2, which still preserves a long Pleistocene sequence overlain by a Neolithic layer that currently remains unexplored. Skoini 3 and 4, to the north, lie some 15m apart, at an altitude of 27m above sea level, on the limestone cliff which overlooks a rather narrow stretch (less than 60m wide) of the Tyrrhenian terrace. Both rockshelters have apsidal openings, rising to a

Figure 11.5. The coast at Skoini, showing the position of Skoini Caves 1-4, viewed from the west (photo A. Darlas).

height of 10m above the current surface of the fill at Skoini 3, and 2.5m at Skoini 4. The opening of Skoini 3 extends for a maximum of 15m along the cliff, though its interior space narrows, barely reaching a maximum length of 10m at the interior. Skoini 4 is even smaller, as its opening extends for a width of 6m and the cave continues inside for a depth of only 4m.

Skoini 3 and 4 yielded evidence for primary burials in pits that had been cut through strata from earlier use in the FN. In both caves, this Neolithic activity occured on top of thick Palaeolithic deposits. The funerary events at both sites included symbolically charged acts of deposition and construction, as a means of reproducing metaphors of the settled space within the cave landscape of the cliff. Repetition of mortuary practices across this cluster of caves probably reflects a pattern of demarcated actions associated with the treatment of the dead, and provides a window into those underlying beliefs surrounding death and the afterlife shared by local FN communities. Parallels between these burials and the elaborate and long-established rites visible within Alepotrypa Cave (Katsarou 2018; Papathanasiou 2018), may suggest that the sharing and exchange of religious knowledge and symbols had integrated more than one community across a wide zone of the Mani coast.

Skoini 3

Excavation at Skoini 3 revealed the double burial of an adult male and an adult female placed against the southern natural sidewall inside the rockshelter (Figure 11.6). The burial was made into a pit, which measured approximately 1m in length and between 0.7m and 0.8m in depth. It was dug into a culturally sterile layer that overlay successive Upper Palaeolithic layers. Interred during a single funerary episode, the bodies were placed in a contracted position, approximately at right angles, with an overlap at the pelvis. The female was placed vertically against the wall of the cave on an almost north-south alignment; she lay on her left side, with her upper body to the north and facing east, and her back turned towards the back of the male, whose body had probably been placed in the pit first. The male, buried in an even more tightly contracted position, was aligned east-west (his head placed west) on his right side, facing southeast towards the side wall of the cave. His feet were positioned within a large pithos that had been accommodated at the southeastern corner of the grave pit, and which had been deposited first (Figures 11.7-9). Small rocks were found scattered on top of the male's chest, and some

Figure 11.6. Skoini 3: location of the FN burial (marked), viewed from the west (photo: A. Darlas).

129

were placed around his body and skull, suggesting a possible intention to mark a boundary for him. Two large fragments broken from the pithos covered his hands (Figure 11.7a).

A *patella* shell and a broken cobblestone were placed inside the male's left hand, which was folded and positioned close to his mouth (Figure 11.7b). Other offerings include two elongated clay beads, and a pumice stone. A small chipped-stone assemblage

Figure 11.7. Skoini 3: revealing the burial context, viewed from the southeast (photo: A. Darlas).

beneath his ribs included a few obsidian blade fragments, flakes and splintered pieces, and fewer flakes in red and brown-yellow flint. A considerable number of ceramic fragments were retrieved from the layer overlying the male remains, including several pieces from two broad-deep handled vessels. Fewer ceramic fragments were mixed with the skeletal remains of the male, and fewer still were recovered from beneath, and around them. No offerings were associated with the female.

Both sets of remains were found articulated. However, while the male's skull was completely preserved, the female's skull was missing (Figure 11.7c). There was no sign of teeth, despite excavation of the periphery of the burial and underlying layers. This absence is problematic, and might provoke speculation that the corpse had been subject to some kind of secondary treatment, perhaps including selective removal of the female skull, although, stratigraphically, there is no sign of later disturbance.

The pithos was found standing in the southeastern corner of the burial pit, installed between the natural cave wall and the apparent edge of the pit. One part of its wall was fragmented, which may explain why it was stabilized in an upright position by a vertical stone slab (0.35m wide) set behind it. Clearly, the placement of the pithos on the floor of the burial pit preceded the interment of the bodies; the bottom of the pithos was fixed at a deeper level than that of the bodies, and the male's feet had been pushed inside, which suggests that the bodies were deposited subsequently (Figure 11.9). While the pithos would have originally measured approximately 1m in height, it survived in situ to a height of only 0.65m. Its associated fragments lay inside the pithos on top of its fill, and above the male's hands (Figure 11.7a). A rough limestone quern was placed on the missing side of the pithos, and a cobble grinder was recovered inside the pithos, below one of the broken fragments. However, some parts of the pithos, including most of its rim and shoulder, were missing from the grave, and no trace of them was found.

The overall picture implies an act of deliberate destruction and selective dispersal. The morphological properties of the pithos imply that it was initially made for storage. So, it could have been in use inside the rockshelter, or elsewhere, up to the time of the burial, and possibly broken during deposition. From a practical point of view, destruction of the sidewall might have helped to accommodate the pithos and the corpses within the small burial pit, or the feet of the male inside the pithos. Simultaneously, the destruction and dispersal of the pithos fragments might have had symbolic connotations.

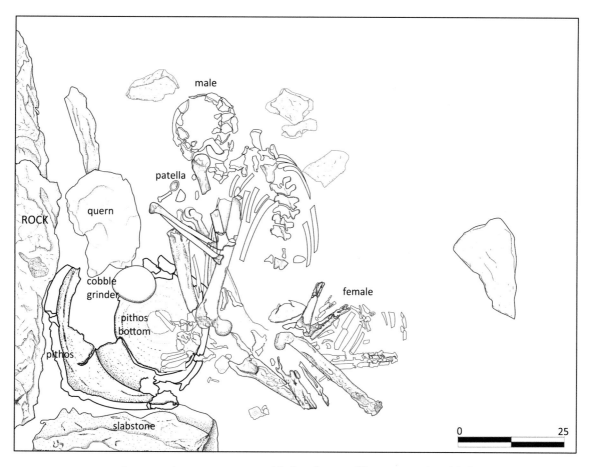

Figure 11.8. Skoini 3: arrangement of the burial context (illustration: D. Chourdakis).

Figure 11.9. Skoini 3: the pithos after removal of human remains, viewed from the west (photo: A. Darlas).

131

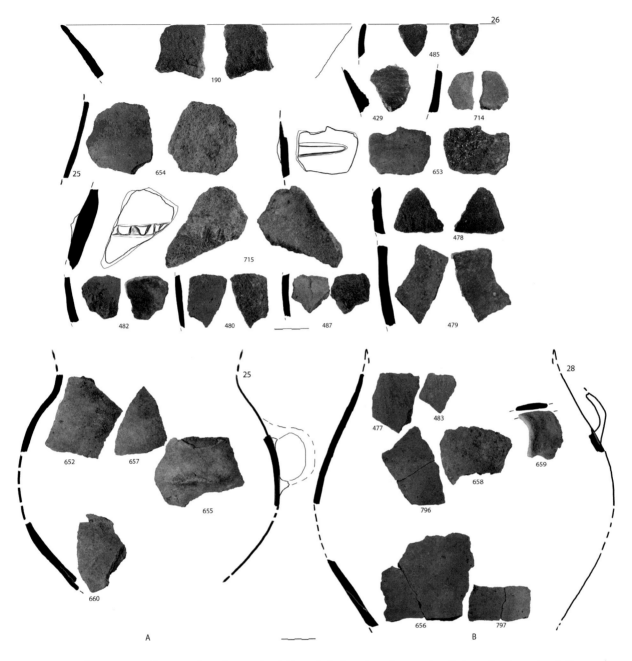

Figure 11.10. Skoini 3: pottery fragments from the upper burial layer, including pieces from two-handled vessels (illustration: S. Katsarou).

The upper part of the pithos fill was composed of small rocks. Further down, the fill appeared, macroscopically, to be formed largely of decomposed organic matter. It contained a fragment of an obsidian blade, another *patella* shell and several small ceramic fragments. Pottery fragments tended to decrease in number with increasing depth through the fill. No trace of burning was observed inside the jar or the burial pit.

The ceramic assemblage associated with the burial at Skoini 3 consisted of a total of 173 sherds (Figures 11.10-13; see Appendixppendix). Spatially, most ceramic fragments came from the layer which overlay and covered the male (Figure 11.10); fewer were retrieved

from among, or below, his skeletal remains (Figures 11.12 and 11.13), and very few derived from inside, and beneath the pithos (Figure 11.11). As noted, no pottery at all was recovered in association with the female remains. The assemblage recovered includes shapes and styles typical of the FN Peloponnese (for which, Bonga 2013; Crouwel 2009; Katsarou 2018; Katsarou and Sampson 1997; Katsipanou-Margeli 2018; Kaznesi and Katsarou 2003; Korres *et al.* 2014; Koumouzelis 1995; Mee 2007b; Valvis 2018; Vitelli 1999; Phelps 2004). More than 80% are of a size smaller than 6cm, and are individual pieces. The less frequent, larger-sized, fragments were recovered above the burial, and included the pieces that were broken off the pithos, and those potsherds partially representing two vessels (Figure 11.10A and B).

Open, shallow or medium-sized containers are equally represented alongside deep, broad vessels, and small jars. Due to extensive fragmentation, and an under-representation of diagnostic pieces (which included only nine plain rims, five flat bases and four strap handles), no complete profiles survived. Nevertheless, some diversity in shape and size is evident. The range of common bowls includes examples with rounded, upright (cat. nos. 425, 485, 702, 706), conical (cat. nos. 190, 460), S-shallow (cat. no. 432), and closely-curved (cat. nos. 458, 669) walls, that vary from narrow (11cm) to very wide (> 30cm). Deeper bowls include examples from upright, incurving (cat. no. 421) and shouldered profiles that can also be as wide as 40cm. Jars (cat. nos. 653, 654, 715) averaged 24cm in width,

with a maximum of 30cm and a minimum of 14cm. Thin walls prevail across all vessel groups, including jars, leaving only the large pithos to stand out as a really thick-walled vessel.

Although some vessels were slipped and polished (for example, cat. nos. 429, 432), the majority, regardless of their shape, were coarse and undecorated. Decorative elements are rare, and, where they are visible, are limited to zones of relief, some with rope impressions, or plastic ribs (cat. nos. 430, 653, 676, 711, 715). Macroscopically distinct tempering is noted using white grits (cat. nos. 653, 684). Formation techniques include typical wall layering with clay slabs or flattened coils, composite bases (cat nos. 455, 671), twisted coils

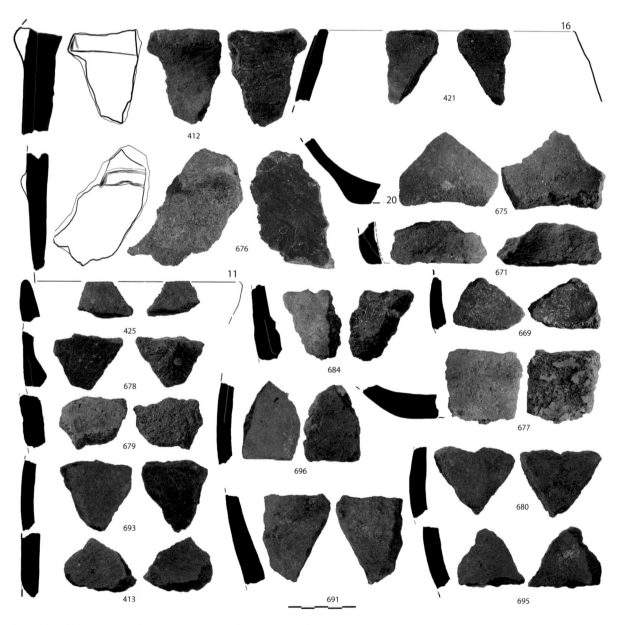

Figure 11.11. Skoini 3: pottery fragments from pithos fill, including pithos fragment (cat. no. 412); from the lower pithos fill (cat. nos. 669, 671): from the upper pithos fill (cat. nos. 413, 421, 425, 675-680, 684, 691, 693, 695, 696) (illustration: S. Katsarou).

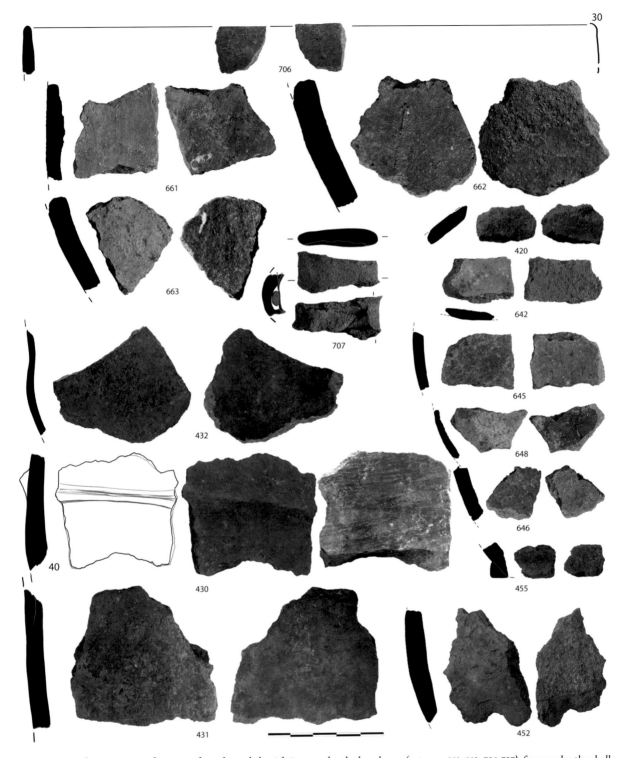

Figure 11.12. Skoini 3: pottery fragments from the male burial. From under the long bones (cat. nos. 661-663, 706-707); from under the skull (cat. no. 420); from the northeast corner and cave wall side (cat. nos. 430-432, 452, 455); from the burial periphery (cat. nos. 642, 645-646, 648) (Illustration: D. Chourdakis, S. Katsarou).

for handle cores (cat. no. 707), smearing (cat. nos. 190, 487) and rustication (cat. no. 672). Random plant impressions on a fragment from a basin (cat. no. 423) suggest possible formation in contact with grass. Reduced cores in almost half the assemblage indicate that incomplete oxidization during firing was common. Use wear includes evidence for soot on the interior surface, possibly from contact with a cooking fire (cat.

nos. 431, 663), as well as an abraded interior in two deep pots (Figure 11.10A and B, especially 655, 656); further explanation of these traces is not possible.

The pithos (Figure 11.14) is worthy of special note for its very elaborate relief decoration, which is formed of plastic ribs arranged in dense horizontal rows that run across the body and through false vertical strap

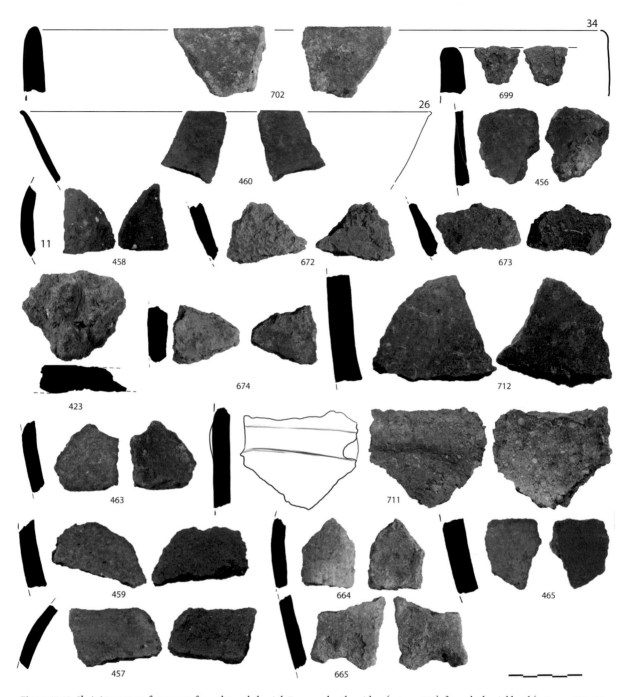

Figure 11.13. Skoini 3: pottery fragments from the male burial. From under the pithos (cat. no. 702); from the burial level (cat. nos. 423, 456-460, 463, 465, 672-674, 699); from under the body (664-665, 711-712) (illustration D. Chourdakis).

handles. Additional layers of clay had been crusted over the exterior of the jar, perhaps to improve its functional properties when in use. Mottling across the handles seems to be a product of firing, typical for the period. The monumental size of the jar, and its elaborate relief, identify another competitive group of potters who projected their individual identities through the syntax and shape of plastic decoration, as has frequently been identified in such containers at other sites (Katsarou and Sampson 1997; Phelps 2004: 116-117; Valvis 2018).

Evidently, the burial was made according to funerary rites that were carefully implemented to fit an established

set of mortuary beliefs. Such choices included double interment, the precise arrangement of bodies, and the sophisticated configuration of the burial, stepping through very specific acts of deposition of items in addition to the bodies, which included the arrangement of the pithos jar at the feet of the dead and possible vessel killing. Given the absence of joining fragments, it is more likely that ceramic fragments recovered from the burial pit were derived from vessels that fell into disuse during an earlier stage of occupation at the rockshelter, perhaps related to domestic activities. Although mixing of these ceramics in the burial fill could have been accidental during shovelling, symbolic intentions

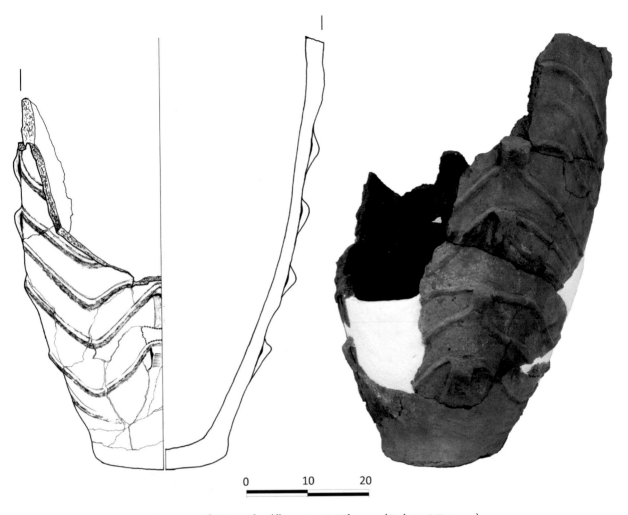

Figure 11.14. Skoini 3: pithos (illustration: D. Bakoyannaki, photo: S. Katsarou).

for their addition cannot be excluded. The two deep, handled and shouldered pots(Figure 11.10A and B) that were distinguished by a number of larger pieces within the layer overlying the male corpse have a more distinct taphonomic profile. Together with evidence for pithos fragmentation, they might be suggestive of a funerary practice involving intentional smashing and selective disposal in the burial.

Skoini 4

A second primary double adult burial occurred in the same chrono-cultural context at Skoini 4, to the north of Skoini 3 (Figure 11.15). Here, the deceased were placed against the northern side wall of the cave, most probably in a burial pit that was dug through the Upper Palaeolithic layer during the FN. Pottery distribution throughout the entire space of the rockshelter indicates extensive occupation at the site before the time of the burial. This occupation should account for a discrete FN layer through which the burial pit had cut before reaching the Palaeolithic level. However, the upper layers of the cave, including that of the FN and part of the Palaeolithic layer, were subject to severe erosion

in later periods. The result was that the FN burial was exposed (solidified and in a poor state of preservation) together with the surface of the Palaeolithic fill that had contained it. This is an important taphonomic indication for recognizing the Neolithic date of the burial within the Palaeolithic stratum. Furthermore, the FN ceramic finds in the burial level comprised a mixture of the original pottery from the burial context and that from the presumed non-burial FN layers that had been cut by the pit. The latter rested on the exposed burial, as the layers within which they had been contained had slowly washed away. Therefore, the FN stratigraphy is now insufficient to enable attribution of the exposed pottery fragments to either the occupation or the burial context. The only intact FN context surviving at Skoini 4 was a stone-lined pit that had been constructed deeper than the grave inside the Palaeolithic layer and, therefore, beneath the level affected by erosion. Artefacts from inside the pit enable taphonomic comparison with artefacts from the exposed surface.

In detail, the burial at Skoini 4 included at least two adults interred in close proximity, although the

Figure 11.15. Skoini 4: location of the Final Neolithic burial (marked), Palaeolithic trench visible at right, viewed from the northwest (photo: A. Darlas).

Figure 11.16. Skoini 4: skeletal remains and the stone-lined pit, viewed from the southwest (photo: A. Darlas).

137

arrangement of the second one is unclear (Figure 11.16). The best preserved of the two, probably male, was oriented roughly almost east-west along the cave wall, with the head turned westward (towards the sea). The body was laid in an extended supine position — maybe slightly on its right side (southwards) — with the knees positioned tightly together, and the right hand probably folded against the pelvis. A boulder recovered above the pelvis area might have been placed intentionally. At least one more individual was laid close to the male, at the south; it is probably a female, however, the very fragmentary preservation makes the identification of sex and posture doubtful.

The construction of the burial pit at Skoini 4, and the practices involved in the formation and arrangement of the bodies, cannot be fully resolved. Nevertheless, the construction of a stone-lined pit was identified at the feet of the probable male, next to the side of the cave. This pit was marked by very few stones forming a narrow mouth at the level of the burial, but opened to an oval interior measuring 75cm by 67cm. It was lined with stones of varying sizes (10cm-30cm) to an approximate depth of 50cm (Figure 11.17); some very large boulders inside the pit (30cm-35cm) might have

been from its lining or fill. Apart from a few FN pottery fragments that were retrieved from its interior (Figure 11.18), this feature contained no other artefact or bones. Some wood charcoal pieces were, however, noted inside its fill. Ceramic fragments from the pit do not exhibit evidence for concretion or stalactite deposition, which was the taphonomic pattern of the exposed potsherds from this cave. Arguably, this observation corroborates the undisturbed nature of the pit deposit. Its position nearby, and in alignment with, the burial verifies it was constructed as an adjunct.

A total of 221 ceramic fragments were collected from the area of the burial, the stone pit, and the overall surface, of Skoini 4 (Figures 11.18 and 11.19; see Appendix). Pottery distribution across the entire space of the cave demonstrates that occupation had started prior to the interment of the burial and the construction of the pit. Of the total assemblage, 21 ceramic pieces were recovered from the stone-lined feature (Figure 11.18) and 71 ceramic fragments were recovered specifically from the burial area (Figure 11.19), although the number of pieces originally included in the burial pit cannot now be determined

Figure 11.17. Skoini 4: the stone-lined pit, viewed from the southwest (photo: A. Darlas).

Figure 11.18. Skoini 4: pottery fragments from the stone-lined pit fill (illustration: S. Katsarou).

due to the stratigraphic disturbance described above. Overall, the fragmentation of ceramics from all areas of the cave is, overwhelmingly, coarse and small (< 6cm), but, as noted, the surfaces of those sherds recovered from the stone-lined pit lack calcite deposits.

Across all areas of Skoini 4, open containers (12cm–33cm wide) were the most frequently represented vessel shape, including carinated (20cm-25cm wide) (cat. nos. 261, 262) and close curved bowls and basins (cat. nos. 224, 261, 262), featuring flat bases (cat. nos. 263, 264), ledges (cat. no. 211) and strap handles (cat. no. 245). Decoration includes patterned-burnishing (cat. nos. 283, 373) and, possibly, impression (cat. no. 246). Technically, there is evidence for base forming by adjoining clay pieces, pinching (cat. nos. 252, 263), smearing (cat. no. 313), and rustication. Reduced firing is extensive. The use of basket-moulding is implied by evidence for impression on the exterior wall of one vessel (cat. no. 281), which looks as if it was from a twined basket. Use wear evidence includes the firing ring on a deep open vessel (cat. no. 245),

and soot deposition attested on the outside (cat. no. 257) as well as the inside surface of some fragments, probably derived from cooking vessels. On a few rim fragments, differential preservation of the surface between rim and body (cat. no. 255) may also be due to use wear, although the identification of function is not possible; neither is identification of the origin of the wear traces associated with roughened or abraded interior surfaces in other fragments.

No distinct vessel feature was noted from the burial area or the pit deposit. The latter yielded the two Pattern Burnished pieces and a sample from open and deep vessels. No burnt ceramics were observed in the pit deposit, despite the presence of some wood charcoal. Overall, small fragmentation, weathered edges and the absence of joins, or associations, between potsherds, prohibits speculation on the deposition of complete vessels intended for the burial or the pit at Skoini 4. Therefore, sherds in the burial context had derived from vessels that had fallen into disuse during previous occupation of the site. However, a symbolic significance

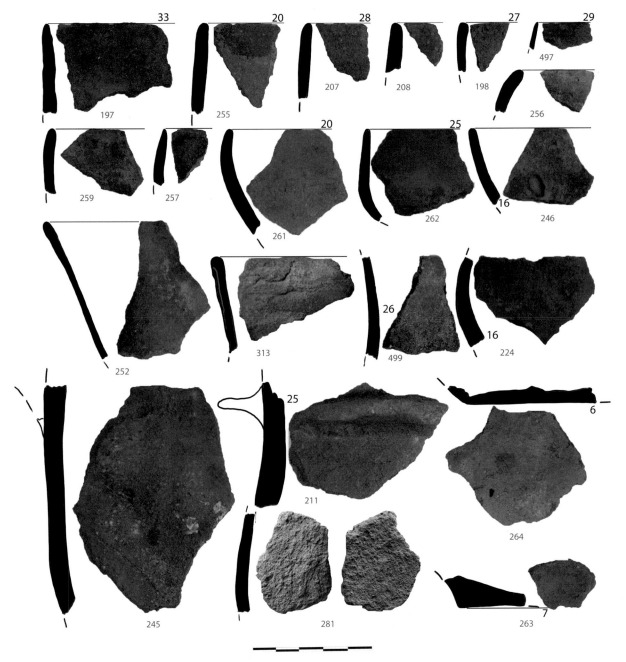

Figure 11.19. Skoini 4: diagnostic pottery fragments from the exposed layer (illustration: S. Katsarou).

for pottery waste added to burial contexts is plausible. More generally, although the state of preservation is less favourable for Skoini 4, the site has provided clear evidence for an established set of mortuary customs, including arrangement of the body, symbolic construction, deposition and sealing.

There is a possible indication of an earlier chronological start in the use of Skoini 4, compared to neighbouring Skoini 3. The suggestion is made on stylistic grounds — as a result of the presence of carinated and Pattern Burnished pieces (cf. Phelps 2004: 106 and 113) — although the sample is small, and may be fortuitous. This earlier start might define the household use of Skoini 4, but it

is unclear whether it should define its burial episode as well. The impression is that Skoini 4 was transformed into a burial place having served for domestic occupation longer than Skoini 3. In general, domestic and funerary activities in the two caves, Skoini 3 and 4, run in parallel and partly overlap, in the FN. The extent of shared vessel properties, ware production techniques and consumption practices, make it likely that there was some direct interconnection between the two sites during household occupation. Cultural homogeneity across the two caves may also reflect diffusion through a wider-reaching network that integrated the Skoini sites into a larger cultural context together with local other caves and open-air centres.

Mortuary practice and community principles at Skoini

The production of burial contexts at Skoini represents only a small part of the demographic spread, human activity, movement and social interaction over the precipitous coast, and the wider region, during the Neolithic. Cave-based activities produced a range of adaptations, possibly site-specific, including ritual performances and practices centred around resource exploitation and the facilitation of domestic tasks (cf. Karkanas 2006; Tomkins 2009), that were able to sustain investment and production and consumption strategies within households and villages. These activities proliferated during the FN and continued until the EBA. It is most probable that they had a temporary, possibly seasonal, character, and persisted as a habitual practice across several generations in every period.

The use of rockshelters at Skoini formed part of this strategy of short-term household exploitation, before they were transformed into burial places. The funerary use at Skoini reveals double burial episodes that were differentiated by location across adjacent sites, and occurred roughly contemporaneously, or within such a very small time gap that is hardly traceable in the course of the cultural phase. The evidence from the two sites reveals that tightly-bound sets of burial traditions related to village communities that developed mortuary facilities at the caves above the coastline in the area of the Gulf of Oitylon, and allows some definition of the symbolic conceptions, and acts of performance, formalized within these caves. Comparison and correlation between the small burial assemblage at Skoini and the major mortuary institution operating already in nearby Alepotrypa Cave to the south for at least a couple of millennia, may have implications for the existence of a pattern of burial rituals and shared conceptions, which was peculiar to these coastal caves and was expressed in contexts of various scales and sizes across them.

Further exploration of this indication certainly requires more targeted investigation among the subterranean caves that preserve Neolithic assemblages, as well as the open caves or rockshelters with Palaeolithic layers that may have been dug into by Neolithic successors for burial purposes, as at Skoini. Potential sites include cave Skoini 2, the third of the cluster which preserves a FN layer on top of a long Pleistocene/Palaeolithic stratigraphic sequence. One might also need to reconsider the chronology of the alleged Upper Palaeolithic female burial excavated at Apidima Cave C, on the coast between the bays of Oitylon and Diros (Pitsios 1999). The report of this burial describes an adult female, tightly flexed, with head missing, which was retrieved in a non-fossilised condition inside loose sediment that lay within the Palaeolithic layer. By comparison to the new evidence, the taphonomic and stratigraphic origin of this burial in the Palaeolithic may now seem open to question.

Returning to Skoini, the funerary practices and accompanying rites reveal beliefs in the animate and transcendental nature of the two caves. It seems that the cliffs of the Mani became the stage on which long-prescribed and structured norms of mortuary practice were played out and experienced. These beliefs were aligning with views that saw cave physicality as liminal and the boundary with the afterlife (Moyes 2012), and were widely shared by farming communities across the rest of the Greek mainland and the Aegean (Faure 1964: 64-69; Fowler, K.D. 2004; Mavridis and Tankosić 2016; Triantaphyllou 2008).

However, rather than reflecting a usual case of funerary treatment in a cave, Skoini stands out for the territorial segregation of the burials. The decision to territorially segregate the deceased at Skoini raises the question of the extent to which individual or group identities were reinforced through the use of different burial grounds in this period. This links Skoini to the wider debate surrounding the notion of ownership at the end of the Neolithic (Halstead 1995; Nowicki 2008: 201). Indeed, a desire for social distinction was increasingly visible in various contexts, and at various levels, of communal life by that time, including projected personal display through funerary behaviour, as noted at Kephala (Coleman 1977), and household competition within large settlements (Souvatzi 2008).

Spatial allocation of the dead in other caves may reflect similar social concerns. Particularly, in inland Laconia, the distribution of burials across adjacent caves is known from Kouveleiki Caves A and B, which are situated 50m apart from each other near Geraki (Kontaxi et al. 1995; Kontaxi and Stravopodi 2003). In the wider region of the Mani coast, the persistence of the practice of accommodating contemporary dead in adjacent clusters seems to be an extensively and deeply embedded theme in those FN communities that expanded over the interior of Alepotrypa Cave and the settlement outside it. Alepotrypa, which was the most densely occupied burial terrain, with an unparalleled number of individuals in the Mediterranean context (Papathanasiou 2018), has provided evidence for social segmentation implemented with ritual monumentality Differentiation was articulated through the formation of mortuary clusters across adjacent natural niches and chambers of the cave and may have reflected different identities, personal or group,, which were critical for embodying the politics of identity by the living and/or stating claims for descent(Katsarou

2018). An increase in social tension might also be implied in this context. Skoini possibly reflects the effects of this wave of transformation towards the projection of social identity and community boundaries, by creating distinction in burial grounds and social topographies through natural monumental landmarks. Taken together with Alepotrypa, and the burial caves of inland Laconia, Skoini may suggest integration of the Mani into a social sphere where distinction of burial territory might have been a means for the definition of identity.

Beyond burial segmentation and its social correlations, the graves at Skoini integrated dense constituent spiritual and conceptual elements which reveal the appropriation of such essential values as communality, wealth, security, history, and overall, reflect the fundamental Neolithic spirit. This perception was ritualised through the symbolic manipulation of food and food culture that are vital elements of farming life (Halstead 2012; Robb 2013; Urem-Kotsou and Kotsakis 2007). This manipulation occurred through everyday ceremonial acts such as disposal, consumption, and feasting at the grave, which permeated Neolithic life at various levels (Cavanagh and Mee 1998; Dietler 2011; Hamilakis 1998; Mavridis and Tankosić 2016; Triantaphyllou 2008). At Skoini, these acts were addressed through salient features intended to emphasise food prosperity for the afterlife: pithos, stone pit, killed vessels, sherd scatter, marine shells, grinding and chipped stone tools, and stone pit. The evidence for foodstuffs comes directly from marine shells — which are commonly consumed on and offered to the dead from the Mesolithic period onward (Cullen 1995: 276) — but might also be implied for other categories.

The pithos and the constructed stone pit are both placed at the feet of the dead from the outset to fulfil the role of containers for food offerings in the grave, and imply the structural roles the theme of food and its associations (cooking, storage, consumption, feasting, and others) had for farmers. Storage jars, for example, accompany burials at many sites; either as urns, such as at Kouveleiki Cave A (Koumouzelis 1995), or as destroyed containers scattered around the human remains (Fowler, K.D. 2004). Alepotrypa Cave, for example, has revealed a large number of pithoid jar fragments in association with mortuary contexts, and provides the clearest evidence that pottery, and specifically jar, destruction and deposition was a funerary ritual in its own right (Katsarou 2018; Katsipanou-Margeli 2018; Psimogiannou 2018). Similarly, pits, which are widely associated with household food in the Greek Neolithic, are transferred to cult and symbolic pit deposits inside grave contexts

throughout the Neolithic and into the Bronze Age (Chapman 2000; Psimogiannou 2012: 188-195).

The disposition of the burial assemblage at Skoini illustrates the grave as an icon of the living household. Food metaphors are constructed in the mortuary sphere for the sake of the dead, whose care becomes the responsibility of the living: the funerary contexts extend the values which revolve around production, and the affluent and conspicuous consumption of wealth, into the afterlife. At Alepotrypa, at this stage, the enactment of rites culminates in the integration of a complete domestic landscape within the burial context, manifest in the deposition of storage jars, and a wide range of domestic accessories, as well as in the construction of clay-lined pits, adjacent to the burial areas (Papathanasiou et al. 2018).

The final act of sealing the graves, and their features, at Skoini under stone rubble and boulders marks the end, and establishes the boundary between the dead and the living. Sealing is a common practice in the Neolithic to symbolically mark the end of life for any structure. Persistence of this act in funerary fills, in both cemeteries and isolated burials, is observed from the Mesolithic in the Franchthi Cave (Cullen 1995). At Alepotrypa, a series of burials are covered with layers of stones, including stone fills of associated pits (Katsipanou-Margeli 2018: 39-43). Once life metaphors have been integrated into the grave and secured, the final sealing of those buried, and their context, stands as a powerful signal of disconnection from life and transition. Finally, just as the living household was capable of safeguarding social and family cohesion, so the funerary household, created with all its necessary distinctions and consumption habits, turned the ancestors of the family into 'spirits' (Fowler, C. 2004: 45), whose veneration is thought to safeguard ties, and amplify tensions, among their descendants (Thomas 2018). However, the symbolism behind the syntax of the bodies at Skoini is beyond our reach. The extended posture of the male at Skoini 4, half leaning on one side, is infrequent compared to the more typical flexed position (Georgiadis 2011), although there are contemporary parallels for various extended positions from Alepotrypa (Papathanasiou 2009: 23), Lerna (Vitelli 2007: 131), the Cave of Lakes at Kastria in the northern Peloponnese (Sampson 1997: 45), and even from various burials in supine positions throughout the Balkans (Borić 2015). Certainly, the flexed position attested at Skoini 3 reflects a widespread norm for primary burials, found in numerous examples at Alepotrypa. The same applies to placement of the dead along the side wall of the caves. Even the head orientation of the males is to the west in both caves. At Skoini 3, the arrangement of the two bodies at right angles with an overlap at the pelvis area is very specific to this episode. All elements seem to underline that highly structured interment associations were meant to be taken care of, in detail.

It is notable that Skoini contains only primary burials — no remains exist from any secondary treatment of the dead. However, the absence of any evidence for the female skull in Skoini 3, even for her teeth, might indicate secondary skull removal, as part of highly-charged post-exhumation veneration rites that were established within FN communities, which can be seen in Ossuary II in Alepotrypa cave (Katsarou 2018) and which are implied by smaller cave ossuaries in other parts of Greece, for example, at Astakos Cave in Aitoloakarnania (Benton 1947).

There is one very significant aspect in both burials at Skoini, which touches on corporate performance, although it is imponderable: it is implied by the burial of two dead individuals in a single event (a couple at Skoini 3, and possibly also at Skoini 4) rather than one single inhumation. The implication of simultaneous death brings into discussion the possibility that dramatic circumstances had determined the fate of the two individuals, or male-female couple, which is an aspect that certainly needs further analytical research. By comparison, a good number of double or multiple primary burials have also been documented in Alepotrypa and its environs (Papathanasiou 2018). Independently of how death occurred, the double inhumation seems to reflect modes of sharing between the two individuals, even to the level of extra-reciprocal attachment or 'dividual' personhood, when each individual is permeable and 'encompasses multiple constituent things and relations received' from the other (Budja 2010: 49).

The definition of the caves at Skoini is more than a cultural attribution of two more burial sites within the wider geographical and social perspective of the Greek Neolithic. It rather requires a contextual look that might be regionally particular, and takes account of local social phenomena and networks to help understand behavioural and ideological links across the farming communities which spread over the Mani coast. Comprehensive examination of human distribution and activities across this wider region also provides insight into the communal identity of those responsible for the creation of the mortuary landscape inside Diros, where the existence of both overland and maritime networks,

and the mobility of people and artefacts throughout the region, is open to speculation but is not yet verified. It also enables clearer understanding of subsistence practices, adaptive decisions, and the ways in which the production of wealth shaped the worldview and life modes of local farmers. One may even assume that configuration of a burial landscape in the Mani, and Laconia more widely, through the transformation of their caves, was reinforced by distinctive local conceptual, social and ritual norms developed alongside mainland practices.

Overall, the coastal caves of the Mani emerge as transcendent, dramatic and protective places during the Neolithic; as spaces for dedication and ritual, and as animate places and institutions of social life, imbued with a long heritage of memory, history and experience. The result is that these supposedly 'marginal' areas (Cavanagh 2004; Mee 2001; 2007: 215; Tomkins 2008) seem distinctly less so. In conclusion, this discussion may generate more general considerations about the changing perception of cave use in the Greek Neolithic. Caves, variably occupied, may have served as communal spaces where people gathered, acted, and shared their worldviews beyond the personal, domestic spaces of the home. Communal buildings are not usually attested to in the Greek Neolithic village (although open areas between houses may have functioned as such; Mee 2010; Pappa et al. 2013), and the degree to which caves may have served as inter-communal arenas of cohesion, perhaps in an institutionalized status, is one aspect of their use that has not yet been adequately explored in the Greek context, although it has been suggested, for example, for the Anatolian Neolithic (Baird et al. 2017). This role may have been made effective through corporate participation in ceremonial and funerary acts which acquired significance from the social sharing of the landscape beyond, or together with household activities (Katsarou 2021). The emergence of group projection by the end of the Neolithic probably affected the nature of cave occupation, rendering them less collective. Although not true for the Mani, other parts of the Peloponnese (cf. Nestor's Cave: Korres et al. 2014) and the mainland, and especially the Cyclades and Minoan Crete (Tomkins 2008), demonstrate that caves retained an influential role in maintaining social cohesion by the time socio-ideological transformations (Alram-Stern 2014; Tomkins 2010) at the end of the period, and through Bronze Age, appointed them to formalized cults that served the power of the emerging political hierarchies.

Appendix. Table of finds

Kalamakia, Upper Cave

Cat. No.	Figure	Context	Description
3	11.4	surface	carinated bowl, oblique parallels in black on red slipped (*Urfirnis*)
6	11.4	surface	carinated bowl, vertical parallels in black on red slipped (*Urfirnis*)

Skoini 3 Cave

Cat. No.	Figure	Context	Description
190	11.10	surface	conical bowl, plain pointed rim, red coarse, reduced core, smeared.
412	11.11	pithos	pithos jar(?), upright body, coarse brown, relief band, wall layering.
413	11.11	pithos fill	conical bowl(?), brown slipped.
420	11.12	burial, skull	shallow bowl(?), close curved body, coarse red, wall layering.
421	11.11	pithos, upper fill	deep bowl, plain rounded rim, coarse red, *d.*16cm.
423	11.13	burial	basin or on-floor feature, flat base (detached), coarse brown, plant impressions.
425	11.11	pithos, upper fill	bowl, rim plain pointed, upright body, coarse brown, reduced core, *d.*11cm.
429	11.10	surface	jar(?), black slipped, polished.
430	11.12	burial, NE corner	deep bowl, red slipped, wall layering, *d.*40cm.
431	11.12	burial, NE corner	deep bowl, lower body, brown slipped, soot, reduced core.
432	11.12	burial, NE corner	shallow bowl, S-body, black slipped.
452	11.12	burial, side stone	jar, brown slipped.
455	11.12	burial, side stone	jar(?), coarse brown, reduced core, added triangular stripe (detached).
456	11.13	burial	bowl, lower body, red slipped, reduced core, wall layering.
457	11.13	burial	jar, red slipped, reduced core, wall layering.
458	11.13	burial	shallow bowl, close curved body, coarse brown, reduced core, *d.*11cm.
459	11.13	burial	bowl, upright body, brown slipped.
460	11.13	burial	conical bowl, plain pointed rim, brown slipped, reduced core, *d.*26cm.
463	11.13	burial	shallow bowl, black slipped, grey body, wall layering.
465	11.13	burial	shallow bowl, red slipped.
477	11.10	surface	small jar, Vessel B.
478	11.10	surface	bowl, brown slipped, reduced core.
479	11.10	surface	bowl, brown slipped/polished, reduced core.
480	11.10	surface	jar, red slipped, reduced core.
482	11.10	surface	shallow bowl, red slipped, soot.
483	11.10	surface	small jar, Vessel B.
485	11.10	surface	shallow bowl, plain pointed rim, brown slipped, reduced core, *d.*26cm.
487	11.10	surface	jar, brown slipped, reduced core, smeared.
642	11.12	burial, periphery	shallow bowl(?), flat base, coarse orange, reduced core
645	11.12	burial, periphery	jar, upright body, coarse grey.
646	11.12	surface	jar, coarse brown, reduced core, wall layering.
648	11.12	surface	bowl, red slipped, wall layering.
652	11.10	surface	collared bowl A (shoulder; with 655, 657, 660), brown slipped/polished, reduced core.

653	11.10	surface	jar, brown slipped, plastic rib, soot, limestone grits.
654	11.10	surface	shouldered jar, brown slipped, reduced core.
655	11.10	surface	shouldered bowl, Vessel A.
656	11.10	surface	small jar, Vessel B.
657	11.10	surface	collared bowl A (shoulder; with 652, 655, 660), brown slipped/polished, reduced core.
658	11.10	surface	small jar, Vessel B.
659	11.10	surface	small jar, Vessel B, flat vertical handle.
660	11.10	surface	collared bowl A.
661	11.12	burial, legs	jar, brown slipped, wall layering.
662	11.12	burial, legs	bowl, slipped grey.
663	11.12	burial, legs	jar, slipped grey, reduced core.
664	11.13	under burial	shallow bowl (with 665), close curved body, brown slipped, wall layering.
665	11.13	under burial	shallow bowl (with 664), brown slipped, wall layering.
669	11.11	pithos, lower fill	shallow bowl, lower body, black slipped.
671	11.11	pithos, lower fill	flat base (detached exterior stripe), coarse brown.
672	11.13	burial	jar, coarse orange, reduced core, rusticated outside(?).
673	11.13	burial	bowl, lower body, brown slipped, wall layering.
674	11.13	burial	jar, coarse grey, reduced core.
675	11.11	pithos fill	jar, flat base, coarse grey, reduced core, wall layering, *d*.20cm.
676	11.11	pithos fill	deep jar, upright body, coarse brown, reduced core, plastic rib, wall layering.
677	11.11	pithos fill	jar, flat base, coarse brown, reduced core, wall layering.
678	11.11	pithos fill	bowl, S-body, brown slipped.
679	11.11	pithos fill	jar, coarse brown.
680	11.11	pithos fill	jar, coarse grey, reduced core.
684	11.11	pithos fill	jar, coarse brown, reduced core.
691	11.11	pithos fill	jar, coarse brown, wall layering.
693	11.11	pithos fill	jar, coarse brown, reduced core.
695	11.11	pithos fill	jar, coarse black, reduced core.
696	11.11	pithos fill	jar, coarse black, reduced core.
699	11.13	burial, side stone	jar, plain pointed rim, upright body, coarse black, reduced core.
702	11.13	under pithos	bowl, plain pointed rim, upright body, coarse brown, *d*.34cm.
706	11.12	under burial, legs	bowl, plain pointed rim, upright body, coarse grey, reduced core, *d*.30cm.
707	11.12	under burial, legs	deep jar, flat vertical handle, coarse brown, reduced core, coil.
711	11.13	under burial	deep jar, coarse brown, reduced core, relief zone, wall layering.
712	11.13	under burial	deep jar, coarse brown, reduced core.
714	11.10	surface	shouldered bowl, coarse grey.
715	11.10	surface	shouldered jar, brown coarse, roped relief, reduced core
796	11.10	surface	small jar, Vessel B.
797	11.10	surface	small jar, Vessel B.
Vessel A	11.10	surface	shouldered bowl (652, 655, 657, 660), flat vertical handle (detached) brown slipped/polished, sandwich core, wall layering, *d*.25cm.
Vessel B	11.10	surface	small jar (477, 483, 656, 658-659, 796-797), flat vertical handle, red-brown coarse, reduced core, wall layering, *d*.28cm.

Skoini 4 Cave

Cat. No.	Figure	Context	Description
197	11.19	surface	broad jar, plain pointed rim, upright walls, grey coarse, *d*.33cm.
198	11.19	surface	bowl, plain rounded rim, red slipped, *d*.27cm.
207	11.19	surface	bowl, plain pointed rim, upright walls, brown coarse, *d*.28cm.
208	11.19	surface	bowl, plain rounded rim, upright walls, brown slipped, reduced core.
211	11.19	surface	deep bowl, concave walls, horizontal ledge, brown coarse, reduced core, *d*.25cm.
224	11.19	surface	shallow bowl, close curved walls, red coarse, reduced core, *d*.16cm.
245	11.19	surface	deep bowl, flat vertical handle (detached), red-brown coarse, firing ring, reduced core.
246	11.19	surface	shallow bowl, plain rounded, rim, brown coarse, *d*.16cm.
252	11.19	surface	conical bowl, thickened rounded rim, brown-grey coarse, reduced core, pinching.
255	11.19	surface	bowl, plain rounded rim, upright walls, grey coarse, exterior rim worn, reduced core, *d*.20cm.
256	11.19	surface	bowl, incurving rim, brown coarse.
257	11.19	surface	shallow bowl, plain pointed rim, S-walls, brown coarse, soot.
259	11.19	surface	bowl, plain rounded rim, brown coarse.
261	11.19	surface	conical bowl, carinated rim, red coarse, sandwich core, *d*.20cm.
262	11.19	surface	carinated bowl, plain pointed rim, red slipped, reduced core, *d*.25cm.
263	11.19	surface	flat base, red coarse, pinching, *d*.7cm.
264	11.19	surface	flat base, brown coarse, reduced core, *d*.6cm.
281	11.19	surface	bowl, brown coarse, reduced core, mat molded.
313	11.19	surface	conical bowl, plain flat rim, brown coarse, smeared.
364	11.18	pit	jar, brown slipped.
366	11.18	pit	shouldered jar, brown slipped, reduced core.
367	11.18	pit	jar, red coarse, reduced core.
368	11.18	pit	jar, brown slipped.
370	11.18	stone structure	jar, brown coarse, reduced core.
371	11.18	stone structure	bowl, brown slipped, reduced core.
373	11.18	stone structure	bowl, concave walls, grey-brown slipped/pattern burnished, reduced core.
375	11.18	stone structure	jar, red coarse, reduced core.
378	11.18	inside the pit	jar, brown coarse.
379	11.18	inside the pit	bowl, brown slipped/polished.
382	11.18	inside the pit	bowl, concave walls, red-brown slipped/polished.
383	11.18	inside the pit	bowl, concave walls, brown slipped/pattern burnished.
497	11.19	surface	bowl, plain pointed rim, incurving walls, red coarse, *d*.29cm.
499	11.19	surface	bowl, concave walls, red coarse, reduced core, smeared, *d*.26cm.

Bibliography

Alram-Stern, E. 2014. Times of change: Greece and the Aegean during the 4th millennium BC, in B. Horejs and M. Mehofer (eds) *Western Anatolia before Troy. Proto-Urbanisation in the 4th Millennium BC? Proceedings of the International Symposium Held at the Kunsthistorisches Museum Wien, Vienna, Austria, 21-24 November 2012* (Oriental and European Archaeology 1): 305-327. Vienna: the Austrian Academy of Sciences.

Baird, D., A. Fairbairn and L. Martin 2017. The animate house, the institutionalization of the household in Neolithic central Anatolia. *World Archaeology* 49(5): 753-776.

Benton, S. 1947. Hagios Nikolaos near Astakos in Akarnania. *The Annual of the British School at Athens* 42: 156-183.

Boyd, M. and K. Holmgren 2018. Speleothems from Alepotrypa Cave: towards climate reconstruction, in A. Papathanasiou, W.A. Parkinson, D.J. Pullen, M.L. Galaty and P. Karkanas (eds) *Neolithic Alepotrypa Cave in the Mani, Greece: in Honor of George Papathanassopoulos*: 400-406. Oxford: Oxbow Books.

Bonga, L. 2013. Late Neolithic Pottery from Mainland Greece, ca. 5,300–4,300 B.C. Unpublished PhD dissertation, Temple University.

Borić, D. 2015. Mortuary practices, bodies, and persons in the Neolithic and Early-Middle Copper Age of South-East Europe, in C. Fowler, I. Harding and D. Hofmann (eds) *The Oxford Handbook of Neolithic Europe* (Oxford Handbooks): 927–958. Oxford: Oxford University Press.

Budja, M. 2010. The archaeology of death: from 'social personae' to 'relational personhood'. *Documenta Praehistorica* 37: 43–54.

Cavanagh, W.G. 1996. The Neolithic pottery, in W. Cavanagh, J. Crouwel, R.W.V. Catling and G. Shipley (eds) *Continuity and Change in a Greek Rural Landscape. The Laconia Survey Volume II. Archaeological Data* (The British School at Athens Supplementary Volume 27): 1-3. London: the British School at Athens.

Cavanagh, W.G. 2004. WYSIWYG: Settlement and territoriality in southern Greece during the Early and Middle Neolithic periods. *Journal of Mediterranean Archaeology* 17(2): 165-189.

Cavanagh, W.G. and J.H. Crouwel 2002. The survey area in the prehistoric periods, in W. Cavanagh, J. Crouwel, R.W.V. Catling and G. Shipley (eds) *Continuity and Change in a Greek Rural Landscape. The Laconia Survey Volume I. Methodology and Interpretation* (The British School at Athens Supplementary Volume 26): 121-150. London: the British School at Athens.

Cavanagh, W. and C. Mee 1998. *A Private Place: Death in Prehistoric Greece* (Studies in Mediterranean Archaeology 125). Jonsered: Paul Åström.

Chapman, J. 2000. Pit-digging and structured deposition in the Neolithic and Copper Age. *Proceedings of the Prehistoric Society* 66: 61-87.

Coleman, J.E. 1977. *Keos I. Kephala: A Late Neolithic Settlement and Cemetery*. Princeton: the American School of Classical Studies at Athens.

Crouwel, J. 2009. Prehistoric Geraki: work in progress (2005), in W.G. Cavanagh, C. Gallou and M. Georgiadis (eds) *Sparta and Laconia: from Prehistory to Pre-Modern. Proceedings of the Conference Held in Sparta, Organised by the British School at Athens, the University of Nottingham, the 5th Ephoreia of Prehistoric and Classical Antiquities and the 5th Ephoreia of Byzantine Antiquities 17-20 March 2005* (The British School at Athens Studies 16): 67-76. London: the British School at Athens.

Cullen, T. 1985. Social implications of ceramic style in the Neolithic Peloponnese, in W.D. Kingery (ed.) *Ancient Technology to Modern Science* (Ceramics and Civilization, Volume I): 77-100. Columbus: the American Ceramic Society.

Cullen, T. 1995. Mesolithic mortuary ritual at Franchthi cave, Greece. *Antiquity* 69(263): 270–289.

Darlas, A. 2007. Η παλαιολιθική κατοίκηση της Μάνης, in E. Konsolaki-Giannopoulou (ed.) *ΕΠΑΘΛΟΝ: Αρχαιολογικό Συνέδριο προς τιμήν του Αδώνιδος Κ. Κύρου, Πόρος, 7-9 Ιουνίου 2002, Τόμος Α'*: 23-48. Athens: Municipality of Poros.

Darlas, A. 2012a. Παλαιολιθικά σπήλαια της Μάνης (2002). *Αρχαιολογικόν Δελτίον* 56-59(2001-2004)(Chr. B'6): 491-492.

Darlas, A. 2012b. Παλαιολιθικά σπήλαια της Μάνης (2003-2004). *Αρχαιολογικόν Δελτίον* 56-59(2001-2004) (Chr. B'6): 519–521.

Darlas, A. 2012c. Γεωμορφολογική εξέλιξη και κατοίκηση των σπηλαίων της Δυτικής Μάνης κατά το Ανώτερο Πλειστόκαινο και το Ολόκαινο, in N. Zacharias, M. Georgakopoulou, K. Polykreti, Y. Facorellis, and T. Vakoulis (eds) *Πρακτικά 5ου Συμποσίου της Ελληνικής Αρχαιομετρικής Εταιρείας, Αθήνα, 8-10 Οκτωβρίου 2008*: 237–253. Athens: Papazisis.

Darlas, A. and H. De Lumley 2004. La grotte de Kalamakia (Aréopolis, Grèce). Sa contribution à la connaissance du Paléolithique moyen de Grèce, in Le Secrétariat Du Congrès (ed.) *Section 5: Le Paléolithique Moyen / The Middle Palaeolithic. General Sessions and Posters. Acts of the XIVth Union International de Sciences Préhistoriques et Protohistoriques Congress, Liège, 2–8 September 2001* (British Archaeological Reports International Series 1239): 225-234. Oxford: Archaeopress.

Darlas, A. and E. Psathi 2016. The Middle and Upper Palaeolithic in the western coast of the Mani peninsula (southern Greece), in K. Harvati and M. Roksandic (eds) *Palaeoanthropology of the Balkans and Anatolia: Human Evolution and its Context* (Vertebrate Paleobiology and Paleoanthropology Series): 95-117. Dordrecht: Springer.

De Lumley, H. and A. Darlas 1994. Grotte de Kalamakia (Aréopolis, Peloponnèse). *Bulletin de Correspondance Hellénique* 118(2): 535–559.

Dietler, M. 2011. Feasting and fasting, in T. Insoll (ed.) *The Oxford Handbook of the Archaeology of Ritual and Religion*: 179–194. Oxford: Oxford University Press.

Dufaure, J.J. 1975. Le relief du Péloponnèse. Unpublished PhD dissertation (Thèse d'état), Paris-Sorbonne University (Paris IV).

Efstathiou-Manolakou, I. 2009. Archaeological investigations in the caves of Laconia, in W.G. Cavanagh, C. Gallou and M. Georgiadis (eds) *Sparta and Laconia: from Prehistory to Pre-Modern. Proceedings of the Conference Held in Sparta, Organised by the British School at Athens, the University of Nottingham, the 5th Ephoreia of Prehistoric and Classical Antiquities and the 5th Ephoreia of Byzantine Antiquities 17-20 March 2005* (The British School at Athens Studies 16): 5-20. London: the British School at Athens.

Faure, P. 1964. *Fonctions des cavernes crétoises* (École française d'Athènes, Travaux et mémoires des anciens membres étrangers de l'École et de divers savants 14). Paris: de Boccard.

Fowler, C. 2004. *The Archaeology of Personhood. An Anthropological Approach* (Themes in Archaeology). London and New York: Routledge.

Fowler, K.D. 2004. *Neolithic Mortuary Practices in Greece* (British Archaeological Reports International Series 1314). Oxford: Archaeopress.

Georgiadis, M. 2011. Honouring the dead in Mesolithic and Neolithic Peloponnese: a few general observations, in H. Cavanagh, W. Cavanagh and J. Roy (eds) *Honouring the Dead in the Peloponnese. Proceedings of the Conference Held at Sparta, 23–35 April 2009* (Centre for Spartan and Peloponnesian Studies Online Publication 2): 163–181. Nottingham: Centre for Spartan and Peloponnesian Studies, University of Nottingham.

Halstead, P. 1995. From sharing to hoarding: the Neolithic foundations of Aegean Bronze Age society, in R. Laffineur and W.-D. Niemeier (eds) *POLITEIA. Society and State in the Aegean Bronze Age. Proceedings of the 5th International Aegean Conference/ 5e Rencontre égéenne internationale, University of Heidelberg, Archäologisches Institut, 10-13 April 1994* (Aegaeum 12): 11–21. Liège and Austin: the University of Liège and University of Texas at Austin.

Halstead, P. 2012. Feast, food and fodder in Neolithic-Bronze Age Greece. Commensality and the construction of value, in S. Pollock (ed.) *Between Feasts and Daily Meals: Toward an Archaeology of Commensal Spaces* (eTopoi: Journal for Ancient Studies Special Volume, 2): 21-51. Berlin: Edition Topoi.

Hamilakis, Y. 1998. Eating the dead: mortuary feasting and the politics of memory in the Aegean bronze age societies, in K. Branigan (ed.) *Cemetery and Society in the Aegean Bronze Age* (Sheffield Studies in Aegean Archaeology 1): 115-132. Sheffield: Sheffield Academic Press.

Karkanas, P. 2006. Late Neolithic household activities in marginal areas: the micromorphological evidence from the Kouveleiki caves, Peloponnese, Greece. *Journal of Archaeological Science* 33(11): 1628-1641.

Katsarou. S. 2018. When do the dead become dead? Mortuary projects from Ossuaries I and II, Alepotrypa Cave, in A. Papathanasiou, W.A. Parkinson, D.J. Pullen, M.L. Galaty and P. Karkanas (eds) *Neolithic Alepotrypa Cave in the Mani, Greece: in Honor of George Papathanassopoulos*: 91-126. Oxford: Oxbow Books.

Katsarou, S. and A. Sampson 1997. Φάσεις I-III. Η νεολιθική κεραμική, in A. Sampson (ed.) *Το Σπήλαιο των Λιμνών στα Καστριά Καλαβρύτων: Μία προϊστορική θέση στην ορεινή Πελοπόννησο* (Εταιρεία Πελοποννησιακών Σπουδών 7): 77-273: Athens: the Society of Peloponnesian Studies.

Katsarou, S. 2021. The dawn of ancient Greek cave cult: Prehistoric cave sanctuaries, in S. Katsarou and A. Nagel (eds) *Cave and Worship in Ancient Greece. New Approaches in Landscape and Ritual*: 17-48. New York: Routledge.

Katsipanou-Margeli, B. 2018. The stratigraphic and pottery sequence of Trench B1 at Alepotrypa Cave: a first approach to the investigation of ceramic and chronological associations, in A. Papathanasiou, W.A. Parkinson, D.J. Pullen, M.L. Galaty and P. Karkanas (eds) *Neolithic Alepotrypa Cave in the Mani, Greece: in Honor of George Papathanassopoulos*: 33-90. Oxford: Oxbow Books.

Kaznesi, A. and S. Katsarou 2003. Η Νεολιθική κεραμική από τη Β Κουβελέικη σπηλαιά Αλεποχοριού Λακωνίας. *Αρχαιολογικά Ανάλεκτα εξ Αθηνών* 32-34(1999-2001): 27-36.

Kontaxi, C., E. Kotjabopoulou and E. Stravopodi 1995. Προκαταρκτική έκθεση ανασκαφών στη Α' Κουβελέικη Σπηλιά Αλεποχωρίου Λακωνίας. *Αρχαιολογικά Ανάλεκτα εξ Αθηνών* 22(1989): 21-30.

Kontaxi, C. and E. Stravopodi 2003. Ανασκαφή της Β Κουβελέικης Σπηλαιάς Αλεποχωρίου Λακωνίας. *Αρχαιολογικά Ανάλεκτα εξ Αθηνών* 32-34(1999-2001): 19-26.

Korres, G.S., A. Sampson and S. Katsarou 2014. Τὸ σπήλαιον Νέστορος στὴν Βοϊδοκοιλιὰ Πύλου. Ἡ ἔρευνά του καὶ ἡ προκαταρκτικὴ ἐξέταση τῶν παλαιοτέρων καὶ νεωτέρων εὑρημάτων, in I.K. Giannaropoulou (ed.) *Πρακτικά τοῦ Δ' Τοπικοῦ Συνεδρίου Μεσσηνιακῶν Σπουδῶν, Καλαμάτα, 8-11 Ὀκτωβρίου 2010* (Πελοποννησιακά – Παράρτημα 31): 49-90. Athens: the Society of Peloponnesian Studies.

Koumouzelis, M. 1995. Η Κεραμική από την Α' Κουβελέϊκή σπηλιά Αλεποχωρίου Λακωνίας. *Αρχαιολογικά Ανάλεκτα εξ Αθηνών* 22(1989): 143-159.

Mavridis, F. and Ž. Tankosić 2016. Early Bronze Age burial deposits at the Ayia Triada Cave at Karystos, Euboia: tentative interpretations. *Hesperia: the Journal of the American School of Classical Studies at Athens* 85(2): 207-242.

Mee, C. 2001. Nucleation and dispersal in Neolithic and Early Helladic Laconia, in K. Branigan (ed.) *Urbanism in the Aegean Bronze Age* (Sheffield Studies in Aegean Archaeology 4): 1-14. Sheffield: Sheffield Academic Press.

Mee, C. 2007. The production and consumption of pottery in the Neolithic Peloponnese, in C. Mee and J. Renard (eds) *Cooking up the Past: Food and Culinary Practices in the Neolithic and Bronze Age Aegean*: 200-224. Oxford: Oxbow Books.

Mee, C. 2010. Cohesion and diversity in the Neolithic Peloponnese: what the pottery tells us, in W. Cavanagh and S. Hodkinson (eds) *Being Peloponnesian. Proceedings from the Conference Held at the University of Nottingham 31st March–1st April 2007* (Centre for Spartan and Peloponnesian Studies Online Publication 1): 1–11. Nottingham: Centre for Spartan and Peloponnesian Studies, University of Nottingham.

Mee, C., B. Cavanagh and J. Renard 2014. The Middle–Late Neolithic transition at Kouphovouno. *The Annual of the British School at Athens* 109: 65-95.

Moyes, H. (ed.) 2012. *Sacred Darkness: A Global Perspective on the Ritual Use of Caves.* Boulder: University Press of Colorado.

Nowicki, K. 2008. The Final Neolithic (Late Chalcolithic) to Early Bronze Age transition in Crete and the southeast Aegean islands: changes in settlement patterns and pottery, in V. Isaakidou and P. Tomkins (eds) *Escaping the Labyrinth: the Cretan Neolithic in Context* (Sheffield Studies in Aegean Archaeology 8): 201-228. Oxford: Oxbow Books.

Papathanasiou, A. 2009. Mortuary behaviour in the Alepotrypa Cave: assessments from the study of the human osteological material, in W.G. Cavanagh, C. Gallou and M. Georgiadis (eds) *Sparta and Laconia: from Prehistory to Pre-Modern. Proceedings of the Conference Held in Sparta, Organised by the British School at Athens, the University of Nottingham, the 5th Ephoreia of Prehistoric and Classical Antiquities and the 5th Ephoreia of Byzantine Antiquities 17–20 March 2005* (The British School at Athens Studies 16): 21-28. London: the British School at Athens.

Papathanasiou, A. 2018. The people of Alepotrypa, in A. Papathanasiou, W.A. Parkinson, D.J. Pullen, M.L. Galaty and P. Karkanas (eds) *Neolithic Alepotrypa Cave in the Mani, Greece: in Honor of George Papathanassopoulos*: 260-271. Oxford: Oxbow Books.

Papathanasiou, A., W.A. Parkinson, D.J. Pullen, M.L. Galaty and P. Karkanas (eds) 2018. *Neolithic Alepotrypa Cave in the Mani, Greece: in Honor of George Papathanassopoulos.* Oxford: Oxbow Books.

Papathanasopoulos, G.A. 2011. *Το Νεολιθικό Διρό: Σπήλαιο Αλεπότρυπα Τόμος I.* Athens: Melissa Editions.

Pappa, M., P. Halstead, K. Kotsakis, A. Bogaard, R. Fraser, V. Isaakidou, I. Mainland, D. Mylona, K. Skourtopoulou, S. Triantaphyllou, C. Tsoraki, D. Urem-Kotsou, S.M. Valamoti and R. Veropoulidou 2013. The Neolithic site of Makriyalos, northern Greece: a reconstruction of the social and economic structure of the settlement through a comparative study of the finds, in S. Voutsaki and S.M. Valamoti (eds) *Diet, Economy and Society in the Ancient Greek World. Towards a Better Integration of Archaeology and Science. Proceedings of the International Conference held at the Netherlands Institute at Athens on 22–24 March 2010* (Pharos Supplement 1): 77–87. Leuven: Peeters.

Pentedeka, A. 2018. The Alepotrypa Cave pottery assemblage: a ceramic petrology approach, in A. Papathanasiou, W.A. Parkinson, D.J. Pullen, M.L. Galaty and P. Karkanas (eds) *Neolithic Alepotrypa Cave in the Mani, Greece: in Honor of George Papathanassopoulos*: 163–178. Oxford: Oxbow Books.

Phelps, B. 2004. *The Neolithic Pottery Sequence in Southern Greece* (British Archaeological Reports International Series 1259). Oxford: Archaeopress.

Pitsios, T. K. 1999. Paleoanthropological research at the cave site of Apidima and the surrounding region (South Peloponnese, Greece). *Anthropologischer Anzeiger* 57(1): 1-11.

Psimogiannou, K. 2012. Creating identities in the mortuary arena of the Greek Final Neolithic: a contextual definition of practices in central and southern Greece. *Documenta Praehistorica* 39: 185-201.

Psimogiannou, K. 2018. Patterns of pottery consumption, destruction and deposition at Alepotrypa cave: the case of Chamber Z during the Neolithic period, in A. Papathanasiou, W.A. Parkinson, D.J. Pullen, M.L. Galaty and P. Karkanas (eds) *Neolithic Alepotrypa Cave in the Mani, Greece: in Honor of George Papathanassopoulos*: 127-157. Oxford: Oxbow Books.

Pullen, D. 2018. Caves and the landscape of Late Neolithic to Early Helladic I Greece: Comparing excavation and survey data from the Peloponnese, in S. Dietz, F. Mavridis, Ž. Tankosić and T. Takaoğlu (eds) *Communities in Transition. The Circum-Aegean Area during the 5th and 4th Millennia BC* (Monographs of the Danish Institute at Athens 20): 314-322. Oxford: Oxbow Books.

Pullen, D.J., M.L. Galaty, W.A. Parkinson, W.E. Lee and R.M. Seifried 2018. The Diros Project, 2011-2013: surface survey and site collection in Diros Bay, in A. Papathanasiou, W.A. Parkinson, D.J. Pullen, M.L. Galaty and P. Karkanas (eds) *Neolithic Alepotrypa Cave in the Mani, Greece: in Honor of George Papathanassopoulos*: 407-425. Oxford: Oxbow Books.

Robb, J. 2013. Material culture, landscapes of action, and emergent causation: a new model for the origins of the European Neolithic. *Current Anthropology* 54(6), 657-683.

Sampson, A. 1997. *Το Σπήλαιο των Λιμνών στα Καστριά Καλαβρύτων: Μία προϊστορική θέση στην ορεινή Πελοπόννησο* (Society of Peloponnesian Studies Monograph Series 7). Athens: the Society of Peloponnesian Studies.

Souvatzi, S. 2008. *A Social Archaeology of Households in Neolithic Greece: An Anthropological Approach.* Cambridge and New York: Cambridge University Press.

Thomas, J. 2018. The Neolithic body, in P. Bickle and E. Sibbesson (eds) *Neolithic Bodies* (Neolithic Studies Group Seminar Papers 15): 132-143. Oxford: Oxbow Books.

Tomkins, P. 2008. Time, space and the reinvention of the Cretan Neolithic, in V. Isaakidou and P. Tomkins (eds) *Escaping the Labyrinth: the Cretan Neolithic in Context* (Sheffield Studies in Aegean Archaeology 8): 21-48. Oxford: Oxbow Books.

Tomkins, P. 2009. Domesticity by default. Ritual, ritualization and cave-use in the Neolithic Aegean. *Oxford Journal of Archaeology* 28(2): 125-153.

Tomkins, P. 2010. Neolithic antecedents. On the origins of the Aegean Bronze Age, in E.H. Cline (ed.) *The Oxford Handbook of the Bronze Age Aegean (ca. 3000-1000 B.C)*: 31-49. Oxford: Oxford University Press.

Tourloukis, V., N. Thompson, C. Garefalakis, P. Karkanas, G.E. Konidaris, E. Panagopoulou and K. Harvati 2016. New Middle Palaeolithic sites from the Mani Peninsula, southern Greece. *Journal of Field Archaeology* 41(1): 68-83.

Triantaphyllou, S. 2008. Living with the dead: a reconsideration of mortuary practices in the Greek Neolithic, in V. Isaakidou and P. Tomkins (eds) *Escaping the Labyrinth: the Cretan Neolithic in Context*

(Sheffield Studies in Aegean Archaeology 8): 136–154. Oxford: Oxbow Books.

Urem-Kotsou, D. and K. Kotsakis 2007. Pottery, cuisine and community in the Neolithic of north Greece, in C. Mee and J. Renard (eds) *Cooking up the Past: Food and Culinary Practices in the Neolithic and Bronze Age Aegean*: 225-246. Oxford: Oxbow Books.

Valvis. G. 2018. Pithoi with relief decoration from Alepotrypa Cave, in A. Papathanasiou, W.A. Parkinson, D.J. Pullen, M.L. Galaty and P. Karkanas (eds) *Neolithic Alepotrypa Cave in the Mani, Greece: in Honor of George Papathanassopoulos*: 158-162. Oxford: Oxbow Books.

Vitelli, K.D. 1993. *Franchthi Neolithic Pottery. Volume 1: Classification and Ceramic Phases 1 and 2* (Excavations at Franchthi Cave, Greece 8). Bloomington and Indianapolis: Indiana University Press.

Vitelli, K.D. 1999. *Franchthi Neolithic Pottery. Volume 2: the Later Neolithic Ceramic Phases 3 to 5* (Excavations at Franchthi Cave, Greece 10). Bloomington and Indianapolis: Indiana University Press.

Vitelli, K.D. 2007. *Lerna V. The Neolithic Pottery from Lerna.* Princeton: the American School of Classical Studies at Athens.

Waterhouse, H. and R. Hope Simpson 1960. Prehistoric Laconia: part I. *The Annual of the British School at Athens* 55: 67-107.

Attica during the Final Neolithic and the Early Bronze Age: Regional Ceramic Traditions and Connections with Neighbouring Areas

Margarita Nazou

Introduction

Situated between mainland and island-defined archaeological entities, Attica has traditionally been treated as a transitional borderland between what is perceived as 'Helladic' culture, versus that perceived as 'Cycladic' culture (Figure 12.1). This can be easily explained by looking at the history of chronological and cultural schemes in the prehistoric Aegean (Table 12.1). In the early 20th century AD, a 'tripartite' evolutionary scheme (Early-Middle-Late) was introduced by Evans (1906) for Crete, and later adapted by Wace and Blegen (1918) for the Greek mainland, and by Harland (1924: 71) for the Cyclades. This ordering of data was based on the correlation of seriated ceramic typologies with stratigraphic contexts. An alternative classification of the Aegean data into 'cultures' and 'groups', was attempted in an effort to avoid the problems caused by equating a chronological period with a specific style of material culture. The need for separate geographical, chronological and cultural terminologies led Renfrew (1972: 53) to propose an alternative classification of the Aegean data into cultures, which could be defined in space and time, and need not correspond directly with chronological periods. He was later criticised (Coleman 1979a, 1979b; Manning 1995: 21) because his groups, in general, seem simply to replicate the existing tripartite chronological scheme under a new name. Thus, confusion has been created among researchers by the concurrent and interchangeable use of the tripartite chronological systems and the cultural groups, as in many studies there is no clear reference to the respective chronological or cultural phenomena. Only in the case of the Cyclades are Renfrew's 'cultures' and 'groups' still popular, somewhat re-defined by Doumas (1977) and Rambach (2000). However, their use by most researchers as groups of archaeological data is not accompanied by consideration of the processes behind their creation. An exceptional study, which led towards an interpretation of Cycladic cultural groups as something more than data clusters, is Broodbank's application of the theoretical framework of island archaeology (2000). Behind the identified Cycladic cultures, he was able to distinguish different ways in which islanders engaged with their material world over a period of substantial change from the earliest colonists to the end of the Early Bronze Age (EBA).

In the case of Attica, the existing ordering of archaeological data is problematic in many respects. Even though Attica is neither geographically nor culturally peripheral in the prehistoric Aegean, previous research has tried to force its data into both the Helladic and the Cycladic chronological schemes and 'cultures'. This causes two main problems: on the one hand, the existing chronological and cultural schemes create terminological ambiguity in the presentation of the archaeological evidence. For example, the terms Early Helladic (EH), Early Cycladic (EC) and Early Helladic/Early Cycladic (EH/EC) are all used to describe the EBA in Attica, and thus chronologies valid for other areas are imposed on the archaeological evidence of this region. An independent consideration of the evidence from Attica would aim towards the creation of a chronological framework primarily from the region's archaeological evidence, and only secondarily in relation to that of neighbouring regions. This is now possible, as many sites are known from the region (for gazetteers, see Nazou 2014: 343-370 and Fachard et al. 2020a; 2020b: xii-xiii), even if mostly from preliminary accounts. On the other hand, and perhaps more importantly, the existing cultural schemes leave the study region's cultural patterns unexplored. An independent chronology should therefore be accompanied by a consideration of the cultural character of the study region during the Final Neolithic (FN)-EBA periods, and would also have to include the areas which seem to be in close cultural contact with Attica. For example, Kea and especially its northern part (which includes the sites of Kephala, Paouras and Ayia Irini) is traditionally grouped with the Cycladic islands, but is, in fact, in closer contact with the eastern coast of Attica than the southern Cyclades (Coleman 1977: 100-108; Wilson 1987). The case of Aegina is also problematic, as it is usually treated as a part of the Mainland cultural sphere, and especially that of the northeastern Peloponnese during the EB III period (Berger and Gauss 2016: 218-219), even though, in earlier periods, it also had very close cultural links with the rest of the Saronic islands and Attica, namely during the FN (Weisshaar 1994: 685-686; Whitbread and Mari 2014: 86-87) and in EB II (Berger 2003: 170-174). This has also been claimed for the southern part of Euboea during the FN (Sampson 1981: 129; Phelps 2004: 121). Ultimately, it can be argued that Attica during the 4th and 3rd millennia BC is an interaction zone, open to

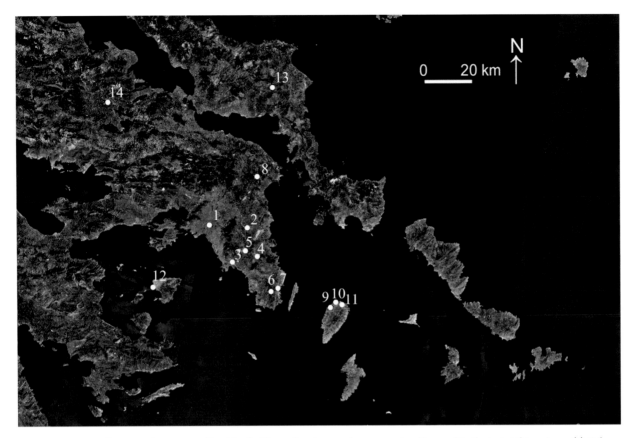

Figure 12.1. Map of Attica and its surrounding islands, illustrating the most important sites discussed in the text: Athens, Agora (1); Yalou (2); Kontra Gliate (3); Merenda (4); Koropi (5); Kitsos Cave (6); Thorikos (7); Tsepi (8); Ayia Irini (9); Kephala (10); Parouras (11); Kolonna (12); Tharrounia and Skoteini Cave (13); and Sarakenos Cave (14). Map after NASA World Wind, modified by author.

its neighbouring regions, and with cultural connections that are equally open to many directions. It is precisely this close, but varying, interaction of Attica with its neighbouring areas and islands, that the current paper aims to investigate through the ceramic evidence.

As mentioned above, most discussions of social and cultural interactions in the southern Aegean have so far assumed a peripheral role for Attica during the Final Neolithic and the Early Bronze Age. This is mainly an accident of investigation, resulting from a lack of systematic research focusing on the stylistic character of FN-EBA material culture excavated at sites within this region. But it is now clear that Attica was densely settled during the 4th and 3rd millennia BC, and there are numerous finds that indicate complexity of social organization. To name only a few of the impressive discoveries in Attica from the last two decades, an EB I silver metallurgical workshop has been excavated at the site of Lambrika near Koropi (Kakavogianni *et al.* 2008: 47-49), and further evidence for copper and silver metallurgy has been excavated from FN-EB I Merenda (Kakavogianni *et al.* 2008: 49-50; Kakavogianni *et al.* 2016: 445-447), FN-EB I Koropi (Kakavogianni *et al.* 2008: 50) and FN-EB I Yalou (Ginalas *et al.* 2015: 344-345). In terms of settlement patterns, the largest and more fertile agricultural plain, the Mesogaia, is densely inhabited with a number of large villages, as indicated by rescue

excavations both at Koropi (Kakavogianni and Douni 2009: 389-393) and at Spata (Kakavogianni and Douni 2009: 383-386). On the western Attic coast, the settlements of Asteria and Kontopigado flourished during EB I-EB II and offer good evidence for pottery production (Kaza-Papageorgiou 2009: 434-440). Last, but not least, the well published cemetery at Tsepi Marathon (Pantelidou Gofa 2005; 2016) best illustrates burial customs in eastern Attica during the FN-EB I periods.

Among the archaeological evidence from Attica, pottery is the most abundant artefact type, and its presence at all the excavated sites provides considerable research potential for detailed inter-site comparisons. The detailed data on FN-EBA ceramic styles has been extensively presented and discussed elsewhere (Nazou 2014). In this paper, we would like to return to the issues of the definition of Attic styles in comparison to those of other regions, and contextualise Attica within the broader patterns of FN-EB II southern Aegean ceramics. The relationship of stylistic change to economic, social and cultural interaction between prehistoric communities will be explored, and possible factors that triggered stylistic changes in pottery will be investigated. In the conclusion, we will discuss the issues pertaining to the definition of Attica as a region and the fluidity of its sociocultural borders.

Attica's ceramic styles in the broader Southern Aegean context

The Final Neolithic period

The evidence from the study of FN ceramic fabrics in Attica, so far, seems to indicate local production of the bulk of the pottery. By the term 'local' we mean ceramic production in, or within the vicinity of, most large settlements/villages by one or several potters associated with the village, being members of the residential community. The use of multiple 'local' fabrics is attested in Attica, in settlements like Kontra Gliate (Nazou 2014: 172-174) as well as Kolonna on Aegina (Nazou 2014: 292), and is most likely associated with different *chaînes opératoires* co-existing in this period (though we still need to define their precise chronological extent).

Ceramic exchange is limited in this period, with the exception of the Kitsos Cave (Courtois 1981: 375), but there are abundant stylistic similarities in the repertoires of forms and decoration across Attica and its neighbouring regions. There are very good stylistic connections with central Euboea and Boeotia. For example, there are parallels for most of the Attic forms (Figure 12.2) from Tharrounia (Sampson 1993a: 110, 113, 115-116) and the Sarakenos Cave (Sampson 2008:

236-238). There do not seem to be as many similarities with the Argolid, i.e., at FN Lerna (Vitelli 2007: 117-125) and Franchthi (Vitelli 1999: 64-95). Rolled rim bowls and Pattern Burnished wares are reported from these sites, but the repertoire comprises mainly Heavy Burnished, painted and Crusted bowls, as well as large asymmetrical vessels ('drums'), examples of which have not been recovered in Attica. Whether this is attributed to chronological, regional and/or contextual differences has not yet been sufficiently clarified (see below for the 'Athens North Slope' phase). Finally, FN Attic sites such as the Agora, the Kitsos Cave, Kontra Gliate and Thorikos, seem to be well connected with sites on the northern Cycladic islands, such as Kephala on Kea (Coleman 1977: 100-102), although not so much with Ayia Irini I, which is most likely later in date (Wilson 1999: 7). There is very little FN pottery published from the central and southern Cyclades[1] and, therefore, the links between Attica and the rest of the Cycladic islands are unclear.

Therefore, Renfrew's definition of an 'Attica-Kephala culture' has stood the test of time, even though some clarifications and amendments to his original definition can be suggested (Table 12.1). Renfrew initially restricted this culture to Attica, Euboea, and the northwestern Cyclades. However, many researchers extend this culture to include a very large stylistic zone,

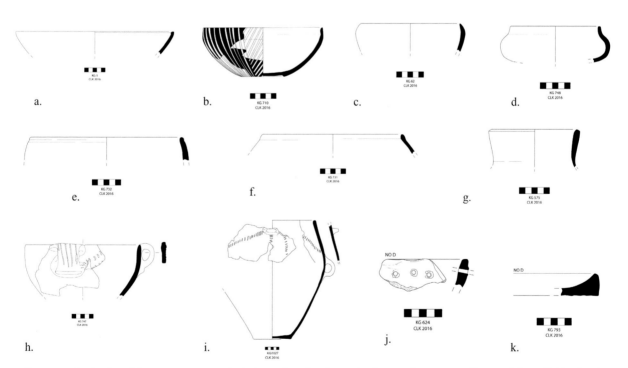

Figure 12.2. A selection of the most common FN Attic shapes, based on the study of pottery from Kontra Gliate: straight-walled bowl with rolled rim (a); Pattern Burnished convex bowl with rolled rim (b); carinated bowl (c); collared bowl (d); hole-mouth jar (e); necked jar (f) collared jar (g); handled jar (h); pithoid jar (i); cheese-pot (j); pan (k).

[1] It remains unclear how early in the FN period the Grotta-Pelos styles originated. This question has also been discussed by Alram-Stern (2014: 306).

the so-called 'Aegina-Attica-Kephala group', whose boundaries spread to the whole of central and southern Greece and the Cyclades, and with a chronological range covering the greater part of the FN period (Alram-Stern 1996: 157; Demoule and Perlès 1993: 398). It has indeed been confirmed that the Pattern Burnished style is not restricted to Attica, Euboea, Kea and the Saronic islands; rather this style was produced concurrently in many areas, in countless varieties and combinations (Mari 1993: 147; contra Phelps 2004: 106-108). In fact, the extension of the 'Attic-Kephala culture' over such a large geographic area is a result of researchers seizing familiar ceramic types, such as the Pattern Burnished style, to roughly date sites in regions not previously intensively studied. The problem is mainly caused by the limited study of sites of this date in other regions, and the absence of other distinctive types of material culture on which local cultural group definitions can be based. Relying on only a few similarities in pottery decoration, the definition of FN cultural groups remains tentative. There are, indeed, close stylistic similarities between Attica, the northern Cyclades, Boeotia and central and southern Euboea, but there are fewer connections with Thessaly, the Peloponnese, and the southern Cyclades. Having acknowledged the problems of designating cultural groups in the FN, there still seems to be validity in the traditional definition of three 'cultures': the 'Rachmani culture' in Thessaly (Alram-Stern 1996: 96), the 'Attic-Kephala culture' in Attica and the surrounding islands, and the 'Grotta-Pelos culture' in the south-central Cyclades. Alram-Stern (2014: 305)

has argued that the 'Rachmani' and the 'Attic-Kephala culture' are contemporary.

The relationships between Attica and Crete may be reconsidered in the light of the evidence from Kephala Petras. Papadatos and Tomkins (2013: 358-361) have identified a significant amount of imported pottery at the site; about 10% of the assemblage from a FN building is of a White Mica Schist fabric that does not have convincing mineralogical parallels on Crete. Moreover, the reconstructed forms are typologically similar to examples from Attica (the Kitsos Cave) and Kea (Kephala and Ayia Irini). A different picture emerges from the recently published data from Knossos: a few stylistic connections between Crete and southern Greece are highlighted, but it seems that there are more connections with the eastern Aegean and Anatolia (Tomkins 2007: 35, 41, 44). It remains to be confirmed through analytical study whether the pottery of the White Mica Schist fabric at Kephala Petras on Crete is, indeed, imported from Attica and/or Kea, in which case the argument for long-range maritime interaction among these areas would be validated.

The recent ceramic evidence from Attica adds to the ongoing debate around the identification of two chronological phases within the FN (French 1972: 17; Maran 1998; Phelps 2004: 112-121). The distinction of two FN phases has been based, mainly, on the variation of pottery styles, and using the few absolute chronological dates available. The first phase is called

Table 12.1. Final Neolithic chronological and cultural schemes in the Aegean, according to the researcher.

Studies	Chronological Term	Period in Years	Geographical Area	'Culture'
Renfrew 1972; Phelps 1975; Diamant 1985	Final Neolithic	4100-3200 BC	Attica, Euboea and the northwestern Cyclades	'Attica-Kephala'
Treuil et al. 1989	Late Neolithic (Chalcolithic)	4900/4700-4100/3800/3400 BC	southern Aegean	no term
Demoule and Perlès 1993	Phase 5 of the Neolithic	5800/5700-4800/4600 BP	central and southern Greece, the Adriatic coast and the Cyclades	'Aegina-Attica-Kephala'
Sampson 1989, 2006; Coleman 1992; Zachos 2008	Late Neolithic II	4300/4200-3300/3200 BC	Euboea, central and southern Greece, Cyclades and eastern Aegean islands	no term
Dousougli 1992; Weisshaar 1994	Chalcolithic	4200/4000-3200 BC	Peloponnese, central Greece and Cyclades (southwest Aegean)	'Attica-Kephala'

the 'Attic-Kephala', with predominant styles being the Pattern Burnished, Crusted and Red Monochrome wares, as well as incised scoops. It should be noted that the use of the term 'Attic-Kephala' for both a cultural group and a chronological phase creates confusion in the literature, as it is unclear whether the stylistic uniformity of pottery excavated from Attica and the surrounding islands is a cultural or chronological phenomenon, or both. The second phase is known as 'late Chalcolithic' (Maran 1998: 152) or the 'Athens North Slope' phase (French 1972: 17). The pottery of this phase is characterised by thick-walled vessels, rolled rim bowls and dark polished decoration, known as Heavy Burnished Ware This phase was identified at Franchthi (Franchthi Ceramic Phase (FCP) 5.2), where it is characterised by Heavy Burnished shapes (Vitelli 1999: 83), and Lerna (Vitelli 2007: 117-126). Vitelli dates both the Franchthi and the Lerna FN phases somewhere in the middle of the FN, based on radiocarbon dates from Franchthi. It is problematic that this phasing is not associated with stratified deposits; therefore, this typological variation could also be related to differences in regional styles, or in the nature of the deposits.

It is worth discussing the rolled rim bowls in more detail, as these are considered important in the chronology of the FN across the Aegean. In his study of pottery styles from southern Greece, Phelps (2004: 118) highlights the 'Kum Tepe Ib' bowl, or rolled-rim bowl, as indicative of a later horizon in the FN. He and Renfrew consider that the rolled-rim bowls with Pattern Burnished decoration are typological indicators of a transitional phase between the early and the late phases of the Final Neolithic (Phelps 2004: 122). Spitaels (1982: 42) also suggests that angular profiles for bowls, along with pattern-burnishing and rolled rims, constitute typological features of a later phase of the Final Neolithic. The rolled-rim bowls can perhaps be used to distinguish earlier from later FN pottery, but one should not rely exclusively on this type as a chronological criterion, as it persists into EB I (French 1972: 18-19).

Johnson (1999: 325) highlights two other pottery types as good chronological indicators for the late phase of the FN: the tunnel lug, set at or below the rim of vessels with or without rolled rims, and the necked jar or bowl with fluted or channelled belly. Indeed these two features co-occur in Attica only in the material from the North Slope of the Athenian Acropolis (Immerwahr 1971: pl. 6.70-75 and 83-84) and Deposit 39 at Tsepi Marathon (Figure 12.3 and 12.4). The published pottery from Deposit 39 of the prehistoric cemetery at Tsepi has ample evidence for bowls with tunnel lugs (Pantelidou Gofa 2016: pl. 54: 1550) and necked jars with channelled bellies (Pantelidou Gofa 2016: pl. 72: 1563, 1586, 1730 and 1768).

The wide distribution of these few distinctive pottery types most likely indicates inter-regional contacts. Another frequently cited example is the 'Bratislava lid'. This form has been excavated from south-eastern Thessaly, Epirus and Attica (Pantelidou Gofa 2005: 314-316; 2016: 164-166) and its distribution stretches from the Carpathian Basin to the southern Aegean (Forsén 2010: 56, 58; Maran 1998: 40-41, 344-346). At Tsepi, this vessel is suggested to be imported, though unfortunately it was not sampled for petrographic analysis (Pantelidou-Gofa 2016: 164). These pots were most likely part of an eating and drinking set which was used from the northern Balkans to central Greece (Alram-Stern 2014: 313).

The site of Merenda has produced radiocarbon dates compatible with a later phase in the FN (Maniatis et al. 2016: 58). However, Coleman (2011: 19-20) has argued that the FN pottery published so far from Merenda does not seem to support the existence of a discrete later phase within the FN. The authors mention the existence of two wares, a Red Burnished Ware used mostly for bowls, and a Black Burnished Ware used mostly for small necked jars (Kakavogianni et al. 2016: 443-444). Few objects are illustrated in the recent publications, of which a jar with a tunnel lug below the neck (Dimitriou 2020; Kakavogianni et al. 2016: 444, fig.

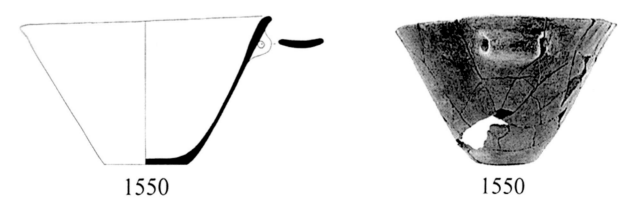

Figure 12.3. Large bowls with tunnel lugs set below the rim (after Pantelidou Gofa 2016: pls. 54-55, no. 1550). Not to scale.

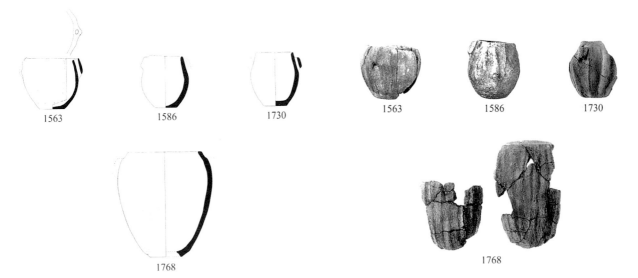

Figure 12.4. Jars with fluted or channelled bellies (after Pantelidou Gofa 2016: pls. 72-73, nos. 1563, 1586, 1730 and 1768). Not to scale.

9) could be considered a 'transitional' characteristic of an FN-EB I phase, as defined in the discussion above. The publication of the pottery will further clarify the stylistic character of this assemblage.

A final problem concerns the synchronisation of different regions in the southern Aegean during the FN. The case of Euboea is especially problematic. Its pottery styles have been studied by Sampson (1981), but the chronological relationship of the Euboean FN to the rest of the southern Aegean has not been clarified. The main problem is that the FN phases identified by Sampson do not coincide with Phelps' early and late FN (Phelps 2004: 121). Sampson (1981: 128-129) initially distinguished an early FN (FN I) and a late FN (FN II) period in his thesis, based on typological differences observed in Euboean pottery. His FN I is characterised by black burnished surface treatments, some of which are also ribbed, fruitstands and buttons on handles (Sampson 1981: 133-137). His FN II comprises red burnished shallow bowls with rolled rims and pattern burnished decoration. Relief decorated wares (rope pattern) are most common in his FN II (Sampson 1981: 147-156). Sampson's study did not distinguish any phases in his FN II. Therefore, from the data presented in Sampson's thesis, it would seem that his FN I, or at least a part of it, is contemporary with Phelps' LN. Another problem is that the Black Burnished Fluted Ware occurring at FN I Seimen Mnima (Sampson 1981: 137, table 9a) is most likely a late FN feature according to Johnson (1999: 329).

Sampson's later studies led to the suggestion of a new chronological system without, however, reassessing the data presented in his early study. This results in contradictions in his revised chronology. More specifically, he suggested reuniting the Late and Final Neolithic periods, and proposed to use the term LN I

for the Late Neolithic, and LN II for the Final Neolithic (Sampson 1989). Based on the stratigraphy of the Skoteini Cave at Tharrounia, he also distinguished two subphases within his LN II period: LN IIa and LN IIb (Sampson 1993a). Generally, stratigraphic observations in caves can be difficult to interpret, given the complex formation processes of cave strata, which are often disturbed by continuous use of the same areas. At Skoteini, the LN IIa and LN IIb phases were identified stratigraphically, but there is only one radiocarbon date for the entire LN II, associated with the end of the LN IIa (Sampson 1993a: 286). It was argued that, at Skoteini, the cheese pots, the scoops, the rolled rim bowls and the rows of vertically pierced lugs appear in the higher strata and the superficial layer of sections A and Γ and belong to a short phase named Tharrounia 4, dated to LN IIb (Sampson 1993a: 286). The Pattern Burnished sherds, occurring mostly in strata associated with the LN IIa, are fewer in the LN IIb strata, but they co-exist with LN IIb pottery types. The uncertainty of Sampson's phasing at Skoteini is evident in his statement that 'there is no clear distinction between the early and the late part of the LN II' (Sampson 1993a: 286). The faunal analysis also confirms that the LN IIb strata at Skoteini were mixed, containing remains from later periods (Kotjabopoulou and Trantalidou 1993: 394).

The above discussion has clarified the distribution of FN styles in Attica, and discussed the remaining uncertainties of the temporal and spatial distributions of FN pottery styles in the southern Aegean. The suggestions of previous research on the interpretation of FN pottery styles are clearer. The small variety of decorated wares (of which the Pattern Burnished style is the most popular) and the predominance of coarse wares was, at first, interpreted as a technological decline in pottery production (Immerwahr 1971: 5). To explain the decline in the quality of decorated tableware, Halstead (1995: 18) suggests a reduced social significance of pottery for hospitality, or that the significance of hospitality was now marked by vessels made from other materials. Moreover, the fashion for burnished pottery was linked by some researchers with the value attached to metal objects (Immerwahr 1971: 9). It is also likely that other crafts, such as basketry, influenced the decorative motifs used on pottery (Keller 1982: 50).

Demoule and Perlès (1993: 401) note that, throughout the FN, an increase in coarse wares and rapidly produced decoration is observed in all areas of the southern Aegean. FN pottery was being produced in larger quantities than in the previous Neolithic periods, and pottery styles are similar across several regions. Such changes could have been caused by a gradual change in the role of pottery into domestic and utilitarian uses (Demoule and Perlès 1993: 401), as pottery became an essential part of FN household equipment. Therefore, FN stylistic similarities could be attributed to reduced specialisation related to household production.

To conclude, there is a fundamental problem in studying FN pottery in the southern Aegean: most styles are only defined in fairly broad terms, and are similar across several regions throughout the 4th millennium BC, which indicates a high degree of conservatism in ceramic styles and hinders the identification of local cultural groups. It was argued above that there is a high degree of stylistic homogeneity among FN

assemblages in Attica, southern Euboea, the northern Cyclades and the Saronic Gulf, which indicates close cultural contacts and interaction. The data suggest shared ceramic technologies and cultural norms; with some exceptions, pottery exchange is limited. Beyond this region, the similarities are more generic, but also relatively poorly defined, based on relatively few well-studied assemblages.

Early Bronze Age I

During EB I, the ceramic fabrics studied macroscopically from Attica are compatible with local geology (Nazou 2014: 304), but there is now more imported pottery with volcanic inclusions at sites such as Kontra Gliate and Thorikos, most likely from the Saronic Gulf (Aegina). The presence of Talc Ware at Thorikos (Nazou 2014: 304) indicates connections with the western Cycladic islands, probably via Kea, although the fact that different sources for Talc Ware on Skyros and Poros in the Saronic Gulf have recently been suggested (Sotirakopoulou 2016: 16-17) complicates the issue of the presence of Talc Ware in Attica. The Attic EB I pottery known so far has a variety of stylistic connections: the repertoires from sites such as Lithares in Boeotia (Tzavella-Evjen 1984: 150-165) and Kaloyerovrysi in central Euboea (Sampson 1993b: 30-44), provide good parallels for Attic forms (Figure 12.5). The material from Deposit 39 at Tsepi provides evidence for the early occurrence of a shape that would become the 'hallmark' (Pullen 2011: 65) of the 'Talioti' assemblage in the Argolid; the characteristic

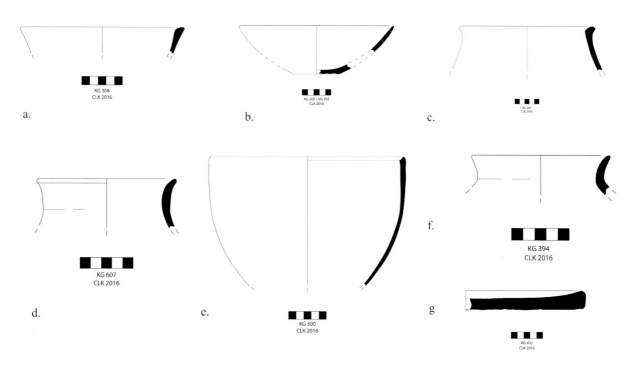

Figure 12.5. A selection of the most common EB I Attic shapes, based on the study of pottery from Kontra Gliate: straight bowl (a); convex bowl (b); necked jar (c); collared jar (d); cooking bowl (e); globular jar or pyxis (f); pan (g).

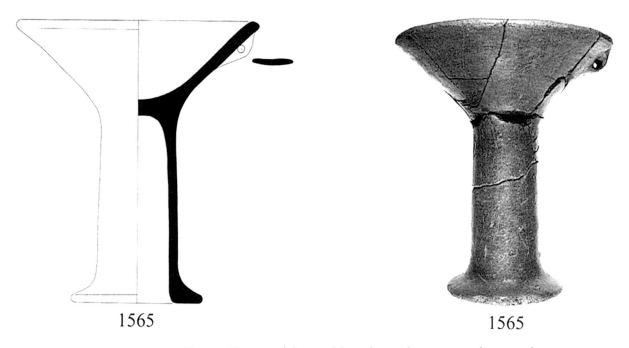

Figure 12.6. A restored fruitstand from Tsepi (after Pantelidou Gofa 2016: pls. 48-49, no. 1565). Not to scale.

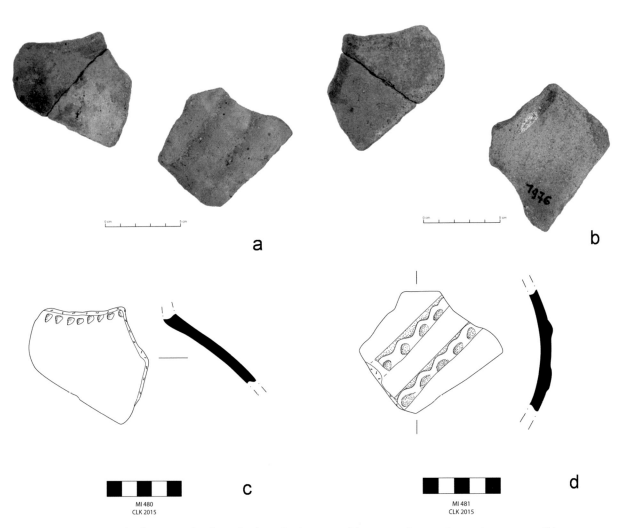

Figure 12.7.. Sherds associated with pyxides from Thorikos Mine 3 (photos: E. Rodriguez-Alvarez; drawings: C. Kolb).

'fruitstands' (Figure 12.6), which are reported in great numbers and complete (Pantelidou Gofa 2016: pls 44-50). It is notable that the Tsepi fruitstands possess a different profile[2] to, and most likely date earlier than, those occurring in the Argolid, at Talioti (Dousougli 1987: 204), and Tsoungiza in the Corinthia (Pullen 2011: 72). The pyxides (Figure 12.7) from Thorikos Mine 3 (Nazou 2014: 138), as well as Tsepi (Pantelidou Gofa 2005: 303-305), indicate stylistic connections with the Cyclades, though some variations of the shape seem to be Attic inventions with no parallels from the Cyclades.

EB I ceramic styles in the southern Greek mainland remain poorly defined, because we lack publications of well-stratified deposits; a notable exception is Pullen's (2011) publication of Tsoungiza. There is both an ambiguity surrounding the definitions of this period in previous research, and a lack of broader studies examining EB I ceramic production and consumption across several regions. In more detail, based on the stratigraphy of his excavations at Korakou, Blegen (1921: 121) first subdivided the EBA on the Greek mainland into three sub-periods, broadly modelled on, and contemporary with, the Minoan EBA sequence. Subsequent excavations at Zygouries (Blegen 1928) and Eutresis (Caskey and Caskey 1960; Goldman 1931) allowed the clarification of the nature of pottery styles attributed to the EH I period; ceramic assemblages contain a large quantity of coarse wares (pithoi, jars) and cooking vessels, along with finer decorated (burnished/polished, incised, impressed) tableware, mainly bowls. In an effort to disaggregate styles/cultures from chronological phases, Renfrew defined the 'Eutresis culture' on the southern Greek mainland and the 'Grotta-Pelos culture' in the Cyclades. The 'Eutresis culture' encompassed several regions, namely Corinthia, Boeotia and Attica (Renfrew 1972: 100). It was unclear, at the time of its description, whether sites in Thessaly, the eastern Aegean islands, the Peloponnese and Kythera, which produced red slipped pottery, should also be included in this culture (Renfrew 1972: 100). As far as the Cycladic cultural sequence is concerned, Renfrew's second cultural group, the 'Grotta-Pelos culture' of the south-central Cyclades, spans both the FN and the EB I periods (Renfrew 1972: 150). He also defined the 'Kampos group' of the south-central Cyclades, dated to the late EB I/early EB II. The characteristic pottery forms of the 'Kampos group' are a specific type of frying pan, a footed bowl or 'fruitstand', and the 'bottle' (Renfrew 1972: 153). Doumas (1977) tried to further subdivide the Cycladic cultural sequence, but his suggestions have generally not been followed. Later on, Rambach's (2000: 247) detailed study of the Early

Cycladic chronological sequence placed the 'Kampos group' at the end of EC I, rather than early EC II.

An addition to Renfrew's cultural sequence in the southern mainland was the 'Talioti' pottery group, distributed in the Argive Plain and southern Corinthia (Dousougli 1987). The chronology of the 'Talioti' group is a matter of debate. Dousougli (1987: 207-208) initially dated the group to the end of EB I, based on typological and stratigraphic comparisons among the sites of Makrovouni, Kefalari Magoula, and Talioti. Following this chronology, it could be suggested that two separate phases can be distinguished in the EH I period of Boeotia, Corinthia and the Argolid (Forsén 2010: 59). Several assemblages (from Asine, Eutresis and Perachora) have produced red slipped or unslipped and polished or Dark Burnished wares. These could date to the early EH I period, whereas the 'Talioti' group represents the late EH I period (Forsén 2010: 59). However, Maran (1998: 9) and Pullen (2008: 22) disagree, and believe that the 'Talioti' group represents the entire EH I period in the northeastern Peloponnese.

In contrast to the FN, when there are several common pottery styles in use across the southern Aegean, the EB I saw increasing regional diversity. Early Minoan I styles comprise jugs, pyxides, zoomorphic shapes decorated with painted motifs, and the so-called 'Pyrgos chalices', decorated with pattern-burnish, perhaps continuing a Neolithic tradition (Dickinson 1994: 103). This rich variety of Cretan tableware contrasts with the styles known from the southern Greek mainland, where the main forms produced are bowls and jars (with only a few jugs and cups reported) and the main surface treatments are plain slipped or burnished (Dickinson 1994: 103). The 'Talioti' fruitstand, decorated with incisions, impressions, and/or plastic decoration (Dousougli 1987: 184), is similar to the 'Pyrgos chalice'. Different styles are reported from the Cyclades, where there seems to be a preference for dark burnished and incised surfaces. The most common shapes are the rolled-rim bowl with the tubular lug, collared jars and 'pyxides', examples of which are known mostly from graves (Broodbank 2008: 60; Doumas 1977: 16, fig. 3). The 'frying pan', decorated with incised and stamped motifs, appears at the end of EB I in the Cyclades, but also occurs on the Greek mainland (Coleman 1985; Renfrew 1972: 536-537). Frying pans are mainly considered as a 'Cycladic' pottery form (Pullen 2008: 22), as most examples are known from Cycladic graves. However, it is difficult to argue with certainty about the origin of the type, and one wonders about the stylistic connections between the 'frying pan' and the 'Bratislava lid'. The variations in shape and decoration of examples of the 'frying pan' indicate the existence of different regional styles (Coleman 1985).

---

[2] With high and narrow pedestals and straight rims, as opposed to the spreading pedestals and overhanging, or thickened, rims of examples in the Argolid

Interpretations of EB I pottery styles mainly revolve around two issues: the specialisation of pottery production and the interpretation of ceramic exchange. It has been argued that in Crete, from the beginning of EM I, there are signs of a shift in ceramic production, characterised by the development of a new and distinctive range of styles, by marked regionality in material expression, by increasingly elaborate *chaînes opératoires*, and by rising productive intensity and output (Wilson and Day 1994: 84). It has also been suggested that in Crete, independent full-time specialists were producing a range of distinctive products, consumed across one or several regions on the island (Wilson and Day 1994: 84-85). Such a phenomenon has not yet been suggested for the rest of the southern Aegean. As far as ceramic exchange is concerned, in the late EB I, it seems that there are intense contacts between northern Crete and the southern Cyclades. The identification of imported pots, or imported ceramic technologies, on Crete has been considered indicative of population movement (Day *et al.* 1998).

In order to interpret the increasing volume of evidence on EB I styles in the southern Aegean, discussed above, a re-examination of old and new material is required, using the same criteria for inter-site comparisons. Regional styles and inter-regional contacts need to be systematically defined and interpreted.

Early Bronze Age II

The EB II period provides the most evidence for connections between Attica and other areas of the southern Aegean. Renfrew's term 'international spirit' is used to indicate the intensification of multidirectional trading links, and the complex interplay of styles, in this period (Broodbank 2008: 64). In other words, during EB II in the southern Aegean there was abundant exchange of raw materials and finished products; many areas share the same pottery forms and decorative techniques, and trade seems to have played an important role in stylistic interaction. Attica participated in the EB II 'international spirit', and Attic communities had drinking customs similar to those of other areas, especially the southern Greek mainland and the Cyclades.

The southern Greek mainland is characterised by the occurrence of *Urfirnis* and Yellow Mottled wares, associated mainly with tableware shapes, such as the askos, the sauceboat, the saucer and the jug. At Lerna, a site with the most intensively studied and documented assemblage, a wide form repertoire of 23 different pottery shapes has been identified, of which several occur in different sizes (Wiencke 2000: 318). Renfrew (1972: 101) stresses the occurrence of painted decoration at Lerna. The sauceboat, the jug, and large storage vessels, sometimes decorated with applied rope bands, are characteristic types also in the Cyclades (Broodbank 2008: 61). The surface treatments of previous periods, such as incision, remain popular, but a wider range of decorative techniques appears in Early Cycladic II, such as impression and the use of dark-painted designs on light surfaces (Broodbank 2008: 61).

Several of these styles occur in Attica, indicating shared ceramic traditions with other regions. There is evidence for the standard drinking set of askoi, jugs, saucers and sauceboats (Douni 2015: 174-188; Nazou 2014: 219). These shapes are encountered in the Argolid, Boeotia and the Cyclades. It is unclear whether other ceramic types which have a wide distribution across Attica and its neighbouring regions were produced in one specific region, or in several; some shapes seem to be more common in specific regions. For example, the tankard with the wavy rim (Nazou 2014: 229) occurs in Attica and Boeotia, and the pedestalled goblet (Nazou 2014: 144) in Corinthia, Attica and the northern Cyclades (Figure 12.8). Two distinctive Attic drinking forms, the cups and the collared bowls, are reported in large

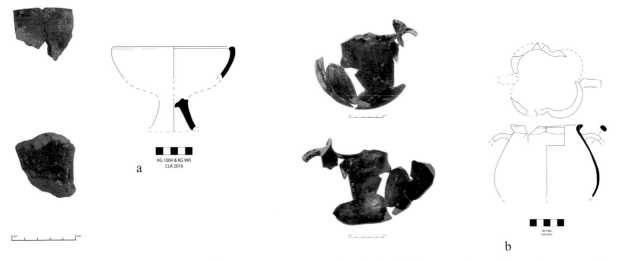

Figure 12.8. Pedestalled goblet from Kontra Gliate (a) and tankard with wavy rim from Thorikos (b) (photos: E. Rodriguez-Alvarez; drawings: C. Kolb).

numbers from Attica, and have few parallels in other regions (Nazou 2014: 142, 229). Finally, the site of Koropi was most likely a production centre for Buff Yellow Slipped and Yellow Mottled wares (Douni 2015: 491), which could have been imported to Ayia Irini, and perhaps further away, in the Cycladic islands.

Cretan pottery has a rather different stylistic character in this period than the rest of the Southern Aegean, and stylistic differences among different regions in Crete become more evident (Wilson 2008: 87). The study and publication of EM II assemblages has been combined with a series of analytical studies (Day et al. 1999; Whitelaw et al. 1997; Wilson and Day 1994), which allow the identification of production centres and the interpretation of regional styles.

It is widely accepted that EB II saw technological advances in pottery production, such as the use of finer clays and higher firing temperatures (Broodbank 2008: 60), and this may have been accompanied by changes in the organisation of production. Excavations at Proskynas in Lokris yielded large constructions for the storage and processing of clay and evidence for possible kilns in an area of the settlement associated with pottery and stone vessel production (Zachou 2004). The study of an early EB II assemblage from Kouphovouno has suggested the existence of part-time specialist potters based in each of the main settlements in Laconia, which supplied a network of smaller sites (Mee 2009: 51). This has also been argued for the Argolid, based on the study of pottery from Lerna (Wiencke 2000: 637). Wiencke (1989: 506) proposed that potters specialised in the production of pithoi travelled in the Argolid to cover the demand for these vessels during Lerna IIIC. Another suggestion for specialisation at Lerna is based on the mass production of sauceboats (Wiencke 1989: 506). In Attica, the use of finer clays, fired at high temperatures to achieve a blue-greyish ('Yellow Mottled') slip, is widely attested in the EB II; there is no evidence to argue convincingly for the production of particular wares at particular sites only, although Koropi, so far, presents the best evidence in terms of the association of the Buff Yellow Slipped and Yellow Mottled with the largest number of shapes (Douni 2015: 431, 439).

In the Cyclades, the range of shapes and decoration expands in this period, and stylistic sub-groups could reflect the increasing definition of local networks in parts of the Cyclades, as population grew (Broodbank 2008: 61). Broodbank (2008: 61) stresses three characteristics of the EC II ceramic repertoire. First, drinking and pouring vessels become prominent, perhaps indicating increased social consumption of liquids, such as wine. This was also suggested to interpret the increased variety of ceramic shapes at Lerna for storing and pouring liquids, indicating changes in diet and social behaviour and an emphasis on communal feasting and drinking (Pullen 2008: 30;

Wiencke 2010: 661). Second, increasing skeuomorphism of metallic forms is observed in ceramic details and this feature, combined with a taste for lustrous surfaces, may indicate an increased use of metal vessels, which have not survived in the archaeological record (Broodbank 2008: 61). Third, non-Cycladic parallels, and in some cases prototypes, can be identified for several important locally- manufactured shapes, such as sauceboats (Broodbank 2008: 61). As mentioned above, Attic Yellow Mottled sauceboats were most likely being exported to Ayia Irini (Wilson 1999: 76-78), and perhaps further away to sites such as Dhaskalio-Kavos (Sotirakopoulou 2016: 397); thus, Attic ceramic styles, and perhaps also drinking customs, may have influenced Cycladic styles.

Maritime exchange is central to the discussion of imported pottery in the southern Aegean. Distinctive styles, such as the Syros frying pans, decorated with ships and female genitalia, seem to be iconological styles, related to the construction of maritime identity and the knowledge and power that could be obtained by maritime journeys (Broodbank 2000: 249-256). In the Cyclades, small sites usually have a lower percentage of imports, ranging between 5% and 10% of total assemblage, but at larger sites, such as Ayia Irini and Dhaskalio-Kavos, the percentage of imported pottery is larger, from c. 25% to almost 50% of the total assemblage, respectively (Broodbank 2008: 65). At Kavos, vessels imported from distant areas are lighter (e.g., sauceboats), whereas bulky vessels are imported from neighbouring islands (Broodbank 2008: 61). As far as long-range pottery exchange is concerned, Cycladic imports, such as sauceboats and Melian liquid storage vessels, are rare, but occur at Knossos (Wilson 2008: 307) and, more abundantly, at the port of Poros (Wilson et al. 2008). There are also long-range exports to the Cyclades from the southern mainland, such as Urfirnis and Yellow Mottled sauceboats (Broodbank 2008: 65).

A last issue concerns the identification of areas of intense stylistic contact and/or exchange in the southern Aegean through the study of EB II pottery. For example, Kythera and northwestern Crete seem to be in close contact during EB II (Broodbank and Kiriatzi 2007). Further north, Manika in Euboea has been argued to have strong connections with the Cyclades in this period (Sampson 1988: 115). However, the majority of the pottery from Manika and especially the frying pans are not particularly close to Cycladic forms (Sampson 1988: 117). The close relationships between Kea and southeastern Attica were first highlighted by Wilson (1987). The importance of EB II maritime interaction is also evident in the case of Thorikos, which seems to be in closer contact with northern Kea than the rest of Attica; the study of the pottery from Mine 3 highlights the relationships between Thorikos and Ayia Irini, as the closest parallels for the EB II pottery are from Ayia Irini II and III (Nazou 2014: 232, 239).

Late Early Bronze Age II (Lefkandi I-Kastri group)

It should be stressed that the Lefkandi I-Kastri group is not just a regional variant, occurring in the eastern-central part of the southern Aegean; it also represents new ways of doing things: new technology (wheel-made), new shapes/styles, new external influences, and new or refocused social practices are embodied in these new pottery types (Manning 2010: 16). The distinctiveness of the group most likely indicates a new fashion in tableware, related to western Anatolian styles and metal prototypes (Nakou 2007). Moreover, the coastal distribution of the group indicates that the new technology and ideas were most likely transferred through maritime interaction.

The changes in pottery technology, shapes and style distribution during this period are most likely associated with wider changes in economic and social networks at the end of EB II in the southern Aegean. It has been suggested that, in this period, the Cyclades are incorporated into Anatolian trade networks (Broodbank 2000: 313). It is also interesting that ceramic exchange between EM IIb sites in northern Crete and the southern Cyclades stops, whereas raw materials continue to be imported (Tomkins and Schoep 2010: 70). Apart from the occurrence of the shallow bowl or deep plate (not wheel-made) in the late phase of EM II A at Knossos, none of the other shapes associated with the Lefkandi I-Kastri group occur in Crete (Wilson 2008: 94). However, skeuomorphism has been noted for EM IIb pottery, and the often metallic finish of so-called 'Vasiliki Ware' could be associated with a taste for metal vessels (Wilson 2008: 95). A new phenomenon is the appearance of 'Minoanising' pottery at Kastri on Kythera, suggesting that people from western Crete settled on Kythera at this time, and that Kythera was thoroughly incorporated into western Cretan networks (Broodbank and Kiriatzi 2007).

The changes that occurred at the end of the EB II period in Attica remain to be clarified. It should be stressed that only Thorikos and Raphina adopted some of the Lefkandi I-Kastri shapes; the coastal location of these sites facilitated access to new ceramic styles and technologies. Moreover, there are many stylistic similarities, and much pottery exchanged, between Thorikos, Ayia Irini and Kolonna (Nazou 2014: 232, 239, 245-246). The presence of the tableware forms of the Lefkandi I-Kastri group at Raphina and Thorikos, indicates the participation of these communities in a broader southern Aegean maritime network.

In the next section, the changes in Attic ceramic styles will be discussed in terms of their possible relationship with changes in pottery technology, socioeconomic interaction and cultural identity.

Interpreting stylistic change: technological changes, economic and social interaction and cultural identity

Changes in ceramic technology

Material science approaches to limestone-tempered pottery (Hoard *et al.* 1995: 831) have shown that, once spalling is controlled, limestone-tempered pottery offers many benefits compared with sand- and grog-tempered pottery, especially for large cooking pots. It produces a more workable clay body, which allows for a thinner and more globular vessel, and a fired clay body that is more resistant to mechanical and, possibly, thermal stresses. The fact that calcite-tempered pottery becomes more common in the Final Neolithic period most likely indicates a shift in pottery technology, which could be associated with a more extensive use of pottery in cooking and other household activities. In Attica, pottery forms of the calcite-tempered fabric from the Athenian Agora and the Thorikos acropolis (Nazou 2014: 265, 278) show evidence for use over fire. The volume of calcite-tempered fabric drops in EB I, and it is uncommon during EB II (Nazou 2014: 299, 304, 307); it was most likely replaced by other tempers. For example, at Thorikos Mine 3, the pans that would have been suitable for cooking are of the local metamorphic and imported talc fabrics (Nazou 2014: 255).

Compared to the FN, the EBA saw innovations in ceramic technology. First, we see changes in clay recipes, as potters used better levigated clays. Moreover, asymmetrical forms such as askoi and sauceboats became more common. These fine tablewares were fired at higher, and better controlled, temperatures, which is evident from the occurrence of consistent buff, yellow and blue colours. These changes in technology and forming seem, particularly, to be employed in the manufacture of vessels linked to new drinking customs.

Economic and social interaction

It has been established that similar pottery traditions existed among FN communities in Attica and the surrounding islands. This is highlighted by Phelps, who argues: 'The sea that washed the shores of southern Euboea and southern Attica must have formed a small maritime cultural *koine* in the Final Neolithic (LNII) period, stretching from Eretria to Laurion. The six or seven settlements lining Karystos Bay, perched on small headlands, were all within sight and easy walking or rowing distance of each other. They faced southwards towards Thorikos on the mainland and Kephala on Kea. And they shared the same type of pottery' (Phelps 2004: 121). It was exactly this similarity in pottery styles that led Renfrew to identify his 'Attic-Kephala' culture, implying that these communities were interacting, most likely through maritime journeys.

The ethnographic record confirms that the knowledge of pottery production is often transferred from the elderly to the younger members of the same household or extended family (Arnold 1989: 176; Miller 1985: 77-78). There are also cases of transfer of knowledge from one area to another, such as through the marriage of a potter into another village (Miller 1985: 111). It could be suggested that increased social interaction in the southern Aegean through the FN-EB II periods may have resulted in closer contacts among potters in different prehistoric communities. This phenomenon, in combination with the intensification of maritime exchange, could be responsible for the formation of areas of close stylistic interaction; the data is indicative of close stylistic similarity and/or exchange between Kea and south-eastern Attica during the FN-EB II. This reinforces the argument that Kea was in closer contact with eastern Attica than the central and southern Cyclades (Broodbank 2008: 67; Wilson 1987). In the case of rapid change in pottery fashion, such as the 'Anatolian' shapes of the 'Lefkandi I-Kastri group', it is possible that specialists in the new technologies would be invited by their neighbours to teach the skills necessary to produce desirable products. In the case of the use of the wheel, learning the new skill would have required close interaction, possibly involving the temporary or permanent re-location of potters to new areas.

Sociocultural identity

Although always implied by the archaeologist's definition of cultural groups, the association of pottery styles with sociocultural groups and/or identity can be hard to demonstrate (Nazou 2014: 55-66). While the study of EB II pottery styles can be informative on social and cultural interaction in the southern Aegean, the pottery data should be contextualised with reference to the information obtained from other materials. It has been stressed that pottery as a cultural marker does not coincide with other types of material culture in the EH II period, such as, for example, the corridor house (Pullen 2008: 31). It is also argued that ceramics were not as socially valued as other materials, such as metals, which most likely generated regular contact between the Cycladic islands and Attica.

Attica is a particularly suitable case study for the investigation of southern Aegean interaction networks between mainland and island areas (Wilson 1987; Nazou 2010). The conceptualisation of the archaeological construction of cultural identity in previous research has been dominated by arguments about Cycladic colonies in Attica (Marinatos 1972; Mylonas 1959). This has resulted in a degree of inattention toward the dynamic role that Attic communities played in southern Aegean social and cultural interactions. Recent studies (Douni 2015; Nazou 2014) document the

more complex patterns represented by a rich body of data on FN-EBA pottery production and consumption in Attica and the surrounding islands. Along with the emerging evidence for metallurgical practice in south-eastern Attica already from the FN, the 'predominance' and 'influence' of Cycladic communities on Attica, implied by most cultural reconstructions of the FN-EB II periods, is now challenged. However, instead of looking for traces of distinct cultural identities in the archaeological record, which are hard to isolate and demonstrate convincingly, research should focus on the exploration of differential patterns of social and cultural interaction among prehistoric communities in the southern Aegean.

Conclusions: the fluidity of borders in Attica during the 4th and 3rd millennia BC and the need to define micro-regions of economic and social interaction

Some fifty years ago, when Renfrew wrote *The Emergence of Civilisation* (1972), there was very little data available for a synthesis of Attic material culture patterns; what there was provided by a few sites in Attica and neighbouring islands (e.g., Agios Kosmas, Kolonna, Kephala and Ayia Irini), not systematically published. There was also a tendency to see the few sites in Attica in terms of what was previously known from a few key sites in neighbouring, slightly better documented, regions. This is evident in Mylonas' (1959: 155-156) interpretation of the material and cultural affiliations of Ayios Kosmas to the Cyclades. Mylonas was following the prevailing cultural historical theoretical assumptions, and interpreted Agios Kosmas' material styles in terms of 'people'. Since then, processual and post-processual studies have debated the problematic assumptions which underlie material culture, style and identity.

Challenging these assumptions requires a more thorough documentation of more sites in Attica, a greater appreciation of the variability of each ceramic assemblage (and, even more broadly, in each material culture assemblage), as well as the potential variety of reasons for this variability. Such an approach must be threefold: along with producing new data through the study of unpublished ceramic assemblages, we should be contextualising them with reference to previously published pottery, and interpreting them in relation to changes in the region's social and cultural dynamics. Moreover, the integration of the islands closest to Attica, such as southern Euboea, the Saronic Gulf islands and the northern Cyclades, is essential in order to break the mainland-island division that has so far dominated research approaches to Attica.

The study of FN-EBA pottery styles from Attica and its neighbouring islands suggests that, to some degree, there is continuous variation across the region; it is not possible to talk of a single coherent ceramic style zone which is constant across Attica, and changes abruptly at its borders. The borders of Attica are, when one looks closely, difficult to establish in any geographically 'given' sense. Whatever features one takes (e.g., mountain ranges, shores), they were variably permeable, and in different ways; sometimes as a result of innovations in maritime or terrestrial transport technology (e.g., equid domestication and their use for transportation), but also to flexible socially constituted boundaries, which we are, essentially, using material culture patterns to try to map and understand. That the extent and constitution of style zones in different periods change, even to the limited degree that we can define them, at least alerts us to the variety of situationally variable causal factors which must underlie those patterns.

On the other hand, there is considerable variation within Attica; it is not, in any period examined here, a cohesive and standardised cultural region. Similarly, the differential links beyond its shores, and (unsurprisingly) often to the geographically nearest islands, indicate that the shores never acted as effective boundaries. To establish whether, in any period, there was greater coherence within Attica, with more change at those shores, or much more continuous variation, both across land and sea, will require the filling in of geographical gaps by the publication of significantly more pottery at the site level, and will also require the application of a standardised systematic methodology for description, in order to be able to create regional syntheses.

While, of course, it is important to pay attention to the variability of pottery types in order to understand site and micro-regional specific styles, we should also rationalise and standardise the many different, often site-specific, schemes developed by researchers, in order to resolve the big picture of regional connections between Attica and the southern Greek mainland. Moreover, systematic macroscopic observations must become standard practice in the study of prehistoric Attic pottery, in order to enable the broad distinction of local from imported pottery at Attic sites. While the provenience of material needs to be established firmly through compositional analyses, with such common lithologies across large swathes of Attica and the surrounding islands, simple petrographic or chemical analyses may not provide much more certainty than systematic macroscopic examination. Yet, more recent detailed approaches, focusing on the technologies of paste preparation, may well allow the definition of micro-regional proveniences. Moreover, a more detailed analysis of forming and firing technology is essential in defining site-specific or micro-regional styles. But to do this will require larger assemblages which are better defined chronologically, better documented both stratigraphically and contextually, and more intensively studied, from a larger number of sites to establish site-

and phase-specific clay preparation recipes, and build a picture of the compositional signatures of site-specific, local and regional pottery-making traditions. Some sites (or sites representing localised regions), such as Kolonna on Aegina, play a disproportionate role in the production and circulation of specific wares, whether in specific periods, or over the longer term. In fact, the study of Attic pottery reveals the regional importance of Aegina within, and beyond, the shores of the Saronic Gulf. Another micro-region with geographically-based linkage, which seems to have diachronic importance, is south-eastern Attica-Kea-Karystia.

To conclude, the volume of archaeological data dated to the 4th and 3rd millennia BC from Attica has grown considerably in recent decades, and will continue to grow. Excavations have revealed a plethora of new FN-EBA sites in the study region. These rich archaeological datasets are comprised largely of excavated pottery. Future studies of this pottery, apart from the refinement of typological observations, could focus on the identification of possible micro-regions through space and time and, through the systematic study of large assemblages, help to distinguish chronological, local and functional variations, and sample-size biases, in different assemblages. The micro-region of southeastern Attica, Kea and southern Euboea has already been highlighted, by documenting the similarity of pottery styles and ceramic exchange during the FN-EBA (Nazou 2014; Wilson 1987). This approach could be further pursued, to enable further clarification of the economic and social dynamics of Attica and its surrounding islands.

Bibliography

Alram-Stern, E. 1996. *Die Ägäische Frühzeit. 2. Serie, Forschungsbericht 1975-1993. 1. Band. Das Neolithikum in Griechenland mit Ausnahme von Kreta und Zypern* (Veroffentlichungen Der Mykensichen Kommission 16). Vienna: the Austrian Academy of Sciences.

Alram-Stern, E. 2014. Times of change: Greece and the Aegean during the 4th millennium BC, in B. Horejs and M. Mehofer (eds) *Western Anatolia before Troy. Proto-Urbanisation in the 4th Millennium BC? Proceedings of the International Symposium Held at the Kunsthistorisches Museum Wien, Vienna, Austria, 21-24 November 2012* (Oriental and European Archaeology 1): 305-327. Vienna: the Austrian Academy of Sciences.

Arnold, D.E. 1989. Patterns of learning, residence, and descent among potters in Ticul, Yucatan, Mexico, in S. Shennan (ed.) *Archaeological Approaches to Cultural Identity*: 174–184. London: Unwin Hyman.

Berger, L.M. 2003. Die Frühhelladisch II Keramik von Ägina Kolonna und ihre Stellung im Ägäischen Raum. Unpublished PhD dissertation, University of Salzburg.

Berger, L. and W. Gauss 2016. Early Bronze Age Aegina Kolonna: a view from a southwest Aegean centre, in E. Pernicka, S. Ünlüsöy and S.W.E. Blum (eds) *Early Bronze Age Troy: Chronology, Cultural Development and Interregional Contacts. Proceedings of an International Conference held at the University of Tübingen May 8-10, 2009* (Studia Troica Monographien 8): 209-228. Bonn: Rudolf Habelt.

Blegen, C.W. 1921. *Korakou. A Prehistoric Settlement near Corinth.* Boston: the American School of Classical Studies at Athens.

Blegen, C.W. 1928. *Zygouries. A Prehistoric Settlement in the Valley of Cleonae.* Cambridge: Harvard University Press.

Broodbank, C. 2000. *An Island Archaeology of the Early Cyclades.* Cambridge: Cambridge University Press.

Broodbank, C. 2008. The Early Bronze Age in the Cyclades, in C.W. Shelmerdine (ed.) *The Cambridge Companion to the Aegean Bronze Age*: 47-76. Cambridge: Cambridge University Press.

Broodbank, C. and E. Kiriatzi 2007. The first 'Minoans' of Kythera revisited: technology, demography, and landscape in the Prepalatial Aegean. *American Journal of Archaeology* 111(2): 241-274.

Caskey, J.L. and E.G. Caskey 1960. The earliest settlement at Eutresis supplementary excavations, 1958. *Hesperia: the Journal of the American School of Classical Studies at Athens* 29(2): 126-167.

Coleman, J. 1977. *Keos I. Kephala: A Late Neolithic Settlement and Cemetery.* Princeton: the American School of Classical Studies at Athens.

Coleman, J.E. 1979a. Chronological and cultural divisions of the Early Cycladic period: a critical approach, in J.L. Davis and J.F. Cherry (eds) *Papers in Cycladic Prehistory* (University of California Los Angeles Institute of Archaeology Monograph 14): 48-50. Los Angeles: University of California, Los Angeles Institute of Archaeology.

Coleman, J.E. 1979b. Remarks on "terminology and beyond", in J.L. Davis and J.F. Cherry (eds) *Papers in Cycladic Prehistory* (University of California Los Angeles Institute of Archaeology Monograph 14): 64-65. Los Angeles: University of California Los Angeles Institute of Archaeology.

Coleman, J.E. 1985. 'Frying pans' of the Early Bronze Age Aegean. *American Journal of Archaeology* 89(2): 191-219.

Coleman, J.E. 2011. The Petromagoula-Doliana group and the beginning of the Aegean Early Bronze Age, in D. Katsonopoulou (ed.) *Helike IV: Ancient Helike and Aigialeia. Protohelladika: the Southern and Central Greek Mainland*: 13-44. Athens: the Helike Society.

Courtois, L. 1981. Étude physico-chemique de la céramique, in N. Lambert (ed.) *La Grotte préhistorique de Kitsos (Attique): missions, 1968-1978: l'occupation néolithique: les vestiges de temps paléolithiques, de l'antiquité et de l'histoire récente* (Recherche sur les grandes civilisations 7): 373-389. Paris: the French School at Athens.

Day, P.M., D.E. Wilson and E. Kiriatzi 1998. Pots, labels and people: burying ethnicity in the EM I cemetery at Aghia Photia, Siteias, in K. Branigan (ed.) *Cemetery and Society in the Aegean Bronze Age* (Sheffield Studies in Aegean Archaeology 1): 133-149. Sheffield: Sheffield Academic Press.

Day, P.M., E. Kiriatzi, A. Tsolakidou, and V. Kilikoglou 1999. Group therapy in Crete: a comparison between analyses by NAA and Thin Section Petrography of Early Minoan pottery. *Journal of Archaeological Science* 26(8): 1025-1036.

Demoule, J-P. and C. Perlès 1993. The Greek Neolithic: a new review. *Journal of World Prehistory* 7(4): 355-416.

Dickinson, O. 1994. *The Aegean Bronze Age.* Cambridge: Cambridge University Press.

Doumas, C. 1977. *Early Bronze Age Burial Habits in the Cyclades* (Studies in Mediterranean Archaeology 48). Gothenburg: Paul Åström.

Dimitriou, K. 2020. Η κεραμική του τέλους της Νεολιθικής και των αρχών της Πρώιμης Εποχής του Χαλκού από τον οικισμό της Μερέντας στο Μαρκόπουλο, in Papadimitriou, N., J.C. Wright, S. Fachard, N. Polychronakou-Sgouritsa and E. Andrikou (eds) *Athens and Attica in Prehistory. Proceedings of the International Conference, Athens, 27-31 May 2015*: 221-229. Oxford: Archaeopress.

Douni, K. 2015. La céramique du Bronze Ancien II en Attique. Unpublished PhD dissertation, University of Panthéon-Sorbonne (Paris 1).

Dousougli, A. 1987. Makrovouni-Kefalari Magoula-Talioti. Bemerkungen zu den Stufen FHI und II in der Argolis. *Prähistorische Zeitschrift* 62(2): 164–220.

Evans, A.J. 1906. *Essai de classification des époques de la civilisation minoenne: résumé d'un discours fait au Congrès d'archéologie à Athènes.* London: Quaritch.

Fachard, S. N. Papadimitriou, E. Andrikou and A. Mari. 2020a. Catalogue of prehistoric sites in Attica, in N. Papadimitriou, J.C. Wright, S. Fachard, N. Polychronakou-Sgouritsa and E. Andrikou (eds). *Athens and Attica in Prehistory. Proceedings of the International Conference, Athens, 27-31 May 2015*: v-xi. Oxford: Archaeopress.

Fachard, S. N. Papadimitriou, E. Andrikou and A. Mari. 2020b. Site distribution maps, in Attica, in N. Papadimitriou, J.C. Wright, S. Fachard, N. Polychronakou-Sgouritsa and E. Andrikou (eds). *Athens and Attica in Prehistory. Proceedings of the International Conference, Athens, 27-31 May 2015*: xii-xv. Oxford: Archaeopress.

Forsén, J. 2010. Mainland Greece, in E.H. Cline (ed.) *The Oxford Handbook of the Bronze Age Aegean (ca. 3000-1000 BC)*: 53-65. Oxford: Oxford University Press.

French, D.H. 1972. Notes on Prehistoric Pottery Groups from Central Greece. Athens: unpublished typescript.

Ginalas, M., M. Stathi and Z. Zgouleta 2015. Προϊστορικός οικισμός στην περιοχή Γυαλού Σπάτων, in A.D. Stephanis (ed.) *Πρακτικά ΙΕ΄ Επιστημονικής Συνάντησης ΝΑ Αττικής*: 337-352. Kalyvia: the Society for the Study of Southeast Attica.

Goldman, H. 1931. *Excavations at Eutresis in Boeotia*. Cambridge, Mass.: Harvard University Press.

Halstead, P. 1995. From sharing to hoarding: the Neolithic foundations of Aegean Bronze Age society, in R. Laffineur and W.-D. Niemeier (eds) *POLITEIA. Society and State in the Aegean Bronze Age. Proceedings of the 5th International Aegean Conference/ 5e Rencontre égéenne internationale, University of Heidelberg, Archäologisches Institut, 10-13 April 1994* (Aegaeum 12): 11–21. Liège and Austin: the University of Liège and University of Texas at Austin.

Harland, J.P. 1924. Aegean (Bronze Age) chronology and terminology. *American Journal of Archaeology* 28(1): 69-72.

Hoard, R.J., M.J. O'Brien, M.G. Khorasgany and V.S. Gopalaratnam 1995. A materials-science approach to understanding limestone-tempered pottery from the Midwestern United States. *Journal of Archaeological Science* 22(6): 823-832.

Immerwahr, S. 1971. *The Athenian Agora, Volume XIII. The Neolithic and Bronze Ages*. Princeton: the American School of Classical Studies at Athens.

Johnson, M. 1999. Chronology of Greece and south-east Europe in the Final Neolithic and Early Bronze Age. *Proceedings of the Prehistoric Society* 65: 319-336.

Kakavogianni, O. and K. Douni 2009. Μικρές έρευνες και ανασκαφές σε προϊστορικές θέσεις στα Μεσόγεια, 1994-2004, in V. Vasilopoulou and S. Katsarou-Tzeveleki (eds) *Από τα Μεσόγεια στον Αργοσαρωνικό. Β΄ Εφορεία Προϊστορικών και Κλασικών Αρχαιοτήτων. Το έργο μιας δεκαετίας, 1994-2003. Πρακτικά Συνεδρίου, Αθήνα, 18-20 Δεκεμβρίου 2003*: 383-398. Markopoulo: Municipality of Markopoulo, Mesogeia.

Kakavogianni, O., K. Douni and F. Nezeri 2008. Silver metallurgical finds dating from the end of the Final Neolithic period until the Middle Bronze Age in the area of the Mesogeia, in I. Tzachili (ed.) *Aegean Metallurgy in the Bronze Age. Proceedings of an International Symposium held at the University of Crete, Rethymnon, Greece, on November 19-21, 2004*: 45-57. Athens: Ta Pragmata.

Kakavogianni O., E. Tselepi, K. Dimitriou, C. Katsavou and K. Douni 2016. The Neolithic and Early Bronze Age settlement in Merenta, Attica, in its regional context, in Z. Tsirtsoni (ed.) *The Human Face of Radiocarbon: Reassessing Chronology in Prehistoric Greece and Bulgaria, 5000-3000 cal BC* (Travaux de la Maison de l'Orient et de la Méditerranée 69): 437-451. Lyon: House of the Orient and the Mediterranean-Jean Pouilloux.

Kaza-Papageorgiou, K. 2009. Άλιμος, Ελληνικό και Γλυφάδα: νέα ευρήματα προϊστορικών και ιστορικών χρόνων από ανασκαφές σε ιδιωτικούς και δημόσιους χώρους, V. Vasilopoulou and S. Katsarou-Tzeveleki (eds) *Από τα Μεσόγεια στον Αργοσαρωνικό. Β΄ Εφορεία Προϊστορικών και Κλασικών Αρχαιοτήτων. Το έργο μιας δεκαετίας, 1994-2003. Πρακτικά Συνεδρίου, Αθήνα, 18-20 Δεκεμβρίου 2003*: 433-449. Markopoulo: Municipality of Markopoulo, Mesogeia.

Keller, D.R. 1982. Final Neolithic pottery from Plakari, Karystos, in P. Spitaels (ed.) *Studies in South Attica 1* (Miscellanea Graeca 5): 47-67. Ghent: Belgian Archaeological Mission in Greece.

Kotjabopoulou, E. and K. Trantalidou 1993. Faunal analysis of the Skoteini Cave, A. Sampson (ed.) *Σκοτεινή Θαρρουνίων. Το σπήλαιο. Ο οικισμός και το νεκροταφείο*: 392-434. Athens: Ministry of Culture, Ephorate of Paleoanthropology-Speleology.

Maniatis, Y. Oberlin, C. and Z. Tsirtsoni 2016. "Balkans 4000": the radiocarbon dates from archaeological contexts, in Z. Tsirtsoni (ed.) *The Human Face of Radiocarbon: Reassessing Chronology in Prehistoric Greece and Bulgaria, 5000-3000 cal BC* (Travaux de la Maison de l'Orient et de la Méditerranée 69): 41-65. Lyon: House of the Orient and the Mediterranean-Jean Pouilloux.

Manning, S.W. 1995. *The Absolute Chronology of the Aegean Early Bronze Age. Archaeology, Radiocarbon and History* (Monographs in Mediterranean Archaeology 1). Sheffield: Sheffield Academic Press.

Manning, S.W. 2010. Chronology and terminology, in E.H. Cline (ed.) *The Oxford Handbook of the Bronze Age Aegean (ca. 3000-1000 BC)*: 11-28. Oxford: Oxford University Press.

Maran, J. 1998. *Kulturwandel auf dem griechischen Festland und den Kykladen im späten 3. Jahrtausend v. Chr.: Studien zu den kulturellen Verhältnissen in Südosteuropa und dem zentralen sowie östlichen Mittelmeerraum in der späten Kupfer- und frühen Bronzezeit* (Universitätsforschungen zur prähistorischen Archäologie 53). Bonn: Rudolf Habelt.

Mari, A. 1993. Αγγεία με στιλβωτή διακόσμηση, in A. Sampson (ed.) *Σκοτεινή Θαρρουνίων. Το σπήλαιο. Ο οικισμός και το νεκροταφείο*: 135-151. Athens: Ministry of Culture, Ephorate of Paleoanthropology-Speleology.

Marinatos, S. 1972. Ανασκαφαί Μαραθώνος. *Πρακτικά της εν Αθήναις Αρχαιολογικής Εταιρείας* 1970: 5-28.

Mee, C. 2009. Interconnectivity in Early Helladic Laconia, in W.G. Cavanagh, C. Gallou and M. Georgiadis (eds) *Sparta and Laconia: from Prehistory to Pre-Modern. Proceedings of the Conference Held in Sparta, Organised by the British School at Athens, the University of Nottingham, the 5th Ephoreia of Prehistoric and Classical Antiquities and the 5th Ephoreia of Byzantine Antiquities 17-20 March 2005* (The British School at Athens Studies 16): 43-53. London: the British School at Athens.

Miller, D. 1985. *Artefacts as Categories: A Study of Ceramic Variability in Central India* (New Studies in

Archaeology). Cambridge: Cambridge University Press.

Mylonas, G.E. 1959. *Aghios Kosmas: An Early Bronze Age Settlement and Cemetery in Attica*. Princeton: Princeton University Press.

Nakou, G. 2007. Absent presences: metal vessels in the Aegean at the end of the third millennium, in P.M. Day and R.C.P. Doonan (eds) *Metallurgy in the Early Bronze Age Aegean* (Sheffield Studies in Aegean Archaeology 7): 224-244. Oxford: Oxbow Books.

Nazou, M. 2010. Grey areas in past maritime identity? The case of Final Neolithic–Early Bronze Age Attica (Greece) and the surrounding islands. *Shima: the International Journal of Research into Island Cultures* 4(1): 3-15.

Nazou, M. 2014. Defining the Regional Characteristics of Final Neolithic and Early Bronze Age Pottery in Attica. Unpublished PhD dissertation, University College London.

Pantelidou Gofa, M. 2005. *Τσέπι Μαραθώνος: Το πρωτοελλαδικό νεκροταφείο* (Βιβλιοθήκη της εν Αθήναις Αρχαιολογικής Εταιρείας 235). Athens: the Archaeological Society of Athens.

Pantelidou Gofa, M. 2016. *Τσέπι Μαραθώνος. Ο αποθέτης 39 του προϊστορικού νεκροταφείου* (Βιβλιοθήκη της εν Αθήναις Αρχαιολογικής Εταιρείας 310). Athens: the Archaeological Society of Athens.

Papadatos, Y. and P. Tomkins 2013. Trading, the longboat, and cultural interaction in the Aegean during the late fourth millennium B.C.E.: the view from Kephala Petras, East Crete. *American Journal of Archaeology* 117(3): 353-381.

Rambach, J. 2000. *Kykladen I und II: Die frühe Bronzezeit Band 1: Grab- und Siedlungsbefunde. Band 2: Frühbronzezeitliche Beigabensittenkreise auf den Kykladen: relative Chronologie und Verbreitung* (Beiträge zur ur- und frühgeschichtlichen Archäologie des Mittelmeer-Kulturraumes 33/34). Bonn: Rudolf Habelt.

Phelps, B. 2004. *The Neolithic Pottery Sequence in Southern Greece* (British Archaeological Reports International Series 1259). Oxford: Archaeopress.

Pullen, D. 2008. The Early Bronze Age in Greece, in C.W. Shelmerdine (ed.) *The Cambridge Companion to the Aegean Bronze Age*: 19-46. Cambridge: Cambridge University Press.

Pullen, D.J. 2011. *Nemea Valley Archaeological Project, Volume 1. The Early Bronze Age Village on Tsoungiza Hill*. Princeton: the American School of Classical Studies at Athens.

Renfrew, A.C. 1972. *The Emergence of Civilisation: the Cyclades and the Aegean in the Third Millennium BC*. London: Methuen.

Sampson, A. 1981. *Η Νεολιθική και η Πρωτοελλαδική Ι στην Εύβοια* (Αρχείον Ευβοϊκών Μελετών, Παράρτημα 24). Athens: the Society of Euboean Studies.

Sampson, A. 1988. *Μάνικα ΙΙ: Ο πρωτοελλαδικός οικισμός και το νεκροταφείο*. Athens: Municipality of Chalkis.

Sampson, A. 1989. Some chronological problems of the end of the Neolithic and the Early Bronze Age, in Y. Maniatis (ed.) *Archaeometry. Proceedings of the 25th International Symposium*: 709-718. Amsterdam: Elsevier.

Sampson, A. 1993a. *Σκοτεινή Θαρρουνίων: το σπήλαιο, ο οικισμός και το νεκροταφείο*. Athens: Eleftheroudakis.

Sampson, A. 1993b. *Καλογερόβρυση, ένας οικισμός της Πρώιμης και Μέσης Χαλκοκρατίας στα Φύλλα της Εύβοιας*. Athens: Morfi.

Sampson, A. 2008. *The Sarakenos Cave at Akraephnion, Boeotia, Greece, Volume I: the Neolithic and the Bronze Age*. Athens: University of the Aegean/Polish Academy of Arts and Sciences.

Sotirakopoulou, P. 2016. *The Pottery from Dhaskalio. The Sanctuary on Keros and the Origins of Aegean Ritual: the Excavations of 2006-2008, Volume IV*. Cambridge: McDonald Institute for Archaeological Research.

Spitaels, P. 1982. Final Neolithic pottery from Thorikos, in P. Spitaels (ed.) *Studies in South Attica 1* (Miscellanea Graeca 5): 9-45. Ghent: Belgian Archaeological Mission in Greece.

Tomkins, P. 2007. Neolithic: strata IX-VIII, VII-VIB, VIA-V, IV, IIIB, IIIA, IIB, IIA and IC groups, in N. Momigliano (ed.) *Knossos Pottery Handbook. Neolithic and Bronze Age (Minoan)* (The British School at Athens Studies 14): 9-48. London: the British School at Athens.

Tomkins, P. and I. Schoep 2010. Crete, in E.H. Cline (ed.) *The Oxford Handbook of the Bronze Age Aegean (ca. 3000-1000 BC)*: 66-82. Oxford: Oxford University Press.

Tzavella-Evjen, H. 1984. *Λιθαρές*. Athens: the Archaeological Receipts and Expropriations Fund.

Vitelli, K.D. 1999. *Franchthi Neolithic Pottery. Volume 2: the Later Neolithic Ceramic Phases 3 to 5* (Excavations at Franchthi Cave, Greece 10). Bloomington and Indianapolis: Indiana University Press.

Vitelli, K.D. 2007. *Lerna V. The Neolithic Pottery from Lerna*. Princeton: the American School of Classical Studies at Athens.

Whitbread, I. and A. Mari 2014. Provenance and proximity: a technological analysis of Late and Final Neolithic ceramics from Euripides Cave, Salamis, Greece. *Journal of Archaeological Science* 41: 79-88.

Wace, A.J.B. and C.W. Blegen 1918. The pre-Mycenaean pottery of the mainland. *The Annual of the British School at Athens* 22: 175-189.

Weisshaar, H.-J. 1994. Keramik des südwest-ägäischen Chalkolithikums von Ägina, in C. Dobiat and D. Vorlauf (eds) *Festschrift für Otto-Herman Frey zum 65. Geburtstag* (Marburger Studien zur Vor- und Frühgeschichte 16): 675-689. Marburg: Hitzeroth.

Whitelaw, T., P. Day, E. Kiriatzi, V. Kilikoglou and D. Wilson 1997. Ceramic traditions at EM IIB Myrtos, Fournou Korifi, in R. Laffineur and P. Betancourt (eds) *TEXNH: Craftsmen, Craftswomen and Craftsmanship in the Aegean Bronze Age. Proceedings of the 6th international Aegean Conference/ 6e Rencontre égéenne internationale,*

Philadelphia, Temple University, 18-21 1996 (Aegaeum 16): 265-274. Liège: the University of Liège.

Wiencke, M.H. 1989. Change in Early Helladic II. *American Journal of Archaeology* 93(4): 495-509.

Wiencke, M.H. 2000. *Lerna IV. The Architecture, Stratification and Pottery of Lerna III*. Princeton: the American School of Classical Studies at Athens.

Wiencke, M.H. 2010. Lerna, in E.H. Cline (ed.) *The Oxford Handbook of the Bronze Age Aegean (ca. 3000-1000 BC)*: 660-670. Oxford: Oxford University Press.

Wilson, D.E. 1987. Kea and east Attike in Early Bronze II: beyond pottery typology, in J.M. Fossey (ed.) *Συνεισφορά McGill I. Papers in Greek Archaeology and History, in Memory of Colin D. Gordon* (McGill Monographs in Classical Archaeology and History 6): 35-49. Amsterdam: J.C. Gieben.

Wilson, D.E. 1999. *Keos IX. Ayia Irini: Periods I-III. The Neolithic and Early Bronze Age Settlements. Part I. The Pottery and Small Finds.* Mainz: Philipp von Zabern.

Wilson, D.E. 2008. Early Prepalatial Crete, in C.W. Shelmerdine (ed.) *The Cambridge Companion to the Aegean Bronze Age*: 77-104. Cambridge: Cambridge University Press.

Wilson, D.E. and P.M. Day 1994. Ceramic regionalism in Prepalatial central Crete: the Mesara imports at EM I-EM IIA Knossos. *The Annual of the British School at Athens* 89: 1-87.

Wilson, D.E., P.M. Day, and N. Dimopoulou-Rethemiotaki 2008. The gateway port of Poros-Katsambas: trade and exchange between north-central Crete and the Cyclades in EB I-II, in N. Brodie, J. Doole, G. Gavalas and C. Renfrew (eds) *Horizon. A Colloquium on the Prehistory of the Cyclades*: 261-270. Cambridge: McDonald Institute for Archaeological Research.

Zachou, E. 2004. Die frühbronzezeitliche Siedlung in Proskynas/Lokris in E. Alram-Stern (ed.) *Die Ägäische Frühzeit. 2. Serie. Forschungsbericht 1975-2002. 2. Band, Tiel 1 und 2. Die Frühbronzezeit in Griechenland mit Ausnahme von Kreta* (Veröffentlichungen der Mykenischen Kommission 21): 1267-1283. Vienna: the Austrian Academy of Sciences.

The Study of Mycenaean Pottery from Cyprus:
A Short Story of the 1895 British Museum Excavations at Site D, Kourion[1]

Angelos Papadopoulos

Prologue

Professor Chris Mee engaged with the study of pottery throughout his career, including in his work with material from the Bronze Age Dodecanese, Cyprus and the Greek Mainland. He was an expert in this field, yet when I arrived at Liverpool in 2002 to study under his supervision, it was not to better understand ceramics, but rather the iconography of warfare in the Bronze Age Aegean (and what a mentor he was). Following a successful doctoral defence, I moved to Cyprus to continue my research, hoping to identify there a bridge between Near Eastern and Aegean iconography. Evidently, this hypothesis quickly fainted away, to be rapidly replaced by a growing interest in the imported Mycenaean pottery discovered on the island.[2]

In this short contribution in memory of Professor Mee, I present some preliminary observations on, and methodological problems and considerations regarding, the Mycenaean pottery from the tomb groups excavated during the late 19th century AD from the site of Kourion (Site D, Episkopi-Bamboula) in Cyprus and today held in the British Museum, London and the Cyprus Museum, Nicosia.

Setting the stage

The excavation of Kourion Site D (Episkopi-Bamboula) was carried out during a period of intense foreign archaeological interest in Cyprus. It suffered from many of the same difficulties of procedure and recording that characterised other early Mediterranean excavations, and the objects recovered were subject to a division between parties which saw many of the most significant finds from the site transported overseas. As such, understanding what exactly was found, and recognising the importance of the site in the wider context of Cypriot prehistory, has proved to be challenging.

The late Professor Paul Åström, reflecting on the perennial problem of looting and the destruction of Cyprus' unique cultural heritage, noted that 'archaeological activities in Cyprus at the end of the nineteenth century have been characterized by Stanley Casson as "the gold rush" and by John L. Myres as a "mischievous pastime". It was a time when many antiquities were taken out of the country in various ways legally and illegally. In one instance some soldiers smuggled a limestone sculpture through the customs and into a boat by pretending it was a drunken soldier' (Åström 2000: 8-9).

Nevertheless, these early excavations on Cyprus were important, for they related directly to the progress of Greek archaeology and the so-called 'Mycenaean question' surrounding the characterisation and dating of the Mycenaean culture of mainland Greece. In *The Mycenaean Age* (1897), Tsountas and Manatt argued that the birth of the Greek world was to be found not in the 'Homeric Age', but in the Mycenaean culture of the 16th to 12th centuries BC (see also, Steel 2001). In their discussion, they recognised the work of Sir Charles Newton, Keeper of the Greek and Roman Antiquities at the British Museum, 1861-1886, who had identified links between finds made at Mycenae, and others from Rhodes and Cyprus. It was he, they held, who had 'laid the real foundation of Mycenaean archaeology' (Tsountas and Manatt 1897: 5).[3]

[1] Acknowledgments: the current chapter is based on a long-term project, and I would like to express my sincere thanks to a number of people for their assistance and advice. First and foremost, I am grateful to Dr Despina Pilides (former Curator of the Department of Antiquities, Cyprus) for inviting me to participate to the Enkomi Digitisation Project, for it was this that triggered my interest in Late Bronze Age Cyprus. I am indebted, also, to the former Director of the Department, Dr Maria Hadjikosti, who granted me permission to study and publish the Episkopi-Bamboula material, as well as the curators, conservators, photographers and staff of the Cyprus Museum for facilitating my research. Dr Lesley Fitton (Keeper, Department of Greece and Rome) and Dr Thomas Kiely (Cyprus Curator) of the British Museum have provided me access to information, artefacts and archives for which I am grateful. The financial assistance provided by the Institute for Aegean Prehistory and the British School at Athens allowed me to work between Greece, the UK and Cyprus. Many thanks to my dear friend and colleague Dr. David Smith (University of Liverpool) for the great care he has afforded to my text. The images illustrated in Figure 13.1 were made by Mr Nikos Sepetzoglou. It goes without saying that all mistakes and omissions remain my own.

[2] Late Bronze Age Cyprus was included among Professor Mee's numerous research interests. In 1998, together with Louise Steel, he published *The Cypriote Collections in the University of Liverpool and the Williamson Art Gallery and Museum* (Mee and Steel 1998), and his contribution to *The Cambridge Companion to the Aegean Bronze Age*, edited by Cynthia Shelmerdine, explored themes including interregional trade and the use of Mycenaean pottery in Cyprus (Mee 2008).

[3] Several objects from the Aegean, and others locally made in imitation of Aegean prototypes, are known from various sites on Cyprus (Steel 2001). More recent excavations on the island, like those of the New Swedish Cyprus Expedition at Hala Sultan Tekke (the

Excavating in Cyprus

With the annexation of Cyprus to Great Britain in 1878,[4] British archaeologists became eligible to carry out excavations on the island. In 1892, a bequest of £2000 made by Miss Emma Turner to the British Museum 'for the purpose of excavation, exploration, or survey of sites in Europe, Asia or Africa in furtherance of the study of the antiquities of Greece, Rome or Egypt or the Biblical Antiquities' (Kiely 2009; 2010b; 2019; Kiely and Ulbrich 2012) prompted a rush of systematic excavation as part of the eponymous Turner Bequest expedition. This included work at the sites of Amathous, excavated by Arthur H. Smith and John Myres from November 1893 to March 1894; Kourion, excavated by Henry Beauchamp Walters from January to April 1895; and Enkomi, excavated by Alexander Stuart Murray, Percy Christian, and Arthur H. Smith from March to September 1896.[5] The results of this work were published in 1900, although discussion is limited only to those tomb groups which were subsequently given to the British Museum.

Excavations at Kourion (Figure 13.1) lasted for three months. Myres and Ohnefalsch-Richter record that 'the special feature of the excavations was the discovery of a necropolis dating to the Mycenaean period, which apparently confirms the statement of Strabo that "Kurion had originally been founded by a colony from Argos"' (1899: 180) (Figure 13.2). The Bronze Age site (Site D) was first excavated by Charles Christian and John Williamson between the 11th and 23rd February (Tombs 17-58), and then from the 18th until the 27th March (Tombs 86-109), under the supervision of Henry Beauchamp Walters, then Curator of the British Museum. Charles Christian was the Director of the Imperial Ottoman Bank in Larnaca and acted as an agent for the British Museum in London, arranging excavation permits among his other duties (Kiely 2009). John Williamson, a prominent English resident in Cyprus, Head of the English Club at Limassol, and employee of the English-Cyprus Copper Mine Company, fulfilled a similar role.

Surviving correspondence, stored at the Cyprus State Archives and the British Museum, provide useful

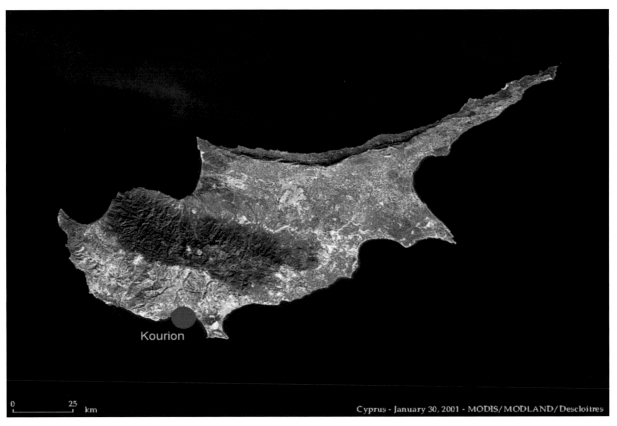

Figure 13.1. Map of Cyprus showing the location of Kourion (after d-maps.com)

Söderberg Expedition), have continued to recover low quantities of imported Mycenaean pottery (Fischer and Bürge 2018; 2019).
[4] It was subsequently recognised as an English protectorate in 1914, and became a colony in 1922.
[5] The quality and quantity of material recovered from the excavations at Enkomi led to further excavations at the sites of Maroni (1897), Hala Sultan Tekke (Vyzakia, 1897-1898), Kouklia (1897) and Klavdia-Tremithos (1899).

insight into the bureaucracy which surrounded these works, and particularly, the division of their spoils. In a letter dated 24th April 1895, the District Commissioner of Limassol, Roland L.N. Michell, informed the Chief Secretary to Government of Cyprus, Harry Langhorne Thompson, about the division of objects. The number of those tombs that yielded material which would constitute the share of the Government was recorded (see Table 13.1). A further letter, dated 30th April 1895, notes the existence of books illustrating the objects found at the recent excavations. On the 19th of June, Williamson requested permission for a Captain A. Young 'to ship 4 cases with the BM [British Museum] share from the Curium Excavations addressed to the Principal Librarian'. The Chief Secretary subsequently agreed, but demanded a list of the contents of these boxes and a statement of their estimated value, to be handed to customs officials. A list of artefacts recovered from each tomb was provided by Williamson, and placed inside Boxes I and II. No value estimate was included. Interestingly, in the record for Box II, Williamson mentions 'one cardboard box cont[aining] the gold that fell to lot of the C.M [Cyprus Museum]', and a small quantity of objects with no numbers. This latter group appears not to have included any Mycenaean pottery.

The system by which the finds from Kourion were divided up, and the fact that the British Museum received a majority 'lion's share' including large quantities of very high-quality objects, was a function of the historical, social and political framework within which the work was carried out. The British authorities on Cyprus, in an attempt to safeguard the antiquities of the island from illegal excavation and export abroad, had maintained the so-called Ottoman Law of 1874. This legislation required that, at the end of excavation, the material recovered would be divided equally between the owner of the excavated plot, the State, and the excavator. Even with subsequent amendments in 1905,

Table 13.1. *The tombs attributed to the Cyprus Museum (in-filled), based on data from Folder 5/95, Cyprus State Archives (source: A. Papadopoulos).*

2	27	51	76	97
5	29	54	79	100
7	32	58	82	103
12	35	60	84	105
13	40	64	85	108
19	41	66	87	111
20	46	71	91	113
23	49	74	93	116

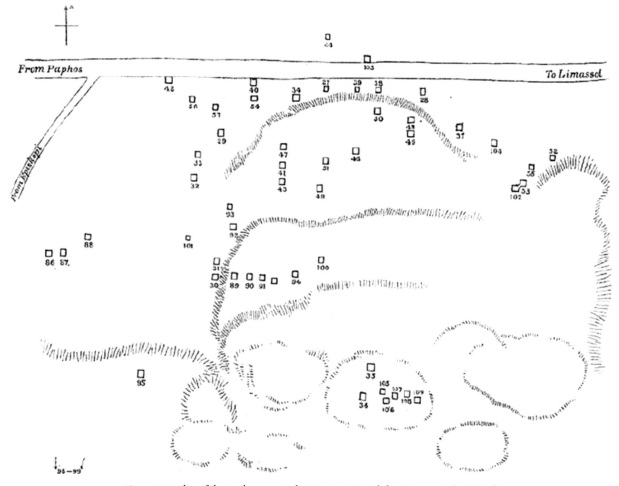

Figure 13.2. *Plan of the tombs excavated at Kourion Site D (after Murray* et al. *1900: 61)*

and again in 1927 (coinciding with the arrival to the island of the Swedish Cyprus Expedition, SCE), however, this legislation failed to curtail illegal export, or ensure amicable division of material excavated legitimately. Indeed, in 1931, the law proved so favourable to foreign excavators that the Swedish Cyprus Expedition was able to export to Sweden approximately half of all the finds that it had recovered during its own work (Göransson 2012; Wright 2001).

Primary and secondary sources

In addition to the author's understanding of 19th century AD excavations on Cyprus,[6] there exists a considerable body of surviving archival material in Cyprus and the United Kingdom, through which it has been possible to analyse the British Museum's early excavations on Cyprus. These resources include:

The Kourion Excavation Diary (1895): this notebook was maintained during the excavation of the site and includes various comments and observations made by the excavators in the field. Many of the lines which describe the finds have been struck through at a later date, apparently in relation to the donation of so-called 'duplicate vessels' to particular individuals (Kiely 2009). Those items that became part of the Cyprus Museum share were marked with letter 'N', most likely a reference to 'Nicosia', to reflect their intended destination. Those pages on the right-hand side of the notebook are reserved for notation and, later, the addition of British Museum inventory numbers. Those on the left-hand side of the notebook contain basic site sketches and plans.

A Catalogue of the Cyprus Museum by John Myres and Max Ohnefalsch-Richter (1899): this rather impressive first catalogue records the Cyprus Museum share of the finds from the British Museum excavations. The authors attempt to organise their discussion chronologically, and in relation to their tomb group provenance, although, as noted by Myres and Onhnefalsch-Richter, this proved challenging in practice.

Excavations in Cyprus by Alexander Murray, Arthur Smith, and Henry Walters (1900): the preliminary results of the excavations at Enkomi, Kourion, and Amathous were published by Murray and colleagues in 1900. The authors detail the background of the excavations, provide photographs, and drawings of the artefact and sketches and plans of the sites under investigation, as well as a synthesis of the excavated data. However, the conclusions drawn are limited, and make no reference to the Cyprus Museum share at all. The volume also makes clear the greater quality, and

archaeological significance, of those finds held at the British Museum, with an emphasis on the Mycenaean and Egyptian imports.

The Cyprus State Archives: the Cyprus State Archives contain a very large volume of material related both to the bureaucracy of excavation, the nature of the material recovered, and the logistics of export. It is particularly informative on the contents of the tombs and the share of the Cyprus Museum. The Archives include correspondence between the Cypriot authorities and the representatives of the British Museum, applications and correspondence from those British Museum personnel based on Cyprus, and various catalogues, permissions, communicae and guidelines issued by the Cypriot authorities, including the requirement for the provision of the aforementioned list of artefacts to be included within the boxes to be exported.

The index cards of the Department of Antiquities, Cyprus: these cards provide information on the stored collections of the Cyprus Museum.[7] They refer, primarily, to the so-called Old Collection (comprised of material recovered prior to 1935), and for each object typically include a date of discovery, acquisition or donation, a provenance (where available), dimensions, materiality, and a basic description.

Despite these resources, there are a number of significant obstacles to understanding the context of deposition and the context of discovery of much of the Kourion material, understanding what exactly was recovered, and identifying the current location of surviving pieces. To be more specific:

1. The tombs from Site D and, indeed, those from all areas of the excavation at Kourion, seemed to have been looted in antiquity. In several instances, and as noted by the excavators, excavation yielded only very small numbers of offerings.

2. It seems to be clear that the excavators targeted the acquisition of certain categories of artefact (and particularly imports from the Aegean region), while others, particularly among the pottery assemblage, were neither recorded nor collected. This recovery bias is evidenced by the majority presence within the collections of both the British Museum and the Cyprus Museum of largely intact, or very well preserved, vessels.[8]

---

[6] The result, largely, of previous work with the Cyprus Museum Enkomi Project, for which, see Pilides (2019).

[7] These are available at the Curator's office at the Cyprus Museum. I would like to express my gratitude to the former curator of the Cyprus Museum and Ephor of Antiquities, Dr Despina Pilides, for allowing me access to the index cards and for time spent discussing the various difficulties of this dataset, and its use.

[8] A small number of sherds belonging to pictorial kraters are exceptional in this regard.

3. There was no attempt made by the excavators to accurately record human remains encountered during excavation, with the result that no calculations are possible to determine the Minimum Number of Individuals (MNI) buried in the Kourion tombs excavated by the British Museum, or to establish relationships between individuals and objects.[9]

4. The material record has been skewed by the post-excavation distribution of various 'duplicates' through sales, or as gifts. Rather than forming genuine duplicates, it is likely that they were considered disposable on aesthetic, rather than scientific, criteria, as was common practice in the late 19th and early 20th century AD. In many cases, the details of these duplicates are not recorded in the excavation notebooks.

5. Study of the handwritten catalogue of the contents of the tombs demonstrates clearly that the details of those finds delivered to the Cyprus Museum were recorded hastily and carelessly, and raises the possibility that errors were introduced during the writing of the catalogue. The lack of detail provided in the descriptions lead to further problems in the later identification of several of those artefacts stored in the Cyprus Museum.

6. In the years following the division of the Kourion material between the Cyprus and British Museums, the material at the Cyprus Museum was neither well organised, nor stored safely, as noted by Myres and Onhnefalsch-Richter (1899: v-vii).[10] This raises the possibility that some of the Cyprus Museum share has been subject to post-excavation loss as a result of damage.

7. The data recorded on the index cards at the Cyprus Museum is limited and, generally, the provenance of the artefacts is either unrecorded or uncertain (typically signified with a question mark, '?'), as are the dates of their excavation and/or discovery.

More generally, there appears to be very little concordance between sources on the quantity and quality of objects recorded. In the case of Tomb 41, for example (see Table 13.2), the three main sources of information exhibit very little agreement, especially when considered against the surviving material from the Cyprus Museum *apotheke*.

Some observations on the Mycenaean pottery from Kourion

The Cyprus Museum share of the Aegean pottery recovered from the Site D tombs, as it survives, appears to consist of shapes and surface treatments typical of southwestern Cyprus and known from other sites on the island and elsewhere in the Eastern Mediterranean (see Figure 13.3 for characteristic shapes from Site D). This group includes drinking vessels and containers for liquids and solids, including examples of alabastra, stirrup jars, shallow one-handled cups, kraters for mixing wine and water, and piriform or pithoid jars. The same shapes have also been found within the wider area of Kourion (Benson 1972).[11]

With the exception of a shallow semi-globular cup with vertical handle (A1530), no examples of kylikes, or other drinking shapes, have been identified among the Cyprus Museum share, although they are known from nearby tombs that now constitute part of the British Museum share. The lack of rhyta among the Cyprus Museum share is also not indicative of their presence across the site as a whole, since, again, examples of these cult vessels are visible among the British Museum share.

Among the Cyprus Museum share of storage and transport vessels from Site D are two small stirrup jars, A1586 and A1616. The decoration of A1586 suggests a possible central Cretan provenance, while the fabric of A1616 could be indicative of its manufacture in western Crete.[12] Another large stirrup jar bearing Linear B script, originating from Site D Tomb 50 and now located at the British Museum (inv. no. 1896,0201.265; Kiely 2011: 50.1), has been proven by petrographic analysis to also derive from Crete (Haskell *et al.* 2011); fragments from the same vase were identified by Daniel in Site D Tomb 26 during the excavations of the University of Pennsylvania (Benson 1972; Karageorghis 2009; Kiely 2009; Vermeule and Karageorghis 1982). A number of small piriform jars (A1668, A1665 and A1689) may have contained liquids or perhaps pastes, as was the case with alabastron A1729.

Of the pictorial pottery, joined fragments A2025a-e-g, most likely form part of a krater (perhaps FS 53-55), and preserve part of a chariot scene. This includes a typical Late Bronze Age chariot with leather(?)-covered box, pulled by two horses, and a selection of geometric motifs typical of the Mycenaean decorative tradition of *horror vacui*. The interior surface includes a partially-preserved sign in the Cypro-Minoan script, which

---

[9] A handwritten note from Percy Christian (brother of Charles) concerning Tomb 47 in the excavation diary of the Enkomi Excavations (1896) highlights this issue: 'we had a very interesting tomb with about 4 ft. of human bones, but very little else except a porcelain flask...and a short sword...we got several skulls from this one with a diadem still adhering which I preserved as it was...I will send you as many skulls as I can perfect' (see Tatton-Brown 2001). My sincere thanks to Dr Thomas Kiely for allowing me access to the Enkomi excavation diary.

[10] Similar problems have been noted by the researchers who studied the material from Hala Sultan Tekke (Åström *et al.* 1976).

[11] See also the Digital Kourion project of the University of Pennsylvania Museum of Archaeology and Anthropology (2021).

[12] I am indebted to Dr. Kostas Paschalidis (National Archaeological Museum, Athens) for providing me with this information. It should be noted that this is work in progress.

Table 13.2. The contents of Tomb 41 based on all available sources (source: A. Papadopoulos).

Cyprus State Archives	Kourion Excavation Diary	Catalogue of the Cyprus Museum	Cyprus Museum
Alabaster vase	Alabaster vase	Alabaster vase	
Small marble vase	(?)	Small marble vase	
Stone mortar	Mortar of basalt on three legs	Mortar of basalt	
Stone vase	Stone vase with thick flutings	Stone vase with thick flutings, like a mould	
Fragments of vase			
	Pseudamphora with bands and chevron patterns	Two Mycenaean pseudoamphorae	
(?)Mycenaean vase, broken	Mycenaean stamnos – broken – network pattern on shoulder	Mykenaean ' stamnos ' with network pattern	
	Do plain red ware		
	Alabastron with black rings on drab		Alabastron (A1729)
	Small vase with two small handles		
	Small vase of black ribbed ware		
(?)Vase in fragments	Vase in fragments – diamond and chevron patterns on shoulder		
	Two gold rings	Two gold rings	
	Two gold beads	Two gold beads	
	Stone bead as before		
			Pithoid jar (A1668)
			Pithoid jar (A1689)
			Pithoid jar (A1690)
		Small jar	

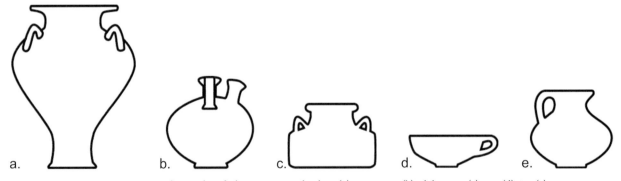

Figure 13.3. Ceramic shapes identified at Kourion: pithoid jar (a); stirrup jar (b); alabastron (c); cup (d); jug (e)
(illustration: Nikos Sepetzoglou).

cannot be safely identified (Hirschfeld 2006: 90, no. 17). The index card accompanying these fragments states that it was delivered as a gift by one 'Cl. Pierides', having been recovered, originally, from Kourion (Karageorghis 1963: 6-7, no. 4, pl. 6). Although impossible to prove with certainty, it is very tempting to consider this as a vessel recovered from Kourion, and particularly from the British Museum excavations there, given the aforementioned focus of those excavators on the

retrieval of intact examples, or large fragments, of pictorial kraters.[13]

Kourion has certainly yielded other examples of imported Mycenaean pictorial pottery of very high

---

[13] It is noteworthy that two further pictorial krater fragments from the Cyprus Museum (A2025e and A2025i), allegedly come from the area of Kourion, yet this identification too is problematic.

quality. The so-called 'Window Krater', particularly, has a fascinating recent biography, with fragments having first been identified during the British Museum excavations in Tombs 53 and 102, and by Daniel in 1937 in Tombs 17 and 17A (Benson 1972: 20-21, no. 26; Daniel 1940: 10, pl. IVd); the latter fragments bearing depictions of window frames and women holding lilies.[14] This vessel has formed the subject of various studies (see, for example, Benson 1972: 20-21, no. 26; Karageorghis 1957), and its decorative scheme seems to be unique among the pictorial repertoire. Indeed, the depiction of women stood at the windows of buildings is a motif that is frequently (and perhaps almost exclusively) encountered on the mural paintings of the LH IIIB palaces of mainland Greece (Papadopoulos 2018).

The pictorial krater appears to constitute a special category of Late Helladic object imported from the Aegean for consumption by an eastern Mediterranean clientele; an unapologetically 'exotic' shape whose pictorial decoration elevated the performative component of its use. There are no known examples of these kraters in gold or silver. They seem, therefore, to have been exclusively ceramic products, allowing the socio-economic middle classes of Late Bronze Age Cyprus to incorporate them within a variety of status-focused activities (Steel 1998; 2004). The chariot motif, particularly, can be considered a symbol of prestige and military and/or hunting prowess, and is more occasionally present in narrative scenes that can be interpreted as mythological in character (Feldman and Sauvage 2010; also, Vermeule and Karageorghis 1982).

Epilogue

This study illuminates a previously obscure Mycenaean ceramic component of Cyprus' Late Bronze Age archaeological record, and the potential opportunities and difficulties associated with both its future study, and the study of other similar material groups. Some of this material is presented and discussed for the first time. Much of the material from old excavations on Cyprus remains unpublished and, even where this is not the case, vessels are commonly published individually, rather than as groups (see Åström 1972a; 1972b; Foster 1979; Karageorghis 1963; Vermeule and Karageorghis 1982), in a trend which, ultimately, serves only to limit our understanding.

Despite the many, and varied, problems encountered during the study of the material from Kourion Site D, its benefits are clear, and particularly as they related to the methodological approach taken toward old material. Careful collection of the finds from Site D, will allow the creation of new burial datasets for improved archaeological and statistical analyses, such as those presented by Keswani (1989; 2004) and Kiely (2010a). Similarly, a more detailed pottery record will inform existing hypotheses on the distribution and appreciation of certain vessel types, of the sort offered by van Wijngaarden (2001) in his study of the distribution of Mycenaean pictorial kraters at Enkomi.[15] The publication of new, or largely unknown, pottery allows for new insight into the geographical distribution of pottery categories. The presence of Aegean (as well as Cypriot) pottery can also inform the study of local chronologies, trade and exchange mechanisms, and patterns of consumption (Crewe 2009; Papadimitriou 2012; 2017).

The study of the cemetery at Kourion Site D represents one part of a long series of research projects focused on the study of the 19th century AD British Museum excavations on the island of Cyprus. Incorporating the restudy of material from the Late Bronze Age sites of Hala Sultan Tekke, Enkomi and Maroni, the shares from the British Museum and the Cyprus Museum, and the study of other objects in museums around Europe, it is envisaged that this work will deliver new insight into prehistoric Cyprus.

Bibliography

Åström, P. 1972a. *The Swedish Cyprus Expedition IV.1B. The Middle Cypriote Bronze Age.* Lund: the Swedish Cyprus Expedition.

Åström, P. 1972b. *The Swedish Cyprus Expedition IV.1C. The Late Cypriote Bronze Age: Architecture and Pottery.* Lund: the Swedish Cyprus Expedition.

Åström, P. 2000. *A Century of International Cyprological Research* (12th Annual Lecture on the History and Archaeology of Cyprus). Nicosia: the Bank of Cyprus Cultural Foundation.

Åström, P., D.M. Bailey and V. Karageorghis 1976. *Hala Sultan Tekke I. Excavations 1897-1971* (Studies in Mediterranean Archaeology 45.1). Gothenburg: Paul Åström.

Benson, J.L. 1972. *Bamboula at Kourion: the Necropolis and the Finds Excavated by J.F. Daniel* (University Museum Monograph 32; Haney Foundation Series 12). Philadelphia: University of Pennsylvania Press.

Crewe, L. 2009. Feasting with the dead? Tomb 66 at Enkomi, in T. Kiely (ed.) *Ancient Cyprus in the British*

---

[14] In 1969, following negotiations between the Cyprus and British Museums, it was agreed that all the sherds should be accessioned into the collection at Nicosia, to preserve them as a group and allow for restoration. This example demonstrates the willingness of the curators of the great museum to provide solutions to the many difficulties surrounding scholarship and the borrowing and exhibition of cultural property. For further discussion on the issue of bringing the pieces together, see Karageorghis (2009).

[15] Here Van Wijngaarden (2001) argues that the distribution of these mixing vessels is a function of various mechanisms of consumption intended to enhance the social status of their owner(s).

Museum. *Essays in Honour of Veronica Tatton-Brown* (British Museum Research Publication 180): 27-48. London: the British Museum.

Daniel, J. 1940. The Achaeans at Kourion. *The University Museum Bulletin* 8(1): 3-14.

Feldman, M. and C. Sauvage 2010. Objects of prestige? Chariots in the Late Bronze Age Eastern Mediterranean and Near East. *Egypt and Levant* 20: 67-181.

Fischer, P.M. and T. Bürge 2018. The New Swedish Cyprus Expedition 2017: excavations at Hala Sultan Tekke (The Söderberg Expedition). Preliminary results, with contributions by M. Ausiayevich, B. Placiente Robedizo, V. Barrera Alarcón, L. Recht and D. Kofel. *Opuscula. Annual of the Swedish Institutes at Athens and Rome* 11: 29-79.

Fischer, P.M. and T. Bürge 2019. The New Swedish Cyprus Expedition 2018: excavations at Hala Sultan Tekke (The Söderberg Expedition). Preliminary results, with contributions by J. Tracz and D. Kofel. *Opuscula. Annual of the Swedish Institutes at Athens and Rome* 12: 287-326.

Foster, K.P. 1979. *Aegean Faience of the Bronze Age.* New Haven: Yale University Press.

Göransson, K. 2012. The Swedish Cyprus Expedition. The Cyprus collections in Stockholm and the Swedish excavations after the SCE. *Cahiers du Centre d'Études Chypriotes* 42: 399-421.

Haskell, H.W., R.E. Jones, P.M. Day and J.T. Killen 2011. *Transport Stirrup Jars of the Bronze Age Aegean and East Mediterranean* (Prehistory Monographs 33). Philadelphia: INSTAP Academic Press.

Hirschfeld, N. 2006. Vases marked for exchange: the not-so-special case of pictorial pottery, in E. Rystedt and B. Wells (eds) *Pictorial Pursuits: Figurative Painting on Mycenaean and Geometric Pottery. Papers from Two Seminars at the Swedish Institute at Athens in 1999 and 2001* (Skrifter utgivna av Svenska institutet i Athen 4o, 53): 83-96. Stockholm: the Swedish Institute at Athens.

Karageorghis, V. 1957. The Mycenaean 'Window-Crater' in the British Museum. *Journal of Hellenic Studies* 77(2): 269-271.

Karageorghis, V. 1963. *Corpus Vasorum Antiquorum. Cyprus. Fasc. 1. Cyprus Museum [Nicosia], Larnaca District Museum (Cyprus Museum). Cyprus Museum Fasc. 1.* Nicosia: Department of Antiquities, Cyprus.

Karageorghis, V. 2009. Cypriote archaeology in the Bloomsbury area. Ancient Cyprus in the British Museum, in T. Kiely (ed.) *Ancient Cyprus in the British Museum. Essays in Honour of Veronica Tatton-Brown* (British Museum Research Publications 180): 1-6. London: the British Museum.

Keswani, P. 1989. Dimensions of social hierarchy in Late Bronze Age Cyprus: an analysis of the mortuary data from Enkomi. *Journal of Mediterranean Archaeology* 2(1): 49-86.

Keswani, P. 2004. *Mortuary Ritual and Society in Bronze Age Cyprus* (Monographs in Mediterranean Archaeology). London: Equinox.

Kiely, T. 2009. The Kourion Notebook in the British Museum. Excavating an old excavation, in T. Kiely (ed.) *Ancient Cyprus in the British Museum. Essays in Honour of Veronica Tatton-Brown* (British Museum Research Publication 180): 63-100. London: the British Museum.

Kiely, T. 2010a. Prestige goods and social complexity at Episkopi-Bamboula, in A. Jasink and L. Bombardieri (eds) *Researches in Cypriote History and Archaeology. Proceedings of the Meeting held in Florence April 29-30th 2009* (Periploi. Collana di Studi egei e ciprioti 2): 53-74. Florence: Firenze University Press.

Kiely, T. 2010b. Charles Newton and the archaeology of Cyprus. *Cahiers du Centre d'Études Chypriotes* 40 : 231-251.

Kiely, T. 2011. Episkopi-Bamboula. The rise and fall of a Late Cypriot urban settlement, in A. Demetriou (ed.) *Πρακτικά του Δ´ Διεθνούς Κυπρολογικού Συνεδρίου, Λευκωσία 29 Απριλίου-3 Μαΐου 2008. Τόμος Α´ 1 Αρχαίο Τμήμα*: 549-560. Nicosia: Society of Cypriot Studies.

Kiely, T. 2019. Poachers turned gamekeepers? The British Museum's archaeological agents in Cyprus in the 1890s, in D. Pilides (ed.) *The Tombs of Egkomi. British Museum Excavations*: 9-52. Nicosia: Department of Antiquities, Cyprus.

Kiely, T. and A. Ulbrich 2012. Britain and the archaeology of Cyprus. I. The long 19th century. *Cahiers du Centre d'Études Chypriotes* 42: 305-356.

Mee, C. and L. Steel 1998. *Corpus of Cypriote Antiquities 17: the Cypriote Collections in the University of Liverpool and the Williamson Art Gallery and Museum* (Studies in Mediterranean Archaeology 20.17). Jonsered: Paul Åström.

Mee, C. 2008. Mycenaean Greece, the Aegean and beyond, in C.W. Shelmerdine (ed.) *The Cambridge Companion to the Aegean Bronze Age*: 362-386. Cambridge: Cambridge University Press.

Murray, A.S., A. Smith and H. Walters 1900. *Excavations in Cyprus (Bequest of Miss E.T. Turner to the British Museum).* London: Trustees of the British Museum.

Myres, J.L. and M. Ohnefalsch-Richter 1899. *A Catalogue of the Cyprus Museum, with a Chronicle of Excavations Undertaken since the British Occupation and Introductory Notes on Cypiote Archaeology.* Oxford: Clarendon Press.

Papadimitriou, N. 2012. Regional or 'international' networks? A comparative examination of Aegean and Cypriot imported pottery in the Eastern Mediterranean. *Talanta. Proceedings of the Dutch Archaeological and Historical Society* 44 (Special issue: Recent Research and Perspectives on the Late Bronze Age Eastern Mediterranean): 92-136.

Papadimitriou, N. 2017. Κυπριακό και αιγαιακό εμπόριο κατά την 2η χιλιετία π.Χ.: μια συγκριτική εξέταση, in N. Papadimitriou and M. Toli (eds) *ΑΡΧΑΙΑ ΚΥΠΡΟΣ.*

Πρόσφατες εξελίξεις στην αρχαιολογία της ανατολικής Μεσογείου: 159-188. Athens: Museum of Cycladic Art.

Papadopoulos, A. 2018. The iconography of LH IIIA-B pictorial kraters and wall-paintings: a view from the Eastern Mediterranean, in A. Vlachopoulos (ed.) *ΧΡΩΣΤΗΡΕΣ / PAINTBRUSHES. Wall-Painting and Vase-Painting of the Second Millennium BC in Dialogue. Proceedings of the International Conference on Aegean Iconography Held at Akrotiri, Thera, 24-26 May 2013*: 523-531. Athens: University of Ioannina and the Hellenic Ministry of Culture and Sports, Archaeological Receipts and Expropriations Fund.

Pilides, D. (ed.) 2019. *The Tombs of Egkomi. British Museum Excavations.* Nicosia: Department of Antiquities, Cyprus.

University of Pennsylvania Museum of Archaeology and Anthropology 2021. Digital Kourion, viewed 10 September 2021, < https://www.penn.museum/sites/kourion/>.

Steel, L. 1998. The social impact of Mycenaean imported pottery in Cyprus. *The Annual of the British School at Athens* 93: 285-296.

Steel, L. 2001. The British Museum and the invention of the Late Cypriot Bronze Age, in V. Tatton-Brown (ed.) *Cyprus in the 19th century AD. Fact, Fancy and Fiction* (Papers of the 22nd British Museum Classical Colloquium, December 1998): 160–167. Oxford: Oxbow Books.

Steel, L. 2004. A reappraisal of the distribution, context and function of Mycenaean pottery in Cyprus, in J.

Balensi, J.-Y. Monchambert and S. Müller Celka (eds) *La Céramique mycénienne de l'Égée au Levant. Hommage à Vronwy Hankey. Table ronde internationale, Maison de l'Orient et de la Méditerranée, 20 mars 1999* (Travaux de la Maison de l'Orient de la Méditerranée 41): 69-85. Lyon: House of the Orient and the Mediterranean-Jean Pouilloux.

Tatton-Brown, V. 2001. Excavations in ancient Cyprus. Original manuscripts and correspondence in the British Museum, in V. Tatton-Brown (ed.) *Cyprus in the 19th century AD. Fact, Fancy and Fiction* (Papers of the 22nd British Museum Classical Colloquium, December 1998): 168-183. Oxford: Oxbow Books.

Tsountas, Ch. and J.I. Manatt 1897. *The Mycenaean Age: A Study of the Monuments and Culture of Pre-Homeric Greece.* Boston and New York: Houghton, Mifflin and Company.

Van Wijngaarden, G.J. 2001. The cultural significance of Mycenaean pictorial kraters. *Pharos. Journal of the Netherlands Institute at Athens* 9: 75-95.

Vermeule, C. and V. Karageorghis 1982. *Mycenaean Pictorial Vase Painting.* Cambridge: Harvard University Press.

Wright G. 2001. Archaeology and Islamic law in Ottoman Cyprus, in V. Tatton-Brown (ed.) *Cyprus in the 19th century AD. Fact, Fancy and Fiction* (Papers of the 22nd British Museum Classical Colloquium, December 1998): 261-266. Oxford: Oxbow Books.

Filling a Gap:
First Steps in the Discovery of Early Helladic III Laconia[1]

Aris Papayiannis

To Yiannis Yiannoukos,
who left us so unexpectedly

In 1993, Jeremy Rutter noted that, based on the lack of diagnostic Early Helladic (EH) III pottery from the southern Peloponnese, 'there appears to have been a substantial lacuna in Laconian and Messenian prehistory equivalent to most of the duration of Lerna IV' (Rutter 1993: 773; see also Dickinson 1992; Zavvou 2012: 3, 6). The intensive Laconia Survey similarly failed to recognise any EH III pottery, prompting Bill Cavanagh and Joost Crouwel to suggest that the region witnessed 'realignment, indeed abandonment, of settlement at the end of the EH II period' (Cavanagh and Crouwel 2002: 130). The late third millennium BC 14C date of 'Middle Helladic' (MH) grave H0705 at Kouphovouno (2286-2040 cal. BC) shows that the site was probably used during the EH III period (Cavanagh and Mee 2011: 46). But, where is the EH III material culture?[1]

A shaft-hole axe of EH III-MH type found in association with EH pottery on the surface of the hill of Ai-Lias near Chrysapha may indicate EH III activity there (Carter and Ydo 1996: 181, 172; Shipley 1996: 436, site U502). Possible late EH III or transitional EH III-MH I pottery from Ayios Stephanos, including one EH III or MH pattern-painted sherd, sheds no further light on the matter; Janko favours a model of southern Peloponnesian depopulation at the end of EH II (Runnels and Van Andel 1987: 314), as a result of socio-political collapse and/or climate change,[2] and the arrival of groups from Asia Minor at the end of EH III (Janko 2008: 565-566).[3] Of course, the change or even collapse, of EH II social structures need not necessarily lead to general dereliction. It has been suggested (Rutter 1993: 773; 2001: 125) that the absence of categorical EH III may be explained by the persistence of EH II culture in the southern Peloponnese until the EH III-MH transition; a view described by Dickinson as a 'counsel of despair' (Boyd 2002: 2; Dickinson 1982: 133).

On the other hand, EH III pottery 'can be very difficult to recognize when heavily worn and highly fragmentary' (Rutter 1993: 772). Prior to 2011, the categorical Laconian EH III ceramic assemblage consisted of three Dark-on-Light Painted sherds[4] and one Light-on-Dark Painted.[5] Dark-on-Light Painted pottery is the 'trademark' of the EH III northeastern Peloponnesian ceramic tradition, while Light-on-Dark is more typical of central Greece, although it has been suggested that the Argive Light-on-Dark is produced in Corinthia, Megara and Aegina (Alram-Stern 2004: 363; Rutter 1982: 460; 1995: 619-623). As the most readily identifiable EH III ceramic category, it is not surprising that the period has been represented in Laconia solely by pattern-painted material. It has been suggested that the absence of a painted pottery tradition may, in fact, be responsible for the absence of EH III phase in the southern Peloponnese (Spencer 2007: 27, n.3).[6] This view may be closer to the truth, given that pattern-painted is the scarcest ceramic category at the only excavated EH III site in the region: Karavas. EH III is a 'low-visibility' period, in both surface and excavation assemblages (Forsén 1992: 27; Rutter 1983: 138-139). This is due to a number of factors (Spencer 2007: 28-29): diagnostic surface treatments are less likely to survive on survey material; diagnostic feature sherds resemble MH types;

---

[1] This paper provides important new evidence on the question of the existence of an EH III gap in Laconia; an issue which the late Professor Mee tackled in his 2011 article, with Bill Cavanagh, 'Minding the gaps'. The rescue excavation was carried out as part of work on the 'Leuktron-Sparta' branch of the 'Corinth-Tripolis Kalamata' highway during the winter periods of 2011 and 2012. I would like to thank the former director of the then 5th Ephorate of Prehistoric and Classical Antiquities, Adamantia Vasilogamvrou, for allowing me to publish the Early Helladic material. I would also like to deeply thank Professor Jerry Rutter and Dr Walter Gauss, for discussing some of this material with me and for sharing their valuable opinion. Thanks also to Dr David Smith for his invitation to contribute to the current volume and for thoroughly checking my draft, and to those alongside whom I worked at Karavas under sometimes difficult conditions: Stelios ('Kritikos') Papadakis, Nikos Tzavaras, Stratis Karteroulis and Yiannis Yiannoukos. Maria Koulogeorgiou and Eirini Koulogeorgiou prepared the excavation drawings, which have been digitally processed by the author. All photographs were taken by the author, unless otherwise stated.
[2] On the 4.2 millennium BP climatic event, see Meller *et al.* (2015). On the influence of modern fears into the interpretations of such crises, see O'Brien (2013).
[3] Very late EH III or early MH activity is also suggested in the Armakas Cave (Efstathiou-Manolakou 2009: 12; Zavvou 2012: 3, 6).
[4] Two from Palaiopyrgi (Banou 1999; 2012: 50) and one from Vouno Panayias (Banou 1999: fig. 7.9, pl. 13c bottom left).
[5] From Ayios Georgios (Banou 1999: 71, fig. 6.7, pl. 13a),
[6] Waterhouse and Hope Simpson (1960: 168) suggested that the lack of EH III pottery from Laconia was 'only a chance result'.

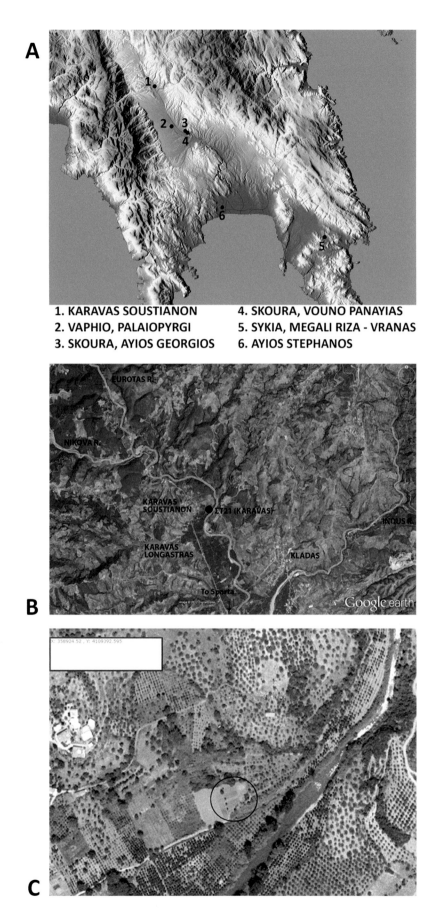

1. KARAVAS SOUSTIANON
2. VAPHIO, PALAIOPYRGI
3. SKOURA, AYIOS GEORGIOS
4. SKOURA, VOUNO PANAYIAS
5. SYKIA, MEGALI RIZA - VRANAS
6. AYIOS STEPHANOS

Figure 14.1. Map of the EH III sites of Laconia (A); satellite image of the Karavas area at an altitude of 10km (B); satellite image of the Karavas area at an altitude of 1km (C) (Sources: A: base map: http://maps-for-free.com; B: Google Earth; C: Ελληνικό Κτηματολόγιο, http://gis.ktimanet.gr/wms/ktbasemap/default.aspx).

there is a general dearth of well-published, stratified EH III contexts; many prototypes of MH pottery types first appear in EH III, with the result that these EH III features may be confused and misinterpreted as MH; the short duration of the period may result in thin archaeological deposits and less deposited pottery; and, finally, the strongly regional character of EH III pottery makes it difficult to recognise the diagnostic features of any local ceramic traditions.

In 2011, Cavanagh and Mee (2011:48) inquired: 'are the EH I and EH III gaps still there and is it possible to fill them?', and concluded that, 'as far as EH I is concerned, there is reason to hope'. By strange coincidence, it was at the same time that the work at Karavas was being undertaken, and the publication of the results of the 2011-2012 excavations at the site now offers opportunity for the further clarification of EH III in Laconia. The site ('ΣΤ21', Figures 14.1 and 14.2a) is located at Mouhteika, approximately 6km north of Sparta and east of the modern settlement of Karavas Soustianon, in an intensively cultivated area flanked by hills at the northern edge of the fertile Karavas Plain. The river Eurotas flows about 70m to the south, passing through a narrow ravine which contains the ruins of the Ottoman period Kopana Bridge and an ancient quarry (Shipley 1996: 339-343, sites E49 and E89). The upper course of the river follows the main natural land route that connects the shores of the Laconian Gulf with the mountainous central Peloponnese. To the northwest of Sparta, the ancient road which Pausanias walked, followed the western bank of the Eurotas (Pausanias, iii. 20. 8-21.3). The excavation lies on the same bank, where the road from Sparta was divided to avoid the gorge, following a northwestern branch, to Pellana-Asea, and an eastern-northeastern branch to Megalopolis (Armstrong et al. 1992; Shipley 1996: 339, 352).

The site faces the sun, open to the south and southwest, and descends gently towards the river. This inclination must have been somewhat greater in antiquity, having been altered more recently by fluvial deposition which is visible for a distance of approximately 25m from the site. The hill which overlooks the site offers protection from the cold, northern winds blowing from the Arcadian Mountains. The southwestern slope of the hill, and the area of the excavation immediately below it, yielded Mycenaean pottery at the surface, along with a few sherds of the first millennium BC: some probably Archaic, some certainly Roman.

The excavation covered an area of approximately 715m2 (0.07ha). Construction of the northern abutment of the new road bridge required the total excavation of the southern part of the site (Figure 14.3a, southeast of line). Recent levelling activities meant that the original ground level could not be accurately determined,

although it is unlikely to have been much higher than its current elevation.[7] The natural, sterile soil is yellowish-green and compact. Archaeological levels were encountered at a minimum depth of 0.75m, at the north of the site.[8] They were covered by a deposit of brown, fine-grained soil containing a small number of worn Classical black-glazed and Roman sherds. The latter derived from a Roman bath located c. 40m to the north.

The site yielded evidence for at least four major use phases: Early Helladic, (LH IIIB2 late –) LH IIIC Early, Archaic-Classical and Modern. The most recent phase is agricultural and has resulted in the disturbance of underlying deposits. The probable Archaic occupation (Figure 14.3a) included a minimum of two subphases. At least one very large open space is represented by a series of four walls, the construction of which disturbed both EH and LH deposits, material from which was subsequently redeposited as levelling fill. The major architectural phase belongs to a settlement of very late LH IIIB2-LH IIIC Early date. Buildings during this phase were arranged across a series of terraces running toward the river, and appear to have been abandoned and left to ruin. Much of this Mycenaean occupation layer lies directly above the natural soil, and may well have destroyed earlier EH contexts. The earliest occupation phase at Karavas belongs to the Early Helladic (Figure 14.3b). Activity during the Final Neolithic and EH I phase is not yet clear, although EH II and EH III are securely represented. There is no evidence of Middle Helladic occupation.

The Early Helladic remains (Figure 14.3)

The southeastern corner of the excavation revealed a thin layer[9] of brown-dark brown soil immediately above the sterile, beneath Mycenaean Rooms I (Locus 168) and III (Locus 169).[10] Both contained EH III pottery (Figure 14.10c and 14.10g). A small assemblage of EH II pottery, and a larger volume of EH III, was recovered alongside a discoid loomweight in a similar layer (Locus 183)[11] beneath Wall 1b (Figures 14.5a and 14.5b). The fill of Pit 11,[12] partly cut into the sterile soil, contained a small number of charcoal fragments, a few medium-sized stones, and the remains of two storage jars and a number of other vessels. It seems likely that Pit 11

---

[7] At depths of 0.5m (north), 0.7m (northwest), 0.93m (southeast), 1m (south) and 1.21m (southwest). All vertical measurements were taken from a single datum point (215.98m above sea level).
[8] Archaeological remains in the centre of the excavated area were located at a depth of 1.05m and, in the south of the site, at a depth of 1.72m.
[9] This measured 0.2m thick at most, at a depth of between 1.93 and 2.13m (Locus 168).
[10] The earth of Locus 168 was rather hard, due to the beaten earth floor of Room I, while that of Locus 169 was somewhat softer.
[11] Locus 183 was identified at a depth of 1.78m to 2m.
[12] Pit 11 measured 0.83m in diameter at the rim, and 0.4m in diameter at its base. Locus 193 was identified at a depth of 1.90m to 2.25m.

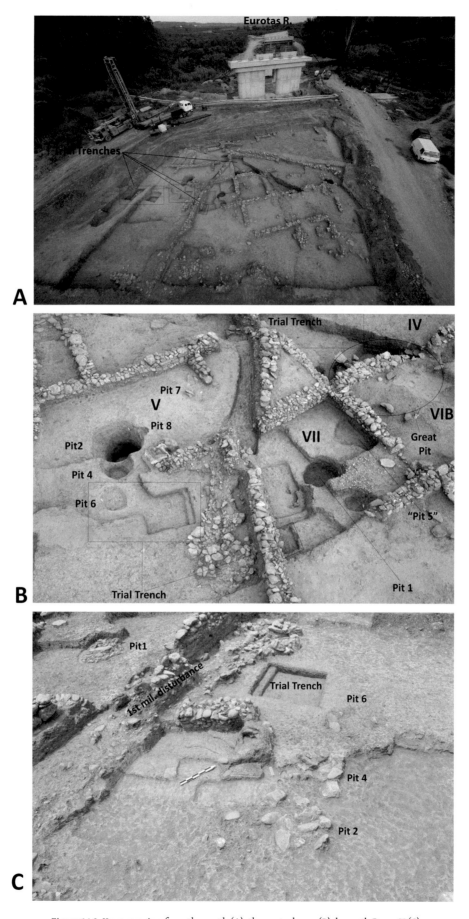

Figure 14.2. Karavas: view from the north (A); the central area (B); beneath Room V (C)
(Photos A and B: V. Georgiadis).

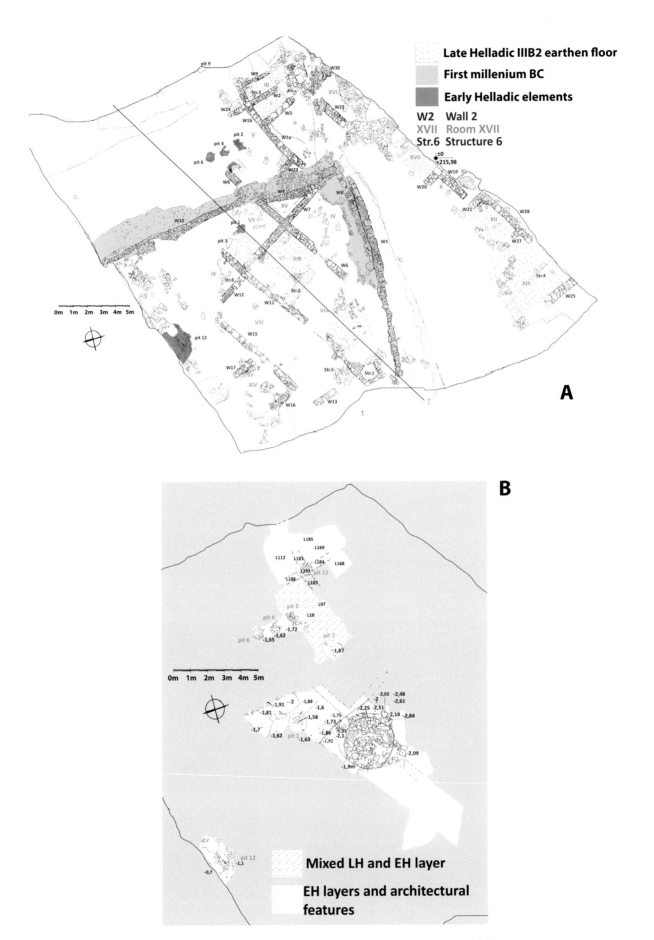

Figure 14.3. Plan of the excavation (A) and plan of the Early Helladic layers (B).

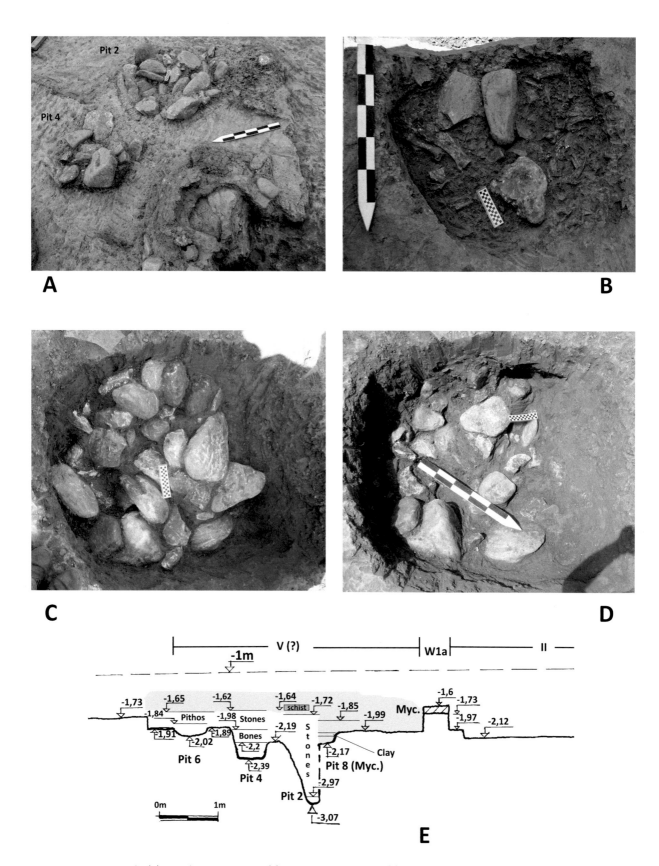

Figure 14.4. Pits 2 and 4 (A); Pit 4 during excavation (B); Pit 2 during excavation (C); Pit 2 during excavation with inverted askos A25 (D); and section of Room V and Pits 6, 4 and 2 underneath it. Mycenaean layer is grey (E).

was constructed to support a storage vessel. A layer of brown soil located east of Wall 24, and continuing to the eastern limit of excavation, yielded small and very small stones, charcoal, EH and LH ceramics, and a further discoid weight. This layer lay immediately above an EH layer (Locus 112; 0.15m deep) of compact blackish-brown soil containing a number of very small charcoal fragments, one obsidian blade and two animal bones.[13] Locus 112 corresponded to Locus 186, which was identified immediately beneath Wall 24.[14]

Neither the floor, nor the eastern limit, of Mycenaean Room V was located (Figure 14.3a-b). If it was closed to the east by Wall 24, then its floor must have been split across two levels.[15] Whatever the case, the deepest layer beneath Room V yielded an assemblage of EH and LH material. A total of three conical pits (Pits 6, 4, and 2) were excavated here, arranged in a north-south oriented row, from the shallowest to the deepest. The fill of Pit 6 (Figures 14.2, 14.3 and 14.4e) consisted of very dark brown to blackish soil, with charcoal and few small stones. The upper part of the fill yielded large body fragments of a pithos or pithoid vessel,[16] while its lower part contained charcoal and some EH pottery.[17] Like Pit 11, Pit 6 may have been built to support a storage vessel.

Pit 4 (Figures 14.2, 14.3a-b, 14.4a-b, e),[18] located 0.3m from Pit 6, was partly covered by medium-sized stones (from a depth of 1.44m to 1.98m), which sealed a layer of brown to dark brown soil containing charcoal, much animal bone, one obsidian tool and some EH III sherds (from a depth of 1.98m to 2.2m). The deepest of the three pits, Pit 2 (Figures 14.2, 14.3a-b and 14.4a, c-e)[19] was packed with large stones and a very thin, clayey soil. At approximately mid-depth in the west of the pit, excavation yielded an inverted EH IIB Late askoid jug (acc. no. A25, at a depth of 2.25m to 2.35m) held in place by a body sherd from a pithos (Figures 14.4d and 14.10a).[20] Only a handful of sherds were retrieved from this layer, the base of which was identified at a depth of 2.97m. From the base of this layer, lying immediately above a 0.1m deep deposit of fine-grained greenish-yellow soil, was an EH III body sherd from a large, Black

Burnished vessel. Pit 4 abuts Pit 2 and may be slightly later than it. In any case, it is clear that the excavators of the later pit were aware of the older one and respected it. A much shallower, cylindrical pit (Pit 7; Figures 14.2b, 14.3a and 14.5c)[21] was excavated 1.5m to the east. It contained brown to dark brown fine-grained soil, small- and medium-sized fluvial stones, many charcoal fragments and sherds from at least four vessels.

At the northern limit of the excavated area, part of a further pit, Pit 12, was investigated (Figures 14.3 and 14.5a). Measuring approximately 2m in diameter and 0.45m in depth,[22] it extended north beyond the limit of excavation. A small modern arboricultural pit had been inserted into its eastern side. Pit 12 was filled with a greyish-dark brown soil containing much charcoal and yielded a substantial quantity of early EH III pottery, including pithoi, Black Burnished bass bowls, an ouzo cup (acc. no. K73, Figure 14.10s) and a one-handled cup or kantharos. Some well-preserved EH II sherds were also collected, as well as a trapezoidal schist pendant (acc. no. Λ25).

The largest volume of Early Helladic material was recovered in the central part of the site (Figure 14.4). Immediately beneath the floor of Room VII (Figure 14.6a-b, d), excavation revealed a rather hard, brown, fine-grained fill containing mixed EH and LH pottery.[23] Beneath that, a layer of softer soil[24] yielded almost exclusively EH pottery, with some positively identified EH II sherds, a number of animal bones — some with traces of burning — and one obsidian cutting tool. An intermittent thin layer of red clay could perhaps be the remains of an EH floor surface, although this is not certain. This red clay layer lay directly above the sterile soil.[25]

The excavation of Level 5,[26] revealed an intriguing rectilinear depression, oriented north-northwest to south-southeast, and destroyed at its eastern limit by the construction of the later Wall 10 and its foundation trench (Figures 14.2b, 14.3b and 14.6e-f). Measuring 3m by 1.2m, the depression possessed vertical walls and consisted of two parts: a wider, trapezoidal area to the north,[27] that continued into an unexplored area, and a narrower, deeper, rectilinear part which has its bottom at, or just below, a depth of 1.91m.[28] These two areas

---

[13] Locus 80 identified at a depth between 1.59m/1.63m and 1.85m; Locus 112 was identified at a depth between 1.85m and 2m.

[14] Locus 112, at a depth between 1.77m and 2m.

[15] A lower western part, at a depth of approximately 1.85m, and an eastern part, at a depth of 1.62m or higher, to cover the EH Pit 4.

[16] Locus 91, at a depth of 1.65m to 1.84m.

[17] Pit 6 measured 0.82m diameter at the rim and 0.7m in diameter at its base. Locus 120 was identified at depths between 1.84m and 2m.

[18] Pit 4 measured 0.84m diameter at the rim and 0.44m diameter at its base. Locus 114 was identified at depths between 1.62m and 2.39m.

[19] Pit 2 measured 1m in diameter at the rim and 0.6m in diameter at its base. Locus 104 was identified at depths between 1.72m and 3.07m.

[20] This EH IIB Late askoid jug has parallels from Pelikata (Heurtley 1938: 19; Souyoudzoglou-Haywood 1999: 98), Voidokoilia (Korres 1981: 153, fig. 113δ), Epidauros (Proskynitopoulou 2011: 146) and Ayios Dhimitrios IIb (which corresponds to Lerna IIID) (Zachos 2008: 73-74, 87, fig. 61).

[21] Pit 7 measured 1.2m in diameter. Locus 121 was identified at depths between 1.85m and 2.12m.

[22] Loci 47 and 224 (depth from 0.7m to 1.1m).

[23] Level 3 / Locus 76 (depth from 1.56m to 1.63m).

[24] Level 4 / Locus 105 (depth from 1.63m to 1.75/-1.68m).

[25] At a depth of 1.63m/1.75m, except in the case of Pit 5, where it lay on soil at a depth of 1.74m.

[26] Locus 113 (at a depth of 1.68/-1.75m to 1.97/2.11m).

[27] Measuring 1m by 0.85m/1.75m, at a depth of 1.7m.

[28] 1.6m by 0.7/0.85m. We reached a depth of 2m attempting to securely identify the natural. A number of white calcareous features were considered natural, rather than anthropogenic.

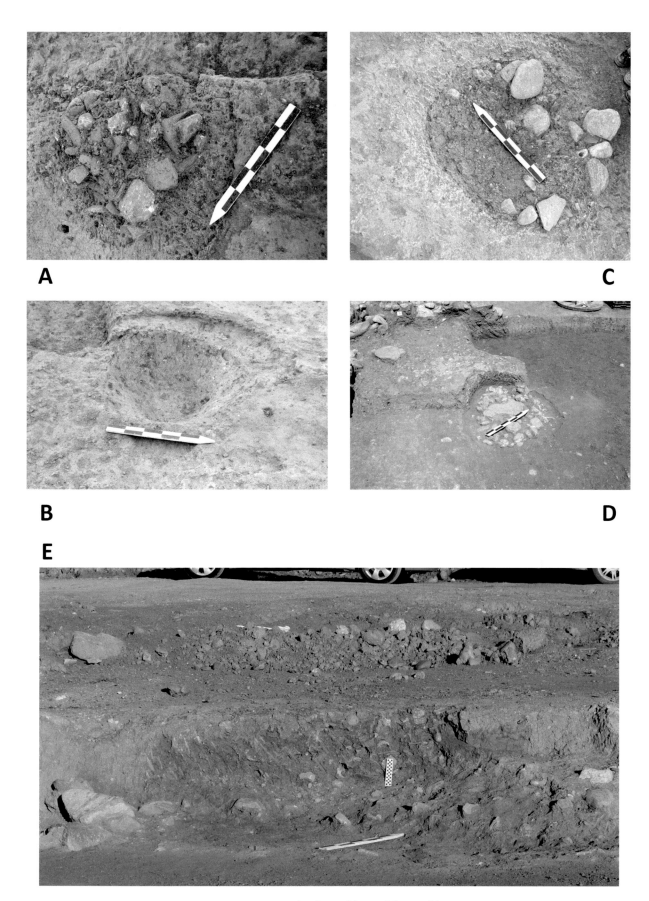

Figure 14.5. Pit 11 (A, B); Pit 7 (C); Pit 1 (D); Pit 12 (E).

communicated via a step.[29] The natural soil where this depression was opened emerges at a depth of 1.62m in the northwest and 1.88m in the southwest. The latter must have been higher. The soil was blackish brown, even from Level 4, and yielded a large quantity of very small charcoal fragments (increasing in frequency with depth), several small stones, fragments of architectural clay and, in obsidian, a cutting tool and probable arrowhead. The pottery assemblage was clearly EH II, and included bowls with incurving rims, a sauceboat, a cup with ring handle, a fragment of a lid or frying pan and an askos handle with incised zig-zags. An EH III Dark-On-Light handle fragment (acc. no. K46a; Figure 14.10r) included in this group should derive from deposits disturbed by the later Wall 10.

Cylindrical Pit 1[30] was identified sunk through EH II layers (Locus 76, Locus 105 and Locus 113) in the centre of the excavated area, below the floor of Room VII (Figures 14.2, 14.3, 14.5d and 14.6a-c). It was filled with a large number of small- and medium-sized stones and pebbles, less tightly packed than those in Pit 2, interspersed with a thin, orange, clayey soil. Some stones evidenced thermal stress, and adjoining clay may also have been heat affected. The western part of the fill yielded part of an EH III tankard (K14, Figure 14.10d) and several fragments of an extremely fragile, low-fired, wide-mouthed vessel in a porous red fabric.[31]

An unusual cut feature (measuring 1.35m by 0.65m) was located parallel to the later Wall 7, the fill of which consisted of black-brown soil, charcoal, architectural clay with wattle impressions, EH pottery and two lithic tools in flint and obsidian (Figures 14.2b and 14.6a-c).[32] It was initially identified as a pit,[33] but was later revealed to be connected to the upper EH III layers beneath Room VIB.

On completion of the first phase of excavation, a southeast-northwest oriented trial trench was opened to clarify the architectural sequence in Rooms IV and VIA (Figures 14.2a-b and 14.8a). Underneath Room IV, three EH III levels[34] were identified, overlaid by a very late LH IIIB2 phase (Level 3). In the southeast of this trench, the natural soil was encountered at a depth of c. 2m.[35] In the northwest, however, there was a much greater depth of archaeological material. This deposit (2.02-2.6m) consisted of a dark brown soil, charcoal, much burnt earth and architectural clay, and an assemblage of EH III pottery consisting, principally, of pithoid vessels, but also including smaller and finer shapes, and a number of EH II sherds, including one handle from an askos similar to A25. The sterile soil appeared at a depth of between 2.61m and 2.84m (Figure 14.9a).

To the north, pure EH levels were identified immediately below the floor of the Mycenaean Room VIB (Figures 14.3b and 14.7). The soil from Level 4[36] was brown and relatively clear, while that of Level 5[37] was darker brown with much charcoal, coarse sand and fragments of architectural clay evidencing various degrees of burning and hardening (from grey-black to yellowish and reddish). It also contained a few bones. Level 6[38] consisted of a dark brown–black soil, much charcoal, and fragments of raw or lightly-burnt clay, along with EH III (and possibly also EH II) pottery. With increased depth, these layers evidenced increasing volumes of charcoal and architectural clay, from underneath the floor of Room VIB up to the emergence of a layer of stones which was termed the 'mantle'.[39]

This 'mantle' (Figures 14.3b, 14.7a and 14.8a-c) consisted principally of tightly-packed small- and medium-sized river stones. A smaller number (n=5) of larger stones were positioned at a slightly lower depth, at the northern edge of the layer.[40] The mantle was slightly ovoid in plan (measuring c. 2.4m-2.6m by 3m) and followed the natural inclination of the slope.[41] Within the mantle a smaller stone circle — rather an ellipse (0.9m by 1.2m) — can be discerned. In this inner circle, a series of three flat stones, approximately 0.3m long, were set vertically in a row (oriented northwest to southeast) at a distance of c. 0.3m, and projected above the mantle by a maximum of 0.4m (Figures 14.8b-c and 14.7a crosshatched). A closer look revealed that the mantle had subsided vertically for at least 0.2m at its northwestern part (Figure 14.8a), leaving the outer row of at least six stones, resting on the natural sterile soil, at its initial depth of 1.9m. Right outside the mantle, to the west (at a depth of 2.09m), east (at a depth of 1.73/2.04m) and south (at a depth of 2.03/2.18m), three concentrations of schist slabs and stones lay at approximately the same elevation and descended towards the mantle, having probably being progressively washed down into the depression of the pit from a higher point (Figures 14.7a, 14.8a-

---

[29] Measuring 0.35m by 0.85m, located at a depth of 1.81m.
[30] Measuring 1m in diameter, Locus 103 (depth from 1.58m to 2.26m).
[31] Π14, at a depth between 1.58m and 1.71m.
[32] Already from Level 3, at a depth between 1.56m and 1.63m.
[33] 'Pit 5', Locus 110, at a depth between 1.63m and 1.86m. Locus 110 extended to southwest beneath Wall 7 at a depth of 1.92m.
[34] Levels 4-6, Loci 88, 98 and 106.
[35] The natural sterile soil emerged at a depth of 2m (close to Wall 7) and some 0.2m-0.3m lower to the west-northwest, where a few scattered stones emerged at a depth of 2.1m.

[36] Loci 189, 197, at a depth between 1.73m/1.78m and 1.96m.
[37] Locus 199, at a depth between 1.96 and 2.13m.
[38] Locus 211, at a depth between 2.13m and 2.4/2.55m. Judging from its filling, 'Pit 5' (Locus 110), a feature dug in the sterile beneath Room VII, but open to southwest, seems to be part of Level 6 / Locus 211 of the EH layers beneath Room VIB, although Locus 211 laid 0.2-0.3m deeper and was covered by Levels 4 and 5.
[39] From a depth of 1.73m/1.78m to 2.4m/2.55m.
[40] At a depth between 2.36m and 2.59m.
[41] It emerges at a depth of 1.9m at the northwest, 2.1m at the north, 2.25m at the southeast, and 2.4m at the south.

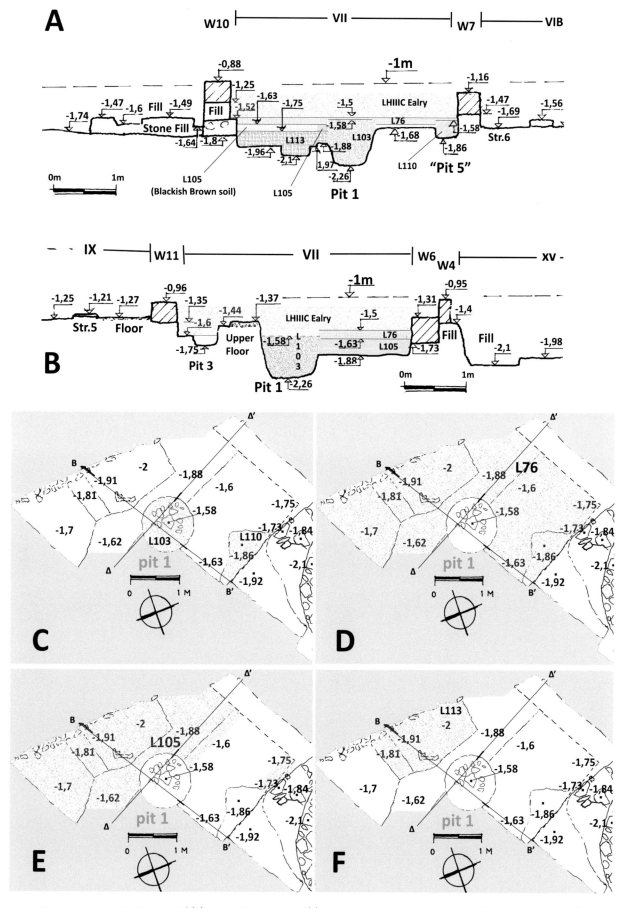

Figure 14.6. Room VII. Section B-B′ (A); Room VII. Section Δ-Δ′(B); successive EH II and EH III layers underneath Room VII (C-F).

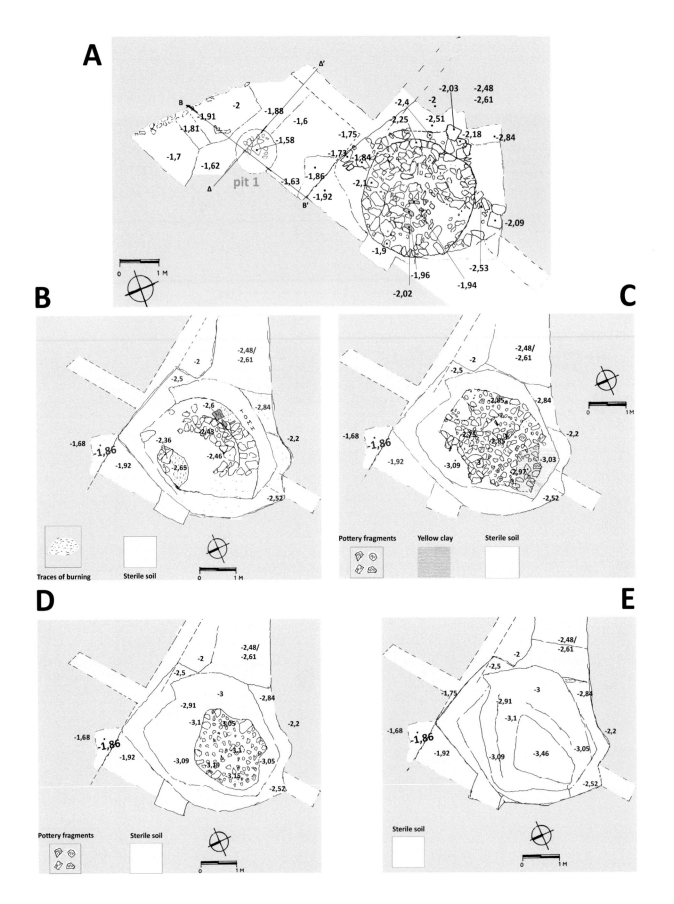

Figure 14.7. Plan of successive EH III layers in the Great Pit underneath Room VIB.

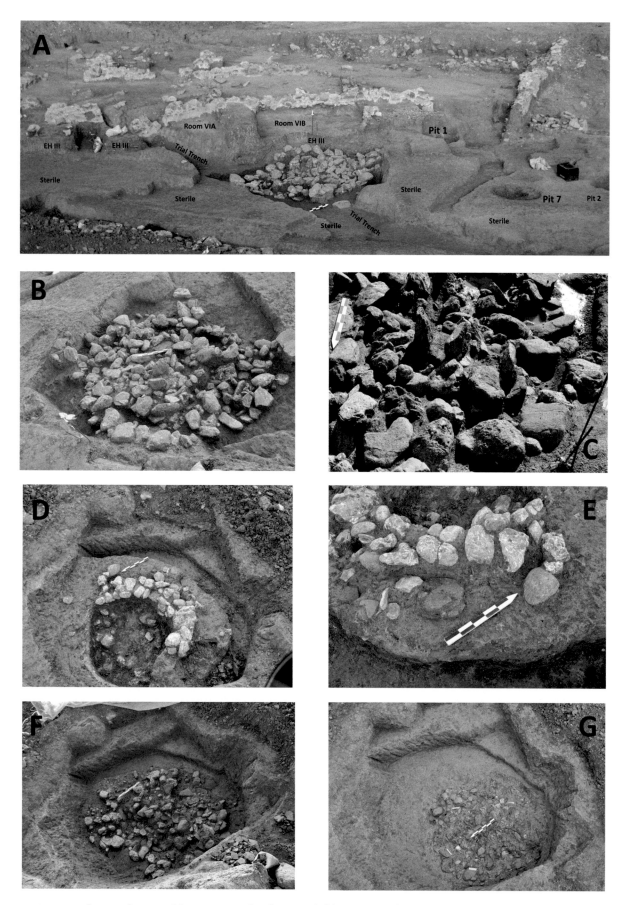

Figure 14.8. The central section of the excavation after the removal of the Mycenaean layers. Great Pit and mantle, viewed from the south – southeast (A); the mantle and the three upright stones (B-C); the 'activity level' with the curvilinear wall and the mudbrick (D-E); successive layers of stones and pottery (F-G).

b and 14.9a).[42] The fill from the mantle was markedly different from the layers above and below,[43] consisting of a brown soil with fragments of architectural clay and some with traces of soot, but no charcoal. The EH II and EH III pottery belonged primarily to storage vessels, with a lower number from drinking vessels.

Immediately below the mantle was a curvilinear wall, preserved only as a single course and formed of two parallel rows of small- to medium-sized stones and one large limestone block (Figures 14.7b and 14.8d-e).[44] To the north of this wall was an ovoid deposit of ash and fired earth, measuring 1.2m by 0.6m.[45] The pottery assemblage is characterised by the numerous fragments of pithoid vessels.

South of the wall,[46] excavation revealed a single rectangular parallelepiped mudbrick, placed horizontally.[47] This brick (Figures 14.7b in dark grey, 14.8d-e), burnt on its upper surface, is smaller than those noted from Lerna III (Wiencke 2000: 274) and corresponds to Banks' second category of mid-sized bricks from Lerna IV:2-3 (Banks 2013: 9). It is not clear whether it was burnt in situ, functioning as a form of hearth, or whether it served as a small platform. A number of small stones were found scattered immediately outside the southwestern part of the wall, fallen from it at the level of the upper surface of the mudbrick, indicating once more that 2.6m was the approximate depth of the surface of an activity area on both sides of the wall. A pair of stones set vertically (Figures 14.7b, dark grey and 14.8e) appear to have served to delimit the area of this mudbrick feature. The soil here (Locus 233) was dark brown with plenty of charcoal and fragments of burnt clay.

Levels 8 and 9[48] included larger volumes of pottery, burnt architectural clay (including one fragment bearing branch impressions), scattered stones and charcoal. Close to the south half of the wall of the pit, the earth was, in places, very fine grey, and included fewer stones and no burnt clay. The pottery from this area (Figure 14.10i-j, l, o-p) was primarily EH III and included pithoi with plastic and impressed decoration, narrow-necked jars with impressed decoration (Lerna IV Form XVII, see Rutter 1995: 404-426) and trianguloid

handles, as well as bowls with horizontal handles or lugs (Lerna IV Form XIII, see Rutter 1995: 376-388) and Black- or Dark Burnished drinking vessels. A smaller number of worn EH II sherds from sauceboats, bowls with incurving rims, and an askos similar to A25, were also identified.

A small number of animal bones were recovered to the south-southwest, where the concentration of charcoal, burnt earth and burnt architectural clays increased sharply. Immediately beneath this deposit was a discrete area of ash and charcoal (0.1m by 0.3m), and a large spread of yellow clay[49] containing flecks of charcoal, very small pebbles, and a number of high-quality EH III sherds (Figure 14.7c). This layer covered part of a substantial ovoid deposit[50] (Figures 14.7c and 14.8f) of small and medium river cobbles and fine brown soil with some charcoal, measuring c. 0.25m deep at the south and c. 0.5m deep at the north. Excavation here yielded fragments of architectural clay, bone, and pottery, including a fragment from an EH III narrow-necked jar with impressed decoration (Lerna IV Form XVII, see Rutter 1995: 404-426). Of particular note is the recovery of a small sphere of raw clay and a sherd with a black, probably organic, residue on its interior.

After the removal of this discard of stones and pottery, the natural, sterile soil emerged levelled under most of its eastern periphery at a depth of 3m-3.1m, seemingly the bottom/floor of this large pit (Figures 14.7d and 14.8g). The rest of the area was covered by brown, fine grained soil[51] with abundant fragments of charcoal, few bones, and many fragments of burnt architectural clay and burnt earth.[52] The concentration of burnt clay and earth in the west of Levels 8, 9 and 11 is interesting. Particularly, the western area contained much more burnt clay and burnt earth in Levels 8-9 (at a depth of 2.62m to 2.9m) and now in Level 11 (at a depth of 3.23m to 3.35m) than the rest of the layers. The pottery from Level 11/Locus 236 included many fragments from large, pithoid vessels, as well as a narrow-necked jar with impressed and incised decoration (acc. no. 63a; Figure 14.10h), an askos, and a pattern-painted tankard (acc. no. K68; Figure 14.10q).

The underlying Level 12[53] was composed of a second deposit of small (–medium) sized stones and pottery measuring 1.96m by 1.9m (Figures 14.7d and 14.8g). In addition to the more common pithos fragments, the pottery assemblage included a higher percentage

---

[42] I would like to thank geoarchaeologist Dr Nancy Krahtopoulou for this observation.

[43] Locus 227 (depth 1.9m/2.4m to 2.58m) and the upper part of Locus 232 (depth from 1.9m/2.4m to 2.62m/2.7m). The depth of the mantle was from 1.9m/2.1m/2.4m to 2.59m/2.7m.

[44] At a depth between 2.46m/2.52m and 2.72m. This block had a minimum width of 0.39m and a maximum width of 0.47m.

[45] At a depth between 2.55m/2.65m and 2.72m.

[46] Level 8 / Locus 233, at a depth between 2.6m and 2.66m.

[47] Π33. This brick measured 0.3m by 0.29m by 0.09m, and was located a depth of 2.6m to 2.69m.

[48] Locus 229 (at a depth of 2.9m to 3.02/3.09m), Locus 230 (at a depth of 2.6m to 2.86m/3.03m) and Locus 234 (at a depth of 2.9m/3.03m to 3m/3.05m).

[49] Locus 234, measuring 1.3m by 0.95m.

[50] Level 10, Locus 235. This deposit measured 2.9m by 2.5m, and was identified at a depth between 2.75m/3m and 3m/3.23m.

[51] Level 11, Locus 236, identified at a depth between 3m/3.23m and 3.05m/3.35m.

[52] The latter two were especially numerous in the western - southwestern part.

[53] Locus 237, identified at a depth between 3.05m/3.35m and 3.36m/3.43m.

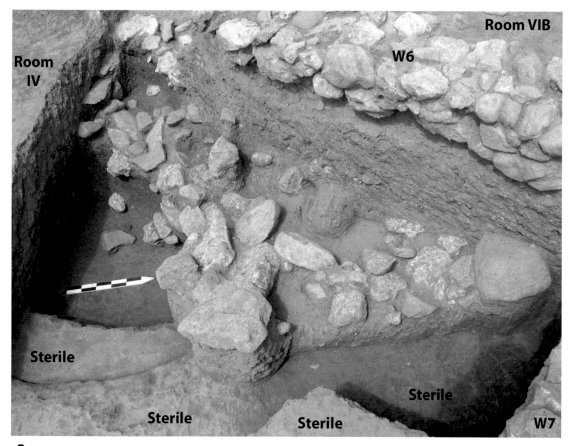

A

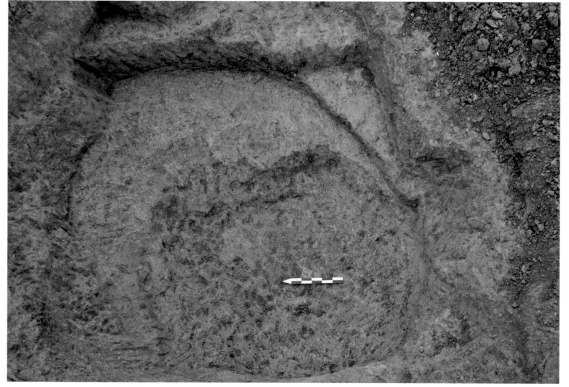

B

Figure 14.9. Remains below Room IV. The southern part of the Great Pit with the stones of the mantle and the southern concentration of stones descending towards the former (A); the Great Pit after the completion of the excavation (B).

of smaller shapes, narrow-necked jars bearing either Fine Impressed or plastic and incised decoration and fragments of Black Burnished bass-bowls (Figure 14.10b, f, k, m). The soil was brown with some charcoal and many fragments of burnt constructional clay, especially in the centre of the layer. The final Level 13[54] was markedly different, consisting of light brown, sandy soil, noticeably clearer than every other level, with barely any charcoal or small stones and significantly less pottery. Levels 12 and 13 formed the basal fill of a large, roughly circular, depression dug in the west of the pit (Figures 14.7e and 14.9b).[55] The upper 0.1m of this pit-like construction was filled with the earth of Level 11/Locus 236.

Although study of the ceramic assemblage from Karavas is ongoing, it is possible to identify four major EH III phases in the deep stratigraphy (1.73m) below Room VIb. The earliest major phase, Phase 1 (Figures 14.7c-e, 14.8f-g and 14.9b) is represented by those deposits identified below the curvilinear wall: Levels 9(lower)-13 (depths from c. 2.66m to 3.46m) and is wholly subterranean. It is composed of a number of stone deposits, and successive layers of fine-grained earth containing charcoal, burnt architectural clay and pottery. It is possible — though still uncertain — that in these layers we might recognise chronologically distinct episodes of discard and filling within the pit.

Phase 2 (Levels 8-9(upper); Figures 14.7b and 14.8d-e) is represented by the probable activity or occupation surface[56] that belonged to Level 8. A curvilinear wall divides this into two contexts ('north' and 'south'), each of which bears traces of burning and perhaps some form of hearth or utilitarian surface. Level 8 was c. 0.4-0.85m beneath the level of the sterile soil, and yielded no in situ portable artifacts. However, the dark brown soil which overlay this activity area included some charcoal, several fragments of architectural clay and a large number of pithoid sherds.

Phase 3 (Level 7, depth from 1.9m/2.4m to 2.6m; Figures 14.7a and 14.8b-c) is represented by the stone mantle. This layer must initially have reached approximately the same level as the sterile soil in the northern part, but it had subsided vertically, for at least 0.2m, due to settlement of the underlying soil. The rest of the stone layer was, from the beginning, below ground level. Three parallel, upright, flat stones, projecting above the stone layer by a maximum of 0.4m, must have acted as markers. The use of upright slabs in this manner finds a direct parallel from Lerna IV:3.[57]

Phase 4 is represented by the 0.65-0.8m thick soil layer overlying the mantle (Levels 4-6, depth from 1.73m/1.78m to 2.4m/2.55m). Comprised of a progressively darker brown-black soil, burnt architectural clay and charcoal, it must represent a destruction deposit reflecting the gradual erosion of anthropogenic deposits surrounding the depression, as evidenced by the aforementioned similarity of the soil from immediately above the mantle and from the so-called 'Pit 5', and by the three concentrations of stones descending from the mouth of the depression towards the mantle.

The successive layers comprising the fill of this large pit contain quantities of building material, sherds from storage and drinking vessels, ash, charcoal and a few animal bones — the latter perhaps evidence of in-situ food preparation. Two lithic implements found in 'Pit 5' represent the only stone tools recovered.

The Great Pit Complex, including 'Pit 5', was roughly synchronous with Pit 1. Both Pits 1 and 5 were dug into EH II remains (including the rectilinear depression) below Room VII. Other certain EH III features include Pits 2 and 4 and the EH III levels beneath, and northeast of, Rooms I and III and Pit 12. An EH III layer was also traced to the southwest of the Great Pit, beneath Room VIA. This was rather thick (0.5-0.7m)[58] compared to those thin, fragmentary EH layers recognised elsewhere on the site, and consisted of brown to dark brown earth with much charcoal, little gravel and some EH III pottery (Figure 14.10n).

The Early Helladic architecture at Karavas

Clear evidence of Early Helladic architecture is practically absent from Karavas, likely as a direct result of Mycenaean levelling activity. The presence of pits while suggestive, is not absolute proof of permanent occupation, although Pit 11 appears to have held a storage vessel and was, presumably, located within an interior room or roofed area. The same may be true for Pit 6.

The EH III sequence revealed beneath Room VIB is complex, and includes both stone built and cut-and-filled features (Figure 14.7).[59] At least one trapezoidal space[60] has been identified, although it is not clear whether its inner sides belong to a single construction phase. Within the limits of this space was an ovoid cut

---

[54] Locus 238, identified at a depth between 3.36m/3.43m and 3.46m.
[55] This depression possessed a diameter of 2.5m by 2.3m at the rim, and 1.5m by 1.95m at the base. It had a depth of c. 0.35-0.4m (identified between 3.05m/3.1m and 3.46m).
[56] At a depth of c. 2.6m to 2.65m.
[57] See Bothros B-166 (Banks 2013: 281-282). This bothros measured

1.25m by 1.5m, and a depth of 1.1m. Unfortunately, it was not drawn or photographed.
[58] At a depth between 1.75m to 2.24m/2.42m.
[59] The natural soil — truncated by the Mycenaean occupation — emerged at depths of 1.68m, 1.75m, and 2m at the eastern side, 1.9m at the northern side, 2m and 2.48m at the southern side, and 2.2m at the western side.
[60] Measuring c. 2.9m (east), 2.8m (southeast), 2.8m (southwest), 5.4m (north).

feature measuring 3.5m (northwest to southeast) by 3.35m (northeast to southwest), with vertical walls with preserved heights of 0.5m (east), 0.45m (north), 1.2m (northwest) and 0.15m (south). It was certainly bigger than the slightly ovoid stone mantle, which covered the area that corresponds to the level the curved wall.

It is possible that these features represent the remains of a pit-chamber or, more plausibly, the subterranean or semi-subterranean room of a house made, in all likelihood, of wattle-and-daub (Batzelas 2008; Yiannouli 2006).[61] Such subterranean or semi-subterranean structures are known from Neolithic and Early Helladic southern Greece,[62] although the type is more common in Neolithic and Early Bronze Age Thessaly, northern Greece and the Balkans. Thus, we must look to the north, and to earlier periods, to better understand their architecture and identify parallels.

If the identification is correct, then the large, ovoid pit must have formed a subterranean room (its floor at a depth of 1.35m below the sterile soil) within a hut, or a series of huts, of rectilinear plan.[63] It is possible, of course, that these rectilinear and curvilinear features represent chronologically distinct constructions. At the Early Neolithic site of Revenia in Pieria, the large Pit 11 (measuring 3.25m by 2.95m by 1.05m) offers a similar profile: rectilinear on top and round towards the base, and has been identified as part of a rectilinear house (Batzelas 2008: 70; Besios and Adaktylou 2006: 361). The absence of postholes at EH Karavas is not surprising, given their general absence from other suspected or definite pit- or semi-subterranean houses. At Stavroupolis Ia (Middle Neolithic III), this absence was interpreted by the excavators as a result of the common roofing of groups of pits, and a similar technique may account for their absence at our site (Batzelas 2008: 81; Grammenos and Kotsos 2002: 323; 2004: 17-18).

Those remains exposed beneath Room VII (Figures 14.2b, 14.3b and 14.6) are more easily interpreted. Despite the destruction of its eastern section, and the fact that it was not fully explored to the north, the rectilinear area[64] dug 0.3m into the natural soil and

accessed through a narrowing stepped passage,[65] seems certain to represent a semi-subterranean rectangular structure (with preserved dimensions of 2.95m by 1.75m-0.7m) of EH II date. Theocharis (1952: 96-98) uncovered a similar horseshoe-shaped 'hut' at Palaia Kokkinia, Piraeus, dated to EH I, which measured 1.48m by 2.3m by 0.45m and was accessed by a ramp measuring 1.25m wide.[66] It is interesting that the entrance of the structures at Karavas and Palaia Kokkinia share a similar (unconventional) northern orientation.[67] This makes their identification as dwellings difficult. Ethnographically (Papayiannis 2013: 70, 166, pl. 1), wattle-and-daub dwellings (for humans and animals) in Greece have possessed entrances oriented towards the sun (east, south, or southwest). The only exception seems to be in the courtyards and dwellings of some transhumant pastoralists, which face north to provide respite from the summer heat. Storage structures offer no clear preference in orientation; indeed, a northerly orientation would better preserve their contents. The transhumant Sarakatsani are known to prefer semi-subterranean, cool and relatively humid huts for the storage of cheese (Papayiannis 2013: 162). It is possible, therefore, that the EH II semi-subterranean or sunken-floor building beneath Room VII served a storage function.

Pappa (2008: 323-329) identifies the (Neolithic) pit-house as a roofed pit used by one or more individuals for sleeping, refuge and protection. She sets a minimum area of 2m² of roofed space per person, and suggests that activities like cooking, work and social interaction could have taken place within the pit or outside it. Naturally, the EH III large ovoid pit falls into this very broad definition, although its identification as a domestic pit house is uncertain.

Elia's criteria are much more analytic (Batzelas 2008: 6; Elia 1982: 141). A domestic pit-house should include *sufficient space* for housing a family; relatively vertical walls and a flat bottom; evidence for the existence of a superstructure and/or roof; built features at the interior (e.g., a hearth, storage facilities); benches or similar for work or sleep; artifacts connected to household activities (such as vessels, tools and symbolic artifacts).

The first and second criteria, albeit general, are met by both possible pit-houses. The third is also met, excluding the presence of postholes. The fourth criterion is met

---

[61] I would like to thank E. Yiannouli, N. Krahtopoulou and Kleonicki Tserga for separately discussing with me the possibility that the Great Pit was a pit-house.

[62] Briefly reviewed by Batzelas (2008: 26-29). For recent discoveries in Attica, see Smith (2017: 122) and Tsonos (2017).

[63] Pit 7 at Revenia (Pieria) was also considered to be the subterranean room of a house, because of its vertical walls (Urem-Kotsou *et al.* 2015: 164).

[64] Pit-houses or semi-subterranean houses with rectilinear plans are known from Late Mesolithic-Early Neolithic Ostrovul Corbului in southeast Romania (Bailey 2000: 62-64; Whittle 1996: 27); Early Neolithic Revenia at Korinos, Pieria (Besios and Adaktylou 2006: 360); Late Neolithic I Tataria (Pit 7) at Mavrachades, Karditsa (Krahtopoulou *et al.* 2020); and Late Neolithic Zagliveri, Thessaloniki (Batzelas 2008: 103; Grammenos and Kotsos 2003).

[65] Pit-houses or semi-subterranean houses with stepped access are known from Late Neolithic Ia Pit 44 at Thermi 2, Thessaloniki (Batzelas 2008: 91-92; Pappa 2008: 74-87); Late Neolithic II Makriyialos IIa at Pieria (Pappa 2008: 292-298, 233-287); and Early Bronze Age Melissochori at Larissa (Batzelas 2008: 61; Toufexis 2003: 507-508).

[66] Pit-houses or semi-subterranean houses with ramps are known from the Sultanian culture of Israel and Jordan during the Pre-Pottery Neolithic A (PPNA) (Cauvin 2004: 33).

[67] The same may be true for the two steps in the northwestern side of Pit 44 at Thermi 2 (Pappa 2008: 74-87).

by the EH III case, through the presence of the wall and possible hearths. If we consider the horizontally placed brick as a form of a small mantel or platform, and not a hearth, we may cover the fifth criterion as well. The last criterion may be met by the presence of large quantities of pottery.

In practice, though, it is open to question whether many of those criteria can be met, because of the very nature of these underground constructions: it is difficult to be certain if their fill represents a destruction or abandonment layer, or simply garbage. Two things are, nevertheless, certain: there are currently no examples of complete vessels from any context and at least one activity area can confidently be recognised within the stratigraphy of the EH III Great Pit.

Finally, it is worth noting that the 'mason's foot' of 0.3m recognised by Walter and Felten (1981: 20-21) in the architecture of the EH II corridor building known as the 'Weisses Haus' ('White House') at Kolonna, appears to have been in use at Karavas, and can be recognised in the size of the mantle (8-9 by 10 mason's feet), the size of its 'inner circle' (3 by 4 mason's feet), the length of the three upright stones, the space between them (1 mason's foot) and the dimensions of the brick (1 by 1 by 1/3 mason's feet). The foot continues in use as the basic measuring instrument among the Sarakatsani, and other traditional groups (Chatzimichali 1957: 196-198, 278-279; Papayiannis 2013: 52-54).

Initial remarks on the EH III pottery from Karavas

The study of the Early Helladic pottery from Karavas is still underway, although it is possible to offer some preliminary observations on the character of the EH III material. The pottery is exclusively handmade, and can be divided into the following shape categories:

A. Open, drinking shapes: including bass bowls (Lerna IV Form XII, see Rutter 1995: 355-376; Figure 14.10b-c), neck-handled tankards (Lerna IV Form II, see Rutter 1995: 279-281) and shoulder-handled tankards (Lerna IV Form III, see Rutter 1995: 281-301; Figure 14.10d). There is also one ouzo cup (Lerna IV Form VIII: see Rutter 1995: 334-341; Figure 14.10s) and a low pedestal foot, perhaps from a Black Burnished two-handled cup (Lerna IV Form X, see Rutter 1995: 345-348; Figure 14.10f).

B. Other open forms: including cooking vessels (wide-mouthed jar) (Lerna IV Form XXI; Figure 14.10p) and bowls with horizontal handles or lugs (Lerna IV Form XIII, see Rutter 1995: 376-388).

C. Closed forms: including narrow-necked jars (Lerna IV Form XVII, see Rutter 1995: 404-426; Figure 14.10h-k, m-n) and pithoi or pithoid vessels.

D. One unpainted lid (Lerna IV Form XXII, type 1, see Rutter 1995: 454-457; Figure 14.10g) has also been recognised.

Drinking vessels are predominantly Dark Burnished (black to mottled brown-black) and unpainted, with the best examples being dark black and highly lustrous (Figure 14.10b, f). There is no evidence of Fine Gray Burnished ceramics.

Lugs are rare. Excluding the seven examples of H-shaped lugs from narrow-necked jars (below), only four examples were recovered: two single knob lugs, including one 'horn-shaped' lug on the shoulder of a wide-mouthed jar (Figure 14.10p) and a lower one; one double knob lug; and one small crescentic ledge lug (Figure 14.10e).

Plastic and impressed or incised decoration is represented by single plastic finger-impressed bands on pithoi of Rutter's first variant (Rutter 1995: 636; Figure 14.10l) and plastic bands with multiple, carefully executed and closely spaced, diagonal slashes (Figure 14.10m-o). Most examples belong to large, closed vessels (possibly narrow-necked jars). They are always found in groups of parallel bands and belong to Rutter's third variant, with the exception of one pithos fragment of the second variant (Rutter 1995: 636-637; Figure 14.10o).

Pattern Painted decoration is very rare, and is represented only by a Dark-on-Light painted strap handle — perhaps from a one-handled cup (Lerna IV Form IV, type 1?) or tankard (Lerna IV Form I or III; acc. no. K46a, Figure 14.10r) — and a rim-shoulder fragment from a large shoulder-handled tankard (Lerna IV Form III, type 2?) (acc. no. K68, Figure 14.10q). The ouzo cup (acc. no. K73, Figure 14.10s) may have been painted, although its surface is worn.[68] Pattern Painted sherds are so few, that it seems reasonable to conclude that they arrived at Karavas as imports.

Fine Impressed decoration (Figure 14.10h-k) is more common, and is represented by multiple rows of very carefully executed impressions which, in one case, were coupled with incisions marking the borders of the impressed area. It is found exclusively on narrow-necked jars and is also associated with H-shaped lugs, which points to a shape similar to Lerna IV Form XVII, type 3 (see Rutter 1995: 416-418). The half-disks at both ends of these lugs are always a little oblique. The decoration is restricted to the upper body of the vessel, where it appears as diagonal bands (Figure 14.10h) on the shoulder, or as simple rings below the shoulder-neck transition. One sherd has traces

---

[68] Low numbers of ouzo cups appear in pottery classes other than Dark-on-Light Painted (see Rutter 1995: 336).

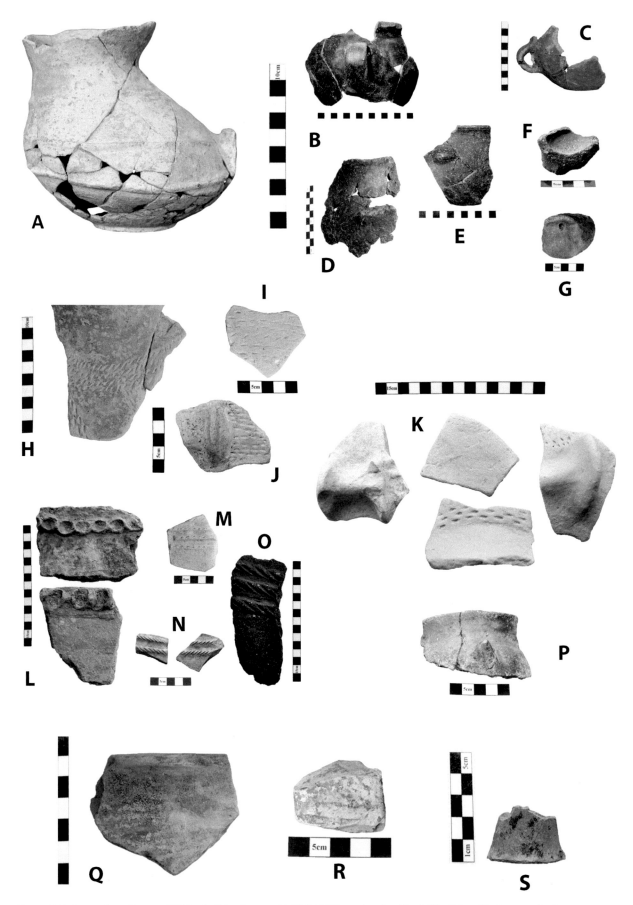

Figure 14.10. Pottery from Karavas: EH IIB askoid jug (acc. no. A25) (A); EH III unpainted and Dark (Black) Burnished pottery (B-G); EH III narrow-necked jars with H-shaped lugs and Fine Impressed decoration (H-K); EH III pottery with plastic and impressed or incised decoration (L-O); EH III wide-mouthed jar with knob lug (P); EH III Pattern Painted sherds (Q-R); and EH III Early ouzo-cup (S).

of a thin red slip (Figure 14.10i). This combination of narrow-necked jars with H-shaped lugs and Fine Impressed decoration constitutes a distinctive feature of the EH III pottery of Karavas. It is interesting to note that all examples of narrow-necked jars with Fine Impressed decoration (and most of those with plastic incised bands) were recovered from the Great Pit. The Lerna IV:3 narrow-necked jars P991 and P1376, which together represent the only Fine Incised examples of the shape at Lerna (see Rutter 1982: 474-476), may, in the light of the evidence from Karavas, be identified as Laconian imports (see Figure 14.10h, k lower; Rutter 1982: 468, nos. 29-30; 1995: 200-201, 262, 629).[69] A similar fragment is known from the Asea Valley (Forsén 2003: 173, no. 104). Fine Impressed decoration from EH III Karavas is markedly distinct from the Fine Incised and Impressed pottery characteristic of the northwest Peloponnese and also found in northeast Peloponnese, Aegina and southern Thessaly (Alram-Stern 2004: 368-369; Maran 1998: 277-282; Rutter 1982; 1995: 627-632).

The preliminary study of the pottery has also resulted in the recognition of the local EH III drinking (-offering) set, which employed narrow-necked jars for offering, and bass bowls and tankards for drinking. The ouzo cup, the kantharos, and the probable two-handled cup are not well-represented. The repertoire of drinking shapes visible at EH III Karavas thus develops from the Lefkandi I/Kastri group, rather than from Laconian EH II.[70] Distinctly local, however, is the appearance of these shapes with unpainted well-burnished surfaces, perhaps intended as lustrous black, as Rutter (1995: 19-20) notes for the Solidly Painted and Burnished class of Lerna IV. It is possible that this group was utilized for ceremonial drinking at Karavas. Communal drinking behaviours at Lerna IV:1-2 appear to have employed narrow-necked jars with plastic and impressed decoration and ouzo cups, while at Lerna IV:3 they included narrow-necked jars with variant pattern-decoration, a giant kantharos, and small kantharoi. These kantharoi replaced the earlier use of the ouzo cup and appear to mark a shift in practice (and serving size). The scarcity of small capacity ouzo cups or similar at Karavas is striking and may indicate the observation of practices distinct from those at Lerna.[71] With caution, the study of the EH III pottery of Karavas represents a first step towards understanding the peculiarities and preferences of local ceramic production.

A brief discussion of site size and topography

The excavation at Karavas yielded EH III material over an area of roughly 400m2 (0.04ha). Further pottery was recovered from a small trial trench, opened hastily by a bulldozer, some 20m to the east, which, if it also proves to be of EH III date, could suggest a minimum size estimate for the site of 760 m2 (0.08ha). This estimate is well below that of even the smallest EH III-MH II sites mentioned by Spencer, and closer to the smallest EH II settlements (<0.2ha) which, in the case of the southern Argolid, are considered rural farmsteads and hamlets, and are generally abandoned at the end of the period (Jameson et al. 1994: 542-547; Spencer 2007: 35-51). Systematic survey of the hill may increase this estimate, or it may be the case that settlement was dispersed in small clusters, as seems to have been the case in the Pylian hinterland during EH III (Stocker 2003: 402).

All of those Laconian sites with evidence of EH III activity also provide evidence of occupation during EH II. Both Karavas and Vranas (Zoumboulakis plot) are abandoned prior to the beginning of the MH period, while occupation at Skoura and Palaiopyrgi, in contrast, continues for some part of it. Following its abandonment during EH II, Ayios Stephanos is reoccupied during the EH III-MH I transition, and survives throughout the MH period (Banou 2000: 177-183, 189-194; 2012: 41; Janko 2008; Vasilogamvrou and Maltezou 2016). We can see that 60% (3 of 5) of the EH III sites survive into the MH period, while just 30% (3 of 10) of EH II sites identified by the Laconia Survey are reoccupied during the MH (Cavanagh and Crouwel 2002: 136-137).

The occupation of Karavas continues from EH II to EH III, probably because it meets the conditions given by Spencer (2007: 51): 'access to a rich and extensive catchment of arable land and, possibly even more importantly, reliable water resources.' The numerous pithos fragments recovered from the Great Pit of Karavas point to the storage of surplus. Furthermore, the narrow passage from where the Eurotas flows could easily be closed with a fishing net, and it is possible that the two perforated schist discs are, in fact, net weights. On the other hand, it is equally easy to control the movement of humans.

All definite EH III sites in Laconia share some topographical features: they enjoy ready access to potable water;[72] they have a catchment with multiple resources, including fertile plain for cereal cultivation, hilly hinterland for the cultivation of other crops such as vines and olive trees, as well as for animal husbandry, hunting, and the provision of firewood and timber,

---

[69] P991 was formerly identified as a probable Cycladic import. I am grateful to Jerry Rutter for the observation.

[70] On EH II feasting equipment, see Pullen (2011); on EH III drinking equipment and behavior, see Rutter (2008).

[71] The possibility that the large vessels could have contained beer is intriguing, though speculative (Rutter 2008).

[72] This would have been the Eurotas River in the case of Karavas, and a spring for Ayios Stephanos and the two sites at Skoura (Banou 1999: 65).

and a riverine and a riparian environment that offers fishing and hunting opportunities; some sites (such as Karavas, Skoura and Vranas) seem to be strategically positioned on the fringe between the plain and the hilly hinterland, in order to have immediate access to both; they are directly related to a prominent hill; and, finally, EH III site distribution (Figure 14.1a) appears to show a preference for locations close to the Eurotas[73] and the most important overland route between the southeastern Peloponnesian coast and the central uplands.[74] Karavas sits on top of this route, controlling the crossroad leading from the Eurotas Valley to the Megalopolis plateau (northwest) and the Tripolis plateau (northeast). Palaiopyrgi overlooks large part of the middle Eurotas Plain, and is in visual contact with Skoura (Banou 2012: 43, fig. 3; Janko 2008: 555). Vranas is situated on the natural passage that connects the Molaoi Plain to the west with Epidauros Limera and the Myrtoon Sea. Ayios Stephanos lies at the head of Laconian Gulf, on the coastal sea route connecting the Maleas and Mani peninsulas. Two important land routes end here: the Eurotas route, which is accessible over the mid-course of the river through the hilly terrain via Krokeai; and, to the east, following the foothills of Mount Parnon, via the area of Vranas, to Epidauros Limera (Janko 2008: 554). Strategic placement on major land routeways, such as the 'cross-Phocis' route, the 'cross-Boeotian' route, and the route that links the eastern Corinthian Gulf to the Myrtoon Sea, seems to be a very important factor in the choice of site location during EH III and the early Middle Helladic elsewhere on the mainland (Spencer 2007: 53). To these could now be added the route linking the Laconian Gulf with the Peloponnesian hinterland, providing further hints to the importance of routes of movement and communication in an era with very strong provisional character (Alram-Stern 2004: 363; Maran 1998: 282-283; Spencer 2007: 30-31).

Bibliography

Alram-Stern, E. (ed.) 2004. *Die ägäische Frühzeit. 2. Serie. Forschungsbericht 1975 - 2002, 2. Band. Teil 2: Die Frühbronzezeit in Griechenland, mit Ausnahme von Kreta* (Veröffentlichungen der Mykenischen Kommission 21). Vienna: the Austrian Academy of Sciences.

Armstrong, P., W.G. Cavanagh and G. Shipley 1992. Crossing the river: observations on routes and bridges in Laconia from the Archaic to Byzantine periods. *The Annual of the British School at Athens* 87: 293-310.

Bailey, D.W. 2000. *Balkan Prehistory. Exclusion, Incorporation and Identity*. London: Routledge.

Banks, E.C. 2013. *Lerna VI. The Settlement and Architecture of Lerna IV.* Princeton: the American School of Classical Studies at Athens.

Banou, E. 1999. New evidence on Early Helladic Laconia. *The Annual of the British School at Athens* 94: 63-79.

Banou, E. 2000. Middle Helladic Laconia: new evidence. *Studi Micenei ed Egeo-Anatolici* 42(2): 175-199.

Banou, E. 2012. The Eurotas valley and the Helos plain in the Early Helladic period. Addressing some key issues on the basis of topography and pottery, in C. Mee and M. Prent (eds) *Early Helladic Laconia. Proceedings of the Round Table Conference held 16 January 2010 at the Netherlands Institute at Athens. Pharos. Journal of the Netherlands Institute at Athens* 18(1): 39-52.

Batzelas, C. 2008. Σπίτια Βυθισμένα στη Γη: Νεολιθικές Υπόσκαφες Οικίες στη Θεσσαλία. Ένα Παράδειγμα από το Μακρυχώρι Λάρισας. Unpublished MA dissertation, University of Thessaly.

Besios, M. and Adaktylou, F. 2006. Νεολιθικός οικισμός στα «Ρεβένια» Κορινού. *Το Αρχαιολογικό Έργο στη Μακεδονία και στη Θράκη* 18(2004): 357-366.

Boyd, M.J. 2002. *Middle Helladic and Early Mycenaean Mortuary Practices in the Southern and Western Peloponnese* (British Archaeological Reports International Series 1009). Oxford: Archaeopress.

Cavanagh, W.G. and J.H. Crouwel 2002. The survey area in the prehistoric periods, in W. Cavanagh, J. Crouwel, R.W.V. Catling and G. Shipley (eds) *Continuity and Change in a Greek Rural Landscape. The Laconia Survey Volume I. Methodology and Interpretation* (The British School at Athens Supplementary Volume 26): 121-150. London: the British School at Athens.

Cavanagh, W.G. and C. Mee 2011. Minding the gaps in Early Helladic Laconia, in W. Gauss, M. Lindblom, R.A.K. Smith and J.C. Wright (eds) *Our Cups are Full. Pottery and Society in the Aegean Bronze Age. Papers presented to Jeremy B. Rutter on the Occasion of his 65th Birthday* (British Archaeological Reports International Series 2227): 40-50. Oxford: Archaeopress.

Carter, T. and M. Ydo 1996. The chipped and ground stone, in W. Cavanagh, J. Crouwel, R.W.V. Catling, and G. Shipley (eds) *Continuity and Change in a Greek Rural Landscape. The Laconia Survey Volume II. Archaeological Data* (The British School at Athens Supplementary Volume 27): 141-182. London: the British School at Athens.

Cauvin, J. 2004. *Γέννηση των Θεοτήτων, Γέννηση της γεωργίας. Η επανάσταση των συμβόλων στη νεολιθική εποχή*. Herakleion: University of Crete.

Chatzimichali, A. 1957. *Σαρακατσάνοι*. Athens: Kakoulidis.

Cullen, T. (ed.) 2001. *Aegean Prehistory. A Review* (American Journal of Archaeology Supplement 1). Boston: Archaeological Institute of America.

---

[73] With the exception of Vranas, and acknowledging that low ceramic visibility, and lack of understanding of its local features, is likely to have biased the picture. Vouno Panayias is located 400m from the river, while Ayios Georgios is located 600m north of Vouno Panayias (Banou 1999: 63-65).

[74] Spencer's (2007: 50) observation that late EH and MH sites in Laconia are concentrated 'along the coastline', should obviously be limited to MH I-II.

Dickinson, O.T.P.K. 1982. Parallels and contrasts in the Bronze Age of the Peloponnese. *Oxford Journal of Archaeology* 1(2): 125-138.

Dickinson, O.T.P.K. 1992. Reflections on Bronze Age Laconia, in J.M. Sanders (ed.) ΦΙΛΟΛΑΚΩΝ. *Lakonian Studies in Honour of Hector Catling*: 109-114. London: the British School at Athens.

Efstathiou-Manolakou, I. 2009. Archaeological investigations in the caves of Laconia, in W.G. Cavanagh, C. Gallou and M. Georgiadis (eds) *Sparta and Laconia: from Prehistory to Pre-Modern. Proceedings of the Conference Held in Sparta, Organised by the British School at Athens, the University of Nottingham, the 5th Ephoreia of Prehistoric and Classical Antiquities and the 5th Ephoreia of Byzantine Antiquities 17-20 March 2005* (The British School at Athens Studies 16): 5-20. London: the British School at Athens.

Elia, R. 1982. A Study of the Neolithic Architecture of Thessaly, Greece. Unpublished PhD dissertation, Boston University.

Forsén, J. 1992. *The Twilight of the Early Helladics: A Study of the Disturbances in East-Central and Southern Greece towards the End of the Early Bronze Age* (Studies in Mediterranean Archaeology and Literature Pocket-book 116). Jonsered: Paul Åström.

Forsén, J. 2003. Early and Middle Helladic pottery, in J. Forsén and B. Forsén (eds) *The Asea Valley Survey: An Arcadian Mountain Valley from the Palaeolithic Period until Modern Times* (Skrifter utgivna av Svenska institutet i Athen, 4o, 51): 167-176. Stockholm: the Swedish Institute at Athens.

Grammenos, D.B. and Kotsos, S. 2002. *Σωστικές Ανασκαφές στο Νεολιθικό Οικισμό Σταυρούπολης Θεσσαλονίκης Μέρος I* (Δημοσιεύματα του Αρχαιολογικού Ινστιτούτου Βόρειας Ελλάδας 2). Thessaloniki: the Archaeological Institute of Northern Greece.

Grammenos, D.B. and Kotsos, S. 2003. Ανασκαφή στον νεολιθικό οικισμό του Ζαγκλιβερίου νομού Θεσσαλονίκης. *Μακεδονικά* 33(2001-2002): 49-75.

Grammenos, D.B. and Kotsos, S. 2004. *Σωστικές ανασκαφές στο Νεολιθικό Οικισμό Σταυρούπολης Θεσσαλονίκης Μέρος II (1998-2003)* (Δημοσιεύματα του Αρχαιολογικού Ινστιτούτου Βόρειας Ελλάδας 6). Thessaloniki: the Archaeological Institute of Northern Greece.

Heurtley, W.A. 1938. Excavations in Ithaka, II. *The Annual of the British School at Athens* 35(1934-1935): 1-44.

Jameson, M.H., C.N. Runnels and T.H. van Andel 1994. *A Greek Countryside: the Southern Argolid from Prehistory to the Present Day*. Stanford: Stanford University Press.

Janko, R. 2008. Summary and historical conclusions, in W.D. Taylour and R. Janko (eds) *Ayios Stephanos. Excavations at a Bronze Age and Medieval Settlement in Southern Laconia* (The British School at Athens Supplementary Volume 44): 551-610. London: the British School at Athens.

Korres, G.S. 1981. Ανασκαφή Βοϊδοκοιλιάς Πυλίας. *Πρακτικά της εν Αθήναις Αρχαιολογικής Εταιρείας* 134(1979): 138-155.

Krahtopoulou, A., F. Sofianou, N. Alexiou, C. Papakosta, M. Charouli, F. Kostopoulou and I. Christophoridou 2020. Από τη Νεότερη Νεολιθική στη Μέση Εποχή του Χαλκού στους Μαυραχάδες και τον Άγιο Θεόδωρο της Καρδίτσας, in A. Mazarakis Ainan (ed.) *Αρχαιολογικό Έργο Θεσσαλίας και Στερεάς Ελλάδας 5. Πρακτικά επιστημονικής συνάντησης Βόλος 26.2 έως 1.3.2015. Τόμος I: Θεσσαλία*: 127-140. Volos: Ministry of Culture and Sport, Archaeological Receipts and Expropriations Fund.

O'Brien, S. 2013. Parables of decline: popular fears and the use of crises in Aegean archaeological interpretation, in E.M. van der Wilt and J. Martínez Jiménez (eds) *Tough Times: the Archaeology of Crisis and Recovery. Proceedings of the Graduate Archaeology at Oxford Conferences in 2010 and 2011* (British Archaeological Reports International Series 2478): 13-22. Oxford: British Archaeological Reports.

Maran, J. 1998. *Kulturwandel auf dem griechischen Festland und den Kykladen im späten 3. Jahrtausend v. Chr.: Studien zu den kulturellen Verhältnissen in Südosteuropa und dem zentralen sowie östlichen Mittelmeerraum in der späten Kupfer- und frühen Bronzezeit* (Universitätsforschungen zur prähistorischen Archäologie 53). Bonn: Rudolf Habelt.

Meller, H., H.W. Arz, R. Jung and R. Risch (eds) 2015. *2200 BC – Ein Klimasturz als Ursache für den Zerfall der Alten Welt? 7. Mitteldeutscher Archäologentag vom 23. bis 26. Oktober 2014 in Halle (Saale)* (Tagungen des Landesmuseums für Vorgeschichte Halle 12/I). Halle: the State Museum of Prehistory.

Pappa, M. 2008. Οργάνωση του Χώρου και Οικιστικά Στοιχεία στους Νεολιθικούς Οικισμούς της Κεντρικής Μακεδονίας: Δ.Ε.Θ. – Θέρμη – Μακρύγιαλος. Unpublished PhD dissertation, Aristotle University of Thessaloniki.

Papayiannis, A. 2013. Κτηνοτροφικές Πρακτικές στον Προϊστορικό και τον Παραδοσιακό Ελλαδικό Χώρο. Unpublished MA dissertation, University of Crete.

Proskynitopoulou, R. 2011. *Αρχαία Επίδαυρος, Εικόνες μιας αργολικής πόλης από την προϊστορική εποχή έως την ύστερη αρχαιότητα: Αρχαιολογικά ευρήματα και ιστορικές μαρτυρίες*. Athens: Ministry of Culture, Archaeological Receipts and Expropriations Fund.

Pullen, D. 2011. Picking out pots in patterns: feasting in Early Helladic Greece, in W. Gauss, M. Lindblom, R.A.K. Smith and J. Wright (eds) *Our Cups are Full: Pottery and Society in the Aegean Bronze Age. Papers Presented to Jeremy B. Rutter on the Occasion of his 65th Birthday* (British Archaeological Reports International Series 2227): 217–226. Oxford: Archaeopress.

Runnels, C.N. and T.H. Van Andel 1987. The evolution of settlement in the southern Argolid, Greece: an economic explanation. *Hesperia: the Journal of the American School of Classical Studies at Athens* 56(3): 303-334.

Rutter, J.B. 1982. A group of distinctive pattern-decorated Early Helladic III pottery from Lerna and its implications. *Hesperia: the Journal of the American School of Classical Studies at Athens* 51(4): 459-488.

Rutter, J. 1983. Some thoughts on the analysis of ceramic data generated by site surveys, in D.R. Keller and D.W Rupp (eds) *Archaeological Survey in the Mediterranean Area* (British Archaeological Reports International Series 155): 137-142. Oxford: British Archaeological Reports.

Rutter, J.B. 1993. Review of Aegean Prehistory II: the Prepalatial Bronze Age of the southern and central Greek mainland. *American Journal of Archaeology* 97(4) 745-797.

Rutter, J.B. 1995. *Lerna III. The Pottery of Lerna IV.* Princeton: the American School of Classical Studies at Athens.

Rutter, J. 2001. The Prepalatial Bronze Age of the southern and central Greek mainland, in T. Cullen (ed.) *Aegean Prehistory: A Review* (American Journal of Archaeology Supplement 1): 95-155. Boston: Archaeological Institute of America.

Rutter, J.B. 2008. The Anatolian roots of Early Helladic III drinking behavior, in H. Erkanal, H. Hauptmann, V. Şahoğlu and R. Tuncel (eds) *The Aegean in the Neolithic, Chalcolithic and the Early Bronze Age. Proceedings of the International Symposium, Oct. 13-16, 1997, Urla - İzmir, Turkey* (Ankara University Research Centre for Maritime Archaeology 1): 461-481. Ankara: Ankara University Press.

Shipley, G. 1996. Site catalogue of the survey, in W. Cavanagh, J. Crouwel, R.W.V. Catling, and G. Shipley (eds) *Continuity and Change in a Greek Rural Landscape. The Laconia Survey Volume II. Archaeological Data* (The British School at Athens Supplementary Volume 27): 315-438. London: the British School at Athens.

Smith, D.M. 2017. Recent research in Early Helladic southern Greece. *Archaeological Reports* 63: 107-129.

Souyoudzoglou-Haywood, C. 1999. *The Ionian Islands in the Bronze Age and Early Iron Age, 3000-800 BC.* Liverpool: Liverpool University Press.

Spencer, L.C. 2007. Pottery Technology and Socio-Economic Diversity on the Early Helladic III to Middle Helladic II Greek Mainland. Unpublished PhD dissertation, University College London.

Stocker, S. 2003. Pylos Regional Archaeological Project, part V. Deriziotis Aloni: a small Bronze Age site in

Messenia. *Hesperia: the Journal of the American School of Classical Studies at Athens* 72(4): 341-404.

Theocharis, D. 1952. Ἀνασκαφὴ ἐν Παλαιᾷ Κοκκινιᾷ Πειραιῶς. *Πρακτικά της εν Αθήναις Αρχαιολογικής Εταιρείας* 106(1951): 93-127.

Toufexis, G. 2003. Μελισσοχώρι. *Αρχαιολογικόν Δελτίον* 52(1997)(Chr. Β΄2): 507-508.

Tsonos, I. 2017. Η κατοίκηση στη νεολιθική Ανατολική Αττική: Το παράδειγμα της νεολιθικής εγκατάστασης στη θέση Σαμάρθι στα Καλύβια Θορικού. Unpublished MA dissertation, University of Thessaly.

Urem-Kotsou, D., A. Papaioannou, T. Silva, F. Adaktylou and M. Besios 2015. Οικισμός αρχαιότερης και μέσης νεολιθικής στα Ρεβένια Κορινού. Πρώτα αποτελέσματα της μελέτης της κεραμικής. *Το Αρχαιολογικό Έργο στη Μακεδονία και στη Θράκη* 25(2011): 163-172.

Vasilogamvrou, A. and A. Maltezou 2016. Συκέα Μολάων. Θέση Μεγάλη Ρίζα-Βρανά, αγροτεμάχιο Π. Ζουμπουλάκη. *Αρχαιολογικόν Δελτίον* 65(2010)(Chr. Β΄1a): 552.

Walter, H. and F. Felten 1981. *Alt-Ägina III,1. Die vorgeschichtliche Stadt. Befestigungen. Häuser. Funde.* Mainz: von Zabern.

Waterhouse, H. and Hope Simpson, R. 1960. Prehistoric Laconia: part 1. *The Annual of the British School at Athens* 55: 67-107.

Whittle, A. 1996. *Europe in the Neolithic: the Creation of New Worlds* (Cambridge World Archaeology). Cambridge: Cambridge University Press.

Wiencke, M.H. 2000. *Lerna IV. The Architecture, Stratification and Pottery of Lerna III.* Princeton: the American School of Classical Studies at Athens.

Yiannouli, E. 2006. Σκέψεις για τις οικίες-ορύγματα υπό το φως των δεδομένων της Θεσσαλίας, in A.Mazarakis Ainan (ed.) *Αρχαιολογικό Έργο Θεσσαλίας και Στερεάς Ελλάδας I. Πρακτικά επιστημονικής συνάντησης, Βόλος 27.2 - 2.3.2003. Τόμος I. Θεσσαλία:* 27-41. Volos: Ministry of Culture and The University of Thessaly.

Zachos, K. 2008. *Ayios Dhimitrios. A Prehistoric Settlement in the Southwestern Peloponnese: the Neolithic and Early Helladic Periods* (British Archaeological Reports, International Series 1770). Oxford: Archaeopress.

Zavvou, E. 2012. Early Helladic Laconia after the time of H. Waterhouse and R. Hope Simpson, in C. Mee and M. Prent (eds) *Early Helladic Laconia. Proceedings of the Round Table Conference held 16 January 2010 at the Netherlands Institute at Athens. Pharos. Journal of the Netherlands Institute at Athens* 18(1): 1-37.

Ceramic Surprises from LH IIIC Aigeira[1]

Jeremy Rutter

Introduction

The site of ancient Aigeira in eastern Achaea occupies the summit and upper slopes of a steep hill close to the southern shore of the Corinthian Gulf, almost exactly due south of Delphi and the nearby (and often visible) prehistoric sites of Kirrha and Krisa on the opposite side of the gulf in Phocis, some 30-35km away. The prehistoric focus of settlement that has thus far been explored at Aigeira is situated on the western acropolis at a maximum elevation of 415m above sea level, and across gently sloping terraces to the north, east, and south. The highest of these terraces, to the east, forms a saddle linking the western acropolis to a much smaller, and more heavily eroded, eastern acropolis. Excavations between 1975 and 1980, directed by the late Wilhelm Alzinger and supervised by Sigrid Deger-Jalkotzy on behalf of the Austrian Institute of Archaeology at Athens, cleared almost all of the western acropolis (see Alzinger *et al.* 1985). They exposed a small Postpalatial Mycenaean settlement below a poorly preserved Archaic to Classical sanctuary, the whole surrounded by a fortification wall first built in Mycenaean times but periodically modified thereafter down to the Late Roman and, probably, even later periods (Gauss 2015). The topography of the western acropolis, and the stratigraphy, chronology and material remains of the Late Helladic (LH) IIIC settlement on top of it, have been summarised on several occasions since the mid-1980s, as has the evidence for sporadic occupation of this part of the site during the Chalcolithic, Early Helladic (EH) I, and Early Helladic III to Middle Helladic (MH) I periods (see Alram-Stern 2003, 2007; Alram-Stern and Deger-Jalkotzy 2006; Arena 2020; Deger-Jalkotzy 2003; Deger-Jalkotzy and Alram-Stern 1985; Gauss 2015; Moschos 2009; Mountjoy 1999: 399). As a result, there is no need to further review that evidence here. The bulk of the Mycenaean remains belong to two phases, heretofore termed phases 1a and 1b, the first of which

is datable to an early stage (but not the earliest!) of LH IIIC Early (Deger-Jalkotzy 2003; Kardamaki 2015; Mühlenbruch 2020: 122, table 13.1: LH IIIC Early 2 = Tiryns Architectural Horizons 19b0-19c = Mycenae Architectural Phase X; Rutter 1977: 2 'Phase 2'; 2007: 293, table 4: phase 2; Vitale 2006). The second of these phases ended in a wholesale destruction by fire of the acropolis settlement, an event datable to the very end of LH IIIC Early or to an initial stage of LH IIIC Middle (Arena 2020: 38-39; Deger-Jalkotzy 2003: 58-67). Occupation of the acropolis continued following this disastrous fire in what the excavators have termed 'phase 2'. The finds of this terminal Bronze Age occupational phase were often scrappy, however, and from contexts badly disturbed by later activity, with the result that phase 2's definition in ceramic, and hence chronological, terms has proved rather problematic, as has any understanding of precisely when the Postpalatial settlement was finally abandoned (Deger-Jalkotzy 2003: 67-73; Gauss 2009; Mountjoy 1999: 399 and n. 204).

Fresh excavations of the Mycenaean remains located at the easternmost point on the western acropolis, as well as in the saddle area not far to the southeast, were undertaken from 2012 to 2016 by the Austrian Institute under the direction of Walter Gauss.[2] The results of the first three seasons of this work have been detailed already within two extensive preliminary reports, and will not be repeated in detail here (Gauss 2015; Gauss *et al.* 2013; 2015). Instead, my focus will be on several new insights into the rather unusual ceramic assemblages that can now be seen to represent an LH IIIC occupation lengthier than originally imagined, as well as more readily subdivided into distinct chronological stages in its later history.

The LH IIIC ceramic sequence at Aigeira

The Mycenaean stratigraphy in those portions of the western acropolis excavated in the 1970s rarely exceeded 0.75m in depth, and its shallower contexts were often badly disturbed, especially in the eastern half of the roughly 820m2 (*c.* 0.08ha) that constitutes the surface area of this acropolis (Alram-Stern 2003: 17-18, figs. 2-33). In contrast, contemporary stratigraphy recently located immediately inside the circuit of the

[1] I am very grateful to Bill Cavanagh for the invitation to participate in the workshop held at the British School at Athens in honor of Chris Mee's many contributions to our understanding of Aegean prehistory. Chris was a good friend, a generous colleague, and an inspirational teacher: it is a privilege and a genuine pleasure to dedicate this paper to him for all that he taught us about the prehistoric pottery of the Peloponnese. For the accompanying line drawings, I am beholden to Tina Ross and Christina Kolb. For the photographs, and much helpful support and advice, I am deeply indebted to Walter Gauss and Rudolphine Smetana. For permission to illustrate archived materials from one of its official excavations, I thank the Austrian Institute of Archaeology at Athens. I would also like to express my appreciation to David Smith for all of his editorial assistance.

[2] For a summary of the results of some testing of the stratification in the saddle area between 1972 and 1975, prior to the commencement of work on the western acropolis, see Gauss (2009).

preserved fortification wall at the eastern end of the acropolis, extended to a depth of *c.* 1.20m in some places. In the northern portion of the saddle, the LH IIIC deposit was measured at a depth of over 2m from the lowermost to the uppermost of the recognised floor levels, and would be significantly deeper if the undisturbed fills below the earliest floors, and above the latest, were to be taken into account. These extremely fortunate circumstances of preservation have allowed us to define no less than five distinct ceramic phases represented in the two areas. The first two of these phases correspond with phases 1a and 1b of the earlier excavators, while the last three have allowed us to subdivide, and more closely define, the previously rather nebulous, phase 2. I will henceforth refer to our newly defined phases with the prefix 'APP', standing for Aigeira Pottery Phase (Table 15.1).

From the two main zones excavated since 2012, we have inventoried some 950 pieces of LH IIIC pottery from well-stratified contexts (Table 15.2). The vast majority, to be sure, consist of single feature sherds (rims, handles, bases, spouts, and decorated body fragments), most of them small, and many of them heavily worn. But they also include *c.* 20 complete profiles, of which about half provided a fully restorable decorative schema. About three-quarters of these inventoried pieces (725 in total) came from the saddle, while just one quarter (roughly 225 pieces) were found immediately inside the LH IIIC

fortification wall, some 20m to the west-northwest and over 5m higher in elevation. But while three-quarters of the saddle pieces belong to APP 1 and APP 2 (equivalent to phase 1a and phase 1b of the previous excavators), these phases are represented by only a little less than half of the acropolis fragments. The saddle yielded virtually all of our inventoried APP 3 material, but less than a third of our total of APP 4 pieces, and provided no evidence at all of APP 5. Instead, two-thirds of the APP 4 sherds, and all of those of APP 5, came from the easternmost acropolis. This variability in the LH IIIC stratigraphy, along with the overall dearth of APP 4 and APP 5 material (together totalling less than one-sixth of inventoried pieces), suggests that it may be necessary to undertake additional testing of LH IIIC levels across the broader saddle zone (an area far more extensive than the 820m2 of the western acropolis) in order to achieve a genuinely holistic appreciation of ceramic development throughout Aigeira's *c.* 120-year LH IIIC occupation (*c.* 1170/1160-1050/1040 BC).

Having the good fortune to find deep and well-stratified deposits belonging to the LH IIIC settlement was only part of the reason for our being able to confidently distinguish such a large number of ceramic phases across the two excavation zones. At least as important was the precision of the excavation technique: digging by the square metre unit, as well as by natural stratigraphy, into deposits which varied from the neatly

Table 15.1. LH IIIC chronological table placing Aigeira Pottery Phases (APP 1-5) relative to phases at other LH IIIC settlement sites (modified form of Rutter 2007: table 4). For the especially important sites of Mycenae and Tiryns in the Argolid, see now Mühlenbruch (2020: 122, table 13.1).

Mountjoy's 1999 Phases of LH IIIC	Rutter 1977, 1978	Mycenae [Argolid]	Lefkandi [Euboea]	Aigeira (Eastern Achaia)	Kalapodi [Phokis]	Kynos (Livanates) [Lokris]
LH IIIC Early	2	Early	1a	APP 1		
	3	Tower	1b	APP 2	Horizon 1	
LH IIIC Middle	4 early	Developed		APP 3	Horizon 2	
			2a		Horizon 3	
	4 late	Advanced		APP 4	Horizon 4	Phase 5 [earthquake/fire]
			2b		Horizon 5	
LH IIIC Late	5 early	Final		APP 5 (?)	Horizon 6	Phase 4 [earthquake]
			3			
"Sub-Mycenaean"	5 late		Skoubris Cemetery		Horizon 7	Phase 3 (?)

Table 15.2. Aigeira 2012-2016: Late Helladic IIIC pottery from well-stratified contexts: counts of inventoried pieces by excavation area.

Aigeira Pottery Phase [APP]	Area of Excavation		TOTALS
	Northwest Saddle	Easternmost Acropolis	
APP 1	262 (= 36.1%)	7 (= 3.1%)	269 (= 28.3%)
APP 2	279 (= 38.5%)	103 (= 45.8%)	382 (= 40.2%)
APP 3	151 (= 20.8%)	1 (= 0.4%)	152 (= 16.0%)
APP 4	33 (4.6%)	73 (= 32.4%)	106 (= 11.2%)
APP 5	0	41 (= 18.2%)	41 (= 4.3%)
TOTALS	725 (100.0%)	225 (100.0)	950 (100.0%)

horizontal to the sharply sloping. All excavated earth was dry-sieved, representative samples of all strata were also water-sieved, and all features and baulk profiles were meticulously recorded in both drawings and photographs. It is this kind of precision, to cite just one example, that allowed us to securely identify our single greatest concentration of fully mendable pots (Figure 15.1) as a dumped fill of debris from the great destruction by fire on the acropolis, rather than as the in situ floor deposit that we initially understood it to be (Gauss *et al.* 2015: 16-19).

Previous publications of the pottery of APP 1 and 2, assignable to two successive stages of LH IIIC Early, have proved sufficiently numerous, detailed, and accurate that no significant corrections to them are necessary (Deger-Jalkotzy 2003: 55-67; Deger-Jalkotzy and Alram-Stern 1985: 398-404; Gauss *et al.* 2015: 23-25). APP 1 represents the earliest phase of Mycenaean settlement so far detected on either the acropolis or the saddle. Its repertoire of tableware is dominated

by solidly coated deep bowls, linearly decorated semiglobular cups and basins, pattern-decorated kraters, and plain kylikes and dippers. Commonly occurring large, closed shapes, such as hydrias, amphoras, and jugs, may be solidly coated, linearly decorated, or plain, but are rarely pattern-decorated. Smaller closed shapes, such as stirrup jars, alabastra, and amphoriskoi, on the other hand, are typically pattern-decorated; most of the small stirrup jars are likely to be imports. Pattern-decorated open shapes other than kraters consist of a few deep bowls and occasional mugs or stemmed bowls. The presence of a few carinated cups (FS 240) and occasional solidly coated carinated kylikes (FS 267), and the absence of any linearly decorated or patterned high-stemmed kylikes with conical bowls (FS 275), are of chronological significance. This material is contemporary with Lefkandi phase 1a or with, what I have, since 1977, termed LH IIIC phase 2 (Deger-Jalkotzy 2003: 55-58, 64-67, fig. 2; Mountjoy 1999: 38-41, table II; Mühlenbruch 2020: 122, table 13.1: LH IIIC Early 2; Rutter 1977: 2).

Q610-420/091-6

Q610-420/091-1

Q610-420/091-8
(KLQ 12)

Q610-420/120-1
(KLQ)

Q610-420/090-2
(KLQ 11)

Q610-420/120-2

Figure 15.1. Largely mendable vessels from a dumped fill of APP 2 date at the easternmost end of Aigeira's western Acropolis.

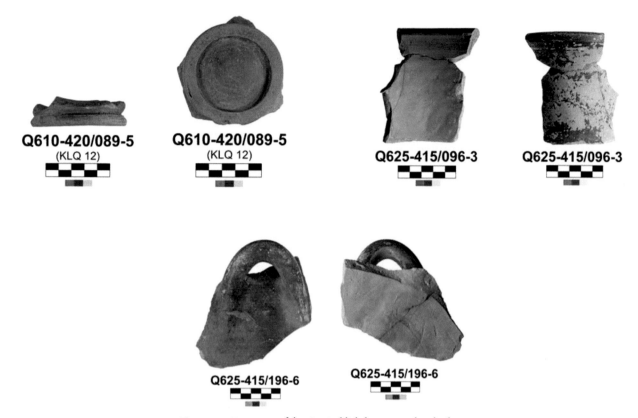

Q610-420/089-5
(KLQ 12)

Q610-420/089-5
(KLQ 12)

Q625-415/096-3

Q625-415/096-3

Q625-415/196-6

Q625-415/196-6

Figure 15.2. Fragments of the Fine Reddish-brown Handmade class.

The pottery of APP 2 is very similar to that of the preceding APP 1, differing only in the appearance of small numbers of linear- and pattern-decorated kylikes, the former being either short-stemmed with carinated bodies (for example, Fig. 15.15, no. Q625-415/013-001) or higher-stemmed with relatively shallow conical bodies. Thanks to the violent destruction of the settlement at the end of this phase, both on the acropolis and, seemingly, also on the saddle below, the quantity of pottery assignable to APP 2, and especially the quantity of fully restorable pots, is substantially higher than for any other LH IIIC phase represented at Aigeira. APP 2 may be securely dated to the end of LH IIIC Early — LH IIIC phase 3 in my own terminology — ending slightly earlier than the end of Lefkandi phase 1b (Table 15.1; Deger-Jalkotzy 2003: 58-67, figs. 3-4; Mountjoy 1999: 38-41, table II; 2007: 221-222, fig. 1; Rutter 1977).

The LH IIIC ceramic repertoire at Aigeira exhibits a number of peculiarities that have been abundantly documented during excavations at the site since 2012, and that merit more attention than they have thus far received. The earliest of these is a class of pottery that has been variously described by previous specialists working on the site as 'rotbrauner Hartware' (Fine Reddish Brown Hard-Fired Ware: Deger-Jalkotzy 2003: 56, 64, figs. 2.14-2.15; Deger-Jalkotzy and Alram-Stern 1985: 411-412, fig. 14 no. 1) or 'Macroscopic Group 13' (MG 13: Gauss 2009: 165-166, fig. 8). The fine fabric, aptly characterised by Walter Gauss (2009), ranges in colour from red to reddish

yellow (2.5-5YR 5/6-6/8) in the fracture, shading to light reddish brown to pink (2.5-5YR 6-7/3-4) at the unpainted surface, and contains few, if any, visible inclusions, with the exception of some very fine sparkling grits and occasional small bits of shell (Figure 15.2). The range of shapes (Figure 15.3) consists, for the most part, of large closed vessels with pronounced necks (amphoras, hydrias, occasional transport stirrup jars, and probably also some four-handled jars), basins with horizontal strap handles attached just below markedly swollen lips, and so-called truncated stemmed bowls: deep bowls with the thickened rims typical of stemmed bowls but with ring bases (Mountjoy 1986: 92; 1999: 762 and nos. 72-73, fig. 295 no. 78; Phialon 2018: 458-459 and nos. 248-250). Virtually all closed shapes in this fabric have solidly coated exteriors, the undersides of the slightly raised bases often also being completely coated.[3] Almost all of the deep bowls are solidly coated inside and out, but the basins and rare kraters often have a linear exterior combined with a coated interior. The paint ranges from a metallic black through to very dark reddish brown to red. What is most striking about the vessels produced in

---

[3] Some raised bases have a simple thin band at their edge, although their undersides otherwise remain unpainted (for example, Figure 15.3, no. Q625-415/094-011). In 2015, the discovery of a few linearly decorated closed body sherds showed that at least a few large, closed shapes might be linearly decorated on their bodies as well (for example, Q630-415/044-015). Patterned decoration in this fabric, however, is extremely rare; thus far, I have seen only one deep bowl body sherd in this fabric that bears a pattern (Q630-415/045-004; the pattern is stemmed spirals, FM 51).

this fabric is the fact that they are typically coil-made, although in some cases, the necks, rims, and raised bases of large, closed shapes appear to have been wheel-finished, or perhaps even wheel-thrown, and then added to hand-built bodies (Gauss *et al.* 2015: 24 n. 42, 25 fig. 14.8). Abundant parallels for such solidly coated, large, closed vessels have recently been reported from very early LH IIIC contexts at Kontopigado near Athens (Kaza-Papageorgiou *et al.* 2011: 215, 251-252 fig. 16 nos. 112-116). The frequency of this fabric in APP 1 deposits is striking, and plenty of such vessels were still in use during APP 2, but thereafter the amount of this material, except in the form of increasingly more worn, and hence softer, residual sherds, declined sharply. In view of its frequency, and its distinctive combination of decoration and mode of manufacture, I would like to propose calling this class 'Fine Reddish-brown Handmade', modified by the adjectives monochrome or linear as may be appropriate. There is little doubt but that vessels in this fabric are imports to Aigeira (Gauss *et al.* 2015: 23), but their place of production is uncertain (Rutter 2020: 212). Similarly decorated large closed vessels and deep bowls with thickened rims are, apparently, common among the pottery dated to LH IIIA2 from the Corycian Cave on the other side of the Corinthian Gulf, as well as from Krisa and Delphi (Mountjoy 1999: 759 n. 70, 760 fig. 295 nos.75

and 78, 762 nos. 75 and 78; Phialon 2018: 458-459, 480 no. 6091, 481 no. 6092, 484 no. 6107, 491 no. 6129, figs. 41-42, 50, 66), but, to my knowledge, none of those sites has yielded any assemblage of such vessels from LH IIIB or early LH IIIC contexts (Livieratou 2020: 101, 103).

From the same APP 1 contexts on the saddle as those large quantities of the proposed Fine Reddish-brown Handmade material came a concentration of decoratively and technologically related vessels made using an altogether different clay recipe that resulted in a distinctively different appearance. The fired fabric is medium fine, very pale (10YR 8/3-1.25Y 8/2), and quite soft; those vessels produced in it are, again, handmade, but are rendered much more awkwardly than those of the superbly potted Fine Reddish-brown Handmade class. Examples of this separate class of relatively fine handmade vessels appear to have been either entirely coated with a dark paint or else very simply banded, although precise identification of their decoration is now made problematic by a paint that adhered so poorly to the clay ground beneath that the vessels in question often look practically plain, with only specks of their original banding or monochrome coating preserved. The shapes represented in this vaguely Corinthian-looking, but poorly levigated (and ultimately totally

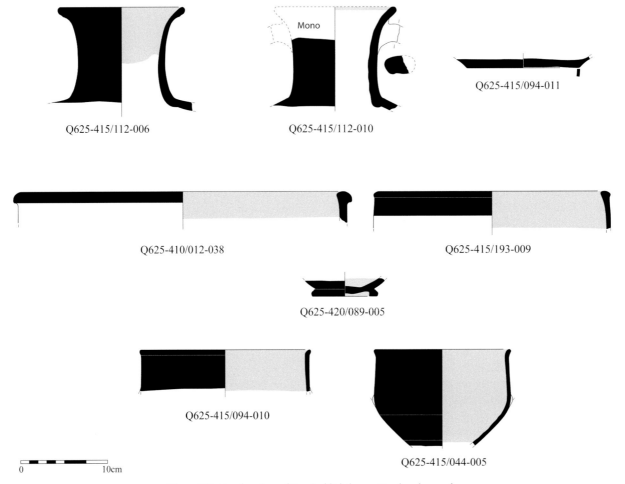

Figure 15.3. Line drawings of Fine Reddish-brown Handmade vessels.

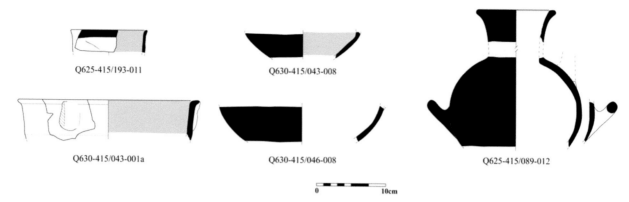

Q625-415/193-011

Q630-415/043-008

Q630-415/043-001a

Q630-415/046-008

Q625-415/089-012

0   10cm

Figure 15.4. Line drawings of Soft, Medium Fine Pale Handmade vessels.

impractical) fabric are quite varied: a semiglobular cup and basin with linear decoration, as well as a solidly coated deep bowl, carinated kylix, and small hydria (Figure 15.4). It is difficult to view these wretchedly made containers as anything but a potting experiment by a rather unskilled artisan, possibly trying their hand with unfamiliar raw materials. The fact that this class of Soft, Medium Fine Pale Handmade vessels failed to survive into APP 2 is hardly surprising. But its existence during APP 1 is one of several indications that at least some of the initial settlers of LH IIIC Aigeira are likely to have been either strangers to the area or simply strangers to potting (Rutter 2020: 213).

The class of handmade pottery of LH IIIC date for which Aigeira is best known, of course, is that commonly referred to as Handmade Burnished Ware (HBW in English, HGK in German), initially published by Deger-Jalkotzy in 1977 and frequently discussed and supplemented by new finds since then (Deger-Jalkotzy 1977; Gauss *et al.* 2013: 77-78, figs. 7 no.2 and fig. 8 no. 3; 2015: 23, 25 fig. 14.1; Jung 2006: 43-46; Lis 2009; 2018: 141; Rutter 2020: 213). The class is medium coarse to coarse, dark-surfaced, handmade and burnished, and was present in substantial quantities among the material recovered during the recent excavations of 2012-2016, including in the form of several complete profiles (Figure 15.5). We may now state with confidence that this class of pottery first appeared at Aigeira in the earliest LH IIIC strata of APP 1, and continued to be produced and used throughout the rest of the LH IIIC sequence at the site. Although more than 100 different vessels in this class are now known from Aigeira, no more than three distinct shapes appear to be represented: first, a small to medium-sized jug with a low, flaring neck whose rim in some cases slopes up slightly from the upper attachment of a vertical strap handle to a very broad and simple, troughed spout opposite the handle (Figures 15.1, 15.5 and 15.6 no. Q610-420/120-002); second, a medium-sized to large jar with a profile not unlike that of the jug, but with a somewhat higher and symmetrical neck, and with two horizontal loop handles set on the shoulder, the backs of which often feature a single broad horizontal groove (Figures

15.1, 15.5 and 15.7 no. Q610-420/091-006). The bases of these two closed forms may be either simply flattened, or else provided with an extra coil of clay at the bottom to fashion a hollowed and slightly raised base, or even a clumsily rendered ring foot. Whether simple or more elaborate, these bases are invariably somewhat convex, with the result that the vessels wobble, rather than sit in a stable position, when placed on a horizontal surface. This inherent instability seems very odd for a shape that was obviously designed to dispense liquid contents.

The third shape represented in this class is a dipper or ladle, supplied with a single high-swung handle and a body that can be quite variable in both shape and size (Figures 15.5 and 15.7 no. Q625-415/013-003). The horizontal-handled jars (Figures 15.1, 15.5 and 15.7 no. Q610-420/091-006) have necks that are wide enough to have allowed their makers to burnish their interiors. Many of the jugs (Figures 15.1, 15.5, 15.6 no. Q610-420/120-002 and 15.15 no. Q625-415/013-002), however, have necks that are too narrow for this purpose, with the result that many body sherds can be assigned to one or the other shape by the presence or absence of an interior burnish. The two shapes appear to be equally common, and may have been intended to function as pairs. The dippers, on the other hand, are markedly less common. In addition, the surfaces of the dippers sometimes lack the burnish (Figure 15.7 no. Q625-415/013-003) that is an invariable feature of the exteriors of the jugs and jars. Given that the dippers sometimes have round bottoms, in addition to disproportionately large handles that make them even less stable than the jug and jar, it is possible that all three shapes may have been hung on pegs when not in use.

None of these Dark Burnished shapes bear any kind of decoration. Perhaps their oddest feature, however, is that relatively few of them exhibit any clear signs of use, particularly in the form of the secondary burning that discolours the surfaces of ordinary cooking pots. Moreover, the LH IIIC population at Aigeira had ready access to standard Mycenaean cooking shapes that do feature abundant traces of secondary burning (Figure

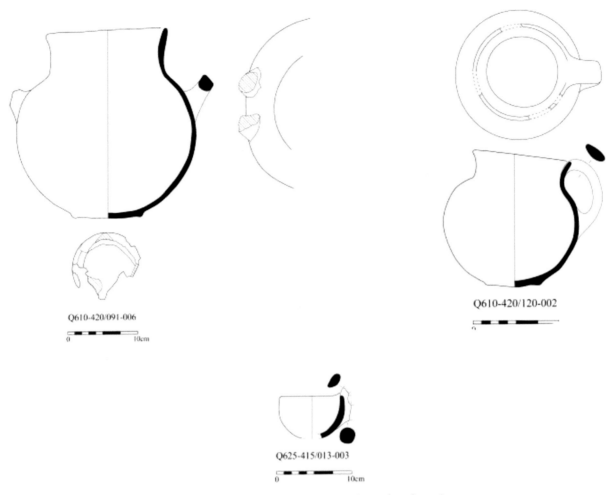

Q610-420/091-006

Q610-420/120-002

Q625-415/013-003

Figure 15.5. Line drawings of Handmade Burnished Ware (HBW) vessel types.

Q610-420/120-2

Q610-420/120-2

Q610-420/120-2

Figure 15.6. Handmade Burnished Ware wide-mouthed jug.

15.8). Most common among these cooking pots are strap-handled wide-mouthed jugs (FS 65) of various sizes, but also attested are a few cooking kraters (probably spouted, FS 298), at least one two-handled cooking amphora (FS 66), and a small number of cooking vessels with tripod legs that are probably imported. So, what were these handmade and burnished jugs, jars, and dippers used for, if not for cooking? The shape range of this class at Aigeira is distinctly unusual, as

Reinhard Jung made clear a decade ago (Jung 2006: 43-46). Could it be that the three shapes in question were display pieces of some sort, or that they were used in particular social or ceremonial contexts?[4]

_____

[4] Excavations at Mount Lykaion in Arcadia, undertaken in 2018 as part of the long-term *synergasia* co-directed by Dr. Anna Karapaniotou of the Ephoreia of Antiquities in Tripolis and Dr. David Romano and Dr. Mary Voyatzis of the University of Arizona, uncovered at least two examples of dark-surfaced Handmade and Burnished jugs (inv.

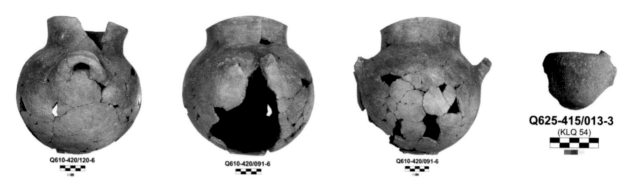

Figure 15.7. Handmade Burnished Ware shoulder-handled amphora and Handmade Unburnished Ware dipper or ladle.

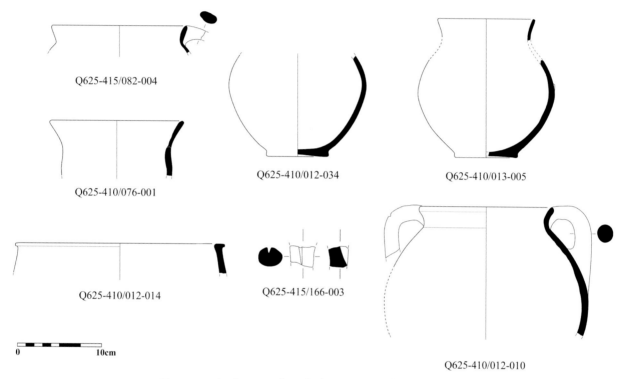

Figure 15.8. Line drawings of standard Mycenaean cooking ware vessels.

The deep LH IIIC stratification identified in the northernmost part of the saddle has preserved multiple strata that can be assigned to a phase of occupation we term APP 3; one that is barely represented in the somewhat shallower sequence of LH IIIC strata at the east end of the acropolis. As was the case for the earlier transition from APP 1 to APP 2, the typological shifts in shapes and painted patterns between APP 2 and APP 3 are relatively minor, but a major change is apparent in

the fabrics represented. The amount of Fine Reddish-brown Handmade pottery declined precipitously. It was replaced, especially for the manufacture of large open and closed shapes,[5] by a medium fine to medium coarse, pale-surfaced fabric that is clearly the Aigeiran equivalent of what has been called 'White Ware' at Lefkandi, and numerous other LH IIIC sites in Central Greece and the Cyclades, but that is much less frequently attested in the northeastern Peloponnese (Figure 15.9).[6] At Lefkandi, this fabric first appeared in the local phase 2a, but only became truly popular there in phases 2b and 3, and is therefore diagnostic of both LH IIIC Middle and

nos. C-Z-866-Find Z759 and C-Z-882-10) that appear to me to be indistinguishable from those recovered at Aigeira. The jugs from Mount Lykaion were found in a context directly adjacent to the man-made Architectural Feature at the base of the stratification within the ash altar at its highest point (Voyatzis 2019: 134-139 and nos. 11-12, figs. 5-6). They were located in direct association with a number of unpainted and wheelmade carinated kylikes (FS 267) of advanced LH IIIB or early LH IIIC date (for example, inv. no. C-Z-882-09), as well as other Mycenaean vessels. Although the Mount Lykaion material remains to be fully studied, I am extremely grateful to Dr. Romano and Dr. Voyatzis for permission to mention this startling new discovery, in advance of its formal publication.

[5] These include basins, kraters, amphoras, hydrias, and large jugs, mostly linear and occasionally either plain or pattern-decorated, but never solidly coated on the exterior.
[6] For examples from Aigeira, see Deger-Jalkotzy and Alram-Stern (1985: 419), Mountjoy (1999: 399), and Gauss et al. (2013: 74 fig. 6.1, 75 and n. 14; 2015: 16 and n. 13); for Corinth, see Rutter (1979: 390 and n. 37); for Lefkandi, see Popham et al. (2006: 151, 169, 175, 178-179, 189, 193, 227 and n. 93); for Perati, see Lis et al. (2020).

Late (Table 15.1). At Perati, roughly 20% of the more than 1200 complete vessels recovered from the 219 tombs of the LH IIIC cemetery are thought to have been produced in this fabric (Lis *et al.* 2020: 1-3), which appears first in tombs of Perati I/II and becomes progressively more popular through phase II and into phase III (Lis *et al.* 2020: 12, table 1). Nine of the 12 White Ware vessels from Perati sampled for Instrumental Neutron Activation Analysis (INAA) by Hans Mommsen and his team at Bonn in 1996, and subsequently subjected to macroscopic analysis by Bartek Lis, have been identified as local products. Three of the White Ware samples, however, turned out to be NAA outliers and thus imports to the site (Lis *et al.* 2020: 12, table 1), a finding that suggests that White Ware is likely to have been produced at quite a number of different locales (Lis *et al.* 2020: 3). Where such discrete production centres may have been located remains to be determined, as do the varying distribution patterns of their products (Lis *et al.* 2020: 11, fig. 29). The essentials of the clay recipe and inclusions that resulted in what has been termed White Ware may end up marking a novel production technology introduced into the central and western Aegean from Cyprus, as suggested over 20 years ago by Sigrid Deger-Jalkotzy (Deger-Jalkotzy 1994: 19; Popham *et al.* 2006: 227 n. 93). Aside from its much paler fracture and surface coloration, and significantly coarser fabric, White Ware differs from the earlier Fine Reddish-brown Handmade class in having very cursorily treated surfaces, and typically dull rather than lustrous paint. More specifically, White Ware surfaces are simply smoothed or wiped. The solidly painted exterior surfaces of Fine Reddish-brown Handmade vessels are highly lustrous, having been either burnished, wheel-polished, or very finely wiped. One has the impression that White Ware vessels took much less time to produce than did Fine Reddish-brown Handmade containers.

If White Ware vessels were produced locally at those sites where they have been found in quantity, there are likely to be significant differences in their mineralogical as well as chemical compositions, but no large-scale petrographic or chemical studies of this class have been undertaken except in the case of Perati. At both Lefkandi and Aigeira, this class eventually included not only those large shapes already mentioned, but also a far larger number of smaller ones, such as semiglobular cups, deep bowls, and stirrup jars (Evely 2006: 331 s.v. 'White Ware'), than produced in its Fine Reddish-brown Handmade predecessor. In the absence of more comprehensive studies of these two ceramic classes, it is probably inadvisable to speculate here as to what the rapid (or even sudden) replacement of one by the other at the beginning of Aigeira's version of LH IIIC Middle might signify.

I have already drawn attention to the handmade rather than wheel-thrown (or wheel-finished) character of several different classes of both fine and coarse pottery at LH IIIC Aigeira during the APP 1-3 phases. We have also noted that a substantial number of other vessels understood to be locally produced tablewares (whether monochrome painted, simply banded, patterned, or plain) as well as some of the local cooking pots in standard Mycenaean shapes (Figure 15.8; mostly wide-mouthed jugs made in a sandy, quartz-rich fabric lacking any kind of post-shaping finish) were also handmade using a coiled technique. Unfortunately, because so many of our inventoried pieces consist of small and quite heavily worn sherds, we have not yet determined how to properly quantify this phenomenon. We are largely dependent on the preservation of clear indications of junctions between distinct coils (visible 'coil joins') or on the survival of fragments large

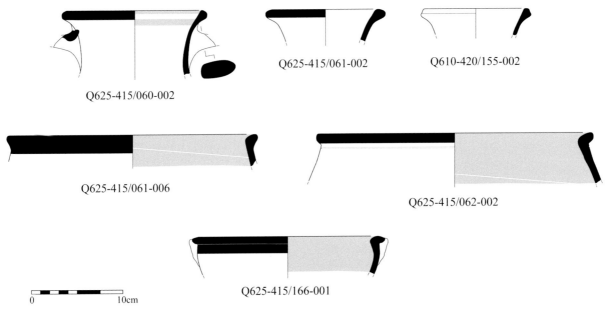

Q625-415/060-002

Q625-415/061-002

Q610-420/155-002

Q625-415/061-006

Q625-415/062-002

Q625-415/166-001

0   10cm

Figure 15.9. Line drawings of White Ware vessels.

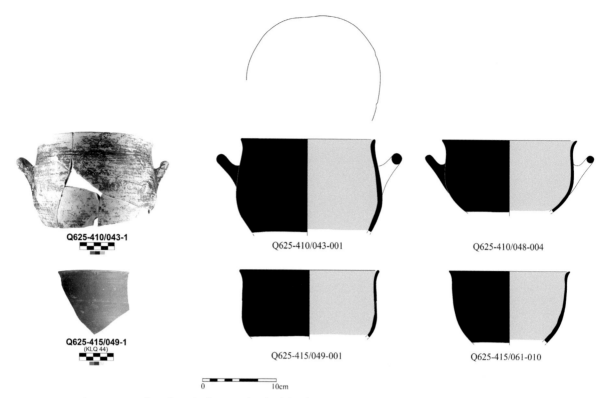

Q625-410/043-1

Q625-410/043-001

Q625-410/048-004

Q625-415/049-1
(KLQ 44)

Q625-415/049-001

Q625-415/061-010

0   10cm

Figure 15.10. Coil-made and subsequently wheel-finished deep bowls, solidly coated and usually burnished.

enough to have preserved substantially different wall thicknesses of a given pot at the same point in its elevation. Examples of such coil-made vessels include the following: monochrome deep bowls of APPs 2 and 3 with clear coil joins visible in the lower body (Figure 15.10 nos. Q625-410/043-001, Q625-410/048-004 [APP 2]; Q625-415/049-001, Q625-415/061-010 [APP 3]); a wide-mouthed cooking jug of APP 2 exhibiting a similar coil join at the point where the flaring rim was attached (Figure 15.8 no. Q625-410/076-001 [APP 2]); and a bridge-spouted, pattern-decorated krater (FS 298), the wall thickness of which varies significantly at the same level (Figure 15.11; Gauss *et al.* 2015: 16, 18 fig. 6.1). This last pot features a clear coil join on the interior. After its primary forming, it was wheel-finished, and then its solidly painted interior was burnished. It was one of three largely mendable pattern-decorated kraters from the same dumped fill of APP 2 date; neither one of the other two (Figure 15.1 no. Q610-420/091-8 and Q610-420/120-1) exhibited any features of handmade manufacture. Within the local tableware repertoire, dippers, semiglobular cups, and carinated cups also show signs of coil manufacture. But, like the kraters, not all were coil-made and, of those that were, most were then wheel-finished.

By far the most common shapes in all stages of the LH IIIC sequence at Aigeira were the solidly coated deep bowl (Figure 15.10 no. Q625-410/043-001) and the semiglobular cup with a simple rim band (Figure 15.1 no. Q610-420/090-002; Gauss *et al.* 2015: 16, 18 fig. 6.2). Alongside those of more typical form, in APPs 2 and

3 especially, numerous examples of the two shapes exhibit astonishingly thin-walls (deep bowls: Figure 15.12; cups: Q625-410/048-002; Q625-415/076-004; Q625-415/077-009(b); Q625-415/085-020). I suspect that most of the extra-thin-walled specimens of these shapes were coil-made and subsequently pared in order to reduce their weight and improve the quality of their firing, but further study of these pieces, in particular, is required in order to substantiate this notion.

Determining with any degree of accuracy what percentages of the tableware and cooking pottery in use during APPs 1 through 3 at Aigeira were handmade, handmade before being wheel-finished, or wheel-thrown, is likely to prove difficult, given the material's poor state of preservation. Some categories of the handmade material are probably imported (for example, the Fine Reddish-brown Handmade class of APPs 1 and 2), but most of them appear to be local products, as must certainly be the numerous tubs and vats that functioned, essentially, as built-in furniture, and also the vast majority of the large numbers of pithoi used for storage at the site. Yet, there seems to have been plenty of typical wheel-thrown Mycenaean tableware and cooking pottery in use as well. The overall picture is one of a thorough mixture of handmade as well as wheel-thrown[7] ceramic products in contemporary use, and is highly

---

[7] Among the wheel-thrown pieces should be noted the numerous vessels that were wheel-thrown in sections, subsequently joined at major points of transition in the vessel profile (e.g., at the base of the neck on large, closed shapes; at the junction of bowl and stem on plain and decorated kylikes and some solidly coated stemmed bowls).

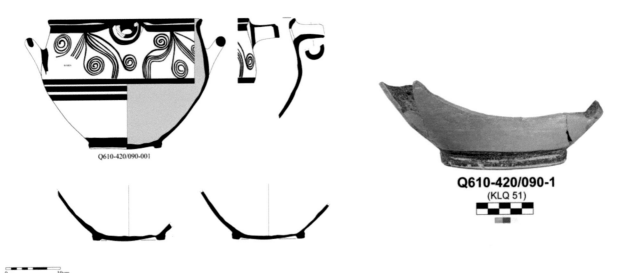

Figure 15.11. Coil-made and subsequently wheel-finished and pattern-decorated krater with solidly coated and burnished interior, of APP 2 date.

unusual in my own experience; the task of identifying the multiple possible combinations of coil-building and wheel-finishing techniques (see, for example, Choleva 2012; 2015a; 2015b; 2018a; 2018b; 2018c; Lis 2016; 2017; Vitale 2018) is one that, undoubtedly, requires specialised training to recognise and describe appropriately. The chief aim of this presentation is simply to communicate that the range of different pottery production methods represented at LH IIIC Aigeira appears to be more heterogenous than is the case for most other Bronze Age Aegean pottery assemblages with which I am familiar, not only in the shaping of pots but also in the preparation of the desired clay mixtures with highly variable amounts and ranges of non-plastic inclusions. I suspect that this may reflect the presence at the site of a larger number of local potters, and hence may indicate that pottery production had become a household craft at Aigeira during this period.

For now, it is possible only to offer a few brief comments on the pottery assemblages of APPs 4 and 5, since neither one of these phases is as well documented as the three which precede them. APP 4 is represented by floor levels in both the saddle and east acropolis excavation zones. Even though material of this phase is comparatively scant, the typological features that distinguish it from the preceding APP 3 are more numerous, and more pronounced, than those that separate the previous pairs of phases. To begin with, deep bowls may look quite different in terms of both shape and decoration. A linear deep bowl with a medium rim band is significantly smaller than before, and has a hollowed raised base instead of the usual ring foot (Figure 15.13 no. Q610-420/050-003; Gauss *et al.* 2015: 15, 17 fig. 5.1). It has, in fact, adopted the linear decoration, rim band, foot profile, and size of a semiglobular cup, but its surviving handle and the scar of a second show clearly that it was

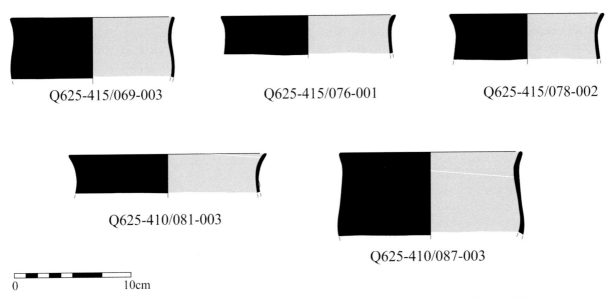

Figure 15.12. Line drawings of exceptionally thin-walled, solidly coated deep bowls, possibly coil-made and then carefully pared so as to reduce their wall thickness.

210

a deep bowl. A second example of this shape, with a rim diameter of just 7cm, is even more unusual: aside from its aberrant size and handmade production, it features a reserved band on the interior rim decorated with continuous dashes (Figure 15.13 nos. Q610-420/085-013 and Q610-420/085-015). Several other solidly coated deep bowls of this phase feature reserved interior rim bands, either plain or dotted (Figure 15.13 nos. Q610-420/087-008, Q625-415/031-002 and Q610-420/089-001; Mountjoy 2007: 222-224, 229 fig. 1; Rutter 1977; 1979). White Ware continues, but now includes both smaller forms like deep bowls and cups (Figure 15.14 nos. Q610-420/083-004 and Q630-410/019-001), and occasional novel shapes such as trefoil-mouthed jugs (Figure 15.14 no. Q625-415/055-017; Mountjoy 2007: 222, 231 fig. 3.1), sometimes supplied with a twisted vertical loop handle (Figure 15.14 no. Q610-420/087-009). Small, closed shapes become more common, and include an occasional example of a stirrup jar or lekythos with dense multiple banding typical of western Achaean

versions of these forms in later LH IIIC Middle and Late (Figure 15.14 no. Q610-420/087-010; Moschos 2002: 23-25, fig. 4; 2009: 349 table 1, 354, 385-387 (Achaean Phases 3(late)-5); Mountjoy 1999: 404-405; Stockhammer 2009: 350-351, fig. 5.4). Fine Unpainted pottery seems to have disappeared altogether by APP 4. This phase lines up well with the Advanced sub-phase of LH IIIC Middle in the Argolid (Table 15.1). A small APP 4 assemblage excavated from a floor deposit in the northern saddle area consists of a Handmade Burnished jug (Figure 15.15 no. Q625-415/013-002; Gauss et al. 2013: 77, fig. 7.2), a Handmade Unburnished round-bottomed dipper (Figures 15.5 and 15.7 no. Q625-415/013-003; Gauss et al. 2015: 23, 25 fig. 14.1), and a linear carinated kylix (FS 267) of a decorative type that had been in use at Aigeira since at least APP 2 (Figure 15.15 no. Q625-415/013-001; Gauss et al. 2013: 77, fig. 7.1).

Stratified APP 5 pottery has been identified only at the eastern end of the acropolis, just inside the fortification

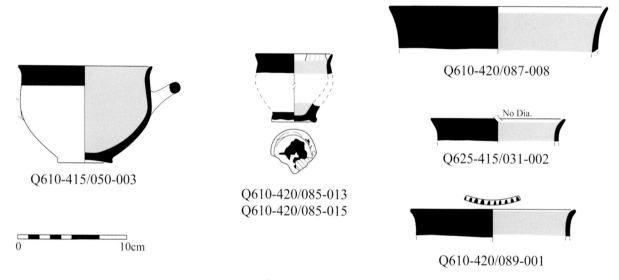

Figure 15.13. Line drawings of atypical deep bowls of APP 4.

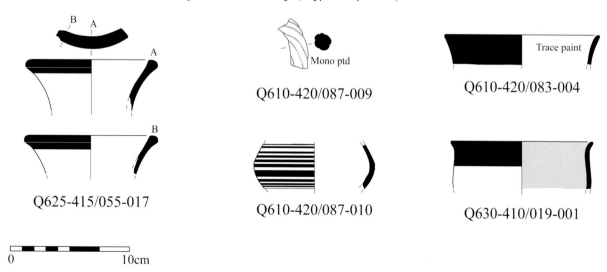

Figure 15.14. Line drawings of atypical White Ware and other diagnostic fragments of APP 4.

Figure 15.15. Handmade Burnished (HMB) jug (Q625-415/013-2) and linear carinated kylix (Q625-415/013-1) of APP 4 from the northern saddle area; solidly coated deep bowl (Q615-415/010-001) of APP 5 from the easternmost end of the western acropolis.

Figure 15.16. Varieties of LH IIIC pithos decoration from Aigeira.

wall. A single complete profile, belonging to a smaller-than-normal deep bowl provided with a hollowed and raised foot rather than a true ring base (Figure 15.15 no. Q615-415/010-001; Gauss et al. 2013: 75, fig. 6.2), is solidly coated, except for a thin reserved line at the very bottom of the foot. The extremely scant sherd material of APP 5 includes later LH IIIC types already attested in the preceding phase, but with the exception of the somewhat higher foot on the single fully preserved deep bowl profile, nothing sets this material apart from that of APP 4. As at so many other settlement sites of the Postpalatial Late Bronze Age on the southern Greek mainland, this terminal LH IIIC ceramic stage at Aigeira

was so poorly attested that it is simply impossible, at present, to determine in detail how it may differ from its predecessor (cf. Rutter 1979: 383 [Corinth])!

Discussion

What, then, does the more fully documented Postpalatial pottery sequence at Aigeira have to teach us that we did not already know? Let us keep in mind that Aigeira was never a palatial site, and is not located in the traditional Peloponnesian and Central Greek heartlands of Mycenaean culture. On present evidence, it may have been newly occupied shortly after the palatial destructions in the Argolid, Messenia, and east-central Greece by people who were probably migrants, if not necessarily refugees, from one or more of those more centrally-located and culturally dominant regions. Their initial repertoire of ceramic containers was an altogether typical one for regions to the east, such as the Corinthia, the Argolid, western Attica, and western Euboea, with the single exception of the odd Aigeiran version of the Handmade Dark Burnished class that is, so far, paralleled only in the substantial fragments of jugs of a similar form from the site of Mt. Lykaion (see note 4, above; Jung 2006: 43-46). The new settlers at Aigeira evidently made their own pottery, but also acquired substantial quantities of it from non-local producers; especially examples of the Fine Reddish-brown Handmade class of APP 1 and 2, but also a large percentage of Pattern Painted kraters, deep bowls, and stirrup jars. That is to say, much of the finer and better-made pottery was, for some time, being imported. Some three to four decades after the site's reoccupation, at a rough estimate, an important change occurred, as Fine Reddish-brown Handmade ceased to be imported and White Ware versions of most of the same shapes began to circulate. Where this White Ware was produced is presently unknown, but there is no good reason to imagine that it should not have been local. For the next three, and perhaps as many as five, decades, Aigeira's inhabitants continued to make, and use, a range of shapes that stayed very much the same. Toward the end of that period, however, the shape and decorative repertoires of the tableware rather quickly became impoverished, possibly because the population of the settlement had decreased significantly...and then the site appears to have simply been abandoned, although how and why continues to be a mystery. At least until the end of what we have termed APP 4, during which the fortification wall at the east end of the acropolis was either first built or, at least, significantly thickened (Gauss 2015: 149-155, 160 fig. 1, 161 fig. 3), the people living at Aigeira seem to have remained reasonably prosperous and in touch with stylistic developments in areas to the east and, increasingly toward the end of the phase, to the west. The ceramic assemblage, overall, is remarkably conservative in its shape repertoire from beginning to end. Also striking is the minimal attention devoted to decoration, other than on those kraters and occasional kalathoi used for the mixing of wine and water at significant social occasions, or the small, closed shapes that appear to have been largely reserved for deposition with the dead (Mountjoy 1999: 404-405, 416-421, 425-430, 432-439, figs. 146-157). As a consequence, telling time at Aigeira with the aid of pottery necessarily relies heavily on significant changes in fabrics and on distinctions in vessel-shaping technology. While the drinking and eating vessels used by individuals were strikingly uniform in design and decoration (that is, their cups, dippers, kylikes, and bowls), those vessels intended for use by groups of people, such as nuclear families or wider kinship groupings or social circles (including kraters, kalathoi, and perhaps also the containers of perfumed oils and unguents), were more lavishly and distinctively decorated. No two kraters in contemporaneous use at the site appear to have been decorated with exactly the same patterns, so far as we can tell, whereas scores of cups and bowls are decorated almost identically. The only other functional ceramic type to be decorated in the post-palatial village of Aigeira consisted of gigantic storage jars, or pithoi, the relatively simple plastic and impressed or incised ornament (Figure 15.16) of which may have served to mark the hands of individual producers, rather than to reflect the choices of the social groups who may have commissioned pattern-painted fine ware vessels intended for communal use. The plentiful evidence for LH IIIC pithoi from the 1970s excavations at Aigeira, presently under study for final publication by Eva Alram-Stern, may have much to tell us, as may detailed study of the variety of local fabrics and vessel-shaping methods employed in the production of smaller shapes.

Addendum

A new volume in the series of Aigeira site publications was published after a preliminarily edited version of this article had been proofread and resubmitted: Aigeira 2. Die Mykenische Akropolis. Grabungen 1975-1980. Stratigraphie und Bebauung (Alram-Stern 2020). This volume contains an illustrated catalogue of the most completely preserved LH IIIC pots recovered on the acropolis of Aigeira during the 1975-1980 excavations (Deger-Jalkotzy 2020), and a second illustrated catalogue devoted to the numerous pithos fragments (Alram-Stern 2020: 189-226). It was not possible to include here references to specific comparanda which exist in these two contributions, although exist they do, and readers interested in exploring them are directed toward the volume.

Bibliography

Alram-Stern, E. 2003. Aigeira – acropolis: the stratigraphy, in S. Deger-Jalkotzy and M. Zavadil (eds) *LH IIIC Chronology and Synchronisms. Proceedings of the International Workshop Held at the Austrian Academy of Sciences at Vienna, May 7th and 8th, 2001* (Österreichische Akademie der Wissenschaften Philosophisch-Historische Klasse Denkschriften 310, Veröffentlichungen der Mykenischen Kommission 20): 15-21. Vienna: the Austrian Academy of Sciences.

Alram-Stern, E. 2007. Characteristic small finds of LH IIIC from Aigeira and their context, in S. Deger-Jalkotzy and M. Zavadil (eds) *LH III C Chronology and Synchronisms II: LH III C Middle. Proceedings of the International Workshop Held at the Austrian Academy of Sciences at Vienna, October 29th and 30th, 2004*

(Österreichische Akademie der Wissenschaften Philosophisch-Historische Klasse Denkschriften 362, Veröffentlichungen der Mykenischen Kommission 28): 15-25. Vienna: the Austrian Academy of Sciences.

Alram-Stern, E. 2020a. Aigeira 2. *Die Mykenische Akropolis. Grabungen 1975-1980. Stratigraphie und Bebauung.* Vienna: the Austrian Academy of Sciences.

Alram-Stern, E. and S. Deger-Jalkotzy (eds) 2006. *Die österreichischen Ausgrabungen von Aigeira in Achaia, Aigeira I. Die Mykenische Akropolis. Faszikel 3. Vormykenische Keramik, Kleinfunde, Archäozoologische und Archäobotanische Hinterlassenschaften, Naturwissenschaftliche Datierung* (Veröffentlichungen der Mykenischen Kommission 24. Sonderschriften des Österreichischen Archäologischen Institutes 43). Vienna: the Austrian Academy of Sciences.

Alzinger, W., E. Alram-Stern and S. Deger-Jalkotzy 1985. Aigeira-Hyperesia und die Siedlung Phelloë in Achaia. Österreichische Ausgrabungen auf der Peloponnes 1972-1983. Teil I: Akropolis. *Klio: Beiträge zur Alten Geschichte* 67: 389-451.

Arena, E. 2020. Mycenaean Achaea before and after the collapse, in G.D. Middleton (ed.) *Collapse and Transformation. The Late Bronze Age to Early Iron Age in the Aegean*: 35-43. Oxford: Oxbow Books.

Choleva, M. 2012. The first wheelmade pottery at Lerna: wheel-thrown or wheel-fashioned? *Hesperia: the Journal of the American School of Classical Studies at Athens* 81(3): 343-381.

Choleva, M. 2015a. L'Apparition et la Diffusion du Tour du Potier dans le Monde Égéen. Unpublished PhD dissertation, University of Panthéon-Sorbonne (Paris 1).

Choleva, M. 2015b. Περιστρέφοντας τον κεραμικό τροχό στο Παλαμάρι Σκύρου: Νέες τεχνολογικές πρακτικές και κεραμικές παραδόσεις στο Αιγαίο της Πρώιμης Εποχής του Χαλκού, in L. Parlama, M.D. Theochari, C. Romanou and S. Bonatsos (eds) *Ο οχυρωμένος προϊστορικός οικισμός στο Παλαμάρι Σκύρου: Διεπιστημονική συνάντηση για το έργο έρευνας και ανάδειξης, Αθήνα, 23-24 Οκτωβρίου 2012*: 143-166. Athens: the Scientific Committee of Palamari Skyros.

Choleva, M. 2018a. Παράγοντας έναν τεχνίτη για τον τροχό στο προϊστορικό Αιγαίο της 3ης χιλιετίας π.Χ: προς μια κοινωνική θεώρηση της τεχνικής πράξη. *Krisi* 3(2018/1): 53-94.

Choleva, M. 2018b. Craft behaviours during a period of transformation: the introduction and adoption of the potter's wheel in Central Greece during the Early Bronze Age, in I. Caloi and C. Langohr (eds) *Technology in Crisis. Technological Changes in Ceramic Production during Periods of Trouble* (Aegis 16): 45-74. Louvain: Louvain University Press.

Choleva, M. 2018c. L'histoire d'un savoir-faire. La transmission du tour de potier et l'émergence de nouvelles traditions technologiques dans le monde égéen préhistorique. *Annales de la Fondation Fyssen* 33: 192-215.

Deger-Jalkotzy, S. 1977. *Fremde Zuwanderer im spätmykenischen Griechenland. Zu einer Gruppe handgemachter Keramik aus den Myk. IIIC Siedlungsschichten von Aigeira* (Österreichische Akademie der Wissenschaften Philosophisch-Historische Klasse Sitzungsberichte 326). Vienna: the Austrian Academy of Sciences.

Deger-Jalkotzy, S. 1994. The post-palatial period of Greece: an Aegean prelude to the 11th century B.C. in Cyprus, in V. Karageorghis (ed.) *Proceedings of the International Symposium 'Cyprus in the 11th Century B.C.' Organized by the Archaeological Research Unit of the University of Cyprus and the Anastasios G. Leventis Foundation, Nicosia, 30–31 October, 1993*: 11-29. Nicosia: A.G. Leventis Foundation.

Deger-Jalkotzy, S. 2003. Stratified pottery deposits from the Late Helladic IIIC settlement at Aigeira/Achaia, in S. Deger-Jalkotzy and M. Zavadil (eds) *LH IIIC Chronology and Synchronisms. Proceedings of the International Workshop Held at the Austrian Academy of Sciences at Vienna, May 7th and 8th, 2001* (Österreichische Akademie der Wissenschaften Philosophisch-Historische Klasse Denkschriften 310, Veröffentlichungen der Mykenischen Kommission 20): 53-75. Vienna: the Austrian Academy of Sciences.

Deger-Jalkotzy, S. (2020) Mykenische Ganzgefässe und Grossfragmente in Situ, in E. Alram-Stern. *Aigeira 2. Die Mykenische Akropolis. Grabungen 1975-1980. Stratigraphie und Bebauung*: 237-284. Vienna: the Austrian Academy of Sciences.

Deger-Jalkotzy, S. and E. Alram-Stern. 1985. Die mykenische Siedlung, in W. Alzinger *et al.* Aigeira-Hyperesia und die Siedlung Phelloë in Achaia. Österreichische Ausgrabungen auf der Peloponnes 1972-1983. Teil I: Akropolis. *Klio: Beiträge zur Alten Geschichte* 67: 391-426.

Evely, D. (ed.) 2006. *Lefkandi IV. The Bronze Age: the Late Helladic IIIC Settlement at Xeropolis* (The British School at Athens Supplementary Volume 39). London: the British School at Athens.

Gauss, W. 2009. The last Mycenaeans at Aigeira and their successors, in S. Deger-Jalkotzy and A.E. Bächle (eds) *LH III C Chronology and Synchronisms III: LH III C Late and the Transition to the Early Iron Age. Proceedings of the International Workshop Held at the Austrian Academy of Sciences at Vienna, February 23rd and 24th, 2007* (Österreichische Akademie der Wissenschaften Philosophisch-Historische Klasse Denkschriften 384, Veröffentlichungen der Mykenischen Kommission 30): 163-182. Vienna: the Austrian Academy of Sciences.

Gauss, W. 2015. Überlegungen zur mykenischen Befestigungsmauer und 'Unterstadt' von Aigeira, in S. Nawracala and R. Nawracala (eds) ΠΟΛΥΜΑΘΕΙΑ: *Festschrift für Hartmut Matthäus anlässlich seines 65. Geburtstages*: 149-162. Aachen: Shaker.

Gauss, W., R. Smetana, J.B. Rutter, J. Dorner, P. Eitzinger, C. Klein, A. Kurz, A. Lätzer-Lasar, M. Leibetseder,

C. Regner, H. Stümpel, A. Tanner, C. Trainor and M. Trapichler 2013. Aigeira 2012. Bericht zu Aufarbeitung und Grabung. *Jahreshefte des Österreichischen Archäologischen Institutes in Wien* 82: 69-91.

Gauss, W., R. Smetana, J.B. Rutter, C. Regner, K. Rusch, H. Stümpel, W. Rabbel, F. Ruppenstein, J. Heiden, M. Leibetseder, A. Tanner, and C. Hinker 2015. Aigeira 2013-2014. Bericht zu Aufarbeitung und Grabung. *Jahreshefte des Österreichischen Archäologischen Institutes in Wien* 84: 11-50.

Jung, R. 2006. *Χρονολογία Comparata. Vergleichende Chronologie von Südgriechenland und Süditalien von ca. 1700/1600 bis 1000 v.u.Z.* (Veröffentlichungen der Mykenischen Kommission 26). Vienna: the Austrian Academy of Sciences.

Kardamaki, E. 2015. Conclusions from the new deposit at the Western Staircase terrace at Tiryns, in A-L. Schallin and I. Tournavitou (eds) *Mycenaeans up to Date: the Archaeology of the Northeastern Peloponnese – Current Concepts and New Directions* (Skrifter utgivna av Svenska Intitutet i Athen, 4°, 56): 79-97. Stockholm: the Swedish Institute at Athens.

Kaza-Papageorgiou, K., E. Kardamaki, P. Kouti, E. Markopoulou and N. Mouka 2011. Κοντοπήγαδο Ἀλίμου Ἀττικῆς. Οἰκισμός των ΠΕ καί ΥΕ χρόνων καί ΥΕ ἐργαστηριακή ἐγκατάσταση. *Ἀρχαιολογική Ἐφημερίς* 150(2011): 197-274.

Lis, B. 2009. Handmade and burnished pottery in the Eastern Mediterranean at the end of the Bronze Age: towards an explanation for its diversity and geographical distribution, in C. Bachhuber and R.G. Roberts (eds) *Forces of Transformation: the End of the Bronze Age in the Mediterranean: Proceedings of an International Symposium Held at St. John's College, University of Oxford, 25th-26th March 2006* (British Association for Near Eastern Archaeology Monograph 1): 152-163. Oxford: Oxbow Books.

Lis, B. 2016. A foreign potter in the Pylian kingdom? A reanalysis of the ceramic assemblage of Room 60 in the Palace of Nestor at Pylos. *Hesperia: the Journal of the American School of Classical Studies at Athens* 85(3): 491-536.

Lis, B. 2017. Variability of ceramic production and consumption on the Greek mainland during the middle stages of the Late Bronze Age: the waterpots from the Menelaion, Sparta. *Oxford Journal of Archaeology* 36(3): 243-266.

Lis, B. 2018. Hand-made pottery groups in mainland Greece during the 13th and 12th c. BC as a sign of economic crisis?, in I. Caloi and C. Langohr (eds) *Technology in Crisis. Technological Changes in Ceramic Production during Periods of Trouble* (Aegis 16): 139-150. Louvain: Louvain University Press.

Lis, B., H. Mommsen, J. Maran, and S. Prillwitz 2020. Investigating pottery production and consumption patterns at the Late Mycenaean cemetery of Perati. *Journal of Archaeological Science:*

Reports 32, 102453. https://doi.org/10.1016/j.jasrep.2020.102453.

Livieratou, A. 2020. East Lokris-Phokis, in G.D. Middleton (ed.) *Collapse and Transformation: the Late Bronze Age to Early Iron Age in the Aegean*: 97-106. Oxford: Oxbow Books.

Moschos, I. 2002. Western Achaea during the LH IIIC period. Approaching the latest excavation evidence, in E. Greco (ed.) *Gli Achei e l'identità etnica degli Achei d'occidente. Atti del Convegno Internazionale di Studi, Paestum, 23-25 febbraio 2001* (Fondazione Paestum, Tekmeria 3): 15-41. Paestum and Athens: Pandemos and The Italian School of Archaeology at Athens.

Moschos, I. 2009. Evidence of social re-organization and reconstruction in Late Helladic IIIC Achaea and modes of contacts and exchange via the Ionian and Adriatic Sea, in E. Borgna and P. Cassola Guida (eds) *Dall'Egeo all'Adriatico: organizzazioni sociali, modi di scambio e interazione in età postpalaziale (XII-XI sec. a.C.) Atti del Seminario internazionale (Udine, 1-2 dicembre 2006)*: 345-414. Rome: Quasar.

Mountjoy, P.A. 1986. *Mycenaean Decorated Pottery: A Guide to Identification* (Studies in Mediterranean Archaeology 73). Gothenburg: Paul Åström.

Mountjoy, P.A. 1999. *Regional Mycenaean Decorated Pottery*. Rahden: Marie Leidorf.

Mountjoy, P.A. 2007. A definition of LH III C Middle, in S. Deger-Jalkotzy and M. Zavadil (eds) *LH III C Chronology and Synchronisms II: LH III C Middle. Proceedings of the International Workshop Held at the Austrian Academy of Sciences at Vienna, October 29th and 30th, 2004* (Österreichische Akademie der Wissenschaften Philosophisch-Historische Klasse Denkschriften 362, Veröffentlichungen der Mykenischen Kommission 28): 221-242. Vienna: the Austrian Academy of Sciences.

Mühlenbruch, T. 2020. The Argolid, in G.D. Middleton (ed.) *Collapse and Transformation: the Late Bronze Age to Early Iron Age in the Aegean*: 121-135. Oxford: Oxbow Books.

Phialon, L. 2018. L'habitat de Krisa (Chrysso-Haghios Georgios) à l'âge du Bronze: un réexamen de la topographie du site et de la céramique. *Bulletin de Correspondance Hellénique* 142(2): 403-536.

Popham, M., E. Schofield and S. Sherratt. 2006. The pottery, in D. Evely (ed.) *Lefkandi IV. The Bronze Age: the Late Helladic IIIC Settlement at Xeropolis* (The British School at Athens Supplementary Volume 39): 137-231. London: the British School at Athens.

Rutter, J.B. 1977. Late Helladic III C pottery and some historical implications, in E.N. Davis (ed.) *Symposium on the Dark Ages in Greece, Sponsored by the Archaeological Institute of America, New York Society and Hunter College, City University of New York, April 30, 1977*: 1-20. New York: Hunter College.

Rutter, J.B. 1979. The last Mycenaeans at Corinth. *Hesperia: the Journal of the American School of Classical Studies at Athens* 48(4): 348-392.

Rutter, J.B. 2007. How different is LH IIIC Middle at Mitrou? An initial comparison with Kalapodi, Kynos, and Lefkandi, in S. Deger-Jalkotzy and M. Zavadil (eds) *LH III C Chronology and Synchronisms II: LH III C Middle. Proceedings of the International Workshop Held at the Austrian Academy of Sciences at Vienna, October 29th and 30th, 2004* (Österreichische Akademie der Wissenschaften Philosophisch-Historische Klasse Denkschriften 362, Veröffentlichungen der Mykenischen Kommission 28): 287-300. Vienna: the Austrian Academy of Sciences.

Rutter, J.B. 2020. Late Palatial versus early Postpalatial Mycenaean pottery (c. 1250-1150 BC): ceramic change during an episode of cultural collapse and regeneration, in G.D. Middleton (ed.) *Collapse and Transformation: the Late Bronze Age to Early Iron Age in the Aegean*: 209-219. Oxford: Oxbow Books.

Stockhammer, P. 2009. New evidence for Late Helladic IIIC Late pottery from Tiryns, in S. Deger-Jalkotzy and A.E. Bächle (eds) *LH III C Chronology and Synchronisms III: LH III C Late and the Transition to the Early Iron Age. Proceedings of the International Workshop Held at the Austrian Academy of Sciences at Vienna, February 23rd and 24th, 2007* (Österreichische Akademie der Wissenschaften Philosophisch-Historische Klasse Denkschriften 384, Veröffentlichungen der Mykenischen Kommission 30): 345-358. Vienna: the Austrian Academy of Sciences.

Vitale, S. 2006. The LH IIIB-LH IIIC transition on the Mycenaean mainland: ceramic phases and terminology. *Hesperia: the Journal of the American School of Classical Studies at Athens* 75(2): 177-204.

Vitale, S. 2018. The troubled century? Potting practices and socio-political changes at Mitrou, east Lokris between the end of the 14th and the beginning of the 12th c. BC, in I. Caloi and C. Langohr (eds) *Technology in Crisis. Technological Changes in Ceramic Production during Periods of Trouble* (Aegis 16): 151-176. Louvain: Louvain University Press.

Voyatzis, M. 2019. Enduring rituals in the Arcadian mountains: the case of the Sanctuary of Zeus at Mt. Lykaion, in I.S. Lemos and A. Tsingarida (eds) *Beyond the Polis: Rituals, Rites and Cults in Early and Archaic Greece (12th-6th Centuries BC)* (Études d'archéologie 15): 133-146. Brussels: Research Centre in Archaeology and Heritage (CReA-Patrimoine).

Coarse Labours Long Continued: Cooking Vessels, Culinary Technology and Prehistoric Foodways at Phylakopi, Melos[1]

David Michael Smith

Introduction

What remains of Phylakopi today occupies a heavily eroded headland on the northwest coast of the Cycladic Island of Melos; the crest of a prehistoric promontory across which the settlement expanded during the course of the Bronze Age, and below which a modest harbour provided ready access to the maritime networks which linked Melos to the rest of the Cycladic archipelago and the wider Aegean.

The site, and particularly the cemeteries in its hinterland, had attracted the attention of looters and antiquarians since the early 19th century AD (Hogarth 1904: 24; Ross 1845: iii, 13; Smith 1895-1896: 75; 1896-1897: 8; Weil 1876: 246), although its first systematic investigation was begun under the aegis of the British School at Athens in May 1896.[2] By the beginning of June 1899, four years of excavation had exposed a complex Early Cycladic (EC) to Late Cycladic (LC) sequence of fills, floors and standing architecture across an area of *c.* 1.8ha, and to a maximum depth of *c.* 6.5m.[3] The volume of pottery generated by this work was extraordinary. Campbell Edgar, the project's de facto ceramicist, records a daily yield of between forty and

fifty 'basketfuls' during 1898 (Edgar 1897-1898: 37) and between 10,000 and 20,000 sherds during 1899 (Edgar 1898-1899: 14).[4] During 1898, all of this material was held for inspection.[5] By 1899, however, the regular recurrence of the same shapes and designs prompted greater selectivity, and the retention of a far smaller percentage of the total count. Those consignments of pottery which arrived to the National Archaeological Museum at Athens at the close of each excavation season were, then, only a representative selection of the total recovered, subject to further selection bias as work on Melos progressed and thinned again during post-excavation study at Athens between 1897 and the beginning of 1904 (see Edgar 1904: 81). Much that survived is addressed only cursorily within the final publication of the excavation; coarse and undecorated pieces, as might be expected, attracted least attention.[6]

The material from the 1896-1899 excavation in the collection of the National Archaeological Museum at Athens has, since 2010, been the subject of a comprehensive programme of restudy in advance of full publication (see recently, Barber 2017).[7] The great

[1] Thanks, first and foremost, are due to Dr Robin Barber for his invitation to study various of the pottery groups from the early British School excavations at Phylakopi, and to the staff of the National Archaeological Museum at Athens for their kindness and cooperation over many seasons of work. Robin's call was relayed to me by Chris, and so it seems entirely fitting that the results of that study should form the focus of this contribution in his memory.

[2] An illegal three-day excavation had earlier been mounted in the southwest of the settlement by Georgios Ghiouroukis, later foreman for the British School excavation during 1896-1897, under the employ of Athenian antiquities dealer Athanasios Rhousopoulos (Smith 1896-1897: 8). This work is also noted in the excavation daybook for 1896 (1896: 5, n.1). A total of four daybooks were drafted by Duncan Mackenzie, corresponding to each year of work during the period from 1896 to 1899, and are today held in the archive of the British School at Athens. References to entries in the daybooks made below (henceforth, *Daybooks*) include the excavation year and the pagination of the original text, rather than the pagination of the unpublished typescript of these volumes completed by Colin Renfrew in 1963.

[3] A number of different dating conventions have been applied to the EC-LC remains at Phylakopi, including the tripartite 'City' sequence of Atkinson and colleagues, and the Phase A-F sequence defined during the 1974-1977 excavation. A separate sequence has also been defined for the LH remains in the area of the so-called Sanctuary (Renfrew 1985: 76). To minimise confusion, the following chapter retains the standard EC-LC convention. There is continued disagreement over the internal chronology of Phylakopi and its relationship to that of other Cycladic sites, particularly in regard to the later EC and early MC period, although in the context of this study, the impact of that uncertainty is negligible, and the discussion will not be repeated here.

[4] The estimates for 1898 and 1899 represent a considerable increase in the quantity of pottery recovered, relative to the total from previous seasons (Edgar 1904: 81). No record survives of the content of these 'baskets', save those noted in the 1898 preliminary report for metre-deep layers in Square Q (later redesignated Square F5): '3-400 fragments of Mycenaean ware, ordinary types and ornamentation; 20 fragments of local ware, chiefly from *pithos* with impressed bands in relief' and Squares F-G: '400 Mycenaean fragments, including many long-footed kylikes, 9 fragments of painted local ware, a few plain cups and 100 coarse fragments from pithoi with impressed bands, tripod pots, etc' (1897-1898: 47). The total sherd counts for these baskets are 320-420 and >510, respectively. This total correlates well with the recovery of several hundred fragments of EC pottery from the thirteenth layer (6-6.50m) of the J1 trial trench (Edgar 1897-1898: 39). At 300-500 sherds per basket, a yield of 40 baskets provides a very coarse estimate of 12,000-25,000 sherds per day during 1898. Extrapolating, a total yield for all seasons (105 field days in total) can be calculated at 1.26-2.625m sherds; at the lower estimate, the 1898 and 1899 seasons (34 and 35 days, respectively) alone could have delivered *c.* 828,000.

[5] 'The cleaned heaps, kept separate according to the depth at which each was found, were...looked through, a liberal selection was made for further study, and a rough record kept of what was thrown aside' (Edgar 1897-1898: 37).

[6] Sherds were initially marked in-field in pencil with the square and depth from which they derived. These 'excavation marks' survive only rarely on the coarse pottery and remain legible only in exceptional cases, with the result that much of the material under discussion lacks context.

[7] The assemblage has been further modified since its arrival at Athens. In 1902, some 800 'restored pots and fragments and [a] small selection of obsidian and other objects' from the British School

Figure 16.1. Map of selected sites discussed within the text.

excavations were presented to the Ashmolean Museum, Oxford (Sherratt 2000: 3, 216-359) and a smaller number of sherds to the Fitzwilliam Museum, Cambridge (Lamb 1936: 1-5, 14-15). A total of 43 vessels and sherds were presented to the British Museum by the British School in 1903 (Forsdyke 1925: 64-69; a very small number still within the School collection are identified as having come from Phylakopi). A group of *c.* 12 vessels and sherds from the Ashmolean group were subsequently presented to the Classical Museum of University College Dublin in 1910 by Hogarth (Haywood 2003: 12-13; Souyoudzoglou-Haywood 2007: 63), and an assemblage of 69 sherds from the personal collection of Thomas Atkinson was bequeathed to Winchester College in 1949. Over time, small numbers of vessels have travelled to the United States. These include a number of those previously presented to the Ashmolean Museum, which were acquired in exchange by the Metropolitan Museum of Art, New York in 1911 (Richter 1912); some within the collection of David Robinson (today at the University of Mississippi; see Robinson 1934: pl. VIII.1, pl. IX.7) and others at the Museum of Fine Art, Boston gifted by the National Museum at Athens in August 1914 (see Fairbanks 1928: 66-70, pl. XIX). At least one unpublished Middle Minoan cup (P.2128) in the collection of the Ella Riegel Memorial Museum at Bryn Mawr College is inked on its base with the word 'Phylakopi'. The veracity of the identification is unclear; it may have entered the collection during the late 1950s (Marianne Weldon, personal communication) and, although no record of the donor exists, several more 'Cycladic' sherds, including another attributed to Phylakopi (P.2000), were bequeathed to the museum by Mrs. H. Lamar Crosby, wife of the American Classicist Henry Lamar Crosby. A small collection of sherds from the site reached the Royal Museum of Art and History, Brussels, in 1901 (Mayence and Verhoogen 1949), although the route by which they travelled is unclear, as it is for those today in the Akademisches Kunstmuseum, Bonn (Kaiser 1976). Some 32 sherds, and a small number of other objects, were first loaned, and subsequently bequeathed, to the World Museum Liverpool by John Droop (see Mee and Doole 1993), although these likely derive from the 1911 season.

value of this study lies not only in the presentation of previously unpublished material, but in the opportunity it affords to contextualise that material with reference to subsequent work both on Melos, and throughout the Cyclades,[8] and to better position Phylakopi and its heavily modified, and often acontextual, material record, within more recent models of agency, identity, materiality and practice.

Food production, consumption and exchange have been shown to be uniquely susceptible to manipulation in the creation and negotiation of identity, and provides a potentially rewarding framework within which to address the legacy coarse assemblage. The following

This list is not exhaustive. The presence of old glue on breaks without corresponding joins at Athens suggests the existence of joins with some of this dispersed material.

[8] A supplementary excavation season undertaken on behalf of the British School by Richard Dawkins and John Droop in 1911 saw trial trenches opened across the northern sector with the aim of clarifying the ceramic sequence established by the earlier excavation. The 1911 pottery assemblage has since been published by Barber (1974; 2008). A modest EC ceramic assemblage was recovered during trial excavations by the Greek Archaeological Service to the west of the site in 1964 (Zapheiropoulou 1969) and is published by Renfrew and Evans (2007: 155-157). Material recovered by the 21st Ephorate of Prehistoric and Classical Antiquities during work at the site, between 2003 and 2008, remains unpublished (Marthari 2012).

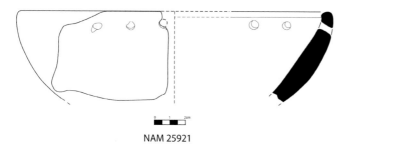

NAM 25921

NAM 25922

Figure 16.2. Perforated rim sherds belonging to Early Cycladic cheese-pots (acc. nos. NAM 25921 and 25922).
Drawing by Kalliope Theodoropoulou

contribution incorporates preliminary observations from study of the Phylakopian cooking assemblage to explore patterns of dietary choice, culinary technology and commensal practice at the site from its foundation during the Early Bronze Age to its abandonment at the very end of the Late Bronze Age, and their value to our understanding of shifting cultural influence in the Cyclades and those wide networks within which Melos operated.

The Early Cycladic period

Phylakopi is first occupied during late EC I (Nikolakopoulou 2019a: 34 table 1.1; Renfrew 2007a: 10 table 2.2). This phase, and the site's subsequent EC II occupation, are represented almost exclusively by diffuse fill deposits. [9]

Petrographic analyses have indicated that much of the pottery used at Phylakopi during EC I and EC II was manufactured on Melos (Vaughn and Williams 2007: 120-125), although low numbers of sherds identify the existence of networks connecting the island with Thera, and one or more of the islands of the so-called Keros Triangle (including Keros-Dhaskalio, Naxos, Ios and Amorgos; see Renfrew 2016: 397; Sotirakopoulou 2016: 14), and, in the distinctive talc fabric, perhaps Siphnos or Poros (see Sotirakopoulou 2016: 15-17; Vaughn and Wilson 1993). In the absence of secure early contexts, understanding how such relationships may have been manifested in diet and dining is now a very difficult proposition.

Pans and hearths

One shape that can be placed into the early part of the EC with some certainty is the (so-called) 'cheese-pot': a coarse, often shallow pan, typically smoothed at the interior only, and characterised by an irregular line of perforations through the vessel wall below the rim (Figure 16.2). Common throughout the Aegean, and extremely long-lived, the cheese-pot is visible in

the Cyclades already during the first phase of the Late Neolithic settlement at Ftelia (*c.* 5000 BC; Doukaki 2018; Sampson 2018) and remains in use perhaps into early EC II (see Broodbank 2007: 225).[10] The shape is recorded by Edgar within the fill of the J1,9 deep sounding, from which a large proportion of the earlier EC material was recovered at Phylakopi (1904: 84)[11] and four examples, all represented by rim fragments, are now preserved at the National Archaeological Museum; manufactured in fabrics consistent with a Melian provenance and varying in their rim diameters between 40 and 44cm. That the shape appears to survive as late at Phylakopi as anywhere else in the Cyclades (EC I-II) may hint at an absence of culinary innovation, or the conscious preservation of existing culinary tradition, within the first generations of the settlement.

The cheese-pot convention, as noted elsewhere, may prove to be a misnomer, given the absence of conclusive evidence of an association with cheese-making.[12] Indeed, the shape may have been relatively

---

[9] A single stone wall below the area of the later megaron, identified during the 1974–77 excavation, is apparently of EC I–II date (Renfrew et al. 2007: 49).

[10] The cheese-pot is also attested during the Late Neolithic at Grotta (Hadjianastasiou 1988: 17) and Saliagos (Evans and Renfrew 1968: fig. 40.2). It becomes widespread during the Final Neolithic (e.g., at Akrotiri: Sotirakopoulou 2008: 124; Antiparos Cave: Mavridis 2010: 23; Mavrispilia: Belmont and Renfrew 1964: pl. 127, fig. 9; Koukounaries: Katsarou and Schilardi 2004: 39; Katsarou-Tzeveleki and Schilardi 2008: 69-70; Kephala: Coleman 1977: 17-18; Mikrogiali: Televantou 2006: 2; Akrotiraki, Pitti Plot: Papadopoulou 2013: 41, fig. 3a; Paoura and Sykamias: Coleman 1972: 358-359; Zas Cave: Zachos and Dousougli, forthcoming; Ayios Sostis: Gropengiesser 1987: 40, fig. 4.19). Probable Early Cycladic examples are known from Kouphonisi (Karantzali 1996: 124), Palati (Karantzali 1996: 20) and Kat'Akrotiri (Yiannouli 2002), while those from Keros may be transitional EC I-II (Broodbank 2007: 165; Sotirakopoulou 2004a: 1334). The shape is being treated as a FN-EC II index for the forthcoming publication of the Keros Survey (Jill Hilditch, personal communication). For additional mainland and Aegean examples, see Georgiadis (2012: 50) and Sotirakopoulou (2008: 124).

[11] Room J1,9 was also investigated during the 1974-1977 excavations (Renfrew et al. 2007: 39-41). One cheese-pot sherd among the 1896-1899 material preserves a faint excavation mark which appears to read '3.5'. This would represent the upper limit of the uppermost layer of the sounding in which EC I-II material was recognised. It may also suggest recovery elsewhere on the site.

[12] Organic residue analysis has identified plant oil (18C unsaturated and 16C fatty acids) on an early example of the shape from Ftelia (Decavallas 2014; 2018: 261). The detection of plant oils on archaeological ceramics, however, has been shown to be problematic (Decavallas 2014: 246; Roumpou et al. 2007: 167; 2013: 37), as has the identification of the form in which it may have been present: as oil proper, as a by-product of the preparation of meals or medicines, as

multifunctional. It is considered a cooking pot or oven at Markiani I (Karantzali 2006: 106-107) and, where burnt, as a baking pan at Akrotiri (Sotirakopoulou 2008: 123). The absence of 'significant' burning on examples from Ayia Irini has prompted Wilson to posit an alternative use (1999: 13-14, nos. I-94-108). Sooting and burning at the exterior of those examples from Phylakopi makes clear their use on, or above, the fire. Burnishing at the interior may represent an attempt to improve heating efficiency and/or reduce the permeability of the vessel wall as a function of the presence of primarily liquid, oily or fatty (rather than dry) contents (see Schiffer 1990; also, Skibo 2012: 47-50). The same treatment may have prevented dough adhering to the interior wall (see Sarpaki 1987: 215; 2001). The perforations (0.4-0.5cm in diameter) which characterise the shape are commonly associated with the use of an organic cover.[13] One cheese-pot among the Phylakopi assemblage exhibits perforation through the vessel wall which has proved only partially successful. This phenomenon has been recognised elsewhere (Georgiadis 2012: 52) and suggests a degree of redundancy in their provision, although, for Phylakopi at least, it is impossible now to determine whether the rate of failure to perforate is generally consistent over time, or whether it reflects a gradual change in function for a traditional vessel form.

The disappearance of the cheese-pot from the Melian-Cycladic repertoire by the later EC II, and the parallel increase in the visibility of baking pan variants, is suggestive of a functional overlap between the two forms.[14] The more typical EC pan form can be recognised at least by EC III (see Renfrew and Evans 2007: 175, fig. 5.14.11; cf. Dhaskalio A Type A pan-hearth). One possible example of an EC pan with low wall and pushed-in rim (see, for example, Sotirakopoulou 2016: 99; Wilson 1999: 45-46) has been recognised at the National Archaeological Museum, although the identification is uncertain. Pans with cut-out or pushed-in rims may be considered to be more specialised, the modification perhaps serving to improve handling when full. Wilson (1999: 45) suggests that such vessels may have functioned as settling pans, perhaps for milk; at Dhaskalio C, at least some examples were utilised for copper metallurgy (see Sotirakopoulou 2016: 223), although there is, currently, no evidence that they were used for similar at Phylakopi.

Cooking pots

Coarse, open jars served as the cooking vessel of choice from the inception of the settlement, and represented a major component of its earlier EC ceramic assemblage.[15] The ubiquity and simplicity of the shape likely accounts for its relative underrepresentation among the material now in the National Archaeological Museum.

No complete example survives among the 1896-1899 assemblage. Interior surfaces may be smoothed or burnished, presumably for the same reasons as those of the pans noted above. Exterior surfaces may be plain or slipped, smoothed and/or occasionally scored.[16] Unpierced crescentic, semi-circular, and trapezoidal lug handles are commonly pressed onto the wall immediately below the exterior rim, sometimes with corresponding finger impressions at the interior, and sometimes burnt or sooted at the underside. A number of flat bases, burnt at interior and exterior, can probably be assigned to the same type. Several preserve mat-impressions[17] and, while the majority of mat-impressed bases were considered to be contemporary with Edgar's EC III-MC Geometric class (EMP and SMP; Barber 2008: 59-60; Edgar 1904: 95), they are present at Phylakopi from at least EC II (Cherry and Davis 2007: 410, table 10.1).[18]

Low pedestal bases are added to the shape at Phylakopi by EC III (Dawkins and Droop 1911: 7, no. 209; Renfrew and Evans 2007: 174, no. P104) in a development recognised too at EC II late Akrotiri (Müller 2009: 42). Low numbers of disembodied pedestal bases are present among the 1896-1899 material which have good parallels at Ayia Irini II (for example, Wilson 1999: 33, no. II-143), although the type survives into MC early. A small number of perforated pedestal bases may be EC III, based on parallels from Akrotiri Phase A (for example, Nikolakopoulou 2019b: 84, no. 424).

The addition of the pedestal base should be understood to have conveyed some benefit for existing cooking practices, although how far it reflects difference in

---

an additive to improve surface burnish (Decavallas 2014: 243) or as a sealing agent to reduce permeability of the vessel wall (Heron and Evershed 1993: 257-258).

[13] See, for example, Cultraro (2013: 108).

[14] The disc/plate seen at Markiani I (Karantzali 2006: 107) may represent a precursor to the larger EC II pan types, although it is extremely rare (Dhaskalio A, Type G pan-hearth: Sotirakopoulou 2016: 40; Kato Akrotiri: Yiannouli 2002: 28-29).

[15] Notably from the basal layers of the J1,9 sounding (5m-6.50m; *Daybooks* 1898: 24). Cheese-pots were also included among this group (Edgar 1904: 84).

[16] A common phenomenon characterised by multiple relatively deep, parallel (though often multidirectional) lines created by a heavy brush or other tool while the vessel is still soft (see, for example, Coleman 1977: 10; Sotirakopoulou 2016: 25; Yiannouli 2002: 13). The treatment may be more functional than aesthetic.

[17] For mat impressions more generally, see Carington Smith (1975, 1977) and Labriola (2008).

[18] Additional examples of certain (AE511) and possible (AE569c and AE1205) EC III date are present within the collections of the Ashmolean Museum (Sherratt 2000: 357-359) and the British Museum (no. 1903.0716.41, Forsdyke 1925: 67, no. A361). The absence from Phylakopi of EC I examples is likely an artefact of the low diagnostic count among the 1974-1977 'course thin' and 'course thick' classes (Renfrew and Evans 2007: 139), particularly given their earlier identification at Markiani I (J. Renfrew 2006) and Ayia Irini I (Wilson 1999: 13). The latest published examples from Phylakopi belong to LC I.

cuisine or cooking technique with those flat-based versions which remained in use is unclear. A large low pedestal would have had the effect of lowering the vessel's centre of gravity and would, thereby, have delivered it an additional stability (see Wilson 1999: 32). It is possible, too, that it would have improved heat transmission from exterior to interior through the lower body for vessels placed directly in the fire, increasing internal temperature, reducing fuel requirements, and improving cooking time.

It is equally possible that some bases derive not from cooking jars, but from examples of the smaller one-handled cooking jug, of a type present at Akrotiri, and at Kastro on Paros, during the very late EC (see Müller *et al.* 2015: 38; Nikolakopoulou 2019a: 207; Overbeck 1989a: 2 and fig. 44; Rubensohn 1917: 31; Sotirakopoulou 2008: 127). An extremely heavy example with a flat base and pulled spout in a red-brown micaceous fabric (Figure 16.3; also, Atkinson *et al.* 1904: pl. XXXV.14), is likely to be EC, but is not readily paralleled. These vessels may have sat in the fire during use, or they may have been suspended at an angle above it (see Nikolakopoulou 2019a: 207), as the recipe dictated.[19]

Hearths or braziers

The restudy of the 1896-1899 assemblage has yielded a surprising number of raised portable hearth or brazier fragments. The earliest of these, a rimless type in talc fabric, should belong to EC II.[20] To a late stage of the EC should belong multiple examples of a red slipped and burnished variant on a conical base, currently designated Phylakopi Type A (Figure 16.4). The shape has not previously been recognised on Melos, although it can be paralleled at Dhaskalio C (Sotirakopoulou 2016: 227-228) and Akrotiri MC Phase A (Doumas 2014: 13, fig. 10c; Nikolakopoulou 2019b: 112, no. 554; Sotirakopoulou 2008: 128, fig. 14.15). No single fragment is taller than 10cm and, in the absence of a complete profile, it is difficult to estimate an original height.[21] These objects were probably furnished with horizontal handles to aid portability (Nikolakopoulou 2019a: 112, no. 554; Sotirakopoulou 2008: 128, fig. 14.15),[22] although none of the Phylakopi examples preserve handle roots or scars. The Type A hearth-brazier

NAM 5814 (not to scale)

Figure 16.3. Early Cycladic heavy one-handled cooking jug with pinched spout (acc. no. NAM 5814).

is produced in a coarse volcanic fabric consistent with Melian manufacture, and is coated with a thick, burnished dark red slip which runs across the upper surface of the pan and terminates immediately below the exterior rim. The underside is always plain and more or less roughly smoothed. Rim diameters are grouped closely between *c.* 42cm and 46cm (with a single, smaller outlier at *c.* 34cm) and profiles are, generally, shallow and flaring.

The Type B hearth-brazier, currently represented by a single fragment, differs from Type A in that it appears to rest on narrow, wide tripod legs, and may be compared to similar examples from Mount Kynthos (Plassart 1928: 34, fig. 33) and perhaps Ayia Irini III (Wilson 1999: 113, no. III-178). A third variant, Type C, is currently recognised in a further fragment which lacks a cut-out, but possesses a circular perforation through its side wall. Whether the distinction between Type A and C is simply an artefact of preservation is currently unclear. As a group, these objects may also be compared with a rimless type with concave pan from EC II Skarkos (Marthari 1999: 20-21, fig. 9; Sotirakopoulou 2008: 128) and with the so-called tripod tables of Poliochni Blue-Green (Bernabò Brea 1964: 578).[23]

The restricted application of burnished slip may well be functional, given the appearance of heavy red slip on other flat based pan-hearths at Phylakopi and Ayia Irini (Wilson 1999: 58). The burn patterns on these objects, again, display some variation. Burning on the underside

---

[19] One example from Kastro (Type H5 deep globular pedestalled jar, Nikolakopoulou 2019a: 206) was found in-situ with other similar vessels on the floor of Room 3, covered by a stone lid and containing the bones of small animals (Overbeck 1989: 13; Rubensohn 1917). This would seem certain to represent part of a meal. If the lid was used during cooking, then the jug must have been set flat, rather than tilted. Alternatively, the lid may simply have been placed afterward, to keep the contents of the jug warm, or dust and insect free.

[20] Talc Ware is most common at Phylakopi during EC II, but is represented at the site throughout the EC period (Renfrew and Evans 2007: 138, 168-169).

[21] One example from Akrotiri A is estimated at *c.* 27cm (see Nikolakopoulou 2019b: pl. XXIV, no. 554).

[22] Also, compare the EM IIA baking pan on low wide feet from the Southeast Kitchen at Myrtos (Warren 1972: 51, 112-113).

[23] These tables are burnished only across their upper surface and red-slip, though rare, is attested. On material networks linking the Cyclades and the northern Aegean during the Early Bronze Age, see Sotirakopoulou (1997).

NAM 26006

Figure 16.4. Early Cycladic Phylakopi Type A hearth-brazier, with large curvilinear cut-out at exterior wall (acc. no. NAM 26006).

indicates use over a small fire. Burning on the upper surface of the pan — almost always with an unburnt 'halo' close to the rim — could reflect the burning of foodstuffs or oil, or the spreading of coals, ashes or embers. The shallow concavity of the pan suggests a relatively low carrying capacity, unless ashes and embers were heaped up around (and over?) the food itself. The unburnt halo seen on the interior of the pan might plausibly result from the use of a large lid or inverted bowl which would have, effectively, transformed these braziers into an oven, concentrating heat in the centre of the pan and protecting its periphery from damage or discolouration.[24]

These objects are not easily categorised as secondary hearths, despite the low visibility of fixed hearths at Early Cycladic Phylakopi.[25] They may have been intended for open air use, although one example from

Dhaskalio C was recovered within a probable upper floor collapse deposit which also yielded a second baking pan or hearth with *kerbschnitt* decoration, and a large quantity of carbonised seeds, shells, and olive wood charcoal (see Renfrew *et al.* 2013: 144-149). It seems probable, then, that they were (also?) used inside the house, perhaps for subsidiary processing or cooking activities away from the primary kitchen space. A similar use of upper floor rooms can also be seen at MC Ayia Irini IV (see Overbeck 1989b: 155).

The Middle Cycladic period

The MC settlement at Phylakopi is far better represented than that of the preceding EC period, although the general absence of published remains from other of the Cycladic islands makes it extremely difficult to accurately assess the nature of its intra-Cycladic relationships.[26] From the very beginning of the MC period at Phylakopi, however, there is evidence for contact with Crete (Hood 2007: 250) which sees the introduction of Cretan shapes, and perhaps new modes of cooking, to Melos.

---

[24] Compare the modern *gastra* or *ponitse* (Efstratiou 1992; Hruby 2008).

[25] The only certain EC fixed hearth at Phylakopi dates late in the period (Trench ΠC Floor 8, Renfrew *et al.* 2007: 46-47, pl. 7a) and consists of two flat stones overlain by a deposit of charcoal and burnt earth. The presence of a built 'grain bin' (not sampled) and a quern and mortar in the same room suggest a kitchen or food preparation area. No cooking vessels are explicitly identified within the associated pottery assemblage (ΠC layers 105-116), although a handful of bowls, deep- and hole-mouthed jars might plausibly have served as such. A second late EC or early MC hearth is perhaps described by Hogarth (1904: 20-21). A fragment belonging to a coarse fixed terracotta hearth of probable EC date has now been identified among the 1896-1899 assemblage.

[26] Relatively few excavated Middle Cycladic ceramic assemblages are well published, and still fewer coarse groups (see Sotirakopoulou 2004b; 2010). The most comprehensive are those of the early and late MC phases at Ayia Irini (Davis 1986; Overbeck 1989b) and the recently published MC sequence from Akrotiri (Nikolakopoulou 2009; 2013; 2019a; 2019b; Nikolakopoulou *et al.* 2008; Roumpou *et al.* 2013). See also Kordatzaki *et al.* (2018) for MC material from Therasia, and Marthari (2001) for material from early MC Ftellos.

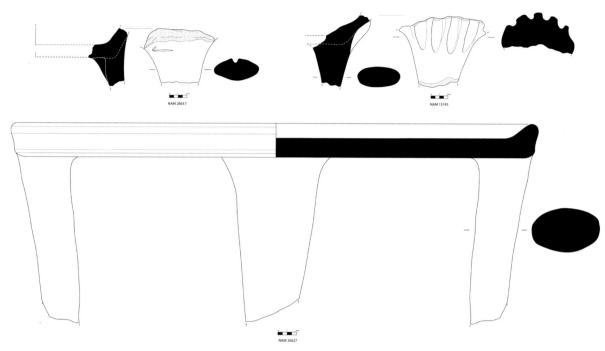

Figure 16.5. Middle Cycladic tripod cooking shapes, including coarse tripod cooking tray (acc. no. NAM 26627).

Cooking pots

Locally-manufactured wide-mouthed jars with everted rims continue to form a fundamental component of the cooking pot repertoire at Phylakopi into the MC period[27] and seem clearly to reflect the survival of EC cooking techniques and recipes at the site. Given that the shape is largely represented by rim fragments, the relative frequency of flat- or pedestal-based variants is not clear. At other sites, however, there is a shift away from the use of pedestal-based cooking shapes after the beginning of the MC.[28]

The occasional application of plastic studs at the shoulder of these vessels suggests, perhaps, a new concern with the aesthetic of even coarse cooking pots during the period. Other jar types seem to also have served as cooking vessels, albeit less frequently, although whether this was as a result of convention or functionality is not clear.[29] During the late MC, a tradition of cooking pot manufacture in Cycladic White fabric is apparent at Panaghia Koimisis on Therasia (Kordatzaki *et al.* 2018), although there is no evidence of such within the Cycladic White assemblage from Phylakopi.

Tripod cooking jars and trays

The characteristic Minoanising cooking pot shape, the tripod cooking jar, very likely arrives at Phylakopi, as elsewhere in the Cyclades, during the earlier Middle Cycladic (see Barber 2007: 231; Nikolakopoulou 2019a: 53). It appears on Crete during EM I at Phaistos (Todaro 2005: 44), and perhaps Debla (Warren, Tzedhakis, and Greig 1974: 329), and an Anatolian(ising) type is visible at Ayia Photia by EM IIA (see Davaras and Betancourt 2004; 2012; Shank 2005: 105). It may well be that similarly early versions of the tripod cooking pot found their way into the Cycladic archipelago during the EC period, although there is, simply, very little evidence for their presence prior to the early MC.[30]

As might be expected, the tripod cooking pot is represented at Phylakopi primarily by a modest assemblage of disembodied legs,[31] circular-ovoid in section (more or less flattened), with or without vertical slashes or grooves at the shoulder which, in addition to any aesthetic value, should have improved the strength of the join of the leg to the body and facilitated firing to the core. Such legs are difficult to date in isolation. Similar slashing is visible throughout the MC and LC period on legs from Ayia Irini (for example, Overbeck 1989b: 25), from the MC late-LC early cemetery at

---

[27] See particularly, Barber's coarse Type 17 wide-mouthed jar (Atkinson et al. 1904: pl. XXXV.15; Barber 2007: 225).
[28] See, for example, the pedestal-based Type H7 and flat-based Type H8 funnel-mouthed cooking jug at Akrotiri (Nikolakopoulou 2019a: 207-208). A similar change seems to be evident on examples of the wide-mouthed jar at Ayia Irini (see Gorogianni et al. 2017: 59-63).
[29] For example, Barber's Type 16a jar (2007: 222, no. 294), and a 'low-necked' type from Ayia Irini IV (Overbeck 1989b: 91).

[30] A single tripod leg fragment from Markiani IV (EC III early?) is identified as part of a cooking pot (Eskitzioglou 2006: 143) and disembodied legs, perhaps to be associated with cooking shapes, are noted from other EC sites (see Sotirakopoulou 2016: 125, with references).
[31] Plentiful at the site, according to Mackenzie (*Daybooks* 1898: 24) and from later excavations (see Barber 2007: 231; 2008: 160).

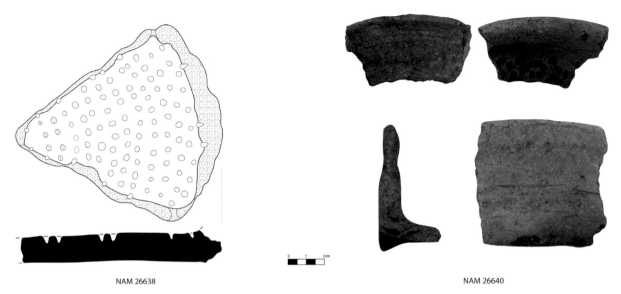

NAM 26638

NAM 26640

*Figure 16.6. Late Cycladic griddle pans of mainland type, including probable 'low-walled' (acc. no. NAM 26638) and 'high-walled'
(acc. no. NAM 26640) variants. Drawing by Kalliope Theodoropoulou.*

Skarkos (Marthari 2009: 52-53, fig. 28),[32] and at LC I Akrotiri (Doumas 2014: 45, fig. 40a; Marinatos 1969: 23, fig. 14). Among the 1896-1899 assemblage is a leg in a probable Melian fabric with a single perforation through its upper thickness. The technique, presumably also designed to aid firing, is unusual and may be Cretan in origin (Sandy MacGillivray, personal communication); a similar example is known among the LB I material from Daskalio Cave on Kalymnos (Benzi 2011: 19, fig. 3G). Both closing, globular (Type A) and open, straight-walled (Type B) variants are represented Phylakopi, and continue in use into the LC period.[33] Most are produced in a fabric consistent with Melian manufacture, although a small number may be imported from other Cycladic islands, and fewer still may be Cretan.[34]

Experimental analyses undertaken by Müller and colleagues (2013: 6) suggest that the more open Type B profile would have been suited to boiling, while the smaller, globular Type A would have been suited to simmering (also Lis 2015; Morrison *et al.* 2015). This, presumably, was the manner in which they were utilised at Phylakopi, though evidently not as an absolute replacement to the wide-mouthed cooking jar. Both types appear to be depicted in use together, presumably to prepare components of the same meal, in an outdoor setting in the Cauldron Scene from the North-East Bastion at LC I Ayia Irini (see Morgan 1998; 2020: 395-399; Wright 2004).[35] Several of the examples

from Phylakopi bear scrape marks at the interior indicative of stirring, or of the use of ladles or scoops during serving.

A related Cretan shape, the tripod cooking tray, arrives to the Cyclades during the later MC (for example, Davis 1986: 87-88), although not, it seems, to the settlement at Akrotiri. Indeed, it appears to be far less common in the Cyclades than the tripod cooking pot (a pattern which also seems to be true of Crete; see Betancourt 1980: 7). The difficulty of distinguishing the shape from flat-based trays or tripod cooking pots (where legs alone survive) has no doubt contributed to its poor visibility, but its rarity may also owe something to the fact that raised variants of the pan hearth-brazier could have served the same function. The tripod cooking jar may have offered a technical advantage over the flat- or pedestal-based cooking pot for the preparation of traditional Melian cuisine, but when faced with the tripod tray — a shape that, effectively, replicated what was already available — it is possible that it was simply met with indifference. The relative popularity of the tripod tray at Ayia Irini V (Gorogianni 2016: 143, table 8.3d) might, plausibly, be attributed to its novelty, but based on its rarity at Ayia Irini during Period VI, it failed to capture the market. The identification of the shape at Phylakopi has, previously, proved somewhat uncertain (see Bosanquet and Welch 1904: 212; Davis and Cherry 2007: 279; Earle 2019: 236, no. 182), although it can now be recognised, unequivocally, among the 1896-1899 assemblage (Figure 16.5).

---

[32] The tripod cooking pots here seem to have been used specifically for the preparation and presentation of funerary meals.

[33] See Betancourt (1980). A further Type B example comes from the 1911 excavation (Barber 1974: pl. 6f).

[34] A very small number of both types appear in fabrics which may be consistent with a Cretan manufacture, including shale temper (a fabric previously identified at Phylakopi; see Vaughn and Williams 2007: 108).

[35] Abramovitz's identification of an individual bringing venison(?) to

these tripod vessels from a 'red table (?)' (1980: 62) is intriguing, given the survival of the red slipped and burnished hearth-braziers (discussed above) into the end of the MC period (see Nikolakopoulou 2019b: 426, no. 1783).

Pans and hearths

Circular, low-walled, flat-based, pans are visible at Phylakopi, as they are elsewhere, during the MC, although they appear in very low numbers among the 1896-1899 assemblage, and MC examples are difficult to distinguish from those of early LC date.[36] There is some considerable variation in profile, surface treatment and rim diameter (24-48cm) even among the small number now at the National Archaeological Museum. That pans of this type were sometimes used in closed ovens is evidenced by an in situ example from the Room of the Oven at Ayia Irini IVb (Overbeck 1989b: 103), although no similar installation has been recognised at Phylakopi.

Hearth-braziers on raised or conical bases also remain in use. The MC period sees the introduction to Phylakopi of a new type, on a low pedestal base, seen also at Akrotiri C (Nikolakopoulou 2019b: 298, no. 1284) and Ayia Irini IV (Overbeck 1989b: 27, pl. 38, G-22). The recovery context of the latter example, from an accumulated deposit above the floor in the kitchen above Building CJ, would seem to support its association with food preparation (for context, Overbeck 1989b: 24-26). Only one example of the type (NAM 26643) has been recognised among the early material from Phylakopi. At a total height of 4.4cm, it is much lower than the earlier Type A-C hearth-braziers, and lacks the characteristic, red slipped and burnished surface treatment of the latter, being apparently undecorated. The pattern of heavy burning preserved at the interior suggests that it was filled to capacity with fuel during use.

A small number of additional rim fragments belong to wide shallow circular pans or deep convex bowls with loop handles pressed on over the rim. An association with food preparation is suggested by their well-finished interior surfaces and the presence of burning at the exterior. The manner in which they were used is not clear, although one possible interpretation is that they functioned as parching trays or similar.[37]

The Late Cycladic period

The early part of the Late Cycladic period, LC I, saw continued, and apparently increased, interaction between Phylakopi and the settlements of Crete to the south. There is evidence of destruction and rebuilding at the site during late LC I-LC II (recently, Brodie 2009)

and, subsequently, an increased visibility of mainland material culture, and cultural engagement, during LC/LH III, which has been associated with the arrival of culturally Mycenaean mainland groups, but which might conceivably have been Melian-led and somewhat more nuanced. This engagement, in any case, is reflected too in the Phylakopian cooking assemblage.

Cooking pots

Cooking pots with flat or raised bases remain in use at Phylakopi to the end of the Late Cycladic period. Although they are not clearly distinguishable from MC types within the 1896-1899 assemblage, stratified examples are known from the 1974-1977 excavation. Examples with plain inturned rims and pedestal bases are attested during LC I (Davis and Cherry 2007: 279, 295) and the recent publication of cooking vessels from PK Pit 1 makes clear the survival of jars with both plain inturned and everted rims and flat and raised bases into LH IIIB1 (Earle 2019: 241-242). Small two-handled cooking jars with everted rims are present during LH IIIB-C (Mountjoy 1985: 196, no. 379; 206-207, no. 543; 2007: 322, no. 222) as, perhaps, is a larger version of the same (Mountjoy 1985: 196, no. 380). The relative (low) frequency of these vessels, as for the MC period, has certainly been skewed by parsing, underreporting, and by the difficulty of distinguishing flat- or pedestal-based and tripod types from rim or handle fragments, although at least five individual vessels (in Melian Purple Gritty and Dark Red Micaceous fabrics) are represented in PK Pit 1, and they should probably be considered to have been common.

Tripod cooking pots

Tripod cooking pots continue to be used at Phylakopi throughout the Late Cycladic. Cretan types are certainly present during the early LC period.[38] During LH III, examples of Aeginetan type (see Gauss et al. 2017: 51-54; Marabea 2019: 461-465, Kanakia Type 1B) also appear, distinguished by their low, globular body, short everted rim and vertical loop handles which join at the rim and the shoulder (for example, Atkinson et al. 1904: pl. XXXV.17). At Kolonna on Aegina, the shape is visible from LH IIIA2 until the decline of the settlement during LH IIIC Early (see Felten 2007: 18-19). At Phylakopi, examples of the type from the area of the West Shrine (for example, Mountjoy 1985: 196, no. 376) should be dated by context to LH IIIC Early-Middle (Sanctuary Phase 2b/3a, Renfrew 1985: 86, table 3.3); the latest possible example deriving from the very last episode of use in the building (NLd space 3, Renfrew 1985: 74; see Barber 1974: 42; Earle 2019;

---

[36] Large, coarse low-walled cooking trays are noted at Akrotiri from Phase A (Nikolakopoulou 2019a: 205-206; Nikolakopoulou et al. 2008: 313). Ayia Irini IV has yielded a variety of types (for example, Overbeck 1989b: 86, 112-113, 121, 136, 173), including possible Minoan imports. Baking pans are recorded among the LC I material from the 1974-1977 excavation (Cherry and Davis 2007: 279).

[37] There are possible parallels for the shape at Ayia Irini (Overbeck 1989b: 101, no. AR-4; Davis 1986: 42, no. U-56).

[38] See Davis and Cherry (2007: 277, Type 11a-b). A single possible example of an imported Minoan-style cooking dish (otherwise rare in the Cyclades) is also noted (see Davis 1986: 105; Davis and Cherry 2007: 295, 303).

NAM 26631

Figure 16.7. Rectangular pan on low feet, a possible local version of the Late Helladic-type 'souvlaki tray' (acc. no. NAM 26631).

Mountjoy 1985: 84, 111). Such vessels seem to have formed a major export category from Aegina during LH IIIB-C (Marabea 2019: 448) at a time when Phylakopi appears to witness a decline in contacts with the mainland (see Barber 1981: 11; also, Gauss and Kiriatzi 2011: 244-247; Mountjoy 2007: 338-344; Spanos 2006).

A single example of the small one-handled tripod cooking pot (see Marabea 2019: 460), of probable LC I-II date, has also now been recognised among the 1896-1899 assemblage. Although unlikely to be sufficient to hold portions enough for a familial group, it would have had capacity for single or double servings, or may have served for the preparation of individual ingredients as part of a larger meal.

Griddle pan

Arguably the most important cooking shape to emerge from the current study is the mainland-type griddle pan (Figure 16.6). The shape is well-attested across the LH III Greek mainland (Hruby 2008; 2017)[39] and is also known on Crete at Phaistos (Borgna 1997: 197), Palaikastro (Dawkins 1902: 325) and Kastelli (Hallager and Hallager 2011: 356-357), but it has not previously been recognised in the Cyclades. A flat base from Ayia Irini VI (Schofield 2011: 40, no. 262) resembles

the finger-impressed variant known from Iklaina in Messenia (cf. Gulizio and Shelmerdine 2017: fig. 4.4, no. P2972) although it would seem too early in date to be related.[40]

Of the few fragments now recognised from Phylakopi, two (NAM 26638 and NAM 26639) derive from the base of the vessel, which is characterised by the presence of numerous, likely upward-facing, indentations, of which none perforate fully. As such, they can only be identified with the 'low-walled' type. A third example (NAM 26640), however, seems to derive from the 'high-walled' variant. Preliminary petrographic analysis conducted on this latter fragment by Jill Hilditch as part of the current study, had raised the possibility that it was an Aeginetan import, although a local origin now seems more likely. To my knowledge, no example of the shape has been published from Aegina to date.[41]

Cereal and olive oil residues have been recognised on a griddle pan from Midea in the Argolid (Tzedakis and Martlew 1999: 126) which suggests that the shape may have been used in the cooking of bread; in this interpretation, the holes could have functioned as 'wells' in which hot oil could pool, thereby helping to prevent

---

[39] To those examples listed by Hruby (with references) can be added others from Kontopigado (see Kaza-Papageorgiou and Kardamaki 2012: 189-190, fig. 24).

[40] The type may appear as early as MH III at Iklaina, although this early date has been questioned and all other securely-dated examples seem to belong to LH III (see Hruby 2017: 22-23).
[41] A small number of probable Melian exports are visible at Kolonna during the late MC period (Phase I and J) and into the early Late Helladic (LH I-II; see Gauss and Smetana 2008: 335-338).

dough from sticking (Hruby 2017: 21). The functional difference between the low-walled and high-walled types is not clear, although Hruby has suggested that high-walled examples may have been better suited for use in exposed locations (2017: 22); the form preventing contamination of food by ash blowing around the fire. Thus, we may be looking at 'indoor' and 'outdoor' types. The shape has been identified with elite dining practices on the mainland, and the exclusiveness of the shape in the Cyclades may support a similar association at Phylakopi. The absence of contextual information makes it difficult to be certain how, and where, these pans were used, although one fragment preserves an excavation mark which places its findspot close to the LC/LH III megaron.

Souvlaki tray

A single fragment of a pan on low feet may represent a local version of the mainland 'souvlaki tray'. Although the identification is tentative, both the dimensions and the general features of the pan — a straight vertical wall, perpendicular flat pan, low narrow leg and probably rectangular form — are consistent with the shape. The characteristic indented rim which might have confirmed the identification in our example is, unfortunately, missing. Uniquely, the shoulder of the foot is both perforated and slashed in the manner more typical of the tripod cooking jar (Figure 16.7).

Canonical examples of the footed souvlaki tray are known from Mycenae (Wardle 1969: 294; Wardle et al. 1973: 327) and Gla (Iakovidis 2001: 109) and belong to LH III; a variant type on a flat base is known from other sites, including LC I Akrotiri (Doumas 2014: 48, fig. 44c). As implied by the name, the shape is generally considered to have been used for the grilling of meat (Hruby 2017: 23), although residue analysis has proved inconclusive (see Tzedakis and Martlew 2008). As with the griddle pan, the recovery contexts of mainland examples suggest an elite association for the shape.

Spit supports

Two fragments of scalloped spit support attest an alternative method of grilling meat at Phylakopi (Bosanquet and Welch 1904: 212, fig. 189). Both are assigned by Scheffer (1984: 158) to her Type A (MC late to LC) — the most common form and, apparently, the earliest — which is characterised by the presence of holes, rather than handles, to enable the supports to be lifted out of the coals. The shape is attested in the Cyclades at Ayia Irini from the developed MC period (Ayia Irini IVc) to LH IIIA (see Georgiou 1986: 23-28; Overbeck 1989b: 77, no. AG-16) and at LC I Akrotiri, including in an extraordinary example with bucrania terminals (see Marinatos 1969: pl. 38; Doumas 2014: 46, fig. 42). The shape is rare, although it is attested beyond

the Cyclades on Crete, mainland Greece, and in eastern Anatolia (also, Kaiser 2009: 160-161); indeed, the earliest example listed by Scheffer derives from Aphrodisias (EB III), while examples from Pylos, Khania and Palaikastro belong to LH/LM III (1984: 160). Like other of the shapes noted above, the scalloped spit support has been associated with feasting, rather than more everyday consumptive practices, although whether it arrived to Phylakopi with other specialist shapes during LH III, or whether it represents an earlier grilling tradition, is not clear.

Not how, but what: archaeozoological and archaeobotanical remains from Phylakopi

Perhaps unsurprisingly, there exists very little faunal data from the 1896-1899 or 1911 excavation seasons. Animal bone was evidently encountered across the site and two deposits, in C5,15 (*Daybooks* 1897: 37) and E3,17 (*Daybooks* 1898: 4-5) are specifically identified as probable kitchen waste, without the provision of any further detail on quantity, burning, articulation, breakage or species. That in C5, and a further deposit of animal bone in A5,6 (*Daybooks* 1896: 11), are likely MC in date,[42] while that in E3,17 may belong to LC II (see Brodie 2009: 68). The possible remnants of a funerary meal[43] were recovered in association with an EC III child burial identified in H4,3 (Barber 1974: 6-8; Dawkins and Droop 1911: 7).

There is also relatively little contextual data published for the substantial faunal assemblage recovered during the 1974-1977 excavation. An unidentified bone assemblage is recorded in association with a quern and a plastered hearth from a MC floor sequence below Rooms J1,13 and 14 (Trench ΠC, Renfrew et al. 2007: 45) although faunal data are presented only in aggregate form by Gamble (1979; 1982) and the inferential difficulties arising therefrom are noted by Winder (2007). Of a total of c. 11,000 bone fragments, around 70% (n = 7819) could not be assigned to a species. The remaining 30% belonged almost exclusively to sheep (*Ovis aries*), goat (*Capra hircus*), pig (*Sus domesticus*) and cattle (*Bos taurus*; Gamble 1982: 166, table 13.6). A handful of other species are represented in extremely low numbers: the domestic dog (*Canis familiaris*) appears in all periods (Gamble 1982: 166, table 13.3); the red deer

---

[42] That from A5,6 was identified at a depth of 4.10m in a deposit which also contained a 'vase with meander pattern in lustreless black on a pale yellow slip'. That from C5,15 was identified at a depth of 3.20m in association with two Melian bowls and a hoard of plain handleless cups (also Smith 1896-1897: 22). That from E3,17 was identified at a depth of 0.5m in a deposit described by Mackenzie as comprised of the 'debris upon which the Mycenaean settlement was built'.

[43] Two ovicaprid teeth, a knucklebone, and two fragments of skull from a 'small animal', as well as two fragments of limpet (Dawkins and Droop 1911: 7).

(*Cervus elaphus*)[44] is visible during the MC period; the beech marten (*Martes foina*), rabbit (*Oryctolagus sp.*) and donkey are present only during the LC period (Gamble 1985: 479, 482, table D.1).[45] Wild boar (*Sus scrofa*) is represented by a small number of unworked tusks (Bosanquet and Welch 1904: 192; Renfrew and Cherry 1985: 329). A very small number of unidentified bird bones derive from the area of the sanctuary (Gamble 1985: 482, table D.1).

The major domesticate taxa are likely to have been exploited within a mixed, non-intensive, system which provided meat and secondary products. The representation of prey species (red deer, boar, rabbit and bird) within the faunal assemblage may conceivably reflect a very modest role for hunting or trapping within the repertoire of subsistence practices utilised by the inhabitants of Phylakopi, although deer antler and boar tusk may have equally arrived to the settlement as raw materials or culturally-valued objects in their own right.[46] Small game species such as rabbit and beech marten may have been snared for food or pelts, although they appear in such low (relative) numbers, that they might just as easily represent occasional kills by dog, fox, or other predatory species. The intramural presence of the beech marten may be explained by its willingness to exploit domestic waste and livestock as a food source (see Bakaloudis *et al.* 2012; Marco 1995).[47] The dog probably served a pastoral role as a shepherd dog or livestock guardian, or as a guard animal. The low visibility of prey species at Phylakopi would seem to argue against the use of the dog as a hunt animal. Higgs (1968: 117) has suggested that the tendency of the goat to withstand dogs would have made them unsuitable for use with goats or mixed herds, although modern breeds continue to be used in Greece in exactly this way. There is no evidence (in the form of mortality profiles, MNI data or butchery marks) to indicate consumption of dog meat at Phylakopi or any other Bronze Age Cycladic site. It has been recognised as a systematic practice (rather than a famine response) at EH II Koropi (Hadjikoumis 2016), although if knowledge of the practice was transmitted through those social and economic networks which linked the wider Cyclades with Attica during the period, it seems to have been rejected as a socio-dietary strategy.[48]

Evidence for the exploitation of aquatic resources at Phylakopi is equally meagre, no doubt in part to the vulnerability of ichthyofaunal remains to taphonomic loss and sampling methodology (Berg 2013: 5; Cherry 2007: 15-16; also, Mylona 2003; Powell 1996: 39).[49] Nothing at all is recorded of the fish remains encountered during the 1896-1899 excavations, while the 1974-1977 assemblage was composed entirely of 'small' (unidentified) species (Gamble 1979: 127; 1985: table D.1), with tuna and other migratory fish entirely absent. A profile such as this might, with caution, be understood to demonstrate a preference for inshore (medio- and infralittoral) or land-based fishing, as seems to have been typical of other settlements of the Bronze Age Cyclades. Of the fishing equipment which might support the inference, Phylakopi has yielded very little. Probable net and line weights in stone are visible from the later EC period, though they are sometimes difficult to identify with certainty (Bosanquet and Welch 1904: 200-201; Cherry and Davis 2007: 430, table 10.6; Renfrew and Cherry 1985: 357), and a single barbless copper-alloy fishhook from the surface of a street in Square G2 should belong to LC I-II (Bosanquet and Welch 1904: 190; Hogarth 1904: 16; Smith, forthcoming). No netting tools or leisters have been recognised, and Phylakopi lacks the conditions necessary to preserve organic in-shore traps or baskets (see Powell 1996: 94-101; Mylona 2014: 5; Alfaro and Mylona 2014: 156-157).

A fairly modest malacological assemblage attests broader exploitation of the inshore ecological zone, although the data are, again, rather inconsistent and taxonomic variation relatively low. By far the largest number of shells from Phylakopi belong to limpet (*Patella coerulea*). Their consumption at the site can be recognised with some confidence from at least the late EC period.[50] LC levels in Trench Pla (Square G5) have yielded limpet in larger quantities, most notably in a discrete deposit of several hundred shells lying upon, and within, a floor surface of LC II date (Floor 13, Renfrew *et al.* 2007: 73, pl. 14c).[51] This group, located

---

[44] The red deer is identified by the presence of antler only.

[45] The beech marten is identified by a single humerus (LC I, Trench PK) and a mandible and vertebra (LC III, East Shrine); the donkey by a group of foot bones (LC III, Trench NLe Space C).

[46] At least two of the boar tusks can be placed into LH IIIB-C. A LH III date increases the likelihood that these objects arrived to Phylakopi as raw material or as objects in their own right (see Trantalidou 2008).

[47] Aristotle (*Hist. An*, 9.6) records that martens had a taste for honey and presented a significant threat to beehives.

[48] The absence of burning on dog remains from Koropi suggests that they were cooked in the pot, rather than roasted on the fire (Hadjikoumis 2016: 240). If Hadjikoumis is correct in characterising cynophagy as a socio-political practice utilised by emergent elites at the supra-household level (2016: 241-242), it may be the absence

of requirement, or suitable context, which saw it rejected in the islands. The general rejection of dog as a food stuff would seem to be supported by the rarity of dog bone, and of bones with cut marks, at Akrotiri (Trantalidou 2008: 48). For evidence of cynophagy elsewhere in Greece during later history, see Snyder and Klippel (2003).

[49] Cherry's (2007) analysis of retrieval efficiency suggests an in-trench recovery rate of only 13% for all animal bone, by weight, rising to c. 40%, by weight, with the use of dry-sieving and exhibiting a bias against small elements from small species (see also, Gamble 1979: 127).

[50] The two fragments of limpet shell identified with the late EC child burial in H4/3 (Barber 1974: 6-8; Dawkins and Droop 1911: 7) may have served a symbolic function as one element of a conceptual meal. Certainly, the unique inclusion of a feeding bottle with the child suggests a focus on food provision. The practice here finds parallel in the inclusion of limpet with the dead at Chalandriani (see Hekman 2003: 161).

[51] From the same trench, an undefined quantity of limpet is noted within the makeup of LH IIIA-B Floor 9, and 100 shells are noted from the fill directly below it (Renfrew *et al.* 2007: 68), while a further undefined quantity are noted from LH IIIA(?) Floor 12 (Renfrew *et al.*

immediately adjacent to a temporary hearth or fire, is best interpreted as the accumulated remains of one or more meals.[52] A further 33 limpet shells, without context and with their apices broken, are recorded from the early excavations (Bosanquet and Welch 1904: 201; Sherratt 2000: 182-183, pl. 229, AE1988a-b). Bosanquet and Welch considered this damage to be evidence of their use as jewellery. Species other than limpet seem to have been preferred for personal adornment (see Karali 1999: 33-42) however, and similar damage might conceivably be natural (see Theodoropoulou 2014: 84), or the result of percussive force applied to weak or cracked shells during harvesting or processing (see Taylor 2016). Indeed, broken apices are visible among the shells of the Floor 13 'kitchen deposit'.

While marine gastropods, by weight, offer a lower protein content, and a lower total calorific yield, than meat, the energy costs associated with their harvest and preparation are exceptionally low, and they represent an important secondary source of calories and vitamins, particularly in late winter and early spring (Karali-Giannakopoulou 1990: 412; Theodoropoulou 2007: 78). The apparent absence of burnt shell may identify a preference at Phylakopi for the consumption of limpet raw, boiled or stewed, rather than roasted directly on coals (see Forbes 1976: 135).[53] It is possible that they were consumed in a seafood soup (*Kakavia*) of the type recognised in House A.1 at LM IB Papadiokampos on Crete (see Brogan *et al.* 2013: 129; Morrison *et al.* 2015: 116-118). The recipe here included limpet, topshell (*Monodonta turbinata*) and crab,[54] and there is evidence for similar from elsewhere in the Cyclades. Large quantities of unburnt limpet (*Patella luscitanica* and *coerulea*) and topshell (*Monodonta turbinata*) are identified in a probable kitchen space at EC III Markiani (Karali-Giannakopoulou 2006: 242-243).[55] These same species dominate the assemblage at EC Korphi t'Aroniou (Doumas 1966: 45, pl. 32a), and

limpet is also present at EC Skarkos (Marthari 1990: 100). At later MC Ayia Irini, both *Patella sp.* and *Murex trunculus* are common (Davis 1986: 110)[56] and, at LC I Akrotiri, only *Murex spp.* appears in greater quantity than limpet (*Patella coerulea*, *aspera* and *vulgata*) and topshell (*Monodonta turbinata*), respectively; examples here are, again, largely unburnt. Given the shared ecology and broader Cycladic popularity of limpet and topshell (as complementary ingredients?), the absence of topshell from Phylakopi is curious and, if not a function of recovery bias (as is entirely possible), may reflect a Melian culinary preference.

Other species present at Phylakopi include cowrie (probably *Luria lurida*), cone shell (*Conus mediterraneus*), spiny oyster (*Spondylus gaederopus*), murex (*Murex trunculus*) and triton (*Charonia sp.*) (Renfrew and Cherry 1985: 326-328). The species of two additional bivalve fragments could not be identified.[57] Both cowrie and cone shell are toxic if ingested. Tritons are certainly edible (Apostolakou *et al.* 2014: 329; Marinatos 1972: 36), although as a deeper-sea species they carry a relatively high retrieval cost, and the shell is known to have been adapted for a variety of other uses (Apostolakou *et al.* 2014; Karali 1999: 19-24). Only four triton shells are known from Phylakopi, of which only one exhibits damage consistent with a deliberate attempt to release suction during meat extraction,[58] thus it is unclear whether the shells were retained after the meat was consumed, or whether they were simply recovered dead (see Theodoropoulou 2014). Spondylus and murex are also edible. However, while the unworked nature of two murex from LH IIIB and LH IIIC deposits in the West Shrine may indicate consumption, spondylus appears only in modified form and was probably collected for its shell or acquired as a manufactured item (see Renfrew and Cherry 1985: 326-327). The low representation of both species suggests occasional, rather than systematic, exploitation, although the cultic context in which these few remains were found is unlikely to be representative of typical subsistence practices.

There is currently no evidence at Phylakopi for the consumption of crab, sea urchin,[59] squid, octopus, or other cephalopods, although the exploitation of these species can be recognised at other contemporary Cycladic sites.[60] Similarly, there is no evidence that

---

2007: 72).

[52] The few catalogued objects associated with Floor 13 include fragments from at least two tripod cooking pots (P786 and P788) and a tub (P1818) (Davis and Cherry 2007: 277, 285), as well as an andesite quern (SF138) and grindstone (SF137) (Cherry and Davis 2007: 430, 433).

[53] Their use as bait is also possible, although this seems to have resulted in a more careless approach to the extraction of meat (see Coleman 1977: 132).

[54] This meal was recovered in-situ from a flat based cooking jar in House A.1 Room 8. A further 2kg of limpet were identified in a cooking dish on the building's South Porch (perhaps left soaking to remove sand and grit prior to cooking). Two further scatters of unburnt limpet from Room 5 are identified as food for the pot; more diffuse spreads of burnt and unburnt limpet, crab and topshell are identified as the remains of multiple meals. The total yield of shellfish from Rooms 5 and 8 of House A.1 is extraordinary (*c.* 40-50kg; Brogan *et al.* 2013: 127-129; Sofianou and Brogan 2009: 7-9).

[55] Space 5, Trench 2,1, layer 20. A total of 1999 *Patella* and 286 *Monodonta turbinata* are recorded for Trench 2, and similarly large volumes of both are noted from undefined contexts in Trench 1 (2146 and 170, respectively; see Karali-Giannakopoulou 2006: 244, table 9.11).

[56] The popularity of both species at LN Saliagos (Shackleton 1968: 122-138) is suggestive of a long-lived culinary pairing.

[57] *Pinna sp.*, *Glycimerus sp.*, and pecten are common at other Cycladic sites.

[58] Two come from the LH IIIC sanctuary (Renfrew and Cherry 1985: 327-328, pl. 62) and a further two, undated, are reported by Bosanquet and Welch (1904: 201), of which one has a broken lower end (NM12015; see Karali 1999: 23) which may be the result of meat extraction or post-mortem damage.

[59] Traditionally consumed raw, see Forbes (1976: 135).

[60] Urchin are recorded at Markiani (Karali-Giannakopoulou 2006: 243) and Skarkos (Marthari 1990: 100); cuttlefish are noted at Skarkos (Marthari 1990: 100) and at Neolithic Saliagos (Evans and Renfrew

NAM 26492   NAM 26493   NAM 26494

Figure 16.8. Middle-Late Cycladic pithoi with spigots (acc. nos. NAM 26492, 26493 and 26494).

the inhabitants of Phylakopi consumed land snails, a traditional dish in autumn and spring (Forbes 1976), although they are attested at EC Skarkos (Marthari 1990: 100) and LC I Akrotiri (*Helix cincta* Müller; see Karali-Giannakopoulou 1990; Trantalidou 2008).

Archaeobotanical remains

Low quantities of carbonised cereal, including barley, (wild?) oat and wheat,[61] have been recovered at Phylakopi (J. Renfrew 1982: 156). The domestic grape (Vitis vinifera) constitutes the only directly-attested fruit crop and the consumption of wine or grape juice is supported by the presence of a number of MC-LC pithoi with spigots now recognised among the 1896-1899 assemblage (Figure 16.8).[62] There is no direct evidence for the cultivation of fig, although it is visible at EC Dhaskalio (Margaritis 2013: 391) and LC I Akrotiri. Neither is there direct evidence of the domesticated olive (Olea Europaea L.), or its wild counterpart. Indirectly, however, the excavation daybook records from a heavily eroded room close to the cliff edge at the north of Square E2 a concentration of pithos fragments containing 'a greenish yellow substance like the sediment of [olive] oil' (*Daybooks* 1898: 5). This space may represent an oil store or, given the presence of two mortars in association, a more general-purpose pantry or food preparation area.

Legumes are represented by a large-seeded vetch, which J. Renfrew (1982: 156) suggests may be common vetch (*Vicia sativa*), but which could be Spanish vetchling (*Lathyrus clymenum*) (Sarpaki and Jones 1990: 365). The vetch (and indeed oats, if wild) could have entered the settlement as a contaminant of the wheat and barley crop, although common vetch is grown in the Cyclades today as a fodder crop (Halstead and Jones 1989) and may well have served as such in the Bronze Age. Spanish vetchling, alternatively, seems to have been cultivated for human consumption at LC I Akrotiri, where it also appears as fava. On modern Melos, wheat and barley are combined to produce a glutinous loaf which is both lighter and more readily digested than barley bread (J. Renfrew 1982: 156). The preference for a more glutinous recipe is interesting given the functional qualities of the Mycenaean griddle pan noted above, and perhaps also those of the earlier Phase B-C hearth-braziers. It is possible that barley may have been consumed as a beverage.[63]

Finally, it is worth noting that the current study has failed to yield any trace of apiculture (hives, smokers and so forth) at Phylakopi, despite its presence at Ayia Irini by middle MC (see Overbeck 1989b: 108 no. AT-32, 110 no. AU-6, 111 no. AV-11) and perhaps at Akrotiri by LC I (see recently, Papageorgiou 2016).

Concluding remarks

Understanding diachronic culinary practice within the successive settlements at Phylakopi is, now, an extremely difficult prospect, and identifying contemporary variation within the separate households of the settlement all but impossible. In broad terms, change in the character of the cooking shape repertoire over time suggests a willingness among at least some of the site's inhabitants to adopt new cooking technologies, although perhaps not necessarily any great evolution in the recipes employed.

1968: 80).

[61] Apparently, Emmer (see Margaritis 2013: 398).

[62] Nikolakopoulou (2002: 127-129) notes traces of beeswax on examples of the shape from LC I Akrotiri which may represent an addition to help prevent evaporation through the vessel wall, one intended to improve flavour, and/or evidence of the practice of mixing wine and honey.

[63] Suggested, perhaps, by the addition of a plastic barley head to the rim of a fine cup at Ayia Irini IV (Overbeck 1989b: 182).

It seems likely that Melian-Cycladic traditions underpinned diet and dining throughout much of the settlement's history. Particularly, the appearance at late EC Phylakopi of the Type A hearth-brazier suggests a connection between the earliest settlement and those at Akrotiri and Dhaskalio and, perhaps, evidence of shared culinary practice. The widespread adaptation of the cooking pot shape during the earlier MC may be indictive of a similar relationship.

During the later MC period, as elsewhere in the archipelago, we can see the integration into the repertoire at Phylakopi of cooking shapes from Crete at the same time as we see Cretan shapes utilised for serving and consumption. This most clearly by the introduction of tripod cooking vessels, and the rare appearance of the tripod cooking tray, which was perhaps largely eschewed by the settlement's inhabitants in favour of then long-lived Melian alternatives.

The identification of a number of new mainland shapes during the LC period, including some not previously recognised in the Cyclades, provides an important perspective on the 'Mycenaean' character of the settlement at Phylakopi during its later stages. This mainland repertoire includes shapes which are generally considered to represent restricted-use equipment, and suggests that some at LC Phylakopi recognised a social value in performative consumption, although the identity of their owners, 'elite' or otherwise, and the context of their use, remains unclear. In this respect, cuisine and cooking may have adopted new meaning at Phylakopi during the LC period, although the low visibility of the period elsewhere in the archipelago makes it difficult to judge how far Melian practices may have been exceptional.

That the Phylakopian diet included a wide variety of terrestrial and marine resources seems clear, and of the latter at least, we can recognise consumption of limpet, perhaps as part of a seafood stew, during LC II. Similar recipes, incorporating cereals, or herbs recovered from the settlement's hinterland, might have been prepared in the deep cooking jars visible at Phylakopi from its earliest inception and in the Cretan and mainland vessels which appeared later. At various stages, dedicated shapes were utilised for the grilling of meat and the cooking of flatbreads; oil and wine filled pithoi in the settlement's storerooms.

This paper has presented an initial attempt to tease out something of the character of cooking pottery and culinary technology at Phylakopi from an incomplete and often difficult dataset and, in so doing, has demonstrated the very significant potential of legacy excavation material to address new questions or reframe old ones. One hopes that the forthcoming full and proper publication of the 1896-1899 assemblage might prompt more of the same.

Bibliography

Abramovitz, K. 1980. Frescoes from Ayia Irini, Keos. Parts II-IV. *Hesperia: the Journal of the American School of Classical Studies at Athens* 49(1): 57-85.

Alfaro, C. and D. Mylona 2014. Fishing for purple shellfish (*Muricidae*) in ancient Greece: acquisition technology and first steps in purple dye production, in C. Alfaro, M. Tellenbach and J. Ortiz (eds) *Production and Trade of Textiles and Dyes in the Roman Empire and Neighbouring Regions. Actas del IV Symposium Internacional sobre Textiles y Tintes del Mediterráneo en el mundo antiguo, Valencia, 5 al 6 de noviembre, 2010* (Purpureae Vestes 4): 149-165. Valencia: University of Valencia.

Apostolakou, S., P.P. Betancourt, T.M. Brogan, D. Mylona and C. Sofianou 2014. Tritons revisited, in G. Touchais, R. Laffineur and F. Rougemont (eds) *PHYSIS: L'environnement naturel et la relation homme-milieu dans le monde Égéen Protohistorique. Actes de la 14e Rencontre égéenne internationale, Paris, Institut National d'Histoire de l'Art (INHA), 11-14 décembre 2012* (Aegaeum 37): 325–332. Leuven: Peeters.

Atkinson, T.D., R.C. Bosanquet, C.C. Edgar, A.J. Evans, D.G. Hogarth, D. Mackenzie, C. Smith and F.B. Welch 1904. *Excavations at Phylakopi in Melos* (Society for the Promotion of Hellenic Studies Supplementary Paper no. 4). London: Macmillan.

Bakaloudis, D.E., C.G. Vlachos, M.A. Papakosta, V.A. Bontzorlos and E.N. Chatzinikos 2012. Diet composition and feeding strategies of the stone marten (*Martes foina*) in a typical Mediterranean ecosystem. *The Scientific World Journal* 2012: 1-11.

Barber, R. 1974. Phylakopi 1911 and the history of the later Cycladic Bronze Age. *The Annual of the British School at Athens* 68: 1-53.

Barber, R. 1981. The Late Cycladic period: a review. *The Annual of the British School at Athens* 76: 1-21.

Barber, R. 2007. The Middle Cycladic pottery, in C. Renfrew, N. Brodie, C. Morris and C. Scarre (eds) *Excavations at Phylakopi in Melos 1974-77* (The British School at Athens Supplementary Volume 42): 181-248. London: the British School at Athens.

Barber, R. 2008. Unpublished pottery from Phylakopi. *The Annual of the British School at Athens* 103: 43-222.

Barber, R. 2017. Phylakopi on Melos and the National Archaeological Museum, in M. Lagogianni-Georgakarakos (ed.) *Odysseys*: 71-78. Athens: Archaeological Receipts Fund.

Belmont, J.S. and Renfrew, C. 1964. Two prehistoric sites on Mykonos. *American Journal of Archaeology* 68(4): 395-400.

Benzi, M. 2011. Daskalio (Vathy), Kalymnos: a Late Bronze I sacred cave in the East Aegean, in W. Gauss, M. Lindblom, R.A.K. Smith and J.C. Wright (eds) *Our Cups are Full. Pottery and Society in the Aegean Bronze Age. Papers presented to Jeremy B. Rutter on the Occasion of his 65th Birthday* (British Archaeological

Reports International Series 2227):13-24. Oxford: Archaeopress.

Berg, I. 2013. Marine creatures and the sea in Bronze Age Greece: ambiguities of meaning. *Journal of Maritime Archaeology* 8(1): 1-27.

Bernabò Brea, L. 1964. *Poliochni. Città Preistorica nell'Isola di Lemnos.* I. Rome: L'Erma di Bretschneider.

Betancourt, P.P. 1980. *Cooking Vessels from Minoan Kommos. A Preliminary Report* (Occasional Paper 7). Los Angeles: Institute of Archaeology, University of California.

Borgna, E. 1997. Kitchen-ware from LM IIIC Phaistos: cooking traditions and ritual activities in LBA Cretan societies. *Studi Micenei ed Egeo-Anatolici* 39: 189-217.

Bosanquet, R.C. and F.B. Welch 1904. The minor antiquities, in T.D. Atkinson, R.C. Bosanquet, C.C. Edgar, A.J. Evans, D.G. Hogarth, D. Mackenzie, C. Smith and F.B. Welch 1904. *Excavations at Phylakopi in Melos* (Society for the Promotion of Hellenic Studies Supplementary Paper no. 4): 190-214. London: Macmillan.

Brodie, N. 2009. A reassessment of Mackenzie's second and third cities at Phylakopi. *The Annual of the British School at Athens* 104: 49-72.

Brogan, T., C. Sofianou, J.E. Morrison, D. Mylona, and E. Margaritis 2013. Living off the fruits of the sea: new evidence for dining at Papadiokampos, Crete, in S. Voutsaki and S.M. Valamoti (eds) *Diet, Economy and Society in the Ancient Greek World. Towards a Better Integration of Archaeology and Science. Proceedings of the International Conference held at the Netherlands Institute at Athens on 22–24 March 2010* (Pharos Supplement 1): 123-132. Leuven: Peeters.

Broodbank, C. 2007. The pottery, in C. Renfrew, C. Doumas, L. Marangou and G. Gavalas (eds) *Keros, Dhaskalio Kavos: the Investigations of 1987-88* (Keros Volume 1): 115-237. Cambridge: McDonald Institute for Archaeological Research.

Carington Smith, J. 1975. Spinning, Weaving and Textile Manufacture in Prehistoric Greece: from the Beginning of the Neolithic to the End of the Mycenaean Ages, with Particular Reference to the Evidence Found on Archaeological Excavations. Unpublished PhD dissertation, University of Tasmania.

Carington Smith, J. 1977. Appendix 2: cloth and mat impressions, in J. Coleman. *Keos I. Kephala: A Late Neolithic Settlement and Cemetery*: 114-127. Princeton: the American School of Classical Studies at Athens.

Cherry, J.F. 2007. Appendix A: a retrieval experiment at Phylakopi: some questions of sample design and efficient collection techniques, in C. Renfrew, N. Brodie, C. Morris and C. Scarre (eds) *Excavations at Phylakopi in Melos 1974-77* (The British School at Athens Supplementary Volume 42): 13-18. London: the British School at Athens.

Cherry, J.F. and J.L. Davis 2007. The other finds, in C. Renfrew, N. Brodie, C. Morris and C. Scarre (eds)

Excavations at Phylakopi in Melos 1974-77 (The British School at Athens Supplementary Volume 42): 401-455. London: the British School at Athens.

Coleman, J. 1972. Investigations in Keos: part II. A conspectus of the pottery. *Hesperia: the Journal of the American School of Classical Studies at Athens* 41(3): 357-401.

Coleman, J. 1977. *Keos I. Kephala: A Late Neolithic Settlement and Cemetery.* Princeton: the American School of Classical Studies at Athens.

Cultraro, M. 2013. Food preparation and consumption in the Early Bronze Age of the northern Aegean: evidence from Poliochni, Lemnos, in G. Graziadio, R. Guglielmino, V. Lenuzza and S. Vitale (eds) *Φιλική Συναυλία. Studies in Mediterranean Archaeology for Mario Benzi* (British Archaeological Reports International Series 2460): 103-111. Oxford: Archaeopress.

Davaras, C. and P.P. Betancourt 2004. *The Hagia Photia Cemetery I. The Tomb Groups and Architecture* (Prehistory Monographs 14). Philadelphia: INSTAP Academic Press.

Davaras, C. and P.P. Betancourt 2012. *The Hagia Photia Cemetery II. The Pottery* (Prehistory Monographs 34). Philadelphia: INSTAP Academic Press.

Davis, J.L. 1986. *Keos V. Ayia Irini: Period V.* Mainz: Philipp Von Zabern.

Davis, J.L. and J.F. Cherry 2007. The Cycladic pottery from Late Bronze I levels, in C. Renfrew, N. Brodie, C. Morris and C. Scarre (eds) *Excavations at Phylakopi in Melos 1974-77* (The British School at Athens Supplementary Volume 42): 265-306. London: the British School at Athens.

Dawkins, R.M. 1902. Excavations at Palaikastro II. *The Annual of the British School at Athens* 9: 297-328.

Dawkins, R.M. and J.P. Droop 1911. Excavations at Phylakopi in Melos, 1911. *The Annual of the British School at Athens* 17: 1-22.

Decavallas, O. 2014. Plant oils from Neolithic Aegean pottery. Chemical proof of the exploitation of oleaginous plants and the question of 'early' oil production, in G. Touchais, R. Laffineur and F. Rougemont (eds) *PHYSIS: L'environnement naturel et la relation homme-milieu dans le monde Égéen Protohistorique. Actes de la 14e Rencontre égéenne internationale, Paris, Institut National d'Histoire de l'Art (INHA), 11-14 décembre 2012* (Aegaeum 37): 244-249. Leuven: Peeters.

Decavallas, O. 2018. Organic residue analysis on pottery from Ftelia, Mykonos: vessels and their contents, in A. Sampson and T. Tsourouni (eds) *Ftelia on Mykonos. Neolithic Networks in the Southern Aegean Basin, Volume II* (University of the Aegean Laboratory of Environmental Archaeology Monograph Series 7): 259-263. Athens: University of the Aegean.

Doukaki, A. 2018. The vases of cheesepot type from Ftelia, Mykonos, in A. Sampson and T. Tsourouni (eds) *Ftelia on Mykonos. Neolithic Networks in the*

Southern Aegean Basin, Volume II (University of the Aegean Laboratory of Environmental Archaeology Monograph Series 7): 59-81. Athens: University of the Aegean.

Doumas, C.G. 1966. Κορφή τ' Αρωνιού. *Αρχαιολογικόν Δελτίον* 20(1965)(Α΄): 41-64.

Doumas, C.G. 2014. *Food for Thought. Dietary Habits in the Bronze Age City at Akrotiri, Thera (3200-1600 BC).* Athens: Society for the Promotion of Studies on Prehistoric Thera.

Earle, J. 2019. Mycenaeans on Melos? Reassessing a Late Bronze Age ceramic deposit at Phylakopi. *Hesperia: the Journal of the American School of Classical Studies at Athens* 88: 215-282.

Edgar, C.C. 1897-1898. Excavations in Melos, 1898. III. The pottery. *The Annual of the British School at Athens* 4: 37-48.

Edgar, C.C. 1898-1899. Excavation in Melos, 1899. C. The pottery. *The Annual of the British School at Athens* 5: 14-19.

Edgar, C.C. 1904. IV. The pottery, in T.D. Atkinson, R.C. Bosanquet, C.C. Edgar, A.J. Evans, D.G. Hogarth, D. Mackenzie, C. Smith and F.B. Welch 1904. *Excavations at Phylakopi in Melos* (Society for the Promotion of Hellenic Studies Supplementary Paper no. 4): 80-176. London: Macmillan.

Efstratiou, N. 1992. Production and distribution of a ceramic type in highland Rhodope: an ethnoarchaeological study. *Origini. Preistoria e protostoria delle civiltà antiche* 16: 311-327.

Eskitzioglou, P. 2006. The pottery of phase IV, in L. Marangou, C. Renfrew, C. Doumas and G. Gavalas (eds) *Markiani, Amorgos. An Early Bronze Age Fortified Settlement, Overview of the 1985-1991 Investigations* (The British School at Athens Supplementary Volume 40): 139-168. London: the British School at Athens.

Evans, J.D. and C. Renfrew 1968. *Excavations at Saliagos near Antiparos* (The British School at Athens Supplementary Volume 5). Athens and London: the British School at Athens and Thames and Hudson.

Fairbanks, A. 1928. *Museum of Fine Arts, Boston: Catalogue of Greek and Etruscan Vases I: Early Vases, Preceding Athenian Black-Figured Wares.* Cambridge: Harvard University Press.

Felten, F. 2007. Aegina-Kolonna: the history of a Greek acropolis, in F. Felten, W. Gauss and R. Smetana (eds) *Ägina-Kolonna Forschungen und Ergebnisse I. Middle Helladic Pottery and Synchronisms. Proceedings of the International Workshop held at Salzburg October 31st - November 2nd, 2004* (Ägina-Kolonna 1; Denkschriften der Gesamtakademie 42; Contributions to the Chronology of the Eastern Mediterranean 14): 11-34. Vienna: the Austrian Academy of Sciences.

Forbes, M.H.C. 1976. Farming and foraging in prehistoric Greece: a cultural ecological perspective. *Annals of the New York Academy of Sciences* 268(1): 127-142.

Forsdyke, E.J. 1925. *Catalogue of the Greek and Etruscan Vases in the British Museum. Volume 1, Part 1. Prehistoric Aegean Pottery.* London: the British Museum.

Gamble, C. 1979. Surplus and self-sufficiency in the Cycladic subsistence economy, in J. Davis and J. Cherry (eds) *Papers in Cycladic Prehistory* (Institute of Archaeology, University of California, Los Angeles Monograph 14): 122-134. Los Angeles: Institute of Archaeology, University of California.

Gamble, C. 1982. Animal husbandry, population and urbanisation, in C. Renfrew and M. Wagstaff (eds) *An Island Polity. The Archaeology of Exploitation in Melos*: 161-171. Cambridge: Cambridge University Press.

Gamble, C. 1985. Appendix D. Formation processes and the animal bones from the Sanctuary at Phylakopi, in C. Renfrew *The Archaeology of Cult. The Sanctuary at Phylakopi* (The British School at Athens Supplementary Volume 18): 479-483. London: the British School at Athens.

Gauss, W. and E. Kiriatzi 2011. *Ägina-Kolonna Forschungen und Ergebnisse V. Pottery Production and Supply at Bronze Age Kolonna, Aegina. An Integrated Archaeological and Scientific Study of a Ceramic Landscape* (Denkschriften der Gesamtakademie 65; Contributions to the Chronology of the Eastern Mediterranean 27). Vienna: the Austrian Academy of Sciences.

Gauss, W. and R. Smetana 2008. Aegina Kolonna and the Cyclades, in N. Brodie, J. Doole, G. Gavalas and C. Renfrew (eds) *Horizon. A Colloquium on the Prehistory of the Cyclades*: 325-338. Cambridge: McDonald Institute for Archaeological Research.

Gauss, W., E. Kiriatzi, M. Lindblom, B. Lis and J.E. Morrison 2017. Aeginetan Late Bronze and Early Iron Age cooking pottery, in J.A. Hruby and D.A. Trusty (eds) *From Cooking Vessels to Cultural Practices in the Late Bronze Age Aegean*: 46-56. Oxford: Oxbow Books.

Georgiadis, M. 2012. *Kos in the Neolithic and Early Bronze Age. The Halasarna Finds and the Aegean Settlement Pattern* (Prehistory Monographs 38). Philadelphia: INSTAP Academic Press.

Georgiou, H.S. 1986. *Keos VI. Ayia Irini: Specialized Domestic and Industrial Pottery.* Mainz: Philipp von Zabern.

Gorogianni, E. 2016. Keian, Kei-noanised, Kei-cenaeanised? Interregional contact and identity in Ayia Irini, Kea, in E. Gorogianni, P. Pavúk and L. Girella (eds) *Beyond Thalassocracies. Understanding Processes of Minoanisation and Mycenaeanisation in the Aegean*: 136-154. Oxford: Oxbow Books.

Gorogianni, E., N. Abell and J. Hilditch 2017. Aegean fusion cuisine: Ayia Irini, Kea as cultural 'middle ground', in J.A. Hruby and D.A. Trusty (eds) *From Cooking Vessels to Cultural Practices in the Late Bronze Age Aegean*: 57-71. Oxford: Oxbow Books.

Gropengiesser, H. 1987. Siphnos, Kap Agios Sostis: Keramische prähistorische Zeugnisse aus dem Gruben- und Hüttenrevier II. *Mitteilungen des*

Deutschen Archäologischen Instituts, Athenische Abteilung 102: 1-54.

Gulizio, J. and C.W. Shelmerdine 2017. Mycenaean cooking vessels from Iklaina, in J.A. Hruby and D.A. Trusty (eds) *From Cooking Vessels to Cultural Practices in the Late Bronze Age Aegean*: 27-38. Oxford: Oxbow Books.

Hadjikoumis, A. 2016. Every dog has its day: cynophagy, identity and emerging complexity in Early Bronze Age Attica, Greece, in N. Marom, R. Yeshurun, L. Weissbrod and G. Bar-Oz (eds) *Bones and Identity. Zooarchaeological Approaches to Reconstructing Social and Cultural Landscapes in Southwest Asia*: 225-245. Oxford: Oxbow Books.

Hadjianastasiou, O. 1988. A Late Neolithic settlement at Grotta, Naxos, in E.B. French and K.A. Wardle (eds) *Problems in Greek Prehistory. Papers Presented at the Centenary Conference of the British School of Archaeology at Athens, Manchester, April 1986*: 11-20. Bristol: Bristol Classical Press.

Halstead, P. and G. Jones 1989. Agrarian ecology in the Greek islands: time stress, scale and risk. *The Journal of Hellenic Studies* 109: 41-55.

Hallager, E. and B.P. Hallager 2011. *The Greek-Swedish Excavations at the Agia Aikaterini Square, Kastelli, Khania, 1970-1987 and 2001. Volume III.1-2. The Late Minoan IIIB:2 Settlement* (Skrifter utgivna av Svenska institutet i Athen, 4o, 47). Stockholm: the Swedish Institute at Athens.

Haywood, C. 2003. *The Making of the Classical Museum: Antiquarians, Collectors and Archaeologists*. Dublin: Classical Museum, University College Dublin.

Hekman, J.J. 2003. The Early Bronze Age Cemetery at Chalandriani on Syros (Cyclades, Greece). Unpublished PhD dissertation, University of Groningen.

Heron, C. and R.P. Evershed 1993. The analysis of organic residues and the study of pottery use. *Archaeological Method and Theory* 5: 247-284.

Higgs, E.S. 1968. Appendix VII. Saliagos animal bones, in J.D. Evans and C. Renfrew. *Excavations at Saliagos near Antiparos* (The British School at Athens Supplementary Volume 5): 114-117. Athens and London: the British School at Athens and Thames and Hudson.

Hogarth, D. 1904. The excavation, in T.D. Atkinson, R.C. Bosanquet, C.C. Edgar, A.J. Evans, D.G. Hogarth, D. Mackenzie, C. Smith and F.B. Welch 1904. *Excavations at Phylakopi in Melos* (Society for the Promotion of Hellenic Studies Supplementary Paper no. 4): 5-24. London: Macmillan.

Hood, M.S.F. 2007. Appendix F. The Middle Minoan pottery, in C. Renfrew, N. Brodie, C. Morris and C. Scarre (eds) *Excavations at Phylakopi in Melos 1974-77* (The British School at Athens Supplementary Volume 42): 248-264. London: the British School at Athens.

Hruby, J. 2008. You are how you eat: Mycenaean class and cuisine, in L. Hitchcock, R. Laffineur, and J.L. Crowley (eds) *Dais: the Aegean Feast*: 151-157. Liège and Austin: the University of Liège and University of Texas at Austin.

Hruby, J. 2017. Finding haute cuisine: identifying shifts in food styles from cooking vessels, in J.A. Hruby and D.A. Trusty (eds) *From Cooking Vessels to Cultural Practices in the Late Bronze Age Aegean*: 15-26. Oxford: Oxbow Books.

Iakovidis, S.E. 2001. *Gla and the Kopais in the 13th Century BC* (Βιβλιοθήκη της εν Αθήναις Αρχαιολογικής Εταιρείας 221). Athens: the Archaeological Society at Athens.

Kaiser, B. 1976. *Corpus Vasorum Antiquorum. Deutschland. Band. 40. Bonn, Akademisches Kunstmuseum, Band 2*. Munich: Beck.

Kaiser, I. 2009. Miletus IV: the locally produced coarse wares, in C. Macdonald, E. Hallager and W-D. Niemeier (eds) *The Minoans in the Central, Eastern and Northern Aegean – New Evidence. Acts of a Minoan Seminar 22-23 January 2005 in collaboration with the Danish Institute at Athens and the German Archaeological Institute at Athens* (Monographs of the Danish Institute at Athens 8): 159-165. Aarhus: Aarhus University Press.

Karali, L. 1999. *Shells in Aegean Prehistory* (British Archaeological Reports International Series 761). Oxford: Archaeopress.

Karali-Giannakopoulou, L. 1990. Sea shells, land snails and other marine remains from Akrotiri, in D. Hardy and A.C. Renfrew (eds) *Thera and the Aegean World, III.2: Earth Sciences. Proceedings of the Third International Congress, Santorini, Greece, 3-9 September 1989*: 410-415. London: the Thera Foundation.

Karali-Giannakopoulou, L. 2006. The organic materials. B. The molluscs, in L. Marangou, C. Renfrew, C. Doumas and G. Gavalas (eds) *Markiani, Amorgos. An Early Bronze Age Fortified Settlement, Overview of the 1985-1991 Investigations* (The British School at Athens Supplementary Volume 40): 242-244. London: the British School at Athens.

Karantzali, E. 1996. *Le Bronze Ancien dans les Cyclades et en Crète: Les relations entre les deux régions. Influence de la Grèce Continentale* (British Archaeological Reports International Series 631). Oxford: British Archaeological Reports.

Karantzali, E. 2006. The pottery of phases I and II and a note on the pottery from the Bastion Area, in L. Marangou, C. Renfrew, C. Doumas and G. Gavalas (eds) *Markiani, Amorgos. An Early Bronze Age Fortified Settlement, Overview of the 1985-1991 Investigations* (The British School at Athens Supplementary Volume 40): 101-130. London: the British School at Athens.

Katsarou, S. and D.U. Schilardi 2004. Emerging Neolithic and Early Cycladic settlements in Paros: Koukounaries and Sklavouna. *The Annual of the British School at Athens* 99: 23-48.

Katsarou-Tzeveleki, S. and D.U. Schilardi 2008. Some reflections on EC domestic space arising from observations at Koukounaries, Paros, in N. Brodie, J. Doole, G. Gavalas and C. Renfrew (eds) *Horizon. A Colloquium on the Prehistory of the Cyclades*: 61-70. Cambridge: McDonald Institute for Archaeological Research.

Kaza-Papageorgiou, K. and E. Kardamaki 2012. Κοντοπήγαδο Άλιμου. Ο Οικισμός ΥΕ χρόνων. *Αρχαιολογική Εφημερίς* 151(2012): 141-199.

Kordatzaki, G., K. Sbonias, F. Farinetti and I. Tzachili 2018. Technological and provenance analysis of an Early and Middle Cycladic pottery assemblage from Therasia, Greece. *The Annual of the British School at Athens* 113: 1-17.

Labriola, L. 2008. First impressions: a preliminary account of mat-impressed pottery in the prehistoric Aegean, in H, Erkanal, H. Hauptmann, V. Şahoğlu and R. Tuncel (eds) *The Aegean in the Neolithic, Chalcolithic and the Early Bronze Age. Proceedings of the International Symposium, Oct. 13-16, 1997, Urla - İzmir, Turkey* (Ankara University Research Centre for Maritime Archaeology 1): 309-322. Ankara: Ankara University Press.

Lamb, W. 1936. *Corpus Vasorum Antiquorum. Great Britain. Fascicule 11. Cambridge, Fitzwilliam Museum, Fascicule 2.* Oxford: Oxford University Press.

Lis, B. 2015. From cooking pots to cuisine. Limitations and perspectives of a ceramic-based approach, in M. Spataro and A. Villing (eds) *Ceramics, Cuisine and Culture. The Archaeology and Science of Kitchen Pottery in the Ancient Mediterranean World*: 104-114. Oxford: Oxbow Books.

Marabea, C. 2019. Late Bronze Age Aiginetan coarse pottery at Kanakia, Salamis: a macroscopic study. *Hesperia: the Journal of the American School of Classical Studies at Athens* 88(3): 447-525.

Marco, M. 1995. Presence and distribution of the stone marten, *Martes foina* Erxleben, 1777, on the island of Crete (Greece). *Hystrix: the Italian Journal of Mammalogy* 7(1-2): 73-78.

Margaritis, E. 2013. Foodstuffs, fruit tree cultivation and occupation patterns at Dhaskalio, in C. Renfrew, O. Philaniotou, N. Brodie, G. Gavalas and M.J. Boyd (eds) *The settlement at Dhaskalio. The Sanctuary on Keros and the Origins of Aegean Ritual Practice: the Excavations of 2006-2008, Volume I*: 389-404. Cambridge: McDonald Institute for Archaeological Research.

Marinatos, S. 1969. *Excavations at Thera II (1968 Season)* (Βιβλιοθήκη της εν Αθήναις Αρχαιολογικής Εταιρείας 64). Athens: the Archaeological Society at Athens.

Marinatos, 1972. *Excavations at Thera V (1971 Season)* (Βιβλιοθήκη της εν Αθήναις Αρχαιολογικής Εταιρείας 64). Athens: the Archaeological Society at Athens.

Marthari, M. 1990. Σκάρκος: Ενας πρωτοκυκλαδικός οικισμός στην Ίο, in R. Misdrachi-Kanon (ed.) *Διαλέξεις 1986-1989*: 97-100. Athens: N.P. Goulandris Foundation, Museum of Cycladic Art.

Marthari, M. 1999. *Το Αρχαιολογικό Μουσείο της Ιου.* Athens: 21st Ephorate of Prehistoric and Classical Antiquities.

Marthari, M. 2001. Η Θήρα από την Πρώιμη στη Μέση Εποχή του Χαλκού. Τα Αποτελέσματα των Ανασκαφών στον Φτέλλο και τον Άγιο Ιωάννη τον Ελεήμονα, in M. Danezis (ed.) *Σαντορίνη: Θήρα, Θηρασιά, Ασπρονήσι*: 105-119. Athens: Adam.

Marthari, M. 2009. Middle Cycladic and early Late Cycladic cemeteries and their Minoan elements: the case of the cemetery at Skarkos on Ios, in C. Macdonald, E. Hallager and W.-D. Niemeier (eds) *The Minoans in the Central, Eastern and Northern Aegean - New Evidence. Acts of a Minoan Seminar 22-23 January 2005 in collaboration with the Danish Institute at Athens and the German Archaeological Institute at Athens* (Monographs of the Danish Institute at Athens 8): 41-58. Aarhus: Aarhus University Press.

Marthari, M. 2012. Φυλακωπή. *Αρχαιολογικόν Δελτίον* 56-59(2001-2004)(Chr., Β′6): 142-144.

Mavridis, F. 2010. Salvage excavations in the Cave of Antiparos, Cyclades: prehistoric pottery and miscellaneous finds. A preliminary report. *Aegean Archaeology* 9: 7-34.

Mayence, F. and V. Verhoogen 1949. *Corpus Vasorum Antiquorum. Belgique. Fascicule 3. Bruxelles: Musées Royaux d'Art et d'Histoire, Fascicule 3.* Brussels: the Royal Museums of Art and History.

Mee, C. and J. Doole 1993. *Aegean Antiquities on Merseyside. The Collections of Liverpool Museum and Liverpool University* (National Museums and Galleries on Merseyside Occasional Papers, Liverpool Museum No. 7). Liverpool: National Museums and Galleries on Merseyside.

Morgan, L. 1998. The wall paintings of the north-east bastion at Ayia Irini, Kea, in A.G. Mendoni and A.I. Mazarakis Ainian (eds) *Kea-Kythnos: History and Archaeology*: 201-210. Athens and Paris: Research Centre for Greek and Roman Antiquity, National Hellenic Research Foundation and de Boccard.

Morgan, L. 2020. *Keos XI. Wall Paintings and Social Context: the Northeast Bastion at Ayia Irini.* Philadelphia: INSTAP Academic Press.

Morrison, J.E., C. Sofianou, T.M. Brogan, J. Alyounis and D. Mylonas 2015. Cooking up new perspectives for Late Minoan IB domestic activities: an experimental approach to understanding the possibilities and probabilities of using ancient cooking pots, in M. Spataro and A. Villing (eds) *Ceramics, Cuisine and Culture. The Archaeology and Science of Kitchen Pottery in the Ancient Mediterranean World*: 115-124. Oxford: Oxbow Books.

Mountjoy, P. 1985. The pottery, in C. Renfrew, *The Archaeology of Cult. The Sanctuary at Phylakopi* (The British School at Athens Supplementary Volume 18): 151-208. London: the British School at Athens.

Mountjoy, P. 2007. The Mycenaean and Late Minoan I-II pottery, in C. Renfrew, N. Brodie, C. Morris and

C. Scarre (eds) *Excavations at Phylakopi in Melos 1974-77* (The British School at Athens Supplementary Volume 42): 307-370. London: the British School at Athens.

Mountjoy, P. 2009. The Late Minoan II-III and Mycenaean pottery from the 1911 excavation at Phylakopi on Melos. *The Annual of the British School at Athens* 104: 73-135.

Müller, N. S. 2009. Technology of Bronze Age Cooking Vessels from Akrotiri, Thera. Unpublished PhD dissertation, University of Sheffield.

Müller, N.S., A. Hein, V. Kilikoglou and P.M. Day 2013. Bronze Age cooking pots: thermal properties and cooking methods. *Préhistoires Méditerranéennes (en ligne)* 4: 1-10. < http://journals.openedition.org/pm/737 >.

Müller, N.S., V. Kilikoglou and P.M. Day 2015. Home-made recipes: tradition and innovation in Bronze Age cooking pots from Akrotiri, Thera, in M. Spataro and A. Villing (eds) *Ceramics, Cuisine and Culture. The Archaeology and Science of Kitchen Pottery in the Ancient Mediterranean World*: 37-48. Oxford: Oxbow Books.

Mylona, D. 2003. Archaeological fish remains in Greece: general trends of the research and a gazetteer of sites, in E. Kotjabopoulou, Y. Hamilakis, P. Halstead, C. Gamble and P. Elefanti (eds) *Zooarchaeology in Greece. Recent Advances* (The British School at Athens Studies 9): 193-200. Athens: the British School at Athens.

Mylona, D. 2014. Aquatic animal resources in prehistoric Aegean, Greece. *Journal of Biological Research-Thessaloniki* 21(2): 1-11.

Nikolakopoulou, I. 2002. Storage, Storage Facilities and Island Economy: the Evidence from LC I Akrotiri, Thera. Unpublished PhD dissertation, University of Bristol.

Nikolakopoulou, I. 2009. "Beware Cretans bearing gifts" — tracing the origins of Minoan influence at Akrotiri, Thera, in C. Macdonald, E. Hallager and W.-D. Niemeier (eds) *The Minoans in the Central, Eastern and Northern Aegean – New Evidence. Acts of a Minoan Seminar 22-23 January 2005 in collaboration with the Danish Institute at Athens and the German Archaeological Institute at Athens* (Monographs of the Danish Institute at Athens 8): 31-34. Aarhus: Aarhus University Press.

Nikolakopoulou, I. 2013. Middle Minoan III beyond Crete: the evidence from Thera, in C.F. MacDonald and C. Knappett (eds) *Intermezzo. Intermediacy and Regeneration in Middle Minoan III Palatial Crete* (The British School at Athens Studies 21): 213-219. London: the British School at Athens.

Nikolakopoulou, I. 2019a. *Akrotiri, Thera. Middle Bronze Age Pottery and Stratigraphy, Volume I. Stratigraphy, Ceramic Typology and Technology, Weaving Equipment* (Βιβλιοθήκη της εν Αθήναις Αρχαιολογικής Εταιρείας 318). Athens: the Archaeological Society at Athens.

Nikolakopoulou, I. 2019b. *Akrotiri, Thera. Middle Bronze Age Pottery and Stratigraphy, Volume II. The Pottery Catalogue. Plates and Drawings* (Βιβλιοθήκη της εν Αθήναις Αρχαιολογικής Εταιρείας 319). Athens: the Archaeological Society at Athens.

Nikolakopoulou, I., F. Georma, A. Moschou and P. Sofianou 2008. Trapped in the middle: new stratigraphic and ceramic evidence from Middle Cycladic Akrotiri, Thera, in N. Brodie, J. Doole, G. Gavalas and C. Renfrew (eds) *Horizon. A Colloquium on the Prehistory of the Cyclades*: 311-324. Cambridge: McDonald Institute for Archaeological Research.

Overbeck, J.C. 1989a. *The Bronze Age Pottery from the Kastro at Paros* (Studies in Mediterranean Archaeology and Literature Pocket-book 78). Jonsered: Paul Åström.

Overbeck, J.C. 1989b. *Keos VII. Ayia Irini: Period IV. Part I: the Stratigraphy and The Find Deposits*. Mainz: Philipp von Zabern.

Papadopoulou, Z. 2013. Αρχαιομεταλλουργικές μελέτες στη νότια Σίφνο: ευρήματα, ερωτήματα, προοπτικές, in *Πρακτικά του Δ' Διεθνούς Σιφναϊκού Συμποσίου: Σίφνος 25-26 Ιουνίου 2010*: 29-36. Athens: the Society of Siphnian Studies.

Papageorgiou, I. 2016. Truth lies in the details: identifying an apiary in the miniature wall painting from Akrotiri, Thera. *The Annual of the British School at Athens* 111: 95-120.

Plassart, A. 1928. *Exploration Archéologique de Délos. Fascicule XI: les sanctuaires et les cultes du mont Cynthe*. Paris: de Boccard.

Powell, J. 1996. *Fishing in the Prehistoric Aegean* (Studies in Mediterranean Archaeology and Literature Pocket-book 137). Jonsered: Paul Åström.

Renfrew, C. 1985. *The Archaeology of Cult. The Sanctuary at Phylakopi* (The British School at Athens Supplementary Volume 18). London: the British School at Athens.

Renfrew, C., 2007a. The development of the excavation and the stratigraphy of Phylakopi, in C. Renfrew, N. Brodie, C. Morris and C. Scarre (eds) *Excavations at Phylakopi in Melos 1974-77* (The British School at Athens Supplementary Volume 42): 5-18. London: the British School at Athens.

Renfrew, C. 2016. Reflections on the pottery from Dhaskalio, in P. Sotirakopoulou. *The Pottery from Dhaskalio. The Sanctuary on Keros and the Origins of Aegean Ritual: the Excavations of 2006-2008, Volume IV*: 393-398. Cambridge: McDonald Institute for Archaeological Research.

Renfrew, C. and J.F. Cherry 1985. The finds, in C. Renfrew. *The Archaeology of Cult. The Sanctuary at Phylakopi* (The British School at Athens Supplementary Volume 18): 299-360. London: the British School at Athens.

Renfrew, C. and R.K. Evans 2007. The Early Bronze Age pottery, in C. Renfrew, N. Brodie, C. Morris and C. Scarre (eds) *Excavations at Phylakopi in Melos 1974-77* (The British School at Athens Supplementary

Volume 42): 129-180. London: the British School at Athens.

Renfrew, C., C. Scarre, T. Whitelaw and N. Brodie 2007. The excavated areas, in C. Renfrew, N. Brodie, C. Morris and C. Scarre (eds) *Excavations at Phylakopi in Melos 1974-77* (The British School at Athens Supplementary Volume 42): 19-90. London: the British School at Athens.

Renfrew, C., W. Megarry, G. Gavalas and M.J. Boyd 2013. The terrace structure east of the summit: Trenches I, II and XV, in C. Renfrew, O. Philaniotou, N. Brodie, G. Gavalas and M.J. Boyd (eds) *The settlement at Dhaskalio. The Sanctuary on Keros and the Origins of Aegean Ritual Practice: the Excavations of 2006-2008, Volume I*: 93-140. Cambridge: McDonald Institute for Archaeological Research.

Renfrew, J. 1982. Early agriculture in Melos, in C. Renfrew and M. Wagstaff (eds) *An Island Polity. The Archaeology of Exploitation in Melos*: 156-160. Cambridge: Cambridge University Press.

Renfrew, J. 2006. The leaf, mat and cloth impressions, in L. Marangou, C. Renfrew, C. Doumas and G. Gavalas (eds) *Markiani, Amorgos. An Early Bronze Age Fortified Settlement, Overview of the 1985-1991 Investigations* (The British School at Athens Supplementary Volume 40): 195-199. London: the British School at Athens.

Richter, G. 1912. Cretan pottery. *The Metropolitan Museum of Art Bulletin* 7(2): 28-35.

Ross, L. 1845. *Reisen auf den griechischen Inseln des Ägäischen Meeres, Volume 3*. Stuttgart and Tübingen: Halle and C.A. Schwetschke and Sohn.

Robinson, D.M. 1934. *Corpus Vasorum Antiquorum. United States of America. Fascicule 4. The Robinson Collection, Baltimore, MD. Fascicule 1*. Cambridge: Harvard University Press.

Roumpou, M., K. Psaraki, V. Aravantinos and C. Heron 2007. Early Bronze Age cooking vessels from Thebes, in C. Mee and J. Renard (eds) *Cooking up the Past. Food and Culinary Practice in the Neolithic and Bronze Age Aegean*: 158-173. Oxford: Oxbow Books.

Roumpou, M., N.S. Müller, N. Kalogeropoulos, P. Day, I. Nikolakopoulou and V. Kilikoglou 2013. An interdisciplinary approach to the study of cooking vessels from Bronze Age Akrotiri, Thera, in S. Voutsaki and S.M. Valamoti (eds) *Diet, Economy and Society in the Ancient Greek World. Towards a Better Integration of Archaeology and Science. Proceedings of the International Conference held at the Netherlands Institute at Athens on 22–24 March 2010* (Pharos Supplement 1): 33-46. Leuven: Peeters.

Rubensohn, O. 1917. Die prähistorischen und frühgeschichtlichen Funde auf dem Burghügel von Paros. *Mitteilungen des Deutschen Archäologischen Instituts, Athenische Abteilung* 42: 1-98.

Sampson, A. 2018. The Neolithic settlement at Ftelia, Mykonos. An intra-site analysis, in A. Sampson and T. Tsourouni (eds) *Ftelia on Mykonos. Neolithic Networks in*

the Southern Aegean Basin II (University of the Aegean Laboratory of Environmental Archaeology Monograph Series 7): 1-14. Athens: University of the Aegean.

Sarpaki, A. 1987. The Palaeoethnobotany of the West House, Akrotiri, Thera. A Case Study. Unpublished PhD dissertation, University of Sheffield.

Sarpaki, A. 2001. Processed cereals and pulses from the Late Bronze Age site of Akrotiri, Thera: preparations prior to consumption: a preliminary approach to their study. *The Annual of the British School at Athens* 96: 27-40.

Sarpaki, A. and G. Jones 1990. Ancient and modern cultivation of *Lathyrus clymenum* L. in the Greek islands. *The Annual of the British School at Athens* 85: 363-368.

Schiffer, M.B. 1990. The influence of surface treatment on heating effectiveness of ceramic vessels. *Journal of Archaeological Science* 17(4): 373-381.

Scheffer, C. 1984. Aegean Bronze Age spit supports with scalloped tops. *Opuscula Atheniensia. Annual of the Swedish Institute at Athens* 15: 155-162.

Schofield, E. 2011. *Keos X. Ayia Irini: the Western Sector*. Mainz: Philipp von Zabern.

Shackleton, N.J. 1968. Appendix IX. The mollusca, the crustacea, the echinodermata, in J.D. Evans and C. Renfrew. *Excavations at Saliagos near Antiparos* (The British School at Athens Supplementary Volume 5): 122-138. Athens and London: the British School at Athens and Thames and Hudson.

Shank, E. 2005. New evidence for Anatolian relations with Crete in EM I–EM IIA, in R. Laffineur and E. Greco (eds) *Emporia: Aegeans in the Central and Eastern Mediterranean. Proceedings of the 10th International Aegean Conference/10e Rencontre égéenne internationale, Athens, Italian School of Archaeology, 14-18 April 2004* (Aegaeum 25): 103-106. Liège: the University of Liège.

Sherratt, S. 2000. *Catalogue of Cycladic Antiquities in the Ashmolean Museum: the Captive Spirit*. Oxford: Oxford University Press.

Skibo, J.M. 2012. *Understanding Pottery Function*. Springer: New York.

Smith, C. 1895-1896. Excavations in Melos. *The Annual of the British School at Athens* 2: 63-76.

Smith, C. 1896-1897. Excavations in Melos, 1897. *The Annual of the British School at Athens* 3: 1-30.

Smith, D. *forthcoming*. The metal and metallurgical objects, in R. Barber and D. Evely (eds) *Phylakopi, Melos, 1896-99: the Finds in the National Archaeological Museum, Athens*.

Snyder, L.M. and W.E. Klippel 2003. From Lerna to Kastro: further thoughts on dogs as food in ancient Greece; perceptions, prejudices and reinvestigations, in E. Kotjabopoulou, Y. Hamilakis, P. Halstead, C. Gamble and P. Elefanti (eds) *Zooarchaeology in Greece. Recent Advances* (The British School at Athens Studies 9): 221-231. London: the British School at Athens.

Sofianou, C. and T. Brogan 2009. The excavation of House A.1 at Papadiokampos. *Kentro* 12: 6-9.

Sotirakopoulou, P. 1997. Κυκλάδες και βόρειο Αιγαίο: οι σχέσεις τους κατά το δεύτερο ήμισυ της 3ης χιλιετίας π.Χ, in C. Doumas and V. La Rosa (eds) *Η Πολιόχνη. Η Πρώιμη Εποχή του Χαλκού στο Βόρειο Αιγαίο*: 522-542. Athens: the Italian School of Archaeology at Athens.

Sotirakopoulou, P. 2004a. Early Cycladic pottery from the investigations of the 1960s at Kavos-Daskaleio, Keros, in E. Alram-Stern (ed.) *Die Ägäische Frühzeit. 2. Serie. Forschungsbericht 1975–2002. 2. Band, Teil 1 und 2: Die Frühbronzezeit in Griechenland. mit Ausnahme von Kreta* (Veröffentlichungen der Mykenischen Kommission 21): 1303-1342. Vienna: the Austrian Academy of Sciences.

Sotirakopoulou, P. 2004b. Η ,απουσία' της Μεσοκυκλαδικής περιόδου από τις Κυκλάδες. Νέα στοιχεία από την Αμοργό. *Αρχαιολογική Εφημερίς* 143: 53-80.

Sotirakopoulou, P. 2008. Akrotiri, Thera: the Late Neolithic and Early Bronze Age phases in light of recent excavations at the site, in N. Brodie, J. Doole, G. Gavalas and C. Renfrew (eds) *Horizon. A Colloquium on the Prehistory of the Cyclades*: 121-134. Cambridge: McDonald Institute for Archaeological Research.

Sotirakopoulou, P. 2010. The Cycladic Middle Bronze Age: a 'Dark Age' in Aegean Prehistory or a dark spot in archaeological research, in A. Philippa-Touchais, G. Touchais, S. Voutsaki and J. Wright (eds) *MESOHELLADIKA. The Greek Mainland in the Middle Bronze Age. Actes du colloque international organisé par l'Ecole française d'Athènes, en collaboration avec l'American School of Classical Studies at Athens et le Netherlands Institute in Athens, Athènes, 8-12 mars 2006* (Bulletin de Correspondance Hellénique Supplément 52): 825-839. Paris: de Boccard.

Sotirakopoulou, P. 2016. *The Pottery from Dhaskalio. The Sanctuary on Keros and the Origins of Aegean Ritual: the Excavations of 2006-2008, Volume IV*. Cambridge: McDonald Institute for Archaeological Research.

Souyoudzoglou-Haywood, C. 2007. Henry Browne, Greek archaeology and 'The Museum of Ancient History', University College, in J.V. Luce, C. Morris and C. Souyoudzoglou-Haywood (eds) *The Lure of Greece. Irish Involvement in Greek Culture, Literature, History and Politics*: 55-69. Dublin: Hinds.

Spanos, S. 2006. Ἡ κυκλαδικὴ κεραμικὴ στὴν Πελοπόννησο καὶ τὴν Ἀττικὴ κατὰ τὴν Μεσοελλαδικὴ καὶ τὴν Ὑστεροελλαδικὴ περίοδο, in T. Gritsopoulos, K.L. Kotsonis and I.K. Giannaropoulou (eds) *Πρακτικά του Ζ' Διεθνούς Συνεδρίου Πελοποννησιακών Σπουδών, Πύργος, Γαστούνη, Αμαλιάδα, 11-17 Σεπτεμβρίου 2005. Τόμος Α': Ολομέλεια - Ἀρχαιότης* (Πελοποννησιακά Παράρτημα 27): 203-224. Athens: the Society of Peloponnesian Studies.

Taylor, D. 2016. Impact damage and repair in shells of the limpet Patella vulgate. *Journal of Experimental Biology* 219: 3927-2935.

Televantou, C. 2006. Προϊστορική Άνδρος, in N. Stampolidis (ed.) *Γενέθλιον. Αναμνηστικός Τόμος για τη συμπλήρωση 20 χρόνων λειτουργίας του Μουσείου Κυκλαδικής Τέχνης*: 1-16. Athens: the Museum of Cycladic Art.

Theodoropoulou, T. 2007. La mer dans l'assiette: l'exploitation des faunes aquatiques dans l'alimentation en Égée pré- et protohistorique, in C. Mee and J. Renard (eds) *Cooking up the Past. Food and Culinary Practice in the Neolithic and Bronze Age Aegean*: 71-88. Oxford: Oxbow Books.

Theodoropoulou, T. 2014. Dead from the sea: worn shells in Aegean prehistory, in K. Szabo, C. Dupont, V. Dimitrijević, L. Gómez Gastélum and N. Serrand (eds) *Archaeomalacology: Shells in the Archaeological Record* (British Archaeological Reports International Series 2666): 77-90. Oxford: Archaeopress.

Todaro, S. 2005. EM I - MM IA ceramic groups at Phaistos: towards the definition of a prepalatial ceramic sequence in south central Crete. *Creta Antica* 6: 11-46.

Trantalidou, K. 2008. Archaeozoological research at the Akrotiri excavation. The animal world in everyday life and ideology. *ΑΛΣ. Περιοδική έκδοση της Εταιρείας Στήριξης Σπουδών Προϊστορικής Θήρας* 6: 26-69.

Tzedakis, Y. and H. Martlew 1999. *Minoans and Mycenaeans: Flavours of their Time*. Athens: Kapon Editions.

Tzedakis, Y. and H. Martlew 2008. Archaeology meets science: the background, in Y. Tzedakis, H. Martlew and M. Jones (eds) *Archaeology Meets Science. Biomolecular Investigations in Bronze Age Greece*: xiv-xxi. Oxford: Oxbow Books.

Vaughn, S.J. and D. Williams 2007. The pottery fabrics, in C. Renfrew, N. Brodie, C. Morris and C. Scarre (eds) *Excavations at Phylakopi in Melos 1974-77* (The British School at Athens Supplementary Volume 42): 91-128. London: the British School at Athens.

Vaughn, S.J. and D.E. Wilson 1993. Interregional contacts in the Aegean in Early Bronze II: the talc ware connection, in C. Zerner (ed.) *Wace and Blegen. Pottery as Evidence for Trade in the Aegean Bronze Age, 1939-1989. Proceedings of the International Conference held at the American School of Classical Studies at Athens, Athens, December 2-3, 1989*: 169-186. Amsterdam: J.C. Gieben.

Wardle, K.A. 1969. A group of Late Helladic IIIB 1 pottery from within the citadel at Mycenae. *The Annual of the British School at Athens* 64: 261-297.

Wardle, K.A., J. Crouwel and E. French 1973. A group of Late Helladic IIIB 2 pottery from within the citadel at Mycenae: 'The Causeway Deposit'. *The Annual of the British School at Athens* 68: 297-348.

Warren, P. 1972. *Myrtos: An Early Bronze Age Settlement in Crete* (The British School at Athens Supplementary Volume 7). London: the British School at Athens and Thames and Hudson.

Warren, P., J. Tzedhakis and J.R.A. Greig 1974. An Early Minoan settlement in western Crete. *The Annual of the British School at Athens* 69: 299-342.

Weil, R. 1876. Von den griechischen Inseln. *Athenische Mitteilungen* 1: 235-252.

Wilson, D.E. 1999. *Keos IX. Ayia Irini: Periods I-III. The Neolithic and Early Bronze Age Settlements*. Mainz: Philipp von Zabern.

Winder, N. 2007. A multidimensional approach to the animal bone data, in C. Renfrew, N. Brodie, C. Morris and C. Scarre (eds) *Excavations at Phylakopi in Melos 1974-77* (The British School at Athens Supplementary Volume 42): 465-484. London: the British School at Athens.

Wright, J. 2004. The Mycenaean feast: an introduction. *Hesperia: the Journal of the American School of Classical Studies at Athens* 73: 121-132.

Yiannouli, E. 2002. Kat'Akrotiri on Amorgos: surface pottery from an Early Cycladic acropolis. *The Annual of the British School at Athens* 97: 1-47.

Zachos, K. and A. Dousougli, forthcoming. Attica and the Cyclades from the Chalcolithic to the Early Bronze Age, in M. Marthari (ed.) *The Aegean Early Bronze Age. New Evidence.*

Zapheiropoulou, P. 1969. Αρχαιότητες και Μνημεία Σάμου και Κυκλάδων. *Αρχαιολογικόν Δελτίον* 23(1968)(Chr. Β΄2): 375-383.

Ritual Pyres in Minoan Peak Sanctuaries.
Reality and Popular Myths

Iphiyenia Tournavitou

Fire, one of the most fascinating — for some, the most fascinating — element of nature, the source of light, the source of life, and the ultimate, most impressive, destroyer of all forms of life, is a crucial element in most religious practices, both in the Aegean and beyond it. Although there is no specific evidence for the existence of fire worship in Minoan Crete, or the ancient Greek world in general (Burkert 1993: 79, 147, 149), fire has played an important role in numerous ancient and modern religions (Burkert 1993: 77-79, 145, 149, 262; Megas 2005: 54-57, 137-139, 149-150, 164, 207-208, 213-214, 240-246, 259-261, 270-271, 274, 277, 282, 287-289; Nilsson 1923: 144, 146-148; Platon 1951: 151-152, 159; Psilakis 2005: 58, 74, 136, 188-189, 247, 277-278, 330, 332-333).

In the ancient Greek world, centuries after the collapse of the Minoan and Mycenaean civilisations, fire was the ultimate medium for the purification of, the ultimate redemption of, body and soul (Burkert 1993: 145, 175-177, 180-181). In ancient Greek lore, fire purified and offered immortality (Burkert 1993: 148, 180-181, 436-437). Fire festivals in Greek antiquity are usually associated with the worship of deities like Hera, Artemis and Demeter, and demigods like Heracles, while the use of fire is widely attested in purification rites, and in the sacrificial offering of animals to deities or the dead. According to Nilsson (1923: 144, 146-148; 1950: 75), festivals involving pyres were mostly attested in central Greece. During the festival of Artemis Laphria at Patras/Kalydon, and at Prinias on Crete, live animals were thrown into the pyre; at Mount Kithairon and at Tithorea in Phocis, parts of sacrificed bovids were also thrown into pyres; at Hymapolis in Phocis, effigies of human figures and other objects were thrown into the fire and, at the festivals of Hera in Boeotia, *xoana* of the goddess herself. Large pyres were also featured in a number of other festivals, including the pyre of Heracles on the summit of Mount Oite, and the festival in honour of the Kouretes at Messene (Burkert 1993: 77-78, 137-138, 144-149, 262).

In the modern Greek world, pyres had, and still have, a special role in customs that are often peripheral to official religion. Pyres, in towns and mountaintops, are mostly associated with physical and moral purification, both collective and personal; with health and healing; with the aversion of evil; with the fertility of the earth and the fertility of people and animals; with

communication with the divine; and with the passing from one cycle of nature to another, and even the influencing of this cycle. The activities accompanying these fires include mostly communal, usually circular, dances, jumping over the fire, or treading on the burning embers of the pyre (Megas 2005: 214, 240-246, 259, 261; Psilakis 2005: 188, 247), the throwing of objects or offerings into the flames, and animal sacrifice (Megas 2005: 259-261, 271; Psilakis 2005: 247).

On the mountaintops of Crete, on Mount Psiloritis and Mount Kophinas, during the two-day pilgrimage for the festival of Ύψωσις του Τιμίου Σταυρού (the Exaltation of the Holy Cross), fires were lit at the *Mitata*,[1] located halfway up the mountains, to protect resting pilgrims against the cold; fires also accompanied their final ascent, during the night. A pyre was also built close to the entrance of the small, rural, chapel at the top of the mountain, for those who could not fit inside (Psilakis 2005: 328-333, 335). On the eve of the festival of Μεταμόρφωση του Σωτήρος Αφέντη Χριστό (Transfiguration of Our Lord and Saviour Jesus Christ), a large fire was lit on Mount Juktas, for protection against the cold (Psilakis 2005: 278). The large fires lit on the eve of the feast during the four major summer festivals of Προφήτης Ηλίας (Prophet Elijah), Άγιο Παντελεήμονα (Saint Panteleimon), Μεταμόρφωση του Σωτήρος (the Transfiguration of the Saviour) and Ύψωση του Τιμίου Σταυρού (the Exaltation of the Holy Cross) — which, in Crete, are celebrated largely on mountaintops — are also meant to emphasise the sanctity of the site, and to illuminate the location where the festivities take place (Psilakis 2005: 277-278).

During the festival of Ayios Antonios on Crete, large fires built in the cave-like churches dedicated to the saint, represent an attempt to influence the cycle of nature, and the change of the seasons in the middle of winter (Psilakis 2005: 58). Ancient rites associated with the changing of the seasons, and the harnessing, the purifying, the healing and apotropaic power of fire, are reflected in the fires lit for the feast of Άι Γιάννη (Saint John), at the summer solstice (Megas 2005: 259-260; Psilakis 2005: 247). Similar notions pervade the ritual mountaintop fires lit during the festival of Προφήτης Ηλίας (Prophet Elijah), in July, when pilgrims

---

[1] These are temporary shelters for shepherds, which also served for cheesemaking.

dance around the pyre, and throw incense and/or frankincense into the flames as an offering to the saint (Megas 2005: 270-271). In the festival in honour of Constantine the Great and his mother, Eleni, the treading of the fire by the *Anastenarides* in Macedonia, involves music and the sacrifice of an animal, usually a sheep. The treading of the fire by initiates, who seem to be in a trance, is an act which embodies notions of moral purification, regeneration and, above all, communication with the divine (Megas 2005: 241, 244-245, n. 1); a notion, apparently, familiar to the pilgrims celebrating the fire festivals on mountaintops (Psilakis 2005: 277).

Ritual pyres in Minoan peak sanctuaries

One of the most popular, and most disputed, theories regarding ritual practices on Minoan peak sanctuaries, concerns the existence, and the importance, of ritual pyres. It has been suggested that these pyres formed the focus of elaborate rituals, during which, pottery, figurines, parts of sacrificed animals, and other offerings were cast into the fire. Deposits containing ashes, animal bones, and votives made of clay or other materials, located in natural hollows or rock crevices at peak sanctuary sites, have been interpreted as the result of the periodic, ritual clearance of the sacred area of the sanctuary, after the completion of these rituals (Bergquist 1988: 32; Burkert 1993: 77-79; Karetsou 1977: 334, 342; 1979: 410-411, 413-414, 417-418; Marinatos 1986: 14-15, 36-37, 39, 49; 1993: 118-119; Myres 1903: 357-358, 360, 378, 380; Peatfield 1983: 277; 1992: 66; Platon 1951: 102-103, 114, 151, 157-158; Rutkowski 1986: 91; Watrous 1995: 394; 1996: 92).

Despite the scarcity of published archaeological evidence on the matter, a large corpus of scholarly theory has developed during the past century or so, which has come to dominate modern research. In view of the negative evidence from the excavations of the only two unlooted peak sanctuaries thus far identified, at Atsipades Korakias on Crete and Ayios Georgios sto Vouno on Kythera, it is high time for a detailed re-evaluation of the subject of 'ritual' pyres.

The theory

The extensive use of ritual pyres in Minoan peak sanctuaries, first proposed by Myres ('bonfires') based on the evidence from the excavation at Petsophas Siteias (Myres 1903: 357-358, 360, 378, 380), and then adopted by Platon in the first synthetic study of the peak sanctuaries then known (Platon 1951: 96-160), has enjoyed widespread acceptance. The finds recovered from the Juktas peak sanctuary in the 1970s, more than 25 years later (Karetsou 1977: 334, 342; 1979: 410-411, 413-414, 417-418), reinforced scholarly opinion about

the validity of the old theory, and the fixed nature of ritual practices in peak sanctuaries in general. The theory was subsequently embraced by Rutkowski (1988: 74), who developed the concept of the so-called 'canonical' peak sanctuary. In more recent times, Kyriakidis (2005: 137), in a comprehensive study of the published views on Minoan peak sanctuaries, appears to concur with the unconditional acceptance of ritual pyres.

Despite the consensus in favour of ritual pyres, some scholars have disputed not only the necessity, but also the existence, of the ritual. Peatfield, who initially favoured the latter, went so far as to propose the existence of an island-wide 'network of sacred pyres', and the existence of a single, uniform, cult pattern at all Minoan peak sanctuaries (Peatfield 1983: 277; 1992: 61). He eventually recanted, on account of the incontrovertible archaeological evidence from the excavation of the sanctuary at Atsipades Korakias. Having acknowledged the almost complete absence of layers with carbonised matter and animal bones at the site, he went on to dispute the published data for ash layers as untrustworthy, and concluded that the archaeological evidence concerning smaller sanctuaries of the Protopalatial period was, at best, ambiguous, or altogether non-existent (Peatfield 1992: 66).

Among those scholars who have consistently expressed doubts over the ubiquity and uniformity of the ritual, Dietrich was the first to suggest that 'the fire ritual at Petsophas is too thinly documented' (1969: 269) to support the model, while Nowicki (1994: 34) maintained that: '...the figurines available for study do not seem to be burnt. The whole idea of "the bonfire", which has appeared so often in later studies on the Minoan peak sanctuaries, must be reconsidered, at least for the Pre- and perhaps also for the Proto-palatial period'. Both Nowicki and Watrous expressed their disagreement with Peatfield's earlier view about the homogeneity of the peak sanctuary cult (Nowicki 1994: 40, n. 55; Watrous 2001: 194), while Marinatos (1993: 119) disputed the existence of a single network of ritual pyres. Finally, while Jones, in his synthetic study of peak sanctuaries and sacred caves, acknowledges evidence of fires at more than half of the peak sanctuaries on Crete, he also notes that the data for the existence of pyres are not particularly abundant, and that the frequency of the custom is, in reality, unknown (Jones 1999: 32-33).

Re-examination of the evidence

The consideration of ritual pyres in Minoan peak sanctuaries should address three essential issues: the existence of pyres, their distribution, and the diachronic nature of the practice. The activities accompanying the suggested use of pyres (the burning of votives and animal parts, preparation of food, consumption of communal meals, singing, dancing or fire-leaping), should reveal the ultimate *raison d'être* of the practice; that is, whether they answered symbolic or ritual concerns (such as health, fertility, the aversion of evil, and communion with the divine), or whether they addressed more practical needs, such as providing protection from the elements, or enhancing the visibility of the site, especially at night.

The archaeological remains directly associated with the existence and/or popularity of ritual pyres include built structures (hearths/altars) with evidence of burning, ashes and ash layers containing burnt organic material, traces of burning on pottery, bone, shell and other objects, and pictorial representations of pyres in a peak sanctuary setting.

Built structures with evidence of burning

Evidence for the existence of 'pyres', be it the remains of built structures or altars, or areas with burnt soil marking the location of fires and/or pyres, in either the Protopalatial or Neopalatial period, has been ascertained at fewer than 20% of the 26 acknowledged peak sanctuaries, including three of the four largest and most important sanctuaries in Crete (Juktas, Kophinas Monophatsiou, and Petsophas Siteias; see Appendix).

Built structures used as altars are, in fact, very rare in the Minoan peak sanctuaries, the only exceptions being the built, stepped altar at Juktas (Karetsou 1976: 231-232; 1977: 330; 1981: 138, 141), and a possible altar or offering table at Gonies Maleviziou-Philioremos (Alexiou 1966: 322; 1969: 484), probably hypaethral (Rutkowski 1986: 80; 1988: 79-81). Hypaethral structures described as altars have also been identified at three other sites, including a stone structure at Vrysinas Rethymnis.[2] The evidence for the existence of an altar at the second site, Prinias Siteias, is admittedly rather flimsy,[3] and equally unconvincing is the evidence for an altar at the sanctuary of Pyrgos Maleviziou (Pera Korphi).[4] At none of these three sites is there any reference to traces of burning on the structures; that

includes the altar at Juktas, where the deposit of black burnt earth and ashes containing a large number of pottery vessels, votives and animal bones in the vicinity of the altar, belongs, according to the excavator, to the Protopalatial period ('ash-altar') (Karetsou 1980b: 247, 258; 1981: 146).

Extensive areas with black or reddish soil, presumably burnt, identify the location of one or more pyres at Juktas (Jones 1999: 57-58 table 9; Karetsou 1976: 232, 234; 1977: 342; 1980a: 419-420; 1980b: 235, 241-242, 247; 1982: 341-342), at Petsophas Siteias (Jones 1999: 57-58 table 9; Myres 1903: 357-358; Platon 1951: 120; Rutkowski 1991: 19), and at Kophinas Monophatsiou (Davaras 1963: 287; Jones 1999: 57-58 table 9; Rutkowski 1988: 83). More uncertain are the references to a burnt deposit of soil, ashes, and animal bones located in an ovoid hollow at the top of the hill on Vigla Siteias (Jones 1999: 57-58 table 9; Rutkowski 1988: 90), and to a burnt deposit of black soil, ashes and figurines identified in the vicinity of one of the Minoan walls at Modi Siteias (Jones 1999: 57-58 table 9; Rutkowski 1988: 84-85, wall 5). Finally, and despite earlier arguments to the contrary (Chrysoulaki 1999: 311-312; Rutkowski 1988: 89), the most recent study concerning ritual practices at Traostalos Siteias, suggests that the main pyre at the top of the hill, and the pyre at the north end of the plateau, should, in fact, be associated with Venetian activities at the site (Vokotopoulos 2017: 6-7).

At Ayios Georgios sto Vouno, the archaeological evidence for fires, ritual or not, is extremely thin on the ground, and often ambiguous in character (Figure 17.1). Traces of pyres have been identified at only two locations, both on Terrace 2, at the top of the mountain; the most important and most easily accessible terrace in the sanctuary (Figure 17.1; Tournavitou 2014: 533 table 17, 1134-1135, distribution map 18). Only one of the two locations preserves any credible evidence for the existence of a pyre dated to the Minoan period: a layer, 0.35-0.38m thick, with sporadic traces of burning, in the south part of the area between the two churches (Sakellarakis 2011: 173; Tournavitou 2014: 134-150, 533 table 17, distribution map 18-Layer 2, 92/Area 2/4).

Despite the undoubtedly Neopalatial character of the deposit, the accompanying pottery assemblage does not include any conical cups or braziers, or, for that matter, any sherds with traces of burning. The fragmentary pottery material associated with the pyre has yielded a notably small number of tripod cooking pots, none of which bore any evidence of having been in contact with a burning fire, and an interesting array of, mostly semiglobular, cups. The latter included two specimens of the shallow semiglobular type with a short, everted rim (K259 and K260, see Tournavitou 2014: 42, 321, 323 fig. 16, 633 pl. 5), which seems to have closer affinities with the Menelaion material, dated to the LM IB-LM

---

[2] According to Rutkowski (1986: 80), 'excavations have brought to light ... part of a stone altar, which has survived to a height of 0.30m'.

[3] According to Rutkowski (1988: 87), 'It is thought that between the crack and the northern group of rocks (on the main terrace), an altar must have stood near a rock that was partly damaged when the modern datum was being built. In the centre of terrace I, stands a rock measuring 0.8m by 1.5m and about 1.5m high, which, according to Davaras, might have been used as an altar. Davaras noted that a funnel had been made in it, for carrying away the blood of the sacrificial animals. Judging from the position of this rock, we may take it that this was the most sacred rock in the cult area'.

[4] According to Rutkowski (1988: 87-88), 'Near the cult building is a stone in which a rectangle has been hollowed out. It may have been a sacrificial table put into secondary use... One half of a pair of limestone horns of consecration was found near the building, and may have come from an altar erected before the building on terrace I'.

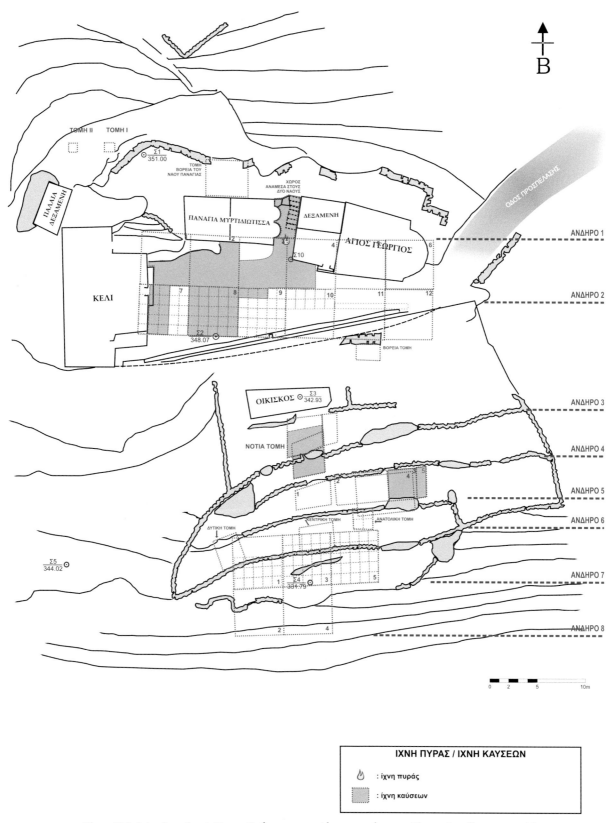

Figure 17.1. Ayios Georgios sto Vouno, Kythera: areas with pyres and areas with remains of burnt material.

IIIA1 period (Catling 1996: 73 fig. 2.4 [LM IB]; 73 fig. 2.5 [LM II-IIIA1], Cretan imports). The closest parallels at Kastri are dated to the LM IB period (Coldstream 1972a: 192 ω175-176; Coldstream 1972b: 243 Tomb J no. 7. Similar specimens, but with a deeper profile, are also known, for example, Coldstream 1972a: 124 ι13, and 140 ξ1 and 16). The non-monochrome interior should perhaps be construed as a further indication of Helladic influence. Outside Kythera, similar cups at Knossos, Palaikastro, and Ayios Stephanos in Laconia,

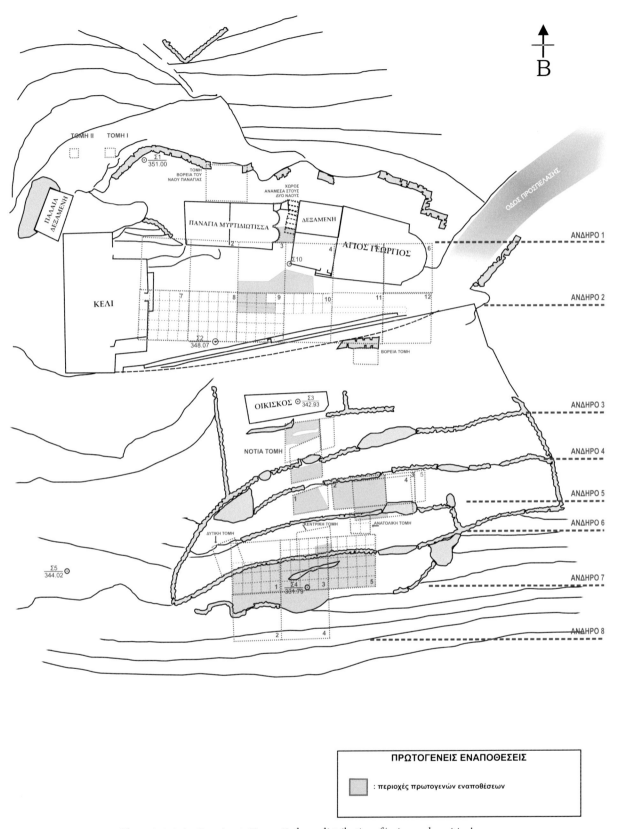

Figure 17.2. Ayios Georgios sto Vouno, Kythera: distribution of 'primary deposition' areas.

are dated to the transitional MM IIIB/LM IA and LM IA-LM IB periods (Bernini 1995: 70 fig. 10.20 [LM IA]; Betancourt 1990: fig. 60.1708 and 1723 [MM III], fig. 70.2020 and 2028 [MM III/LM IA]; Catling *et al.* 1979: 51-52 fig. 37.257 [LM IB]; Cummer and Schofield 1984: 60 no. 244, pl. 30.244 [LMIB]; Popham 1984: pl. 141.4 [MMIIIB/LMIA], pl. 141.2 and 6; Warren 1991: 329 fig. 10c [MMIIIB/LMIA]; fig 10e and f [LM I]; fig 10i and j [MM IIIB/LM IA]). Other such specimens are attested both in Laconia and in Messenia during the MH/MM

IIIB and the LH/LM I periods (Mountjoy 1999: 257 fig. 84.29, 258, 314-315 [Epidauros Limera]; 313 fig. 105.5 [Pylos]; Rutter and Rutter 1976: 40 ill. 12.414 and 416 [period III-MM IIIB, LM IA early]). Another specimen, exemplifying a simpler version of the semiglobular cup, with an incurving rim (K261: Tournavitou 2014: 44, 321, 323 fig. 16), is also at home in the LM I/LM IB repertoire. Similar cups, attested at Kastri and Crete, are dated both to the MM IIIB and the LM I periods (Coldstream 1972a: 106 ζ19 [MM IIIB]). Although specimens with an incurving rim have not been recorded at the settlement of Kastri, they have been attested in the Knossos area during the LM IA period (Catling *et al.* 1979: 51-52 fig. 37.254; Popham 1977: pl. 30a and d).

The same deposit also yielded a fragment of a deep semiglobular, almost cylindrical cup, with a flaring rim (K262: Tournavitou 2014: 43-44, 321, 323 fig. 16), which belongs to a group without close typological parallels, but with close affinities to the LM I tradition. Finally, another specimen (K331: Tournavitou 2014: 45, 331, 333 fig. 20, 635 pl. 7), belongs to a small group of sherds with In-and-Out decoration, typical of Kytheran LM IB (Tournavitou 2014: 45). The pottery material from Kastri has yielded a total of 26 In-and-Out specimens, all dated to the LM IB period (Coldstream 1972a: 142 nos. ζ49-62, 190 nos. ω142-155; 1972c: 293). The decoration on specimen K331 consists of a sea anemone, which forms part of an apparently marine style composition, perfectly in tune with the LM IB style on the island (Coldstream 1972a: 142 ξ53, 190 ω147 and ω152; 1972b: 253 Tomb J no. 4 [LMIB]; 1972c: 297), where the anemone is attested as a primary or secondary motif on semiglobular and shallow In-and-Out cups (see also, Dimopoulou 1999: pl. XLIXc; MacGillivray *et al.* 1989: 424, 425 fig. 6; Sapouna-Sakellaraki 1988-1989: pl. 5, figs. 3.A1 and 3.A4; pl. 6, fig. 5.B5; pl. 12, fig. 14.17.4; pl. 21, fig. 26.21.2; pl. 23, fig. 30.22.7). The same applies to an open vessel discovered in the same location, also decorated with a marine style composition (coral) (K1234: Tournavitou 2014: 125-126, 497, 498 fig. 107, 662 pl. 34).

The pottery material from the pyre also includes a single straight-sided cup, with a flaring rim, almost cylindrical walls, and Dark-on-Light decoration, that can also be assigned to the LM IA/LM IB period (K241: Tournavitou 2014: 38, 317 fig. 14, 318). The only, rather remote, parallels from the Minoan tombs at Kastri are the so-called 'tumblers' of LM IA and LM IB date (Coldstream 1972b: 245 Tomb E nos. 11-13 and 16 [LM I], 254 Tomb J no. 12 [LM I]; 1972c: 285, 294). Other specimens include a semiglobular miniature footed cup (K352: Tournavitou 2014: 47, 335, 336 fig. 21, 635 pl. 7) (Figure 17.3), decorated with a relatively well preserved floral composition, depicting two lilies, a plain version of the lily with two volutes and two stamens and,

possibly, part of a third, in a splayed arrangement. This type of composition, although rare on Kythera, is also attested on the miniature conical rhyton from the sanctuary (K803: Tournavitou 2014: 81, 422, 425 fig. 69, 646 pl. 18), and is securely dated to the LM IB period. The motif of splayed flowers is rarely attested in the LM IB period on Kythera (Bevan *et al.* 2002: 85 fig. 17.144 [LM IB]; Coldstream 1972a: 190 ω147, 191 ω154, 195 ω221 [LM IB]), where all surviving examples of lilies appear on semiglobular cups. The same applies to the material from Ayia Irini on Kea (Cummer and Schofield 1984: 127, no. 1570, pl. 86.1570 [LMIB]). Flowers, typically in the form of bunched lilies or crocuses, are most commonly attested on Kythera during LM IB (Coldstream 1972a: 130 μ15, 133 μ50, 194 ω208). The motif of splayed flowers is, however, rare on the island during the LM IB period (Bevan *et al.* 2002: 85 fig. 17.144 [LM IB]; Coldstream 1972a: 190 ω147, 191 ω154, 195 ω221 [LM IB]), and all surviving examples of lilies appear on semiglobular cups. At Ayia Irini, the only

Figure 17.3. Semiglobular miniature footed cup, K352 (92/4/2) (after Tournavitou 2014: 336 fig. 21). Scale 1:1.

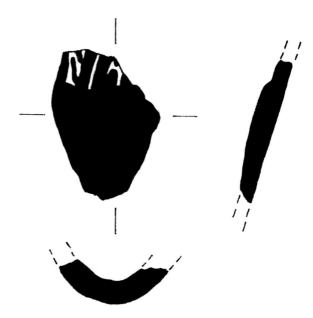

Figure 17.4. Miniature conical rhyton, K809 (92/4/13) (after Tournavitou 2014: 425 fig. 69). Scale 1:1.

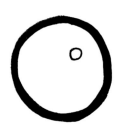

Figure 17.5. Miniature footed cup-rhyton, K859 (92/4/6) (after Tournavitou 2014: 434 fig. 75). Scale 1:1.

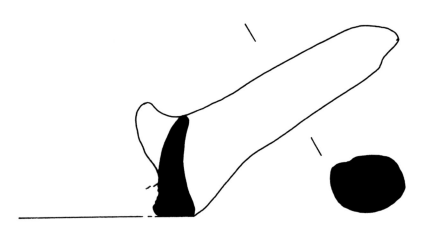

Figure 17.6. Brazier, K979 (92/4/13) (after Tournavitou 2014: 453 fig. 83). Scale 1:1.

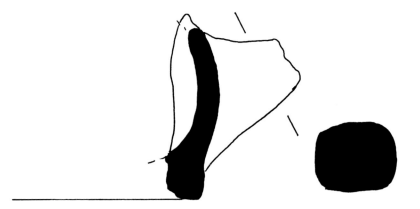

Figure 17.7. Brazier, K980 (92/4/13) (after Tournavitou 2014: 453 fig. 83). Scale 1:1.

published specimen depicting lilies is of Mycenaean provenance (Cummer and Schofield 1984: 80 no. 676, pl. 59.676). At the Menelaion in Laconia, the single preserved example is also dated to the LM IB period (Catling 1996: 73 fig. 2.1 [LMIB]). This latter version of

the lily, although not attested at Kastri, is probably a product of the local style.

Finally, the same deposit has yielded two fragmentary rhyta, a miniature conical rhyton (K809: Tournavitou 2014: 83, 84, 423, 425 fig. 69, 646 pl. 18) (Figure 17.4),

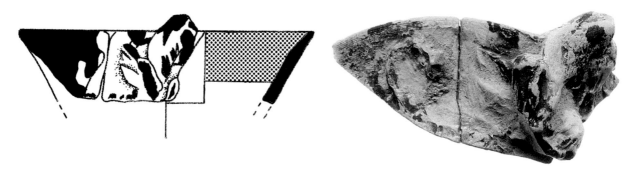

Figure 17.8. Straight-sided cup with plastic decoration, K151 (93/A17/5 and 93/A20/9) (after Tournavitou 2014: 308 fig. 10 and 631 pl. 3). Scale 1:1 (left only).

and a miniature cup-rhyton of the footed kind (K859: Tournavitou 2014: 90, 92, 433, 434 fig. 75, 651 pl. 23) (Figure 17.5), both decorated with floral compositions in the form of dense, oblique branches with leaves, entirely consistent with the LM IB ceramic tradition on Kythera (Coldstream 1972a: 129 μ9, 133 μ50, 191 ω154, 194 ω208 [LM IB]), but also with LM IB floral compositions from the Menelaion (Catling 1996: 70, 73 fig. 2.1 [LM IB]), Ayia Irini (Cummer and Schofield 1984: 116 pl. 80.s, 126 nos. 1559 and 1564, pl. 85.1559 and 1564 [LM IB]) and Palaikastro and Gournia on Crete (Boyd Hawes 1908: 41 fig. 21 [LM IA]; Sackett and Popham 1970: 218 fig. 9, pl. 57 [LMIB]).

The remains of the second pyre at Ayios Georgios sto Vouno, located on Terrace 2, in the area to the south of the southern wall of the Ayios Georgios church (Figure 17.1), are associated with architectural remains of the post-Minoan/post-Mycenaean period and a large quantity of post-Bronze Age pottery, which have contaminated the original Minoan deposit (Tournavitou 2014: 134-135, table 17). In contrast to the material from the first pyre location, the prehistoric pottery was here both Protopalatial and Neopalatial in date.

The pottery associated with this deposit included a relatively modest number of tripod cooking pots, none of which featured any evidence of burning, and six fragmentary braziers (K957: Tournavitou 2014: 98, 450, 452 fig. 82; K979: Tournavitou 2014: 98, 451, 453 fig. 83, 654 pl. 26; K980: Tournavitou 2014: 98, 451, 453 fig. 83, 454, 654 pl. 26; K982: Tournavitou 2014: 98, 453 fig. 83, 454, 654 pl. 26; K983 and K984: Tournavitou 2014: 98-100, 453 fig. 83, 454, 654 pl. 26) (Figures 17.6 and 17.7), of which two, K983 and K984, preserved distinct traces of burning on the interior. The closest parallels, attested at Ayia Irini, are dated almost exclusively to the LM I period (Georgiou 1986: 28-29, pls. 6, 17). The same deposit also included six straight-sided cups (K151: Tournavitou 2014: 33-

34, 304, 308 fig. 10, 631 pl. 3; K152: Tournavitou 2014: 34, 304, 306, 308 fig. 10; K161: Tournavitou 2014: 34, 306, 308 fig. 10; K222: Tournavitou 2014: 35-37, 314, 316 fig. 13; K223: Tournavitou 2014: 35-37, 314-315, 316 fig. 13; K255: Tournavitou 2014: 39, 319, 320 fig. 15, 321), the dates of which are equally divided between the Protopalatial (K151, K152, and K161) and the Neopalatial periods (K222, K223, and K255). One of the Protopalatial specimens, K151 (Figure 17.8), is exceptional, with intriguing plastic decoration against the exterior of

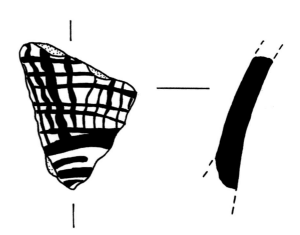

Figure 17.9. Conical rhyton, K811 (93/A35/13) (after Tournavitou 2014: 425 fig. 69).

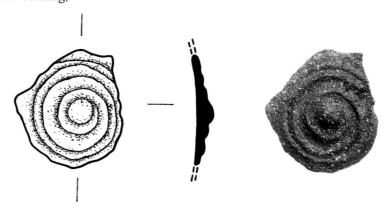

Figure 17.10. Miniature open vessel with plastic decoration depicting a snail in relief, K1073 (93/A35/1-Πηλ. 6) (after Tournavitou 2014: 473 fig. 94 and 657 pl. 29). Scale 1:1 (left only).

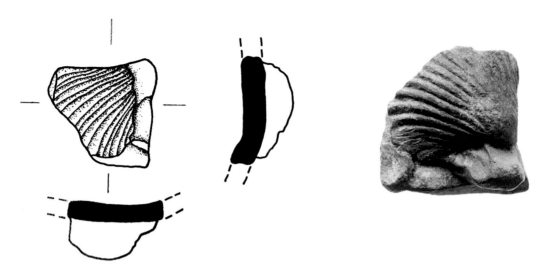

Figure 17.11. Sherd with plastic marine decoration depicting a cockleshell, K1075 (93/A47/11)
(after Tournavitou 2014: 473 fig. 94 and 657 pl. 29). Scale 1:1 (left only).

the rim almost identical to that of a similar type of cup discovered at Anemospilia and dated to the MM IIB-MM IIIA period (Sakellarakis and Sakellarakis 1997: 545-546, fig. 547). Similar examples in faience were recorded in the Temple Repositories at Knossos, and in Grave Circle B at Mycenae (Sakellarakis and Sakellarakis 1997: 291). One of the Neopalatial specimens (K255) bears In-and-Out decoration of a rather early date (MM IIIB/early LM IA), contemporary with its first appearance at Knossos (Popham 1984: pl. 144.4 and 6).

Other exceptional specimens include a fragmentary conical rhyton (K811: Tournavitou 2014: 85, 423, 425 fig. 69, 647 pl. 19) (Figure 17.9), which can safely be placed in the LM IB period, despite the lack of exact parallels; a fragmentary miniature cup-rhyton; a footed cup of LM IB date (K860: Tournavitou 2014: 90, 92, 433, 436 fig. 76; see also, Betancourt 2001: pl. 34.b, middle vase in middle row [LM IB]; Coldstream 1972b: 243-244 Tomb E, nos. 3-4 [LM IB]; Cummer and Schofield 1984: 70 no. 410, pl. 30.410 [LM IB]; 91 no. 999, pl. 30.999 [LM IB]; 98 no. 112, pl. 71.1112 [LM IB]; Koehl 2006: 61-62, Type IV, narrow-stemmed; Macdonald 1990: 86 fig. 8 [LM IB]; Warren 1981: 83 fig. 33, 84 fig. 34, 85 fig. 37 [LM IB]); a fragmentary miniature tripod vessel (K1025: Tournavitou 2014: 104, 460, 461 fig. 87, 655 pl. 27), and four fragmentary vessels with marine decoration (K1073: Tournavitou 2014: 111, 112, 113, 471, 473 fig. 94, 657 pl. 29; K1074: Tournavitou 2014: 113, 471, 473 fig. 94, 657 pl. 29; K1075: Tournavitou 2014: 113, 471, 473 fig. 94, 657 pl. 29; K1076: Tournavitou 2014: 113, 471, 473 fig. 94, 657 pl. 29) (Figures 17.10 and 17.11). Three of these specimens (K1074, K1075 and K1076) which seem to belong to the same vase, were part of an originally larger marine composition. The appliqué cockleshell on one of these specimens (K1075) (Figure 17.11) represents the most popular shell motif in the Minoan repertoire, attested on Crete throughout the MM and LM I periods. Although cockleshells became particularly popular

in the Minoan plastic repertory during the MM II and MM III periods, they declined in popularity during the succeeding LM I period (Foster 1982: 100, 113, 114-117 table 14, 145).

The two remaining specimens (K1074 and K1076) preserve parts of the tail and the body of naturalistically rendered appliqués representing fish. The fish are rather similar in appearance to the faience flying fish in the Temple Repositories at Knossos, and to the dolphin tail as reconstructed by Gill (1985: 64, fig. 4, 66 fig. 7). The size of the preserved examples suggests that they might have been part of a relief scene on a vase or utensil similar to that on the well-known specimen from Phaistos (Foster 1982: 92, n. 76). Although the close association of the marine style with Minoan cult has been adequately demonstrated (Mountjoy 1985; Sakellarakis 1996: 87, n. 58; Sapouna-Sakellaraki 1988-1989: 48), its relationship to the religious context of the peak sanctuary on Kythera is rather weak, given the small number of extant specimens with marine decoration. The fourth specimen (K1073; Figure 17.10), is decorated with a snail in relief, and probably represents parts of a small (possibly miniature) open vessel, made of Red Micaceous Ware. This specimen preserved strong traces of burning on both faces; an indication that the vase to which it belonged had, probably, been thrown into a fire.

In the same deposit were also recorded 19 intact conical cups (K6-7; K9-K14; K20-K28; K30-K31: Tournavitou 2014: 26-31, 285-287, 288-289 figs. 1 and 2, 629 pl. 1), mostly of Neopalatial date (14 examples, 74% of total), one juglet with floral decoration of LM I date (K872: Tournavitou 2014: 94, 437, 440 fig. 77) (Figure 17.12), and nine fragmentary monochrome carinated cups (K360-K362; K367; K370; K372-K375; Tournavitou 2014: 48-49, 337, 338 fig. 22, 635 pl. 7), all perfectly at home in the MM IB-MM IIA period. These specimens from the sanctuary at Ayios

Georgios sto Vouno are, in fact, closer to the classic MM IB version of the shape. At Kommos, the shape, which appears at the same time as at Kythera (MM IB), acquires its canonical, metallic, form during the MM IIA period

Figure 17.12. *Juglet with floral decoration, K872 (93/A16/3-A3) (after Tournavitou 2014: 440 fig. 77). Scale 1:1.*

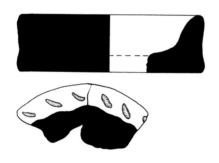

Figure 17.13. *Disc/plate, K427 (93/A16/2) (after Tournavitou 2014: 350 fig. 28). (Scale 1:2)*

(Betancourt 1990: 29, 31, 35-36). It should be noted, however, that the specimens from the sanctuary are not exactly comparable with the majority of carinated cups from the major centres in Crete (MacGillivray 1998: 72-73, fig. 2.11, 'tall-rimmed angular cup'). They seem to be typologically closer to another version of the carinated cup, the so-called 'short-rimmed angular cup' (MacGillivray 1998: 73-74, fig. 2.12) and especially to the Type 1 (MM IB) and Type 2 (MM IB-MM IIA) variants from Knossos.

Other specimens include three fragmentary semiglobular basins (K400, K401 and K403: Tournavitou 2014: 52, 341-342, 343 fig. 24, 636 pl. 8), three kalathoi of LM I date (K416-K418: Tournavitou 2014: 53, 346, 347 fig. 27), six discs/plates (K426: Tournavitou 2014: 54, 348, 350 fig. 28, 637 pl. 9; K427: Tournavitou 2014: 55, 348, 350 fig. 28, 637 pl. 9; K428: Tournavitou 2014: 56, 348, 350 fig. 28; K432: Tournavitou 2014: 56, 349, 350 fig. 28, 637 pl. 9; K433: Tournavitou 2014: 54, 349, 350 fig. 28, 637 pl. 9; K434: Tournavitou 2014: 55, 349, 350 fig. 28) (Figures 17.13 and 17.14), a fragment of a MM IB-MM III sieve or incense burner with polychrome decoration (K995: Tournavitou 2014: 100, 101, 455, 456 fig. 84), and a variety of, mostly large, Neopalatial storage vessels (MM IIIB-LM I), consisting principally of pithoid jars and jugs or amphorae (Tournavitou 2014: 134-150, 533-539 tables 17 and 18).

Ashes and ash layers containing burnt organic material

Instances of burnt material from pyres, in hollows and rock-crevices, are either more common, or more frequently mentioned by the excavators. Published accounts, nevertheless, do not venture beyond general statements, and fail to provide pertinent information on the size, depth, and content of these deposits.

Ash deposits in hollows and crevices of the bedrock are attested, according to Jones (1999: 57-58 table 9, 59-74 table 10), at 15 (or 58%) of the 26 acknowledged peak sanctuaries in Crete.[5] At Atsipades Korakias, although there is very little archaeological evidence to support the existence of ritual pyres, animal sacrifice or the preparation of food (given a lack of animal bones and

Figure 17.14. *Disc/plate, K428 (93/A16/8) (after Tournavitou 2014: 350 fig. 28). Scale 2:1.*

---

[5] These are Vigla Siteias, Juktas, Gonies Maleviziou-Philioremos, Ziros Siteias-Korphi tou Mare, Thylakas Mirabellou, Kophinas Monophatsiou, Maza Pediados, Modi Siteias, Xykephalo Siteias, Petsophas Siteias, Plagia Siteias, Prinias Siteias, Pyrgos Maleviziou, Traostalos Siteias, and Vrysinas Rethymnis (Davaras 1974: 210; Rutkowski 1988: 90; see Appendix).

seeds), the excavator mentions the existence of a small deposit with carbonised material in a bedrock niche on the Upper Terrace, and traces of ash in the soil from the upper layers, presumably modern (Peatfield 1992: 66). Material from these deposits consists mostly of fragmentary pottery and figurines, as well as other categories of votives (Jones 1999: 59-74 table 10).

At Ayios Georgios sto Vouno, burnt material (including charcoal, burnt wood, and ash) is mostly attested on Terrace 2, in ten of the 15 extant layers (Tournavitou 2014: 135, 533 table 17, distribution map 18) (Figure 17.1). In this case too, the association of the burnt material with the Minoan peak sanctuary is, often, extremely tenuous, on account of post-Minoan disturbance (Sakellarakis 2011: 164-205; Tournavitou 2014: 135-136, 533 table 17). It is, moreover, noteworthy that almost the entire quantity of burnt wood, and one of the two ash deposits, are attested in disturbed layers where the majority of the pottery is dated to the historical period (Tournavitou 2014: 533 table 17), making their connection to the Minoan peak sanctuary equally tenuous. In the ten layers with mostly, or exclusively, Minoan material, the quantity of carbonised and burnt is minimal

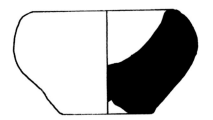

Figure 17.15. Miniature bird's-nest bowl, K1031 (93/A1/2) (after Tournavitou 2014: 463 fig. 88).

(Tournavitou 2014: 533 table 17). It is also worth noting that the only observable concentrations of tripod cooking pots and braziers (Tournavitou 2014: distribution maps 8 and 13) are attested in four different layers, three of which have been identified as 'primary deposition' areas, that also yielded only minute quantities of burnt material (Tournavitou 2014: 533 table 17). Unfortunately, only four of the layers with burnt material from fires or pyres are associated with areas of 'primary deposition' of votive material (Tournavitou 2014: 135–136, 533 tables 17 and 18) (Figures 17.1 and 17.2), a fact that undermines the proposed connection between pyres and ritual depositions in rock crevices.

Figure 17.16. Detail of the so-called 'Sanctuary Rhyton' from Zakros (after Dimopoulou-Rethemiotaki 2005: 165. Drawing by Th. Fanourakis).

Judging by the general distribution of the pottery material in these layers, it seems that there are no significant concentrations (Tournavitou 2014: 533 table 17). The only types of vessels present in numbers that exceed 50% of their total count, are miniature bird's-nest bowls (2 of 2 examples, 100% of total), perforated vessels used as sieves or incense burners (4 of 6 examples, c. 67% of total), miniature tripod vessels (4 of 7 examples, c. 57% of total), discs/plates (30 of 56 examples, c. 54% of total), and fruitstands (1 of 2 examples, 50% of total). All are quite rare shapes in the sanctuary and of a clearly symbolic or ritual character. Braziers (16 of 42 examples, c. 38% of total), lids (9 of 24 examples, c. 38% of total), pithoid jars (56 of 170 examples, c. 33% of total), and kalathoi (4 of 13 examples, c. 31% of total), are represented in less significant quantities, ranging between 30 and 40% of the total count of each vessel type (Tournavitou 2014: 533 table 17). With the exception of the basins (4 of 17 examples, c. 24% of total), all of the remaining types of vessels, including the conical cups, the straight-sided cups, the tripod cooking pots, the juglets, storage vessels, the rhyta, the cup-rhyta, or even vessels with plastic decoration, in other words the most numerous and/or significant vessel types in the sanctuary, are attested in extremely low, and occasionally negligibly low, numbers (19% of total; see Tournavitou 2014: 533 table 17).

Traces of burning on pottery, bone, shell and other objects

Traces of burning on objects and organic matter (pottery, figurines, other types of votive offerings, and animal bones), is directly associated with the activities accompanying the suggested pyres. This association, however, has been almost impossible to test, since the relevant data, largely overlooked in the published reports, are extremely limited. Indeed, information about burning on pottery, and other votive offerings, is almost non-existent.

Myres (1903: 356-387), the first to suggest that offerings were thrown into pyres, fails to mention anything about traces of burning on the extant votive offerings from Petsophas Siteias. Platon (1951: 103, 150-151), who embraced Myre's theory, is forced to admit the absence of 'obvious traces of burning' on figurines from the site. In an attempt to explain this phenomenon, he suggests that they were perhaps 'thrown... when the pyre was being extinguished'. This explanation was later adopted by Rutkowski (1985: 352, 354-355, figs. 4 and 5; 1986: 91; 1991: 53), who suggested that the votives were thrown 'into the embers of the dying fire' (Rutkowski 1991: 53) and that 'sacrificial animals that had previously been killed were perhaps also cast into the dying fire' (Rutkowski 1986: 91).

We know nothing about the state of most of the portable finds from Juktas. There is no information whatsoever concerning traces of burning, not even for those votive offerings (including figurines and stone offering tables) discovered on the step of the built altar (Karetsou 1976: 232; 1981: 146). In her lecture at the Danish Archaeological Institute in Athens (2005), Maria Zeimbekis also noted an absence of burning on the terracotta animal figurines from Juktas. In the discussion that followed this lecture, it was generally acknowledged that the casting of figurines and other objects into pyres at peak sanctuaries was nothing more than a theoretical construct concocted by scholars who have never examined the relevant material.

The only sanctuaries which have yielded pottery and/ or votive offerings with explicit traces of burning are Traostalos Siteias (Chrysoulaki 2001: 60-61; Vokotopoulos 2017: 7), and Korakomouri Sphaka, where, according to the excavators, a large percentage of the votive offerings bear clear traces of burning (Schlager 1995; Tzedakis et al. 1999: 323).

At Ayios Georgios sto Vouno, none of the votive offerings of the Minoan period preserve any traces of burning. This is also true of the finds in the single verifiably Minoan layer preserving the remains of a pyre, the pottery material included (Sakellarakis 2011: 173; Tournavitou 2014: 134, 136, 533 table 17; Layer 2, 92/Area 2/4). As far as the pottery is concerned, the percentage of specimens with traces of burning is really very small, and does not exceed 0.2% of the entire material assemblage at the site (303 of 196,010 sherds and vessels; see Tournavitou 2014: 562 chart 31). The pottery with traces of burning includes ten different vessel types, mostly tripod cooking vessels (270 of 303 examples, c. 89% of total; Tournavitou 2014: 136-137, 556 chart 19, 562 chart 32), conical cups (10 of 303 examples, c. 3% of total; Tournavitou 2014: 136-137, 59 chart 5, 562 chart 32), jugs/amphorae (7 of 303 examples, c. 2% of total), and juglets (6 of 303 examples, c. 2% of total; Tournavitou 2014: 136-137, 560 chart 27, 562 chart 32). The remaining types of vessel are represented by one or two specimens each, and include braziers (K983-984: Tournavitou 2014: 136-137, 561 chart 29, 562 chart 32); a miniature disc/plate (K427); a pithos (K488); a hole-mouth jar (93/B3β); an incense burner (K997); an intact miniature bird's-nest bowl (K1031); a miniature open vessel with plastic decoration (K1073); a small closed vessel with plastic decoration (K1082); and a small closed vessel with floral decoration (K1220)(Tournavitou 2014: 562 chart 32). It is worth noting that in the vast majority of the cases (273 of 303, c. 90% of total), and particularly so in the case of the tripod cooking pots, braziers and the single incense burner, the traces of burning could have been the result of primary use, and were probably not caused by their being thrown or placed onto a pyre (Tournavitou 2014: 136-137, 563 chart 33).

The remaining specimens (30 of 303 examples) represent a very small percentage (c. 10%) of the pottery with traces of burning, and *c.* 0.02% of the total pottery assemblage from the site (30 of 196,010 sherds and vessels). Only two of these vessels, a miniature disc/plate (K427: Tournavitou 2014: 55, 348, 350 fig. 28, 637 pl. 9, 562 chart 32) (Figure 17.13) and an intact miniature bird's-nest bowl (K1031-93/A1/2: Tournavitou 2014: 104-105, 462, 463 fig. 88, 562 chart 32, 655 pl. 27) (Figure 17.15), exhibit a burn pattern potentially consistent with having been placed in a fire or pyre. The vast majority of the remaining sherds (28 of 30 examples, *c.* 93%) had been burnt both inside and out, and had probably been broken before they came into contact with fire (Tournavitou 2014: 136-137, 563 chart 33). This group includes conical cups (*c.* 0.01% of the total shape count) (Tournavitou 2014: 136-137, 549 chart 5), closed storage vessels (10 specimens) (Tournavitou 2014: 136-137, 562 chart 32), as well as specialised vessels, possibly of ritual character (six juglets and two vessels with plastic decoration; Tournavitou 2014: 136-137, 562 chart 32). It is worth noting that the majority of these vessels (16 of 28 examples, *c.* 57% of total) are made of the same Red Micaceous fabric commonly used for vessels designed to come into contact with fire, like the tripod cooking pots, and do not bear any trace of painted decoration (Tournavitou 2014: 136).

The emerging evidence concerning the distribution of this material, and its association with 'primary deposition' areas (Figure 17.2) and with layers preserving burnt material from fires or pyres (including ash and carbonised organic matter) (Figure 17.1) is interesting (Tournavitou 2014: 136-137, 533 table 17, 536 table 18, distribution maps 5, 19-20, 27, 29, 31-33). Of the two miniature vessels that had possibly been placed on a fire, only the disc/plate (K427; Figure 17.13) was discovered in a 'primary deposition' area on Terrace 2 (Figure 17.2) (Tournavitou 2014: 533 table 17; Terrace 2, west part, MM-LM I deposit). This deposit also contained many bronze and clay votive offerings, and many animal bones, but very few traces of burnt material (Tournavitou 2014: 136-137, 533 table 17, 536 table 18, distribution maps 18 and 19). The miniature bird's-nest bowl (K1031), on the other hand, was discovered in a surface layer on Terrace 2, which did include traces of burnt material and many animal bones (Tournavitou 2014: 136-137, 533 table 17; Terrace 2, surface layer south of the Panagia church).

The overwhelming majority of the remaining specimens (26 of 28 examples, *c.* 93% of the total), which had probably been burnt after breakage, were attested in 'primary deposition' areas, especially on Terrace 7 (Figure 17.2), which have otherwise yielded no traces of fire or burnt material (Tournavitou 2014: 136-137, 533 table 17, 536 table 18, distribution maps 18 and 19). It is also worth pointing out that only two of the surviving examples were found in the same layer on Terrace 2: a fragmentary miniature open vessel with plastic

decoration (K1073: Tournavitou 2014: 111, 112, 113, 471, 473 fig. 94, 563 chart 33, 657 pl. 29) (Figure 17.10), and the disc/plate (K427) mentioned above (Figure 17.13). Moreover, of those sherds preserving traces of primary burning, i.e., the tripod cooking pots, the two braziers, and the incense burner, only the incense burner (K997: Tournavitou 2014: 100-101, 455, 456 fig. 84, 562 chart 32; 655 pl. 27) was found in a layer with burnt material from a fire or pyre dated to the Minoan period (Figure 17.1). The two braziers (K983 and K984), as noted, were discovered in the same layer on Terrace 2, where the remains of an apparently post-Bronze Age pyre have been identified (Terrace 2, east part, Minoan deposit).

Faunal remains associated with carbonised organic material are even less well documented. According to Jones, animal bones are attested only at Vrysinas Rethymnis, Juktas, Gonies Malevíziou-Philioremos, Maza Pediados, Traostalos Siteias, and Ayios Georgios sto Vouno on Kythera (6 of 26, or 23% of peak sanctuary sites; Jones 1999: 57 table 9, 59 table 10). While the absence of animal bones from Petsophas Siteias is questioned by Nowicki (1994: 31), animal bones were recorded, according to Rutkowski (1988: 90), at Vigla Siteias.

Only at Juktas (Karetsou 1977: 333; 1979: 410; 1980b: 238, 247, 258) is the precise find spot of animal bones (Room 1, Protopalatial votive pit/altar area), and the species represented, specified. Room 1 apparently contained the bones of domesticated animals and birds, in a thin layer of ash (pyre-layer δ). It was also reported that the votive pits of the Protopalatial period on Terrace 1 included both animal bones and seashells. The layer associated with the pyre in the area of the altar yielded a large quantity of animal bones, mostly sheep and goats, followed in frequency by the remains of larger animals like pigs and bovids. A few bird bones are also noted. The bones of sheep and goats preserved evidence of butchery. At Traostalos Siteias, although the total number of burnt animal bones is small, they are interpreted as remains of sacrifices (Chrysoulaki 1999: 316).

The systematic study of the animal bones from Ayios Georgios sto Vouno is the only one of its kind undertaken to date on a peak sanctuary site. According to Trantalidou (2013: 465-500), the presence of butchery marks on the animal bones from the sanctuary suggests that they most probably represent the remains of meals. The vast majority of the bones recovered from 'primary deposition' areas, an average of *c.* 88%, belong to sheep and goats, followed in frequency by pigs (*c.* 6%), and bovids (*c.* 2%), while bird bones constitute only *c.* 2% of the total and belong, mostly, to partridges and pigeons (76% of all bird remains). Even more importantly, only *c.* 3% of the animal bones in the sanctuary were carbonised, an indication that they had been exposed to the fire long enough to burn completely, presumably as votive offerings.

The exceptionally small number of peak sanctuaries which have yielded votive offerings or pottery with traces of burning, or carbonised animal bones, compared to the much larger number of sanctuaries preserving evidence of burnt deposits, suggests that the use of ritual pyres should be disassociated from the custom of throwing objects, votives/pottery, or parts of animals, into the fire. Only three sites (Traostalos Siteias, Korakomouri Sphakas and Ayios Georgios sto Vouno) have yielded pottery and/or votives with traces of burning, while carbonised animal bones are, again, reported at only three sites (at Maza Pediados, Traostalos Siteias and Ayios Georgios sto Vouno) (c. 12% of peak sanctuaries). In all three cases, carbonised animal bones constitute a very small percentage of the total animal bone assemblage.

Pictorial representations of pyres in a peak sanctuary setting

Finally, as far as the iconographic representation of pyres is concerned, the evidence is extremely limited. The only published evidence involves Shaw's interpretation of the central altar on the so-called Sanctuary Rhyton from Zakros (Shaw 1978: 436-437, fig. 9) (Figure 17.16), the upper level of which is thought to depict wood intended as fuel for the lighting of a fire, and can be used to infer the existence of a real pyre in an open air sanctuary. Judging by the archaeological evidence from a considerable number of peak sanctuaries, the almost total absence of iconographic representations of the ritual use of fire in Minoan art might, nevertheless, be misleading, and should perhaps be attributed to thematic selectivity. Indeed, such iconography has often been recognised as an ineffective medium for the interpretation of prehistoric ritual practice.

Conclusions

Despite the absence of iconographic evidence concerning the use of fire in Minoan peak sanctuaries, and the rarity of objects with traces of burning, there is archaeological evidence confirming the existence of pyres/fires at over 50% of acknowledged Minoan peak sanctuaries (see Appendix). Based on this evidence, the diachronic character of the custom, during the Protopalatial and Neopalatial periods, is also indisputable. The frequency of the custom cannot be ascertained in every case, although, in sanctuaries such as Juktas and Petsophas Siteias, the depth of the deposits, or the number of pyres, suggests repeated and, perhaps, regular use. It is very likely that there was considerable differentiation in the popularity of the custom, even among those sanctuaries where the

existence of a pyre has actually been documented. What does seem certain is that the use of pyres was not part of a homogeneous cult ritual practiced in all the Minoan peak sanctuaries, as has previously been suggested.

The practice of throwing objects into the fire is another matter. Based on published data, it seems that there are only two sites, Traostalos Siteias and Korakomouri Sphakas, which have yielded a statistically significant number of objects with traces of burning. Although information concerning the number and type of objects involved is very limited, the evidence from those two sanctuaries does, at least, seem to confirm the practice. At Ayios Georgios sto Vouno, traces of burning have not been attested on any type of votive object, other than pottery. Even in this case, the traces of burning on the vast majority of the material in question (91% of the total), alludes to the primary use of these objects, i.e. the preparation and/or consumption of food (attested by tripod cooking pots), and the ritual/symbolic transportation of coals/ashes (attested by braziers). Of the remaining 9% of the material, only two specimens (the miniature disc and bird's-nest bowl; Figures 17.13 and 17.15) had probably been placed on a fire or pyre, and could plausibly be considered as part of a symbolic ritual act.

If, therefore, the ritual disposal of pottery, as well as votive offerings and parts of sacrificed animals, was a sporadic practice in Minoan peak sanctuaries, disassociated from ritual pyres then, given the absence of evidence for elaborate food preparation at most sanctuary sites, the activities which accompanied the ritual pyres may have consisted, principally, of actions which are now untraceable in the archaeological record: ritual dancing, fire-leaping or fire-walking, the throwing of flowers, or some combination of the above.

We should always be mindful of the multidimensional, multifarious nature of fire, and of the fact that, in the Greek world, purification of body and soul, as well as healing and fertility, neither defines nor determines the character of pyre rituals. Finally, we should not forget that human beings, both now and in the past, find solace in the warmth and safety of the fire (especially at night), stay up and dance around pyres, leap over their flames, tread on their embers and, occasionally, throw objects in their dying flames, thereby successfully defying time, logic, gods, and religions.

Appendix: acknowledged peak sanctuaries

The status of 24 out of the 26 peak sanctuaries, including Ayios Georgios sto Vouno, is acknowledged by three different scholars (Jones 1999; Peatfield 1992: 59 fig. 1; Rutkowski 1988). Of these 24, a total of 19 have been acknowledged as official peak sanctuary sites by all three scholars: Atsipades Korakias, Vigla Siteias, Vrysinas Rethymnis, Juktas, Gonies Maleviziou-Philioremos, Ziros Siteias, Thylakas Mirabellou, Kalamaki Siteias, Karphi Lasithiou, Kophinas Monophatsiou, Maza Pediados, Modi Siteias, Xykephalo Siteias, Petsophas Siteias, Plagia Siteias, Prinias Siteias, Pyrgos Maleviziou, Spili Vorizi in Ayios Vasileios, and Traostalos Siteias. The remaining five sites have been acknowledged by only two of the scholars concerned: Ambelos Siteias, Demati Monophatsiou, Etiani Kephala Siteias, Keria Maleviziou, and Tapes Mirabellou. Although Korakomouri Sphakas in Siteia is a relatively recently-discovered site (Tzedakis *et al.* 1999: 317-326), it has been described as a peak sanctuary in a number of relatively recent publications (see, for example, Kyriakidis 2005: 14; Nowicki 2008).

Bibliography

Alexiou, St. 1966. Γωνιές Μαλεβιζίου. *Κρητικά Χρονικά* 20: 322.

Alexiou, St. 1969. Γωνιές Μαλεβιζίου. *Αρχαιολογικόν Δελτίον* 22(1967)(Chr. B΄2): 484-485.

Bergquist, B. 1988. The archaeology of sacrifice: Minoan-Mycenaean versus Greek. A brief query into two sites with contrary evidence, in R. Hägg, N. Marinatos and G.C. Nordquist (eds) *Early Greek Cult Practice. Proceedings of the Fifth International Symposium at the Swedish Institute at Athens, 26-29 June, 1986* (Skrifter utgivna av Svenska institutet i Athen, 4o, 38): 21-34. Gothenburg: Paul Åström.

Bernini, L.E. 1995. Ceramics of the early Neo-palatial period at Palaikastro. *The Annual of the British School at Athens* 90: 55-82.

Betancourt, P.P. 1980. *Cooking Vessels from Minoan Kommos. A Preliminary Report* (Occasional Paper 7). Los Angeles: Institute of Archaeology, University of California.

Betancourt, P.P. 1990. *Kommos II. The Final Neolithic through Middle Minoan III Pottery.* Princeton: Princeton University Press.

Betancourt, P.P. 2001. The household shrine in the House of the Rhyta at Pseira, in R. Laffineur and R. Hägg (eds) *POTNIA. Deities and Religion in the Aegean Bronze Age. Proceedings of the 8th international Aegean Conference, Göteborg, Göteborg University, 12-15 April 2000* (Aegaeum 22): 145-149. Liège: the University of Liège.

Bevan, A., E. Kiriatzi, C. Knappett, E. Kappa and S. Papachristou 2002. Excavation of Neopalatial deposits at Tholos (Kastri), Kythera. *The Annual of the British School at Athens* 97: 55-96.

Boyd Hawes, H. 1908. Pottery: Town Style, in H. Boyd Hawes, B.E. Williams, R.B. Seager and E.H. Hall. *Gournia, Vasiliki and other Prehistoric Sites on the Isthmus of Hierapetra, Crete. Excavations of the Wells-Houston-Cramp Expedition, 1901, 1903, 1904*: 39-44. Philadelphia: the American Exploration Society and The Free Museum of Science and Art.

Burkert, W. 1993. *Αρχαία Ελληνική Θρησκεία. Αρχαϊκή και Κλασσική Εποχή.* Athens: Kardamitsa.

Catling, H.W. 1996. Minoan and 'Minoan' pottery at the Menelaion, Sparta, in D. Evely, I.S. Lemos and S. Sherratt (eds) *Minotaur and Centaur. Studies in the Archaeology of Crete and Euboea Presented to Mervyn Popham* (British Archaeological Reports International Series 638): 70-78. Oxford: Tempus Reparatum.

Catling, E.A., H.W Catling and D. Smyth 1979. Knossos 1975: Middle Minoan III and Late Minoan I houses by the acropolis. *The Annual of the British School at Athens* 74: 1-80.

Chryssoulaki, S. 1999. Ιερό κορυφής Τραόσταλου. *Κρητική Εστία* 7: 310-317.

Chryssoulaki, S. 2001. The Traostalos peak sanctuaries: aspects of spatial organisation, in R. Laffineur and R. Hägg (eds) *POTNIA. Deities and Religion in the Aegean Bronze Age. Proceedings of the 8th international Aegean Conference, Göteborg, Göteborg University, 12-15 April 2000* (Aegaeum 22): 57-66. Liège: the University of Liège.

Coldstream, J.N. 1972a. Deposits of pottery from the settlement, in J.N. Coldstream and G.L. Huxley (eds) *Kythera. Excavations and Studies Conducted by the University of Pennsylvania Museum and the British School at Athens*: 77-204. London: Faber and Faber.

Coldstream, J.N. 1972b. Tombs: the finds, in J.N. Coldstream and G.L. Huxley (eds) *Kythera. Excavations and Studies Conducted by the University of Pennsylvania Museum and the British School at Athens*: 220-271. London: Faber and Faber.

Coldstream, J.N. 1972c. Kythera: the sequence of the pottery and its chronology, in J.N. Coldstream and G.L. Huxley (eds) *Kythera. Excavations and Studies Conducted by the University of Pennsylvania Museum and the British School at Athens*: 272-308. London: Faber and Faber.

Cummer, W.W. and E. Schofield 1984. *Keos III. Ayia Irini: House A.* Mainz: von Zabern.

Davaras, K. 1963. Κόφινα. *Αρχαιολογικόν Δελτίον* 17(1961-1962)(Chr. B΄): 287-888.

Davaras, K. 1974. Ανασκαφή ΜΜ ιερού κορυφής Βρύσινα Ρεθύμνης. *Αρχαιολογικά Ανάλεκτα εξ Αθηνών* 7(2): 210-212.

Dietrich, B.C. 1969. Peak cults and their place in Minoan religion. *Historia: Zeitschrift für Alte Geschichte* 18(3): 257-275.

Dimopoulou, N. 1999. The Marine Style ewer from Poros, in P. Betancourt, V. Karageorghis, R. Laffineur and W.-D. Niemeier (eds) *Meletemata: Studies in Aegean Archaeology Presented to Malcolm H. Wiener as he Enters his 65th Year* (Aegaeum 20): 217-226. Liège: the University of Liège.

Dimopoulou-Rethemiotaki, N. 2005. *The Archaeological Museum of Herakleion*. Athens: EFG Eurobank Ergasias S.A. and the John S. Latsis Public Benefit Foundation.

Foster, K.P. 1982. *Minoan Ceramic Relief* (Studies in Mediterranean Archaeology 64). Gothenburg: Paul Åström.

Georgiou, H.S. 1986. *Keos VI. Ayia Irini: Specialised Domestic and Industrial Pottery*. Mainz: Philipp von Zabern.

Gill, M.A.V. 1985. Some observations on representations of marine animals in Minoan art, and their identification, in P. Darcque and J.C. Poursat (eds) *L'iconographie minoenne. Actes de la table ronde d'Athènes, 21–22 avril 1983* (Bulletin de Correspondance Hellénique Supplément 11): 63-81. Athens: the French School at Athens.

Jones, D.W. 1999. *Peak Sanctuaries and Sacred Caves in Minoan Crete: A Comparison of Artifacts* (Studies in Mediterranean Archaeology and Literature, Pocket-book 156). Jonsered: Paul Åström.

Karetsou, A. 1976. Ιερόν Κορυφής Γιούχτα. *Πρακτικά της εν Αθήναις Αρχαιολογικής Εταιρείας* 129(1974): 228-239.

Karetsou, A. 1977. Το ιερό κορυφής του Γιούχτα. *Πρακτικά της εν Αθήναις Αρχαιολογικής Εταιρείας* 130(1975)(Α΄): 230-234.

Karetsou, A. 1979. Το ιερό κορυφής Γιούχτα. *Πρακτικά της εν Αθήναις Αρχαιολογικής Εταιρείας* 131(1976)(Β΄): 408-418.

Karetsou, A. 1980a. Το ιερό κορυφής Γιούχτα. *Πρακτικά της εν Αθήναις Αρχαιολογικής Εταιρείας* 132(1977)(Β΄): 419-420.

Karetsou, A. 1980b. Το ιερό κορυφής Γιούχτα. *Πρακτικά της εν Αθήναις Αρχαιολογικής Εταιρείας* 133(1978): 232-258.

Karetsou, A. 1982. Το ιερό κορυφής Γιούχτα (1979-1980). *Πρακτικά της εν Αθήναις Αρχαιολογικής Εταιρείας* 135(1980): 337-353.

Karetsou, A. 1981. The peak sanctuary of Mt. Juktas, in R. Hägg and N. Marinatos (eds) *Sanctuaries and Cults in the Aegean Bronze Age. Proceedings of the First International Symposium at the Swedish Institute in Athens, 12-13 May, 1980* (Skrifter utgivna av Svenska institutet i Athen, 4o, 28): 137-153. Stockholm: the Swedish Institute at Athens.

Koehl, R.B. 2006. *Aegean Bronze Age Rhyta* (Prehistory Monographs 19). Philadelphia: INSTAP Academic Press.

Kyriakidis, E. 2005. *Ritual in the Bronze Age Aegean. The Minoan Peak Sanctuaries*. London: Duckworth.

Macdonald, C.F. 1990. Destruction and construction in the palace at Knossos: LM IA-B, in D.A. Hardy and A.C. Renfrew (eds) *Thera and the Aegean World III. Proceedings of the Third International Congress, Santorini, Greece, 3-9 September 1989. Volume 3. Chronology*: 82-88. London: the Thera Foundation.

MacGillivray, J.A. 1998. *Knossos: Pottery Groups of the Old Palace Period* (The British School at Athens Studies 5). London: the British School at Athens.

MacGillivray, J.A., A. Sarpaki, J-P. Olivier, J. Weingarten, L.H. Sackett, J. Driessen, R. Bridges and D. Smyth 1989. Excavations at Palaikastro, 1988. *The Annual of the British School at Athens* 84: 417-445.

Marinatos, N. 1986. *Minoan Sacrificial Ritual. Cult Practice and Symbolism* (Skrifter utgivna av Svenska institutet i Athen, 8o, 9). Gothenburg: Paul Åström.

Marinatos, N. 1993. *Minoan Religion. Ritual, Image, and Symbol* (Studies in Comparative Religion). Columbia: University of South Carolina Press.

Megas, G.A. 2005. *Ελληνικές Γιορτές και Έθιμα της Λαϊκής Λατρείας*. Athens: Estia.

Mountjoy, P.A. 1985. Ritual associations for LM IB Marine Style vases, in P. Darcque and J.C. Poursat (eds) *L'iconographie minoenne. Actes de la table ronde d'Athènes, 21-22 avril 1983* (Bulletin de Correspondance Hellénique Supplément 11): 231-242. Athens: the French School at Athens.

Mountjoy, P.A. 1999. *Regional Mycenaean Decorated Pottery*. Rahden: Marie Leidorf.

Myres, J.L. 1903. Excavation at Palaikastro II: § 13. The sanctuary-site of Petsofà. *The Annual of the British School at Athens* 9: 356-387.

Nilsson, M.P. 1923. Fire-festivals in Ancient Greece. *Journal of Hellenic Studies* 43(2): 144-148.

Nilsson, M.P. 1950. *The Minoan-Mycenaean Religion and its Survival in Greek Religion* (2nd revised edition). Lund: C.W.K. Gleerup.

Nowicki, K. 1994. Some remarks on the Pre-and Protopalatial peak sanctuaries in Crete. *Aegean Archaeology* 1:31-48.

Peatfield, A.A.D. 1983. The topography of Minoan peak sanctuaries. *The Annual of the British School at Athens* 78: 273-279.

Peatfield, A.A.D. 1992. Rural ritual in Bronze Age Crete: the peak sanctuary at Atsipadhes. *Cambridge Archaeological Journal* 2(1): 59-87.

Platon, N. 1951. Το ιερόν Μαζά (Καλού Χωριού Πεδιάδος) και τα μινωικά ιερά κορυφής. *Κρητικά Χρονικά* 5(1): 96-160.

Popham, M. 1977. Notes from Knossos, part I. *The Annual of the British School at Athens* 72: 185-195.

Popham, M.R. 1984. *The Minoan Unexplored Mansion at Knossos* (The British School at Athens Supplementary Volume 17). London: Thames and Hudson.

Psilakis, N. 2005. *Λαϊκές τελετουργίες στην Κρήτη. Έθιμα στον κύκλο του χρόνου*. Heraklion: Karmanor.

Rutkowski, B. 1985. Untersuchungen zu bronzezeitlichen Bergheiligtümern auf Kreta. *Germania: Anzeiger der Römisch-Germanischen Kommission des Deutschen Archäologischen Instituts* 63(2): 345-359.

Rutkowski, B. 1986. *The Cult Places of the Aegean*. New Haven: Yale University Press.

Rutkowski, B. 1988. Minoan peak sanctuaries: the topography and architecture, in R. Laffineur (ed.) *Aegaeum 2. Annales d'archéologie égéenne de l'Université de Liège*: 71-99. Liège: the University of Liège.

Rutkowski, B. 1991. *Petsophas. A Cretan Peak Sanctuary* (Studies and Monographs in Mediterranean Archaeology and Civilization I.1). Warsaw: Art and Archaeology.

Rutter, J.B. and S.H. Rutter 1976. *The Transition to Mycenaean. A Stratified Middle Helladic II to Late Helladic IIA Pottery Sequence from Ayios Stephanos in Laconia* (Monumenta Archaeologica 4). Los Angeles: Institute of Archaeology, University of California.

Sackett, L.H. and M. Popham 1970. Excavations at Palaikastro VII. Stratigraphical tests undertaken in 1962 and 1963, part II: pottery from Block N, Area DD and House Gamma, supplementary work at Roussolakkos and trials in outlying areas. *The Annual of the British School at Athens* 65: 203-242.

Sakellarakis, Y. 1996. Minoan religious influence in the Aegean: the case of Kythera. *The Annual of the British School at Athens* 91: 81-99.

Sakellarakis, Y. 2011. Η ἀνασκαφὴ, in Y. Sakellarakis. *ΚΥΘΗΡΑ. Το Μινωικό Ιερό Κορυφής στον Άγιο Γεώργιο στο Βουνό 1: τα Προανασκαφικά και η Ανασκαφή* (Βιβλιοθήκη της εν Αθήναις Αρχαιολογικής Εταιρείας 271): 145-332. Athens: Athens Archaeological Society.

Sakellarakis, Y. and E. Sakellarakis 1997. *Archanes. Minoan Crete in a New Light*. Athens: Ammos.

Sapouna-Sakellaraki, E. 1988-1989. Η κεραμική του θαλάσσιου ρυθμού από τις Αρχάνες και η πιθανή ύπαρξη τοπικού εργαστηρίου. *Κρητικά Χρονικά* 28-29: 28-52.

Schlager, N. 1995. Korakomouri: ein neues MM Höhenheiligtum in Sphaka, Gem. Zakros, und die MM Höhen- und Feldheiligtümer von Ost Sitia. *Jahreshefte der Österreichischen Archäologischen Instituts in Wien* 64: 1-24.

Shaw, J.W. 1978. Evidence for the Minoan tripartite shrine. *American Journal of Archaeology* 82(4): 429-448.

Tournavitou, I. 2011. Συλλογική λατρεία και τελετουργικές πρακτικές σε ένα περιφερειακό ιερό κορυφής. Η περίπτωση των Κυθήρων, in M. Andreadaki-Vlazaki and E. Papadopoulou (eds) *Πεπραγμένα Ι' Διεθνούς Κρητολογικού Συνεδρίου (Χανιά, 1-8 Οκτωβρίου 2006), Τόμος Α3 (Προϊστορικοί χρόνοι: Κεραμική - Τεχνολογία - Τέχνη - Εικονογραφία - Λατρεία - Τελετουργικό - Ιστορία της Αρχαιολογικής Έρευνας)*: 733-752. Chania: Philological Society 'Ο Chrysostomos'.

Tournavitou, I. (Y. Sakellarakis, (ed.)) 2014. *ΚΥΘΗΡΑ. Ο Άγιος Γεώργιος στο Βουνό 4: Κεραμεική της Εποχής του Χαλκού* (Βιβλιοθήκη της εν Αθήναις Αρχαιολογικής Εταιρείας 289). Athens: Athens Archaeological Society.

Trantalidou, K. 2013. Αρχαιοζωολογικά κατάλοιπα και ζητήματα της ορνιθοπανίδας, in Y. Sakellarakis (ed.) *ΚΥΘΗΡΑ. Το Μινωικό Ιερό Κορυφής στον Άγιο Γεώργιο στο Βουνό 3: Τα Ευρήματα* (Βιβλιοθήκη της εν Αθήναις Αρχαιολογικής Εταιρείας 282): 463-563. Athens: Athens Archaeological Society.

Tzedakis, I., S. Chrysoulaki, L. Vokotopoulos and A. Sfyroera 1999. Ιερό κορυφής Κορακομούρι Σφάκας. *Κρητικής Εστίας* 7: 322-326.

Vokotopoulos, L. 2017. Ιερό κορυφής Τραόσταλου Ζάκρου: Λατρευτικές πρακτικές και περίοδοι χρήσης, in *Πεπραγμένα του ΙΒ' Διεθνούς Κρητολογικού Συνεδρίου, Ηράκλειο, 21-25.9.2016. Τμήμα Α*. Heraklion: the Society of Cretan Historical Studies.

Warren, P. 1981. Knossos: Stratigraphical Museum excavations, 1978-1980, part I. *Archaeological Reports* 27(1980-1981): 73-92.

Warren, P. 1991. A new Minoan deposit from Knossos, c. 1600 B.C., and its wider relations. *The Annual of the British School at Athens* 86: 319-340.

Watrous, L.V. 1995. Some observations on Minoan peak sanctuaries, in R. Laffineur and W.-D. Niemeier (eds) *POLITEIA. Society and State in the Aegean Bronze Age. Proceedings of the 5th International Aegean Conference/ 5e Rencontre égéenne internationale, University of Heidelberg, Archäologisches Institut, 10-13 April 1994* (Aegaeum 12): 393-402. Liège and Austin: the University of Liège and University of Texas at Austin.

Watrous, L.V. 1996. *The Cave Sanctuary of Zeus at Psychro: A Study of Extra-Urban Sanctuaries in Minoan and Early Iron Age Crete* (Aegaeum 15). Liège: the University of Liège.

Watrous, L.V. 2001. Crete from the earliest prehistory through the Protopalatial period, in Cullen, T. (ed.) *Aegean Prehistory. A Review* (American Journal of Archaeology Supplement 1): 157-215. Boston: Archaeological Institute of America.

Zeimbekis, M. 1998. The Typology, Forms and Functions of Animal Figures from Minoan Peak Sanctuaries with Special Reference to Juktas and Kophinas. Unpublished PhD Dissertation, The University of Bristol.

Zeimbekis, M. 2005. The Clay Animal Figurines and Figures from the Juktas Peak Sanctuary. Lecture delivered to the Minoan Seminar, held at The Danish Institute at Athens, 27th February 2005.